Teach Yourself Borland® C++ 4.5 in 21 Days

Second Edition

Teach Yourself Borland® C++ 4.5 in 21 Days

Second Edition

Namir Clement Shammas
Craig Arnush
Edward Mulroy

A Division of Macmillan Computer Publishing
201 West 103rd Street, Indianapolis, Indiana 46290

To my nephew, Julian Aziz—Namir Clement Shammas

To Bzrblt, who kept me company—Craig Arnush

To Marie—Edward Mulroy

Copyright © 1995 by Sams Publishing

SECOND EDITION
FIRST PRINTING—1995

International Standard Book Number: 0-672-30598-4

Library of Congress Catalog Card Number: 94-67099

98 97 96 95 4 3 2

Interpretation of the printing code: the rightmost double-digit number is the year of the book's printing; the rightmost single-digit, the number of the book's printing. For example, a printing code of 95-1 shows that the first printing of the book occurred in 1995.

Composed in AGaramond and MCPdigital by Macmillan Computer Publishing

Printed in the United States of America

Trademarks

Publisher
Richard K. Swadley

Acquisitions Manager
Greg Wiegand

Managing Editor
Cindy Morrow

Acquisitions Editor
Grace Buechlein

Development Editor
Dean Miller

Production Editor
Deborah Frisby

Copy Editor
Joe Williams

Editorial and Graphics Coordinator
Bill Whitmer

Editorial Assistants
Carol Ackerman
Sharon Cox
Lynette Quinn

Technical Reviewer
Bob Arnson

Marketing Manager
Gregg Bushyeager

Cover Designer
Dan Armstrong

Book Designer
Alyssa Yesh

Director of Production and Manufacturing
Jeff Valler

Imprint Supervisor
Katy Bodenmiller

Manufacturing Coordinator
Paul Gilchrist

Production Analysts
Angela Bannan
Dennis Clay Hager
Mary Beth Wakefield

Graphics Image Specialists
Brad Dixon
Jason Hand
Clint Lahnen
Dennis Sheehan
Craig Small

Production
Steve Adams
Nick Anderson
Carol Bowers
Michael Brumitt
Ayrika Bryant
Kim Cofer
Terri Edwards
Donna Haigerty
Betty Kish
Louisa Klucznik
Jamie Milazzo
Wendy Ott
Shelly Palma
Chad Poore
Casey Price
Beth Rago
Michelle Self
Susan Shepard
SA Springer
Rebecca Tapley
Dennis Wesner

Indexers
Charlotte Clapp
Jennifer Eberhardt

Overview

Extra Credit Bonus Section

Appendix

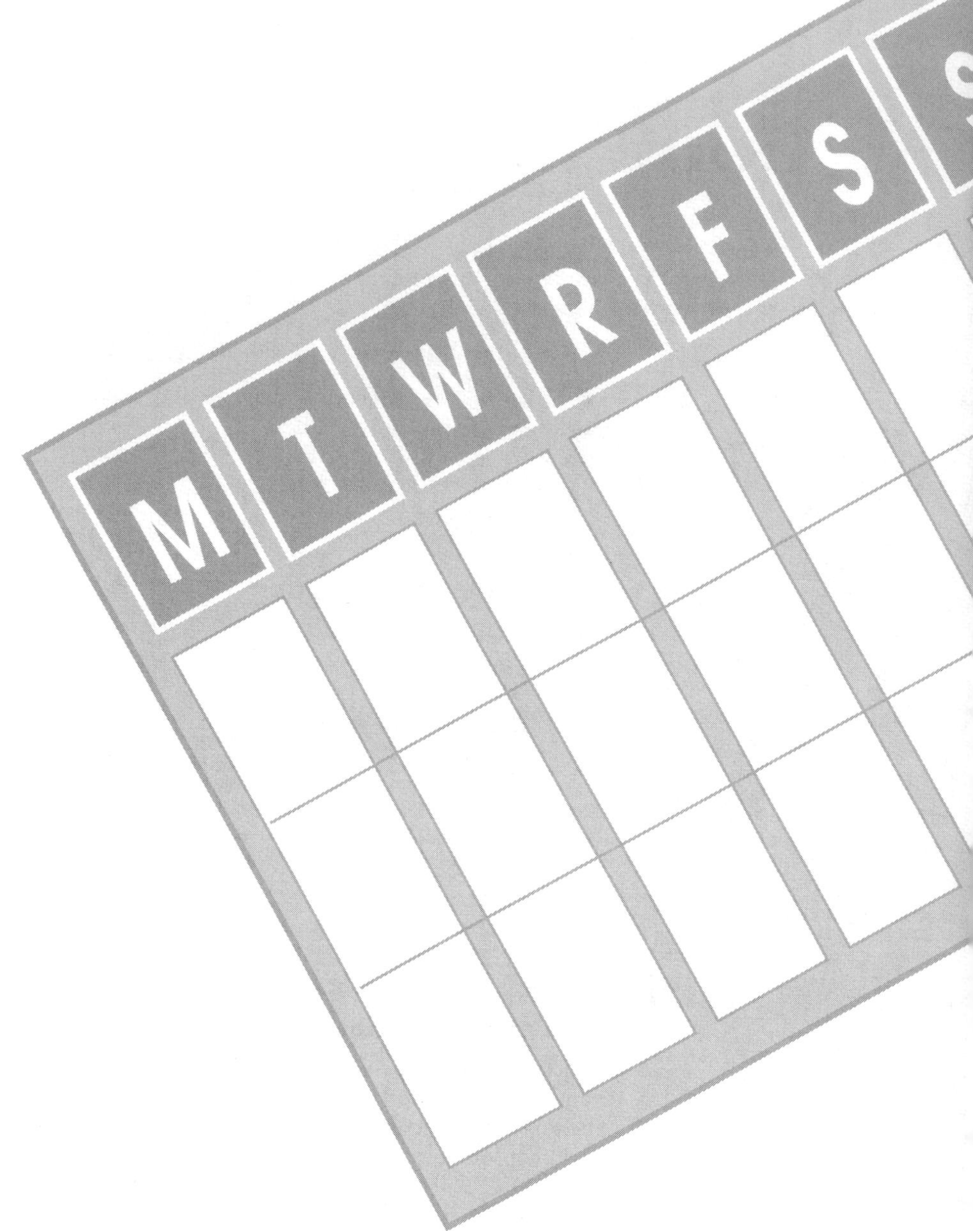
M
T
W
R
F
S
S

Contents

Sams
Learning
Center
SAMS
PUBLISHING

Acknowledgments

I would like to thank Grace Buechlein at Sams Publishing for having the patience to deal with the likes of me. Also, thanks to Dean Miller, who listened to my suggestions and even liked my bugs. My thanks go out to all those at Sams who participated in putting this book together and eventually into your hands. —Craig Arnush

A very special dedication to Ian Spencer who appeared in a crisis, waved his wand, and made the problems disappear. Thanks, Ian. I needed that.

I would like to thank Grace Buechlein, who provided kind, frank guidance; and Peter Aitken, whose responses convinced me to do this. Special thanks to my wife Marie, who has been supportive throughout. —Edward Mulroy

I wish to thank the many people at Sams for encouraging me and working with me on this project. First, I would like to thank Publisher Richard Swadley and Associate Publisher Jordan Gold for their support. Many thanks also to Grace Buechlein, Dean Miller, Joe Williams, and Deborah Frisby for their first-class work. Thanks to all who participated in producing this book. —Namir Clement Shammas

Finally, all of the authors wish to thank Robert Arnson, technical editor for this book. Arnson, who used to work in Borland's Technical Publications department on C++ projects, is now a free-lance writer, editor, and consultant. He's also a member of Team Borland, Borland's group of volunteers who help support Borland products on CompuServe, GEnie, and BIX. His speciality is application frameworks, and he has worked with OWL for more than three years. You can contact him on CompuServe (72662,1376) and GEnie (ARNSON). You can also contact him via Internet mail at `robert.arnson.@channel1.com`.

About the Authors

Namir Clement Shammas is a full-time author of programming books and an expert in object-oriented programming. He has written and coauthored more than 40 books on programming languages such as C++, C, Pascal, and Visual Basic. Among his many books are *Advanced C++*, *Teach Yourself Visual C++ in 21 Days*, and *What Every Borland C++ 4 Programmer Should Know*.

Craig Arnush is an independent software consultant in San Diego and is an expert on Windows. He volunteers his time answering technical questions on the Borland CompuServe forums as a member of Team Borland. Craig can be reached via his CompuServe account at 71333,3052 or via the Internet at `craiga@netcom.com`.

Edward Mulroy is Chief Engineer for RF Data Corporation, a company specializing in communications and embedded work. Since 1990, he has assisted fellow users of C++, C, and Assembler on the Borland CompuServe forums as a member of Team Borland.

Introduction

This book has three major goals: teaching you to program in C++, teaching you to create Windows applications using Borland C++, and teaching you the new features of Borland C++ 4.5 No prior programming experience is required. However, knowing how to program in other languages, such as BASIC or Pascal, certainly helps. This book is not for the faint-hearted because becoming familiar with the new features of a new compiler is hard enough, but also learning to program in C++ and learning to write Windows applications in C++ are two nontrivial tasks!

The book contains 21 chapters, one for each study day. The material is somewhat fast-paced in order to meet the goals of the book. Each chapter contains a Q&A section, a quiz section, and an exercise section. In the back of the book you'll find the answers to the quizzes and to many of the exercises.

Day 1 gives you a brief tour of the Borland C++ IDE, the Windows environment that you use to develop C++ programs. The chapter also presents your first C++ program to demonstrate the basic components of a non-Windows C++ program.

Day 2 looks at C++ program components in more detail. The chapter discusses naming and declaring variables, constants, and functions. The book also provides an early focus on C++ functions because they are important program building blocks.

Day 3 presents the various C++ operators and expressions. Operators enable you to manipulate data and form expressions that support more complex data manipulation.

Day 4 discusses formatted stream input and output, as well the famous `printf` function. The latter function supports versatile formatted output.

Day 5 covers C++ decision-making constructs. These constructs include the various kinds of `if` statements as well as the `switch` statement.

Day 6 discusses C++ loops, including the `for`, `do-while`, and `while` loops. The chapter demonstrates how to use the `for` loop as an open loop. In addition, the chapter discusses skipping loop iterations, exiting loops, and nesting loops.

Day 7 presents arrays in C++. The chapter covers both single-dimensional and multidimensional arrays and discusses how to declare them and initialize them. In addition, the chapter discusses sorting and searching single-dimensional arrays.

Day 8 covers user-defined types and pointers. The chapter discusses enumerated data types, structures, unions, reference variables, and pointers. The text demonstrates how to declare and use pointers with simple variables, arrays, structures, and dynamic memory.

Day 9 focuses on strings and the STRING.H library, which is inherited from C. The chapter covers topics like assigning, concatenating, comparing, converting, and reversing strings. In addition, the chapter discusses searching for characters and substrings in strings.

Day 10 discusses advanced function parameters and mainly covers parameters that are arrays, strings, structures, and pointers to functions. The chapter also discusses the various ways to pass structures as parameters and presents recursive functions.

Day 11 introduces you to the world of object-oriented programming (OOP). The chapter covers the basics of OOP and presents C++ classes. The text discusses the basic components of a C++ class and the rules related to using these components.

Day 12 discusses the basic stream file I/O, which is supported by the C++ stream library. The chapter covers common stream functions, sequential text stream I/O, sequential binary stream I/O, and random-access stream I/O.

Day 13 covers the string class, an alternative to strings, and the functions in STRING.H that work with them. This class conforms to the preliminary strings class from the ANSI C++ committee and is prototyped in the header file CSTRING.H.

Day 14 presents very simple OWL-based Windows applications. Object Windows Library version 2.5, or OWL2, is included with BC++ 4.5. It is a C++ library for use in Windows programming, and using it shortens the time and effort in developing a Windows program. OWL is written in C++ and uses a feature of that language called *templates*, which you also learn on Day 14.

Day 15 focuses on drawing text in a window. The chapter presents both nonscrolling and scrolling windows and illustrates how to draw text (as graphics) in these windows.

Day 16 presents the OWL library classes, which model static text controls, edit controls, and pushbutton controls. The chapter also presents a nontrivial command-oriented line calculator as an example that uses these controls.

Day 17 presents the OWL library classes that model the check box control, the radio button control, and the group control.

Day 18 covers the OWL library class that models list box controls. The chapter discusses both single-selection and multiple-selection list boxes. The programs in the chapter illustrate both kinds of list boxes.

Day 19 presents the OWL library classes, which model the scroll bar control and the combo box control. The chapter also discusses how to create history boxes using combo boxes. In addition, the chapter presents a version of the calculator program that uses the combo boxes.

Day 20 focuses on creating and using dialog boxes. The chapter shows you how to use resource files to define modal and modeless dialog boxes. In addition, the chapter discusses data transfer between a dialog box and its parent window.

Day 21 looks at Multiple Document Interface (MDI) windows. The chapter presents the classes that support MDI-compliant applications and illustrates how to manage MDI-child windows.

The bonus chapters present the new features of Borland C++ 4.5, including AppExpert, ClassExpert, the Resource Workshop, and the debugging tools. In addition, you get a bonus chapter on common dialog boxes.

The book contains Windows programs that illustrate aspects of programming that go beyond the trivial aspects of using various visual controls. Study these programs, as they contain techniques and tricks that can enrich your Windows programming. We all learn to program by looking at examples (including nontrivial ones) and by asking friends questions.

In the back of the book is an explanation of how to obtain a companion disk that includes the source code and the project files presented in this book. You can also download the files from CompuServe; type: `GO SAMS`. The Files can be found in the Sams Programming Library 9.

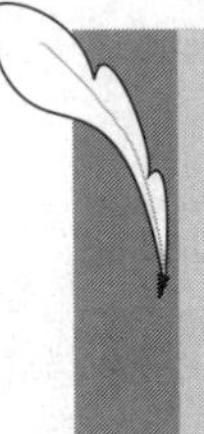

Note: Source code for this book is available on CompuServe in the Programming library of the Sams forum. It is also available via anonymous FTP to

`ftp.netcom.com` in the `pub\cr\craiga` directory.

Happy programming!

WEEK 1

AT A GLANCE

1
2
3
4
5
6
7

The first week of your journey into learning to write Windows applications starts with an introduction to the Borland C++ 4.5 environment—the IDE (integrated development environment). The remaining days in this week present the basics of the C++ language itself. You learn about predefined data types; naming constants, variables, and functions; C++ operators and expressions; managing basic input and output; making decisions; writing loops; and declaring and using arrays. Thus, this week covers the basic components of the C++ language.

Getting Started

WEEK 1

Welcome to the world of C++ and Windows programming. Your journey into this exciting world begins today. Most of the information in today's lesson familiarizes you with the Borland C++ Integrated Development Environment (IDE). You will learn about the following topics:

- The basics and history of C++ programs
- Loading and using the Borland C++ IDE
- EasyWin applications
- Typing and running your first C++ program

The Basics of C++ Programs

You don't need any previous experience in programming to learn Borland C++ with this book; but if you have programmed before, things will be easier. As with other languages, C++ is made up of declarations and statements that specify exact instructions to be executed when the program runs.

C++ was developed by Bjarne Stroustrup at Bell Labs. The language is meant to supersede and build on the popular C language, mainly by adding object-oriented language extensions.

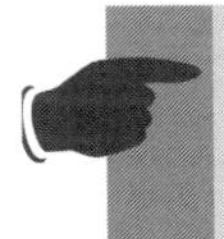

New Term: An *object-oriented language* represents the attributes and operations of objects.

In addition, C++ offers a number of enhancements to C that are not object-oriented. Thus, learning C++ gives you the bonus of becoming very familiar with C. However, unlike C, which has been standardized, C++ is still undergoing the standardization process.

Programming in C++ requires that you become aware of the supporting libraries, which perform various tasks such as input/output, text manipulation, math operations, file I/O (input/output), and so on. In languages such as BASIC, support for such operations is transparent to programs, meaning that it is automatically available to these programs. As a result, many programs come across as single components that are independent of any other programming components. By contrast, programming in C++ makes you more aware of a program's dependency on various libraries. The

advantage of this language feature is that you are able to select between similar libraries, including ones that you develop. Thus, C++ programs are modular. C++ compilers, including Borland C++, use project files and program files. The Borland C++ IDE uses project files to manage the creation and updating of a program.

New Term: *Project files* specify the library. *Program files* create an application.

Loading the Borland C++ IDE

The Borland C++ IDE is the visual interface for the C++ compiler, linker, debugger, and other tools that are used to create, manage, and maintain C++ programs. You can load the IDE by simply clicking the Borland C++ icon or by double-clicking the BCW.EXE program from the File Manager. (The file BCW.EXE is located in the directory \BC45\BIN.)

An Overview of the Borland C++ IDE

The Borland C++ IDE is an MDI-compliant application with the following main components:

- The frame window with the menu system, minimize, and maximize icons. You can resize, move, maximize, and minimize the Borland C++ IDE window. This window has a title that reflects the name of the active window.
- The system menu, which offers numerous options.
- The speed bar, which contains special bitmapped buttons that offer shortcuts to specific commands. The IDE enables you to customize the bitmapped buttons in the speed bar. In addition, these buttons are context sensitive. Their number and type can change, depending on the current task or active window. The IDE supports a nice feature that displays what a bitmapped button does (the text appears in the status line) when you move the mouse over that button.

- The client area, which contains various windows, such as the source-code editing window, the message window, the variable watch window, and so on.
- The status line located at the bottom of the IDE window. This line displays brief online help as you move the mouse over the buttons in the speed bar, offers a brief explanation for the various menu items, displays the cursor location, and shows the status of the insert/overwrite mode.

Figure 1.1 shows a sample session with the Borland C++ IDE.

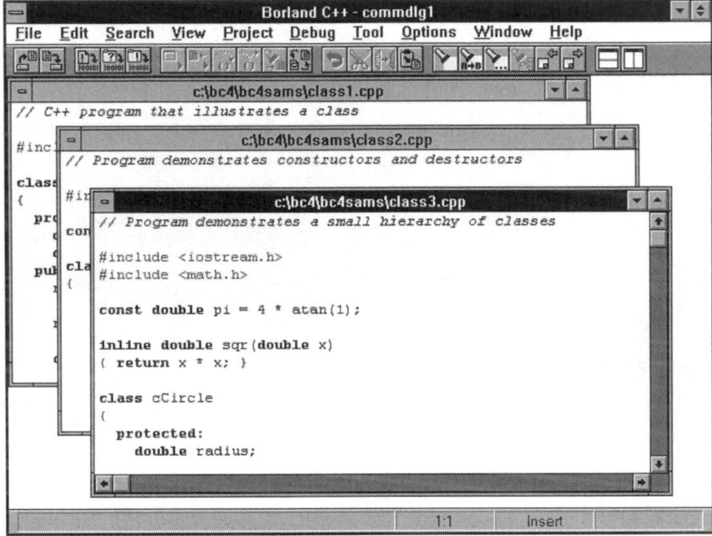

Figure 1.1. *The Borland C++ IDE.*

Note: Because the IDE is meant to accommodate software developers, many of the options will seem advanced to you if you are a novice programmer. However, you only need to be familiar with the options and their related terms. As you become more experienced, these options and terms will become part of your knowledge as a Borland C++ programmer.

1

The File Menu

The File menu provides options to manage files, to print text, and to exit the IDE. Table 1.1 summarizes the options in the File menu. The File menu also includes a dynamic list of the most recently opened source-code files.

Table 1.1. Summary of the options in the File menu.

Command	Shortcut Keys	Function
New		Opens a new edit window.
Open...		Loads an existing source-code file into a new edit window.
Save	Ctrl+K S	Saves the contents of the active edit window.
Save as...		Saves the contents of the active edit window using a new filename.
Save all		Saves all of the opened source-code windows in their respective files.
Print...		Prints the contents of a source code window.
Print setup...		Sets up the printer.
Exit		Exits the IDE.

The New Command

The New option opens a new edit window (also known as a source-code window) and assigns it a default associated filename. The default filename of the first new window you open is NONAME00.CPP. Likewise, the default filename of the second new window is NONAME01.CPP, and so on. The newly opened window is initially empty and has the same window size and location of the last active window. In other words, if the last active window was maximized, the new window will also be maximized.

The Open... Option

The **O**pen... option enables you to load the contents of an existing source-code file into a new edit window. In fact, the IDE is able to load multiple files. The option invokes the Open a File dialog box, shown in Figure 1.2. The dialog box has several list box and combo box controls that enable you to locate the source-code file and then select it. These controls permit you to choose the drive, directory, and filename wildcards that help you to locate the source-code file you seek.

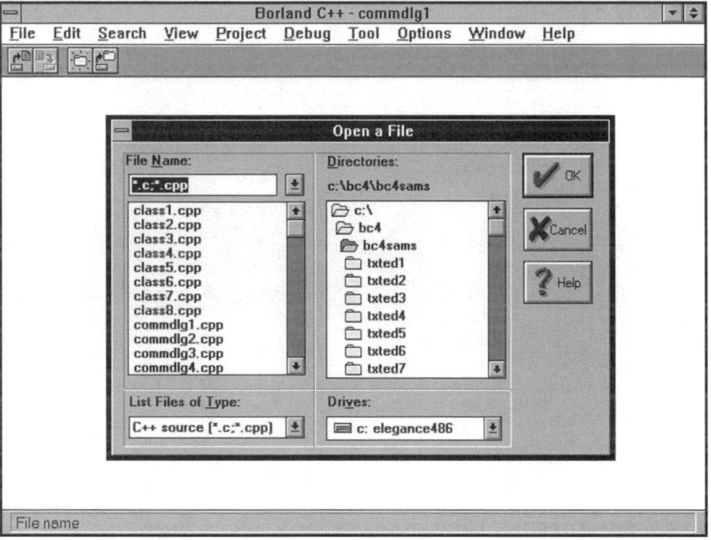

Figure 1.2. *The Open a File dialog box.*

The Save Option

The **S**ave option assists you in saving the contents of the active edit window to its associated file. If you invoke this option with a new edit window, the **S**ave option invokes the Save File As dialog box, shown in Figure 1.3. This dialog box enables you to optionally specify the nondefault filename, as well as the destination drive and directory. The shortcut keys for the **S**ave option are Ctrl+K S.

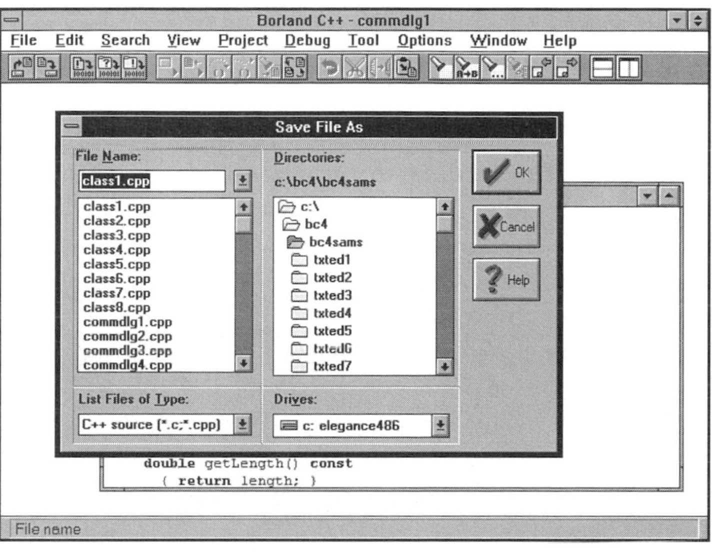

Figure 1.3. *The Save File As dialog box.*

The Save As... Option

The Save **A**s... option enables you to save the contents of the active edit window in a file that is different from the currently associated file. In fact, the new filename becomes the new associated file for the active edit window. The Save **A**s... option invokes the Save File As dialog box, shown in Figure 1.3. If you select an existing file, the option brings up a message dialog box to ask you if you wish to overwrite the contents of the existing file with those of the active edit window.

The Save All Option

The Save A**l**l option writes the contents of all the modified edit windows to their associated files. If the IDE contains new edit windows, this option invokes the Save File As dialog box to save these new windows.

The Print... Option

The **P**rint... option enables you to print the contents of the active edit window. The option brings up the Print Options dialog box, shown in Figure 1.4. This dialog box has check boxes for the following options:

- Print a header and page numbers
- Print line numbers
- Highlight syntax keywords by printing them in bold characters
- Use color (if your printer supports colors)
- Wrap lines
- Left margin edit box option

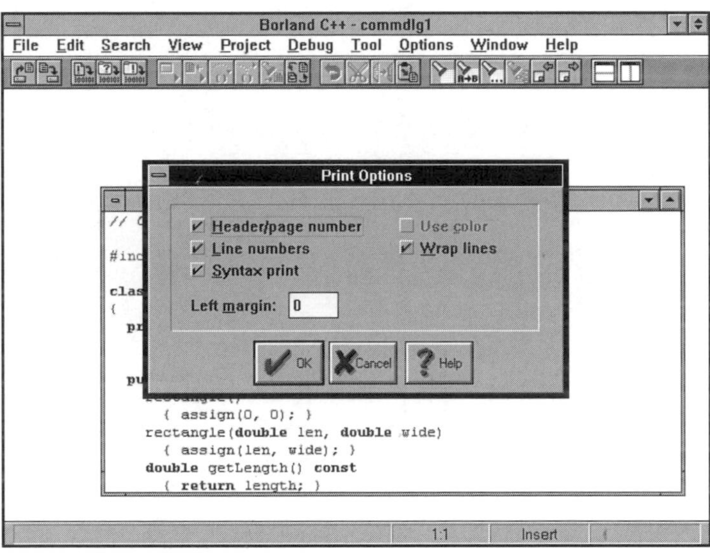

Figure 1.4. *The Print Options dialog box.*

The Print Setup... Option

The Print Setup... option enables you to set up your printer using the **Print...** option before you print. The printer setup option brings up the Setup dialog box, shown in Figure 1.5. (The dialog box in this figure is based on a system that has an HP LaserJet III.) This dialog box contains controls that enable you to specify the following items:

- The paper size.
- The paper source.
- The number of copies to print.

- The amount of printer memory.
- The orientation of the printout.
- The selected font cartridges and fonts.
- Page protection to reserve additional memory for printing a page. This option is available only when you have more than one 1 MB of printer memory.

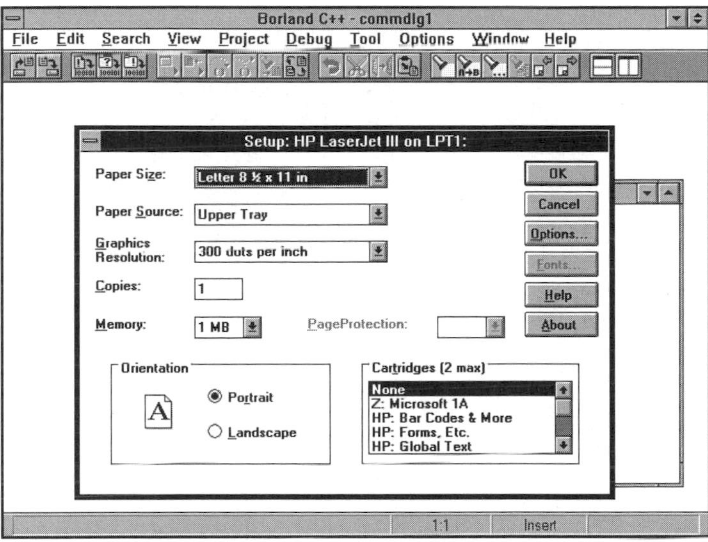

Figure 1.5. *The Setup dialog box.*

The Exit Option

The E**x**it option enables you to exit the Borland C++ IDE altogether. The IDE prompts you for any modified edit window that has not been saved.

The Edit Menu

The Edit menu contains options that enable you to edit the text in the edit windows. Table 1.2 summarizes the options in the Edit menu.

Table 1.2. Summary of the options in the Edit menu.

Command	Shortcut Keys	Function
Undo	Ctrl+Z	Undoes the last editing action.
Redo	Shift+Ctrl+Z	Reverses the action of the last Undo option.
Cu**t**	Ctrl+X	Deletes the selected text and copies it to the Clipboard. The previous contents of the Clipboard are lost.
Copy	Ctrl+C	Copies the selected text to the Clipboard. The previous contents of the Clipboard are lost.
Paste	Ctrl+V	Inserts the contents of the Clipboard at the current cursor location.
Cl**e**ar	Ctrl+Delete	Deletes selected text but does not write it to the Clipboard.
Select all		Selects all of the text in the active edit window.
Buffer list...		Displays the Buffer List dialog box.

The Undo Option

The **U**ndo option enables you to reverse the effect of the last editing task and restore the contents of the active edit window. The shortcut keys for this option are Ctrl+Z. This option enables you to quickly and efficiently deal with editing errors—especially after working long hours.

The Redo Option

The **R**edo option enables you to reverse the action of the **U**ndo option. The shortcut keys for the **R**edo option are Shift+Ctrl+Z. The **R**edo option enables you to switch between two versions of edited source code. This option is beneficial to the truly exhausted programmer who cannot make up his mind about how the source code should look!

The Cut Option

The Cu**t** option deletes selected text and places it in the Clipboard. The previous contents of the Clipboard are lost. The shortcut keys for the Cu**t** option are Ctrl+X.

The Copy Option

The **C**opy option copies the selected text into the Clipboard. The previous contents of the Clipboard are lost. The shortcut keys for the **C**opy option are Ctrl+C.

The Paste Option

The **P**aste option inserts the contents of the Clipboard at the current insertion point. The contents of the Clipboard remain unaffected. Thus you can use the Cu**t** and **P**aste options to move text in the same edit window or across different edit windows. You can also use the **C**opy and **P**aste options to duplicate blocks of text in the same edit window or across different edit windows. The shortcut keys for the **P**aste option are Ctrl+V.

The Clear Option

The C**l**ear option clears the selected text without copying it to the Clipboard. This does not mean that the deleted text is irreversibly lost, because you can use the **U**ndo option to undelete that text. The shortcut keys for the C**l**ear option are Ctrl+Delete.

The Select All Option

The **S**elect All option selects all of the text in the active edit window. You can copy this text to the Clipboard by using the **C**opy option. Then you can write the contents of the Clipboard to another edit window using the **P**aste option.

The Buffer List... Option

The Buffer List... option enables you to examine the list of buffers used with the various edit windows. This option brings up the Buffer List dialog box, shown in Figure 1.6. The dialog box enables you to load a buffer into an edit window. The dialog box contains the list of buffers; those that have changed since they were last loaded have the word `MODIFIED` (placed in parentheses) after them. The dialog box enables you to replace the contents of an edit window without closing the associated file. If the replaced file is not loaded into another edit window, it is hidden. You may use the buffer list later in order to load the hidden buffer into an edit window.

You can use the **Save** pushbutton of the Buffer List dialog box to update the file associated with the selected buffer. This action causes the word `MODIFIED` to disappear from the selected buffer entry. You may also use the **Delete** pushbutton to remove the selected buffer from memory, if that buffer is not in an Edit window.

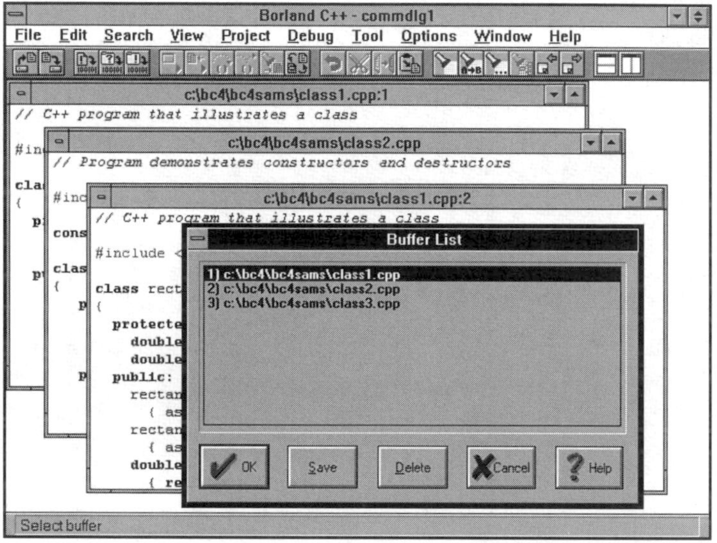

Figure 1.6. *The Buffer List dialog box.*

The Search Menu

The Search menu contains options that enable you to locate various kinds of information, such as text, symbol definitions, function declarations, and program-building errors. Table 1.3 summarizes the options in the Search menu.

Table 1.3. Summary of the options in the Search menu.

Command	Shortcut Keys	Function
Find...	Ctrl+Q F	Searches for text in the active edit window.
Replace...	Ctrl+Q A	Replaces text in the active source-code window.
Search again	F3	Repeats the last Find or Replace operation.

1

Command	Shortcut Keys	Function
Browse symbol...		Locates a symbol in any source code that is part of the current project.
Locate function...		Locates a function.
Previous message	Alt+F7	Selects the previous program-building message and places the cursor at the offending line in an edit window.
Next message	Alt+F8	Selects the next program-building message and places the cursor at the offending line in an edit window.

The Find... Option

The Find... option supports searches for text in the active edit window. This option, which has the shortcut keys Ctrl+Q F, brings up the Find Text dialog box, shown in Figure 1.7. This dialog box has the following controls:

- The **Text to find** combo box control, which enables you either to type in the search text or to recall recently searched text.
- The Options check boxes, which include
    - The **Case sensitive** check box, which enables you to select case-sensitive or case-insensitive text search.
    - The **Whole words only** check box, which enables you to choose between matching entire words or matching any text.
    - The **Regular expression** check box, which turns on or off the use of the BRIEF editor's regular expressions feature. Such expressions result in using the text in the **Text to find** control as the text pattern.
    - The **Direction** diamond-shaped radio button controls. These controls enable you to choose between forward and backward search.
    - The **Scope** diamond-shaped radio button controls. These controls enable you to choose between searching the entire text and limiting the search to the selected text.

- The **Origin** diamond-shaped radio button controls. These controls enable you to choose between searching the entire edit window and searching from the cursor position.

- The **OK**, **Cancel**, and **Help** buttons.

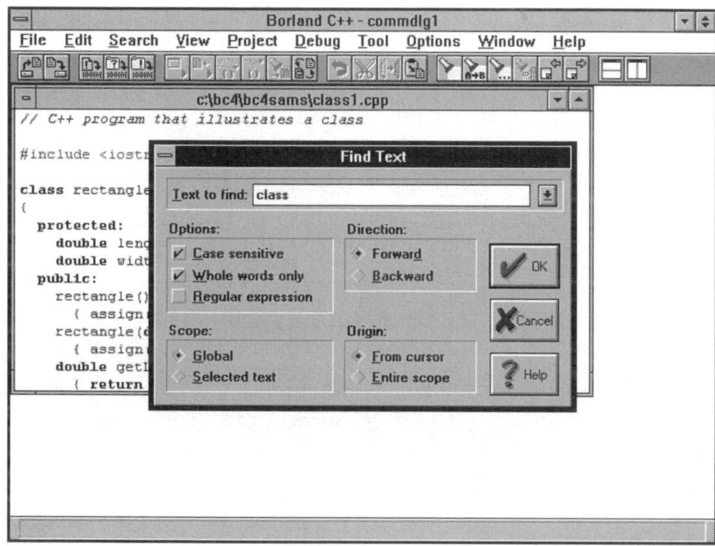

Figure 1.7. *The Find Text dialog box.*

The Replace... Option

The **R**eplace... option supports replacing text in the active edit window. This option, which has the shortcut keys Ctrl+Q A, brings up the Replace Text dialog box, shown in Figure 1.8. This dialog box has the following controls:

- The **Text to find** combo box control, which enables you either to type in the search text or to recall recently searched text.
- The **New text** combo box, which enables you either to enter the replacement text or to select recently used replacement text.
- The Options check boxes, which include
  - The **Case sensitive** check box, which enables you to select case-sensitive or case-insensitive text search.

- The **Whole words only** check box, which enables you to choose between matching entire words or matching any text.
- The **Regular expression** check box, which turns on or off the use of the BRIEF editor's regular expressions. Such expressions result in using the text in the **Text to find** control as a text pattern.
- The **Prompt on replace** check box, which enables you to select whether or not text shall be replaced without your confirmation.
- The **Direction** diamond-shaped radio button controls. These controls permit you to choose between forward and backward search.
- The **Scope** diamond-shaped radio button controls. These controls enable you to choose between searching the entire text and limiting the search to the selected text.
- The **Origin** diamond-shaped radio button controls. These controls enable you to choose between searching the entire edit window and searching from the cursor position.
- The **Change All** pushbutton, which enables you to replace all of the matching text. By contrast, if you click the OK button you will only replace the next matching text.

- The **OK**, **Cancel**, and **Help** buttons.

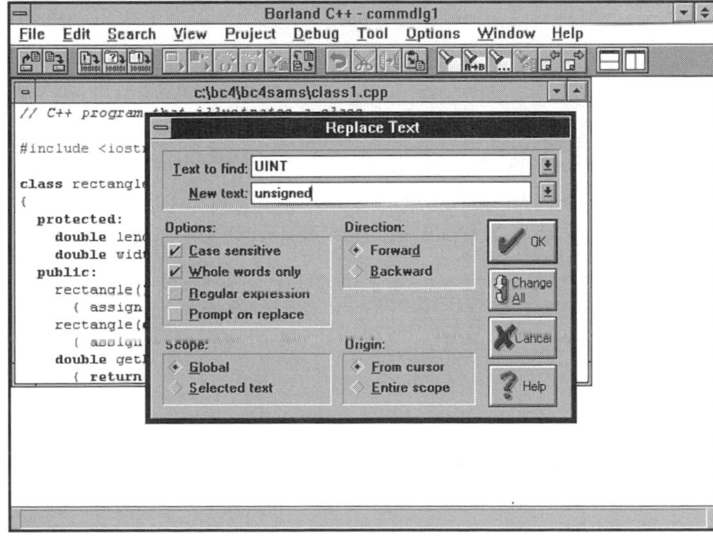

Figure 1.8. *The Replace Text dialog box.*

The Search Again Option

The **S**earch Again option enables you to repeat the last **F**ind... or **R**eplace... option. The shortcut key for this option is the F3 function key.

The Browse Symbol... Option

The **B**rowse Symbol... option enables you to browse the makeup of a symbol, including classes, functions, and variables. These symbols need not be defined in the active edit window, as long as they are defined in one of the current project's source-code files (your files or the library's included files). Figure 1.9 shows a sample symbol-browsing dialog box.

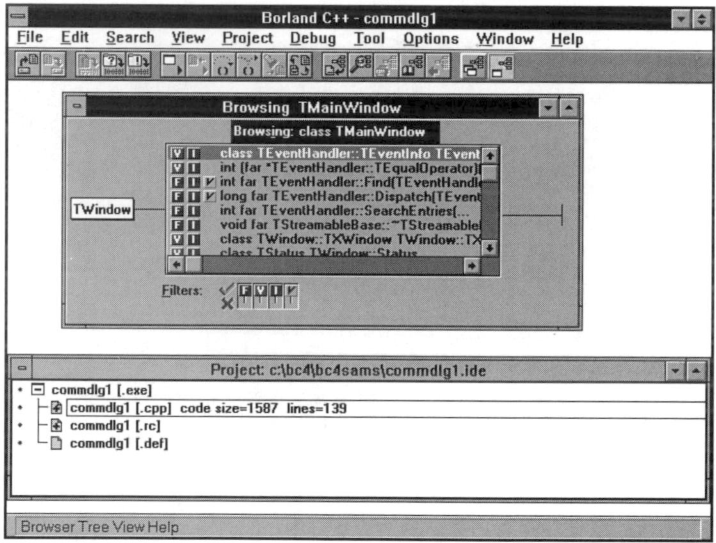

Figure 1.9. *A sample symbol-browsing dialog box.*

The Locate Function... Option

The **L**ocate Function... option enables you to find the definition of a function. This option brings up the Locate Function dialog box, shown in Figure 1.10, which prompts you to enter the name of the function you wish to find. The IDE responds by moving to it in an existing edit window or by displaying the function definition in a new edit window, if need be.

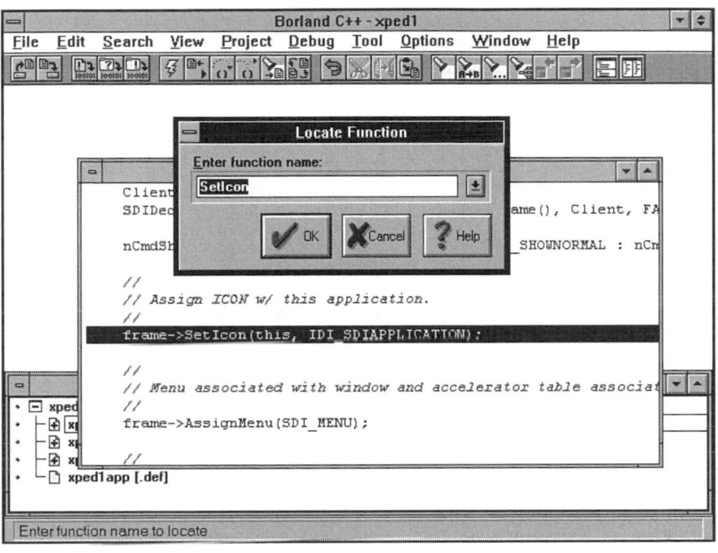

Figure 1.10. *The Locate Function dialog box.*

The Previous Message Option

The **P**revious Message option enables you to zoom in on the offending source-code line that is associated with the previous message in the Message window. The IDE responds to this option by displaying the edit window that contains the offending source-code line. The shortcut keys for this option are Alt+F7.

The Next Message Option

The **N**ext Message option enables you to zoom in on the offending source-code line that is associated with the next message in the Message window. The IDE responds to this option by displaying the edit window which contains the offending source-code line. The shortcut keys for this option are Alt+F8.

The View Menu

The View menu contains options that enable you to view and browse through a wide variety of information. This information goes beyond the declarations in the source-code files of your own project. Table 1.4 summarizes the options in the View menu.

Table 1.4. Summary of the options in the View menu.

Command	Shortcut Keys	Function
ClassExpert		Invokes the ClassExpert utility, which works with project files generated by AppExpert.
Project		Displays the Project window.
Message		Displays the Message window.
Classes		Browses through the classes.
Globals		Browses through global data types, constants, and variables.
Watch		Selects or opens the Watch window.
Breakpoint		Selects or opens the Breakpoints window.
Call stack		Selects or opens the Call Stack window.
Register		Selects or opens the Registers window.
Event log		Selects or opens the Event Log window.
Information...		Displays system or status information.

The ClassExpert Option

The ClassExpert option invokes the ClassExpert utility, which works only with project files created by the AppExpert (which we introduce in the next section). This option invokes the ClassExpert window, which has three panes, as follows:

- The Classes pane, which lists the classes involved in the project created using AppExpert. The information in the other two panes is related to the currently selected class in this pane.
- The Events pane, which lists the command notification, control notifications, virtual functions, Windows messages, and other events that are related to the class selected in the Classes pane.
- The source-code window, in which the selected class is defined.

Figure 1.11 shows a sample ClassExpert window.

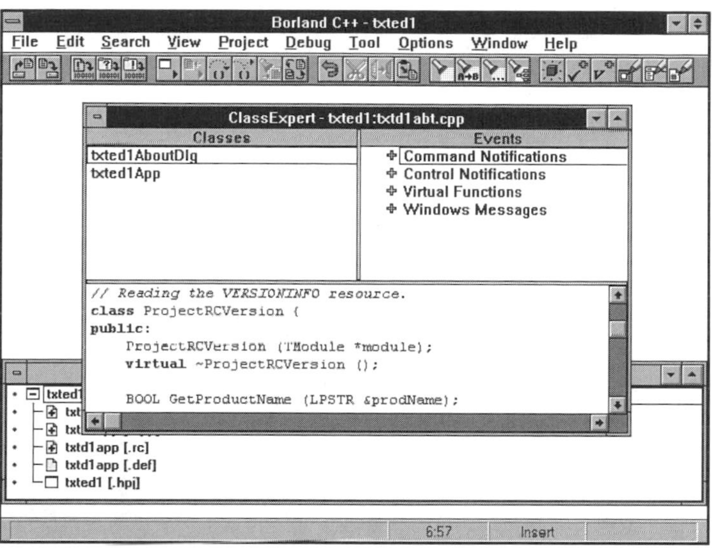

Figure 1.11. *A sample ClassExpert window.*

The Project Option

The **P**roject option selects or opens the Project window, which lists the targets in the nodes in the current .IDE file. The Project window displays the files of a target in the form of a tree-like outline. The outline is made up of nodes that you can expand and collapse (if they have child nodes). Figure 1.12 shows a sample Project window. Each node has a bitmap to its left. If the bitmap graphic has a + sign, then the node has child nodes that are currently hidden. If you click the + sign, you expand that node, and the IDE replaces the + sign with a – sign. The child nodes without + or – signs have no child nodes of their own.

If you click the right mouse button on a node in the Project window, the IDE displays a floating menu that enables you to view various components of the project, manage nodes, and edit project-related components.

The Message Option

The **M**essage option displays, selects, or opens the Message window, which contains the source-code compiler, resource compiler, and linker messages. These messages inform you of the progress of building the .EXE program file. In addition, the Message window contains any warning or error messages generated by the compilers or by the linker.

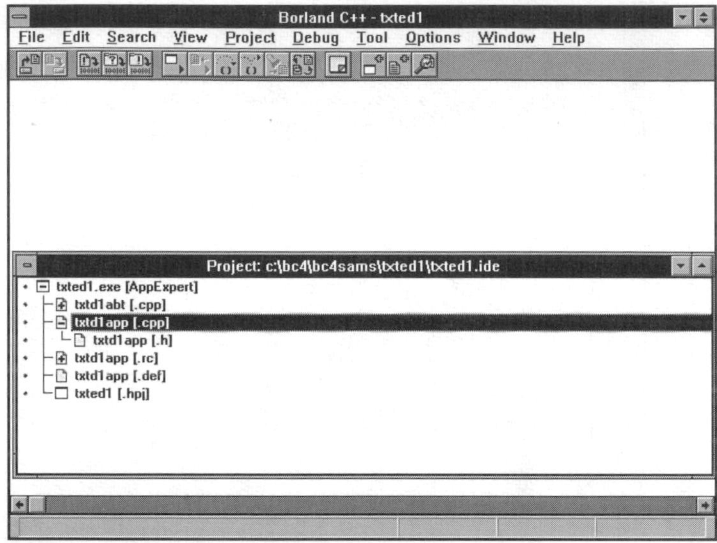

Figure 1.12. *A sample Project window.*

The Classes Option

The **C**lasses option displays the Browsing Objects window, showing a graph of the various classes in the current project and how they are interlinked. Typically, the Browsing Objects window has a vertical and horizontal scroll bar to enable you to scroll through the various classes involved in the current project. Figure 1.13 shows a sample Browsing Objects window that displays the custom application class TWinApp and the application's frame window class, TMainWindow.

The Globals Option

The **G**lobals option displays the Browsing Globals window, which shows the global data types, constants, variables, and functions. Figure 1.14 shows a sample Browsing Globals window. The window identifies each item by using the following special bitmaps:

- The bitmap T indicates that the symbol is a data type.
- The bitmap C signals that the symbol is a constant.
- The bitmap F signifies that the symbol is a function.
- The bitmap V indicates that the symbol is a variable.

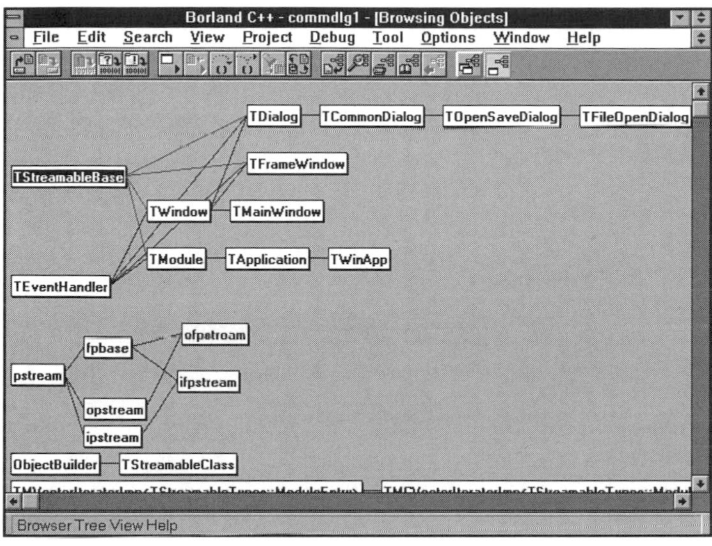

Figure 1.13. *A sample Browsing Objects window.*

The Browsing Globals window contains switches that enable you to filter the viewing of certain global symbols. The window also contains an edit box control that enables you to type in the name of the symbol you want to find. The edit box control filters the symbols with every keystroke you enter.

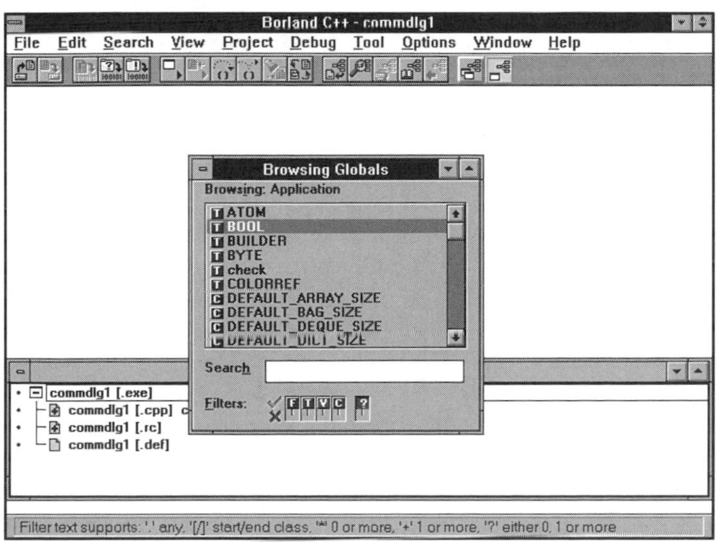

Figure 1.14. *A sample Browsing Globals window.*

The Watch Option

The **W**atch option selects or opens the Watch window. This window lists the currently watched variables in your program. Figure 1.15 shows a sample Watch window. The window displays a check box to the left of each variable. The check box is checked by default to display and update the value in the associated variable. You can uncheck the control to temporarily disable displaying the value of a variable. This task is especially meaningful when the watched variable is not defined in the currently traced function.

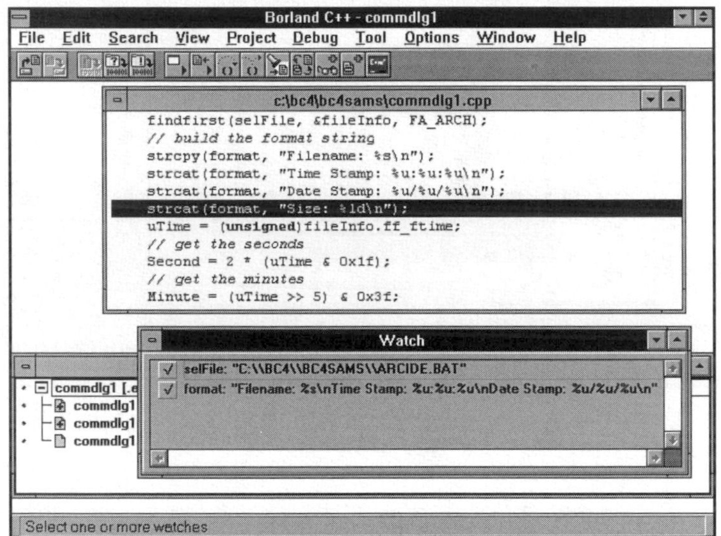

Figure 1.15. *A sample Watch window.*

The Breakpoint Option

The **B**reakpoint option displays the Breakpoints window, which lists the location and type of breakpoints. A *breakpoint* is a program statement at which the program stops to enable you to inspect its variables. Figure 1.16 shows a sample Breakpoints window. The Breakpoints window displays the following information:

- The filename that contains the breakpoint.
- The line number where the breakpoint is located.
- The state of the breakpoint.

- The number of passes (that is, the number of times the statement is executed before the program stops at the breakpoint).

If you double-click any entry in the Breakpoints window, the IDE displays the Breakpoints Properties dialog box. This dialog box enables you to edit the breakpoint's data. We'll cover this dialog box when we discuss managing breakpoints in the Debug menu section.

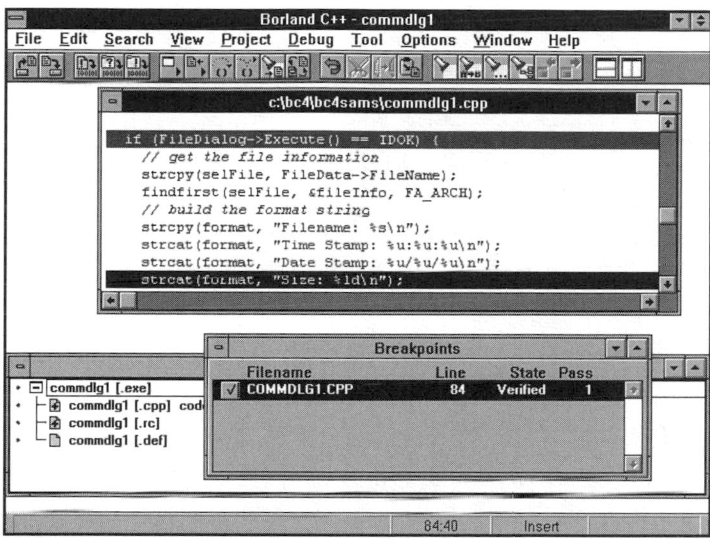

Figure 1.16. *The Breakpoints window.*

The Call Stack Option

The Call **S**tack option displays the Call Stack window, which lists the pending program and the DLL functions that were called (and not yet returned) when the program reached the current breakpoint or the current single-stepped line. Figure 1.17 shows a sample Call Stack window. The DLL functions are referenced by the name of the DLL library, followed by the address of the function.

The Register Option

The **R**egister option displays the Registers window, which reveals the current values in CPU registers. The information in this window helps you perform a low-level debug and trace of a program.

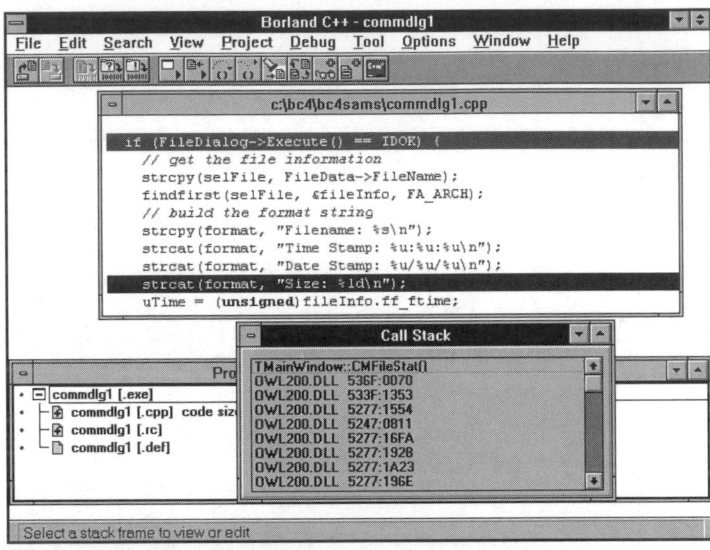

Figure 1.17. *A sample Call Stack window.*

The Event Log Option

The **E**vent Log option displays the Event Log window, which lists the sequence of breakpoint events. Each log entry includes the breakpoint address, followed by text that identifies the related Windows messages, output messages, or exceptions. Figure 1.18 shows a sample Event Log window.

The Information... Option

The **I**nformation... option displays the Information dialog box. This dialog box contains the following information:

- The current directory
- The Windows version and mode
- The MS-DOS version
- The total free memory space
- The largest free memory block
- The percent of USER, GDI, and total free heap space

Figure 1.19 shows a sample Information dialog box.

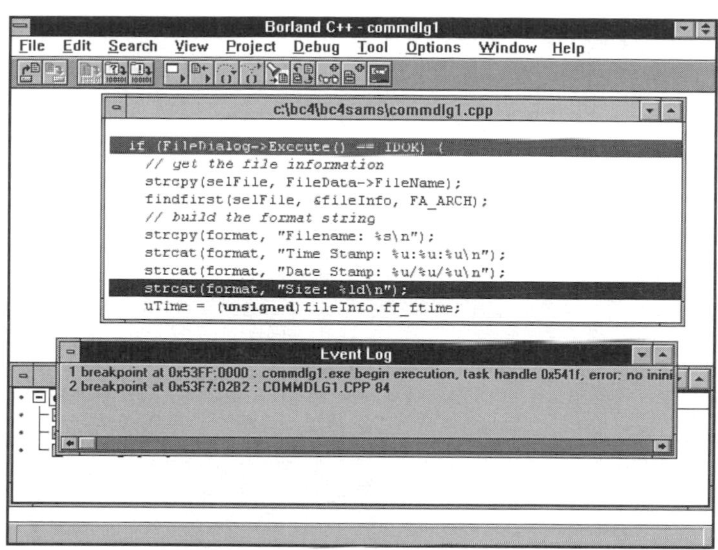

Figure 1.18. *A sample Event Log window.*

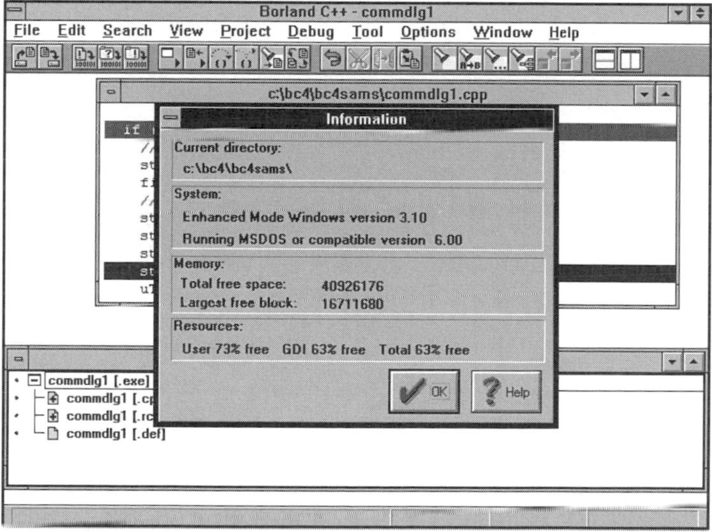

Figure 1.19. *A sample Information dialog box.*

The Project Menu

The Project menu offers options that manage a project to build an executable program or a library. Table 1.5 summarizes the options in the Project menu.

Table 1.5. Summary of the options in the Project menu.

Command	Shortcut Keys	Function
AppExpert...		Invokes the AppExpert utility to generate the files of a project.
New project...		Creates a new project.
Open project...		Opens an existing project and closes the current project.
Close project		Closes the current project.
New target...		Creates a new target in the current project.
Compile	Alt+F9	Compiles the file in the active edit window.
Make all		Updates the project files by compiling and linking the necessary source-code files.
Build all		Unconditionally compiles and links all of the project source-code files.
Generate makefile		Generates a .MAK makefile.

The AppExpert... Option

The AppExpert... option invokes the AppExpert utility, which is a valuable and sophisticated tool for rapid program development. The third extra-credit chapter, “Using the Application Expert,” discusses using the AppExpert.

The New Project... Option

The **N**ew project... option triggers the process that enables you to create a new project without involving the AppExpert utility. This option brings up the New Project dialog box, shown in Figure 1.20. The dialog box enables you to specify the following information:

- The path and name of the new project.
- The target name (that is, the name of the .EXE file).
- The target type, which can be one of the following:
    - A Windows .EXE application.
    - A Windows .DLL dynamic library.
    - An EasyWin .EXE program.
    - A .LIB static library.
    - A .LIB import library.
    - A Windows .HLP help file.
- The application's platform, which can be 16-bit Windows 3.x, Win32, DOS standard or DOS overlay.
- The target's memory model, which can be tiny, small, compact, medium, large, or huge (the tiny and huge memory models are only available for DOS targets).
- A variety of choices related to the libraries included.
- The options to specify child node files with .C or .CPP extension along with an optional .RC resource file and a .DEF definition file. The **Advanced** pushbutton control in the dialog box offers these options through a special dialog box.
- The option to select the path for the project. The **Browse** pushbutton control in the dialog box offers this option.

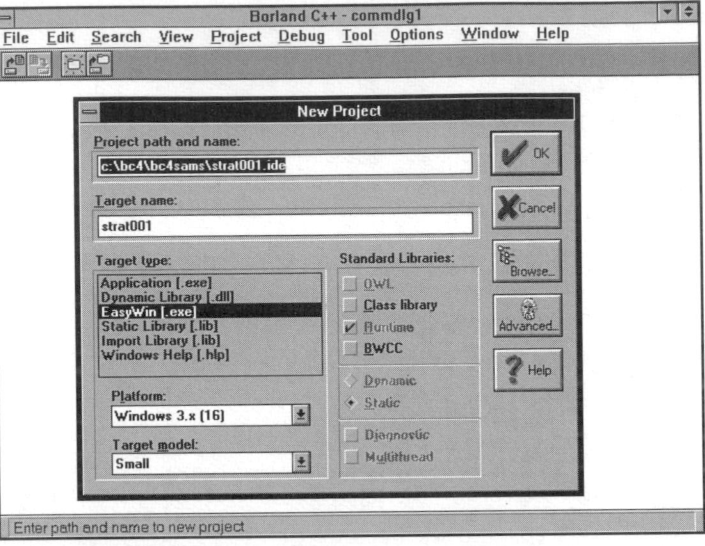

Figure 1.20. *A sample New Project dialog box.*

The Open Project... Option

The **O**pen Project... option enables you to open a new project and automatically close the current one. This option brings up the Open Project File dialog box, which resembles the File Open dialog box. The Project File dialog box enables you to specify the drive, directory, and filename wildcards involved in selecting the .IDE or .PRJ project files. The .IDE project files are new to Borland C++ 4.5 and support multiple targets. The .PRJ project files are available for backward compatibility with previous versions of Borland C++ and are automatically converted to .IDE files.

The Close Project Option

The C**l**ose Project option closes the current project and its edit windows.

The New Target... Option

The New **T**arget... option enables you to add another target to the project. The option first brings up the New Target dialog box, which enables you to enter the name and type of the target. The target type may be AppExpert, Standard, or SourcePool. If you choose the AppExpert target type, the IDE invokes the AppExpert once you

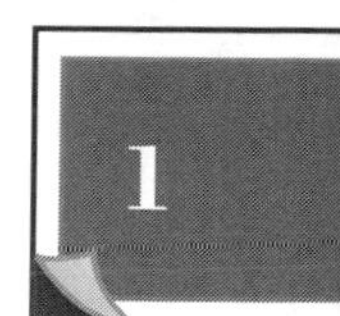

close the New Target dialog box. If you select the Standard target type, the IDE invokes the Add Project dialog box. If you choose the SourcePool target type, the IDE quietly adds a SourcePool target node. The Project window reflects the addition of the new target and indicates its type.

A source pool target contains a set of nodes that are not built in the project. Instead, source pools play the role of templates for creating reference copies, which allow different targets to employ common source code. For example, you can use the source pools in creating a 16-bit .EXE target and a 32-bit .EXE target.

The Compile Option

The **C**ompile option compiles the source code in the active edit window. The option displays the Compile Status dialog box, which informs you of the files being compiled, the number of lines, the number of warnings, and the number of errors. Once the compilation process ends, the Message window displays general messages for the compilation steps and includes warning and error messages generated by the compiler, linker, and other tools. The shortcut key for this option is Alt+F9.

The Make All Option

The **M**ake All option updates the project's target by compiling and linking only those files that have been changed since the previous program make or build operations. The option also uses the Compile Status dialog box to display the progress of the compilation and linking steps. Once this process is terminated, the Message window displays messages that reflect the progress of compiling and linking, along with any warning and error messages.

The Build All Option

The **B**uild All option is similar to the **M**ake All option, except that it systematically recompiles and links all of the project's files.

The Generate Makefile Option

The **G**enerate Makefile option generates a .MAK file. This option opens a new edit window for the .MAK file, creates the contents of the .MAK file, and then displays the contents of the makefile in the new edit window. Listing 1.1 shows a sample COMMDLG1.MAK makefile.

Listing 1.1. The COMMDLG1.MAK file.

```
#
# Borland C++ IDE generated makefile
#
.AUTODEPEND

IDE_TARGET_NAME = steps

#
# Borland C++ tools
#
TLINK    = TLink
TLINK32 = TLink32
IMPLIB  = Implib
TASM    = Tasm
BCC     = Bcc +$(IDE_TARGET_NAME).cfg
BCC32   = Bcc32 +$(IDE_TARGET_NAME).cfg
BRC     = Brc
BRC32   = Brc32

#
# IDE Debug/Release option
#
!if $d(PRJ_DEBUG)

IDE_DBG_LFLAGS = -v
IDE_DBG_CFLAGS = -v

!endif

#
# IDE macros
#


#
# Options
#
IDE_LFLAGS =  -L\BC45\LIB -c -C
IDE_RFLAGS =  -I\BC45\INCLUDE
IDE_BFLAGS =
CLAT_commdlg1dexe =  -ml -WS -D_USEDLL;
LLAT_commdlg1dexe =  -Twe -C -c
RLAT_commdlg1dexe =
BLAT_commdlg1dexe =
CEAT_commdlg1dexe = $(CLAT_commdlg1dexe)
LEAT_commdlg1dexe = $(LLAT_commdlg1dexe)
REAT_commdlg1dexe = $(RLAT_commdlg1dexe)
BEAT_commdlg1dexe = $(BLAT_commdlg1dexe)
CLAT_commdlg1dcpp =
```

```
LLAT_commdlg1dcpp =
RLAT_commdlg1dcpp =
BLAT_commdlg1dcpp =
CEAT_commdlg1dcpp = $(CEAT_commdlg1dexe) $(CLAT_commdlg1dcpp)
LEAT_commdlg1dcpp = $(LEAT_commdlg1dexe) $(LLAT_commdlg1dcpp)
REAT_commdlg1dcpp = $(REAT_commdlg1dexe) $(RLAT_commdlg1dcpp)
BEAT_commdlg1dcpp = $(BEAT_commdlg1dexe) $(BLAT_commdlg1dcpp)
CLAT_commdlg1drc =
LLAT_commdlg1drc =
RLAT_commdlg1drc =
BLAT_commdlg1drc =
CEAT_commdlg1drc = $(CEAT_commdlg1dexe) $(CLAT_commdlg1drc)
LEAT_commdlg1drc = $(LEAT_commdlg1dexe) $(LLAT_commdlg1drc)
REAT_commdlg1drc = $(REAT_commdlg1dexe) $(RLAT_commdlg1drc)
BEAT_commdlg1drc = $(BEAT_commdlg1dexe) $(BLAT_commdlg1drc)

#
# Dependency List
#
Dep_steps = \
   commdlg1.exe

steps : $(IDE_TARGET_NAME).cfg $(Dep_steps)
#  $(MakeNode) steps

Dep_commdlg1dexe = \
   commdlg1.obj\
   commdlg1.res\
   commdlg1.def

commdlg1.exe : $(Dep_commdlg1dexe)
  $(TLINK)   @&&¦
 $(IDE_DBG_LFLAGS) +
 $(IDE_LFLAGS) $(LEAT_commdlg1dexe) +
C:\BC45\LIB\c0wl.obj+
commdlg1.obj
$<,$*
C:\BC45\LIB\bidsi.lib+
C:\BC45\LIB\owlwi.lib+
C:\BC45\LIB\import.lib+
C:\BC45\LIB\crtldll.lib
commdlg1.def
¦
   $(BRC) commdlg1.res $<

commdlg1.obj :  commdlg1.cpp
  $(BCC)   -c $(CEAT_commdlg1dcpp) -o$@ commdlg1.cpp

commdlg1.res :  commdlg1.rc
  $(BRC) $(IDE_RFLAGS) $(REAT_commdlg1drc) -R -FO$@ commdlg1.rc
```

continues

Listing 1.1. continued

```
# Compiler configuration file
$(IDE_TARGET_NAME).cfg :
   Copy &&¦
$(IDE_DBG_CFLAGS)
-I\BC45\INCLUDE
¦ $(IDE_TARGET_NAME).cfg
```

The Debug Menu

The Debug menu provides you with options that enable you to manage debugging and executing your C or C++ source code. Table 1.6 summarizes the options in the Debug menu.

Table 1.6. Summary of the options in the Debug menu.

Command	Shortcut Keys	Function
Run	Ctrl+F9	Runs the program of the current target. If necessary, this option also compiles and links the project source-code files.
Step over	F8	Single-steps through the next statement without tracing the statements of functions that are called in the next statement.
Trace into	F7	Single-steps through the next statement and also traces the statements of functions that are called in the next statement.
Toggle brea**k**point	F5	Toggles making the line at the current cursor location an unconditional breakpoint.
Find execution		Shows the source code at the point of execution.
Pause program		Pauses the program and switches to the debugger.

Command	Shortcut Keys	Function
Terminate program	Ctrl+F2	Stops the program and restarts it from the beginning.
Add watch...	Ctrl+F5	Opens the Watch Properties dialog box to add a variable to watch.
Add breakpoint...		Opens the Breakpoint Properties dialog box to add a breakpoint.
Evaluate/Modify...		Evaluates an expression and modifies the value in a variable.
Inspect...	Alt+F5	Inspects the contents of a variable.
Load symbol table...		Loads DLL symbol table.

The Tool Menu

The Tool menu provides you with access to several programming utilities. The IDE Tools... option in the Options menu enables you to customize the list of programming tools that appear in the Tool menu. Table 1.7 summarizes the default options in the Tool menu.

Table 1.7. Summary of the default options in the Tool menu.

Command	Shortcut Keys	Function
TDW		Invokes the Turbo Debugger for Windows to work with the current target node.
Resource Workshop		Invokes the Resource Workshop utility.
Grep		Runs the Grep utility on the currently selected nodes.
WinSight		Invokes the WinSight utility to monitor Windows messages.

continues

Table 1.7. continued

Command	Shortcut Keys	Function
WinSpector		Runs the WinSpector utility to perform postmortem analysis.
Key map compiler		Compiles the IDE key map file.

The Options Menu

The Options menu enables you to fine-tune the operations of the compiler, linker, editor, and all of the other components of the IDE. Table 1.8 summarizes the options in the Options menu.

Table 1.8. Summary of the options in the Options menu.

Command	Shortcut Keys	Function
Project...		Inspects and edits the setting of the current project.
Environment...		Views and edits the setting of the environment.
Tools...		Adds or deletes (or both) tools in the Tool commands.
Style Sheets...		Edits the options style sheets.
Save...		Configures to save the project, desktop, and environment.

The Project... Option

The **P**roject... option displays the dialog box with the title "Style Sheet: Default Project Options," as shown in Figure 1.21. The Project Option dialog box contains a list of topics that influence the appearance of commenting text and the controls for each topic. The Project Options topics are these:

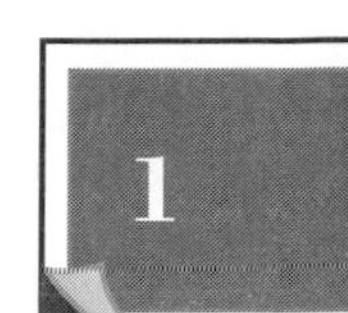

- The Directories topic, which enables you to specify the directories for the include, library, and source code files, as well as to specify the paths for intermediate and final files.
- The Compiler topic, which enables you to fine-tune the compiling of C and C++ source code, specify the preprocessor definitions, manage the inclusion of debug information, and manage precompiled header files.
- The 16-bit Compiler topic, which enables you to manage compiling for 16-bit Windows 3.x applications, select the processor type, and choose the memory model for the compiled files.
- The 32-bit Compiler topic, which enables you to generate 32-bit Windows applications (aimed at Win32s and Windows NT) and specify the processor type.
- The C++ Options topic, which assists you in determining how the C++ compiler interprets your source code to manage new and old C++ language features.
- The Optimizations topic, which enables you to fine-tune the generation of the program or library code to make that code smaller or faster, or to perform general optimization.
- The Messages topic, which enables you to determine the kind of messages emitted during the creation of the program. The options in the Message topic allows you to choose anything from a very strict to a very relaxed level of warnings and errors.
- The Linker topic, which enables you to control the creation of .OBJ, and .LIB files, which are united into the executable .EXE files.
- The Librarian section, which enables you to combine a set of .OBJ files into a .LIB file and control this process.
- The Resources section, which enables you to specify the target Windows version in order to create the right kind of .RES compiled resource file and how it is bound to the .EXE.
- The Make section, which offers options that control the integrated make process.

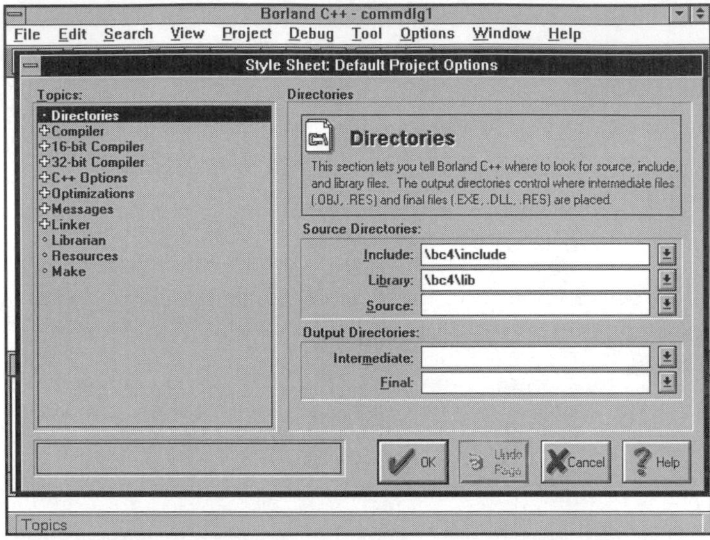

Figure 1.21. *A sample session with the Project Options dialog box.*

The Environment... Option

The **E**nvironment... option brings up the Environment Options dialog box, shown in Figure 1.22, which enables you to customize various aspects of the IDE. These aspects are organized and controlled by the following sections that appear in the dialog box:

- The Editor topic, which controls the operations of the IDE's text editor. The Editor's subtopics allow you to select the default text editor (which is similar to WordStar), select the IDE classical text editor, to emulate the BRIEF editor, to emulate the Epsilon editor, or to customize various aspects of the current text editor.
- The Syntax Highlighting topic, which enables you to determine both the color and style used by the editor to display the source code. The syntax topic offers a few predefined sets of colors and styles.
- The Browser topic, which enables you to determine the default filters for the Browser. In addition, the topic enables you to request the creation of new windows as you traverse through the hierarchy of classes.

- The Debugger topic, which enables you to select between hard mode and soft mode debugging and to select smart mode debugging. (The hard and soft debugging modes determine how the Windows messages are intercepted by the debugger.) In addition, this topic enables you to select the capture of Windows messages, output messages, and breakpoints.
- The Speedbar section, which enables you to customize the location and contents of the speed bar.
- The Preferences section, which provides you with options related to saving various IDE components, such as the editor files, the environment, the desktop, and the project. The section also provides you with options to specify which parts of the desktop to save.
- The Project View section, which provides options that determine the kind of information to include in the Project window—code size, data size, location, name, number of lines, node type, and so on.

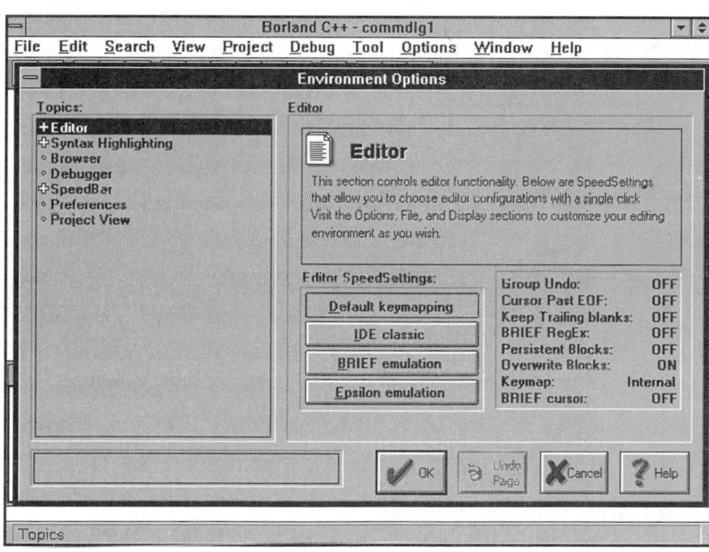

Figure 1.22. *A sample session with the Environment Options dialog box.*

The Tools... Option

The Tools... option enables you to add new menu items to the Tool menu and to delete items from that menu. Figure 1.23 shows the Tools dialog box, which contains

a Tools list box that shows you the available tools. If you click the **Edit** pushbutton, the dialog box brings up the Tools Options dialog box, as shown in Figure 1.24. The latter dialog box enables you to specify the name of the tool, along with its path, command line, menu text, and help hint (which appears in the status line).

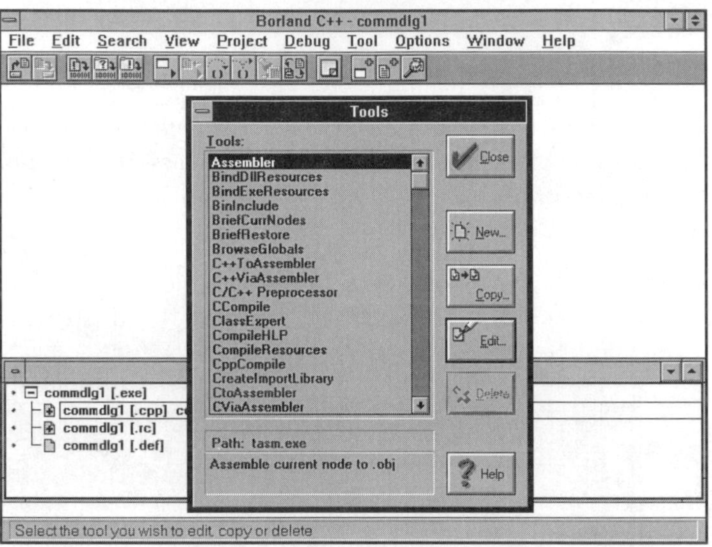

Figure 1.23. *The Tools dialog box.*

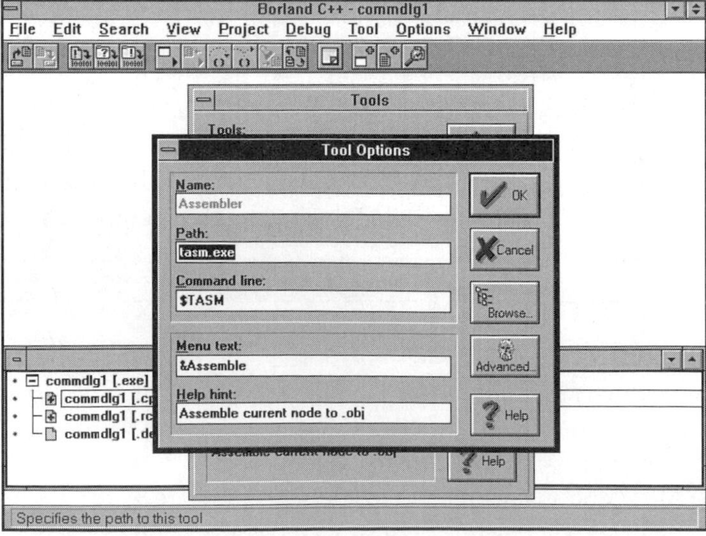

Figure 1.24. *The Tools Options dialog box.*

The Style Sheets... Option

The Style Sheets... option displays the Style Sheet dialog box, shown in Figure 1.25, which enables you to select a configuration for the compile and runtime settings for a project. Each style sheet is a predefined collection of settings that can be affiliated with a node.

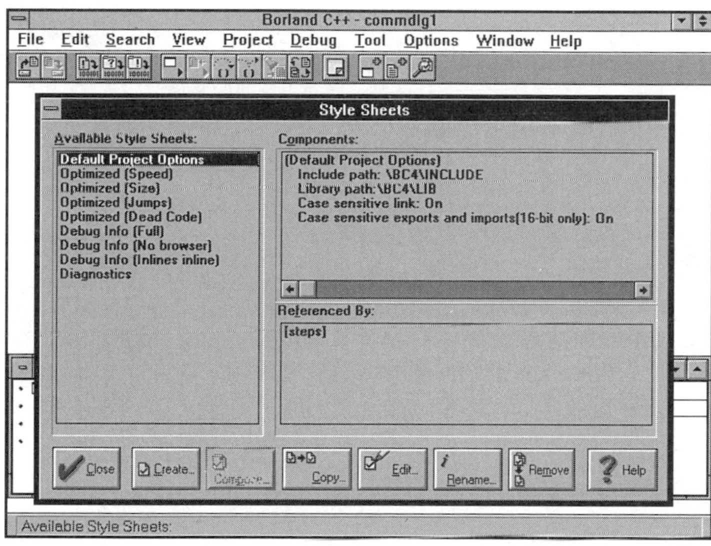

Figure 1.25. *The Style Sheet dialog box.*

The Save... Option

The **S**ave... option enables you to specify to automatically save the desktop, environment, and project file. This option invokes the Save Options dialog box, which offers check boxes for saving these three IDE components.

The Window Menu

The Window menu offers options to manage windows in the IDE client area. These options, which are summarized in Table 1.9, allow you to arrange, close, minimize, and restore some or all of the windows. In addition to the standard options, the Window menu also lists the current windows.

Table 1.9. Summary of the options in the Window menu.

Command	Shortcut Keys	Function
Cascade	Shift+F5	Cascades the windows in the client area of the IDE.
Tile	Shift+F4	Tiles the windows horizontally on the client area of the IDE.
Tile vertical		Tiles the windows vertically on the client area of the IDE.
Arrange icons		Arranges the icons in the client area of the IDE.
Close all		Closes all windows— debugger windows, browser windows, or editor windows.
Minimize all		Minimizes all windows, debugger windows, browser windows, or editor windows.
Restore all		Restores all windows, debugger windows, browser windows, or editor windows.

The Help Menu

The Help menu provides you with the kind of online help you may have gotten from other software. Table 1.10 summarizes the options in the Help menu.

Table 1.10. Summary of the options in the Help menu.

Command	Shortcut Keys	Function
Contents		Displays the table of contents for the online help system.
Keyword search	F1	Displays help regarding the keyword upon which the cursor is situated.
Keyboard		Displays information about the mapping of the keyboard.

Command	Shortcut Keys	Function
Using **h**elp		Displays information to assist you in using the online help system.
About...		Displays information regarding the software version and copyright.

The EasyWin Applications

The Borland C++ IDE enables you to build a special kind of program called an EasyWin application. This application is a cross between an MS-DOS program and a Windows program. The programs in Days 1 through 12 of this book are EasyWin applications that enable you to focus on learning C++ using a DOS-like interface and input/output procedure. The EasyWin window is the standard input and output for C++ programs (compiled as EasyWin applications). The EasyWin window has a simple menu with few options and a few selections.

To create an EasyWin application, perform the following steps:

1. Load the Borland C++ IDE.
2. Choose the Project menu from the menu bar.
3. Select the **N**ew Project command to invoke the New Project dialog box.
4. Enter the path and name of the .IDE project file in the topmost edit box. The dialog box echoes the pathname (as you type it) in the Target name edit box (that is, it makes the program name match the name of the project). You need to edit the target name if the name of the program does not match the name of the .IDE project file. You can use the **Browse...** pushbutton to select the directory that will contain the project files.
5. Click the **Advanced...** pushbutton to invoke the Advanced Options dialog box. Select the check box labeled **.cpp node**. This selection causes the IDE to insert the .CPP node for the EasyWin source-code file. Close the Advanced Options dialog box.
6. Select the **EasyWin [.exe]** item in the Target type list box.
7. Click the **OK** pushbutton to create the new project file.

8. The IDE displays the Project window, which lists the nodes for the various programs. When you first create a project file, the Project window will have only one node.

9. Click the main node to view the files contained in that node. The nodes of EasyWin programs contain only one file, a .CPP file, which has the source code. Double-click the .CPP file to request editing the file. Initially, the source window for the .CPP file is empty.

10. Enter the source code for the EasyWin program.

11. Press the Ctrl+F9 keys to compile, link, and run the EasyWin program. The compiler flags any errors and lists them in the Message window. If the EasyWin program is correct, the IDE will launch it.

You can add more than one program in an .IDE file. We suggest that you group the programs of each of the first twelve days in .IDE files named DAY1.IDE, DAY2.IDE, and so on. Grouping related program files in a single IDE saves space because the .IDE files are not small.

To add another node to an existing .IDE file, you perform the following steps:

1. Load the Borland C++ IDE.
2. Choose the Project menu from the menu bar.
3. Select the New **T**arget command to invoke the New Target dialog box.
4. Enter the name of the new program and click the **OK** pushbutton.
5. The IDE displays the New Project dialog box. Simply click the **OK** pushbutton to add a new program node in the Project window.
6. The IDE displays the Project window, which lists the new nodes for the new program.

Your First C++ Program

The first C++ program presented in this book displays a one-line greeting message. This simple program enables you to see the very basic components of a C++ program.

Listing 1.2 contains the source code for the program HELLO.CPP with numbered lines. Do *not* enter the line numbers when you type in the program. These line numbers serve as reference only. This simple program displays the string `Hello Programmer!` Carry out the following steps to create and run this first C++ program:

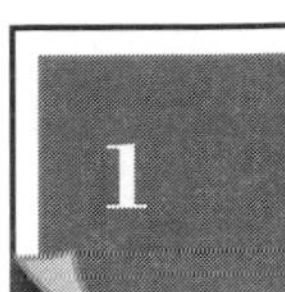

1. Load the Borland C++ IDE if it is not already loaded.
2. Choose the Project menu from the menu bar.
3. Select the **N**ew Project command to invoke the New Project dialog box.
4. Enter `\bc45\bc21day\hello.ide` in the edit box requesting the Project path and name. The dialog box also shows the name `"hello"` in the Target name edit box.
5. Click the **Advanced...** pushbutton to invoke the Advanced Options dialog box. Select the check box labeled **.cpp Node**. Close the Advanced Options dialog box.
6. Select the **EasyWin [.exe]** item in the Target type list box.
7. Click the **OK** pushbutton to create the new project file.
8. The IDE displays the Project window, which lists the node for the hello program.
9. Click the hello.exe node to view the hello.cpp node. Double-click the hello.cpp node to invoke the IDE editor.
10. Enter in the new window the program shown in Listing 1.2.
11. Choose the Save **A**s... command in the File menu. Save the C++ programs as HELLO.CPP in directory \BC45\BC21DAY.
12. Press the Ctrl+F9 keys to compile, link, and run the HELLO.EXE program.

When an EasyWin program ends, the runtime system alters the title of the program's window to include the word *Inactive*. To close the program's window, select the **C**lose command from the system menu, or simply press the Alt+F4 keys.

Listing 1.2. Source code for the program HELLO.CPP.

```
// a trivial C++ program that says hello

#include <iostream.h>

main()
{
  cout << "Hello Programmer!";
  return 0;
}
```

The output of the program appears in Figure 1.26. Notice that the caption of the output window starts with the word *Inactive* to indicate that the program has terminated.

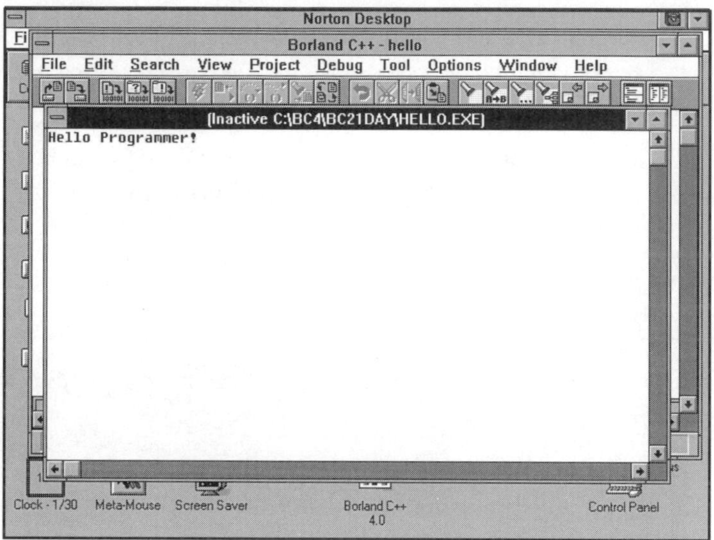

Figure 1.26. *The output of the HELLO.EXE program.*

Examine the short code of the C++ program and notice the following characteristics:

- C++ uses the `//` characters for comments that go to the end of the line. C++ also supports the C-style comments that begin with the `/*` characters and end with the `*/` characters. Line 1 contains a comment that briefly describes the program.

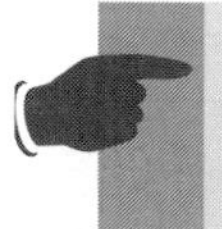

New Term: *Comments* are remarks that you put in the program to explain or clarify certain parts of the program. The compiler ignores comments.

- The C++ program has no reserved keywords that declare the end of a program. In fact, C++ uses a rather simple scheme for organizing a program. This scheme supports two levels of code: global and single-level functions. In

addition, the function `main`, which starts in line 5, plays a very special role because runtime execution begins with this function. Therefore, there can be only a single function `main` in a C++ program. You can place the function `main` anywhere in the code.

- The C++ strings and characters are enclosed in double and single quotes, respectively. Thus, `'A'` is a single character whereas `"A"` is a single-character string. Mixing C++ single-character strings and characters is not allowed.

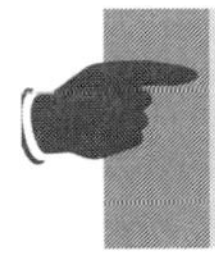

New Term: Strings can have any number of characters, including no characters. A string without any characters is called the *empty string*.

- C++ defines blocks using the `{` and `}` characters. See examples in lines 6 and 9, respectively.
- Every statement in a C++ program must end with a semicolon (`;`).
- C++ contains the `#include` compiler directive. An example of this is in line 3, instructing the Borland C++ compiler to include the IOSTREAM.H header file. C++ extends the notion of streams, which already exists in C. IOSTREAM.H provides the operations that support basic stream input and output. The C++ language does not include built-in I/O routines. Instead, the language relies on libraries specializing in various types of I/O.

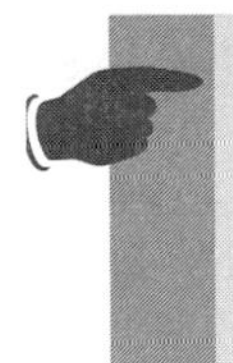

New Term: A *compiler directive* is a special instruction for the compiler. A *header file* contains the declarations of constants, data types, variables, and forward (early) declarations of functions. A *stream* is a sequence of data flowing from one part of a computer to another.

- The C++ program outputs the string `Hello Programmer!` to the standard output stream `cout`, which is the EasyWin window. In addition, the program uses the extractor operator, <<, to send the emitted string to the output stream.
- The function `main` must return a value that reflects the error status of the C++ program. Returning the value `0` signals to the operating system that the program terminated normally.

Exiting the IDE

To exit the IDE, choose the Exit command in the File menu.

Summary

Today's lesson introduced you to the Borland C++ IDE and presented you with the first C++ program. You learned these basics:

- C++ programs are modular and rely on standard and custom libraries.
- The two ways to load the Borland C++ IDE are clicking the Borland C++ icon or double-clicking the BCW.EXE file when using the File Manager (or any similar utility).
- The Borland C++ IDE is a versatile environment for developing, maintaining, and debugging C and C++ programs and libraries for MS-DOS and Windows applications.
- The File menu manages the creation of new files, the opening of files, the saving of files, printing, and exiting the IDE.
- The Edit menu offers options to perform popular editing operations (such as undo, cut, copy, paste, and delete).
- The Search menu enables you to find and replace text, as well as to browse through symbols, locate functions, and visit the offending source-code lines.
- The View menu enables you to view a wide variety of information. Among the viewable information are the project nodes, compiler and linker messages, the hierarchy of the project classes, global symbols, watched variables, the stack of called functions, and the CPU registers.
- The Project menu provides options to create, open, close and manage a project. The project options enable you to compile and link related source code files.
- The Debug menu offers options that enable you to debug and single-step in the source code from within the IDE and watch the values of variables in the Watch window.

- The Tool menu enables quick access to a variety of Windows programming tools, such as the Turbo Debugger for Windows, the message-tracing WinSight utility, the postmortem WinSpector utility, and your own tools.
- The Options menu enables you to fine-tune various aspects of your project—environment, tools, and project style sheets.
- The Window menu is for managing, arranging, closing, and restoring the windows in the IDE desktop.
- The Help menu provides you with the online help.
- The EasyWin applications are Windows applications providing special windows that act as standard input and output devices. EasyWin applications allow you to write DOS-like programs.
- The first C++ program in this book is a simple greeting program that illustrates the basic components of a C++ program. These components include comments, the `#include` directive, and the `main` function.
- You exit the IDE through the E**x**it selection in the File menu.

Q&A

Q Does C++ use line numbers?

A No. We are using line numbers in the listings in this book only for the sake of reference.

Q Does the IDE's editor monitor what I type?

A Yes, it does. In fact, when you type a C++ keyword, the IDE quickly colors that keyword.

Q What happens if I forget to type the second double quote in the first program?

A The compiler tells you that there is an error in the program. You need to add the second double quote and build the project.

Q How do I delete text in the currently edited window?

A Use the Replace selection in the Edit option and specify nothing for the replacement string, or use the Edit menu's cut and clear commands.

Workshop

The Workshop provides quiz questions to help you solidify your understanding of the material covered and exercises to provide you with experience in using what you've learned. Try to understand the quiz and exercise answers before continuing on to the next day's lesson. (Answers are provided in Appendix A, "Answers.")

Quiz

1. What is the output of the following program?

```
// quiz program #1

#include <iostream.h>

main()
{
  cout << "C++ in 21 Days?";
  return 0;
}
```

2. What is the output of the following program?

```
// quiz program #2

#include <iostream.h>

main()
{
  // cout << "C++ in 21 Days?";
  return 0;
}
```

3. What is wrong with the following program?

```
// quiz program #3

#include <iostream.h>

main()
{
```

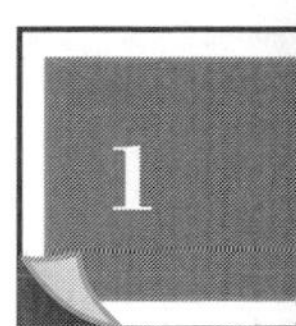

```
   cout << "C++ in 21 Days?"
   return 0;
}
```

Exercise

Write a program that displays the message `I am a C++ Programmer`.

C++ Program Components

WEEK 1

Day 1 presented the Borland IDE and a simple C++ program. Today you will focus on the basic components of C++ programs, including data types, variables, constants, and functions. You will learn about the following topics:

- The predefined data types in Borland C++ 4.5
- Naming items in Borland C++ 4.5
- The `#include` directive
- Declaring variables
- Declaring constants
- Declaring and prototyping functions
- Local variables in functions
- Static variables in functions
- Inline functions
- Exiting functions
- Default arguments
- Function overloading

Predefined Data Types in Borland C++ 4.5

Borland C++ 4.5 offers the `int`, `char`, `float`, `double`, and `void` data types to represent integers, characters, single-precision floating-point numbers, double-precision floating-point numbers, and valueless data, respectively. C++ uses the `void` type with a function's returned values to indicate that the function does not yield a significant result—that is, the function acts as a procedure.

C++ adds more flexibility to data types by supporting data type modifiers. The type modifiers are as follows: `signed`, `unsigned`, `short`, and `long`. Table 2.1 shows the predefined data types in C++ (and includes the type modifiers), along with their sizes and ranges. Notice that `int` and `unsigned int` are system-dependent. The table shows the 16-bit values for the predefined data types in C++.

New Term: *Data type modifiers* alter the precision and the range of values.

Table 2.1. Predefined data types in C++.

Data Type	Byte Size	Range	Examples
`bool`	1	`false` or `true`	`true`, `false`
`char`	1	–128 to 127	`'A','!'`
`signed char`	1	–128 to 127	`23`
`unsigned char`	1	0 to 255	`200,0x1a`
`int`	2	Depends on system –32768 to 32767 for 16-bit	`3000`
`unsigned int`	2	Depends on system 0 to 65535 for 16-bit	`0xffff`, `65535`
`short int`	2	–32768 to 32767	`100`
`unsigned short int`	2	0 to 65535	`0xff`, `40000`
`long int`	4	–2147483648 to 2147483647	`0xfffff`, `-123456`
`unsigned long int`	4	0 to 4294967295	`123456`
`float`	4	3.4E–38 to 3.4E+38 and –3.4E–38 to –3.4E+38	`2.35`, `-52.354`, `1.3e+10`
`double`	8	1.7E–308 to 1.7E+308 and –1.7E–308 to –1.7E+308	`12.354`, `-2.5e+100`, `-78.32544`
`long double`	10	3.4E–4932 to 1.1E+4932 and –1.1E–4932 to –3.4E+4932	`8.5e-3000`

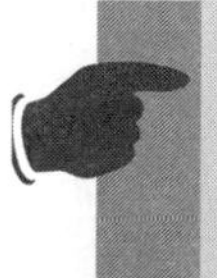

New Term: C++ supports *hexadecimal numbers*. Such numbers begin with the characters `0x`, followed by the hexadecimal value. For example, the number `0xff` is the hexadecimal equivalent of the decimal number 255.

Naming Items in Borland C++ 4.5

Borland C++ 4.5 requires you to observe the following rules with identifiers:

1. The first character must be a letter or an underscore (_).
2. Subsequent characters can be letters, digits, or underscores.
3. The maximum length of an identifier is 32 characters.
4. Identifiers are case-sensitive in C++. Thus, the names `rate`, `RATE`, and `Rate` refer to three different identifiers.
5. Identifiers cannot be reserved words, such as `int`, `double`, or `static` to name just a few.

The following are examples of valid identifiers:

```
X
x
aString
DAYS_IN_WEEK
BinNumber0
bin_number_0
bin0Number2
_length
```

DO	DON'T

DO use descriptive names that have a reasonable length.

DON'T use identifier names that are too short or too long. Short names yield poor readability, and long names are prone to typographical errors.

The *#include* Directive

You will recall that a *directive* is a special instruction for C and C++ compilers. A directive begins with the `#` character and is followed by the directive name. Directives are usually placed in the first column of a line. They can be preceded only by spaces or tab characters. The C++ program in Day 1 contains the `#include` directive. This directive tells the compiler to include the text of a file as if you have typed that text yourself. Thus, the `#include` directive is a better alternative than cutting text from one file and pasting it in another file. Recall from Day 1 that programs use the `#include` directive to include header files.

Syntax

The *#include* Directive

The general syntax for the #include directive is

```
#include <filename>
#include "filename"
```

Examples:

```
#include <iostream.h>
#include "string.h"
```

The filename represents the name of the included file. The two forms differ in how the `#include` directive searches for the included file. The first form searches for the file in the special directory for included files. The second form extends the search to involve the current directory before searching the include directory.

Declaring Variables

Declaring variables requires you to state the data type of the variable and the name of the variable. The word *variable* indicates that you can alter the data of these data containers.

New Term: *Variables* are identifiers used to store and recall information. You can regard a variable as a labeled data container.

Syntax

Declaring Variables

The general syntax for declaring variables is

```
type variableName;
type variableName = initialValue;
type var1 [= initVal1], var2 [= initVal2], ...;
```

Examples:

```
int j;
double z = 32.314;
long fileSize, diskSize, totalFileSize = 0;
```

C++ enables you to declare a list of variables (that have the same types) in a declarative statement, for example:

```
int j, i = 2, k = 3;
double x = 3.12;
double y = 2 * x, z = 4.5, a = 45.7;
```

The initializing values may contain other variables defined earlier.

DO | **DON'T**

DO resist using global variables.

DON'T declare variables within the same program unit with names that are different in character case (such as `rate` and `Rate`).

Let's look at a simple example that uses variables. Listing 2.1 shows the source code for the program VAR1.CPP. The program declares four variables, two of which are initialized during their declarations. The program then assigns values to the uninitialized variables and displays the contents of all four variables. Create the project DAY2.IDE (in the directory \BC45\BC21DAY) and include the VAR1.CPP file as a node. Compile and run the VAR1.EXE program.

Type

Listing 2.1. Source code for the program VAR1.CPP.

```
// C++ program that illustrates simple variables

#include <iostream.h>

main()
{
  int i, j = 2;
  double x, y = 355.0 / 113;

  i = 3 * j;
  cout << "i = " << i << "\n"
       << "j = " << j << "\n";

  x = 2 * y;
  x = x * x;
  cout << "y = " << y << "\n"
       << "x = " << x << "\n";
  return 0;

}
```

Here is a sample session with the program in Listing 2.1:

```
i = 6
j = 2
y = 3.14159
x = 39.4784
```

The program uses the `#include` directive in line 3 to include the stream I/O header file IOSTREAM.H. The function `main` appears in line 5. The function contains the declarations of the `int`-typed variables `i` and `j` in line 7, and the `double`-typed variables `x` and `y` in line 8. The declarations initialize the variable `j` and `y`. The statement in line 10 multiplies the value in variable `j` (which is 2) by 3 and stores the result in variable `i`. The stream output statement in lines 11 and 12 displays the values of variables `i` and `j`. The statement includes strings that label the output.

The statement in line 14 doubles the value in variable `y` and stores it in variable `x`. The statement in line 15 squares the value in variable `x` and assigns the result back to variable `x`. This statement uses the variable `x` on both sides of the equal sign. The stream output statement in lines 16 and 17 displays the values in variables `x` and `y`. The statement in line 18 returns 0 as the result of function `main`.

Declaring Constants

Many languages, such as BASIC (the more recent implementations), Modula-2, Ada, C, Pascal, and C++, support constants. No one can deny that constants enhance the readability of a program by replacing numeric constants with identifiers that are more descriptive. Moreover, using constants enables you to change the value of a program parameter by merely changing the value of that parameter in one location. This capability is more convenient and less prone to generate the errors that may occur when you employ your text editor to replace certain numbers with other numbers.

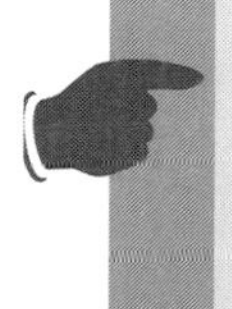

New Term: *Constants* are identifiers that are associated with fixed values. C++ offers constants in two varieties: *macro-based* and *formal*. The macro-based constants are inherited from C and use the `#define` compiler directive.

Syntax

The *#define* Directive

The general syntax for the `#define` directive is

```
#define constantName constantValue
```

The `#define` directive causes the compiler to invoke the preprocessor and perform text substitution to replace the macro-based constants with their values. This text replacement step occurs before the compiler processes the statements in the source file. Consequently, the compiler never sees the macro-based constants themselves—only what they expand to.

Examples:

```
#define ASCII_A 65
#define DAYS_IN_WEEK 7
```

The second type of constant in C++ is the formal constant.

Syntax

The Formal Constant

The general syntax for the formal constant is

```
const dataType constantName = constantValue;
```

The *dataType* item is an optional item that specifies the data type of the constant values. If you omit the data type, the C++ compiler assumes the `int` type.

Examples:

```
const unsigned char ASCII_A = 65;
const DAYS_IN_WEEK = 7;
const char FIRST_DISK_DRIVE = 'A';
```

DO | **DON'T**

DO use uppercase names for constants. This naming style enables you to determine quickly if an identifier is a constant.

DON'T assume that other people who read your code will know what embedded numbers mean. Use declared constants to enhance the readability of your programs.

Using Macro-Based Constants

Now consider an example that uses macro-based constants. Listing 2.2 shows the source code for the program CONST1.CPP. The program prompts you to enter the number of hours, minutes, and seconds since midnight. The program then calculates and displays the total number of seconds since midnight. Add the CONST1.CPP file as a node in the project file DAY2.IDE and remove VAR1.CPP. Compile and run the CONST1.EXE program by pressing Ctrl+F9.

Listing 2.2. Source code for the program CONST1.CPP.

```
// C++ program that illustrates constants

#include <iostream.h>

#define SEC_IN_MIN 60
#define MIN_IN_HOUR 60

main()
{
  long hours, minutes, seconds;
  long totalSec;

  cout << "Enter hours: ";
  cin >> hours;
  cout << "Enter minutes: ";
  cin >> minutes;
  cout << "Enter seconds: ";
  cin >> seconds;

  totalSec = ((hours * MIN_IN_HOUR + minutes) *
               SEC_IN_MIN) + seconds;

  cout <<"\n\n" << totalSec << " seconds since midnight";
  return 0;
}
```

Here is a sample session with the program in Listing 2.2:

```
Enter hours: 10
Enter minutes: 0
Enter seconds: 0


36000 seconds since midnight
```

The program uses the `#include` directive in line 3 to include the header file IOSTREAM.H. Lines 5 and 6 contain the `#define` directive that declares the macro-based constants `SEC_IN_MIN` and `MIN_IN_HOUR`. Both constants have the value 60, but each value has a different meaning. The function `main`, which starts at line 8, declares four `long`-typed variables: `hours`, `minutes`, `seconds`, and `totalSec`.

The function uses pairs of statements to output the prompting messages and receive input. Line 13 contains the stream output statement that prompts you for the number of hours. Line 14 contains the stream input statement. The identifier `cin` is the name of the standard input stream and uses the *insertion operator* >> to read data from the keyboard and to store it in the variable `hours`. The input and output statements in lines 15 through 18 perform a similar task of prompting for input and obtaining keyboard input.

Line 20 contains a statement that calculates the total number of seconds since midnight and stores the result in the variable `totalSec`. The statement uses the macro-based constants `MIN_IN_HOUR` and `SEC_IN_MIN`. As you can see, using these constants enhances the readability of the statement, compared to using the number 60 in place of both constants. Line 23 contains a stream output statement that displays the total number of seconds since midnight (stored in the variable `totalSec`), followed by qualifying text to clarify the output.

Using Formal Constants

Now let's look at a new version of the program, one that uses the formal C++ constants. Listing 2.3 shows the source code for the program CONST2.CPP. This program works like the CONST1.CPP program. Add the CONST2.CPP file as a node in the project file DAY2.IDE. Compile and run the CONST2.EXE program by pressing the Ctrl+F9 keys.

Note: At this point, we assume that you are familiar with the process of creating the .CPP source file, creating the .IDE project file, and adding .CPP files as nodes in the project file. From now on we will not mention creating these files, unless there is a special set of source files in a project.

Listing 2.3. Source code for the program CONST2.CPP.

```
1:  // C++ program that illustrates constants
2:
3:  #include <iostream.h>
4:
5:  const SEC_IN_MIN = 60; // global constant
6:
7:  main()
8:  {
9:    const MIN_IN_HOUR = 60; // local constant
10:
11:   long hours, minutes, seconds;
12:   long totalSec;
13:
14:   cout << "Enter hours: ";
15:   cin >> hours;
16:   cout << "Enter minutes: ";
17:   cin >> minutes;
18:   cout << "Enter seconds: ";
19:   cin >> seconds;
20:
21:   totalSec = ((hours * MIN_IN_HOUR + minutes) *
22:                SEC_IN_MIN) + seconds;
23:
24:   cout <<"\n\n" << totalSec << " seconds since midnight";
25:   return 0;
26: }
```

Here is a sample session with the program in Listing 2.3:

```
Enter hours: 1
Enter minutes: 10
Enter seconds: 20

4220 seconds since midnight
```

The programs in Listings 2.2 and 2.3 are similar. The difference between them is in how they declare their constants. In Listing 2.3, we use the formal C++ constant syntax to declare the constants. In addition, we declare the constant `SEC_IN_MIN` in line 5, outside the function `main`. This kind of declaration makes the constant global. That is, if there were another function in the program, it would be able to use the constant `SEC_IN_MIN`. By contrast, we declare the constant `MIN_IN_SEC` inside the function `main`. Thus, the constant `MIN_IN_SEC` is local to the function `main`.

Declaring and Prototyping Functions

Most programming languages use functions and procedures. C++ does not support formal procedures. Instead, all C++ routines are functions.

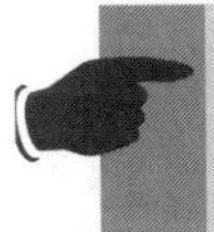

New Term: *Functions* are the primary building blocks that conceptually extend the C++ language to fit your custom programs.

Syntax

Declaring Functions

The general form for the ANSI C style of declaring functions (which is maintained by C++) is

```
returnType functionName(typedParameterList)
```

Examples:

```
double sqr(double y)
{ return y * y; }

char prevChar(char c)
{ return c - 1; }
```

Remember the following rules when declaring C++ functions:

1. The return type of the C++ function appears before the function's name.
2. If the parameter list is empty, you still use empty parentheses. C++ also allows you the option of using the `void` keyword to explicitly state that there are no parameters.
3. The typed parameter list consists of a list of typed parameters that use the following general format:

   ```
   [const] type1 parameter1, [const] type2 parameter2, ...
   ```

   This format shows that the individual parameter is declared like a variable—you state the type first and then the parameter's identifier. The list of parameters in C++ is comma-delimited. In addition, you cannot group a sequence of parameters that have exactly the same data type. You must declare each parameter explicitly. If a parameter has the `const` clause, the

compiler makes sure that the function does *not* alter the arguments of that parameter.

4. The body of a C++ function is enclosed in braces ({}). There is no semicolon after the closing brace.

5. C++ supports passing arguments either by value or by reference. By default, parameters pass their arguments by value. Consequently, the functions work with a copy of the data, preserving the original data. To declare a reference parameter, insert the `&` character after the data type of the parameter. A reference parameter becomes an alias to its arguments. Any changes made to the reference parameter also affect the argument. The general form for reference parameters is

   ```
   [const] type1& parameter1, [const] type2& parameter2, ...
   ```

   If a parameter has the `const` clause, the compiler makes sure that the function does not alter the arguments of that parameter.

6. C++ supports local constants, data types, and variables. Although these data items can appear in nested block statements, C++ does not support nested functions.

7. The `return` keyword returns the function's value.

8. If the function's return type is `void`, you do not have to use the `return` keyword, unless you need to provide an exit route in the middle of the function.

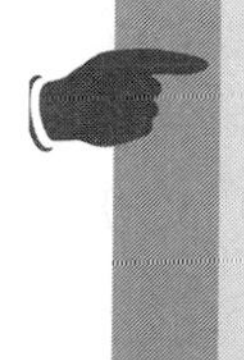

New Term: C++ dictates that you either declare or define a function before you use it. Declaring a function, commonly called *prototyping*, lists the function name, return type, and the number and type of its parameters. Including the name of the parameter is optional. You also need to place a semicolon after the close parenthesis. C++ requires that you declare a function if you call it before you define it.

The following is a simple example of prototyping:

```
// prototype the function square
double sqr(double);

main()
{
```

```
  cout << "5^2 = " << sqr(5) << "\n";
  return 0;
}

double sqr(double z)
{ return z * z; }
```

Notice that the declaration of function sqr only contains the type of its single parameter.

Typically, the declaration of a function is global. You may still prototype a function within its client function. This technique conceals the prototype from other functions.

Calling a function requires that you supply its parameter with arguments. The arguments are mapped onto the parameter by the sequence in which the parameters are declared. The arguments must be data types that match or are compatible with those of the parameters. For example, you may have a function volume, defined as follows:

```
double volume(double length, double width, double height)
{
  return length * width * height;
}
```

To call the function volume, you need to supply double-typed arguments or arguments with compatible types (which, in this case, are all of numeric data types). Here are a number of sample calls to the function volume:

```
double len = 34, width = 55, ht = 100;
int i = 3;
long j = 44;
unsigned k = 33;

cout << volume(len, width, ht) << "\n";
cout << volume(1, 2, 3) << "\n";
cout << volume(i, j, k) << "\n";
cout << volume(len, j, 22.3) << "\n";
```

Note: C++ enables you to discard the result of a function. This kind of function call is used when the focus is on what the function does rather than its return value.

Local Variables in Functions

Good structured-programming techniques foster the notion that functions should be as independent and as reusable as possible. Consequently, functions can have their own data types, constants, and variables to give them this independence.

New Term: The *local variable* in a function exists only when the host function is called. Once the function terminates, the runtime system removes the local variables. Consequently, local variables lose their data between function calls. In addition, the runtime system applies any initialization to local variables every time the host function is called.

DO | **DON'T**

DO use local variables to store and alter the values of parameters that are declared with the `const` clause.

DON'T declare a local variable to have the same name as a global variable that you need to access in the function.

Let's look at an example. Listing 2.4 displays the value of the mathematical function

```
f(X) = X2 - 5 X + 10
```

and its slope at the argument 3.5. The program calculates the slope using the approximation

```
f'(X) = (f(X + h) - f(X - h)) / 2h
```

where `h` is a small increment.

Listing 2.4. Source code for the program VAR2.CPP.

```
// C++ program that illustrates local variables in a function

#include <iostream.h>

double f(double x)
{
  return x * x - 5 * x + 10;
```

continues

Listing 2.4. continued

```
8:  }
9:
10: double slope(double x)
11: {
12:   double f1, f2, incrim = 0.01 * x;
13:   f1 = f(x + incrim);
14:   f2 = f(x - incrim);
15:   return (f1 - f2) / 2 / incrim;
16: }
17:
18: main()
19: {
20:  double x = 3.5;
21:
22:   cout << "f("  << x << ") = " << f(x) << "\n"
23:        << "f'(" << x << ") = " << slope(x) << "\n";
24:
25:   return 0;
26: }
```

Here is a sample session with the program in Listing 2.4:

```
f(3.5) = 4.75
f'(3.5) = 2
```

The program in Listing 2.4 declares three functions, namely `f` (in line 5), `slope` (in line 10), and `main` (in line 18). The function `f` is simple and returns the value of the mathematical function. The function `f` is void of local variables. By contrast, the function `slope` declares the local variables `f1`, `f2`, and `incrim`. This function also initializes the latter variable. Line 13 assigns the value of `f(x + incrim)` to the local variable `f1`. Line 14 assigns the value of `f(x - incrim)` to the local variable `f2`. Line 15 returns the value for function `slope` using the local variables `f1`, `f2`, and `incrim`. The function `main` simply displays the values of the mathematical function and its slope when `x = 3.5`.

Static Variables in Functions

In Listing 2.4, the local variables in the function `slope` lose their values once the function terminates. C++ enables you to declare a local variable as static simply by placing the `static` keyword to the left of its data type. Static variables are usually initialized. This initialization is performed once, when the host function is called for the first time.

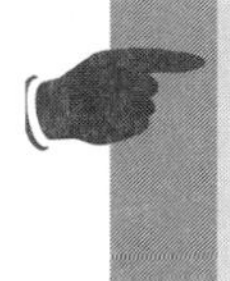

New Term: There are a number of programming techniques that require maintaining the values of local variables between function calls. These special local variables are called *static variables.*

When the host function terminates, the static variables maintain their values. The compiler supports this language feature by storing static variables in a separate memory location that is maintained while the program is running. You can use the same names for static variables in different functions. This duplication does not confuse the compiler because it keeps track of which function owns which static variables.

Let's look at a simple program. Listing 2.5 uses a function with static variables to maintain a moving average. The program supplies its own data and calls that function several times in order to obtain and display the current value of the moving average.

Listing 2.5. Source code for the program STATIC1.CPP.

```
// C++ program that illustrates static local variables

#include <iostream.h>

double mean(double x)
{
  static double sum = 0;
  static double sumx = 0;

  sum = sum + 1;
  sumx = sumx + x;
  return sumx / sum;
}

main()
{
  cout << "mean = " << mean(1) << "\n";
  cout << "mean = " << mean(2) << "\n";
  cout << "mean = " << mean(4) << "\n";
  cout << "mean = " << mean(10) << "\n";
  cout << "mean = " << mean(11) << "\n";
  return 0;
}
```

Here is a sample session with the program in Listing 2.5:

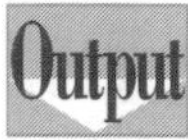

```
mean = 1
mean = 1.5
mean = 2.33333
mean = 4.25
mean = 5.6
```

The program in Listing 2.5 declares the function `mean`, which contains static local variables. Lines 7 and 8 declare the static variables `sum` and `sumx`, respectively. The function initializes both static variables with 0. The statement in line 10 increments the variable `sum` by 1. The statement in line 11 increments the variable `sumx` by the value of parameter `x`. Line 12 returns the updated moving average, obtained by dividing `sumx` by `sum`.

The function `main` issues a series of calls to function `mean`. The stream output statements in lines 17 through 21 display the updated moving average. These results are possible thanks to the static local variables `sum` and `sumx` in function `mean`. If static variables are not supported by C++, you must resort to using global variables—a highly questionable programming choice.

Inline Functions

Using functions requires the overhead of calling them, passing their arguments, and returning their results. C++ enables you to use inline functions that expand into their statements. Thus, inline functions offer faster execution time—especially helpful where speed is critical—at the cost of expanding the code.

Syntax

The *inline* Function

The general syntax for the `inline` function is

```
inline returnType functionName(typedParameterList)
```

Examples:

```
inline double cube(double x)
{ return x * x * x; }

inline char nextChar(char c)
{ return c + 1; }
```

The alternative to using inline functions is the use of the `#define` directive to create macro-based pseudofunctions. Many C++ programmers strongly recommend foregoing this method in favor of inline functions. The justification for this is that inline functions provide type checking. Macros created with the `#define` directive do not.

DO | **DON'T**

DO start by declaring inline functions as ordinary functions when you develop your programs. Non-inline functions are easier to debug. Once your program is working, insert the inline keyword where needed.

DON'T declare inline functions with many statements. The increase in .EXE program size may not be acceptable.

Here is a simple example of a program that uses inline functions. Listing 2.6 contains the source code for the program INLINE1.CPP. This program prompts you for a number, then calculates and displays the square and cube values for your input.

Listing 2.6. Source code for the program INLINE1.CPP.

```
// C++ program that illustrates inline functions

#include <iostream.h>

inline double sqr(double x)
{
  return x * x;
}

inline double cube(double x)
{
  return x * x * x;
}

main()
{
  double x;

  cout << "Enter a number: ";
  cin >> x;

  cout << "square of "  << x << " = " << sqr(x) << "\n"
       << "cube of " << x << " = " << cube(x) << "\n";

  return 0;
}
```

Here is a sample session with the program in Listing 2.6:

```
Enter a number: 2.5
square of 2.5 = 6.25
cube of 2.5 = 15.625
```

The program in Listing 2.6 declares the inline functions `sqr` and `cube`. Each function heading starts with the keyword `inline`. The other aspects of the inline functions resemble short normal functions. The function `main` calls the functions `sqr` and `cube` to display the square and cube values, respectively.

Exiting Functions

Usually you make an early exit from a function because particular conditions do not allow you to proceed with executing the statements in that function. C++ provides the `return` statement to exit from a function. If the function has the `void` type, you then employ the statement `return` and include no expression after the return. By contrast, if you exit a non-`void` function, the return statement should produce a value that indicates the purpose for exiting the function.

Default Arguments

Default arguments are a language feature that is quite simple and yet very powerful. When you omit the argument of a parameter that has a default argument, that argument is automatically used.

Note: C++ permits you to assign default arguments to the parameters of a function.

Using default arguments requires that you follow these rules:

1. Once you assign a default argument to a parameter, you must do so for all subsequent parameters in the same parameter list. You cannot randomly assign default arguments to parameters. This rule means that the parameter list can be divided into two sublists: the leading parameters, which do not have default arguments, and the trailing parameters, which do.
2. You must provide an argument for every parameter that has no default argument.
3. You may omit the argument for a parameter that has a default argument.

4. Once you omit the argument for a parameter with a default argument, the arguments for all subsequent parameters must also be omitted.

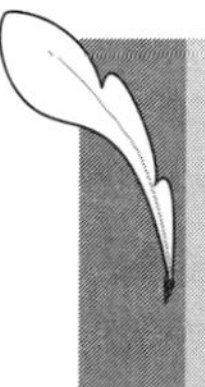

Note: The best way to list the parameters with default arguments is to locate them according to the likelihood of using their default arguments. Place the least-likely-to-be-used arguments first and the most-likely-to-be-used arguments last.

Let's look at a simple example that uses a function with default arguments. Listing 2.7 shows the source code for the program DEFARGS1.CPP. The program prompts you to enter the x and y coordinates of two points. Then the program calculates and displays the distance between the two points and between each point and the origin (0, 0).

Listing 2.7. Source code for the program DEFARGS1.CPP.

```
// C++ program that illustrates default arguments

#include <iostream.h>
#include <math.h>

inline double sqr(double x)
{ return x * x; }

double distance(double x2, double y2,
                double x1 = 0, double y1 = 0)
{
  return sqrt(sqr(x2 - x1) + sqr(y2 - y1));
}

main()
{
  double x1, y1, x2, y2;

  cout << "Enter x coordinate for point 1: ";
  cin >> x1;
  cout << "Enter y coordinate for point 1: ";
  cin >> y1;
  cout << "Enter x coordinate for point 2: ";
  cin >> x2;
  cout << "Enter y coordinate for point 2: ";
```

continues

Listing 2.7. continued

```
26:    cin >> y2;
27:
28:    cout << "distance between points = "
29:         << distance(x1, y1, x2, y2) << "\n";
30:    cout << "distance between point 1 and (0,0) = "
31:         << distance(x1, y1, 0) << "\n";
32:    cout << "distance between point 2 and (0,0) = "
33:         << distance(x2, y2) << "\n";
34:
35:    return 0;
36: }
```

Here is a sample session with the program in Listing 2.7:

```
Enter x coordinate for point 1: 1
Enter y coordinate for point 1: 1
Enter x coordinate for point 2: -1
Enter y coordinate for point 2: 1
distance between points = 2
distance between point 1 and (0,0) = 1.41421
distance between point 2 and (0,0) = 1.41421
```

The program in Listing 2.7 includes not one, but two header files. Line 4 uses the `#include` directive to include the MATH.H header file, which declares the square-root math function, `sqrt`. The program declares the inline `sqr` function in line 6. This function returns the square value of the arguments for parameter `x`. The program also declares the function `distance` with four `double`-typed parameters. The parameters `x2` and `y2` represent the x and y coordinates, respectively, for the second point, whereas the parameters `x1` and `y1` represent the x and y coordinates, respectively, for the first point. Both parameters `x1` and `y1` have the default argument of 0. The function returns the distance between the two points. If you omit the arguments for `x1` and `y1`, the function returns the distance between the point (x2, y2) and the origin (0, 0). If you omit only the argument for the last parameter, the function yields the distance between the points (x2, y2) and (x1, 0).

The function `main` prompts you to enter the x and y coordinates for two points, using the statements in lines 19 through 26. The output statement in lines 28 and 29 calls the function `distance`, providing it with four arguments, namely, `x1`, `y1`, `x2`, and `y2`. Therefore, this call to the function `distance` uses no default arguments. By contrast, the statement in lines 30 and 31 calls the function `distance`, supplying it with only three arguments. This call to the function `distance` uses the default argument for the last parameter. The statement in lines 32 and 33 calls the function `distance`, providing it with only two arguments. This call to the function `distance` uses the two

default arguments for the third and fourth parameters. We can omit the third argument in the second call to the function `distance` and still compile and run the program.

Function Overloading

Function overloading is a language feature in C++ that has no parallel in C, Pascal, or BASIC. This new feature enables you to declare multiple functions that have the same name but different parameter lists. The function's return type is not part of the function signature, because C++ enables you to discard the result type. Consequently, the compiler is not able to distinguish between two functions with the same parameters and different return type when these return types are omitted.

New Term: A parameter list is also called the *function signature.*

Warning: Using default arguments with overloaded functions may duplicate the signature for some of the functions (when the default arguments are used). The C++ compiler is able to detect this ambiguity and generate a compile-time error.

DO	DON'T

DO use default arguments to reduce the number of overloaded functions.

DON'T use overloaded functions to implement different operations.

Let's look at a simple program that uses overloaded functions. Listing 2.8 contains the source code for the program OVERLOAD.CPP. The program performs the following tasks:

- Declares variables that have the `char`, `int`, and `double` types, and initializes them with values

- Displays the initial values
- Invokes overloaded functions that increment the variables
- Displays the updated values stored in the variables

Listing 2.8. Source code for the program OVERLOAD.CPP.

```
// C++ program that illustrates function overloading

#include <iostream.h>

// inc version for int types
void inc(int& i)
{
  i = i + 1;
}

// inc version for double types
void inc(double& x)
{
  x = x + 1;
}

// inc version for char types
void inc(char& c)
{
  c = c + 1;
}

main()
{
  char c = 'A';
  int i = 10;
  double x = 10.2;

  // display initial values
  cout << "c = " << c << "\n"
       << "i = " << i << "\n"
       << "x = " << x << "\n";
  // invoke the inc functions
  inc(c);
  inc(i);
  inc(x);
  // display updated values
  cout << "After using the overloaded inc function\n";
  cout << "c = " << c << "\n"
```

```
40:           << "i = " << i << "\n"
41:           << "x = " << x << "\n";
42:
43:     return 0;
44: }
```


Here is a sample session with the program in Listing 2.8:

```
c = A
i = 10
x = 10.2
After using the overloaded inc function
c = B
i = 11
x = 11.2
```

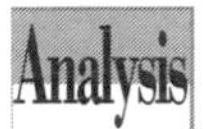

The program in Listing 2.8 declares three versions of the overloaded `void` function `inc`. The first version of function `inc` has an `int`-typed reference parameter, `i`. The function increments the parameter `i` by 1. Because the parameter `i` is a reference to its arguments, the action of function `inc(int&)` affects the argument outside the scope of the function. The second version of function `inc` has a `double`-typed reference parameter, `x`. The function increments the parameter `x` by 1. Because the parameter `x` is a reference to its arguments, the action of function `inc(double&)` affects the argument beyond the scope of the function. The third version of function `inc` has a `char`-typed reference parameter, `c`. The function increments the parameter `c` by 1. The reference parameter affects its arguments outside the scope of the function.

The function `main` declares the variables `c`, `i`, and `x` to have the `char`, `int`, and `double` types, respectively. The function also initializes the variables `c`, `i`, and `x` using the values `'A'`, `10`, and `10.2`, respectively. The statement in lines 30 through 32 displays the initial values in variables `c`, `i`, and `x`. The function `main` invokes the overloaded function `inc` in lines 34 through 36. The call to function `inc` in line 34 ends up calling the function `inc(char&)` because the argument used is a `char`-typed variable. The call to function `inc` in line 35 results in calling the function `inc(int&)` because the argument used is an `int`-typed variable. The call to function `inc` in line 36 invokes the function `inc(double&)` because the argument used is a `double`-typed variable. The output statement in lines 39 through 41 displays the updated values in variables `c`, `i`, and `x`.

Summary

Today's lesson presented the basic components of C++ programs. These components include data types, variables, constants, and functions. You learned these basics:

- The predefined data types in Borland C++ 4.5 include the `int`, `char`, `float`, `double`, and `void` data types. C++ adds more flexibility to data types by supporting data-type modifiers. These modifiers alter the precision and the range of values. The type modifiers are `signed`, `unsigned`, `short`, and `long`.
- Borland C++ 4.5 identifiers can be up to 32 characters long and must begin with a letter or an underscore. The subsequent characters of an identifier may be a letter, digit, or underscore. C++ identifiers are case-sensitive.
- The `#include` directive is a special instruction to the compiler. The directive tells the compiler to include the contents of the specified file as though you typed it in the currently scanned source file.
- Declaring variables requires you to state the data type of the variable and the name of the variable. C++ enables you to initialize a variable when you declare it. You can declare multiple variables in a single declarative statement.
- Declaring constants involves using the `#define` directive to declare macro-based constants or using the `const` keyword to declare formal constants. The formal constants require that you specify the constant's type (the default is `int`, when omitted), the name of the constants, and the associated value.
- The general form for defining functions is

  ```
  returnType functionName(parameterList)
  {
      <declarations of data items>

      <function body>
      return returnValue;
  }
  ```

  You need to prototype a function if it is used by a client function before the prototyped function is defined. The general form for prototyping functions is

  ```
  returnType functionName(parameterList);
  ```

  You can omit the name of the parameters from the parameter list.

- Local variables in a function support the implementation of highly independent functions. Declaring local variables is similar to declaring global variables.
- Static variables in functions are declared by placing the keyword `static` before the data type of the variables. Static variables retain their values between function calls. In most cases, you need to initialize static variables. These initial values are assigned to the static variables the first time the program calls the host function.
- Inline functions enable you to expand their statements in place, like macro-based pseudofunctions. However, unlike these pseudofunctions, inline functions perform type checking.
- You exit functions with the `return` statement. `Void` functions do not need to include an expression after the `return` keyword.
- Default arguments enable you to assign default values to the parameters of a function. When you omit the argument of a parameter that has a default argument, that argument is automatically used.
- Function overloading enables you to declare multiple functions that have the same name but different parameter lists (the parameter list is also called the function signature). The function's return type is not part of the function signature, because C++ enables you to discard the result type.

Q&A

Q Is there a specific style for naming identifiers?

A There are a few styles that have become popular in recent years. The one we use has the identifier begin with a lowercase character. If the identifier contains multiple words, such as `numberOfElements`, make the first character of each subsequent word an uppercase letter.

Q Can C++ functions declare nested functions?

A No. Nested functions actually add a lot of overhead at runtime.

Q When can I use static global variables?

A Global variables need not be declared static, because they exist for the entire program's lifetime, but a global static variable will be visible only in the source module where it's declared.

Workshop

The Workshop provides quiz questions to help you solidify your understanding of the material covered and exercises to provide you with experience in using what you've learned. Try to understand the quiz and exercise answers before continuing on to the next day's lesson. Answers are provided in Appendix A, "Answers."

Quiz

1. Which of the following variables are valid, and which are not? Why?

```
numFiles
n0Distance_02_Line
0Weight
Bin Number
static
Static
```

2. What is the output of the following program? What can you say about the function swap?

```
#include <iostream.h>

void swap(int i, int j)
{
  int temp = i;
  i = j;
  j = temp;
}

main()
{
  int a = 10, b = 3;
  swap(a, b);
  cout << "a = " << a << " and b = " << b;
  return 0;
}
```

3. What is the output of the following program? What can you say about the function swap?

```
#include <iostream.h>
```

```
void swap(int& i, int& j)
{
  int temp = i;
  i = j;
  j = temp;
}

main()
{
  int a = 10, b = 3;
  swap(a, b);
  cout << "a = " << a << " and b = " << b;
  return 0;
}
```

4. What is the problem with the following overloaded functions?

```
void inc(int& i)
{
  i = i + 1;
}

void inc(int& i, int diff = 1)
{
  i = i + diff;
}
```

5. Where is the error in the following function?

```
double volume(double length, double width = 1, double
height)
{
  return length * width * height;
}
```

6. Where is the error in the following function?

```
void inc(int& i, int diff = 1)
{
  i = I + diff;
}
```

7. What is the error in the following program, and how can you correct it?

```
#include <iostream.h>

main()
{
  double x = 5.2;

  cout << x << "^2 = " << sqr(x);
  return 0;
}

double sqr(double x)
{ return x * x ; }
```

Exercise

Create the program OVERLOD2.CPP by adding a second parameter with default arguments to the overloaded `inc` functions in the program OVERLOAD.CPP. The new parameter should represent the increment value, with a default argument of 1.

Operators and Expressions

WEEK

1

The manipulation of data involves expressions that are made up of operands and operators. C++ supports several kinds of operators and expressions.

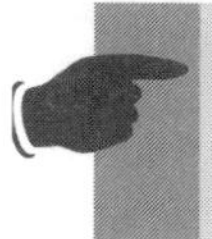

New Term: *Operators* are special symbols that take the values of *operands* and produce a new value.

Each category of operator manipulates data in a specific way. Today you will learn about the following topics:

- Arithmetic operators and expressions
- Increment operators
- Arithmetic assignment operators
- Typecasting and data conversion
- Relational operators and conditional expressions
- Bit-manipulating operators
- The comma operator

Arithmetic Operators

Table 3.1 shows the C++ arithmetic operators. The compiler carries out floating-point or integer division, depending on the operands. If both operands are integer expressions, the compiler yields the code for an integer division. If either or both operands are floating-point expressions, the compiler generates code for floating-point division.

Table 3.1. C++ arithmetic operators.

C++ Operator	Purpose	Data Type	Example
`+`	Unary plus	Numeric	`x = +y + 3;`
`-`	Unary minus	Numeric	`x = -y;`
`+`	Add	Numeric	`z = y + x;`
`-`	Subtract	Numeric	`z = y - x;`
`*`	Multiply	Numeric	`z = y * x;`

C++ Operator	Purpose	Data Type	Example
/	Divide	Numeric	`z = y / x;`
%	Modulus	Integers	`z = y % x;`

Let's look at an example that uses the mathematical operators with integers and floating-point numbers. Listing 3.1 shows the source code for program OPER1.CPP. (We suggest that you place all of today's programs in the DAY3.IDE project file.) The program performs the following tasks:

- Prompts you to enter two integers (one integer per prompt).
- Applies the `+`, `-`, `*`, `/`, and `%` operators to the two integers, storing the results in separate variables.
- Displays the results of the integer operations.
- Prompts you to enter two floating-point numbers (one number per prompt).
- Applies the `+`, `-`, `*`, and `/` operators to the two numbers, storing the results in separate variables.
- Displays the result of the floating-point operations.

Listing 3.1. Source code for the program OPER1.CPP.

```
// simple C++ program to illustrate simple math operations

#include <iostream.h>

main()
{

    int int1, int2;
    long long1, long2, long3, long4, long5;
    float x, y, real1, real2, real3, real4;

    cout << "\nType first  integer : ";
    cin >> int1;
    cout << "Type second integer : ";
    cin >> int2;
    cout << "\n";
    long1 = int1 + int2;
    long2 = int1 - int2;
    long3 = int1 * int2;
    long4 = int1 / int2;
```

continues

Listing 3.1. continued

```
21:     long5 = int1 % int2;
22:     cout << int1 << " + " << int2 << " = " << long1 << '\n';
23:     cout << int1 << " - " << int2 << " = " << long2 << '\n';
24:     cout << int1 << " * " << int2 << " = " << long3 << '\n';
25:     cout << int1 << " / " << int2 << " = " << long4 << '\n';
26:     cout << int1 << " mod " << int2 << " = " << long5 << '\n';
27:     cout << "\n\n";
28:     cout << "Type first  real number : ";
29:     cin >> x;
30:     cout << "Type second real number : ";
31:     cin >> y;
32:     cout << "\n";
33:     real1 = x + y;
34:     real2 = x - y;
35:     real3 = x * y;
36:     real4 = x / y;
37:     cout << x << " + " << y << " = " << real1 << '\n';
38:     cout << x << " - " << y << " = " << real2 << '\n';
39:     cout << x << " * " << y << " = " << real3 << '\n';
40:     cout << x << " / " << y << " = " << real4 << '\n';
41:     cout << "\n\n";
42:     return 0;
43: }
```

Here is a sample session with the program in Listing 3.1:

```
Type first  integer : 10
Type second integer : 5

10 + 5 = 15
10 - 5 = 5
10 * 5 = 50
10 / 5 = 2
10 % 5 = 0


Type first  real number : 1.25
Type second real number : 2.58

1.25 + 2.58 = 3.83
1.25 - 2.58 = -1.33
1.25 * 2.58 = 3.225
1.25 / 2.58 = 0.484496
```

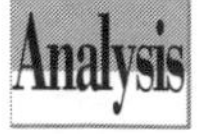

The program in Listing 3.1 declares a set of `int`-typed, `long`-typed, and `float`-typed variables in the function `main`. Some of these variables store your input, and others store the results of the mathematical operations. The output statement in line 12 prompts you to enter the first integer. The input statement in line

13 obtains your input and stores it in the variable `int1`. Lines 14 and 15 perform a similar operation to prompt you for the second integer and store it in variable `int2`.

The program performs the integer math operation in lines 17 through 21 and stores the results of these operations in variables `long1` through `long5`. We declared these variables as `long`-typed to guard against possible numeric overflow. The output statements in lines 22 through 26 display the integer operands, the operators used, and the results.

The output statement in line 28 prompts you to enter the first floating-point number. The input statement in line 29 obtains your input and stores it in the variable `x`. Lines 30 and 31 perform a similar operation to prompt you for the second floating-point number and to store it in variable `y`.

3

New Term: A floating-point number is also known as a *real number*.

The program performs the floating-point math operation in lines 33 through 36 and stores the results of these operations in variables `real1` through `real4`. The output statements in lines 37 through 40 display the operands, the operators used, and the results.

Arithmetic Expressions

The simplest kinds of expressions are the ones that contain literals, such as

```
-12
34.45
'A'
"Hello"
```

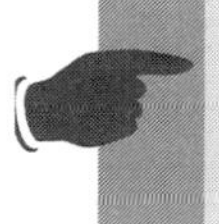

New Term: In general terms, an *arithmetic expression* is part of a program statement that contains a value.

The literal constants `-12` and `35.45` are the simplest arithmetic expressions. The next level of arithmetic expressions includes single variables or constants, such as

```
DAYS_IN_WEEK // a constant
i
x
```

Yet another level of arithmetic expressions contains a single operator with numbers, constants, and variables as operands. Here are a few examples:

```
355 / 113
4 * i
45.67 + x
```

More advanced arithmetic expressions contain multiple operators, parentheses, and even functions, such as

```
(355 / 113) * square(radius)
PIE * square(radius)
((2 * x - 3) * x + 2) * x - 5
(1 + x) / (3 - x)
```

We will discuss the order of executing the operators at the end of today's lesson, after introducing the other types of operators.

Increment Operators

C++ supports the special increment and decrement operators.

New Term: *Increment* (++) and *decrement* (--) *operators* enable you to increment and decrement, respectively, by 1 the value stored in a variable.

Syntax

Increment Operators

The general syntax for the increment operators is

```
variable++   // post-increment
++variable   // pre-increment
```

Examples:

```
lineNumber++;
++index;
```

Syntax

Decrement Operators

The general syntax for the decrement operators is

```
variable--   // post-decrement
--variable   // pre-decrement
```

Examples:

```
lineNumber--;
--index
```

This general syntax demonstrates that there are two ways to apply the ++ and -- operators. Placing these operators to the left of their operand changes the value of the operand *before* the operand contributes its value in an expression. Likewise, placing these operators to the right of their operands alters the value of the operand *after* the operand contributes its value in an expression. If the ++ or -- operators are the only operators in a statement, there is no practical distinction between using the pre- or post- forms.

Here are a few simple examples:

```
int n, m, t = 5;

t++; // t is now 6, same effect as ++t
--t; // t is now 5, same effect as t--
n = 4 * t++; // t is now 6 and n is 20
t = 5;
m = 4 * ++t; // t is now 6 and m is 24
```

The first statement uses the post-increment ++ operator to increment the value of variable t. If you write ++t instead, you get the same result once the statement finishes executing. The second statement uses the pre-decrement -- operator. Again, if we write t-- instead, we get the same result. The next two statements assign 5 to variable t and then use the post-increment ++ operator in a simple math expression. This statement multiplies 4 by the current value of t (that is, 5), assigns the result of 20 to the variable n, and then increments the values in variable t to 6. The last two statements show a different outcome. The statement first increments the value in variable t (the value in variable t becomes 6), then performs the multiplication, and finally assigns the result of 24 to the variable m.

Let's look at a simple program that illustrates the feature of the increment operator. Listing 3.2 shows the source code for the program OPER2.CPP. The program requires no input from you. It simply displays two integers whose values were obtained using the increment operator.

Type

Listing 3.2. Source code for the program OPER2.CPP.

```
/*
   C++ program to illustrate the feature of the increment operator.
   The ++ or -- may be included in an expression.  The value
   of the associated variable is altered after the expression
   is evaluated if the var++ (or var--) is used, or before
   when ++var (or --var) is used.
```

continues

Listing 3.2. continued

```
7:  */
8:
9:  #include <iostream.h>
10:
11: main()
12: {
13:    int i, k = 5;
14:
15:    // use post-incrementing
16:    i = 10 * (k++); // k contributes 5 to the expression
17:    cout << "i = " << i << "\n\n"; // displays 50 (= 10 * 5)
18:
19:    k--; // restores the value of k to 5
20:
21:    // use pre-incrementing
22:    i = 10 * (++k); // k contributes 6 to the expression
23:    cout << "i = " << i << "\n\n"; // displays 60 (= 10 * 6)
24:    return 0;
25: }
```

Here is a sample session with the program in Listing 3.2:

```
i = 50

i = 60
```

The program in Listing 3.2 has the function `main`, which declares two `int`-typed variables, `i` and `k`. The function initializes the variable `k` by assigning it the value 5. Line 16 contains a statement that applies the post-increment operator to the variable `k`. Consequently, the statement multiplies 10 by the initial value in `k`, 5, and assigns the product, 50, to variable `i`. After assigning the result to variable `i`, the program increments the value in variable `k`. The output statement in line 17 displays the value in variable `i`. The statement in line 19 decrements the value in variable `k` back to 5. The statement in line 22 applies the pre-increment operator to the variable `k`. Therefore, the program first increments the value in variable `k` (from 5 to 6) and then multiplies 10 by the updated value in `k`. The program assigns the result of the multiplication, 60, to the variable `i`. The output statement in line 23 displays the current value of variable `i`.

Assignment Operators

As a programmer, you may often come across statements that look similar to this:

```
IndexOfFirstElement = IndexOfFirstElement + 4;
```

```
GraphicsScaleRatio = GraphicsScaleRatio * 3;
CurrentRateOfReturn = CurrentRateOfReturn / 4;
DOSfileListSize = DOSfileListSize - 10;
```

The variable that receives the result of an expression is also the first operand. (Of course, the addition and multiplication are communicative operations. Therefore, the assigned variable can be either operand with these operations.) Notice that we chose relatively long names to remind you of your need to shorten the expression without making the names of the variables shorter.

Note: Remember that the = is an assignment operator. Hence, the left side of the = is assigned to the value or expression on the right side.

New Term: C++ offers *assignment operators* that merge with simple math operators.

You can write the following statements:

```
IndexOfFirstElement += 4;
GraphicsScaleRatio *= 3;
CurrentRateOfReturn /= 4;
DOSfileListSize -= 10;
```

Notice that the name of the variable appears only once. In addition, notice that the statements use the operators +=, *=, /=, and -=. Table 3.2 shows the arithmetic assignment operators. C++ supports other types of assignment operators.

Table 3.2. Arithmetic assignment operators.

Assignment Operator	Long Form	Example
`x += y`	`x = x + y`	`x += 12;`
`x -= y`	`x = x - y`	`x -= 34 + y;`
`x *= y`	`x = x * y`	`scale *= 10;`
`x /= y`	`x = x / y`	`z /= 34 * y;`
`x %= y`	`x = x % y`	`z %= 2;`

Let's look at a program that applies the assignment operators to integers and floating-point numbers. Listing 3.3 shows the source code for the program OPER3.CPP. The program performs the following tasks:

- Prompts you to enter two integers (one integer per prompt).
- Applies a set of assignment and increment operators to the two integers.
- Displays the new values of the integers.
- Prompts you to enter two floating-point numbers (one number per prompt).
- Applies a set of assignment and increment operators to the two numbers.
- Displays the new values of the floating-point numbers.

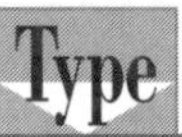

Listing 3.3. Source code for the program OPER3.CPP.

```
// C++ program to illustrate math assignment operators

#include <iostream.h>

main()
{
    int i, j;
    double x, y;

    cout << "Type first  integer : ";
    cin >> i;
    cout << "Type second integer : ";
    cin >> j;
    i += j;
    j -= 6;
    i *= 4;
    j /= 3;
    i++;
    j--;
    cout << "i = " << i << "\n";
    cout << "j = " << j << "\n";

    cout << "Type first  real number : ";
    cin >> x;
    cout << "Type second real number : ";
    cin >> y;
    // abbreviated assignments also work with doubles in C++
    x += y;
    y -= 4.0;
    x *= 4.0;
    y /=  3.0;
    x++;
```

```
33:     y--;
34:     cout << "x = " << x << "\n";
35:     cout << "y = " << y << "\n";
36:     return 0;
37: }
```

Here is a sample session with the program in Listing 3.3:

```
Type first  integer : 55
Type second integer : 66
i = 485
j = 19
Type first  real number : 2.5
Type second real number : 4.58
x = 29.32
y = -0.806667
```


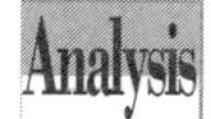

The program in Listing 3.3 contains the function main, which declares two `int`-typed variables (`i` and `j`) and two `double`-typed variables (`x` and `y`) in lines 7 and 8, respectively. The output statement in line 10 prompts you to enter the first integer. The input statement in line 11 receives your input and stores it in the variable i. Lines 12 and 13 are similar to lines 10 and 11—they prompt you for the second integer and store it in variable j.

The program manipulates the values in variables `i` and `j` using the statements in lines 14 through 19. In line 14, the program uses the `+=` operator to increment the value in variable `i` by the value in variable `j`. Line 15 uses the `-=` operator to decrement the value in variable `j` by 6. Line 16 applies the `*=` operator to multiply the value in variable `i` by 4 and to assign the result back to variable `i`. Line 17 utilizes the `/=` operator to divide the value in variable `j` by 3 and to store the result in `j`. Lines 18 and 19 apply the increment and decrement operators to variables `i` and `j`, respectively. The output statements in lines 20 and 21 display the contents of variables `i` and `j`, respectively.

The output statement in line 23 prompts you to enter the first floating-point number. The input statement in line 24 receives your input and saves it in the variable `x`. Lines 25 and 26 are similar to lines 23 and 24; they prompt you for the second floating-point number and store it in variable `y`.

The program manipulates the values in variable `x` and `y` using the statements in lines 28 through 33. In line 28, the program uses the `+=` operator to increment the value in variable `x` by the value in variable `y`. Line 29 uses the `-=` operator to decrement the value in variable `y` by 4. Line 30 applies the `*=` operator to multiply the value in variable x by 4 and to save the result back to x. Line 31 utilizes the /= operator to divide the value in variable y by 3 and to store the result in y. Lines 32 and 33 apply the increment and decrement operators to variable x and y, respectively. The output statements in lines 34 and 35 display the contents of variables x and y, respectively.

The *sizeof* Operator

Frequently your programs need to know the size, in bytes, of a data type or of a variable. C++ provides the sizeof operator, which takes for an argument either a data type or the name of a variable (scalar, array, record, and so on).

Syntax

The *sizeof* Operator

The general syntax for the sizeof operator is

```
sizeof({expression ¦ data_type})
sizeof {expression}
```

Examples:

```
int sizeDifference = sizeof(double) - sizeof(float);
int intSize = sizeof sizeDifference;
```

DO | **DON'T**

DO use sizeof with the name of the variable instead of its data type. This approach is safer because if you alter the data type of the variable, the sizeof operator still returns the correct answer. By contrast, if you use the sizeof operator with the data type of the variable and later alter the variable's type, you create a bug if you do not update the argument of the sizeof operator.

DON'T use numbers to represent the size of a variable. This approach often causes errors.

Let's look at an example that uses the sizeof operator with variables and data types. Listing 3.4 contains the source code for the program SIZEOF1.CPP. The program displays two similar tables that indicate the sizes of the short int, int, long int, char, and float data types. The program displays the first table by applying the sizeof operators to variables of these types. The program displays the second table by directly applying the sizeof operator to the data types.

Type

Listing 3.4. Source code for the program SIZEOF1.CPP.

```
/*
  simple program that returns the data sizes using the sizeof()
  operator with variables and data types.
*/

#include <iostream.h>

main()

{
    short int aShort;
    int anInt;
    long aLong;
    char aChar;
    float aReal;

    cout << "Table 1. Data sizes using sizeof(variable)\n\n";
    cout << "    Data type          Memory used\n";
    cout << "                         (bytes)\n";
    cout << "------------------    ----------";
    cout << "\n     short int              " << sizeof(aShort);
    cout << "\n      integer               " << sizeof(anInt);
    cout << "\n   long integer             " << sizeof(aLong);
    cout << "\n     character              " << sizeof(aChar);
    cout << "\n      float                 " << sizeof(aReal);
    cout << "\n\n\n\n";

    cout << "Table 2. Data sizes using sizeof(dataType)\n\n";
    cout << "    Data type          Memory used\n";
    cout << "                         (bytes)\n";
    cout << "------------------    ----------";
    cout << "\n     short int              " <<  sizeof(short int);
    cout << "\n      integer               " <<  sizeof(int);
    cout << "\n    long integer            " <<  sizeof(long);
    cout << "\n     character              " <<  sizeof(char);
    cout << "\n       float                " <<  sizeof(float);
    cout << "\n\n\n\n";

    return 0;
}
```

Here is a sample session with the program in Listing 3.4:

```
Table 1. Data sizes using sizeof(variable)

    Data type          Memory used
                         (bytes)
------------------    ----------
     short int             2
      integer              2
   long integer            4
     character             1
      float                4



Table 2. Data sizes using sizeof(dataType)

    Data type          Memory used
                         (bytes)
------------------    ----------
     short int             2
      integer              2
    long integer           4
     character             1
       float               4
```

The program in Listing 3.4 declares five variables in the function `main`. Each variable has a different data type and derives its name from its data type. For example, the variable `anInt` is an `int`-typed variable, the variable `aLong` is a `long`-typed variable, and so on.

The statements in lines 17 through 25 display the table of data sizes. The output statements in lines 21 through 25 use the `sizeof` operator with the variables.

The statements in lines 28 through 36 also display the table of data sizes. The output statements in lines 32 through 36 use the `sizeof` operator with the data-type identifiers.

Typecasting

Automatic data conversion of a value from one data type to another compatible data type is one of the duties of a compiler. This data conversion simplifies expressions and eases the frustration of both novice and veteran programmers. With behind-the-scenes data conversion, you do not need to examine every expression that mixes compatible data types in your program. For example, the compiler handles most expressions that mix various types of integers or mix integers and floating-point types. You get a compile-time error if you attempt to do something illegal.

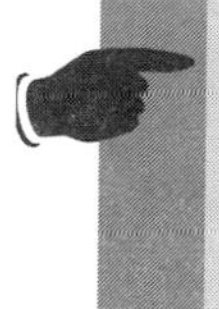

New Term: *Typecasting* is a language feature that enables you to specify explicitly how to convert a value from its original data type into a compatible data type. Thus, typecasting instructs the compiler to perform the conversion you want and not the one the compiler thinks is needed.

Syntax

Typecasting

C++ supports the following forms of typecasting:

```
type_cast(expression)
```

and

```
(type_cast) expression
```

Examples:

```
int i = 2;
float a, b;
a = float(i);
b = (float) i;
```

Let's look at an example that illustrates implicit data conversion and typecasting. Listing 3.5 shows the source code for the program TYPCAST1.CPP. The program declares variables that have the character, integer, and floating-point data types. Then the program performs two sets of similar mathematical operations. The first set relies on the automatic conversions of data types, performed by the compiler. The second set of operations uses typecasting to explicitly instruct the compiler on how to convert the data types. The program requires no input—it provides its own data—and it displays the output values for both sets of operations. The program illustrates that the compiler succeeds in generating the same output for both sets of operations.

Listing 3.5. Source code for the program TYPCAST1.CPP.

```
// simple C++ program that demonstrates typecasting

#include <iostream.h>

main()
{
    short shortInt1, shortInt2;
```

continues

Listing 3.5. continued

```
    unsigned short aByte;
    int anInt;
    long aLong;
    char aChar;
    float aReal;

    // assign values
    shortInt1 = 10;
    shortInt2 = 6;
    // perform operations without typecasting
    aByte = shortInt1 + shortInt2;
    anInt = shortInt1 - shortInt2;
    aLong = shortInt1 * shortInt2;
    aChar = aLong + 5; // conversion is automatic to character
    aReal = shortInt1 * shortInt2 + 0.5;

    cout << "shortInt1 = " << shortInt1 << '\n'
         << "shortInt2 = " << shortInt2 << '\n'
         << "aByte = " << aByte << '\n'
         << "anInt = " << anInt << '\n'
         << "aLong = " << aLong << '\n'
         << "aChar is " << aChar << '\n'
         << "aReal = " << aReal << "\n\n\n";

    // perform operations with typecasting
    aByte = (unsigned short) (shortInt1 + shortInt2);
    anInt = (int) (shortInt1 - shortInt2);
    aLong = (long) (shortInt1 * shortInt2);
    aChar = (unsigned char) (aLong + 5);
    aReal = (float) (shortInt1 * shortInt2 + 0.5);

    cout << "shortInt1 = " << shortInt1 << '\n'
         << "shortInt2 = " << shortInt2 << '\n'
         << "aByte = " << aByte << '\n'
         << "anInt = " << anInt << '\n'
         << "aLong = " << aLong << '\n'
         << "aChar is " << aChar << '\n'
         << "aReal = " << aReal << "\n\n\n";
    return 0;
}
```

Here is a sample session with the program in Listing 3.5:

```
shortInt1 = 10
shortInt2 = 6
aByte = 16
anInt = 4
aLong = 60
aChar is A
aReal = 60.5


shortInt1 = 10
shortInt2 = 6
aByte = 16
anInt = 4
aLong = 60
aChar is A
aReal = 60.5
```

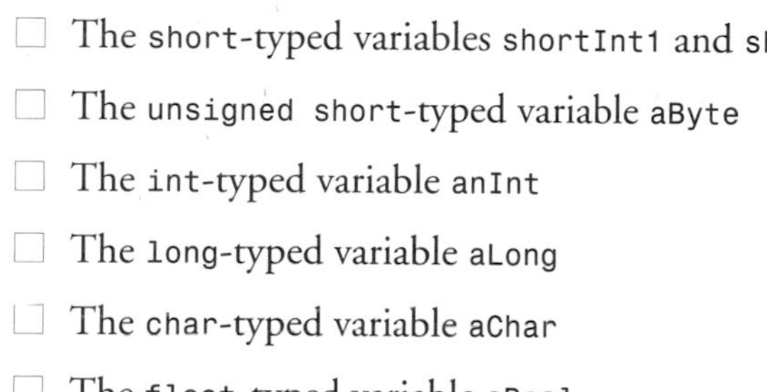

The program in Listing 3.5 declares the following variables in the function `main`:

- The `short`-typed variables `shortInt1` and `shortInt2`
- The `unsigned short`-typed variable `aByte`
- The `int`-typed variable `anInt`
- The `long`-typed variable `aLong`
- The `char`-typed variable `aChar`
- The `float`-typed variable `aReal`

Lines 15 and 16 assign the integers 10 and 6 to variable `shortInt1` and `shortIn2`, respectively. Lines 18 through 22 perform various mathematical operations and assign the results to variables `aByte`, `anInt`, `aLong`, `aChar`, and `aReal`.

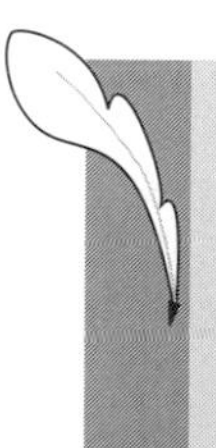

Note: C and C++ treat the `char` type as a special integer. Each `char`-type literal (such as `'A'`), constant, or variable has an integer value that is equal to its ASCII representation. This language feature enables you to store an integer in a `char`-type variable and treat a `char`-type data item as an integer. The statement in line 21 adds the integer 5 to the value of the variable `aLong` and assigns the result, an integer, to the variable `aChar`. The value of the assigned integer, 65, represents the ASCII code for the letter A.

The output statement in lines 24 through 30 displays the values stored in the variables. Notice that the output for variable `aChar` is the letter `A`. If we write the output term for variable `aChar` as `<< (int) aChar`, we get `65`, the ASCII code of the character stored in `aChar`.

The statements in lines 32 through 37 perform similar operations to the statements in lines 18 through 22. The main difference is that the statements in lines 32 through 37 use typecasting to explicitly instruct the compiler on how to convert the result. The output statement in lines 39 through 45 displays the contents of the variables.

Relational and Logical Operators

Table 3.3 shows the C++ relational and logical operators. Notice that C++ does not spell out the operators `AND`, `OR`, and `NOT`. Rather, it uses single- and dual-character symbols. Also notice that C++ does not support the relational `XOR` operator. You can use the `#define` macro directives, shown in the New Term box, to define the `AND`, `OR`, and `NOT` identifiers as macros.

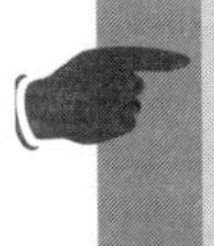

New Term: The *relational operators* (less than, greater than, and equal to) and the *logical operators* (`AND`, `OR`, and `NOT`) are the basic building blocks of decision-making constructs in any programming language.

```
#define AND &&
#define OR ||
#define NOT !
```

Table 3.3. C++ relational and logical operators.

C++ Operator	Meaning	Example
`&&`	Logical `AND`	`if (i > 1 && i < 10)`
`||`	Logical `OR`	`if (c==0 || c==9)`
`!`	Logical `NOT`	`if (!(c>1 && c<9))`
`<`	Less than	`if (i < 0)`
`<=`	Less than or equal to	`if (i <= 0)`
`>`	Greater than	`if (j > 10)`

C++ Operator	Meaning	Example
`>=`	Greater than or equal to	`if (x >= 8.2)`
`==`	Equal to	`if (c == '\0')`
`!=`	Not equal to	`if (c != '\n')`
`?:`	Conditional assignment	`k = (i<1) ? 1 : i;`

Although these macros are permissible in C++, you might get a negative reaction from veteran C++ programmers who read your code. Who says that programming is always objective?

3

Warning: Do *not* use the = operator as the equality relational operator. This common error is a source of logical bugs in a C++ program. You may be accustomed to using the = operator in other languages to test the equality of two data items. In C++, you *must* use the == operator. What happens if you employ the = operator in C++? Do you get a compiler error? The answer is that you may get a compiler warning. Other than that, your C++ program should run. When the program reaches the expression that it is supposed to test for equality, it actually attempts to assign the operand on the right of the = sign to the operand on the left of the = sign. Of course, a session with such a program most likely leads to weird program behavior or even a system hang.

Notice that the last operator in Table 3.3 is the `?:` operator. This special operator supports what is known as the conditional expression.

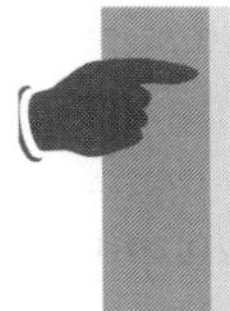

New Term: The *conditional expression* is a shorthand for a dual-alternative simple `if-else` statement. (See Day 5 for more information about the `if` statement.)

For example, the following is an `if-else` statement that can be compressed into a conditional expression:

```
if (condition)
     variable = expression1;
else
     variable = expression2;
```

The equivalent conditional expression is as follows:

```
variable = (condition) ? expression1 : expression2;
```

The conditional expression tests the condition. If that condition is true, it assigns *expression1* to the target variable. Otherwise, it assigns *expression2* to the target variable.

Boolean Expressions

Often, you need to use a collection of relational and logical operators to formulate a nontrivial condition. Here are examples of such conditions:

```
x < 0 || x > 11
(i != 0 || i > 100) && (j != i || j > 0)
x != 0 && x != 10 && x != 100
```

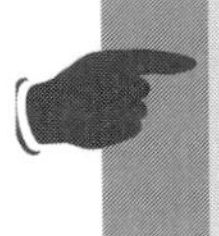

New Term: *Boolean* (also called *logical) expressions* are expressions that involve logical operators and/or relational operators.

DO | **DON'T**

DO double-check to avoid Boolean expressions that are either always true or always false. For example, the expression `(x < 0 && x > 10)` is always false, because no value of `x` can be negative and greater than 10 at the same time.

DON'T use the = operator to test for equality.

Consider now an example that uses relational and logical operators and expressions. Listing 3.6 shows the source code for the program RELOP1.CPP. The program prompts you to enter three integers and then proceeds to perform a battery of tests. The program displays the relational and logical operations, their operands, and their results.

Listing 3.6. Source code for the program RELOP1.CPP.

```
/*
   simple C++ program that uses logical expressions
   this program uses the conditional expression to display
   TRUE or FALSE messages, since C++ does not support the
   BOOLEAN data type.
*/

#include <iostream.h>

const MIN_NUM = 30;
const MAX_NUM = 199;
const int TRUE = 1;
const int FALSE = 0;

main()
{
    int i, j, k;
    int flag1, flag2, in_range,
        same_int, xor_flag;

    cout << "Type first  integer : "; cin >> i;
    cout << "Type second integer : "; cin >> j;
    cout << "Type third  integer : "; cin >> k;

    // test for range [MIN_NUM...MAX_NUM]
    flag1 = i >= MIN_NUM;
    flag2 = i <= MAX_NUM;
    in_range = flag1 && flag2;
    cout << "\n" << i << " is in the range "
         << MIN_NUM << " to " << MAX_NUM << " : "
         << ((in_range) ? "TRUE" : "FALSE");

    // test if two or more entered numbers are equal
    same_int = i == j || i == k || j == k;
    cout << "\nat least two integers you typed are equal : "
         << ((same_int) ? "TRUE" : "FALSE");

    // miscellaneous tests
    cout << "\n" << i << " != " << j << " : "
         << ((i != j) ? "TRUE" : "FALSE");
```

continues

Listing 3.6. continued

```
    cout << "\nNOT (" << i << " < " << j << ") : "
         << ((!(i < j)) ? "TRUE" : "FALSE");
    cout << "\n" << i << " <= " << j << " : "
         << ((i <= j) ? "TRUE" : "FALSE");
    cout << "\n" << k << " > " << j << " : "
         << ((k > j) ? "TRUE" : "FALSE");
    cout << "\n(" << k << " = " << i << ") AND ("
         << j << " != " << k << ") : "
         << ((k == i && j != k) ? "TRUE" : "FALSE");

    // NOTE: C++ does NOT support the logical XOR operator for
    // boolean expressions.
    // add numeric results of logical tests.  Value is in 0...2
    xor_flag = (k <= i) + (j >= k);
    // if xor_flag is either 0 or 2 (i.e. not = 1), it is
    // FALSE therefore interpret 0 or 2 as false.
    xor_flag = (xor_flag == 1) ? TRUE : FALSE;
    cout << "\n(" << k << " <= " << i << ") XOR ("
         << j << " >= " << k << ") : "
         << ((xor_flag) ? "TRUE" : "FALSE");
    cout << "\n(" << k << " > " << i << ") AND("
         << j << " <= " << k << ") : "
         << ((k > i && j <= k) ? "TRUE" : "FALSE");
    cout << "\n\n";
    return 0;
}
```

Here is a sample session with the program in Listing 3.6:

```
Type first  integer : 55
Type second integer : 64
Type third  integer : 87

55 is in the range 30 to 199 : TRUE
at least two integers you typed are equal : FALSE
55 != 64 : TRUE
NOT (55 < 64) : FALSE
55 <= 64 : TRUE
87 > 64 : TRUE
(87 = 55) AND (64 != 87) : FALSE
(87 <= 55) XOR (64 >= 87) : FALSE
(87 > 55) AND(64 <= 87) : TRUE
```

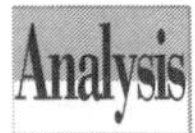

The program in Listing 3.6 declares four global constants. The constants `MIN_NUM` and `MAX_NUM` define a range of numbers used in the logical tests. The constants `TRUE` and `FALSE` represent the Boolean values. The function `main` declares a number of `int` variables that are used for input and various testing. The

statements in lines 21 through 23 prompt you for three integers and store them in the variables `i`, `j`, and `k`, respectively.

The statements in lines 26 through 31 involve testing whether the value in variable `i` lies in the range of `MIN_NUM` and `MAX_NUM`. The statement in line 26 tests if the value in `i` is greater than or equal to the constant `MIN_NUM`. The program assigns the Boolean result to the variable `flag1`. The statement in line 27 tests whether the value in `i` is less than or equal to the constant `MAX_NUM`. The program assigns the Boolean result to the variable `flag2`. The statement in line 28 applies the `&&` operator to the variable `flag1` and `flag2`, and it assigns the Boolean result to the variable `in_range`. The output statement in lines 29 through 31 states what the test is and displays `TRUE` or `FALSE` depending on the value in the variable `in_range`. The statement uses the conditional operator `?:` to display the string `TRUE` if `in_range` has a nonzero value and to display the string `FALSE` if otherwise.

3

The statements in lines 34 through 36 determine whether at least two of the three integers you entered are equal. The statement in line 34 uses a Boolean expression that applies the `==` relational operators and the `||` logical operators. The statement assigns the Boolean result to the variable `same_int`. The output statement in lines 35 and 36 states the test and displays the `TRUE/FALSE` outcome. The output statement uses the conditional operator to display the strings `TRUE` or `FALSE` depending on the value in variable `same_int`.

The statements in lines 39 through 49 perform miscellaneous tests that involve the input values, and they display both the test and the results. Please feel free to alter these statements to conduct different tests.

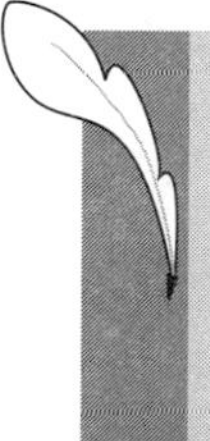

Note: The statements in lines 54 through 60 perform an `XOR` test and display the outcome. The program uses a simple programming trick to implement the `XOR` operator. The statement in line 54 adds the Boolean value of the subexpressions `(k <= i)` and `(j >= k)`. The result is 0 if both subexpressions are false, 1 if only one of the subexpressions is true, and 2 if both subexpressions are true. Because the `XOR` operator is true only if either subexpression is true, the statement in line 57 assigns `TRUE` to the variable `xor_flag` if the previous value is 1. Otherwise, the statement assigns `FALSE` to `xor_flag`. The statements in lines 61 through 63 perform another miscellaneous test.

Bit-Manipulation Operators

C++ is a programming language that is suitable for system development. System development requires bit-manipulating operators.

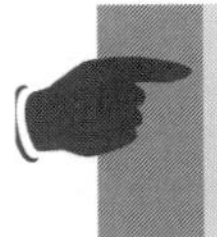

New Term: *Bit-manipulating operators* toggle, set, query, and shift the bits of a byte or a word.

Table 3.4 shows the bit-manipulating operators. Notice that C++ uses the symbols `&` and `¦` to represent the bitwise `AND` and `OR`, respectively. Recall that the `&&` and `¦¦` characters represent the logical `AND` and `OR` operators, respectively. In addition to the bit-manipulating operators, C++ supports the bit-manipulating assignment operators, shown in Table 3.5. (Using bit-manipulating operators is a part of advanced programming that involves fiddling with single bits. As a novice C++ programmer, you most likely will not use these operators in the near future.)

Table 3.4. C++ bit-manipulating operators.

C++ Operator	Meaning	Example
`&`	Bitwise `AND`	`i & 128`
`¦`	Bitwise `OR`	`j ¦ 64`
`^`	Bitwise `XOR`	`j ^ 12`
`~`	Bitwise `NOT`	`~j`
`<<`	Bitwise shift left	`i << 2`
`>>`	Bitwise shift right	`j >> 3`

Table 3.5. C++ bit-manipulating assignment operators.

C++ Operator	Long Form	Example
`x &= y`	`x = x & y`	`i &= 128`
`x ¦= y`	`x = x ¦ y`	`j ¦= 64`
`x ^= y`	`x = x ^ y`	`k ^= 15`

C++ Operator	Long Form	Example
`x <<= y`	`x = x << y`	`j <<= 2`
`x >>= y`	`x = x >> y`	`k >>= 3`

Let us present a C++ program that performs simple bit manipulation. Listing 3.7 contains the source code for the program BITS1.CPP. The program requires no input, because it uses internal data. The program applies the ¦, &, ^, >>, and << bitwise operators and displays the results of the bitwise manipulation.

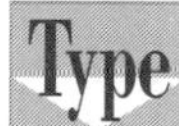

Listing 3.7. Source code for the program BITS1.CPP.

```
// C++ program to perform bit manipulations

#include <iostream.h>

main()
{

     int i, j, k;

     // assign values to i and j
     i = 0xF0;
     j = 0x1A;

     k = j & i;
     cout << j << " AND " << i << " = " << k << "\n";

     k = j ¦ i;
     cout << j << " OR " << i << " = " << k << "\n";

     k = j ^ 0x1C;
     cout << j << " XOR " << 0x1C << " = " << k << "\n";

     k = i << 2;
     cout << i << " shifted left by 2 bits = " << k << "\n";

     k = i >> 2;
     cout << i << " shifted right by 2 bits = " << k << "\n";
     return 0;
}
```

Here is a sample session with the program in Listing 3.7:

```
26 AND 240 = 16
26 OR 240 = 250
26 XOR 28 = 6
240 shifted left by 2 bits = 960
240 shifted right by 2 bits = 60
```

The program in Listing 3.7 declares three `int`-typed variables, `i`, `j`, and `k`. The statements in lines 11 and 12 assign hexadecimal numbers to the variables `i` and `j`, respectively. The statement in line 14 applies the bitwise `AND` operator to the variables `i` and `j`, and it stores the result in variable `k`. The output statement in line 15 displays the operands, the bitwise operator, and the results. The statement in line 17 applies the bitwise `OR` operator to the variable `i` and `j`, and it saves the result to variable `k`. The output statement in line 18 displays the operands, the bitwise operator, and the results. The statement in line 20 applies the bitwise `XOR` operator using the variable `j` and the hexadecimal integer `0x1C`. The output statement in line 21 displays the operands, the bitwise operator, and the results.

The statements in lines 23 through 27 apply the shift-left and shift-right operators to variable `i`. These operators shift the bits of the variable `i` by two bits and assign the result to variable `k`. The effect of the left-shift operator is the same as multiplying the value in the variable `i` by 4. Similarly, the effect of the right-shift operator is the same as dividing the value in the variable `i` by 4.

The Comma Operator

The comma operator requires that the program completely evaluate the first expression before evaluating the second expression. Both expressions are located in the same C++ statement. What does *located in the same C++ statement* mean exactly? Why use this rather unusual operator in the first place? Because the comma operator with its peculiar role does serve a specific and very important purpose in the `for` loop.

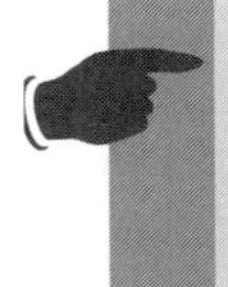

New Term: *Loops* are powerful language constructs that enable computers to excel in achieving repetitive tasks. The *comma operator* enables you to create multiple expressions that initialize multiple loop-related variables.

Syntax

The Comma Operator

The general syntax for the comma operator is

```
expression1, expression2
```

Example:

```
for (i = 0, j = 0; i < 10; i++, j++)
```

You will learn more about the `for` loop in Day 6. For now, this example shows you how to apply the comma operator.

Operator Precedence and Evaluation Direction

Now that you are familiar with most of the C++ operators (there are a few more operators that deal with pointers and addresses), you need to know two related aspects: first, the precedence of the C++ operators; and second, the direction (or sequence) of evaluation. Table 3.6 shows the C++ precedence of the C++ operators that we have covered so far and also indicates the evaluation direction.

Table 3.6. C++ operators and their precedence.

Category	Name	Symbol	Evaluation Direction	Precedence
Monadic				
	Post-increment	`++`	Left to right	2
	Post-decrement	`--`	Left to right	2
	Address	`&`	Right to left	2
	Bitwise `NOT`	`~`	Right to left	2
	Typecast	`(type)`	Right to left	2
	Logical `NOT`	`!`	Right to left	2
	Negation	`-`	Right to left	2

continues

Table 3.6. continued

Category	Name	Symbol	Evaluation Direction	Precedence
Monadic				
	Plus sign	`+`	Right to left	2
	Pre-increment	`++`	Right to left	2
	Pre-decrement	`--`	Right to left	2
	Size of data	`sizeof`	Right to left	2
Multiplicative				
	Modulus	`%`	Left to right	3
	Multiply	`*`	Left to right	3
	Divide	`/`	Left to right	3
Additive				
	Add	`+`	Left to right	4
	Subtract	`-`	Left to right	4
Bitwise Shift				
	Shift left	`<<`	Left to right	5
	Shift right	`>>`	Left to right	5
Relational				
	Less than	`<`	Left to right	6
	Less or equal	`<=`	Left to right	6
	Greater than	`>`	Left to right	6
	Greater or equal	`>=`	Left to right	6
	Equal	`==`	Left to right	7
	Not equal	`!=`	Left to right	7

<table>
<tr><th>Category</th><th>Name</th><th>Symbol</th><th>Evaluation Direction</th><th>Precedence</th></tr>
<tr><td>Bitwise</td><td></td><td></td><td></td><td></td></tr>
<tr><td></td><td><code>AND</code></td><td><code>&</code></td><td>Left to right</td><td>8</td></tr>
<tr><td></td><td><code>XOR</code></td><td><code>^</code></td><td>Left to right</td><td>9</td></tr>
<tr><td></td><td><code>OR</code></td><td><code>|</code></td><td>Left to right</td><td>10</td></tr>
<tr><td>Logical</td><td></td><td></td><td></td><td></td></tr>
<tr><td></td><td><code>AND</code></td><td><code>&&</code></td><td>Left to right</td><td>11</td></tr>
<tr><td></td><td><code>OR</code></td><td><code>||</code></td><td>Left to right</td><td>12</td></tr>
<tr><td>Ternary</td><td></td><td></td><td></td><td></td></tr>
<tr><td></td><td>Cond. express.</td><td><code>?:</code></td><td>Right to left</td><td>13</td></tr>
<tr><td>Assignment</td><td></td><td></td><td></td><td></td></tr>
<tr><td></td><td>Arithmetic</td><td><code>=</code></td><td>Right to left</td><td>14</td></tr>
<tr><td></td><td></td><td><code>+=</code></td><td>Right to left</td><td>14</td></tr>
<tr><td></td><td></td><td><code>-=</code></td><td>Right to left</td><td>14</td></tr>
<tr><td></td><td></td><td><code>*=</code></td><td>Right to left</td><td>14</td></tr>
<tr><td></td><td></td><td><code>/=</code></td><td>Right to left</td><td>14</td></tr>
<tr><td></td><td></td><td><code>%=</code></td><td>Right to left</td><td>14</td></tr>
<tr><td></td><td>Shift</td><td><code>>>=</code></td><td>Right to left</td><td>14</td></tr>
<tr><td></td><td></td><td><code><<=</code></td><td>Right to left</td><td>14</td></tr>
<tr><td></td><td>Bitwise</td><td><code>&=</code></td><td>Right to left</td><td>14</td></tr>
<tr><td></td><td></td><td><code>|=</code></td><td>Right to left</td><td>14</td></tr>
<tr><td></td><td></td><td><code>^=</code></td><td>Right to left</td><td>14</td></tr>
<tr><td></td><td>Comma</td><td><code>,</code></td><td>Left to right</td><td>15</td></tr>
</table>

Summary

Today's lesson presented the various C++ operators and discussed how to use these operators to manipulate data. You learned the following:

- The arithmetic operators include `+`, `-`, `*`, `/`, and `%` (modulus).
- The arithmetic expressions vary in complexity. The simplest expression contains a single data item (literal, constant, or variable). Complex expressions include multiple operators, functions, literals, constants, and variables.
- The increment and decrement operators come in the pre- and post- forms. C++ enables you to apply these operators to variables that store characters, integers, and even floating-point numbers.
- The arithmetic assignment operators enable you to write shorter arithmetic expressions in which the primary operand is also the variable receiving the result of the expression.
- The `sizeof` operator returns the byte size of either a data type or a variable.
- Typecasting enables you to force the type conversion of an expression.
- Relational and logical operators enable you to build logical expressions. C++ does not support a predefined Boolean type and instead considers 0 as false and any nonzero value as true.
- Boolean expressions combine relational and logical operators to formulate nontrivial conditions. These expressions allow a program to make sophisticated decisions.
- The conditional expression offers you a short form for the simple dual-alternative `if-else` statement.
- The bit-manipulation operators perform bitwise `AND`, `OR`, `XOR`, and `NOT` operations. In addition, C++ supports the << and >> bitwise shift operators.
- The bit-manipulation assignment operators offer short forms for simple bit-manipulation statements.

Q&A

Q How does the compiler react when you declare a variable but never assign a value to it?

A The compiler issues a warning that the variable is unreferenced.

Q What is the Boolean expression for checking that the value of a variable, `i`, is in the range of values (for example, defined by variables `lowVal` and `hiVal`)?

A The expression that determines whether the value in variable `i` is located in a range is

```
(i >= lowVal && i <= hiVal)
```

Q What is the Boolean expression for checking that the value of a variable, `i`, is inside the range of values (for example, defined by variables `lowVal` and `hiVal`)?

A The expression that determines whether the value in variable `i` is located inside a range is

```
(i > lowVal && i < hiVal)
```

Workshop

The Workshop provides quiz questions to help you solidify your understanding of the material covered and exercises to provide you with experience in using what you've learned. Try to understand the quiz and exercise answers before continuing on to the next day's lesson. (Answers are provided in Appendix A, "Answers.")

Quiz

1. What is the output of the following program?

```
#include <iostream.h>

main()
{
  int i = 3;
  int j = 5;
  double x = 33.5;
  double y = 10.0;

  cout << 10 + j % i << "\n";
  cout << i * i - 2 * i + 5 << "\n";
  cout << (19 + i + j) / (2 * j + 2) << "\n";
```

```
  cout << x / y + y / x << "\n";
  cout << i * x + j * y << "\n";
  return 0;
}
```

2. What is the output of the following program?

```
#include <iostream.h>

main()
{
  int i = 3;
  int j = 5;

  cout << 10 + j % i++ << "\n";
  cout << --i * i - 2 * i + 5 << "\n";
  cout << (19 + ++i + ++j) / (2 * j + 2) << "\n";
  return 0;
}
```

3. What is the output of the following program?

```
#include <iostream.h>

main()
{
  int i = 3;
  int j = 5;

  i += j;
  j *= 2;
  cout << 10 + j % i << "\n";
  i -= 2;
  j /= 3;
  cout << i * i - 2 * i + j << "\n";
  return 0;
}
```

4. What is the output of the following program?

```
#include <iostream.h>

main()
{
  int i = 5;
  int j = 10;

  cout << ((i < j) ? "TRUE" : "FALSE") << "\n";
  cout << ((i > 0 && j < 100) ?  "TRUE" : "FALSE") << "\n";
  cout << ((i > 0 && i < 10) ? "TRUE" : "FALSE") << "\n";
  cout << ((i == 5 && i == j) ? "TRUE" : "FALSE") << "\n";
  return 0;
}
```

3

Exercises

1. Use the conditional operator to write the function `max`, which returns the greater of two integers.
2. Use the conditional operator to write the function `min`, which returns the smaller of two integers.
3. Use the conditional operator to write the function `abs`, which returns the absolute value of an integer.
4. Use the conditional operator to write the function `isOdd`, which returns 0 if its integer argument is an odd number and yields 1 if otherwise.

Managing I/O

WEEK
1

C++, like its parent language C, does not define I/O operations that are part of the core language. Instead, C++ and C rely on I/O libraries to provide the needed I/O support. Such libraries are mainly aimed at non-GUI (graphical user interface) environments such as MS-DOS. These libraries usually work with EasyWin applications, which is why they are of interest in this book. However, because our primary goal here is to teach you how to write Windows programs, we are keeping the discussion of these I/O libraries to a minimum. Today's short lesson looks at a small selection of input and output operations and functions that are supported by the STDIO.H and IOSTREAM.H header files. You will learn about the following topics:

- Formatted stream output
- Stream input
- The `printf` function

Formatted Stream Output

C++ brings with it a family of extendable I/O libraries. The language designers recognized that the I/O functions in STDIO.H, inherited from C, have their limitations when dealing with classes. (You will learn more about classes in Day 11.) Consequently, C++ extends the notion of streams. Recall that streams, which already exist in C, are a sequence of data flowing from part of a computer to another. In the programs that we have presented thus far, you have seen the extractor operator << working with the standard output stream, `cout`. You also saw the inserter operator >> and the standard input stream, `cin`. In this section, we introduce you to the stream functions `width` and `precision`, which help in formatting the output. The C++ stream libraries have many more functions to additionally fine-tune the output. However, as we stated earlier, because these functions work for non-GUI interfaces, we don't want to overwhelm you with information that is not relevant to Windows programming. The `width` function specifies the width of the output. The general form for using this function with the `cout` stream is

```
cout.width(widthOfOutput);
```

The `precision` function specifies the number of digits for floating-point numbers. The general form for using this function with the `cout` stream is

```
cout.precision(numberOfDigits);
```

Let's look at an example. Listing 4.1 contains the source code for the program OUT1.CPP. (We suggest that you place all of today's programs in the DAY4.IDE project file.) The program, which requires no input, displays formatted integers,

floating-point numbers, and characters using the `width` and `precision` stream functions.

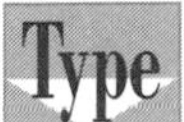

Listing 4.1. Source code for the program OUT1.CPP.

```
1: // Program that illustrates C++ formatted stream output
2: // using the width and precision functions
3:
4: #include <iostream.h>
5:
6: main()
7: {
8:   short    aShort    = 4;
9:   int      anInt     = 67;
10:  unsigned char aByte = 128;
11:  char     aChar     = '@';
12:  float    aSingle   = 355.0;
13:  double   aDouble   = 1.130e+002;
14:  // display sample expressions
15:  cout.width(3); cout << int(aByte) << " + ";
16:  cout.width(2); cout << anInt << " = ";
17:  cout.width(3); cout << (aByte + anInt) << '\n';
18:
19:  cout.precision(4); cout << aSingle << " / ";
20:  cout.precision(4); cout << aDouble << " = ";
21:  cout.precision(5); cout << (aSingle / aDouble) << '\n';
22:
23:  cout << "The character in variable aChar is "
24:       << aChar << '\n';
25:  return 0;
26: }
```

Here is a sample session with the program in Listing 4.1:

```
128 + 67 = 195
355 / 113 = 3.1416
The character in variable aChar is @
```

The program in Listing 4.1 declares a set of variables that have different data types. The statements in lines 15 through 17 use the stream function `width` to specify the output width for the next item displayed by a `cout` statement. Notice that it takes six statements to display three integers. In addition, notice that in line 15 the program uses the expression `int(aByte)` to typecast the `unsigned char` type into an `int`. Without this type conversion, the contents of the variable `aByte` appear as a character instead of a number. If we use the stream output to display integers that have default widths, we can indeed replace the six stream-output statements with a single one.

Lines 19 through 21 contain the second set of stream-output statements for the floating-point numbers. The statements in these lines contain the stream function `precision` to specify the total number of digits to display. Again, it takes six C++ statements to output three floating-point numbers. Once more, if we use the stream output to display numbers that have default widths, we can replace the six stream-output statements with a single one.

Stream Input

Like the standard output stream, C++ offers the standard input stream, `cin`. This input stream can read predefined data types, such as `int`, `unsigned`, `long`, and `char`. Typically, you use the inserter operator >> to obtain input for the predefined data types. The programs that we presented so far use the >> operator to enter a single item. C++ streams enable you to chain the >> operator to enter multiple items. In the case of multiple items, you need to observe the following rules:

1. Enter a space between two consecutive numbers to separate them.
2. Entering a space between two consecutive `char`s is optional.
3. Entering a space between a `char` and a number (or vice versa) is necessary only if the `char` is a digit.
4. The input stream ignores spaces.
5. You can enter multiple items on different lines. The stream-input statements are not fully executed until they obtain all the specified input.

Note: For now, we will postpone discussing the input of character strings. Day 9 covers strings and includes the input of strings.

Let's look at a program that illustrates both the input of multiple items and different combinations of data types. Listing 4.2 shows the source code for the program IN1.CPP. The program performs the following tasks:

- Prompts you to enter three numbers
- Calculates the sum of the three numbers
- Displays the sum and the average of the three numbers you entered

- Prompts you to type in three characters
- Displays your input
- Prompts you to enter a number, a character, and a number
- Displays your input
- Prompts you to enter a character, a number, and a character
- Displays your input

Listing 4.2. Source code for the program IN1.CPP.

```
// Program that illustrates standard stream input

#include <iostream.h>

main()
{
  double x, y, z, sum;
  char c1, c2, c3;

  cout << "Enter three numbers separated by a space : ";
  cin >> x >> y >> z;
  sum = x + y + z;
  cout << "Sum of numbers = " << sum
       << "\nAverage of numbers = " << sum / 2 << "\n";
  cout << "Enter three characters : ";
  cin >> c1 >> c2 >> c3;
  cout << "You entered characters '" << c1
       << "', '" << c2 << "', and '"
       << c3 << "'\n";
  cout << "Enter a number, a character, and a number : ";
  cin >> x >> c1 >> y;
  cout << "You entered " << x << " " << c1 << " " << y << "\n";
  cout << "Enter a character, a number, and a character : ";
  cin >> c1 >> x >> c2;
  cout << "You entered " << c1 << " " << x << " " << c2 << "\n";

  return 0;
}
```

Here is a sample session with the program in Listing 4.2:

```
Enter three numbers separated by a space : 1 2 3
Sum of numbers = 6
Average of numbers = 3
Enter three characters : ABC
```

```
You entered characters 'A', 'B', and 'C'
Enter a number, a character, and a number : 12A34.4
You entered 12 A 34.4
Enter a character, a number, and a character : A3.14Z
You entered A 3.14 Z
```

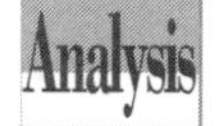

The program in Listing 4.2 declares four `double`-typed variables and three `char`-typed variables. The output statement in line 10 prompts you to enter three numbers. The input statement in line 11 obtains your input and stores the numbers in variables `x`, `y`, and `z`. You need to enter a space character between any two numbers. You can also enter each number on a separate line. The statement stores the first number you enter in variable `x`, the second number in variable `y`, and the third one in variable `z`. This sequence is determined by the sequence in which these variables appear in line 11. The statement in line 12 calculates the sum of the values in variables `x`, `y`, and `z`. The output statement in lines 13 and 14 displays the sum and average of the numbers that you entered.

The output statement in line 15 prompts you to enter three characters. The input statement in line 16 obtains your input and sequentially stores the characters in variables `c1`, `c2`, and `c3`. Your input need not separate the characters with a space. Thus, you can type in characters such as `1A2`, `Bob`, and `1  D  d`. The output statement in lines 17 through 19 displays the characters that you type, separated by spaces.

The output statement in line 20 prompts you to enter a number, a character, and a number. The input statement in line 21 sequentially stores your input in variables `x`, `c1`, and `y`. You need to type a space between the character and either of the numbers only if the character can be interpreted as part of either number. For example, if you want to enter the number 12, the dot character, and the number 55, type `12 . 55`. The spaces around the dot ensure that the input stream does not consider it as a decimal part of either floating-point number. The output statement in line 22 displays the values you entered, separated by spaces.

The output statement in line 23 prompts you to enter a character, a number, and a character. The input statement in line 24 sequentially stores your input in variables `c1`, `x`, and `c2`. You need to enter a space between the characters and the number only if the characters can be interpreted as part of the number. For example, if you want to enter the character `-`, the number `12`, and the digit `0`, type in `- 12 0`. The output statement in line 25 displays the values you entered, separated by spaces.

The *printf* Function

As a novice C++ programmer, you have a wealth of I/O functions from which to choose. In this section, we discuss the formatting features of the function `printf`, which is part of the standard I/O of C. The function is prototyped in the header file STDIO.H.

The `printf` function offers much power and presents formatted controls. The general syntax for the individual formatting instruction is

```
% [flags] [width] [.precision] [F ¦ N ¦ h ¦ l] <type character>
```

The *`flags`* options indicate the output justification, numeric signs, decimal points, and trailing zeros. In addition, these flags also specify the octal and hexadecimal prefixes. Table 4.1 shows the options for the flags in the format string of the `printf` function.

The *`width`* option indicates the minimum number of displayed characters. The `printf` function uses zeros and blanks to pad the output, if needed. When the width number begins with a 0, the `printf` function uses leading zeros, instead of spaces, for padding. When the `*` character appears instead of a width number, the `printf` function obtains the actual width number from the function's argument list. The argument that specifies the required width must come before the argument that is actually being formatted. The following is an example that displays the integer 3 using 2 characters, as specified by the third argument of `printf`:

```
printf("%*d", 2, 3);
```

The *`precision`* option specifies the maximum number of displayed characters. If you include an integer, the precision option defines the minimum number of displayed digits. When the `*` character is used in place of a precision number, the `printf` function obtains the actual precision from the argument list. The argument that specifies the required precision must come before the argument that is actually being formatted. The following is an example that displays the floating-point number 3.3244 using 10 characters, as specified by the third argument of `printf`:

```
printf("%7.*f", 10, 3.3244);
```

The `F`, `N`, `h`, and `l` options are sized options that are used to overrule the argument's default size. The `F` and `N` options are used in conjunction with far and near pointers, respectively. The `h` and `l` options are used to indicate `short int` or `long`, respectively.

Table 4.1. The escape sequence.

Sequence	Decimal Value	Hex Value	Task
`\a`	7	0×07	Bell
`\b`	8	0×08	Backspace
`\f`	12	0×0C	Formfeed
`\n`	10	0×0A	New line
`\r`	13	0×0D	Carriage return
`\t`	9	0×09	Horizontal tab
`\v`	11	0×0B	Vertical tab
`\\`	92	0×5C	Backslash
`\'`	44	0×2C	Single quote
`\"`	34	0×22	Double quote
`\?`	63	0×3F	Question mark
`\000`			1 to 3 digits for octal value
`\Xhhh` and `\xhhh`		0×hhh	Hexadecimal value

The `printf` function requires that you specify a data type character with each `%` format code. Table 4.2 shows the options for the flags in the format string of `printf`. Table 4.3 shows the data type characters used in the format string of `printf`.

Table 4.2. Options for the flags in the format string of the `printf` function.

Format Option	Outcome
-	Justifies to the left within the specified field
+	Displays the plus or minus sign of a value
blank	Displays a leading blank if the value is positive; displays a minus sign if the value is negative

Format Option	Outcome
#	No effect on decimal integers; displays a leading 0X or 0x for hexadecimal integers; displays a leading zero for octal integers; displays the decimal point for reals

Table 4.3. Data type characters used in the format string of `printf`.

Category	Type Character	Outcome
Character	`c`	Single character
	`d`	Signed decimal int
	`i`	Signed decimal int
	`o`	Unsigned octal int
	`u`	Unsigned decimal int
	`x`	Unsigned hexadecimal int (the set of numeric characters used is 0123456789abcdef)
	`X`	Unsigned hexadecimal int; the set of numeric characters used is 0123456789ABCDEF
Pointer	`p`	Displays only the offset for near pointers as OOOO; displays far pointers as SSSS:OOOO
Pointer to int	`n`	
Real	`f`	Displays signed value in the format [-]dddd.dddd
	`e`	Displays signed scientific value in the format [-]d.dddde[+|-]ddd
	`E`	Displays signed scientific value in the format [-]d.ddddE[+|-]ddd

continues

Table 4.3. continued

Category	Type Character	Outcome
	`g`	Displays signed value using either the `f` or `e` formats, depending on the value and the specified precision
	`G`	Displays signed value using either the `f` or `E` formats, depending on the value and the specified precision
String pointer	`s`	Displays characters until the null terminator of the string is reached

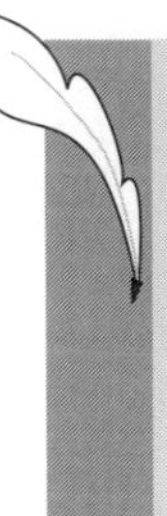

Note: Although the function `printf` plays no role in the output of Windows applications, its sister function, `sprintf`, does. The latter function creates a string of characters that contains the formatted image of the output. We discuss the `sprintf` function in a later lesson, and we use that function later to create a dialog box that contains messages that include numbers.

Consider now a simple example. Listing 4.3 shows the source code for the program OUT2.CPP. We created this program by editing the OUT1.CPP in Listing 4.1. The new version displays formatted output using the `printf` function. The program displays the same floating-point numbers using three different sets of format code.

Listing 4.3. Source code for the program OUT2.CPP.

```
// C++ program that uses the printf function for formatted output

#include <stdio.h>

main()
{
   short    aShort      = 4;
   int      anInt       = 67;
   unsigned char aByte = 128;
   char     aChar       = '@';
   float    aSingle     = 355.0;
   double   aDouble     = 1.130e+002;
   // display sample expressions
   printf("%3d %c %2d = %3d\n",
```

```
15:           aByte, '+', anInt, aByte + anInt);
16:
17:    printf("Output uses the %%lf format\n");
18:    printf("%6.4f / %6.4lf = %7.5lf\n", aSingle, aDouble,
19:                                  aSingle / aDouble);
20:    printf("Output uses the %%le format\n");
21:    printf("%6.4e / %6.4le = %7.5le\n", aSingle, aDouble,
22:                                  aSingle / aDouble);
23:    printf("Output uses the %%lg format\n");
24:    printf("%6.4g / %6.4lg = %7.5lg\n", aSingle, aDouble,
25:                                  aSingle / aDouble);
26:
27:    printf("The character in variable aChar is %c\n", aChar);
28:    printf("The ASCII code of %c is %d\n", aChar, aChar);
29:     return 0;
30: }
```

Here is a sample session with the program in Listing 4.3:

```
128 + 67 = 195
Output uses the %lf format
355.0000 / 113.0000 = 3.14159
Output uses the %le format
3.5500e+002 / 1.1300e+002 = 3.14159e+000
Output uses the %lg format
   355 / 113 = 3.1416
The character in variable aChar is @
The ASCII code of @ is 64
```

The program in Listing 4.3 declares a collection of variables with different data types. The output statement in lines 14 and 15 displays integers and characters using the `%d` and `%c` format controls. Table 4.4 shows the effect of the various format controls in the `printf` statement at line 14. Notice that the `printf` function converts the first item in output from an `unsigned char` to an `int`.

Table 4.4. Effects of the various format controls in the `printf` statement.

Format Control	Item	Data Type	Output
`%3d`	`aByte`	`unsigned char`	Integer
`%c`	`'+'`	`char`	Character
`%2d`	`anInt`	`int`	Integer
`%3d`	`aByte + anInt`	`int`	Integer

The output statement in line 18 displays the variable `aSingle`, the variable `aDouble`, and the expression `aSingle / aDouble` using the format controls `%6.4f`, `%6.4lf` and `%7.5lf`. These controls specify precision values of 4, 4, and 5 digits, respectively, and minimum widths of 6, 6, and 7 characters, respectively. The last two format controls indicate that they display a `double`-typed value.

The output statement in line 21 is similar to that in line 18. The main difference is that the `printf` in line 21 uses the `e` format instead of the `f` format. Consequently, the three items in the `printf` statement appear in scientific notation.

The output statement in line 24 is similar to that in line 18. The main difference is that the `printf` in line 24 uses the `g` format instead of the `f` format. Consequently, the first two items in the `printf` statement appear with no decimal places because they are whole numbers.

The output statement in line 27 displays the contents in the variable `aChar` using the `%c` format control. The output statement in line 28 displays the contents of variable `aChar` twice: once as a character and once as an integer (or, to be more exact, the ASCII code of a character). The `printf` function in line 28 performs this task by using the `%c` and `%d` format controls, respectively.

Summary

Today's lesson examined the basic input and output operations and functions that are supported by the IOSTREAM.H and STDIO.H header files. You learned the following:

- ☐ Formatted stream output uses the `precision` and `width` functions to provide some basic formatting output.
- ☐ Standard stream input supports the insert operator `>>` to obtain input for the predefined data types in C++.
- ☐ The format codes involved in the format string of the `printf` function allow the `printf` function to control the appearance of the output and even perform type conversion.

Q&A

Q How can I chain >> or << operators?

A Each of these operators returns a special stream data type that can be the input for another similar stream operator.

Q Why can't I use the stream I/O operators in Windows applications?

A Windows applications have a fundamentally different way of interacting with you. When an EasyWin program (which emulates a non-GUI MS-DOS application) executes an input statement, it goes into a special mode where it monitors the keyboard input. By contrast, Windows programs (which are GUI applications) are always monitoring the mouse (its movements and its button clicks) and the keyboard, and reporting the current status to the part of Windows that monitors such events. The vast differences between GUI and non-GUI applications render non-GUI input functions useless in GUI applications.

Workshop

The Workshop provides quiz questions to help you solidify your understanding of the material covered and exercises to provide you with experience in using what you've learned. Try to understand the quiz and exercise answers before continuing on to the next day's lesson. Answers are provided in Appendix A, "Answers."

Quiz

1. What is wrong with the following statement?

```
cout << "Enter a number " >> x;
```

2. What happens in the following statement?

```
cout << "Enter three numbers : ";
cin >> x >> y >> x;
```

Exercises

1. Write the program OUT3.CPP, which displays a table of square roots for whole numbers in the range of 2 to 10. Use the MATH.H header file to import the `sqrt` function, which calculates the square root of a `double`-typed argument. Because we have not discussed C++ loops, use repetitive statements to display the various values. Employ the format controls `%3.0lf` and `%3.4lf` to display the number and its square root, respectively.

2. Write the program OUT4.CPP, which prompts you for an integer and displays the hexadecimal and octal equivalent forms. Use the `printf` format controls to perform the conversion between decimal, hexadecimal, and octal numbers.

The Decision-Making Constructs

WEEK 1

Different programming languages offer varying support for decision-making constructs. Some languages provide only simple decision-making constructs, whereas others offer more sophisticated constructs.

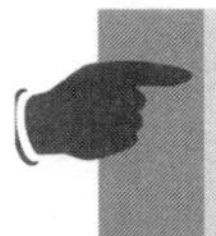

New Term: *Decision-making constructs* allow your applications to examine conditions and choose courses of action.

Today's lesson looks at the decision-making constructs in C++ and covers the following topics:

- The single-alternative `if` statement
- The dual-alternative `if-else` statement
- The multiple-alternative `if-else` statement
- The multiple-alternative `switch` statement
- Nested decision-making constructs

The Single-Alternative *if* Statement

Unlike many programming languages, C++ does not have the keyword `then` in any form of the `if` statement. This language feature may lead you to ask how the `if` statement separates the tested condition from the executable statements. The answer is that C++ dictates that you enclose the tested condition in parentheses.

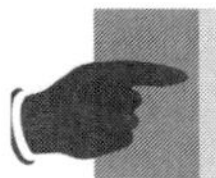

New Term: An `if` statement is a *single-alternative* statement.

Syntax

The Single-Alternative *if* Statement

The general syntax for the single-alternative `if` statement is

```
if (condition)
     statement;
```

for a single executable statement, and

```
if (condition) {
     <sequence of statements>
}
```

for a sequence of executable statements.

Examples:

```
if (numberOfLines < 0)
     numberOfLines = 0;

if ((height - 54) < 3) {
     area = length * width;
     volume = area * height;
}
```

C++ uses the open and close braces `{}` to define a block of statements. Figure 5.1 shows the flow in a single-alternative `if` statement.

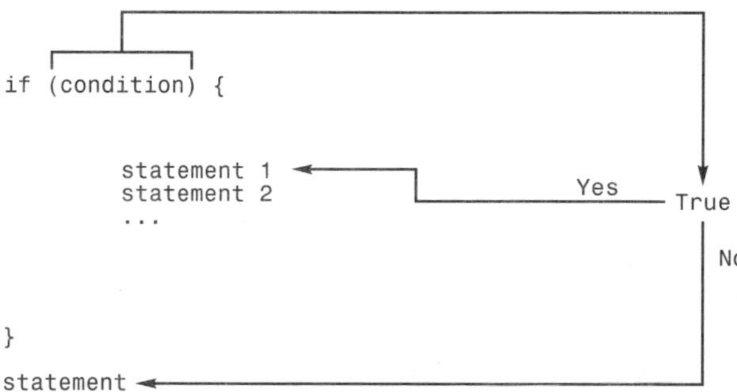

Figure 5.1. *The program flow in the single-alternative* `if` *statement.*

Let's look at an example. Listing 5.1 shows a program with a single-alternative `if` statement. The program prompts you to enter a nonzero number and stores the input in the variable `x`. If the value in `x` is not zero, the program displays the reciprocal of `x`.

Listing 5.1. Source code for the program IF1.CPP.

```
// Program that demonstrates the single-alternative if statement

#include <iostream.h>

main()
{
  double x;
  cout << "Enter a non-zero number : ";
```

continues

5

Listing 5.1. continued

```
9:    cin >> x;
10:   if (x != 0)
11:     cout << "The reciprocal of " << x
12:          << " is " << (1/x) << "\n";
13:   return 0;
14: }
```

Here is a sample session with the program in Listing 5.1:

```
Enter a non-zero number : 25
The reciprocal of 25 is 0.04
```

The program in Listing 5.1 declares the `double`-typed variable `x` in the function `main`. The output statement in line 8 prompts you to enter a nonzero number. The input statement in line 9 stores your input in variable `x`. The `if` statement in line 10 determines whether `x` does not equal zero. If this condition is true, the program executes the output statement in lines 11 and 12. This statement displays the value of `x` and its reciprocal, `1/x`. If the tested condition is false, the program skips the statements in lines 11 and 12 and resumes at the statement in line 13.

The Dual-Alternative *if-else* Statement

In the *dual-alternative* form of the `if` statement, the `else` keyword separates the statements that are used to execute each alternative.

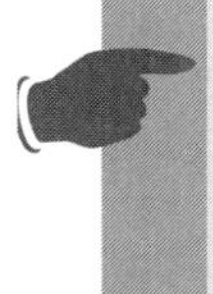

New Term: The *dual-alternative* `if-else` statement provides you with two alternate courses of action based on the Boolean value of the tested condition.

Syntax

The Dual-Alternative *if-else* Statement

The general syntax for the dual-alternative `if-else` statement is

```
if (condition)
    statement1;
else
    statement2;
```

for a single executable statement in each clause, and

```
if (condition) {
     <sequence #1 of statements>
}
else {
     <sequence #2 of statements>
}
```

for a sequence of executable statements in both clauses.

Example:

```
if (moneyInAccount > withdraw) {
  moneyInAccount -= withdraw;
  cout << "You withdrew $" << withdraw << "\n";
  cout << "Balance is $" << moneyInAccount << "\n";
}
else {
  cout << "Cannot withdraw $" << withdraw << "\n";
  cout << "Account has $" << moneyInAccount << "\n";
}
```

Figure 5.2. shows the program flow in the dual-alternative `if-else` statement.

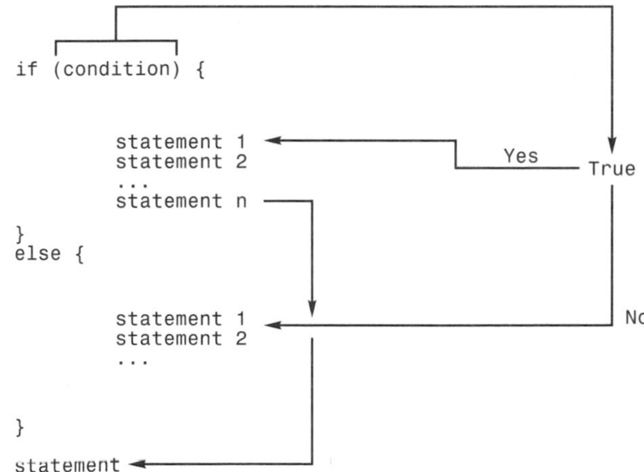

Figure 5.2. *The program flow in the dual-alternative* `if-else` *statement.*

Let's look at an example that uses the dual-alternative `if-else` statement. Listing 5.2 contains the source code for the program IF2.CPP. The program prompts you to enter a character and then determines whether or not you entered a letter. The program output classifies your input as either a letter or a nonletter character.

Listing 5.2. Source code for the program IF2.CPP.

```
1:  // Program that demonstrates the dual-alternative if statement
2:
3:  #include <iostream.h>
4:  #include <ctype.h>
5:
6:  main()
7:  {
8:    char c;
9:    cout << "Enter a letter : ";
10:   cin >> c;
11:   // convert to uppercase
12:   c = toupper(c);
13:   if (c >= 'A' && c <= 'Z')
14:     cout << "You entered a letter\n";
15:   else
16:     cout << "Your input was not a letter\n";
17:   return 0;
18: }
```

Here is a sample session with the program in Listing 5.2:

```
Enter a character : g
You entered a letter
```

The program in Listing 5.2 declares the `char`-typed variable `c` in line 8. The output statement in line 9 prompts you to enter a letter. The input statement in line 10 obtains your input and stores it in variable `c`. The statement in line 12 converts the value in the variable to uppercase by calling the function `toupper` (prototyped in the CTYPE.H header file). This character case conversion simplifies the tested condition in the `if-else` statement at line 13. The `if-else` statement determines if the variable `c` contains a character in the range of *A* to *Z*. If this condition is true, the program executes the output statement in line 14. This statement displays a message stating that you have entered a letter. Alternatively, if the tested condition is false, the program executes the `else` clause statement in line 16. This statement displays a message stating that your input was not a letter.

Potential Problems with the *if* Statement

There is a potential problem with the dual-alternative `if` statement. This problem occurs when the `if` clause includes another single-alternative `if` statement. In this case, the compiler considers that the `else` clause pertains to the nested `if` statement. (A nested `if` statement is one that contains another `if` statement in the `if` and/or `else` clauses. You will learn more about nesting in the next section.) Here is an example:

```
if (i > 0)
     if (i = 10)
          cout << "You guessed the magic number";
else
     cout << "Number is out of range";
```

In this code fragment, when the variable `i` is a positive number other than 10, the code displays the message `Number is out of range`. The compiler treats these statements as though the code fragment meant

```
if (i > 0)
     if (i = 10)
          cout << "You guessed the magic number";
     else
          cout << "Number is out of range";
```

To correct this problem, enclose the nested `if` statement in a statement block:

```
if (i > 0) {
     if (i = 10)
          cout << "You guessed the magic number";
}
else
     cout << "Number is out of range";
```

The Multiple-Alternative *if-else* Statement

C++ enables you to nest `if-else` statements to create a multiple-alternative form. This alternative gives a lot of power and flexibility to your applications.

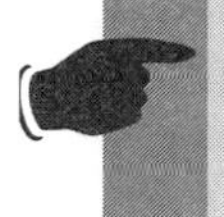

New Term: The *multiple-alternative* `if-else` statement contains nested `if-else` statements.

Syntax

The Multiple-Alternative *if-else* Statement

The general syntax for the multiple-alternative if-else statement is

```
if (tested_condition1)
     statement1; ¦ { <sequence #1 of statement> }
else if (tested_condition2)
     statement2; ¦ { <sequence #2 of statement> }
...
else if (tested_conditionN)
     statementN; ¦ { <sequence #N of statement> }
[else
     statementN+1; ¦ { <sequence #N+1 of statement> }]
```

Example:

```
char op;

int opOk = 1;
double x, y, z;
cout << "Enter operand1 operator operand2: ";
cin >> x >> op >> y;
if (op == '+')
     z = x + y;
else if (op == '-')
     z = x - y;
else if (op == '*')
     z = x * y;
else if (op == '/' && y != 0)
     z = x / y;
else
     opOk = 0;
```

The multiple-alternative `if-else` statement performs a series of cascaded tests until one of the following occurs:

1. One of the conditions in the `if` clause or in the `else if` clauses is true. In this case, the accompanying statements are executed.
2. None of the tested conditions is true. The program executes the statements in the catch-all `else` clause (if there is an `else` clause).

Figure 5.3 shows the program flow in the multiple-alternative `if-else` statement.

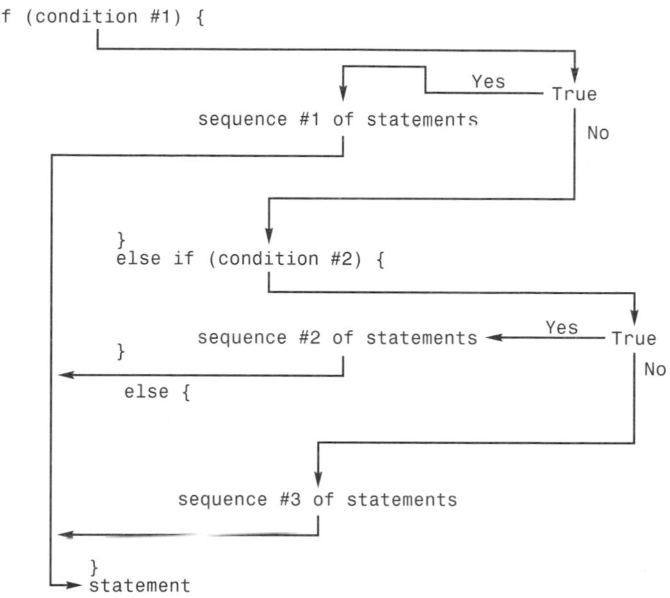

Figure 5.3. *The program flow in the multiple-alternative* `if-else` *statement.*

Consider the following example. Listing 5.3 shows the source code for the program IF3.CPP. The program prompts you to enter a character and uses the multiple-alternative `if-else` statement to determine whether your input is one of the following:

- An uppercase letter
- A lowercase letter
- A digit
- A non-alphanumeric character

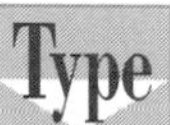

Listing 5.3. Source code for the IF3.CPP program.

```
// Program that demonstrates the multiple-alternative if statement

#include <iostream.h>

main()
{
  char c;
  cout << "Enter a character : ";
```

continues

Listing 5.3. continued

```
9:     cin >> c;
10:    if (c >= 'A' && c <= 'Z')
11:      cout << "You entered an uppercase letter\n";
12:    else if (c >= 'a' && c <= 'z')
13:      cout << "You entered a lowercase letter\n";
14:    else if (c >= '0' && c <= '9')
15:      cout << "You entered a digit\n";
16:    else
17:      cout << "You entered a non-alphanumeric character\n";
18:    return 0;
19: }
```

Here is a sample session with the program in Listing 5.3:

```
Enter a character : !
You entered a non-alphanumeric character
```

The program in Listing 5.3 declares the `char`-typed variable `c` in line 7. The output statement in line 8 prompts you to enter a letter. The input statement in line 9 obtains your input and stores it in variable `c`. The multi-alternative `if-else` statement tests the following conditions:

1. In line 10, the `if` statement determines whether the variable `c` contains a letter in the range of *A* to *Z*. If this condition is true, the program executes the output statement in line 11. This statement confirms that you entered an uppercase letter. The program then resumes at line 18.
2. If the condition in line 10 is false, the program jumps to the first `else if` clause, in line 12. There the program determines whether the variable `c` contains a letter in the range of *a* to *z*. If this condition is true, the program executes the output statement in line 13. This statement confirms that you entered a lowercase letter. The program then resumes at line 18.
3. If the condition in line 12 is false, the program jumps to the second `else if` clause, in line 14. There the program determines whether the variable `c` contains a digit. If this condition is true, the program executes the output statement in line 15. This statement confirms that you entered a digit. The program then resumes at line 18.
4. If the condition in line 14 is false, the program jumps to the catch-all `else` clause in line 16 and executes the output statement in line 17. This statement displays a message telling you that your input was neither a letter nor a digit.

The *switch* Statement

The switch statement offers a special form of multiple-alternative decision-making. It enables you to examine the various values of an integer-compatible expression and choose the appropriate course of action.

Syntax

The *switch* Statement

The general syntax for the switch statement is

```
switch (expression) {
     case constant1_1:
[    case constant1_2: ...]
          <one or more statements>
          break;
     case constant2_1:
[    case constant2_2: ...]
          <one or more statements>
          break;
...
     case constantN_1:
[    case constantN_2: ...]
          <one or more statements>
          break;
     default:
          <one or more statements>
}
```

Example:

```
OK = 1;
switch (op) {
     case '+':
          z = x + y;
          break;
     case '-':
          z = x - y;
          break;
     case '*':
          z = x * y;
          break;
     case '/':
          if (y != 0)
               z = x / y;
          else
               OK = 0;
          break;
     default:
          Ok = 0;
}
```

The rules for using a `switch` statement are

1. The `switch` requires an integer-compatible value. This value may be a constant, variable, function call, or expression. The `switch` statement does not work with floating-point data types.
2. The value after each `case` label *must* be a constant.
3. C++ does not support `case` labels with ranges of values. Instead, *each* value must appear in a separate case label.
4. You need to use a `break` statement after each set of executable statements. The `break` statement causes program execution to resume after the end of the current `switch` statement. If you do not use the `break` statement, the program execution resumes at the subsequent `case` labels.
5. The `default` clause is a catch-all clause.
6. The set of statements in each `case` label or grouped `case` labels need not be enclosed in open and close braces.

Note: The lack of single `case` labels with ranges of values makes it more appealing to use a multiple-alternative `if-else` statement if you have a large contiguous range of values.

Figure 5.4 shows the program flow in the multiple-alternative `switch` statement.

Let's look at an example that uses the `switch` statement. Listing 5.4 contains the source code for the program SWITCH1.CPP that we obtained by editing Listing 5.3. The new program performs the same task of classifying your character input, this time using a `switch` statement.

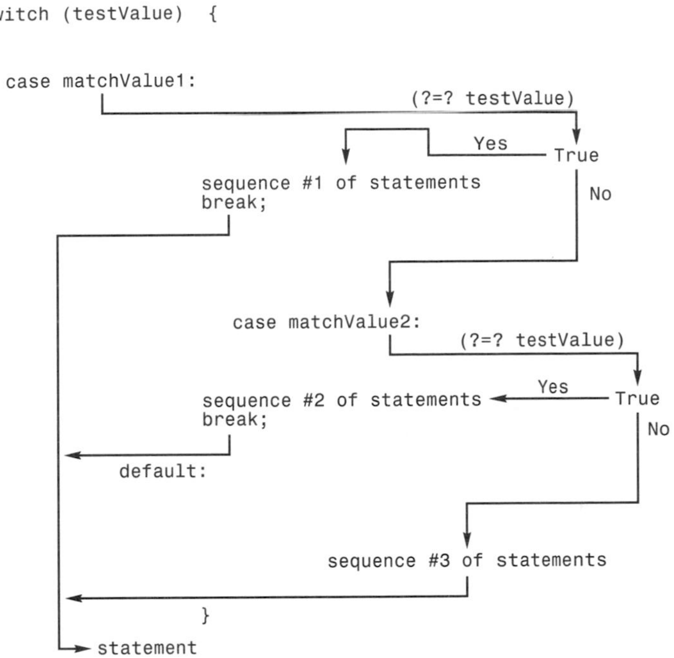

Figure 5.4. *The program flow in the multiple-alternative* `switch` *statement.*

Type Listing 5.4. Source code for the SWITCH1.CPP program.

```
// Program that demonstrates the multiple-alternative switch statement

#include <iostream.h>

main()
{
  char c;
  cout << "Enter a character : ";
  cin >> c;
  switch (c) {
    case 'A':
    case 'B':
    case 'C':
    case 'D':
```

continues

Listing 5.4. continued

```
15:       // other case labels
16:         cout << "You entered an uppercase letter\n";
17:         break;
18:       case 'a':
19:       case 'b':
20:       case 'c':
21:       case 'd':
22:       // other case labels
23:         cout << "You entered a lowercase letter\n";
24:         break;
25:       case '0':
26:       case '1':
27:       case '2':
28:       case '3':
29:       // other case labels
30:         cout << "You entered a digit\n";
31:         break;
32:       default:
33:         cout << "You entered a non-alphanumeric character\n";
34:     }
35:     return 0;
36: }
```

Here is a sample session with the program in Listing 5.4:

```
Enter a character : 2
You entered a digit
```

The program in Listing 5.4 declares the `char`-typed variable `c`. The output statement in line 8 prompts you to enter a character. The statement in line 9 stores your input in variable `c`. The `switch` statement starts at line 10. Lines 11 through 14 contain the `case` labels for the letters *A* through *D*. We omitted the case labels for the rest of the uppercase letters to keep the program short. If the character in variable `c` matches any value in lines 11 through 14, the program executes the output statement in line 16. This statement confirms that you entered an uppercase letter. (Because we reduced the number of `case` labels, the program executes the statement in line 16 only if you enter one of the letters *A* through *D*.) The `break` statement in line 17 causes the program flow to jump to line 35, past the end of the `switch` statement.

If the character in variable `c` does not match any of the `case` labels in lines 11 through 14, the program resumes at line 18, where it encounters another set of `case` labels.

These labels are supposed to represent lowercase characters. As you can see, we reduced the number of labels to shorten the program. If the character in variable `c` matches any value in lines 18 through 21, the program executes the output statement in line 23. This statement confirms that you entered a lowercase letter. (Because we reduced the number of `case` labels, the program executes the statement in line 23 only if you enter one of the letters *a* through *d*.) The `break` statement in line 24 causes the program flow to jump to line 35, past the end of the `switch` statement.

If the character in variable `c` does not match any of the case labels in lines 18 through 21, the program resumes at line 25, where it encounters another set of `case` labels. These labels are supposed to represent digits. Again, you can see that we reduced the number of labels to shorten the program. If the character in variable `c` matches any value in lines 25 through 28, the program executes the output statement in line 30. This statement confirms that you entered a digit. (Because we reduced the number of case labels, the program executes the statement in line 30 only if you enter one of the digits 0 to 3.) The `break` statement in line 31 causes the program flow to jump to line 35, past the end of the `switch` statement.

If the character in variable `c` does not match any `case` label in lines 25 through 28, the program jumps to the catch-all clause in line 32. The program executes the output statement in line 33. This statement tells you that you entered a non-alphanumeric character.

5

Nested Decision-Making Constructs

Often you need to use nested decision-making constructs to manage nontrivial conditions. Nesting decision-making constructs enables you to deal with complicated conditions using a divide-and-conquer approach. The outer-level constructs help you to test preliminary or more general conditions. The inner-level constructs help you deal with more specific conditions.

Let's look at an example. Listing 5.5 shows the source code for the program IF4.CPP. The program prompts you to enter a character. Then the program determines if your input is an uppercase letter, a lowercase letter, or a character that is not a letter. The program displays a message that classifies your input.

Listing 5.5. Source code for the program IF4.CPP.

```
1:  // Program that demonstrates the nested if statements
2:
3:  #include <iostream.h>
4:
5:  main()
6:  {
7:    char c;
8:    cout << "Enter a character : ";
9:    cin >> c;
10:   if ((c >= 'A' && c <= 'Z') || (c >= 'a' && c <= 'z'))
11:     if (c >= 'A' && c <= 'Z')
12:       cout << "You entered an uppercase letter\n";
13:     else
14:       cout << "You entered a lowercase letter\n";
15:   else
16:     cout << "You entered a non-letter character\n";
17:   return 0;
18: }
```

Here is a sample session with the program in Listing 5.5:

```
Enter a character : a
You entered a lowercase letter
```

The program in Listing 5.5 declares the `char`-typed variable `c`. The output statement in line 8 prompts you to enter a character. The statement in line 9 stores your input in variable `c`. The program uses nested `if-else` statements that begin at lines 10 and 11. The outer `if-else` statement determines whether or not the variable `c` contains a letter. If the tested condition is true, the program executes the inner `if-else` statement in line 11. Otherwise, the program resumes at the `else` clause of the outer `if-else` statement and executes the output statement in line 16. This statement tells you that your input was not a letter.

The program uses the inner `if-else` statement to further examine the condition of the outer `if-else` statement. The `if-else` statement in line 11 determines whether the variable `c` contains an uppercase letter. If this condition is true, the program executes the output statement in line 12. Otherwise, the program executes the `else` clause statement in line 14. These output statements tell you whether you entered an uppercase or a lowercase letter. After executing the inner `if-else` statement, the program jumps to line 17, past the end of the outer `if-else` statement.

Summary

Today's lesson presented the various decision-making constructs in C++, including the following:

- The single-alternative `if` statement, such as

```
if (tested_condition)
     statement; ¦ {     <sequence of statements> }
```

- The dual-alternative `if-else` statement, such as

```
if (tested_condition)
    statement1; { <sequence #1 of statements> }
else
    statement1; { <sequence #1 of statements> }
```

- The multiple-alternative `if-else` statement, such as

```
if (tested_condition1)
     statement1; ¦ { <sequence #1 of statement> }
else if (tested_condition2)
     statement2; ¦ { <sequence #2 of statement> }
...
else if (tested_conditionN)
     statementN; ¦ { <sequence #N of statement> }
[else
     statementN+1; ¦ { <sequence #N+1 of statement> }]
```

- The multiple-alternative `switch` statement, such as

```
switch (caseVar) {
    case constant1_1:
    case constant1_2:
    <other case labels>
         <one or more statements>
         break;
    case constant2_1:
    case constant2_2:
    <other case labels>
         <one or more statements>
         break;
    ...
    case constantN_1:
```

5

```
    case constantN_2:
    <other case labels>
         <one or more statements>
         break;

    default:
         <one or more statements>
         break;
}
```

You also learned about the following topics:

- The `if` statements require you to observe the following two rules:
  - The tested condition must be enclosed in parentheses.
  - Blocks of statements are enclosed in pairs of open and close braces.
- Nested decision-making constructs enable you to deal with complex conditions using a divide-and-conquer approach. The outer-level constructs help you in testing preliminary or more general conditions. The inner-level constructs assist in handling more specific conditions.

Q&A

Q Does C++ impose any rules for indenting statements in the clauses of an `if` statement?

A No. The indentation is purely up to you. Typical indentations range from 2 to 4 spaces. Using indentations makes your listings much more readable. Here is the case of an `if` statement with unindented clause statements:

```
if (i > 0)
j = i * i;
else
j = 10 - i;
```

Compare the readability of that listing with this indented version:

```
if (i > 0)
  j = i * i;
else
  j = 10 - i;
```

The indented version is much easier to read.

Q What are the rules for writing the condition of an `if-else` statement?

A There are two schools of thought. The first one recommends that you write the condition so that it is more often true than not. The second school recommends avoiding negative expressions (those that use the relational operator `!=` and the Boolean operator `!`). Programmers in this camp translate this `if` statement,

```
if (i != 0)
    j = 100 / i;
else
    j = 1;
```

into the following equivalent form,

```
if (i == 0)
    j = 1;
else
    j = 100 \ i;
```

even though the likelihood of variable `i` storing 0 might be very low.

Q How do I handle a condition such as the following, which divides by a variable that can possibly be zero?

```
if (i != 0 && 1/i > 1)
    j = i * i;
```

A C++ does not always evaluate the entire tested condition. This partial evaluation occurs when a term in the Boolean expression renders the entire expression false or true, regardless of the values of the other terms. In this case, if variable `i` is 0, the runtime system does not evaluate the term `1/i > 1`. This is because the term `i != 0` is false and would render the entire expression false, regardless of what the second term yields.

Q Is it really necessary to include an `else` or `default` clause in multi-alternative `if-else` and `switch` statements?

A Programmers highly recommend the inclusion of these catch-all clauses to ensure that the multiple-alternative statements handle all conditions.

Workshop

The Workshop provides quiz questions to help you solidify your understanding of the material covered and exercises to provide you with experience in using what you've learned. Try to understand the quiz and exercise answers before continuing on to the next day's lesson. (Answers are provided in Appendix A, "Answers.")

Quiz

1. Simplify the following nested `if` statements by replacing them with a single `if` statement:

```
if (i > 0)
  if (i < 10)
     cout << "i = " << i << "\n";
```

2. Simplify the following `if` statements by replacing them with a single `if` statement:

```
if (i > 0) {
    j = i * i;
    cout << "j = " << j << "\n";
}
if (i < 0) {
    j = 4 * i;
    cout << "j = " << j << "\n";
}
if (i == 0) {
    j = 10 + i
    cout << "j = " << j << "\n";
}
```

3. True or false? The following `if` statements perform the same tasks as the `if-else` statement:

```
if (i < 0) {
     i = 10 + i;
     j = i * i;
     cout << "i = " << i << "\n";
     cout << "j = " << j << "\n";
}
```

```
if (i >= 0) {
      k = 4 * i + 1;
      cout << "k = " << k << "\n";

}

if (i < 0) {
      i = 10 - i;
      j = i * i;
      cout << "i = " << i << "\n";
      cout << "j = " << j << "\n";
}
else {
      k = 4 * i + 1;
      cout << "k = " << k << "\n";
}
```

4. Simplify the following `if-else` statement:

```
if (i > 0 && i < 100)
  j = i * i;
else if (i > 10 && i < 50)
  j = 10 + i;
else if (i >= 100)
  j = i;
else
  j = 1;
```

5. What is wrong with the following `if` statement?

```
if (i > (1 + i * i)) {
  j = i * i
  cout << "i = " << i << " and j = " << j << "\n";
}
```

Exercises

1. Write the program IF5.CPP to solve for the roots of a quadratic equation. The quadratic equation is

$$A X^2 + B X + C = 0$$

5

The roots of the quadratic equation are

```
root1 = (-B +  (B2 - 4AC)) / (2A)
root1 = (-B -  (B2 - 4AC)) / (2A)
```

If the term in the square root is negative, the roots are complex. If the term in the square root term is zero, the two roots are the same and are equal to `-B/(2A)`.

2. Write the program SWITCH2.CPP, which implements a simple four-function calculator. The program should prompt you for the operand and the operator, and display both the input and the result. Include error checking for bad operators and for the attempt to divide by zero.

Loops

WEEK 1

You will recall from Day 3 that loops are powerful language constructs that improve the processing of repetitive tasks. Computers are able to repeat tasks quickly, accurately, and tirelessly. (In this regard, they are better than humans.) Today's lesson presents the following loops in C++:

- The `for` loop statement
- The `do-while` loop statement
- The `while` loop statement
- Skipping iterations
- Exiting loops
- Nested loops

The *for* Loop

The `for` loop in C++ is a versatile loop because it offers both fixed and conditional iterations. The latter feature of the `for` loop deviates from the typical use of the `for` loop in other programming languages, such as Pascal and Basic.

Syntax

The *for* Loop

The general syntax for the `for` loop statement is

```
for (<initialization of loop control variables>;
     <loop continuation test>;
     <increment/decrement of loop control variables>)
```

Example:

```
for (i = 0; i < 10; i++)
     cout << "The cube of " << i << " = " << i * i * i << "\n";
```

The `for` loop statement has three components, each of which are optional. The first component initializes the loop control variables. (C++ enables you to use more than one loop control variable.) The second part of the loop is the condition that determines whether or not the loop makes another iteration. The last part of the `for` loop is the clause that increments and/or decrements the loop control variables.

Note: The C++ `for` loop enables you to declare the loop control variables. Such variables exist in the scope of the loop. This scope is defined by the block of statements that contains the loop.

Let's look at an example. Listing 6.1 contains the source code for the program FOR1.CPP. The program prompts you to define a range of integers by specifying the lower and upper bounds. Then the program calculates the sum of the integers in the range you specify, as well as the average value.

Listing 6.1. Source code for the program FOR1.CPP.

```
// Program that calculates a sum and average of a range of
// integers using a for loop

#include <iostream.h>

main()
{
    double sum = 0.0;
    double sumx = 0.0;
    int first, last, temp;

    cout << "Enter the first integer : ";
    cin >> first;
    cout << "Enter the last integer : ";
    cin >> last;
    if (first > last) {
      temp= first;
      first = last;
      last = temp;
    }
    for (int i = first; i <= last; i++) {
      sum++;
      sumx += (double)i;
    }
    cout << "Sum of integers from "
         << first << " to " << last << " = "
         << sumx << "\n";
    cout << "Average value = " << sumx / sum;
    return 0;
}
```

Here is a sample session with the program in Listing 6.1:

```
Enter the first integer : 1
Enter the last integer : 100
Sum of integers from 1 to 100 = 5050
Average value = 50.5
```

The program in Listing 6.1 declares a collection of `int`-typed and `double`-typed variables in function `main`. The function initializes the summation variables, `sum` and `sumx`, to 0. The input and output statements in lines 12 through 15 prompt you to enter the integers that define a range of values. The program stores these integers in the variables `first` and `last`. The `if` statement in line 16 determines whether the value in variable `first` is greater than the value in variable `last`. If this condition is true, the program executes the block of statements in lines 17 through 19. These statements swap the values in variables `first` and `last`, using the variable `temp` as a swap buffer. Thus, the `if` statement ensures that the integer in variable `first` is less than or equal to the integer in variable `last`.

The program carries out the summation using the `for` loop in line 21. The loop declares its own control variable, `i`, and initializes it with the value in the variable `first`. The loop continuation condition is `i <= last`. This condition indicates that the loop iterates as long as `i` is less than or equal to the value in the variable `last`. The loop increment component is `i++`, which increments the loop control variable by 1 for every iteration. The loop contains two statements. The first statement increments the value in the variable `sum`. The second statement adds the value of `i` (after typecasting it to `double`) to the variable `sumx`.

Note: You can rewrite the `for` loop to move the first loop statement to the loop increment component:

```
for (int i = first; i <= last; i++, sum++)
   sumx += (double)i;
```

The output statement in lines 25 through 27 displays the sum and average of integers in the range you specified.

To illustrate the flexibility of the `for` loop, we created the program FOR2.CPP, shown in Listing 6.2, by editing the program FOR1.CPP. The two programs perform the same tasks and interact identically with the user. The changes we made are in line 10 and lines 21 through 25. Line 10 declares the loop control variable. In line 21, we initialize the variable `i` using the value in the variable `first`. The `for` loop is located at line 22. The loop has no initialization part because we took care of that in line 21. In addition, we removed the loop increment component and compensated for it by applying the post-increment operator to the variable `i` in line 24.

Listing 6.2. Source code for the program FOR2.CPP.

```
1:  // Program that calculates a sum and average of a range of
2:  // integers using a for loop
3:
4:  #include <iostream.h>
5:
6:  main()
7:  {
8:      double sum = 0;
9:      double sumx = 0.0;
10:     int first, last, temp, i;
11:
12:     cout << "Enter the first integer : ";
13:     cin >> first;
14:     cout << "Enter the last integer : ";
15:     cin >> last;
16:     if (first > last) {
17:       temp= first;
18:       first = last;
19:       last = temp;
20:     }
21:     i = first;
22:     for (; i <= last; ) {
23:       sum++;
24:       sumx += (double)i++;
25:     }
26:     cout << "Sum of integers from "
27:          << first << " to " << last << " = "
28:          << sumx << "\n";
29:     cout << "Average value = " << sumx / sum;
30:     return 0;
31: }
```

Here is a sample session with the program in Listing 6.2:

```
Enter the first integer : 10
Enter the last integer : 100
Sum of integers from 10 to 100 = 5005
Average value = 55
```

Open Loops Using the *for* Loops

When we introduced you to the C++ `for` loop, we stated that the three components of the `for` loop are optional. In fact, C++ permits you to leave these three components empty.

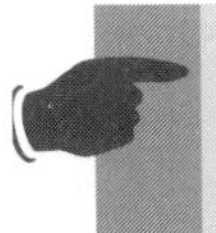

New Term: When you leave the three components of a loop empty, the result is an *open loop*.

It is worthwhile to point out that other languages, such as Ada and Modula-2, do support formal open loops and provide mechanisms to exit these loops. C++ permits you to exit from a loop in the following two ways:

1. The `break` statement causes the program execution to resume after the end of the current loop. Use the `break` statement when you wish to exit a `for` loop and resume with the remaining parts of the program.
2. The `exit` function (declared in the STDLIB.H header file) enables you to exit the program. Use the `exit` function if you want to stop iterating and also exit the program.

Consider the following example. Listing 6.3 contains the source code for the program FOR3.CPP. The program uses an open loop to prompt you repeatedly for a number. The program takes your input and displays it along with its reciprocal value. Then the program asks you whether or not you wish to calculate the reciprocal of another number. If you type in the letter *Y* or *y*, the program performs another iteration. Otherwise, the program ends. If you keep typing *Y* or *y* for the latter prompt, the program keeps running—at least until the computer breaks down!

Listing 6.3. Source code for the program FOR3.CPP.

```
// Program that demonstrates using the
// for loop to emulate an infinite loop.

#include <iostream.h>
#include <ctype.h>

main()
{
   char ch;
   double x, y;

```

```
12:     // for loop with empty parts
13:     for (;;) {
14:        cout << "\nEnter a number : ";
15:        cin >> x;
16:        // process number if non-zero
17:        if (x != 0) {
18:          y = 1/ x;
19:          cout << "1/(" << x << ") = " << y << "\n";
20:          cout << "More calculations? (Y/N) ";
21:          cin >> ch;
22:          ch = toupper(ch);
23:          if (ch != 'Y')
24:             break;
25:        }
26:        else
27:          // display error message
28:          cout << "Error: cannot accept 0\n";
29:     }
30:     return 0;
31: }
```

Here is a sample session with the program in Listing 6.3:

```
Enter a number : 5
1/(5) = 0.2
More calculations? (Y/N) y

Enter a number : 12
1/(12) = 0.0833333
More calculations? (Y/N) y

Enter a number : 16
1/(16) = 0.0625
More calculations? (Y/N) n
```

The program in Listing 6.3 declares the `char`-typed variable `ch` and two `double`-typed variables, `x` and `y`. The function `main` uses the `for` loop, in line 13, as an open loop by eliminating all three loop components. The output statement in line 14 prompts you to enter a number. The input statement in line 15 obtains your input and stores it in variable `x`. The `if-else` statement in line 17 determines if the value in variable `x` is not zero. If this condition is true, the program executes the block of statements in lines 18 through 24. Otherwise, the program executes the `else` clause statement in line 28. This statement displays an error message.

The statement in line 18 assigns the reciprocal of the value in variable `x` to variable `y`. The output statement in line 19 displays the values in variables `x` and `y`. The output statement in line 20 prompts you for more calculations, and requires a Y/N (in either uppercase or lowercase) type of answer. The input statement in line 21 stores your single-character input in variable `c`. The statement in line 22 converts your input into uppercase, using the function `toupper`. (This function is prototyped in the CTYPE.H header file.) The `if` statement in line 23 determines whether the character in variable `c` is not the letter *Y*. If this condition is true, the program executes the `break` statement in line 24. This statement causes the program execution to exit the open loop and to resume at line 30.

The *do-while* Loop

The `do-while` loop in C++ is a conditional loop that tests the iteration condition at the end of the loop. Therefore, the `do-while` loop iterates at least once.

New Term: A *conditional loop* iterates as long as a condition is true. This condition is tested at the end of the loop.

Syntax

The *do-while* Loop

The general syntax for the `do-while` loop is

```
do {
     <sequence of statements>
} while (condition);
```

Example:

The following loop displays the squares of 2 to 10:

```
int i = 2;
do {
     cout << i << "^2 = " << i * i << "\n";
} while (++i < 11);
```

Let's look at an example. Listing 6.4 shows the source code for the program DOWHILE1.CPP, which essentially calculates square root values. The program performs the following tasks:

- Prompts you to enter a number. (If you enter a negative number, the program reprompts you for a number.)
- Calculates and displays the square root of the number you entered.
- Asks you if you wish to enter another number. (If you enter the letter *Y* or *y*, the program resumes at step number 1; otherwise, the program ends.)

Type

Listing 6.4. Source code for the program DOWHILE1.CPP.

```
// Program that demonstrates the do-while loop

#include <iostream.h>

const double TOLERANCE = 1.0e-7;

double abs(double x)
{
  return (x >= 0) ? x : -x;
}

double sqroot(double x)
{
  double guess = x / 2;
  do {
    guess = (guess + x / guess) / 2;
  } while (abs(guess * guess - x) > TOLERANCE);
  return guess;
}

double getNumber()
{
  double x;
  do {
    cout << "Enter a number: ";
    cin >> x;
  } while (x < 0);
  return x;
}

main()
{
   char c;
   double x, y;

   do {
      x = getNumber();
      y = sqroot(x);
      cout << "Sqrt(" << x << ") = " << y << "\n"
           << "Enter another number? (Y/N) ";
      cin >> c;
      cout << "\n";
   } while (c == 'Y' || c == 'y');
   return 0;
}
```

Here is a sample session with the program in Listing 6.4:

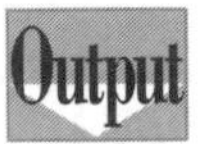

```
Enter a number: 25
Sqrt(25) = 5
Enter another number? (Y/N) y

Enter a number: 144
Sqrt(144) = 12
Enter another number? (Y/N) n
```

The program in Listing 6.4 declares the global constant `TOLERANCE` and the functions `abs`, `sqroot`, `getNumber`, and `main`. The function `abs`, located in line 7, returns the absolute value of `double`-typed arguments.

The function `sqroot`, located in line 12, returns the square root of the parameter `x`. The function sets the initial guess for the square root to `x / 2` in line 14. Then the function uses a `do-while` loop to refine iteratively the guess for the square root. The condition in the `while` clause determines if the absolute difference between the square of the current guess and the parameter `x` is greater than the allowable error (represented by the constant `TOLERANCE`). The loop iterates as long as this condition is true. The function returns the guess for the square root in line 18. The function `sqroot` implements Newton's method for iteratively obtaining the square root of a number.

The function `getNumber`, located in line 21, prompts you for a number and stores your input in the local variable `x`. The function uses a `do-while` loop to ensure that you enter a nonnegative number. The `while` clause in line 27 determines if the value in variable `x` is negative. As long as this condition is true, the `do-while` loop iterates. In line 28, the `return` statement yields the value of `x`.

The function `main`, located in line 31, uses a `do-while` loop to perform the following tasks:

- ☐ Prompts you for a number by calling function `getNumber`. (The statement in line 37 contains the function call and assigns the result to the local variable x.)
- ☐ Calculates the square root of `x` by calling function `sqroot`, and assigns the result to the variable `y`. (The statement that contains this function call is in line 38.)
- ☐ Displays the values in variables `x` and `y`.
- ☐ Asks you if you want to enter another number. (The input statement in line 41 takes your single-character Y/N input and stores it in variable `c`.)

The `while` clause, located in line 43, determines if the variable `c` contains either the letter *Y* or *y*. The `do-while` loop iterates as long as this condition is true.

The program in Listing 6.4 illustrates the following uses for the `do-while` loop:

1. *Iterative calculations.* The loop in function `sqroot` demonstrates this aspect.
2. *Data validation.* The loop in function `getNumber` demonstrates this aspect.
3. *Program continuation.* The loop in function `main` demonstrates this aspect.

The *while* Loop

The `while` loop in C++ is another conditional loop that iterates as long as a condition is true. Thus, the `while` loop may not iterate if the tested condition is initially false.

Syntax

The *while* Loop

The general syntax of the `while` loop is

```
while (condition)
     statement; ¦ { sequence of statements }
```

Example:

```
function power(double x, int n)
{
  double pwr = 1;
  while (n-- > 0)
     pwr *= x;
  return pwr;
}
```

Look at the next example. Listing 6.5 shows the source code for the program WHILE1.CPP. This program performs the same operations as the program FOR1.CPP, in Listing 6.1. The two programs interact with the user in the same way and yield the same results.

Listing 6.5. Source code for the program WHILE1.CPP.

```
// Program that demonstrates the while loop

#include <iostream.h>

main()
{
    double sum = 0;
    double sumx = 0.0;
    int first, last, temp, i;

```

continues

Listing 6.5. continued

```
11:     cout << "Enter the first integer : ";
12:     cin >> first;
13:     cout << "Enter the last integer : ";
14:     cin >> last;
15:     if (first > last) {
16:       temp= first;
17:       first = last;
18:       last = temp;
19:     }
20:     i = first;
21:     while (i <= last) {
22:       sum++;
23:       sumx += (double)i++;
24:     }
25:     cout << "Sum of integers from "
26:          << first << " to " << last << " = "
27:          << sumx << "\n";
28:     cout << "Average value = " << sumx / sum;
29:     return 0;
30: }
```

Here is a sample session with the program in Listing 6.5:

```
Enter the first integer : 1
Enter the last integer : 100
Sum of integers from 1 to 100 = 5050
Average value = 50.5
```

Because the programs in Listings 6.5 and 6.1 are similar, we will focus here on lines 20 through 24, where the main difference between the two programs lies. The statement in line 20 assigns the value of the variable `first` to the variable `i`. The `while` loop starts at line 21. The loop iterates as long as the value in the variable `i` is less than or equal to the value in the variable `last`. The variable `i` plays the role of the loop control variable. The statement in line 22 increments the value in the variable `sum`. The statement in line 23 adds the value in variable `i` to the variable `sumx` and also increments the variable `i`. The statement performs the latter task by applying the post-increment operator to the variable `i`.

Skipping Loop Iterations

C++ enables you to jump to the end of a loop and resume the next iteration using the `continue` statement. This programming feature permits your loop to skip iteration for special values that may cause runtime errors.

Syntax

The *continue* Statement

The general form for using the `continue` statement is

```
<loop-start clause> {
     // sequence #1 of statements
     if (skipCondition)
          continue;
     // sequence #2 of statements
} <loop-end clause>
```

Example (in a `for` loop):

```
double x, y;
for (int i = -10; i < 11; i++) {
  x = i;
  if (i == 1)
     continue;
  y = 1/sqrt(x * x - 1);
  cout << "1/sqrt(" << (x*x-1) << ") = " << y << "\n";
}
```

This form shows that the evaluation of the first sequence of statements in the `for` loop gives rise to a condition tested in the `if` statement. If that condition is true, the `if` statement invokes the `continue` statement to skip the second sequence of statements in the `for` loop.

Let's look at an example. Listing 6.6 shows the source code for the program FOR4.CPP. The program displays the table of values for the function f(X) = $\sqrt{(X^2-9)}$ at integer values between –10 and 10. Because the integers between –2 and 2 yield complex results, which the program avoids, the table does not display the complex values for f(X) between –2 and 2.

Listing 6.6. Source code for the program FOR4.CPP.

```
// Program that demonstrates using the continue statement
// to skip iterations.

#include <iostream.h>
#include <math.h>


double f(double x)
{
  return sqrt(x * x - 9);
}

```

continues

Listing 6.6. continued

```
main()
{
   double x, y;

   cout << "         X";
   cout << "           f(X)\n";
   cout << "________________________________________\n\n";
   // for loop with empty parts
   for (int i = -10; i <= 10; i++) {
     if (i > -3 && i < 3)
       continue;
     x = (double)i;
     y = f(x);
     cout << "       ";
     cout.width(3);
     cout << x << "         ";
     cout.width(7);
     cout << y << "\n";
   }
   return 0;
}
```

Here is a sample session with the program in Listing 6.6:

```
         X           f(X)
________________________________________

       -10        9.53939
        -9        8.48528
        -8         7.4162
        -7        6.32456
        -6        5.19615
        -5              4
        -4        2.64575
        -3              0
         3              0
         4        2.64575
         5              4
         6        5.19615
         7        6.32456
         8         7.4162
         9        8.48528
        10        9.53939
```

The program in Listing 6.6 declares the function `f` to represent the mathematical function f(X). The function `main` declares the `double`-typed variables `x` and `y` in line 15. The output statements in lines 17 through 19 display the table's heading. The `for` loop in line 21 declares its own control variable and iterates between –10 and 10, in increments of 1. The first statement inside the loop is the `if` statement located at line 22. This statement determines if the value in variable `i` is greater than –3 and less than 3. If this condition is true, the program executes the `continue` statement in line 23. Thus, the `if` statement enables the `for` loop to skip error-generating iterations and resume with the next iteration. The statement in line 24 assigns the value in variable `i` to variable `x`. The statement in line 25 calls the function `f` and supplies it with the argument `x`. The statement then assigns the result to variable `y`. The output statements in lines 25 through 30 display the values of the variables `x` and `y`. The statements use the function `width` for simple formatting.

Exiting Loops

C++ supports the `break` statement to exit a loop. The `break` statement makes the program resume after the end of the current loop.

Syntax

The *break* Statement

The general form for using the `break` statement in a loop is

```
<start-loop clause> {
     // sequence #1 of statements
     if (exitLoopCondition)
          break;
     // sequence #2 of statements
} <end-loop clause>
// sequence #3 of statements
```

Example:

```
// calculate the factorial of n
factorial = 1;
for (int i = 1; ; i++) {
  if (i > n)
     break;
  factorial *= (double)i;
}
```

This form shows that the evaluation of the first sequence of statements in the `for` loop gives rise to a condition tested in the `if` statement. If that condition is true, the `if` statement invokes the `break` statement to exit the loop altogether. The program execution resumes at the third sequence of statements.

For a good example that uses the `break` statement, we recommend that you reexamine the FOR3.CPP program in Listing 6.3.

Nested Loops

Nested loops enable you to contain repetitive tasks as part of other repetitive tasks. C++ enables you to nest any kind of loops to just about any level needed. Nested loops are frequently used to process arrays (which are covered in Day 7).

The following is an example that uses nested loops. Listing 6.7 shows the source code for the program NESTFOR1.CPP. The program displays a table for square roots for whole numbers in the range of 1 to 10. The program uses an outer loop to iterate over this range of numbers and employs an inner loop to iteratively calculate the square root.

Listing 6.7. Source code for the program NESTFOR1.CPP.

```
// Program that demonstrates nested loops

#include <stdio.h>

const double TOLERANCE = 1.0e-7;
const int MIN_NUM = 1;
const int MAX_NUM = 10;

double abs(double x)
{
  return (x >= 0) ? x : -x;
}

main()
{
   double x, sqrt;

   printf("  X       Sqrt(X)\n");
   printf("_____________________\n\n");
   // outer loop
```

```
21:    for (int i = MIN_NUM; i <= MAX_NUM; i++) {
22:      x = (double)i;
23:      sqrt = x /2;
24:      // inner loop
25:      do {
26:        sqrt = (sqrt + x / sqrt) / 2;
27:      } while (abs(sqrt * sqrt - x) > TOLERANCE);
28:      printf("%4.1f     %8.6lf\n", x, sqrt);
29:    }
30:    return 0;
31: }
```

Here is a sample session with the program in Listing 6.7:

```
    X        Sqrt(X)
_______________________

   1.0      1.000000
   2.0      1.414214
   3.0      1.732051
   4.0      2.000000
   5.0      2.236068
   6.0      2.449490
   7.0      2.645751
   8.0      2.828427
   9.0      3.000000
  10.0      3.162278
```

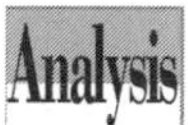

The program in Listing 6.7 includes the header file STDIO.H in order to use the `printf` output function with its powerful formatting capabilities. Lines 5 through 7 define the constants `TOLERANCE`, `MIN_NUM`, and `MAX_NUM` to represent, respectively, the tolerance in square root values, the first number in the output table, and the last number in the output table. The program defines the function `abs` to return the absolute number of a `double`-typed number.

The function `main` declares the `double`-typed variables `x` and `sqrt`. The output statements in lines 18 and 19 display the table's heading. Line 21 contains the outer loop, a `for` loop. This loop declares its control variable, `i`, and iterates from `MIN_NUM` to `MAX_NUM` in increments of 1. Line 22 stores the typecast value of `i` in variable `x`. The statement in line 23 obtains the initial guess for the square root and stores it in variable `sqrt`. Line 25 contains the inner loop, a `do-while` loop that iterates to refine the guess for the square root. The statement in line 26 refines the guess for the square root. The `while` clause in line 27 determines whether or not the refined guess is adequate. The output statement in line 28 displays the formatted values for the variables `x` and `sqrt`.

Summary

Today's lesson covered the C++ loops and topics related to loops. You learned about the following:

- The `for` loop in C++ has the following general syntax:

  ```
  for (<initialization of loop control variables>;
       <loop continuation test>;
       <increment/decrement of loop control variables>)
  ```

  The `for` loop contains three components: the loop initialization, loop continuation condition, and the increment/decrement of the loop variables.

- The conditional loop `do-while` has the following general syntax:

  ```
  do {
       sequence of statements
  } while (condition);
  ```

  The `do-while` loop iterates at least once.

- The conditional `while` loop has the following general syntax:

  ```
  while (condition)
       statement; ¦ { sequence of statements }
  ```

  The `while` loop might not iterate if its tested condition is initially false.

- The `continue` statement enables you to jump to the end of the loop and resume with the next iteration. The advantage of the `continue` statement is that it uses no labels to direct the jump.

- Open loops are `for` loops with empty components. The `break` statement enables you to exit the current loop and resume program execution at the first statement that comes after the loop. The `exit` function (declared in STDLIB.H) enables you to make a critical loop exit by halting the C++ program altogether.

- Nested loops enable you to contain repetitive tasks as part of other repetitive tasks. C++ enables you to nest any kind of loops to just about any level needed.

Q&A

Q How can a `while` loop simulate a `for` loop?

A Here is a simple example:

```
int i;
for (i = 1; i <= 10; i +=2) {
  cout << i << "\n";
```

```
int i = 1;
 while (i <= 10) {
  cout << i << "\n";
  i += 2;
}
```

The `while` loop needs a leading statement that initializes the loop control variable. Also notice that the `while` loop uses a statement inside it to alter the value of the loop control variable.

Q How can a `while` loop simulate a `do-while` loop?

A Here is a simple example:

```
i = 1;
do {
  cout << i << "\n";
  i += 2;
} while (i <- 10);
```

```
i = 1;
while (i <= 10) {
  cout << i << "\n";
  i += 2;
}
```

The two loops have the same condition in their `while` clauses.

Q How can the open `for` loop emulate the `while` and `do-while` loops?

A The open `for` loop is able to emulate the other C++ loops by placing the loop-escape `if` statement near the beginning or end of the loop. Here is how the open `for` loop emulates a sample `while` loop:

```
i = 1;
while (i <= 10) {

  cout << i << "\n"
  i += 2;
}
```

```
i = 1;
for (;;) {
  if(i > 10) break;
  cout << i << "\n"
  i += 2;
}
```

6

Notice that the open `for` loop uses a loop-escape `if` statement as the first statement inside the loop. The condition tested by the `if` statement is the logical reverse of the `while` loop condition. Here is a simple example showing the emulation of the `do-while` loop:

```
i = 1;                          i = 1;
do {                            for (;;) {
  cout << i << "\n"               cout << i << "\n"
  i += 2;                         i += 2;
                                  if (i > 10) break;
} while (i <= 10);              }
```

The open `for` loop uses a loop-escape `if` statement right before the end of the loop. The `if` statement tests the reverse condition as the `do-while` loop.

Q In nested `for` loops, can I use the loop control variable of the outer loops as part of the range of values for the inner loops?

A Yes. C++ does not prohibit such use. Here is a simple example:

```
for (int i = 1; i <= 100; i += 5)
    for (int j = i; j <= 100; j++)
         cout << i * j << "\n";
```

Q Does C++ restrict nesting of the various types of loops?

A No. You can nest any combination of loops in a C++ program.

Workshop

The Workshop provides quiz questions to help you solidify your understanding of the material covered and exercises to provide you with experience in using what you've learned. Try to understand the quiz and exercise answers before continuing on to the next day's lesson. (Answers are provided in Appendix A, "Answers.")

Quiz

1. What is wrong with the following loop?

```
i = 1;
while (i < 10) {
  j = i * i - 1;
  k = 2 * j - i;
  cout << "i = " << i << "\n";
```

```
    cout << "j = " <<  j << "\n";
    cout << "k = " << k << "\n";
  }
```

2. What is the output of the following `for` loop?

```
for (int i = 5; i < 10; i += 2)
     cout << i - 2 << "\n";
```

3. What is the output of the following `for` loop?

```
for (int i = 5; i < 10; )
     cout << i - 2 << "\n";
```

4. What is wrong with the following code?

```
for (int i = 1; i <= 10; i++)
     for (i = 8; i <= 12; i++)
          cout << i << "\n";
```

5. Where is the error in the following loops?

```
for (int i = 1; i <= 10; i++)
  cout << i * i << "\n";
for (int i = 1; i <= 10; i++)
  cout << i * i * i << "\n";
```

6. Where is the error in the following loop?

```
i = 1;
while (1 > 0) {
  cout << i << "\n";
  i++;
}
```

7. The factorial of a number is the product of the sequence of integers from 1 to that number. The following general equation defines the factorial (which uses the symbol `!`):

```
n! = 1 * 2 * 3 * ... * n
```

Here is a C++ program that calculates the factorial of a number. The problem is that for whatever positive value you enter, the program displays a 0 value for the factorial. Where is the error in the program?

```
int n;
double factorial;
```

```
cout << "Enter positive integer : ";
cin >> n;
for (int i = 1; i <= n; i++)
  factorial *= i;
cout << n << "!= " << factorial;
```

Exercises

1. Write the program FOR5.CPP, which uses a `for` loop to obtain and display the sum of odd integers in the range of 11 to 121.
2. Write the program WHILE2.CPP, which uses a `while` loop to obtain and display the sum of the squared odd integers in the range of 11 to 121.
3. Write the program DOWHILE2.CPP, which uses a `do-while` loop to obtain and display the sum of the squared odd integers in the range of 11 to 121.

Arrays

WEEK

1

Arrays are among the most utilized data structures. They enable programs to store data for later processing. Most popular programming languages support static arrays. Many languages also support dynamic arrays.

New Term: An *array* is a group of variables.

Today, you will learn about the following topics related to static arrays:

- Declaring single-dimensional arrays
- Using single-dimensional arrays
- Initializing single-dimensional arrays
- Declaring single-dimensional arrays as function parameters
- Sorting arrays
- Searching arrays
- Declaring multidimensional arrays
- Using multidimensional arrays
- Initializing multidimensional arrays
- Declaring multidimensional arrays as function parameters

Declaring Single-Dimensional Arrays

The single-dimensional array is the simplest kind of array. In a single-dimensional array, each variable is individually accessed using a single index.

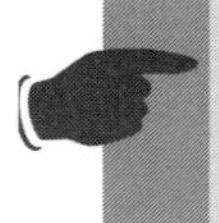

New Term: A *single-dimensional array* is a group of variables that share the same name (the name of the array).

Syntax

A Single-Dimensional Array

The general syntax for declaring a single-dimensional array is

```
type arrayName[numberOfElements];
```

C++ requires you to observe the following rules in declaring single-dimensional arrays:

1. The lower bound of a C++ array is set at 0. C++ does not allow you to override or alter this lower bound.
2. Declaring a C++ array entails specifying the number of members. Keep in mind that the number of members is equal to the upper bound plus one.

The valid range of indices for this form extends between `0` and *`numberOfElements - 1`*.

Examples:

```
int intArray[10];
char name[31];
double x[100];
```

Using Single-Dimensional Arrays

Using a single-dimensional array involves stating both its name and the valid index in order to access one of its members. Depending on where the reference to an array element occurs, it can either store or recall a value. The simple rules to remember are

1. Assign a value to an array element before accessing that element to recall data. Otherwise, you get garbage data.
2. Use a valid index.

DO	DON'T

DO make reasonable checks for the indices that access the arrays.

DON'T assume that indices are always valid.

7

Let's look at an example. Listing 7.1 shows the source code for the program ARRAY1.CPP. The program uses a 30-element numeric array to calculate the average for the data in a numeric array. The program performs the following tasks:

- Prompts you to enter the number of actual data points. (This value must lie in the range of valid numbers indicated by the prompting message.)
- Prompts you to enter the data for the array elements.
- Calculates the average of the data in the array.
- Displays the average value.

Listing 7.1. Source code for the program ARRAY1.CPP.

```
/*
  C++ program that demonstrates the use of one-dimensional
  arrays.  The average value of the array is calculated.
*/

#include <iostream.h>

const int MAX = 30;

main()
{

    double x[MAX];
    double sum, sumx = 0.0, mean;
    int i, n;

    do { // obtain number of data points
        cout << "Enter number of data points [2 to "
             << MAX << "] : ";
        cin >> n;
        cout << "\n";
    } while (n < 2 || n > MAX);

    // prompt user for data
    for (i = 0; i < n; i++) {
        cout << "X[" << i << "] : ";
        cin >> x[i];
    }

    // initialize summations
    sum = n;

    // calculate sum of observations
    for (i = 0; i < n; i++)
        sumx += x[i];

    mean = sumx / sum; // calculate the mean value
```

```
38:     cout << "\nMean = " << mean << "\n\n";
39:     return 0;
40: }
```

Here is a sample session with the program in Listing 7.1:

```
Enter number of data points [2 to 30] : 5

X[0] : 12.5
X[1] : 45.7
X[2] : 25.6
X[3] : 14.1
X[4] : 68.4

Mean = 33.26
```

The program in Listing 7.1 declares the global constant `MAX` as the size of the array used in the program. The function `main` declares the `double`-typed array `x`, in line 13, to have `MAX` elements. The function also declares other nonarray variables in lines 14 and 15.

The `do-while` loop, located in lines 17 through 22, obtains the number of data points that you want to store in the array `x`. The output statement in lines 18 and 19 prompts you to enter the number of data points. The output indicates the range of valid numbers, which is `2 to MAX`. The statement in line 20 obtains your input and stores it in the variable `n`. The `while` clause validates your input. The clause determines if the value in variable `n` is less than 2 or is greater than `MAX`. If this condition is true, the `do-while` loop iterates again to obtain a correct input value.

The `for` loop statement, in lines 25 through 28, prompts you to enter the data. The loop uses the control variable `i` and iterates from 0 to `n-1`, in increments of 1. The output statement in line 26 prompts you to enter the value for the indicated array element. The input statement in line 27 obtains your input and stores it in the element `x[i]`.

The statement in line 31 assigns the integer in variable `n` to the `double`-typed variable `sum`. The `for` loop in lines 34 and 35 adds the values in array `x` to the variable `sumx`. The loop uses the control variable `i` and iterates from 0 to `n-1`, in increments of 1. The statement in line 35 uses the increment assignment operator to add the value in element `x[i]` to the variable `sumx`.

The statement in line 37 calculates the mean value and stores it in variable `mean`. The output statement in line 38 displays the mean value.

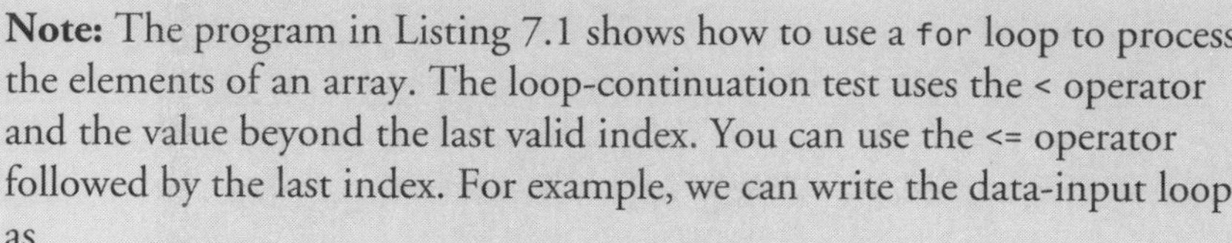

Note: The program in Listing 7.1 shows how to use a `for` loop to process the elements of an array. The loop-continuation test uses the < operator and the value beyond the last valid index. You can use the <= operator followed by the last index. For example, we can write the data-input loop as

```
    // prompt user for data
    for (i = 0; i <= (n - 1); i++) {
        cout << "X[" << i << "] : ";
        cin >> x[i];
    }
```

However, this form is not popular, because it requires an additional operator, whereas the condition `i < n` does not.

DO	DON'T

DO write the loop-continuation expression so that it uses the minimum number of operators. This approach reduces the code size and speeds up loop execution.

DON'T use the <= operator in the loop-continuation condition, unless using the operator helps you write an expression that minimizes the number of operations.

Initializing Single-Dimensional Arrays

C++ enables you to initialize arrays and is flexible about the initialization. You need to enclose the list of initializing values in a pair of open and close braces (`{}`). The list is comma-delimited and may continue on multiple lines. If there are fewer items in the initializing list than there are array elements, the compiler assigns 0 to balance the array elements. By contrast, if the list of initializing values has more items than the number of array elements, the compiler flags a compile-time error.

The next program, Listing 7.2, modifies the last program to supply data internally. Consequently, we eliminate the steps that prompt you for the number of data points and the data itself. The program simply displays the array elements (obtained from the initialization list) and the average value for the data. Although this program does not interact with the user, it offers a version that stores data in the source code. You can edit the program periodically to add, edit, and delete data before recalculating a new average value.

Listing 7.2. Source code for the program ARRAY2.CPP.

```
/*
  C++ program that demonstrates the use of single-dimensional
  arrays.  The average value of the array is calculated.
  The array has its values preassigned internally.
*/

#include <iostream.h>

const int MAX = 10;

main()
{

    double x[MAX] = { 12.2, 45.4, 67.2, 12.2, 34.6, 87.4,
                      83.6, 12.3, 14.8, 55.5 };
    double sum = MAX, sumx = 0.0, mean;
    int n = MAX;

    // calculate sum of observations
    cout << "Array is:\n";
    for (int i = 0; i < n; i++) {
        sumx += x[i];
        cout << "x[" << i << "] = " << x[i] << "\n";
    }

    mean = sumx / sum; // calculate the mean value
    cout << "\nMean = " << mean << "\n\n";
    return 0;
}
```

Here is a sample session with the program in Listing 7.2:

```
Array is:
x[0] = 12.2
x[1] = 45.4
x[2] = 67.2
x[3] = 12.2
```

```
x[4] = 34.6
x[5] = 87.4
x[6] = 83.6
x[7] = 12.3
x[8] = 14.8
x[9] = 55.5

Mean = 42.52
```

Now we will focus on the initialization of the array `x` in Listing 7.2. Line 14 contains the declaration of array `x` and its initialization. The initializing list, which runs to line 15, is enclosed in a pair of braces and has comma-delimited values. The statement in line 16 declares the variables `sum` and `sumx` and initializes these variables to `MAX` and `0`, respectively. The statement in line 17 declares the `int`-typed variable `n` and initializes it with the value `MAX`. The rest of the program resembles parts of the program in Listing 7.1.

If you are somewhat dismayed by the fact that you have to count the exact number of initializing values, then we have some good news for you: C++ enables you to size an array automatically by using the number of items in the corresponding initializing list. Consequently, you don't need to place a number in the square brackets of the array, and you can let the compiler do the work for you.

DO / **DON'T**

DO include dummy values in the initializing list, if the initialized array needs to expand later.

DON'T rely on counting the number of items in the initializing list to provide the data for the number of array elements.

Listing 7.3 shows the source code for the program ARRAY3.CPP. This new version uses the feature of automatic array sizing.

Listing 7.3. Source code for the program ARRAY3.CPP.

```
/*
  C++ program that demonstrates the use of single-dimensional
  arrays.  The average value of the array is calculated.
  The array has its values preassigned internally.
*/

#include <iostream.h>

```

```
9:  main()
10: {
11:
12:     double x[] = { 12.2, 45.4, 67.2, 12.2, 34.6, 87.4,
13:                    83.6, 12.3, 14.8, 55.5 };
14:     double sum,  sumx = 0.0, mean;
15:     int n;
16:
17:     n = sizeof(x) / sizeof(x[0]);
18:     sum = n;
19:
20:     // calculate sum of observations
21:     cout << "Array is:\n";
22:     for (int i = 0; i < n; i++) {
23:         sumx += x[i];
24:         cout << "x[" << i << "] = " << x[i] << "\n";
25:     }
26:
27:     mean = sumx / sum; // calculate the mean value
28:     cout << "\nNumber of data points = " << n << "\n"
29:          << "Mean = " << mean << "\n";
30:     return 0;
31: }
```

Here is a sample session with the program in Listing 7.3:

```
Array is:
x[0] = 12.2
x[1] = 45.4
x[2] = 67.2
x[3] = 12.2
x[4] = 34.6
x[5] = 87.4
x[6] = 83.6
x[7] = 12.3
x[8] = 14.8
x[9] = 55.5

Number of data points = 10
Mean = 42.52
```

Notice that the program in Listing 7.3 does not declare the constant `MAX`, which appears in the previous version (shown in Listing 7.2). How does the program determine the number of array elements? Line 17 shows that the program calculates the number of elements in array `x` by dividing the size of the array `x` (obtained by using `sizeof(x)`) by the size of the first element (obtained by using `sizeof(x[0])`). You can use this method to obtain the size of any array of any data type.

Array Parameters in Functions

C++ enables you to declare function parameters that are arrays. In fact, C++ permits you to be either specific or general about the size of the array parameter. If you want an array parameter to accept arrays of a fixed size, you can specify the size of the array in the parameter declaration. Alternatively, if you want the array parameter to accept arrays with the same basic type but different sizes, use empty brackets with the array parameter.

Syntax

A Fixed-Array Parameter

The general syntax for declaring a fixed-array parameter is

type parameterName[*arraySize*]

Examples:

```
int minArray(int arr[100], int n);
void sort(unsigned dayNum[7]);
```

Syntax

An Open-Array Parameter

The general syntax for declaring an open-array parameter is

type parameterName[]

Examples:

```
int minArray(int arr[], int n);
void sort(unsigned dayNum[]);
```

DO	DON'T

DO use open-array parameters in functions.

DON'T forget to check the upper bounds of an open-array parameter in general-purpose functions.

Let's look at a simple example. Listing 7.4 shows the source code for the program ARRAY4.CPP. The program performs the following tasks:

- Prompts you to enter the number of data points, which ranges from 2 to 10.
- Prompts you to enter the integer values for the arrays.

- Displays the smallest value in the array.
- Displays the largest value in the array.

Listing 7.4. Source code for the program ARRAY4.CPP.

```
// C++ program that passes arrays as arguments of functions

#include <iostream.h>

const int MAX = 10;

main()
{
  int arr[MAX];
  int n;

  // declare prototypes of functions
  int getMin(int a[MAX], int size);
  int getMax(int a[], int size);

  do { // obtain number of data points
    cout << "Enter number of data points [2 to "
        << MAX << "] : ";
    cin >> n;
    cout << "\n";
  } while (n < 2 || n > MAX);

  // prompt user for data
  for (int i = 0; i < n; i++) {
    cout << "arr[" << i << "] : ";
    cin >> arr[i];
  }

  cout << "Smallest value in array is "
       << getMin(arr, n) << "\n"
       << "Biggest value in array is "
       << getMax(arr, n) << "\n";
  return 0;
}


int getMin(int a[MAX], int size)
{
  int small = a[0];
  // search for the smallest value in the
  // remaining array elements
  for (int i = 1; i < size; i++)
    if (small > a[i])
      small = a[i];
```

continues

Listing 7.4. continued

```
45:   return small;
46: }
47:
48: int getMax(int a[], int size)
49: {
50:   int big = a[0];
51:   // search for the biggest value in the
52:   // remaining array elements
53:   for (int i = 1; i < size; i++)
54:     if (big < a[i])
55:       big = a[i];
56:   return big;
57: }
```

Here is a sample session with the program in Listing 7.4:

```
Enter number of data points [2 to 10] : 5

arr[0] : 55
arr[1] : 69
arr[2] : 47
arr[3] : 85
arr[4] : 14
Smallest value in array is 14
Biggest value in array is 85
```

The program in Listing 7.4 declares the global constant `MAX`, in line 5, to size up the array of data. The function `main` declares the `int`-typed array `arr` in line 9. Line 10 contains the declaration of the `int`-typed variable `n`. Lines 13 and 14 declare the prototypes for the functions `getMin` and `getMax`, which return the smallest and biggest values in an `int`-typed array, respectively. The prototype of the function `getMin` indicates that it uses a fixed-array parameter. By contrast, the prototype of the function `getMax` indicates that it uses an open-array parameter. We use both kinds of array parameters for the sake of demonstration.

The `do-while` loop, located in lines 16 through 21, obtains the number of data points you want to store in the array `arr`. The output statement in lines 17 and 18 prompts you to enter the number of data points. The output indicates the range of valid numbers, which runs between 2 and `MAX`. The statement in line 19 obtains your input and stores it in variable `n`. The `while` clause validates your input. The clause determines if the value in variable `n` is less than 2 or is greater than `MAX`. If this condition is true, the `do-while` loop iterates again to obtain a correct input value.

The `for` loop statement in lines 24 through 27 prompts you to enter the data. The loop uses the control variable `i` and iterates from 0 to `n-1`, in increments of 1. The output

statement in line 25 prompts you to enter the value for the indicated array element. The statement in line 26 obtains your input and stores it in the element `arr[i]`.

The output statement in lines 29 through 32 displays the smallest and biggest integers in array `arr`. The statement invokes the functions `getMin` and `getMax`, supplying each one of them with the arguments `arr` and `n`.

The program defines the function `getMin` in lines 37 through 46. The function has two parameters: the `int`-typed, fixed-array parameter `a`, and the `int`-typed parameter `size`. The function declares the local variable `small` and initializes it with `a[0]`, the first element of parameter `a`. The function searches for the smallest value in the parameter `a`, using the `for` loop in line 42. This loop declares the control variable `i`, and iterates from 1 to `size-1`, in increments of 1. The loop contains an `if` statement that assigns the value in element `a[i]` to variable `small`, if the latter is greater than element `a[i]`. The function returns the value in variable `small`. The function `getMin` only accepts `int`-typed arrays that have `MAX` elements.

The program defines the function `getMax` in lines 48 through 57. This function, which is similar to the function `getMin`, has two parameters: the `int`-typed, open-array parameter `a`, and the `int`-typed parameter `size`. The function declares the local variable `big` and initializes it with `a[0]`, the first element of parameter `a`. The function searches for the smallest value in the parameter `a`, using the `for` loop in line 53. This loop declares the control variable `i`, and iterates from 1 to `size-1`, in increments of 1. The loop contains an `if` statement that assigns the value in element `a[i]` to the variable `big`, if the latter is less than element `a[i]`. The function returns the value in the variable `big`. The function `getMax` accepts `int`-typed arrays of any size.

Sorting Arrays

Sorting and searching are the most common nonnumerical operations for arrays. Sorting an array typically arranges its elements in ascending order. The process uses parts or all of the value in each element to determine the precedence of the elements in the array. Searching for data in sorted arrays is much easier than in unordered arrays.

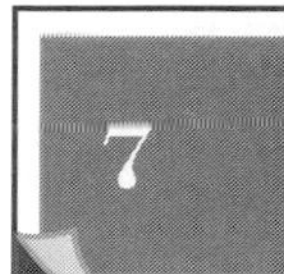

Computer scientists have spent much time and effort studying and creating methods for sorting arrays. A comprehensive discussion of these methods is beyond the scope of this book. We will only mention that some favorite array sorting methods include the QuickSort, Shell-Metzner sort, heap sort, and the new Comb sort. The QuickSort method is the fastest method, in general, but requires some operational overhead. The Shell-Metzner and Comb sort methods do not require similar overhead. The example in this section uses the new Comb sort method, which is more efficient than the Shell-Metzner method.

The Comb sort method uses the following steps, given an array, A, with *N* elements:

1. Initializes the `Offset` value, used in comparing elements, to `N`.
2. Sets the `Offset` value to either `8*Offset/11` or `1`, whichever is bigger.
3. Sets the `InOrder` flag to true.
4. Loops for values 0 to *N*-Offset, using the loop control variable `i`:
   - Assigns `I + Offset` to `J`
   - If `A[I]` is greater than `A[J]`, swaps `A[I]` with `A[J]` and sets the `InOrder` flag to false
5. Resumes at step 2 if `Offset` is not 1 and `InOrder` is false.

Let's look at a program that sorts an array of integers. Listing 7.5 shows the source code for the program ARRAY5.CPP. The program performs the following tasks:

- Prompts you to enter the number of data points.
- Prompts you to enter the integer values for the array.
- Displays the elements of the unordered array.
- Displays the elements of the sorted array.

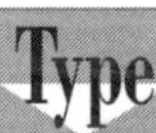

Listing 7.5. Source code for the program ARRAY5.CPP.

```
// C++ program that sorts arrays using the Comb sort method

#include <iostream.h>

const int MAX = 10;
const int TRUE = 1;
const int FALSE = 0;

int obtainNumData()
{
  int m;
  do { // obtain number of data points
    cout << "Enter number of data points [2 to "
        << MAX << "] : ";
    cin >> m;
    cout << "\n";
  } while (m < 2 || m > MAX);
  return m;
}

void inputArray(int intArr[], int n)
```

```
{
  // prompt user for data
  for (int i = 0; i < n; i++) {
    cout << "arr[" << i << "] : ";
    cin >> intArr[i];
  }
}

void showArray(int intArr[], int n)
{
  for (int i = 0; i < n; i++) {
    cout.width(5);
    cout << intArr[i] << " ";
  }
  cout << "\n";
}

void sortArray(int intArr[], int n)
{
  int offset, temp, inOrder;

  offset = n;
  do {
    offset = (8 * offset) / 11;
    offset = (offset == 0) ? 1 : offset;
    inOrder = TRUE;
    for (int i = 0, j = offset; i < (n - offset); i++, j++) {
      if (intArr[i] > intArr[j]) {
        inOrder = FALSE;
        temp = intArr[i];
        intArr[i] = intArr[j];
        intArr[j] = temp;
      }
    }
  } while (!(offset = 1 && inOrder == TRUE));
}

main()
{
  int arr[MAX];
  int n;

  n = obtainNumData();
  inputArray(arr, n);
  cout << "Unordered array is:\n";
  showArray(arr, n);
  sortArray(arr, n);
  cout << "\nSorted array is:\n";
  showArray(arr, n);
  return 0;
}
```

Here is a sample session with the program in Listing 7.5:

```
Enter number of data points [2 to 10] : 10
arr[0] : 55
arr[1] : 68
arr[2] : 74
arr[3] : 15
arr[4] : 28
arr[5] : 23
arr[6] : 69
arr[7] : 95
arr[8] : 22
arr[9] : 33
Unordered array is:
   55     68     74     15     28     23     69     95     22     33

Sorted array is:
   15     22     23     28     33     55     68     69     74     95
```

The program in Listing 7.5 declares the constants `MAX`, `TRUE`, and `FALSE` in lines 5 through 7. The constant `MAX` defines the size of the array used in the program. The constants `TRUE` and `FALSE` define the Boolean values. The program also defines the functions `obtainNumData`, `inputArray`, `showArray`, `sortArray`, and `main`.

The parameterless function `obtainNumData`, defined in lines 9 through 19, prompts you to enter the number of values. The output statement in lines 13 and 14 also specifies the valid range for your input. The statement in line 15 stores your input in the local variable `m`. The function uses a `do-while` loop to ensure that it returns a valid number. The loop iterates as long as the value in variable `m` is less than 2 or greater than `MAX`. The function returns the value in variable `m`.

The function `inputArray`, defined in lines 21 through 28, obtains the data for the tested array. The function has two parameters. The open-array parameter `intArr` passes the input values back to the caller of the function. The parameter `n` specifies how many values to obtain for parameter `intArr`. The function uses a `for` loop, which iterates from 0 to `n-1`, in increments of 1. Each loop iteration prompts you for a value and stores that value in an element of the array `intArr`.

Note: The function `inputArray` illustrates that C++ functions treat array parameters as if they were references to their arguments because these parameters affect the values in the arguments beyond the scope of the functions. In reality, the C++ compiler passes a copy of the address of the array argument to the function when dealing with an array parameter. Armed with the address of the array, C++ functions can then alter the values of the array beyond the scope of these functions. This feature is possible because the function is working with the original array and not a copy.

The function showArray, defined in lines 30 through 37, displays the meaningful data in an array. The function has two parameters. The open-array parameter intArr passes the array values to be displayed by the function. The parameter n specifies how many elements of array *intArr* to display. (Remember that not all of the array elements are used to store your data.) The function uses a for loop, which iterates from 0 to n-1, in increments of 1. Each loop iteration displays the value in an array element. The array elements appear on the same line.

The function sortArray, defined in lines 39 through 57, sorts the elements of an array using the Comb sort method. The function has two parameters. The open-array parameter intArr passes the array values to be sorted by the function. The parameter n specifies how many array elements to sort. The statements in the function sortArray implement the Comb sort method outlined earlier.

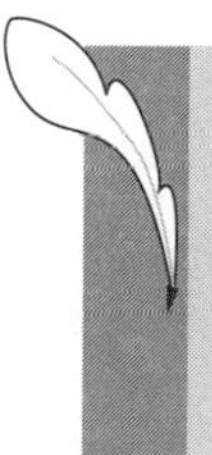

Note: The function sortArray illustrates how array parameters can pass data to and from a function. The function sortArray receives an unordered array, sorts it, and passes the ordered array to the function's caller. The compiler supports this feature by passing a copy of the address of the array to the function. Thus, the function need not explicitly return the array, because it is working with the original data and not a copy.

The function main performs the various program tasks by calling the functions mentioned earlier. The function declares the array arr and the simple variable n in lines 61 and 62, respectively. The statement in line 64 calls function obtainNumData to obtain the number of data points you want to store in the array. The statement assigns the result of the function obtainNumData to variable n. The statement in line 65 calls the function inputArray to prompt you for the data. The function call passes the arguments arr and n. The output statement in line 66 displays a message indicating that the program is about to display the elements of the unordered array. The statement in line 67 calls showArray and passes it the arguments arr and n. This function call displays the elements of the array arr on one line. The statement in line 68 calls the function sortArray to sort the first n elements in array arr. The output

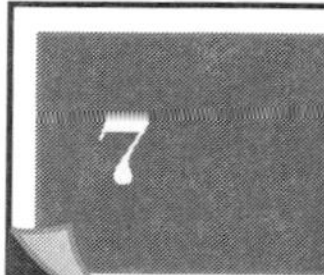

statement in line 69 displays a message indicating that the program is about to display the elements of the sorted array. The statement in line 70 calls `showArray` and passes the arguments `arr` and `n`. This function call displays the elements of the ordered array `arr` on one line.

Searching Arrays

Searching arrays is another important nonnumerical operation. Because arrays can be sorted or unordered, there is a general category of search methods for each. The simplest search method for unordered arrays is the linear search method. The simplest search method for sorted arrays is the versatile binary search method. The search methods for unordered arrays can also be applied to sorted arrays. However, they do not take advantage of the array order.

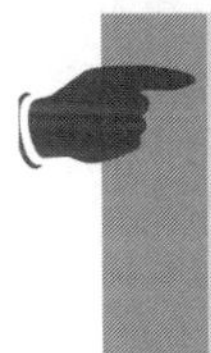

New Term: The *linear search* method sequentially examines the array elements, looking for an element that matches the search value. If the sought value is not in the array, the linear search method examines the entire array's elements.

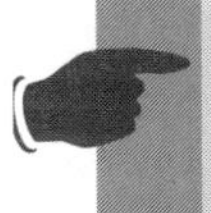

New Term: The binary search method takes advantage of the order in the array. The method searches for a matching value by using the shrinking intervals approach. The initial search interval includes all the array elements (which contain meaningful data). The method compares the median element of the interval with the search value. If the two match, the search stops. Otherwise, the method determines which sub-interval to use as the next search interval. Consequently, each search interval is half the size of the previous one. If the search value has no match in the examined array, the binary method makes far fewer examinations than the linear search method. The binary search method is the most efficient general-purpose search method for sorted arrays.

DO **DON'T**

DO use the unordered-array search method when you are not sure that the array is sorted.

DON'T use sorted-array search methods with unordered arrays. The results of such searches are not reliable.

Let's look at a program that sorts an array of integers. Listing 7.6 shows the source code for the program ARRAY6.CPP. We created this program by adding functions and operations to the program ARRAY5.CPP. The program performs the following tasks:

1. Prompts you to enter the number of data points.
2. Prompts you to enter the integer values for the array.
3. Displays the elements of the unordered array.
4. Asks you if you want to search for data in the unordered array. (If you type characters other than *Y* or *y*, the program resumes at step 8.)
5. Prompts you for a search value.
6. Displays the search outcome. (If the program finds a matching element, it displays the index of that element; otherwise, the program tells you that it found no match for the search value.)
7. Resumes at step 4.
8. Displays the elements of the sorted array.
9. Asks you if you want to search for data in the unordered array. (If you type characters other than *Y* or *y*, the program ends.)
10. Prompts you for a search value.
11. Displays the search outcome. (If the program finds a matching element, it displays the index of that element; otherwise, the program tells you that it found no match for the search value.)
12. Resumes at step 9.

Listing 7.6. Source code for the program ARRAY6.CPP.

```
// C++ program that searches arrays using the linear
// and binary searches methods

#include <iostream.h>

const int MAX = 10;
const int TRUE = 1;
const int FALSE = 0;
const int NOT_FOUND = -1;

int obtainNumData()
{
  int m;
  do { // obtain number of data points
    cout << "Enter number of data points [2 to "
        << MAX << "] : ";
    cin >> m;
    cout << "\n";
  } while (m < 2 || m > MAX);
  return m;
}

void inputArray(int intArr[], int n)
{
  // prompt user for data
  for (int i = 0; i < n; i++) {
    cout << "arr[" << i << "] : ";
    cin >> intArr[i];
  }
}

void showArray(int intArr[], int n)
{
  for (int i = 0; i < n; i++) {
    cout.width(5);
    cout << intArr[i] << " ";
  }
  cout << "\n";
}

void sortArray(int intArr[], int n)
// sort the first n elements of array intArr
// using the Comb sort method
{
  int offset, temp, inOrder;

  offset = n;
  do {
    offset = (8 * offset) / 11;
```

```
    offset = (offset == 0) ? 1 : offset;
    inOrder = TRUE;
    for (int i = 0, j = offset; i < (n - offset); i++, j++) {
      if (intArr[i] > intArr[j]) {
        inOrder = FALSE;
        temp = intArr[i];
        intArr[i] = intArr[j];
        intArr[j] = temp;
      }
    }
  } while (!(offset = 1 && inOrder == TRUE));
}

int linearSearch(int searchVal, int intArr[], int n)
// perform linear search to locate the first
// element in array intArr that matches the value
// of searchVal
{
  int notFound = TRUE;
  int i = 0;
  // search through the array elements
  while (i < n && notFound)
    // no match?
    if (searchVal != intArr[i])
      i++; // increment index to compare the next element
    else
      notFound = FALSE; // found a match
  // return search outcome
  return (notFound == FALSE) ? i : NOT_FOUND;
}

int binarySearch(int searchVal, int intArr[], int n)
// perform binary search to locate the first
// element in array intArr that matches the value
// of searchVal
{
  int median, low, high;

  // initialize the search range
  low = 0;
  high = n - 1;
  // search in array
  do {
    // obtain the median index of the current search range
    median = (low + high) / 2;
    // update search range
    if (searchVal > intArr[median])
      low = median + 1;
    else
      high = median - 1;
```


continues

Listing 7.6. continued

```
  } while (!(searchVal == intArr[median] || low > high));
  // return search outcome
  return (searchVal == intArr[median]) ? median : NOT_FOUND;
}

void searchInUnorderedArray(int intArr[], int n)
// manage the linear search test
{
  int x, i;
  char c;
  // perform linear search
  cout << "Search in unordered array? (Y/N) ";
  cin >> c;
  while (c == 'Y' || c == 'y') {
    cout << "Enter search value : ";
    cin >> x;
    i = linearSearch(x, intArr, n);
    if (i != NOT_FOUND)
      cout << "Found matching element at index " << i << "\n";
    else
      cout << "No match found\n";
    cout << "Search in unordered array? (Y/N) ";
    cin >> c;
  }
}

void searchInSortedArray(int intArr[], int n)
// manage the binary search test
{
  int x, i;
  char c;
  // perform binary search
  cout << "Search in sorted array? (Y/N) ";
  cin >> c;
  while (c == 'Y' || c == 'y') {
    cout << "Enter search value : ";
    cin >> x;
    i = binarySearch(x, intArr, n);
    if (i != NOT_FOUND)
      cout << "Found matching element at index " << i << "\n";
    else
      cout << "No match found\n";
    cout << "Search in sorted array? (Y/N) ";
    cin >> c;
  }
}

main()
{
```

```
    int arr[MAX];
    int n;

    n = obtainNumData();
    inputArray(arr, n);
    cout << "Unordered array is:\n";
    showArray(arr, n);
    searchInUnorderedArray(arr, n);
    sortArray(arr, n);
    cout << "\nSorted array is:\n";
    showArray(arr, n);
    searchInSortedArray(arr, n);
    return 0;
}
```

Here is a sample session with the program in Listing 7.6:

```
Enter number of data points [2 to 10] : 5

arr[0] : 85
arr[1] : 41
arr[2] : 55
arr[3] : 67
arr[4] : 48
Unordered array is:
   85    41    55    67    48
Search in unordered array? (Y/N) y
Enter search value : 55
Found matching element at index 2
Search in unordered array? (Y/N) y
Enter search value : 41
Found matching element at index 1
Search in unordered array? (Y/N) n

Sorted array is:
   41    48    55    67    85
Search in sorted array? (Y/N) y
Enter search value : 55
Found matching element at index 2
Search in sorted array? (Y/N) y
Enter search value : 67
Found matching element at index 3
Search in sorted array? (Y/N) n
```

The program in Listing 7.6 declares the functions `obtainNumData`, `inputArray`, `sortArray`, `linearSearch`, `binarySearch`, `searchInUnorderedArray`, `searchInSortedArray`, and `main`. Because the first three functions are identical to those in Listing 7.5, we will discuss only the remaining functions.

The `linearSearch` function performs a linear search to find the first element in array `intArr` with a value that matches the one in parameter `searchVal`. The function searches the first `n` elements in array `intArr`. The `linearSearch` function returns the index of the matching element in array `intArr` or yields the value of the global constant `NOT_FOUND` if no match is found. The function uses a `while` loop to examine the elements in array `intArr`. The search loop iterates while the value in variable `i` is less than that in variable `n` and while the local variable `notFound` stores `TRUE`. The statement in line 78 returns the function result using the conditional operator.

The `binarySearch` function has the same parameters as the `linearSearch` function and returns the same kind of value. The function uses the local variables `low` and `high` to store the current search interval. The function initializes the variables `low` and `high` using the values 0 and `n-1`, respectively. The `do-while` loop in lines 92 through 100 calculates the index of the median element and compares the median element with the search value. The `if` statement in line 96 performs this comparison, and its clauses update the value of either variable `low` or variable `high`, depending on the outcome of the comparison. The update in either variable shrinks the search interval. The `return` statement in line 102 yields the function's value based on one last comparison between the search value and the median element of the current search interval.

The function `searchInUnorderedArray` manages the search in the unordered array. The function accesses the unordered array using the open-array parameter `intArr`. The function declares local variables that are used to prompt you for and store the search value. The statement in line 116 calls the function `linearSearch` and passes the argument `x` (the local variable that stores the search value), `intArr`, and `n`. The statement assigns the result of function `linearSearch` to the local variable `i`. The `if` statement in line 117 determines whether or not the value in variable `i` is not `NOT_FOUND`. If this condition is true, the output statement in line 118 shows the index of the matching element. Otherwise, the output statement in line 120 displays a no-match-found message.

The function `searchInSortedArray` is very similar to the function `searchInUnorderedArray`. The main difference is that the function `searchInSortedArray` deals with ordered arrays and therefore calls the `binarySearch` function to conduct a binary search on the ordered array `intArr`.

The function `main` invokes these functions to support the program tasks that we described earlier.

Multidimensional Arrays

In a multidimensional array, each additional dimension provides you with an additional access attribute. Two-dimensional arrays (or matrices, if you prefer) are the most popular kind of multidimensional array. Three-dimensional arrays are used less frequently than matrices, and so on.

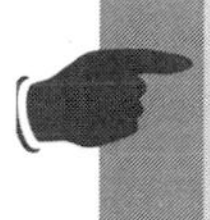

New Term: *Multidimensional arrays* are supersets of the single-dimensional arrays.

Syntax

Two-Dimensional and Three-Dimensional Arrays

The general syntax for declaring two-dimensional and three-dimensional arrays is

```
type array [size1][size2];
type array [size1][size2][size3];
```

As with simple arrays, each dimension has a lower bound index of 0, and the declaration defines the number of elements in each dimension.

Examples:

```
double matrixA[100][10];
char table[41][22][3];
int index[7][12];
```

It is important to understand how C++ stores the elements of a multidimensional array. Most compilers store the elements of a multidimensional array in a contiguous fashion (that is, as one long array). The runtime code calculates where a sought element is located in that long array. To explain the storage scheme of multidimensional arrays, we'll start by employing a convention for referencing the indices of the different dimensions. The following schema specifies the dimension numbering and the concept of high- and low-order dimensions. Here is a six-dimensional array—an extreme case that is a good example:

```
    1     2     3     4     5     6  <-- dimension number
M [20]  [7]  [5]  [3]  [2]  [2]
    higher dimension order -->
```

The first element of the array `M` is `M[0][0][0][0][0][0]` and is stored at the first memory location of array `M`. The array `M` is stored in a contiguous block of 8,400 elements. The location in that contiguous block stores the element at index 1 in the highest dimension number, dimension 6 (that is, `M[0][0][0][0][0][1]`). The location of the next elements in the contiguous block stores the subsequent elements in dimension 6 until the upper limit of dimension 6 is reached. Reaching this limit bumps the index of dimension 5 by 1 and resets the index of dimension 6 to 0. This process is repeated until every element in a multidimensional array is accessed. You can compare this storage scheme to looking at a gasoline pump meter when refueling your car: the right digits turn the fastest, the left digits turn the slowest.

Here is another example that uses a three-dimensional array, `M[3][2][2]`:

```
M[0][0][0]     <-- the starting memory address
M[0][0][1]     <-- 3rd dimension is filled
M[0][1][0]
M[0][1][1]     <-- 2nd and 3rd dimensions are filled
M[1][0][0]
M[1][0][1]     <-- 3rd dimension is filled
M[1][1][0]
M[1][1][1]     <-- 2nd and 3rd dimensions are filled
M[2][0][0]
M[2][0][1]     <-- 3rd dimension is filled
M[2][1][0]
M[2][1][1]     <-- all dimensions are filled
```

Let's consider an example that illustrates basic matrix manipulation. Listing 7.7 shows the source code for the MAT1.CPP program. The program manages a matrix that contains up to 10 columns and 30 rows and performs the following tasks:

- Prompts you to enter the number of rows; the program validates your input.
- Prompts you to enter the number of columns; the program validates your input.
- Prompts you to enter the matrix elements.
- Calculates and displays the average for each column in the matrix.

Listing 7.7. Source code for the program MAT1.CPP.

```
/*
  C++ program that demonstrates the use of two-dimensional arrays.
  The average value of each matrix column is calculated.
*/

#include <iostream.h>

const int MAX_COL = 10;
const int MAX_ROW = 30;

```

```
main()
{
    double x[MAX_ROW][MAX_COL];
    double sum, sumx, mean;
    int rows, columns;

    // get the number of rows
    do {
      cout << "Enter number of rows [2 to "
           << MAX_ROW << "] : ";
      cin >> rows;
    } while (rows < 2 || rows > MAX_ROW);

    // get the number of columns
    do {
      cout << "Enter number of columns [1 to "
           << MAX_COL << "] : ";
      cin >> columns;
    } while (columns < 1 || columns > MAX_COL);

    // get the matrix elements
    for (int i = 0; i < rows; i++)  {
      for (int j = 0; j < columns; j++)  {
          cout << "X[" << i << "][" << j << "] : ";
          cin >> x[i][j];
      }
      cout << "\n";
    }

    sum = rows;
    // obtain the sum of each column
    for (int j = 0; j < columns; j++)  {
      // initialize summations
      sumx = 0.0;
      for (i = 0; i < rows; i++)
        sumx += x[i][j];
      mean = sumx / sum;
      cout << "Mean for column " << j
           << " = " << mean << "\n";
    }
    return 0;
}
```


Here is a sample session with the program in Listing 7.7:

```
Enter number of rows [2 to 30] : 3
Enter number of columns [1 to 10] : 3
X[0][0] : 1
X[0][1] : 2
X[0][2] : 3
```

```
X[1][0] : 4
X[1][1] : 5
X[1][2] : 6

X[2][0] : 7
X[2][1] : 8
X[2][2] : 9

Mean for column 0 = 4
Mean for column 1 = 5
Mean for column 2 = 6
```

The program in Listing 7.7 declares the global constants `MAX_COL` and `MAX_ROW` in lines 8 and 9, respectively. These constants define the dimensions of the matrix that is created in the program. The function `main` declares the matrix `x` to have `MAX_ROW` rows and `MAX_COL` columns. The function also declares other nonarray variables.

The `do-while` loop, in lines 18 through 22, prompts you to enter the number of rows of matrix `x` that will contain your data. The output statement in lines 19 and 20 indicates the range of the valid number of rows. The statement in line 21 stores your input in the variable `rows`.

The second `do-while` loop, in lines 25 through 29, prompts you to enter the number of columns of matrix `x` that will contain your data. The output statement in lines 26 and 27 indicates the range of the valid number of columns. The statement in line 28 saves your input in the variable `columns`.

The nested `for` loops, in lines 32 through 38, prompt you for the matrix elements. The outer `for` loop uses the control variable `i` and iterates from 0 to `rows-1`, in increments of 1. The inner `for` loop uses the control variable `j` and iterates from 0 to `columns-1`, in increments of 1. The output statement in line 34 displays the index of the matrix element that will receive your input. The statement in line 35 stores your input in the matrix element `x[i][j]`.

The process of obtaining the average of each matrix column starts at line 40. The statement in that line assigns the integer in variable rows to the `double`-typed variable `sum`. The program uses another pair of nested `for` loops in lines 42 through 50. The outer `for` loop uses the control variable `j` and iterates from 0 to `columns-1`, in increments of 1. This loop processes each column. The first statement inside the outer `for` loop assigns 0 to the variable `sumx`. The inner `for` loop is located at line 45. This loop uses the control variable `i` and iterates from 0 to `rows-1`, in increments of 1. The inner loop uses the statement in line 46 to add the values of elements `x[i][j]` to the variable `sumx`. The statement in line 47 (which is outside the inner `for` loop) calculates the column average and assigns it to the variable `mean`. The output statement in lines 48 and 49 displays the column number and its average value.

Note: The `for` loop in line 42 redeclares its control variable `j`. (This is not the case with the `for` loop in line 45.) Why? The `for` loop in line 33 also declares the control variable `j`. However, the scope of that loop is limited to the scope of the outer `for` loop. Once the first pair of nested loops finishes executing, the loop control variable `j` is removed by the runtime system.

Initializing Multidimensional Arrays

C++ enables you to initialize a multidimensional array in a manner similar to single-dimensional arrays. You need to use a list of values that appear in the same sequence in which the elements of the initialized multidimensional array are stored. Now you realize the importance of understanding how C++ stores the elements of a multidimensional array. We modified the previous C++ program to use an initializing list that internally supplies the program with data. Consequently, the program does not prompt you for any data. Rather, the program displays the values of the matrix and the average for its columns. Listing 7.8. shows the source code for the MAT2.CPP program.

Type **Listing 7.8. Source code for the program MAT2.CPP.**

```
/*
  C++ program that demonstrates the use of two-dimensional arrays.
  The average value of each matrix column is calculated.
*/

#include <iostream.h>

const int MAX_COL = 3;
const int MAX_ROW = 3;

main()
{
    double x[MAX_ROW][MAX_COL] = {
                                   1, 2, 3, // row # 1
                                   4, 5, 6, // row # 2
                                   7, 8, 9  // row # 3
                                   };
    double sum, sumx, mean;
    int rows = MAX_ROW, columns = MAX_COL;
```

continues

Listing 7.8. continued

```
20:
21:      cout << "Matrix is:\n";
22:      // display the matrix elements
23:      for (int i = 0; i < rows; i++)  {
24:        for (int j = 0; j < columns; j++)  {
25:            cout.width(4);
26:            cout.precision(1);
27:            cout << x[i][j] << " ";
28:        }
29:        cout << "\n";
30:      }
31:      cout << "\n";
32:
33:      sum = rows;
34:      // obtain the sum of each column
35:      for (int j = 0; j < columns; j++)  {
36:        // initialize summations
37:        sumx = 0.0;
38:        for (i = 0; i < rows; i++)
39:          sumx += x[i][j];
40:        mean = sumx / sum;
41:        cout << "Mean for column " << j
42:             << " = " << mean << "\n";
43:      }
44:      return 0;
45: }
```

Here is a sample session with the program in Listing 7.8:

```
Matrix is:
   1    2    3
   4    5    6
   7    8    9

Mean for column 0 = 4
Mean for column 1 = 5
Mean for column 2 = 6
```

The program in Listing 7.8 declares the matrix `x` and initializes its elements with a list of values. Notice that the program declares the constants `MAX_COL` and `MAX_ROW` with values that match the size of the initialized matrix. The declaration statement in lines 13 through 17 shows the elements assigned to each row. The function `main` also initializes the variable `rows` and `columns` with the constants `MAX_ROW` and `MAX_COL`, respectively. The function performs this initialization for two reasons. First, the program no longer prompts you to enter values for the variable `rows` and `columns`. Second, the program is working with a custom-fit size for matrix `x`.

The program uses the nested `for` loops in lines 21 through 30 to display the elements of the matrix `x`. The second pair of nested `for` loops calculates the average for each matrix column. This nested `for` loop is identical to the one in Listing 7.7.

Multidimensional Array Parameters

C++ enables you to declare function parameters that are multidimensional arrays. As with single-dimensional arrays, C++ enables you to be either specific or general about the size of the array parameter. However, in the latter case, you can only generalize the first dimension of the array. If you wish an array parameter to accept arrays of a fixed dimension, you can specify the size of each dimension of the array in the parameter declaration. By contrast, if you want the array parameter to accept arrays of the same basic type but of different first-dimension sizes, use empty brackets for the first dimension in the array parameter.

Syntax

A Fixed-Array Parameter

The general syntax for declaring a fixed-array parameter is

```
type parameterName[dim1Size][dim2Size]...
```

Examples:

```
int minMatrix(int intMat[100][20], int rows, int cols);
void sort(unsigned mat[23][55],
          int rows, int cols, int colIndex);
```

Syntax

An Open-Array Parameter

The general syntax for declaring an open-array parameter is

```
type parameterName[][dim2Size]...
```

Examples:

```
int minMat(int intMat[][100], int rows, int cols);
void sort(unsigned mat[][55],
          int rows, int cols, int colIndex);
```

Let's look at an example. Listing 7.9 shows the source code for the program MAT3.CPP. The program performs the same tasks as program MAT1.CPP in Listing 7.7. We created program MAT3.CPP by editing program MAT1.CPP and placing each program task in a separate function. Thus, program MAT3.CPP is a highly structured version of program MAT1.CPP.

Listing 7.9. Source code for the program MAT3.CPP.

```
/*
  C++ program that demonstrates the use of two-dimensional arrays.
  The average value of each matrix column is calculated.
*/

#include <iostream.h>

const int MAX_COL = 10;
const int MAX_ROW = 30;

int getRows()
{
  int n;
  // get the number of rows
  do {
    cout << "Enter number of rows [2 to "
         << MAX_ROW << "] : ";
    cin >> n;
  } while (n < 2 || n > MAX_ROW);
  return n;
}

int getColumns()
{
  int n;
  // get the number of columns
  do {
    cout << "Enter number of columns [1 to "
         << MAX_COL << "] : ";
    cin >> n;
  } while (n < 1 || n > MAX_COL);
  return n;
}

void inputMatrix(double mat[][MAX_COL],
                 int rows, int columns)
{
  // get the matrix elements
  for (int i = 0; i < rows; i++)  {
    for (int j = 0; j < columns; j++)  {
      cout << "X[" << i << "][" << j << "] : ";
      cin >> mat[i][j];
    }
    cout << "\n";
  }
}

void showColumnAverage(double mat[][MAX_COL],
```

```
                              int rows, int columns)
{
  double sum, sumx, mean;
  sum = rows;
  // obtain the sum of each column
  for (int j = 0; j < columns; j++)  {
    // initialize summations
    sumx = 0.0;
    for (int i = 0; i < rows; i++)
      sumx += mat[i][j];
    mean = sumx / sum;
    cout << "Mean for column " << j
         << " = " << mean << "\n";
  }
}

main()
{
    double x[MAX_ROW][MAX_COL];
    int rows, columns;
    // get matrix dimensions
    rows = getRows();
    columns = getColumns();
    // get matrix data
    inputMatrix(x, rows, columns);
    // show results
    showColumnAverage(x, rows, columns);
    return 0;
}
```

Here is a sample session with the program in Listing 7.9:

```
Enter number of rows [2 to 30] : 3
Enter number of columns [1 to 10] : 3
X[0][0] : 10
X[0][1] : 20
X[0][2] : 30

X[1][0] : 40
X[1][1] : 50
X[1][2] : 60

X[2][0] : 70
X[2][1] : 80
X[2][2] : 90

Mean for column 0 = 40
Mean for column 1 = 50
Mean for column 2 = 60
```

Analysis The program in Listing 7.9 declares the functions `getRows`, `getColumns`, `inputMatrix`, `showColumnAverage`, and `main`. The function `getRows` prompts you for the number of matrix rows that you will be using. The function returns your validated input. Similarly, the function `getColumns` returns the validated number of matrix columns.

The function `inputMatrix` obtains the data for the matrix. The function has three parameters. The parameter `mat` specifies the matrix parameter (with an open first dimension). The parameters `rows` and `columns` specify the number of rows and the number of columns of matrix `mat` that will receive input data.

The function `showColumnAverage` calculates and displays the column averages for the matrix parameter `mat`. The parameters `rows` and `columns` specify the number of rows and the number of columns of matrix `mat` that contain meaningful data.

This function contains the same statements that appeared in the program MAT1.CPP. Program MAT3.CPP uses these functions as shells or wrappers for the statements that perform the various tasks. From a structured programming point of view, program MAT3.CPP is superior to program MAT1.CPP.

The function `main` declares the matrix `x` with `MAX_ROW` rows and `MAX_COL` columns. The function calls the functions `getRows` and `getColumns` to obtain the number of working rows and columns, respectively. The statement in line 73 invokes the function `inputMatrix` and supplies it with the arguments `x`, `rows`, and `columns`. The statement in line 75 calls function `showColumnAverage` and passes it the arguments `x`, `rows`, and `columns`.

Summary

Today's lesson covered various topics related to arrays, including single-dimensional and multidimensional arrays. You learned the following:

- Declaring single-dimensional arrays requires you to state the data type of the array elements, the name of the array, and the number of array elements (enclosed in square brackets). All C++ arrays have a 0 lower bound. The upper bound of an array is equal to the number of elements minus one.
- Using single-dimensional arrays requires you to state the array's name and to include a valid index, enclosed in square brackets.
- The initializing of single-dimensional arrays can be carried out while declaring them. The initializing list of data is enclosed in braces and contains

comma-delimited data. C++ enables you to include fewer data than the size of the array. In this case, the compiler automatically assigns zeros to the elements that you do not explicitly initialize. In addition, C++ enables you to omit the explicit size of the initialized array and instead use the number of initializing items as the number of array elements.

- Declaring single-dimensional arrays as function parameters takes two forms. The first one deals with fixed-array parameters, whereas the second one handles open-array parameters. Fixed-array parameters include the size of the array in the parameter. Arguments for this kind of parameter must match the type and size of the parameter. Open-array parameters use empty brackets to indicate that the arguments for the parameters can be of any size.
- Sorting arrays is an important nonnumerical array operation. Sorting arranges the elements of an array in either ascending or descending order. Sorted arrays are much easier to search. For sorting arrays, the new Comb sort method is very efficient.
- Searching arrays involves locating an array element that contains the same data as the search value. Searching methods are geared toward either unordered or ordered arrays. The linear search method is used for unordered arrays, and the binary search method is used for sorted arrays.
- Declaring multidimensional arrays requires you to state the data type of the array elements, the name of the array, and the size of each dimension (enclosed in separate brackets). The lower index of each dimension is 0. The upper bound of each dimension in an array is equal to the dimension size minus one.
- Using multidimensional arrays requires you to state the array's name and to include valid indices. Each index must be enclosed in a separate set of brackets.
- The initializing of multidimensional arrays can be carried out while declaring them. The initializing list of data is enclosed in braces and contains comma-delimited data. C++ enables you to include fewer data than the total size of the array. In this case, the compiler automatically assigns zeros to the elements that you do not explicitly initialize.
- Declaring multidimensional arrays as function parameters takes two forms. The first one deals with fixed-array parameters, whereas the second one handles parameters with an open first dimension. Fixed-array parameters include the size of each dimension in the array parameter. Arguments for

this kind of parameter must match the type and sizes of the parameter. Open-array parameters use empty brackets for only the first dimension to indicate that the arguments for the parameters have varying sizes for the first dimensions. The other dimensions of the arguments must match those of the array parameter.

Q&A

Q Does C++ permit me to alter the size of an array?

A No. C++ does not allow you to redimension arrays.

Q Can I declare arrays with the basic type `void` (for example, `void array[81];`) to create buffers?

A No. C++ does not allow you to use the `void` type with an array, because the `void` type has no defined size. Use the `char` or `unsigned char` type to create an array that works as a buffer.

Q Does C++ allow me to redeclare an array?

A C++ enables you to redeclare an array to change its basic type, the number of dimensions, and its size if you declare these arrays in nested statement blocks. Here is an example:

```
#include <iostream.h>
const MAX = 100;
const MAX_ROWS = 100;
const MAX_COLS = 20;

main()
{
  // declare variables here?
  {
    double x[MAX];
    // declare other variables?
    // statements to manipulate the single-dimensional
       array x
  }
  {
    double x[MAX_ROWS][MAX_COLS];
    // declare other variables?
```

```
    // statements to manipulate the matrix x
  }
  return 0;
}
```

The function main declares the array x in the first nested statement block. When program execution reaches the end of that block, the runtime system removes the array x and all other variables declared in that block. Then the function redeclares x as a matrix in the second block. When program execution reaches the end of the second block, the runtime system removes the matrix x and all other variables declared in that block. Be aware, however, that the two versions of x are separate entities and should not be considered to share any memory.

Q Are arrays limited to the predefined types?

A Not at all. C++ enables you to create arrays using user-defined types. (See Day 8.)

Workshop

The Workshop provides quiz questions to help you solidify your understanding of the material covered and exercises to provide you with experience in using what you've learned. Try to understand the quiz and exercise answers before continuing on to the next day's lesson. (Answers are provided in Appendix A, "Answers.")

Quiz

1. What is the output of the following program?

```
#include <iostream.h>
const int MAX = 5;
main()
{
  double x[MAX];
  x[0] = 1;
  for (int i = 1; i < MAX; i++)
    x[i] = i * x[i-1];
  for (i = 0; i < MAX; i++)
    cout << "x[" << i << "] = " << x[i] << "\n";
  return 0;
}
```

2. What is the output of the following program?

```
#include <iostream.h>
#include <math.h>
const int MAX = 5;
main()
{
  double x[MAX];
  for (int i = 0; i < MAX; i++)
    x[i] = sqrt(double(i));
  for (i = 0; i < MAX; i++)
    cout << "x[" << i << "] = " << x[i] << "\n";
  return 0;
}
```

3. Where is the error in the following program?

```
#include <iostream.h>
const int MAX = 5;
main()
{
  double x[MAX];
  x[0] = 1;
  for (int i = 0; i < MAX; i++)
     x[i] = i * x[i-1];
  for (i = 0; i < MAX; i++)
     cout << "x[" << i << "] = " << x[i] << "\n";
  return 0;
}
```

Exercise

Write the program ARRAY7.CPP by editing program ARRAY6.CPP and replacing the Comb sort method in the function `sortArray` with an implementation of the Shell-Metzner method.

WEEK 1 IN REVIEW

Before you proceed to the second week of learning about programming with Borland C++ 4.5, let's look at a special example that you will see developed as you work through the next two weeks. The example is a simple number-guessing game, shown in Listing R1.1. The program selects a number at random between 0 and 1,000 and prompts you to enter a number in that range. If your input is greater than the secret number, the program tells you that your guess was higher. By contrast, if your input is less than the secret number, the program tells you that your guess was lower. If you guess the secret number, the game ends with your victory. The program allows you up to 11 guesses. You can end the game at any prompt by entering a negative integer. In this case, the program stops the game and displays the secret number.

Listing R1.1. Source code for program GAME1.CPP.

```
#include <stdlib.h>
#include <iostream.h>
#include <time.h>

// declare a global random number generating function
int random(int maxVal)
{ return rand() % maxVal; }


main()
{
  int n, m;
  int MaxIter = 11;
  int iter = 0;
  int ok = 1;


  // reseed random-number generator
  srand((unsigned)time(NULL));
  n = random(1001);
  m = -1;

  // loop to obtain the other guesses
  while (m != n && iter < MaxIter && ok == 1) {
    cout << "Enter a number between 0 and 1000 : ";
    cin >> m;
    ok = (m < 0) ? 0 : 1;
    iter++;
    // is the user's guess higher?
    if (m > n)
      cout << "Enter a lower guess\n\n";
    else if (m < n)
      cout << "Enter a higher guess\n\n";
    else
      cout << "You guessed it! Congratulations.";
  }
  // did the user guess the secret number
  if (iter >= MaxIter || ok == 0)
    cout << "The secret number is " << n << "\n";
```

```
40:
41:    return 0;
42: }
```

Here is a sample session with the program in Listing R1.1:

```
Enter a number between 0 and 1000 : 500
Enter a lower guess

Enter a number between 0 and 1000 : 250
Enter a higher guess

Enter a number between 0 and 1000 : -1
Enter a higher guess

The secret number is 399
```

The program in Listing R1.1 declares the function `random` to return a random number in the range of 0 to 1,000. The program also declares the function `main`, which conducts the guessing game. The function declares a number of local variables in lines 12 through 15. The statement in line 19 reseeds the random number generator. The statement in line 20 assigns the secret number to the variable `n`. The statement in line 21 assigns –1 to the variable `m`, which stores your guesses.

The `while` loop in lines 24 through 36 conducts the game. The `while` loop determines whether or not the following conditions are all true:

- Your guess (stored in variable `m`) does not match the secret number stored in variable `n`.
- The number of iterations (stored in variable `iter`) are less than the maximum number of iterations (stored in variable `MaxIter`).
- The variable `ok` stores 1.

The first statement in the loop prompts you to enter a number between 0 and 1,000. The statement in line 26 obtains your input and stores it in variable `m`. The statement in line `ok` assigns 0 to the variable `ok` if you entered a negative integer. Otherwise, the statement assigns 1 to variable `ok`. The statement in line 28 increments the variable `iter`.

The multi-alternative `if` statement in lines 30 through 35 compares your input with the secret number and displays the appropriate message reflecting your guess.

The `if` statement in line 38 displays the secret number if you failed to guess it in `MaxIter` iterations or if you entered a negative integer.

WEEK 2 AT A GLANCE

8

9

10

11

12

13

14

This second week continues teaching you about the C++ language. The topics cover the more advanced side of C++. You learn about user-defined data types—especially structures—and about pointers. The week also covers advanced topics on functions and introduces you to object-oriented programming (OOP) in C++. You learn about classes, components, and the rules for using these components. In addition, you learn about basic file I/O using the C++ stream library. Day 13 introduces you to the `string` class, which supports strings using C++ classes. Finally, Day 14 introduces the ObjectWindows Library, a topic you'll cover in great depth in Week 3.

User-Defined Types and Pointers

WEEK 2

Creating user-defined data types is one of the necessary features of a modern programming language. Today's lesson looks at the enumerated data types and structures that enable you to better organize your data. In addition, this lesson discusses using pointers with simple variables, arrays, structures, and dynamic data. Today, you will learn about the following topics:

- The type definition using `typedef`
- Enumerated data types
- Structures
- Unions
- Reference variables
- Pointers to existing variables
- Pointers to arrays
- Pointers to structures
- Using pointers to access and manage dynamic data
- Far pointers

Type Definition in C++

C++ offers the `typedef` keyword, which enables you to define new data type names as aliases of existing types.

Syntax

The *typedef* Keyword

The general syntax for using `typedef` is

```
typedef knownType newType;
```

Examples:

```
typedef unsigned word;
typedef unsigned char byte;
type unsigned char boolean;
```

The `typedef` keyword defines a new type from a known one. You can use `typedef` to create aliases that shorten the names of existing data types or to define names of data types that are more familiar to you. (See the second of the preceding examples, which `typedef`s a `byte` type). In addition, the `typedef` statement can define a new type name that better describes how the data type is used. The third of the preceding examples illustrates this use of `typedef`. You can also use `typedef` to define the name of an array type.

An Array Type Name

The general syntax for defining the name of an array type is

```
typedef baseType arrayTypeName[arraySize];
```

The `typedef` statement defines the *`arrayTypeName`*, whose basic type and size are *`baseType`* and *`arraySize`*, respectively.

Examples:

```
typedef double vector[10];
typedef double matrix[10][30];
```

Thus, the identifiers `vector` and `matrix` are names of data types.

Enumerated Data Types

The rule to follow with enumerated data types is that although the enumerated identifiers must be unique, the values assigned to them need not be unique.

New Term: An *enumerated type* defines a list of unique identifiers and associates values with these identifiers.

An Enumerated Type

The general syntax for declaring an enumerated type is

```
enum enumType { <list of enumerated identifiers> };
```

Examples:

```
enum Boolean { false, true };
enum YesNo { no, yes, dontCare, maybe };
enum weekday { Sunday, Monday, Tuesday,
               Wednesday, Thursday, Friday, Saturday };
```

Here is an example of declaring an enumerated type:

```
enum CPUtype { i8088, i80286, i80386DX, i80386SX,
               i80486DX, i80486SX };
```

C++ associates integer values with the enumerated identifiers. For example, in this type, the compiler assigns 0 to i8088, 1 to i80286, and so on.

C++ is very flexible in declaring an enumerated type. First, the language enables you to explicitly assign a value to an enumerated identifier. Here is an example:

```
enum weekday { Sunday = 1, Monday, Tuesday, Wednesday,
               Thursday, Friday, Saturday };
```

This declaration explicitly assigns `1` to the enumerated identifier `Sunday`. The compiler then assigns the next integer, `2`, to the next identifier, `Monday`, and so on. C++ enables you to explicitly assign a value to each member of the enumerated list. Moreover, these values need not be unique. Here are some examples of the flexibility in declaring enumerated types in C++:

```
// explicit value assignment for every list member
enum colors { black = 1, red = 2, blue = 3, green = 5,
              yellow = 7, white = 11 };

// intermittent value assignment
enum colors { black = 1, red, blue, green = 5,
              yellow = 7, white = 11 };

// duplicate values
enum CPUtype { i8088 = 1, i80286 = 2,
               i80386DX = 3, i80386SX = 3,
               i80486DX = 4, i80486SX = 4 };

enum choiceType { false, true, dontCare = 0 };
```

In the last example, the compiler associates the identifier `false` with `0` by default. However, the compiler also associates the value `0` with `dontCare` because of the explicit assignment.

C++ enables you to declare variables that have enumerated types in the following ways:

1. The declaration of the enumerated type may include the declaration of the variables of that type. The general syntax is

   ```
   enum [enumType] { <list of enumerated identifiers> }
                   <list of variables>;
   ```

   Here is an example:

   ```
   enum weekDay { Sun = 1, Mon, Tue, Wed, Thu, Fri, Sat }
           recycleDay, payDay, movieDay;
   ```

2. The separate declaration of the enumerated type and its variables includes multiple statements to declare the type and the associated variables separately. The general syntax is

```
enum enumType { <list of enumerated identifiers> };
enumType var1, var2, ..., varN;
```

Let's look at an example. Listing 8.1 shows the source code for the program ENUM1.CPP. The program implements a simple one-line, four-function calculator that performs the following tasks:

- Prompts you to enter a number, an operator (+, –, *, or /), and a number.
- Performs the requested operation, if valid.
- Displays the operands, the operator, and the result, if the operation was valid; otherwise displays an error message that indicates the kind of error. (You either entered a bad operator or attempted to divide by 0.)

Type

Listing 8.1. Source code for the program ENUM1.CPP.

```
/*
C++ program that demonstrates enumerated types
*/

#include <iostream.h>

enum mathError { noError, badOperator, divideByZero };

void sayError(mathError err)
{
  switch (err) {
    case noError:
      cout << "No error";
      break;
    case badOperator:
      cout << "Error: invalid operator";
      break;
    case divideByZero:
      cout << "Error: attempt to divide by zero";
  }
}

main()
{
  double x, y, z;
  char op;
  mathError error = noError;

```

continues

Listing 8.1. continued

```
29:    cout << "Enter a number, an operator, and a number : ";
30:    cin >> x >> op >> y;
31:
32:    switch (op) {
33:      case '+':
34:        z = x + y;
35:        break;
36:      case '-':
37:        z = x - y;
38:        break;
39:      case '*':
40:        z = x * y;
41:        break;
42:      case '/':
43:        if (y != 0)
44:          z = x / y;
45:        else
46:          error = divideByZero;
47:        break;
48:      default:
49:        error = badOperator;
50:    }
51:
52:    if (error == noError)
53:      cout << x << " " << op << " " << y << " = " << z;
54:    else
55:      sayError(error);
56:    return 0;
57: }
```

Here is a sample session with the program in Listing 8.1:

```
Enter a number, an operator, and a number : 355 / 113
355 / 113 = 3.14159
```

The program in Listing 8.1 declares the enumerated type `mathError` in line 7. This data type has three enumerated values: `noError`, `badOperator`, and `divideByZero`.

The program also defines the function `sayError` in lines 9 through 21 to display a message based on the value of the enumerated parameter `err`. The function uses the `switch` statement in line 11 to display messages that correspond to the various enumerated values.

The function `main` declares the `double`-typed variables `x`, `y`, and `z` to represent the operands and the result, respectively. In addition, the function declares the `char`-typed variable `op` to store the requested operation, and the enumerated variable `error` to store the error status. The function initializes the variable `error` with the enumerated value `noError`.

The output statement in line 29 prompts you to enter the operands and the operator. The statement in line 30 stores your input in variables `x`, `op`, and `y`, in that order. The function uses the `switch` statement in line 32 to examine the value in variable `op` and perform the requested operation. The `case` labels in lines 33, 36, 39, and 42 provide the values for the four supported math operations. The last `case` label contains an `if` statement that detects the attempt to divide by zero. If this is true, the `else` clause statement assigns the enumerated value `divideByZero` to the variable `error`.

The catch-all `default` clause in line 48 handles invalid operators. The statement in line 49 assigns the enumerated value `badOperator` to the variable `error`.

The `if` statement in line 52 determines whether or not the variable `error` contains the enumerated value `noError`. If this condition is true, the program executes the output statement in line 53. This statement displays the operands, the operator, and the result. Otherwise, the program executes the `else` clause statement that calls the function `sayError` and passes it the argument `error`. This function call displays a message that identifies the error.

Structures

C++ supports structures, and these members can be predefined types or other structures.

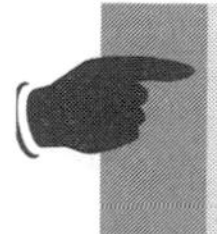

New Term: *Structures* enable you to define a new type that logically groups several fields or members.

Syntax

A Structure

The general syntax for declaring a structure is

```
struct structTag {
     < list of members >
};
```

Examples:

```
struct point {
     double x;
     double y;
};

struct rectangle {
     point upperLeftCorner;
     point lowerRightCorner;
     double area;
};

struct circle {
     point center;
     double radius;
     double area;
};
```

Once you define a `struct` type, you can use that type to declare variables. Here are examples of declarations that use structures that we declared in the syntax box:

```
point p1, p2, p3;
```

You can also declare structured variables when you define the structure itself:

```
struct point {
     double x;
     double y;
} p1, p2, p3;
```

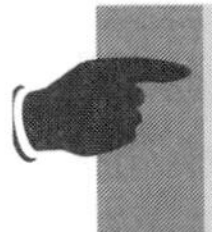

New Term: *Untagged structures* enable you to declare structure variables without defining a name for their structures.

Note: Interestingly, C++ permits you to declare untagged structures. For example, the following structure definition declares the variables `p1`, `p2`, and `p3` but omits the name of the structure:

```
struct {
     double x;
     double y;
} p1, p2, p3;
```

C++ enables you to declare and initialize a structured variable. Here is an example:

```
point pt = { 1.0, -8.3 };
```

Accessing the members of a structure uses the dot operator. Here are a few examples:

```
p1.x = 12.45;
p1.y = 34.56;
p2.x = 23.4 / p1.x;
p2.y = 0.98 * p1.y;
```

Let's consider an example. Listing 8.2 shows the source code for the program STRUCT1.CPP. The program prompts you for four sets of coordinates that define four rectangles. Each rectangle is defined by the *x* and *y* coordinates of the upper-left and lower-right corners. The program calculates the areas of each rectangle, sorts the rectangles by area, and displays the rectangles in the order of their areas.

Type **Listing 8.2. Source code for the program STRUCT1.CPP.**

```
/*
  C++ program that demonstrates structured types
*/

#include <iostream.h>
#include <stdio.h>
#include <math.h>

const MAX_RECT = 4;

struct point {
  double x;
  double y;
};

struct rect {
  point ulc; // upper left corner
  point lrc; // lower right corner
  double area;
  int id;
};

typedef rect rectArr[MAX_RECT];

main()
{
  rectArr r;
  rect temp;
```

continues

Listing 8.2. continued

```
  double length, width;

  for (int i = 0; i < MAX_RECT; i++) {
    cout << "Enter (X,Y) coord. for ULC of rect. # "
         << i << " : ";
    cin >> r[i].ulc.x >> r[i].ulc.y;
    cout << "Enter (X,Y) coord. for LRC of rect. # "
         << i << " : ";
    cin >> r[i].lrc.x >> r[i].lrc.y;
    r[i].id = i;
    length = fabs(r[i].ulc.x - r[i].lrc.x);
    width = fabs(r[i].ulc.y - r[i].lrc.y);
    r[i].area = length * width;
  }

  // sort the rectangles by areas
  for (i = 0; i < (MAX_RECT - 1); i++)
    for (int j = i + 1; j < MAX_RECT; j++)
      if (r[i].area > r[j].area) {
        temp = r[i];
        r[i] = r[j];
        r[j] = temp;
      }

  // display rectangles sorted by area
  for (i = 0; i < MAX_RECT; i++)
    printf("Rect # %d has area %5.4lf\n", r[i].id, r[i].area);
  return 0;
}
```

Here is a sample session with the program in Listing 8.2:

```
Enter (X,Y) coord. for ULC of rect. # 0 : 1 1
Enter (X,Y) coord. for LRC of rect. # 0 : 2 2
Enter (X,Y) coord. for ULC of rect. # 1 : 1.5 1.5
Enter (X,Y) coord. for LRC of rect. # 1 : 3 4
Enter (X,Y) coord. for ULC of rect. # 2 : 1 2
Enter (X,Y) coord. for LRC of rect. # 2 : 5 8
Enter (X,Y) coord. for ULC of rect. # 3 : 4 6
Enter (X,Y) coord. for LRC of rect. # 3 : 8 4
Rect # 0 has area 1.0000
Rect # 1 has area 3.7500
Rect # 3 has area 8.0000
Rect # 2 has area 24.0000
```

Analysis The program in Listing 8.2 includes the header files IOSTREAM.H, MATH.H, and STDIO.H. The program declares the global constant `MAX_RECT` to specify the maximum number of rectangles. Line 11 contains the declaration of structure `point`, which is made up of two `double`-typed members, `x` and `y`. This structure models a two-dimensional point. Line 16 contains the declaration of structure `rect`, which models a rectangle. The structure contains two `point`-typed members, `ulc` and `lrc`, the `double`-typed member `area`, and the `int`-typed member `id`. The members `ulc` and `lrc` represent the coordinates for the upper-left and lower-right corners that define a rectangle. The member `area` stores the area of the rectangle. The member `id` stores a numeric identification number.

The `typedef` statement in line 23 defines the type `recArr` as an array of `MAX_RECT` elements of structure `rect`.

The function `main` declares the `rectArr`-typed array `r`, the `rect`-typed structure `temp`, and the `double`-typed variables `length` and `width`.

The function `main` uses the `for` loop in lines 31 through 42 to prompt you for the coordinates of the rectangles, calculate their areas, and assign their `id` numbers. The output statements in lines 32 and 33, and in lines 35 and 36, prompt you for the *x* and *y* coordinates of the upper-left and lower-right corners, respectively. The input statements in lines 34 and 37 store the coordinates you enter in members `r[i].ulc.x`, `r[i].ulc.y`, `r[i].lrc.x`, and `r[i].lrc.y`, respectively. The statement in line 38 stores the value of the loop control variable `i` in member `r[i].id`. The statement in line 39 calculates the length of a rectangle using the `x` members of the `ulc` and `lrc` members in the element `r[i]`. The statement in line 40 calculates the width of a rectangle using the `y` members of the `ulc` and `lrc` members in the element `r[i]`. The statement in line 41 calculates the area of the rectangle and stores it in member `r[i].area`.

The nested loops in lines 44 through 51 sort the elements of array `r` using the member `area`. The loops implement the simple bubble sort method (which is useful for very small arrays). The `if` statement in line 47 compares the areas of elements `r[i]` and `r[j]`. If the area of rectangle `r[i]` is larger than that of rectangle `r[j]`, the statements in lines 48 through 50 swap all the members of `r[i]` and `r[j]`. The swap uses the structure `temp`. This task illustrates that you can assign all the members of a structure to another structure in one statement.

The `for` loop in lines 54 and 55 displays the rectangles sorted according to their areas. The output statement in line 55 uses the `printf` function to display the rectangle `id` numbers and areas.

Unions

The size of a union is equal to the size of its largest member.

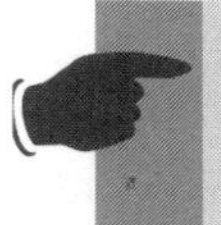

New Term: *Unions* are special structures that store members that are mutually exclusive.

Syntax

Unions

The general syntax for unions is

```
union unionTag {
     type1 member1;
     type2 member2;
     ...
     typeN memberN;
};
```

Example:

```
union Long {
     unsigned mWord[2];
     long mLong;
};
```

The union `Long` stores either two unsigned integers (each requiring two bytes) or a four-byte long integer. In addition, the union `Long` allows you to access the lower or higher words (two-byte integers) of a long integer.

Unions offer an easy alternative for quick data conversion. Unions were more significant in the recent past, when the price of computer memory was much higher and it was feasible to use unions to consolidate memory. Accessing union members involves the dot access operators, just as in structures.

Reference Variables

In Day 2, you learned that you declare reference parameters by placing the `&` symbol after the parameter's type. Recall that a reference parameter becomes an alias to its arguments. In addition, any changes made to the reference parameter affect its argument. In addition to reference parameters, C++ supports reference variables. You can manipulate the referenced variable by using its alias. As a novice C++ programmer,

your initial use of reference variables will most likely be limited. On the other hand, you are probably using reference parameters more frequently. As you advance in using C++, you will discover how reference variables can implement programming tricks that deal with advanced class design. This book discusses only the basics of reference variables.

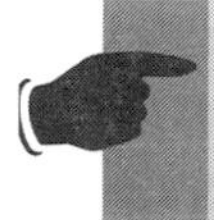

New Term: Like reference parameters, *reference variables* become aliases to the variables they access.

Syntax

A Reference Variable

The general syntax for declaring a reference variable is

```
type& refVar;
type& refVar = aVar;
```

The `refVar` is the reference variable that can be initialized when declared. You must ensure that a reference variable is initialized or assigned a referenced variable before using the reference variable.

Examples:

```
int x = 10, y = 3;
int& rx = x;
int& ry;
ry = y; // take the reference
```

Here is a simple example that shows a reference variable at work. Listing 8.3 shows the source code for the program REFVAR1.CPP. The program displays and alters the values of a variable using either the variable itself or its reference. The program requires no input.

Listing 8.3. Source code for the program REFVAR1.CPP.

```
/*
  C++ program that demonstrates reference variables
*/

#include <iostream.h>

main()
{
```

continues

Listing 8.3. continued

```
9:     int x = 10;
10:    int& rx = x;
11:    // display x using x and rx
12:    cout << "x contains " << x << "\n";
13:    cout << "x contains (using the reference rx) "
14:         << rx << "\n";
15:    // alter x and display its value using rx
16:    x *= 2;
17:    cout << "x contains (using the reference rx) "
18:         << rx << "\n";
19:    // alter rx and display value using x
20:    rx *= 2;
21:    cout << "x contains " << x << "\n";
22:    return 0;
23: }
```

Here is a sample session with the program in Listing 8.3:

```
x contains 10
x contains (using the reference rx) 10
x contains (using the reference rx) 20
x contains 40
```

The program in Listing 8.3 declares the `int`-typed variable `x` and the `int`-typed reference variable `rx`. The program initializes the variable `x` with 10 and the reference variable `rx` with the variable `x`.

The output statement in line 12 displays the value in variable `x` using the variable `x` itself. By contrast, the output statement in lines 13 and 14 displays the value in variable `x` using the reference variable `rx`.

The statement in line 16 doubles the integer in variable `x`. The output statement in lines 17 and 18 displays the new value in variable `x` using the reference variable `rx`. As the output shows, the reference variable accurately displays the updated value in variable `x`.

The statement in line 20 doubles the value in variable `x` by using the reference variable `rx`. The output statement in line 21 displays the updated value in variable `x` using variable `x`. Again, the output shows that the variable `x` and the reference variable `rx` are synchronized.

Overview of Pointers

Each piece of information, both code and data, in the computer's memory resides at a specific address and occupies a specific number of bytes. When you run a program, your variables reside at specific addresses. With a high-level language such as C++, you are not concerned about the actual address of every variable. That task is handled transparently by the compiler and the runtime system. Conceptually, each variable in your program is a tag for a memory address. Manipulating the data using the tag is much easier than dealing with actual numerical addresses, such as 0F64:01AF4.

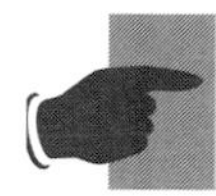

New Term: An *address* is a memory location. A *tag* is the variable's name.

C++ and its parent C are programming languages that are also used for low-level systems programming. In fact, many regard C as a high-level assembler. Low-level systems programming requires that you frequently work with the address of data. This is where pointers, in general, come into play. Knowing the address of a piece of data enables you to set and query its value.

New Term: A *pointer* is a special variable that stores the address of another variable or information.

Warning: Pointers are very powerful language components. They can also be dangerous if used carelessly, because they may hang your system. This malfunction occurs when the pointer happens to have a low memory address of some critical data or function.

Pointers to Existing Variables

In this section, you learn how to use pointers to access the values in existing variables. C++ requires that you associate a data type (including `void`) with a declared pointer. The associated data type may be a predefined type or a user-defined structure.

Syntax

A Pointer

The general syntax for declaring a pointer is

```
type* pointerName;
type* pointerName = &variable;
```

The & operator is the address-of operator (this is not the reference operator, which also uses the & symbol) and is used to take the address of a variable. The address-of operator returns the address of a variable, structure, function, and so on. By contrast, the reference operator creates an alias to a variable using another variable.

Example:

```
int *intPtr; // pointer to an int
double *realPtr; // pointer to a double
char *aString; // pointer to a character
long lv;
long* lp = &lv;
```

You can also declare nonpointers in the same lines that declare pointers:

```
int *intPtr, anInt;
double *realPtr, x;
char *aString, aKey;
```

Note: C++ permits you to place the asterisk character right after the associated data type. You should not interpret this kind of syntax to mean that every other identifier appearing in the same declaration is automatically a pointer:

```
int* intPtr; // pointer to an int
double* realPtr; // pointer to a double
char* aString; // pointer to a character
int *intP, j; // intP is a pointer to int, j is an int
double *realPtr, *doublePtr;  // both identifiers
                              // are pointers to a double
```

DO | **DON'T**

DO initialize a pointer before you use it, just as you do with ordinary variables. In fact, the need to initialize pointers is even more pressing—using uninitialized pointers invites trouble that can lead to unpredictable program behavior or a system hang.

DON'T assume that uninitialized pointers are harmless.

Once a pointer contains the address of a variable, you can access the value in that variable using the `*` operator followed by the pointer's name. For example, if `px` is a pointer to the variable `x`, you can use `*px` to access the value in variable `x`.

DO | **DON'T**

DO include the `*` operator to the left of a pointer to access the variable whose address is stored in the pointer.

DON'T forget to use the `*` operator. Without it, a statement ends up manipulating the address in the pointer instead of the data at that address.

Here is a simple example that shows a pointer at work. Listing 8.4 shows the source code for the program PTR1.CPP. The program displays and alters the values of a variable using either the variable itself or its pointer. The program requires no input.

Type

Listing 8.4. Source code for the program PTR1.CPP.

```
/*
  C++ program that demonstrates pointers to existing variables
*/

#include <iostream.h>

main()
{
  int x = 10;
  int* px = &x;
  // display x using x and rx
  cout << "x contains " << x << "\n";
  cout << "x contains (using the pointer px) "
       << *px << "\n";
  // alter x and display its value using *px
  x *= 2;
  cout << "x contains (using the pointer px) "
       << *px << "\n";
  // alter *px and display value using x
  *px *= 2;
  cout << "x contains " << x << "\n";
  return 0;
}
```

Here is a sample session with the program in Listing 8.4:

```
x contains 10
x contains (using the pointer px) 10
x contains (using the pointer px) 20
x contains 40
```

The program in Listing 8.4 declares the `int`-typed variable `x` and the `int`-typed pointer `px`. The program initializes the variable `x` with 10 and the pointer `px` with the address of variable `x`.

The output statement in line 12 displays the value in variable `x` using the variable `x`. By contrast, the output statement in lines 13 and 14 displays the value in variable `x` using the pointer `px`. Notice that the statement uses `*px` to access the value in variable `x`.

The statement in line 16 doubles the integer in variable `x`. The output statement in lines 17 and 18 displays the new value in variable `x` using the pointer `px`. As the output shows, the pointer accurately displays the updated value in variable `x`.

The statement in line 20 doubles the value in variable `x` by using the pointer `px`. Notice that the assignment statement uses `*px` on the left side of the `=` operator to access the variable `x`. The output statement in line 21 displays the updated value in variable `x` using variable `x`. Again, the output shows that the variable `x` and the pointer `px` are synchronized.

Pointers to Arrays

C++ and its parent language, C, support a special use for the names of arrays. The compiler interprets the name of an array as the address of its first element. Thus, if `x` is an array, the expressions `&x[0]` and `x` are equivalent. In the case of a matrix—call it `mat`—the expressions `&mat[0][0]` and `mat` are also equivalent. This aspect of C++ and C makes them work as high-level assembly languages. Once you have the address of a data item, you've got its number, so to speak. Your knowledge of the memory address of a variable or array enables you to manipulate its contents using pointers.

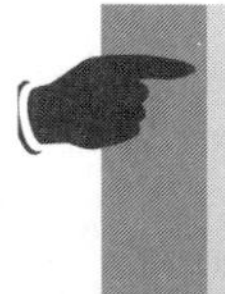

New Term: A *program variable* is a label that tags a memory address. Using a variable in a program means accessing the associated memory location by specifying its name (or *tag*, if you prefer). In this sense, a variable becomes a name that points to a memory location—a pointer.

C++ enables you to use a pointer to access the various elements of an array. When you access the element `x[i]` of array `x`, the compiled code performs two tasks. First, it obtains the base address of the array `x` (that is, where the first array element is located). Second, it uses the index `i` to calculate the offset from the base address of the array. This offset equals `i` multiplied by the size of the basic array type:

```
address of element x[i] = address of x + i * sizeof(basicType)
```

Looking at the preceding equation, assume that we have a pointer `ptr` that takes the base address of array `x`:

```
ptr = x; // pointer ptr points to address of x[0]
```

We can now substitute `x` with `ptr` in the equation and come up with the following:

```
address of element x[i] = ptr + i * sizeof(basicType)
```

In order for C++ and C to be high-level assemblers, they simplify the use of this equation by absolving it from having to explicitly state the size of the basic array type. Thus, you can write the following:

```
address of element x[i] = p + i
```

This equation states that the address of element `x[i]` is the expression `(p + i)`.

Let's illustrate the use of pointers to access one-dimensional arrays by presenting the next program, PTR2.CPP (Listing 8.5). This program is a modified version of the program ARRAY1.CPP that calculates the average value for data in an array. The program begins by prompting you to enter the number of data points and the data itself. Then the program calculates the average of the data in the array. Next, the program displays the average value.

Listing 8.5. Source code for the program PTR2.CPP.

```
/*
   C++ program that demonstrates the use of pointers with
   one-dimension arrays.  Program calculates the average
   value of the data found in the array.
*/

#include <iostream.h>

const int MAX = 30;

main()
```

continues

Listing 8.5. continued

```
{

    double x[MAX];
    // declare pointer and initialize with base
    // address of array x
    double *realPtr = x; // same as = &x[0]
    double sum, sumx = 0.0, mean;
    int n;
    // obtain the number of data points
    do {
        cout << "Enter number of data points [2 to "
             << MAX << "] : ";
        cin >> n;
        cout << "\n";
    } while (n < 2 || n > MAX);

    // prompt for the data
    for (int i = 0; i < n; i++) {
        cout << "X[" << i << "] : ";
        // use the form *(x+i) to store data in x[i]
        cin >> *(x + i);
    }

    sum = n;
    for (i = 0; i < n; i++)
    // use the form *(realPtr + i) to access x[i]
        sumx += *(realPtr + i);
    mean = sumx / sum;
    cout << "\nMean = " << mean << "\n\n";
    return 0;
}
```

Here is a sample session with the program in Listing 8.5:

```
Enter number of data points [2 to 30] : 5

X[0] : 1
X[1] : 2
X[2] : 3
X[3] : 4
X[4] : 5

Mean = 3
```

The program in Listing 8.5 declares the `double`-typed array `x` to have `MAX` elements. In addition, the program declares the pointer `realPtr` and initializes it using the array `x`. Thus, the pointer `realPtr` stores the address of `x[0]`, the first element in array `x`.

The program uses the pointer for `*(x + i)` in the input statement at line 32. Thus, the identifier `x` works as a pointer to the array `x`. Using the expression `*(x + i)` accesses the element number `i` of array `x`, just as using the expression `x[i]` does.

The program uses the pointer `realPtr` in the `for` loop at lines 37 and 38. The expression `*(realPtr + i)` is the equivalent of `*(x + i)`, which in turn is equivalent to `x[i]`. Thus, the `for` loop uses the pointer `realPtr` with an offset value, `i`, to access the elements of array `x`.

The Pointer Increment/ Decrement Method

The preceding C++ program maintains the same address in the pointer `realPtr`. Employing pointer arithmetic with the `for` loop index `i`, we can write a new program version that increments the offset to access the elements of array `x`. C++ provides you with another choice that enables you to access sequentially the elements of an array without the help of an explicit offset value. The method merely involves using the increment or decrement operator with a pointer. You still need to initialize the pointer to the base address of an array and then use the `++` operator to access the next array element. Here is a modified version of the preceding program, a version that uses the pointer increment method. Listing 8.6 shows the source code for the PTR3.CPP program.

Listing 8.6. Source code for the program PTR3.CPP.

```
/*
  C++ program that demonstrates the use of pointers with
  one-dimension arrays.  The average value of the array
  is calculated.  This program modifies the previous version
  in the following way:  the realPtr is used to access the
  array without any help from any loop control variable.
  This is accomplished by 'incrementing' the pointer, and
  consequently incrementing its address.  This program
  illustrates pointer arithmetic that alters the pointer's
  address.

*/

#include <iostream.h>

const int MAX = 30;
```

continues

Listing 8.6. continued

```

main()
{

    double x[MAX];
    double *realPtr = x;
    double sum, sumx = 0.0, mean;
    int i, n;

    do {
        cout << "Enter number of data points [2 to "
             << MAX << "] : ";
        cin >> n;
        cout << "\n";
    } while (n < 2 || n > MAX);

    // loop variable i is not directly involved in accessing
    //  the elements of array x
    for (i = 0; i < n; i++) {
        cout << "X[" << i << "] : ";
        // increment pointer realPtr after taking its reference
        cin >> *realPtr++;
    }

    // restore original address by using pointer arithmetic
    realPtr -= n;
    sum = n;
    // loop variable i serves as a simple counter
    for (i = 0; i < n; i++)
       // increment pointer realPtr after taking a reference
        sumx += *(realPtr++);
    mean = sumx / sum;
    cout << "\nMean = " << mean << "\n\n";
    return 0;

}
```

Here is a sample session with the program in Listing 8.6:

```
Enter number of data points [2 to 30] : 5

X[0] : 10
X[1] : 20
X[2] : 30
X[3] : 40
X[4] : 50

Mean = 30
```

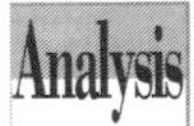

The program in Listing 8.6 initializes the `realPtr` pointer to the base address of array `x`, in line 22. The program uses the `realPtr` pointer in the keyboard input statement in line 38. This statement uses `*realPtr++` to store your input in the currently accessed element of array `x` and then to increment the pointer to the next element of array `x`. When the input loop terminates, the pointer `realPtr` points past the tail of array `x`. To reset the pointer to the base address of array `x`, the program uses the assignment statement in line 42. This statement uses pointer arithmetic to decrease the current address in pointer `realPtr` by `n` times `sizeof(real)`. The statement resets the address in the pointer `realPtr` to access the array element `x[0]`. The program uses the same incrementing method to calculate the sum of data in the second `for` loop in line 47.

Pointers to Structures

C++ supports declaring and using pointers to structures. Assigning the address of a structured variable to a pointer of the same type uses the same syntax as with simple variables. Once the pointer has the address of the structured variable, it needs to use the `->` operator to access the members of the structure.

Syntax

Accessing Structure Members

The general syntax for a pointer to access the members of a structure is

```
structPtr->aMember
```

Example:

```
struct point {
  double x;
  double y;
};

point p;
point* ptr = &p;

ptr->x = 23.3;
ptr->y = ptr->x + 12.3;
```

Here is a sample program that uses pointers to structures. Listing 8.7 shows the source code for the program PTR4.CPP. This program is the version of program STRUCT1.CPP that uses pointers. The program prompts you for four sets of coordinates that define four rectangles. Each rectangle is defined by the *x* and *y* coordinates of the upper-left and lower-right corners. The program calculates the area of each rectangle, sorts the rectangles by area, and displays the rectangles in the order of their areas.

Type

Listing 8.7. Source code for the program PTR4.CPP.

```
/*
  C++ program that demonstrates pointers to structured types
*/

#include <iostream.h>
#include <stdio.h>
#include <math.h>

const MAX_RECT = 4;

struct point {
  double x;
  double y;
};

struct rect {
  point ulc; // upper left corner
  point lrc; // lower right corner
  double area;
  int id;
};

typedef rect rectArr[MAX_RECT];

main()
{
  rectArr r;
  rect temp;
  rect* pr = r;
  rect* pr2;
  double length, width;

  for (int i = 0; i < MAX_RECT; i++, pr++) {
    cout << "Enter (X,Y) coord. for ULC of rect. # "
         << i << " : ";
    cin >> pr->ulc.x >> pr->ulc.y;
    cout << "Enter (X,Y) coord. for LRC of rect. # "
         << i << " : ";
    cin >> pr->lrc.x >> pr->lrc.y;
    pr->id = i;
    length = fabs(pr->ulc.x - pr->lrc.x);
    width = fabs(pr->ulc.y - pr->lrc.y);
    pr->area = length * width;
  }
```

```
45:
46:    pr -= MAX_RECT; // reset pointer
47:    // sort the rectangles by areas
48:    for (i = 0; i < (MAX_RECT - 1); i++, pr++) {
49:      pr2 = pr + 1; // reset pointer pr2
50:      for (int j = i + 1; j < MAX_RECT; j++, pr2++)
51:        if (pr->area > pr2->area) {
52:          temp = *pr;
53:          *pr = *pr2;
54:          *pr2 = temp;
55:        }
56:    }
57:
58:    pr -= MAX_RECT - 1; // reset pointer
59:    // display rectangles sorted by area
60:    for (i = 0; i < MAX_RECT; i++, pr++)
61:      printf("Rect # %d has area %5.4lf\n", pr->id, pr->area);
62:    return 0;
63: }
```

Here is a sample session with the program in Listing 8.7:

```
Enter (X,Y) coord. for ULC of rect. # 0 : 1 1
Enter (X,Y) coord. for LRC of rect. # 0 : 2 2
Enter (X,Y) coord. for ULC of rect. # 1 : 1.5 1.5
Enter (X,Y) coord. for LRC of rect. # 1 : 3 4
Enter (X,Y) coord. for ULC of rect. # 2 : 1 2
Enter (X,Y) coord. for LRC of rect. # 2 : 5 8
Enter (X,Y) coord. for ULC of rect. # 3 : 4 6
Enter (X,Y) coord. for LRC of rect. # 3 : 8 4
Rect # 0 has area 1.0000
Rect # 1 has area 3.7500
Rect # 3 has area 8.0000
Rect # 2 has area 24.0000
```

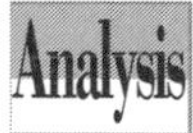

The program in Listing 8.7 declares the pointers `pr` and `pr2` in lines 29 and 30, respectively. These pointers access the structure of type `rect`. The program initializes the pointer `pr` with the base address of array `r`.

The first `for` loop, which begins at line 33, uses the pointer `pr` to access the elements of array `r`. The loop increment part contains the expression `pr++`, which uses pointer arithmetic to make the pointer `pr` access the next element in array `r`. The input statements in lines 36 and 39 use the pointer `pr` to access the members `ulc` and `lrc`. Notice that the statements use the pointer access operator `->` to allow pointer `pr` to access the members `ulc` and `lrc`. The statements in lines 40 through 43 also use the pointer `pr` to access the members `id`, `ulc`, `lrc`, and `area`, using the `->` operator.

The statement in line 46 resets the address stored in pointer `pr` by `MAX_RECT` units (that is `MAX_RECT * sizeof(double)` bytes). The nested loops in lines 48 through 56 use the pointers `pr` and `pr2`. The outer `for` loop increments the address in pointer `pr` by one before the next iteration. The statement in line 49 assigns `pr + 1` to the pointer `pr2`. This statement gives the pointer `pr2` the initial access to the element `i + 1` in array `r`. The inner `for` loop increments the pointer `pr2` by 1 before the next iteration. Thus, the nested `for` loops use the pointers `pr` and `pr2` to access the elements of array `r`. The `if` statement in line 51 uses the pointers `pr` and `pr2` to access the `area` member in comparing the areas of various rectangles. The statements in line 52 through 54 swap the elements of array `r`, which are accessed by pointers `pr` and `pr2`. Notice that the statements use `*pr` and `*pr2` to access an entire element of array `r`.

The statement in line 58 resets the address in the pointer `pr` by subtracting `MAX_RECT - 1`. The last `for` loop also uses the pointer `pr` to access and display the members `id` and `area` of the various elements in array `r`.

This program illustrates that you can completely manipulate an array using pointers only. They are powerful and versatile.

Pointers and Dynamic Memory

The programs presented thus far create the space for their variables at compile-time. When the programs start running, the variables have their memory spaces pre-assigned. There are many applications in which you need to create new variables during the program execution. You need to allocate the memory space dynamically for these new variables at runtime. The designers of C++ have chosen to introduce new operators, which are not found in C, to handle the dynamic allocation and deallocation of memory. These new C++ operators are `new` and `delete`. While the C-style dynamic memory functions `malloc`, `calloc`, and `free` are still available, you should use the operators `new` and `delete`. These operators are more aware of the type of dynamic data that is created than are functions `malloc`, `calloc`, and `free`.

Syntax

The *new* and *delete* Operators

The general syntax for using the `new` and `delete` operators in creating dynamic scalar variables is

```
pointer = new type;
delete pointer;
```

The operator new returns the address of the dynamically allocated variable. The operator delete removes the dynamically allocated memory accessed by a pointer. If the dynamic allocation of operator new fails, it throws an xalloc exception. (See Day 12 for information regarding exception handling.) Therefore, you need to test for a NULL pointer after using the new operator if you suspect trouble.

Example:

```
int *pint;
pint = new int;
*pint = 33;
cout << "Pointer pint stores " << *pint;
delete pint;
```

Syntax

A Dynamic Array

To allocate and deallocate a dynamic array, use the following general syntax:

```
arrayPointer = new type[arraySize];
delete [] arrayPointer;
```

The operator new returns the address of the dynamically allocated array. If the allocation fails, the operator throws an xalloc exception. The operator delete[] removes the dynamically allocated array that is accessed by a pointer.

Example:

```
const int MAX = 10;
int* pint;
pint = new int[MAX];
for (int i = 0; i < MAX; i++)
     pint[i] = i * i
for (i = 0; i < MAX; i++)
     cout << *(pint + i) << "\n";
delete [] pint;
```

DO | **DON'T**

DO maintain access to dynamic variables and arrays at all times. Such access does not need the original pointers that were used to create these dynamic variables and arrays. Here is an example:

```
int* p = new int;
int* q;
*p = 123;
q = p; // q now also points to 123
p = new int; // create another dynamic variable
*p = 345; // p points to 345 whereas q points to 123
```

```
cout << *p << " " << *q << " " << (*p + *q) << "\n";
delete p;
delete q;
```

DON'T forget to delete dynamic variables and arrays at the end of their scope.

There is an important point to make about the difference between the `new`/`delete` operators and the `new[]`/`delete[]` operators. The basic `new` operator allocates only one object of the specified type, and a corresponding `delete` should be used to do away with that object when it's no longer needed. On the other hand, arrays need to use the `new[]` operator in order to make sure that the constructor for the appropriate object is called once for each copy of the array. Similarly, the `delete[]` operator must then be called for that array in order to make sure that the destructor for each object in the array is called.

If a `delete` operator is used to get rid of objects created with the `new[]` operator, the memory will be released properly, but the destructors won't be called. Often, this point doesn't make much of a difference, for example when the objects being created and destroyed don't have constructors or destructors, such as `int`s or `char`s. On the other hand, it's bad practice, and if you use the wrong method on an array of objects that *do* make use of constructors and/or destructors, you could badly cripple your program by failing to let the destructor do any of its necessary cleanup.

Using pointers to create and access dynamic data can be illustrated with the next program, PTR5.CPP (Listing 8.8). This program is a modified version of program ARRAY1.CPP that calculates the average value for data in an array. The program begins by prompting you to enter the actual number of data and validates your input. Then the program prompts you for the data and calculates the average of the data in the array. Next, the program displays the average value.

Type

Listing 8.8. Source code for the program PTR5.CPP.

```
/*
  C++ program that demonstrates the pointers to manage
  dynamic data
*/

#include <iostream.h>

const int MAX = 30;

main()
{
```

```

    double* x;
    double sum, sumx = 0, mean;
    int *n;

    n = new int;
    if (n == NULL)
      return 1;

    do { // obtain number of data points
        cout << "Enter number of data points [2 to "
             << MAX << "] : ";
        cin >> *n;
        cout << "\n";
    } while (*n < 2 || *n > MAX);
    // create tailor-fit dynamic array
    x = new double[*n];
    if (!x) {
      delete n;
      return 1;
    }
    // prompt user for data
    for (int i = 0; i < *n; i++) {
        cout << "X[" << i << "] : ";
        cin >> x[i];
    }

    // initialize summations
    sum = *n;
    // calculate sum of observations
    for (i = 0; i < *n; i++)
        sumx += *(x + i);

    mean = sumx / sum; // calculate the mean value
    cout << "\nMean = " << mean << "\n\n";
    // deallocate dynamic memory
    delete n;
    delete [] x;
    return 0;
}
```

Here is a sample session with the program in Listing 8.8:

```
Enter number of data points [2 to 30] : 5

X[0] : 1
X[1] : 2
X[2] : 3
X[3] : 4
X[4] : 5

Mean = 3
```

The program in Listing 8.8 uses two pointers for dynamic allocations. Line 13 declares the first pointer, which is used to allocate and access the dynamic array. Line 15 declares the pointer to create a dynamic variable.

The statement in line 17 uses the operator `new` to allocate the space for a dynamic `int` variable. The statement returns the address of the dynamic data to the pointer `n`. The `if` statement in line 18 determines whether or not the dynamic allocation failed. If so, the function `main` exits and returns an exit code of 1 (to flag an error).

The `do-while` loop in lines 21 through 26 prompts you to enter the number of data points. The statement in line 24 stores your input in the dynamic variable accessed by pointer `n`. The statement uses the pointer reference `*n` for this access. The `while` clause also uses `*n` to access the value in the dynamic variable. In fact, all the statements in the program access the number of data points using the pointer reference `*n`.

The statement in line 28 creates a dynamic array using the operator `new`. The statement creates a dynamic `double`-typed array with the number of elements that you specify. This feature demonstrates the advantage of using dynamic allocation to create custom-fit arrays. The `if` statement in line 29 determines whether or not the allocation of the dynamic array was successful. If not, the statements in lines 30 and 31 deallocate the dynamic variable accessed by pointer `n` and exit the function with a return value of 1.

The `for` loop in lines 34 through 37 prompts you to enter values for the dynamic array. The statement in line 36 stores your input to the element `i` of the dynamic array. Notice that the statement uses the expression `x[i]` to access the targeted element. This form resembles that of static arrays. C++ treats the expression `x[i]` as equivalent to `*(x + i)`. In fact , the program uses the latter form in the second `for` loop in lines 42 and 43. The statement in line 43 accesses the elements in the dynamic array using the form `*(x + i)`.

The last statements in function `main` delete the dynamic variable and array. The statement in line 48 deallocates the space for the dynamic variable accessed by pointer `n`. The statement in line 49 deletes the dynamic array that is accessed by pointer `x`.

Far Pointers

The architecture of processors such as the family of Intel 80x86 features segmented memory. Each segment is 64 kilobytes in size. Using segments has advantages and disadvantages. This storage scheme supports two kinds of pointers: near pointers and far pointers.

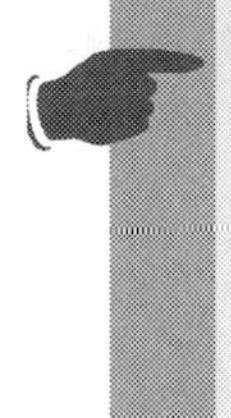

New Term: Within a segment you can use *near pointers* to access data in the same segment. The pointers only store the offset address in the segment and thus require fewer bytes to store their address. By contrast, *far pointers* store the segment and offset addresses, and thus they require more space. Windows applications use far pointers.

To declare far pointers, insert the keyword `far` (or sometimes `__far`) between the pointer's type and the pointer's name.

Summary

Today's lesson introduced you to user-defined data types and covered the following topics:

- You can use the `typedef` declarations to create alias types of existing types and define array types. The general syntax for using `typedef` is

```
typedef knownType newType;
```

- Enumerated data types enable you to declare unique identifiers that represent a collection of logically related constants. The general syntax for declaring an enumerated type is

```
enum enumType { <list of enumerated identifiers> };
```

- Structures enable you to define a new type that logically groups several fields or members. These members can be predefined types or other structures. The general syntax for declaring a structure is

```
struct structTag {
     < list of members >
};
```

- Unions are a form of variant structures. The general syntax for unions is

```
union unionTag {
     type1 member1;
     type2 member2;
     ...
     typeN memberN;
};
```

- Reference variables are aliases of the variables that they reference. To declare a reference variable, place the `&` after the data type of the reference variable or to the left of the variable's name.
- Pointers are variables that store the addresses of other variables or data. C++ uses pointers to offer flexible and efficient manipulation of data and system resources.
- Pointers to existing variables use the `&` operator to obtain the addresses of these variables. Armed with these addresses, pointers offer access to the data in their associated variables. To access the value by using a pointer, use the `*` operator followed by the name of the pointer.
- Pointers access the elements of arrays by being assigned the base address of a class. C++ considers the name of an array as equivalent to the pointer of the base address. For example, the name of the array `X` is treated as `&X[0]`. Pointers can be used to sequentially traverse the elements of an array to store and/or recall values from these elements.
- Pointers to structures manipulate structures and access their members. C++ provides the `->` operator in order to allow a pointer access to the members of a structure.
- Pointers can create and access dynamic data by using the operators `new` and `delete`. These operators enable you to create dynamic variables and arrays. The `new` operator assigns the address of the dynamic data to the pointer used in creating and accessing the data. The operator `delete` assists in recuperating the space of dynamic data when that information is no longer needed.
- Far pointers are pointers that store both the segment and the offset addresses of an item. Near pointers only store the offset address of an item. Far pointers require more storage than near pointers.

Q&A

Q Does C++ support pointers to the predefined type `void`?

A Yes, `void*` pointers are considered typeless pointers and can be used to copy data.

Q Because C++ pointers (including `void*` pointers) have types, can I use typecasting to translate the data accessed by the general-purpose `void*` pointers to non-`void*` pointers?

A Yes. C++ enables you to typecast pointer references. For example:

```
void* p = data;
long *lp = (long*) p;
```

The pointer `lp` uses the typecast to translate the data it accesses.

Q What happens if I delete a dynamic array by using the `delete` operator without following it with the empty brackets?

A The effect of deleting an array with a plain delete operator is undefined. Expect the plain delete operator to leave orphaned dynamic memory.

Q Can a structure contain a pointer to itself?

A Yes. Many structures that model dynamic data structures use this kind of declaration. For example, the following structure models the nodes of a dynamic list with pointer-based links:

```
struct listNode {
  dataType data;
  listNode *next;
};
```

Q Does C++ allow the declaration of a pointer-to-structure type before declaring the structure?

A Yes. This feature makes declaring nodes of dynamic data structure possible.

Q Does C++ allow pointers that access the addresses of other pointers?

A Yes. C++ supports pointers to pointers (also called *double pointers*). To declare such pointers, use two `*` characters, as shown in the following example, which declares the double pointer `p`:

```
int x;
int *px = &x;
int **p = &px;
```

The expression `*p` accesses the pointer `px`, and the expression `**p` accesses the variable `x`.

Workshop

The Workshop provides quiz questions to help you solidify your understanding of the material covered and exercises to provide you with experience in using what you've learned. Try to understand the quiz and exercise answers before continuing on to the next day's lesson. (Answers are provided in Appendix A, "Answers.")

Quiz

1. What is the error in the following declarations?

```
enum Boolean { false, true };
enum State { on, off };
enum YesNo { yes, no };
enum DiskDriveStatus { on , off };
```

2. True or false? The declaration of the following enumerated type is incorrect.

```
enum YesNo ( no = 0, No = 0, yes = 1, Yes = 1 };
```

3. What is the problem with the following program?

```
#include <iostream.h>
main()
{
  int *p = new int;
  cout << "Enter a number : ";
  cin >> *p;
  cout << "The square of " << *p << " = " << (*p * *p);
  return 0;
}
```

Exercises

1. Modify the program PTR4.CPP to create the program PTR6.CPP, which uses the Comb sort method to sort the array of rectangles.
2. Define a structure that can be used to model a dynamic array of integers. The structure should have a member to access the dynamic data and a member to store the size of the dynamic array. Call the structure `intArrStruct`.
3. Define a structure that can be used to model a dynamic matrix. The structure should have a member to access the dynamic data and two members to store the number of rows and columns. Call the structure `matStruct`.

Strings

WEEK
2

The examples presented from Day 1 through Day 8 are predominantly numeric, with a few that involve character manipulation. You may have grown suspicious about the absence of strings in all of these examples. On Day 13 you will learn about the C++ string class. Today's lesson discusses C++ strings. You will learn about the following topics:

- Strings in C++
- String input
- Using the standard string library
- Assigning strings
- Obtaining the length of strings
- Concatenating strings
- Comparing strings
- Converting strings
- Reversing the characters in a string
- Locating characters
- Locating substrings

C++ Strings: An Overview

C++ (and its parent language C) have no predefined string type. Instead, C++, like C, regards strings as arrays of characters that end with the ASCII 0 null character (`'\0'`).

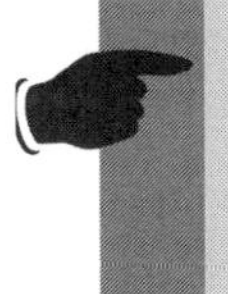

New Term: The `'\0'` character is also called the *null terminator*. Strings that end with the null terminator are sometimes called *ASCIIZ strings*, with the letter Z standing for zero, the ASCII code of the null terminator.

The null terminator *must* be present in all strings and taken into account when dimensioning a string. When you declare a string variable as an array of characters, be sure to reserve an extra space for the null terminator. The advantage of using the null terminator is that you can create strings that are not restricted by any limit imposed by the C++ implementation. In addition, ASCIIZ strings have very simple structures.

Note: The lesson in Day 8 discusses how pointers can access and manipulate the elements of an array. C and C++ make extensive use of this programming feature in manipulating the characters of a string.

DO	DON'T

DO include an extra space for the null terminator when specifying the size of a string.

DON'T declare a string variable as a single-character array. Such a variable is useless.

String Input

The programs that we have presented thus far display string literals in output stream statements; C++ supports stream output for strings as a special case for a nonpredefined data type. (You can say the support came by popular demand.) String output using string variables uses the same operator and syntax. With string input, the inserter operator >> does not work well because strings often contain spaces that are ignored by the inserter operator. Instead of the inserter operator, you need to use the `getline` function. This function reads up to a specified number of characters.

Syntax

The *getline* Function

The general syntax for the overloaded `getline` function is

```
istream& getline(signed char* buffer,
                 int size,
                 char delimiter = '\n');

istream& getline(unsigned char* buffer,
                 int size,
                 char delimiter = '\n');

istream& getline(char* buffer,
                 int size,
                 char delimiter = '\n');
```

The parameter `buffer` is a pointer to the string receiving the characters from the stream. The parameter `size` specifies the maximum number of characters to read. The parameter `delimiter` specifies the delimiting character that causes the string input to stop before reaching the number of characters specified by parameter `size`. The parameter `delimiter` has the default argument of `'\n'`.

Example:

```
#include <iostream.h>
main()
{
  char name[80];
  cout << "Enter your name: ";
  cin.getline(name, sizeof(name)-1);
  cout << "Hello " << name << ", how are you";
  return 0;
}
```

Using the STRING.H Library

The community of C programmers has developed the standard string library STRING.H, which contains the most frequently used string-manipulation functions. The STDIO.H and IOSTREAM.H header file prototype functions also support string I/O. The different C++ compiler vendors have also developed C++-style string libraries. These libraries use classes to model strings. (You will learn more about classes in Day 11.) However, these string libraries *are not yet standard*, whereas the C-style string routines in STRING.H are part of the ANSI C standard. In the next sections, we present several (but not all) of the functions that are prototyped in the STRING.H header file.

Some of the string functions in STRING.H have more than one version. The extra versions that append the characters `_f`, `f`, or `_` work with strings that are accessed using far pointers.

Assigning Strings

C++ supports two methods for assigning strings. You can assign a string literal to a string variable when you initialize it. This method is simple and requires using the = operator and the assigning string.

Syntax

Initializing a String

The general syntax for initializing a string is

```
char stringVar[stringSize] = stringLiteral;
```

Example:

```
char aString[81] = "Borland C++ 4.5 in 21 days";
char name[] = "Namir Shammas";
```

The second method for assigning one ASCIIZ string to another uses the function `strcpy`. This function assumes that the copied string ends with the null character.

Syntax

The *strcpy* Function

The prototype for the function `strcpy` is

```
char* strcpy(char* target, const char* source)
```

The function copies the characters from string source to string target. The function *assumes* that the target string accesses enough space to contain the source string.

Example:

```
char name[41];
strcpy(name,"Borland C++ 4.5");
```

The variable `name` contains the string `"Borland C++ 4.5"`.

The function `strdup` enables you to copy the characters to another string and allocate required space in the target string.

Syntax

The *strdup* Function

The prototype for the function `strdup` is

```
char* strdup(const char* source)
```

The function copies the characters in the source string and returns a pointer to the duplicate string.

Example:

```
char* string1 = "The reign in Spain";
char* string2;

string2 = strdup(string1);
```

This example copies the contents of string1 into string2 after allocating the memory space for string2.

The string library also offers the function strncpy to support copying a specified number of characters from one string to another.

Syntax

The *strncpy* Function

The prototype for the function strncpy is

```
char* strncpy(char* target, const char* source, size_t num);
```

The function copies *num* characters from the source string to the target string. The function performs character truncation or padding, if necessary.

Example:

```
char str1[] = "Pascal";
char str2[] = "Hello there";

strncpy(str1, str2, 6);
```

The variable str1 now contains the string "Hello ".

Note: Using pointers to manipulate strings is a new idea to many novice C++ programmers. In fact, you can use pointers to manipulate the trailing parts of a string by assigning the address of the first character to manipulate. For example, if we declare the string str1 as follows

```
char str1[41] = "Hello World";
char str2[41];
char* p = str1;

p += 6; // p now points to substring "World" in str
strcpy(str2, p);
cout << str2 << "\n";
```

the output statement displays the string "World". This example shows how using pointers can incorporate an offset number of characters.

The Length of a String

Many string operations require information about the number of characters in a string. The STRING.H library offers the function `strlen` to return the number of characters, excluding the null terminator, in a string.

Syntax

The *strlen* Function

The prototype for the function `strlen` is

```
size_t strlen(const char* string)
```

The function `strlen` returns the number of characters in the parameter `string`. The result type `size_t` represents a general integer type.

Example:

```
char str[] = "1234567890";
unsigned i;
i = strlen(str);
```

These statements assign 10 to the variable `i`.

Concatenating Strings

Often, you build a string by concatenating two or more strings. The function `strcat` enables you to concatenate one string to another.

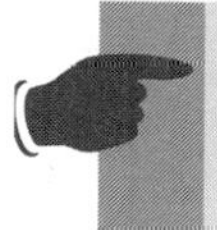

New Term: When you *concatenate* strings, you join or link them together.

Syntax

The *strcat* Function

The prototype for the function `strcat` is

```
char* strcat(char* target, const char* source)
```

The function appends the contents of the source string to the target string and returns the pointer to the target string. The function *assumes* that the target string can accommodate the characters of the source string.

Example:

```
char string[81];
strcpy(string, "Borland");
strcat(string," C++ 4.5")
```

The variable string now contains `"Borland C++ 4.5"`.

The function `strncat` concatenates a specified number of characters from the source string to the target strings.

Syntax

The *strncat* Function

The prototype for the function `strncat` is

```
char* strncat(char* target, const char* source, size_t num)
```

The function appends `num` characters of the source string to the target string and returns the pointer to the target string.

Example:

```
char str1[81] = "Hello I am ";
char str2[41] = "Thomas Jones";

strncat(str1, str2, 6);
```

The variable `str1` now contains `"Hello I am Thomas"`.

DO | **DON'T**

DO use the function `strncat` to control the number of concatenated characters, when you are unsure of the capacity of the target string.

DON'T assume that the target string is always adequate to store the characters in the source string.

Let's look at a program that uses the `getline`, `strlen`, and `strcat` functions. Listing 9.1 contains the source code for the program STRING1.CPP. The program performs the following tasks:

- Prompts you to enter a string; your input should not exceed 40 characters.
- Prompts you to enter a second string; your input should not exceed 40 characters.

- Displays the number of characters in each of the strings you enter.
- Concatenates the second string to the first one.
- Displays the concatenated strings.
- Displays the number of characters in the concatenated strings.
- Prompts you to enter a search character.
- Prompts you to enter a replacement character.
- Displays the concatenated string after translating all the occurrences of the search character with the replacement character.

Listing 9.1. Source code for the program STRING1.CPP.

```
/*
  C++ program that demonstrates C-style strings
*/

#include <iostream.h>
#include <string.h>

const unsigned MAX1 = 40;
const unsigned MAX2 = 80;

main()
{

    char smallStr[MAX1+1];
    char bigStr[MAX2+1];
    char findChar, replChar;

    cout << "Enter first string:\n";
    cin.getline(bigStr, MAX2);
    cout << "Enter second string:\n";
    cin.getline(smallStr, MAX1);
    cout << "String 1 has " << strlen(bigStr)
         << " characters\n";
    cout << "String 2 has " << strlen(smallStr)
         << " characters\n";
    // concatenate bigStr to smallStr
    strcat(bigStr, smallStr);
    cout << "Concatenated strings are:\n"
         << bigStr << "\n";
    cout << "New string has " << strlen(bigStr)
         << " characters\n";
```

continues

Listing 9.1. continued

```
32:     // get the search and replacement characters
33:     cout << "Enter search character : ";
34:     cin >> findChar;
35:     cout << "Enter replacement character : ";
36:     cin >> replChar;
37:     // replace characters in string bigStr
38:     for (unsigned i = 0; i < strlen(bigStr); i++)
39:       if (bigStr[i] == findChar)
40:         bigStr[i] = replChar;
41:     // display the updated string bigStr
42:     cout << "New string is:\n"
43:          << bigStr;
44:     return 0;
45: }
```

Here is a sample session with the program in Listing 9.1:

```
Enter first string:
The rain in Spain stays
Enter second string:
 mainly in the plain
String 1 has 23 characters
String 2 has 20 characters
Concatenated strings are:
The rain in Spain stays mainly in the plain
New string has 43 characters
Enter search character : a
Enter replacement character : A
New string is:
The rAin in SpAin stAys mAinly in the plAin
```

The program in Listing 9.1 includes the STRING.H header file for the string manipulation functions. Lines 8 and 9 declare the global constants `MAX1` and `MAX2`, which are used to size a small string and a big string, respectively. The function `main` declares two strings, `smallStr` and `bigStr`. Line 14 declares the variable `smallStr` to store `MAX1+1` characters. (The extra space is for the null character.) Line 15 declares the variable `bigStr` to store `MAX2+1` characters. Line 16 declares the `char`-typed variable `findChar` and `replChar`.

The output statement in line 18 prompts you to enter the first string. The statement in line 19 uses the stream input function `getline` to obtain your input and to store it in variable `bigStr`. The function call specifies that you can enter up to `MAX2` characters. The output statement in line 20 prompts you to enter the second string.

The statement in line 21 uses the stream input function `getline` to obtain your input and to store it in the variable `smallStr`. The function call specifies that you can enter up to `MAX1` characters.

The output statements in lines 22 through 25 display the number of characters in variables `bigStr` and `smallStr`, respectively. Each output statement calls function `strlen` and passes it a string variable.

The statement in line 27 concatenates the string in the variable `smallStr` to the variable `bigStr`. The output statement in lines 28 and 29 displays the updated string `bigStr`. The output statement in lines 30 and 31 displays the number of characters in the updated string variable `bigStr`. This statement also uses the function `strlen` to obtain the number of characters.

The statement in line 33 prompts you to enter the search character. The statement in line 34 obtains your input and stores it in variable `findChar`. The statement in line 35 prompts you to enter the replacement character. The statement in line 36 obtains your input and stores it in variable `replChar`.

The `for` loop in lines 38 to 40 translates the characters in string `bigStr`. The loop uses the control variable `i` and iterates, in increments of 1, from 0 to `strlen(bigstr)-1`. The `if` statement in line 39 determines whether character number `i` in `bigStr` matches the character in variable `findChar`. If this condition is true, the program executes the statement in line 40. This statement assigns the character in variable `replChar` to character number `i` in variable `bigStr`. This loop shows how you can manipulate the contents of a string variable by accessing each character in that string.

The output statement in lines 42 and 43 displays the updated string `bigStr`.

String Comparison

Because strings are arrays of characters, the STRING.H library provides a set of functions to compare strings. These functions compare the characters of two strings using the ASCII value of each character. The functions are `strcmp`, `stricmp`, `strncmp`, and `strnicmp`.

The function `strcmp` performs a case-sensitive comparison of two strings, using every character possible.

Syntax

The *strcmp* Function

The prototype for the function strcmp is

```
int strcmp(const char* str1, const char* str2);
```

The function compares strings *str1* and *str2*. The integer result indicates the outcome of the comparison.

```
< 0  when str1 is less than str2
= 0  when str1 is equal to str2
> 0  when str1 is greater than str2
```

Example:

```
char string1[] = "Borland C++ 4.5";
char string2[] = "BORLAND C++ 4.5";
int i;

i = strcmp(string1, string2);
```

The last statement assigns a positive number to the variable i, because the string in variable string1 is less than the string in variable string2.

The function stricmp performs a case-insensitive comparison between two strings, using every character possible.

Syntax

The *stricmp* Function

The prototype for the function stricmp is

```
int stricmp(const char* str1, const char* str2);
```

The function compares strings *str1* and *str2* without making a distinction between upper- and lowercase characters. The integer result indicates the outcome of the comparison.

```
< 0  when str1 is less than str2
= 0  when str1 is equal to str2
> 0  when str1 is greater than str2
```

Example:

```
char string1[] = "Borland C++ 4.5";
char string2[] = "BORLAND C++ 4.5";
int i;

i = stricmp(string1, string2);
```

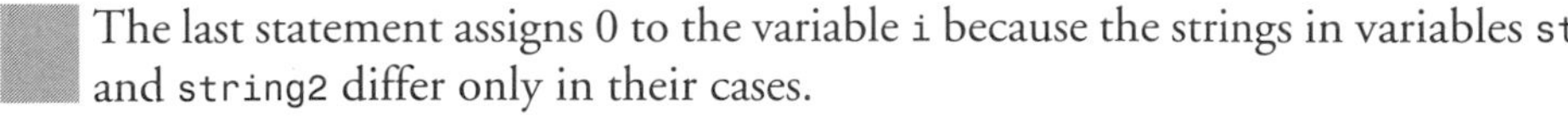

The last statement assigns 0 to the variable `i` because the strings in variables `string1` and `string2` differ only in their cases.

The function `strncmp` performs a case-sensitive comparison on specified leading characters in two strings.

Syntax

The *strncmp* Function

The prototype for the function `strncmp` is

```
int strncmp(const char* str1, const char* str2, size_t num);
```

The function compares the *`num`* leading characters in two strings, *`str1`* and *`str2`*. The integer result indicates the outcome of the comparison, as follows:

```
< 0  when str1 is less than str2
= 0  when str1 is equal to str2
> 0  when str1 is greater than str2
```

Example:

```
char string1[] = "Borland C++ 4.5";
char string2[] = "Borland Pascal";
int i;

i = strncmp(string1, string2, 9);
```

This assigns a negative number to the variable `i` because `"Borland C"` is less than `"Borland P"`.

The function `strnicmp` performs a case-insensitive comparison on specified leading characters in two strings.

Syntax

The *strnicmp* Function

The prototype for the function `strnicmp` is

```
int strnicmp(const char* str1, const char* str2, size_t num);
```

The function compares the *`num`* leading characters in two strings, *`str1`* and *`str2`*, regardless of the character case. The integer result indicates the outcome of the comparison, as follows:

```
< 0  when str1 is less than str2
= 0  when str1 is equal to str2
> 0  when str1 is greater than str2
```

Example:

```
char string1[] = "Borland C++ 4.5";
char string2[] = "BORLAND Pascal";
int i;

i = strnicmp(string1, string2, 7);
```

This assigns 0 to the variable `i` because the strings `"Borland"` and `"BORLAND"` differ only in the case of their characters.

Let's look at an example that compares strings. Listing 9.2 creates an array of strings and initializes it with data. Then the program displays the unordered array of strings, sorts the array, and displays the sorted array.

Listing 9.2. Source code for the program STRING2.CPP.

```
/*
  C++ program that demonstrates comparing strings
*/

#include <iostream.h>
#include <string.h>

const unsigned STR_SIZE = 40;
const unsigned ARRAY_SIZE = 11;
const int TRUE = 1;
const int FALSE = 0;

main()
{

    char strArr[STR_SIZE][ARRAY_SIZE] =
       { "California", "Virginia", "Alaska", "New York",
         "Michigan", "Nevada", "Ohio", "Florida",
         "Washington", "Oregon", "Arizona" };
    char temp[STR_SIZE];
    unsigned n = ARRAY_SIZE;
    unsigned offset;
    int inOrder;

    cout << "Unordered array of strings is:\n";
    for (unsigned i = 0; i < ARRAY_SIZE; i++)
      cout << strArr[i] << "\n";

    cout << "\nEnter a non-space character and press Enter";
    cin >> temp[0];
    cout << "\n";

```

```
    offset = n;
    do {
      offset = (8 * offset) / 11;
      offset = (offset == 0) ? 1 : offset;
      inOrder = TRUE;
      for (unsigned i = 0, j = offset;
           i < n - offset; i++, j++)
        if (strcmp(strArr[i], strArr[j]) > 0) {
          strcpy(temp, strArr[i]);
          strcpy(strArr[i], strArr[j]);
          strcpy(strArr[j], temp);
          inOrder = FALSE;
        }
    } while (!(offset == 1 && inOrder));

    cout << "Sorted array of strings is:\n";
    for (i = 0; i < ARRAY_SIZE; i++)
      cout << strArr[i] << "\n";
    return 0;
}
```

Here is a sample session with the program in Listing 9.2:

```
Unordered array of strings is:
California
Virginia
Alaska
New York
Michigan
Nevada
Ohio
Florida
Washington
Oregon
Arizona
Enter a non-space character and press Enterc
Sorted array of strings is:
Alaska
Arizona
California
Florida
Michigan
Nevada
New York
Ohio
Oregon
Virginia
Washington
```

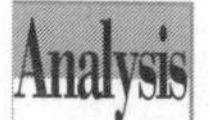

The program in Listing 9.2 declares the global constants `STR_SIZE`, `ARRAY_SIZE`, `TRUE`, and `FALSE` in lines 8 through 11. The constant `STR_SIZE` specifies the size of each string. The constant `ARRAY_SIZE` indicates the number of strings in the array used by the program. The constants `TRUE` and `FALSE` represent the Boolean values employed in sorting the array of strings. The function `main` declares the array `strArr` (actually, the variable `strArr` is a matrix of characters) to have `ARRAY_SIZE` elements and `STR_SIZE` characters per elements. Notice that the declaration states the size of each string in the first dimension and the size of the array in the second dimension. The function also initializes the array `strArr`. The function also declares the variable `temp` as a swap buffer. Lines 21 through 23 declare miscellaneous variables.

The output statement in line 25 shows the title before showing the elements of the unordered array `strArr`. The `for` loop in lines 26 and 27 displays the elements. The loop uses the control variable `i` and iterates, in increments of 1, from 0 to `ARRAY_SIZE-1`. The output statement in line 27 displays the string at element `i`, using the expression `strArr[i]`.

The output and input statements in lines 29 and 30 prompt you to enter a nonspace character. This input enables you to examine the unordered array before the program sorts the array and displays its ordered elements.

The statements in lines 33 through 46 implement the Comb sort method. Notice that the `if` statement in line 40 uses the function `strcmp` to compare elements number `i` and `j`, accessed using the expressions `strArr[i]` and `strArr[j]`, respectively. The statements in lines 41 through 43 swap the elements `i` and `j`, using the function `strcpy` and the swap buffer `temp`.

The output statement in line 48 displays the title before showing the elements of the sorted array. The `for` loop in lines 49 and 50 displays these elements. The loop utilizes the control variable `i` and iterates, in increments of 1, from 0 to `ARRAY_SIZE-1`. The output statement in line 50 displays the string at element `i`, using the expression `strArr[i]`.

Converting Strings

The STRING.H library offers the functions `_strlwr` and `_strupr` to convert the characters of a string to lowercase and uppercase, respectively. Note that these functions are more commonly called `strlwr` and `strupr` (without the leading underscore character) in C textbooks.

Syntax

The *_strlwr* Function

The prototype for the function `_strlwr` is

```
char* _strlwr(char* source)
```

The function converts the uppercase characters in the string *source* to lowercase. Other characters are not affected. The function also returns the pointer to the string *source*.

Example:

```
char str[] = "HELLO THERE";

_strlwr(str);
```

The variable `str` now contains the string `"hello there"`.

Syntax

The *_strupr* Function

The prototype for the function `_strupr` is

```
char* _strupr(char* source)
```

The function converts the lowercase characters in the string *source* to uppercase. Other characters are not affected. The function also returns the pointer to the string *source*.

Example:

```
char str[] = "Borland C++ 4.5";
_strupr(str);
```

The variable `str` now contains the string `"BORLAND C++ 4.5"`.

DO	DON'T

DO make copies for the arguments of functions `strlwr` and `_strupr` if you need the original arguments later in a program.

DON'T always assume that applying the function `_strlwr` and then the function `_strupr` (or vice versa) to the same variable will succeed in restoring the original characters in that variable.

Reversing Strings

The STRING.H library offers the function `strrev` to reverse the characters in a string.

The *strrev* Function

The prototype for the function `strrev` is

```
char* strrev(char* str)
```

The function reverses the order of the characters in string `str` and returns the pointer to the string `str`.

Example:

```
char string[] = "Hello";

strrev(string);
cout << string;
```

This displays `"olleH"`.

Let's look at a program that manipulates the characters in a string. Listing 9.3 shows the source code for the program STRING3.CPP. The program performs the following tasks:

- Prompts you to enter a string.
- Displays your input.
- Displays the lowercase version of your input.
- Displays the uppercase version of your input.
- Displays the character you typed, in reverse order.
- Displays a message that your input has no uppercase character, if this is true.
- Displays a message that your input has no lowercase character, if this is true.
- Displays a message that your input has symmetrical characters, if this is true.

Listing 9.3. Source code for the program STRING3.CPP.

```
/*
  C++ program that demonstrates manipulating the
  characters in a string
*/

#include <iostream.h>
#include <string.h>
```

```

const unsigned STR_SIZE = 40;
const int TRUE = 1;
const int FALSE = 0;

main()
{
    char str1[STR_SIZE+1];
    char str2[STR_SIZE+1];
    int isLowerCase;
    int isUpperCase;
    int isSymmetrical;


    cout << "Enter a string : ";
    cin.getline(str1, STR_SIZE);
    cout << "Input: " << str1 << "\n";
    // copy str1 to str2
    strcpy(str2, str1);
    // convert to lowercase
    strlwr(str2);
    isLowerCase = (strcmp(str1, str2) == 0) ? TRUE : FALSE;
    cout << "Lowercase: " << str2 << "\n";
    // convert to uppercase
    strupr(str2);
    isUpperCase = (strcmp(str1, str2) == 0) ? TRUE : FALSE;
    cout << "Uppercase: " << str2 << "\n";
    // copy str1 to str2
    strcpy(str2, str1);
    // reverse characters
    strrev(str2);
    isSymmetrical = (strcmp(str1, str2) == 0) ? TRUE : FALSE;
    cout << "Reversed: " << str2 << "\n";
    if (isLowerCase)
      cout << "Your input has no uppercase letters\n";
    if (isUpperCase)
      cout << "Your input has no lowercase letters\n";
    if (isSymmetrical)
      cout << "Your input has symmetrical characters\n";
    return 0;
}
```

Here is a sample session with the program in Listing 9.3:

```
Enter a string : level
Input: level
Lowercase: level
Uppercase: LEVEL
Reversed: level
Your input has no uppercase letters
Your input has symmetrical characters
```

The program in Listing 9.3 declares the string variables `str1` and `str2` in the function `main`. Each string stores `STR_SIZE + 1` characters (including the null terminator). The function also declares the flags `isLowerCase`, `isUpperCase`, and `isSymmetrical`.

The output statement in line 22 prompts you to enter a string. The statement in line 23 uses the string input function `getline` to store your input in variable `str1`. The output statement in line 24 echoes your input.

The statement in line 26 copies the characters in variable `str1` to variable `str2`. The statement in line 26 calls the function `strlwr` to convert the characters in variable `str2`. The program manipulates the characters of variable `str2`, while maintaining the original input in variable `str1`. The statement in line 29 calls the function `strcmp` to compare the characters in `str1` and `str2`. The two strings can be equal only if your input has no uppercase characters. The statement uses the conditional operator to assign the constant `TRUE` to the flag `isLowerCase` if the above condition is true. Otherwise, the statement assigns `FALSE` to the flag `isLowerCase`. The output statement in line 30 displays the characters in variable `str2`.

The statement in line 32 calls the function `strupr` and supplies it the argument `str2`. This function call converts any lowercase character in variable `str2` into uppercase. The statement in line 33 calls the function `strcmp` to compare the characters in `str1` and `str2`. The two strings can be equal only if your input has no lowercase characters. The statement uses the conditional operator to assign the constant `TRUE` to the flag `isUpperCase` if that is true. Otherwise, the statement assigns `FALSE` to the flag `isUpperCase`. The output statement in line 34 displays the characters in variable `str2`.

To display the original input in reverse order, the program calls the function `strcpy` to copy the characters of variable `str1` to variable `str2` once more. The statement in line 38 calls the function `strrev` and passes it the argument `str2`. The statement in line 39 calls the function `strcmp` to compare the characters in `str1` and `str2`. The two strings can be equal only if your input has symmetrical characters. The statement uses the conditional operator to assign the constant `TRUE` to the flag `isSymmetrical` if the characters in `str1` and `str2` match. Otherwise, the statement assigns `FALSE` to the flag `isSymmetrical`. The output statement in line 40 displays the characters in variable `str2`.

The program uses the `if` statements in lines 41, 43, and 45 to indicate that your input has special characteristics. The `if` statement in line 41 comments on the fact that your input has no uppercase letter when the value in variable `isLowerCase` is `TRUE`. The `if` statement in line 43 comments on the fact that your input has no lowercase letter when the value in variable isUpperCase is TRUE. The if statement in line 45 comments on the fact that your input has symmetrical characters when the value in variable isSymmetrical is TRUE.

Locating Characters

The STRING.H library offers a number of functions for locating characters in strings. These functions include strchr, strrchr, strspn, strcspn, and strpbrk. These functions enable you to search for characters and simple character patterns in strings.

The function strchr locates the first occurrence of a character in a string.

Syntax

The *strchr* Function

The prototype for the function strchr is

```
char* strchr(const char* target, int c)
```

The function locates the first occurrence of pattern c in the string *target*. The function returns the pointer to the character in string *target* that matches the specified pattern c. If character c does not occur in the string *target*, the function yields a NULL.

Example:

```
char str[81] = "Borland C++ 4.5";
char* strPtr;

strPtr = strchr(str, '+');
```

The pointer strPtr points to the substring "++ 4.5" in string str.

The function strrchr locates the last occurrence of a character in a string.

Syntax

The *strrchr* Function

The prototype for the function strrchr is

```
char* strrchr(const char* target, int c)
```

The function locates the last occurrence of pattern c in the string *target*. The function returns the pointer to the character in string *target* that matches the specified pattern c. If character c does not occur in the string *target*, the function yields a NULL.

Example:

```
char str[81] = "Borland C++ 4.5 is here";
char* strPtr;

strPtr = strrchr(str, '+');
```

The pointer `strPtr` points to the substring `"+ 4.5 is here"` in string `str`.

The function `strspn` yields the number of characters in the leading part of a string that matches any character in a pattern of characters.

Syntax

The *strspn* Function

The prototype for the function `strspn` is

```
size_t strspn(const char* target, const char* pattern)
```

The function returns the number of characters in the leading part of the string *`target`* that matches any character in the string *`pattern`*.

Example:

```
char str[] = "Borland C++ 4.5";
char substr[] = "danrolB ";
int index;

index = strspn(str, substr);
```

This statement assigns 7 to the variable `index` because the characters in `substr` found a match in each of the first seven characters of `str`.

The function `strcspn` scans a string and yields the number of leading characters in a string that is totally void of the characters in a substring.

Syntax

The *strcspn* Function

The prototype for the function `strcspn` is

```
size_t strcspn(const char* str1, const char* str2)
```

The function scans `str1` and returns the length of the leftmost substring that is totally void of the characters of the substring `str2`.

Example:

```
char strng[] = "The rain in Spain";
int i;

i = strcspn(strng," in");
```

This example assigns 8 (the length of "The rain") to the variable i.

The function strpbrk searches a string for the first occurrence of any character in a pattern of characters.

Syntax

The *strpbrk* Function

The prototype for the function strpbrk is

```
char* strpbrk(const char* target, const char* pattern)
```

The function searches the *target* string for the first occurrence of *any character* among the characters of the string *pattern*. If the characters in the pattern do not occur in the string *target*, the function yields a NULL.

Example:

```
char* str = "Hello there how are you";
char* substr = "hr";
char* ptr;

ptr = strpbrk(str, substr);
cout << ptr << "\n";
```

This displays "here how are you", because the 'h' is encountered in the string before the 'r'.

Locating Strings

The STRING.H library offers the function strstr to locate a substring in a string.

Syntax

The *strstr* Function

The prototype for the function strstr is

```
char* strstr(const char* str, const char* substr);
```

The function scans the string *str* for the first occurrence of a string *substr*. The function yields the pointer to the first character in string *str* that matches the parameter *substr*. If the string *substr* does not occur in the string *str*, the function yields a NULL.

Example:

```
char str[] = "Hello there! how are you";
char substr[] = "how";
char* ptr;
```

```
ptr = strstr(str, substr);
cout << ptr << "\n";
```

This displays `"how are you"` because the string search matched `"how"`. The pointer `ptr` points to the rest of the original string, starting with `"how"`.

DO / **DON'T**

DO use the function `strrev` before calling the function `strstr` if you want to search for the last occurrence of a string.

DON'T forget to reverse both the main and the search strings when using the `strrev` function to locate the last occurrence of the search string.

The string library also provides the function `strtok`, which enables you to break down a string into substrings based on a specified set of delimiting characters.

New Term: Substrings are sometimes called *tokens*.

Syntax

The *strtok* Function

The prototype for the function `strtok` is

```
char* strtok(char* target, const char* delimiters);
```

The function searches the target string for tokens. A string supplies the set of delimiter characters. The following example shows how this function works in returning the tokens in a string. The function `strtok` modifies the string target by inserting `'\0'` characters after each token. (Make sure that you store a copy of the original target string in another string variable.)

Example:

```
#include <stdio.h>
#include <string.h>

main()
{
```

```
    char* str = "(Base_Cost+Profit) * Margin";
    char* tkn = "+* ()";
    char* ptr = str;

    printf("%s\n", str);
    // the first call looks normal
    ptr = strtok(str, tkn);
    printf("\n\nThis is broken into: %s",ptr);
    while (ptr) {
        printf(" ,%s",ptr);
        // must make first argument a NULL character
        ptr = strtok(NULL, tkn);
    }
    printf("\n\n");
}
```

This example displays the following when the program is run:

```
(Base_Cost+Profit) * Margin
```

This is broken into `Base_Cost`, `Profit`, `Margin`.

DO	DON'T

DO remember to supply `NULL` as the first argument to the function `strtok` in order to locate thc next token.

DON'T forget to store a copy of the target string in the function `strtok`.

Let's look at an example that searches for characters and strings. Listing 9.4 shows the source code for the program STRING4.CPP. The program performs the following tasks:

- Prompts you to enter the main string.
- Prompts you to enter the search string.
- Prompts you to enter the search character.
- Displays a character ruler and the main string.
- Displays the indices where the search string occurs in the main string.
- Displays the indices where the search character occurs in the main string.

9

Listing 9.4. Source code for the program STRING4.CPP.

```
/*
  C++ program that demonstrates searching for the
  characters and strings
*/

#include <iostream.h>
#include <string.h>

const unsigned STR_SIZE = 40;

main()
{
    char mainStr[STR_SIZE+1];
    char subStr[STR_SIZE+1];
    char findChar;
    char *p;
    int index;
    int count;

    cout << "Enter a string : ";
    cin.getline(mainStr, STR_SIZE);
    cout << "Enter a search string : ";
    cin.getline(subStr, STR_SIZE);
    cout << "Enter a search character : ";
    cin >> findChar;

    cout << "          1         2         3         4\n";
    cout << "01234567890123456789012345678901234567890\n";
    cout << mainStr << "\n";
    cout << "Searching for string " << subStr << "\n";
    p = strstr(mainStr, subStr);
    count = 0;
    while (p) {
      count++;
      index = p - mainStr;
      cout << "Match at index " << index << "\n";
      p = strstr(++p, subStr);
    }
    if (count == 0)
      cout << "No match for substring in main string\n";

    cout << "Searching for character " << findChar << "\n";
    p = strchr(mainStr, findChar);
    count = 0;
    while (p) {
      count++;
      index = p - mainStr;
```

```
48:       cout << "Match at index " << index << "\n";
49:       p = strchr(++p, findChar);
50:     }
51:     if (count == 0)
52:       cout << "No match for search character in main string\n";
53:     return 0;
54: }
```


Here is a sample session with the program in Listing 9.4:

```
Enter a string : here, there, and everywhere
Enter a search string : here
Enter a search character : e
          1         2         3         4
01234567890123456789012345678901234567890
here, there, and everywhere
Searching for string here
Match at index 0
Match at index 7
Match at index 23
Searching for character e
Match at index 1
Match at index 3
Match at index 8
Match at index 10
Match at index 17
Match at index 19
Match at index 24
Match at index 26
```

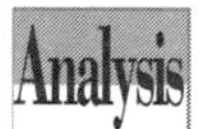

The program in Listing 9.4 declares the strings `mainStr` and `subStr` to represent the main and search strings, respectively. The program also declares the variable `findChar` to store the search character. In addition, the program declares the character pointer `p` and the `int`-typed variables `index` and `count`.

The output statement in line 20 prompts you to enter a string. The statement in line 21 calls the stream input function `getline` and stores your input in variable `mainStr`. The output statement in line 22 prompts you to enter the search string. The statement in line 23 calls the stream input function `getline` and saves your input in variable `subStr`. The output statement in line 24 prompts you to enter the search character. The statement in line 25 obtains your input and stores it in the variable `findChar`.

The output statements in lines 27 through 29 display a ruler, along with your input aligned under the ruler. The output statement in line 30 informs you that the program is searching for the substring you entered. The search begins at the statement in line 31. This statement calls the function `strstr` to locate the first occurrence of string subStr in the string mainStr. The statement in line 32 assigns 0 to the variable count, which keeps track of the number of times the string mainStr contains the string subStr.

The program uses the while loop in lines 33 through 38 to locate all the occurrences of subStr in mainStr. The condition of the while loop examines the address of pointer p. If that pointer is not NULL, the loop iterates. The first statement inside the loop increments the variable count. The statement in line 35 calculates the index of the string mainStr where the last match occurs. The statement obtains the sought index by subtracting the address of pointer p from the address of the first character in the variable mainStr. (Remember that the expression &mainStr[0] is equivalent to the simpler expression mainStr.) The statement assigns the result to the variable index. The output statement in line 36 displays the value in variable index.

The statement in line 37 searches for the next occurrence of the string subStr in mainStr. Notice that this statement calls strstr and supplies it the pointer p as the first argument. The statement also applies the pre-increment operator to pointer p to store the address of the next character. This action ensures that the call to function strstr finds the next occurrence, if any, and is not stuck at the last occurrence. The if statement outside the while loop examines the value in variable count. If it contains zero, the program executes the output statement in line 40 to inform you that no match was found for the search string.

The output statement in line 42 informs you that the program is now searching for the character you specified in the main string. The process of searching for the character in findChar is very similar to searching for the string subStr. The main difference is that searching for a character involves the function strchr.

Summary

Today's lesson presented C++ strings and discussed string manipulation functions that are exported by the STRING.H header file. You learned about the following topics:

- Strings in C++ are arrays of characters that end with the null character (the ASCII 0 character).
- String input requires the use of the getline stream input function. This function requires that you specify the input variable, the maximum number of input characters, and the optional line delimiter.

- The STRING.H header file contains the standard string library for the C language. This library contains many versatile functions that support copying, concatenating, converting, reversing, and searching for strings.
- C++ supports two methods for assigning strings. The first method assigns a string to another when you declare the latter string. The second method uses the function `strcpy` to assign one string to another at any stage in the program. The string library also offers the function `strdup` to copy a string and allocate the needed space.
- The function `strlen` returns the length of a string.
- The `strcat` and `strncat` functions enable you to concatenate two strings. The function `strncat` enables you to specify the number of characters to concatenate.
- The functions `strcmp`, `stricmp`, `strncmp`, and `strnicmp` enable you to perform various types of string comparisons. The function `strcmp` performs a case-insensitive comparison of two strings, using every character possible. The function `stricmp` is a version of the function `strcmp` that performs a case-insensitive comparison. The function `strncmp` is a variant of function `strcmp` that uses a specified number of characters in comparing the strings. The function `strnicmp` is a version of function `strncmp` that also performs a case-insensitive comparison.
- The functions `strlwr` and `strupr` convert the characters of a string into lowercase and uppercase, respectively.
- The function `strrev` reverses the order of characters in a string.
- The functions `strchr`, `strrchr`, `strspn`, `strcspn`, and `strpbrk` enable you to search for characters and simple character patterns in strings.
- The function `strstr` searches for a string in another string. The function `strtok` enables you to break down a string into smaller strings that are delimited by a set of characters that you specify.

Q&A

Q Can a statement initialize a pointer using a string literal?

A Yes. The compiler stores the characters of the string literal in memory and assigns its address to that pointer. Here is an example:

```
char* p = "I am a small string";
```

Q Can a statement declare a constant pointer to a literal string?

A Yes. This kind of declaration resembles the one we mentioned previously. However, because the statement declares a constant pointer, you cannot overwrite the characters of the initializing string literal (you will get a compile-time error). Here is an example:

```
const char* p = "Version 1.0";
```

Use the `const char*` pointer to store fixed messages and titles.

Q Can a statement declare an array of pointers to a set of string literals?

A Yes. This is the easiest method of using an array of pointers to access a collection of messages, titles, or other kinds of fixed strings. Here is an example:

```
char* mainMenu[] = { "File", "Edit", "Search", "View",
                     "Debug", "Options", "Windows", "Help"};
```

Thus, the element `mainMenu[0]` accesses the first string, `mainMenu[1]` accesses the second string, and so on.

Q How can I use `strcmp` to compare strings, starting at a specific number of characters?

A Add the offset value to the arguments of the function `strcmp`. Here is an example:

```
char s1[41] = "Borland C++ 4.5";
char s2[41] = "BORLAND Pascal";
int offset = 7;
int i;
i = strcmp(str1 + offset, str2 + offset);
```

Q How can I use `strncmp` to compare a specific number of characters in two strings, starting at a specific character?

A Add the offset value to the arguments of the function `strcmp`. Here is an example:

```
char s1[41] = "Borland C++ 4.5";
char s2[41] = "BORLAND Pascal";
int offset = 7;
int num = 3;
int i;
i = strncmp(str1 + offset, str2 + offset, num);
```

9

Workshop

The Workshop provides quiz questions to help you solidify your understanding of the material covered and exercises to provide you with experience in using what you've learned. Try to understand the quiz and exercise answers before continuing on to the next day's lesson. (Answers are provided in Appendix A, "Answers.")

Quiz

1. Where is the error in the following program?

```
#include <iostream.h>
#include <string.h>
const int MAX = 10;
main()
{
  char s1[MAX+1];
  char s2[] = "1234567890123456789012334567890";
  strcpy(s1, s2);
  cout << "String 1 is " << s1
       << "\nString 2 is " << s2;
  return 0;
}
```

2. How can you fix the program in the last question using the function `strncpy` instead of `strcpy`?

3. What is the value assigned to variable `i` in the following statements?

```
char s1[] = "Borland C++";
char s2[] = "Borland Pascal";
int i;
i = strcmp(s1, s2);
```

4. What is the value assigned to variable `i` in the following statements?

```
char s1[] = "Borland C++";
char s2[] = "Borland Pascal";
int offset = strlen("Borland ");
int i;
i = strcmp(s1 + offset, s2 + offset);
```

5. True or false? The following function correctly returns 1 if a string does not contain lowercase characters, and yields 0 if otherwise.

```
int hasNoLowerCase(const char* s)
{
  char s2[strlen(s)+1];
  strcpy(s2, s);
  strupr(s2);
  return (strcmp(s, s2) == 0) ? 1 : 0);
}
```

Exercises

1. Write your own version of the function `strlen`. Use a `while` loop and a character-counting variable to obtain the function result.
2. Write another version of the function `strlen`. This time use a `while` loop and a local pointer to obtain the function result.
3. Write the program STRING5.CPP, which uses the function `strtok` to break down the string `"2*(X+Y)/(X+Z) - (X+10)/(Y-5)"` into three sets of tokens, using the token delimiter strings `"+-*/ ()"`, `"( )"`, and `"+-*/ "`.

Advanced Function Parameters

WEEK
2

Functions are the basic building blocks that conceptually extend the C++ language to fit your custom applications. C, the parent language of C++, is more function-oriented than C++. This difference is due to the fact that C++ supports classes, inheritance, and other object-oriented programming features. (More about these in tomorrow's lesson.) Nevertheless, functions still play an important role in C++. In today's lesson, you will learn about the following advanced aspects of C++ functions:

- ☐ Passing arrays as function arguments
- ☐ Passing strings as function arguments
- ☐ Passing structures by value
- ☐ Passing structures by reference
- ☐ Passing structures by pointer
- ☐ Recursive functions
- ☐ Passing pointers to dynamic structures
- ☐ Pointers to functions

Passing Arrays as Arguments

When you write a C++ function that passes an array parameter, you can declare that parameter as a pointer to the basic type of the array.

Syntax

A Pointer-to-Array Parameter

The general syntax for prototyping a function with a pointer-to-array parameter is

```
returnType function(basicType*, <other parameter types>);
```

The general syntax for defining this function is

```
returnType function(basicType *arrParam, <other parameters>)
```

Example:

```
// prototypes
void ShellSort(unsigned *doubleArray, unsigned arraySize);
void QuickSort(unsigned *intArray, unsigned arraySize);
```

On Day 7, we stated that C++ enables you to declare open array parameters using a pair of empty brackets. This kind of declaration is equivalent to using a pointer parameter. C++ programmers use the open array form less frequently than the explicit pointer form, even though using the brackets shows the intent of the parameter more clearly.

DO | **DON'T**

DO use `const` parameters to prevent the host function from altering the arguments.

DON'T forget to include a parameter that specifies the number of array elements to manipulate (when the array-typed arguments are only partially filled with meaningful data).

Let's look at an example. Listing 10.1 shows the source code for the program ADVFUN1.CPP. We created this program by performing minor edits to the program ARRAY5.CPP (found in Listing 7.5 of Day 7). The program performs the following tasks:

- Prompts you to enter the number of data points
- Prompts you to enter the integer values for the array
- Displays the elements of the unordered array
- Displays the elements of the sorted array

Listing 10.1. Source code for the program ADVFUN1.CPP.

```
// C++ program that sorts arrays using the Comb sort method

#include <iostream.h>

const int MAX = 10;
const int TRUE = 1;
const int FALSE = 0;

int obtainNumData()
{
  int m;
  do { // obtain number of data points
    cout << "Enter number of data points [2 to "
        << MAX << "] : ";
    cin >> m;
    cout << "\n";
  } while (m < 2 ¦¦ m > MAX);
  return m;
}

void inputArray(int *intArr, int n)
```

continues

Listing 10.1. continued

```
{
  // prompt user for data
  for (int i = 0; i < n; i++) {
    cout << "arr[" << i << "] : ";
    cin >> *(intArr + i);
  }
}

void showArray(const int *intArr, int n)
{
  for (int i = 0; i < n; i++) {
    cout.width(5);
    cout << *(intArr + i) << " ";
  }
  cout << "\n";
}

void sortArray(int *intArr, int n)
{
  int offset, temp, inOrder;

  offset = n;
  do {
    offset = (8 * offset) / 11;
    offset = (offset == 0) ? 1 : offset;
    inOrder = TRUE;
    for (int i = 0, j = offset; i < (n - offset); i++, j++) {
      if (intArr[i] > intArr[j]) {
        inOrder = FALSE;
        temp = intArr[i];
        intArr[i] = intArr[j];
        intArr[j] = temp;
      }
    }
  } while (!(offset == 1 && inOrder));
}

main()
{
  int arr[MAX];
  int n;

  n = obtainNumData();
  inputArray(arr, n);
  cout << "Unordered array is:\n";
  showArray(arr, n);
  sortArray(arr, n);
  cout << "\nSorted array is:\n";
  showArray(arr, n);
  return 0;
}
```

Here is a sample session with the program in Listing 10.1:

```
Enter number of data points [2 to 10] : 5

arr[0] : 55
arr[1] : 22
arr[2] : 78
arr[3] : 35
arr[4] : 45
Unordered array is:
   55     22     78     35     45

Sorted array is:
   22     35     45     55     78
```

The program in Listing 10.1 is almost identical to that in Listing 7.5 of Day 7. The new program uses slightly different parameters in the functions `inputArray`, `showArray`, and `sortArray`. The first parameter in these functions is a pointer to the `int` type. The function `showArray` prefixes the pointer type with `const`. Such a declaration tells the compiler that the function `showArray` cannot alter the elements of the arguments for the parameter `intArray`.

Using Strings as Arguments

Because C++ treats strings as arrays of characters, the rules for passing arrays as arguments to functions also apply to strings. The following program contains functions that manipulate strings. Listing 10.2 shows the source code for the program ADVFUN2.CPP. The program prompts you to enter a string, then displays the number of characters you typed (the size of the input string) and the uppercase version of your input.

Listing 10.2. Source code for the program ADVFUN2.CPP.

```
/*
  C++ program that declares functions with string parameters
*/

#include <iostream.h>

const unsigned MAX = 40;

char* upperCase(char* str)
{
   int ascii_shift = 'A' - 'a';
   char* p = str;
```

continues

Listing 10.2. continued

```

    // loop to convert each character to uppercase
    while ( *p != '\0') {
        if ((*p  >= 'a') && (*p <= 'z'))
           *p += ascii_shift;
        p++;
    }
    return str;
}

int strlen(char* str)
{
   char *p = str;
   while (*p++ != '\0');
   return --p - str;  //note the semi colon
}

main()
{
     char aString[MAX+1];

     cout << "Enter a string: ";
     cin.getline(aString, MAX);
     cout << "Your string has " << strlen(aString)
          << " characters\n";
     // concatenate bigStr to aString
     upperCase(aString);
     cout << "The uppercase version of your input is: "
          << aString;
     return 0;
}
```

Here is a sample session with the program in Listing 10.2:

```
Enter a string: Borland C++
Your string has 11 characters
The uppercase version of your input is: BORLAND C++
```

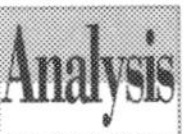

The program in Listing 10.2 declares its own string-manipulating functions: `upperCase` and `strlen`. The function `upperCase` has a single parameter, `str`, which is a pointer to the `char` type. This parameter passes the address of an array of characters. The function converts the characters accessed by the pointer string to uppercase and returns the pointer to the string. The function declares the local variable `ascii_shift` and the local `char`-pointer `p`. The function also initializes the variable `ascii_shift` with the difference between the ASCII values of the letters `A` and `a`. Thus, the `ascii-shift` variable contains the difference in ASCII codes needed to convert a lowercase character into an uppercase character. The function also initializes the local pointer `p` with the address in parameter `str`.

The upperCase function uses the while loop in line 15 to traverse the characters of the string argument. The while clause determines whether the pointer p does not access the null terminator. The if statement in line 16 determines if the character accessed by pointer p is a lowercase letter. If this condition is true, the function executes the statement in line 17. This statement adds the value in variable ascii_shift to the character currently accessed by pointer p. This action converts a lowercase character into uppercase. The statement in line 18 increments the address of pointer p to access the next character. The function returns the address of pointer str.

The function strlen returns the number of characters in the string accessed by the char-pointer parameter str. The function declares the local char-pointer p and initializes it with the address of parameter str. The function uses a while loop with an empty loop statement to locate the null terminator in the string accessed by pointer p. The return statement yields the sought value by taking the difference between the addresses of pointers p and str. The return statement first applies the pre-decrement operator to pointer p to adjust the address of that pointer.

The function main declares the string variable aString. The output statement in line 34 prompts you to enter a string. The statement in line 35 calls the stream input function getline to obtain your input and to store it in variable aString. The output statement in line 36 displays the number of characters you typed. The statement calls the function strlen and passes it the argument aString. The statement in line 39 calls the function upperCase and also passes it the argument aString. The output statement in line 40 displays the uppercase version of your input, which is now stored in variable aString.

Using Structures as Arguments

C++ enables you to pass structures either by value or by reference. In this section, we demonstrate passing structures by value. In the next sections, we show you how to pass structures by reference. The structure's type appears in the function prototype and heading in a manner similar to that of predefined types.

Listing 10.3 shows the source code for the program ADVFUN3.CPP. The program performs the following tasks:

- Prompts you for the *x* and *y* coordinates of a first point
- Prompts you for the *x* and *y* coordinates of a second point
- Calculates the coordinates of the median point between the two points that you entered
- Displays the coordinates of the median point

Listing 10.3. Source code for the program ADVFUN3.CPP.

```
1:  // C++ program that uses a function that passes
2:  // a structure by value
3:
4:  #include <iostream.h>
5:
6:  struct point {
7:    double x;
8:    double y;
9:  };
10:
11: // declare the prototype of function getMedian
12: point getMedian(point, point);
13:
14: main()
15: {
16:   point pt1;
17:   point pt2;
18:   point median;
19:
20:   cout << "Enter the X and Y coordinates for point # 1 : ";
21:   cin >> pt1.x >> pt1.y;
22:   cout << "Enter the X and Y coordinates for point # 2 : ";
23:   cin >> pt2.x >> pt2.y;
24:   // get the coordinates for the median point
25:   median = getMedian(pt1, pt2);
26:   // get the median point
27:   cout << "Mid point is (" << median.x
28:        << ", " << median.y << ")\n";
29:   return 0;
30: }
31:
32: point getMedian(point p1, point p2)
33: {
34:   point result;
35:   result.x = (p1.x + p2.x) / 2;
36:   result.y = (p1.y + p2.y) / 2;
37:   return result;
38: };
```

Here is a sample session with the program in Listing 10.3:

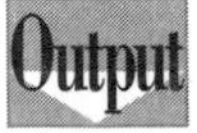

```
Enter the X and Y coordinates for point # 1 : 1 1
Enter the X and Y coordinates for point # 2 : 5 5
Mid point is (3, 3)
```

The program in Listing 10.3 declares the structure `point`, which models a two-dimensional point. This structure has two `double`-typed members, `x` and `y`. Line 12 declares the prototype for the function `getMedian`. The function takes two `point`-typed parameters that are passed by value.

The function main declares the point-typed variables pt1, pt2, and median in lines 16 through 18, respectively. The output statement in line 20 prompts you to enter the *x* and *y* coordinates for the first point. The statement in line 21 obtains your input and stores the coordinates in the members pt1.x and pt1.y. Lines 22 and 23 repeat the same prompting and input process for the second point. The input statement in line 23 stores the values for the second point in members pt2.x and pt2.y. The statement in line 25 calls function getMedian and passes it the arguments pt1 and pt2. The function receives a copy of the arguments pt1 and pt2. The statement assigns the point-typed function result to the variable median. The output statement in lines 27 and 28 displays the *x* and *y* coordinates of the median point (by displaying the x and y members of the variable median).

The function getMedian declares two point-typed parameters, p1 and p2. In addition, the function declares the local point-typed variable result. The statement in line 35 assigns the average of members p1.x and p2.x to member result.x. The statement in line 36 assigns the average of members p1.y and p2.y to member result.y. Notice that these statements use the dot operator to access members x and y of the structures p1, p2, and result. This syntax is used when the function passes a copy or a reference of a structure. The return statement yields the value in the local structure result.

10

Passing Arguments by Reference

C++ enables you to write functions with parameters that pass arguments by reference. This kind of parameter enables you to change the value of the argument beyond the scope of the function. C++ offers two ways to implement such parameters: with pointers and with formal reference parameters. The following sections present functions that pass various kinds of data types by reference.

Passing Structures by Reference

You can pass structures to functions either by using pointers or by using formal reference. Many C++ programmers consider either approach more efficient than passing the structure parameters by copy—you save on the overhead of copying the structure-typed arguments.

Note: Passing a structure by reference enables you to use the dot operator with the reference parameters (as with passing by value). The added advantage is that the reference parameters do not create copies of the original arguments. Thus, they are faster and save memory resources. The down side is that because reference parameters become aliases to their arguments, any changes made to the parameters inside the function affect their arguments. One method to prevent this change is to use `const` reference parameters. Such parameters tell the compiler that the function cannot assign new values to the reference parameters.

DO | **DON'T**

DO pass structures either by formal reference or by pointers when both of the following two circumstances apply: The host function does not alter the arguments, and the function returns values through these structures.

DON'T pass structures by value unless you need to supply the host function with a copy of the data that will be modified by the function.

Let's look at an example. Listing 10.4 shows the source code for the program ADVFUN4.CPP. The program performs the same tasks as the last program, ADVFUN3.CPP. The new version differs only in its implementation.

Type

Listing 10.4. Source code for the program ADVFUN4.CPP.

```
// C++ program which uses a function that passes
// a structure by reference

#include <iostream.h>

struct point {
  double x;
  double y;
};

// declare the prototype of function getMedian
point getMedian(const point&, const point&);

main()
{
  point pt1;
  point pt2;
```

```
  point median;

  cout << "Enter the X and Y coordinates for point # 1 : ";
  cin >> pt1.x >> pt1.y;
  cout << "Enter the X and Y coordinates for point # 2 : ";
  cin >> pt2.x >> pt2.y;
  // get the coordinates for the median point
  median = getMedian(pt1, pt2);
  // get the median point
  cout << "Mid point is (" << median.x
       << ", " << median.y << ")\n";
  return 0;
}

point getMedian(const point& p1, const point& p2)
{
  point result;
  result.x = (p1.x + p2.x) / 2;
  result.y = (p1.y + p2.y) / 2;
  return result;
};
```


Here is a sample session with the program in Listing 10.4:

```
Enter the X and Y coordinates for point # 1 : 1 1
Enter the X and Y coordinates for point # 2 : 9 9
Mid point is (5, 5)
```

The program in Listing 10.4 is very similar to that in Listing 10.3. The new program version uses reference parameters in the function `getMedian`. Thus, the prototype and the function's declaration place the `&` character after the structure type `point`. Using reference parameters, the call to function `getMedian` looks very much like the call to the version in Listing 10.3. Likewise, the implementation of function `getMedian` is similar to the one in Listing 10.3. Both versions use the dot operator to access the members `x` and `y` in the structure `point`.

Passing Structures by Pointers

Using pointers is another efficient way to pass structures. As with the reference parameter types, you can use the `const` declaration to prevent the implementation from changing the structured variables accessed by the pointer parameters.

The next example is, as you might expect, the version of program ADVFUN3.CPP that uses pointer parameters. Listing 10.5 shows the source code for the new version, program ADVFUN5.CPP.

Listing 10.5. Source code for the program ADVFUN5.CPP.

```
// C++ program that uses a function that passes
// a structure by pointer

#include <iostream.h>

struct point {
  double x;
  double y;
};

// declare the prototype of function getMedian
point getMedian(const point*, const point*);

main()
{
  point pt1;
  point pt2;
  point median;

  cout << "Enter the X and Y coordinates for point # 1 : ";
  cin >> pt1.x >> pt1.y;
  cout << "Enter the X and Y coordinates for point # 2 : ";
  cin >> pt2.x >> pt2.y;
  // get the coordinates for the median point
  median = getMedian(&pt1, &pt2);
  // get the median point
  cout << "Mid point is (" << median.x
       << ", " << median.y << ")\n";
  return 0;
}

point getMedian(const point* p1, const point* p2)
{
  point result;
  result.x = (p1->x + p2->x) / 2;
  result.y = (p1->y + p2->y) / 2;
  return result;
};
```

Here is a sample session with the program in Listing 10.5:

```
Enter the X and Y coordinates for point # 1 : 2 2
Enter the X and Y coordinates for point # 2 : 8 8
Mid point is (5, 5)
```

The program in Listing 10.5 uses pointer parameters in the function `getMedian`. The prototype and the implementation of the function uses the `const point*` type for both parameters. The statement in line 25, which calls the function `getMedian`, passes the address of the variable `pt1` and `pt2`, using the `address-of` operator `&`. The implementation of the function `getMedian` uses the `->` operator to access the members `x` and `y` for the pointer parameters `p1` and `p2`.

Recursive Functions

There are many problems that can be solved by breaking them down into simpler and similar problems. Such problems are solved using recursion.

10

New Term: *Recursive functions* are functions that obtain a result and/or perform a task by calling themselves. These recursive calls must be limited in order to avoid exhausting the memory resources of the computer. Consequently, every recursive function must examine a condition that determines the end of the recursion.

New Term: A common example of a recursive function is the *factorial function.* A factorial of a number N is the product of all the integers from 1 to N, with the exclamation point (!) as the mathematical symbol for the factorial function.

The mathematical equation for a factorial is

```
N! = 1 * 2 * 3 * ... * (N-2) * (N-1) * N
```

The recursive version of this equation is

```
N! = N * (N-1)!
(N-1)! = (N-1) * (N-2)!
(N-2)! = (N-2) * (N-3)!
...
2! = 2 * 1!
1! = 1
```

Recursion entails looping to obtain a result. Most recursive solutions have alternate nonrecursive solutions. In some cases, the recursive solutions are more elegant than the nonrecursive ones. The factorial function is an example of a mathematical function that can be implemented using either recursion or a nonrecursive straightforward loop.

DO	DON'T

DO include a decision-making statement in a recursive function to end the recursion.

DON'T use recursion unless its advantages significantly outweigh the alternate nonrecursive solution.

Let us present an example that implements the recursive factorial function. Listing 10.6 shows the source code for the program ADVFUN6.CPP. The program prompts you to enter two positive integers; the first one must be greater than or equal to the second one. The program displays the number of combinations and permutations obtained from the two integers. The number of combinations is given by the following equation:

$${}_{m}C_{n} = m! / ((m - n)! * n!)$$

The number of permutations is given by the following equation:

$${}_{m}P_{n} = m! / (m - n)!$$

Listing 10.6. Source code for the program ADVFUN6.CPP.

```
// C++ program that uses a recursive function

#include <iostream.h>

const int MIN = 4;
const int MAX = 30;

double factorial(int i)
{
  if (i > 1)
```

```
    return double(i) * factorial(i - 1);
  else
    return 1;
}

double permutation(int m, int n)
{
  return factorial(m) / factorial(m - n);
}

double combination(int m, int n)
{
  return permutation(m, n) / factorial(n);
}

main()
{
  int m, n;

  do {
    cout << "Enter an integer between "
         << MIN << " and " << MAX << " : ";
    cin >> m;
  } while (m < MIN || m > MAX);

  do {
    cout << "Enter an integer between "
         << MIN << " and " << m << ": ";
    cin >> n;
  } while (n < MIN || n > m);

  cout << "Permutations(" << m << ", " << n
       << ") = " << permutation(m, n) << "\n";
  cout << "Combinations(" << m << ", " << n
       << ") = " << combination(m, n) << "\n";

  return 0;
}
```

Here is a sample session with the program in Listing 10.6:

```
Enter an integer between 4 and 30 : 10
Enter an integer between 4 and 10 : 5
Permutations(10, 5) = 30240
Combinations(10, 5) = 252
```

The program in Listing 10.6 declares the recursive function `factorial` and the functions `permutation`, `combination`, and `main`. The program also declares the global constants `MIN` and `MAX`, which specify the limits of the first integer you enter.

The function factorial has a single parameter, the int-typed parameter i. The function returns a double-typed value. The if statement in line 10 compares the value of parameter i with 1. This comparison determines whether to make a recursive call, in line 11, or to return the value 1, in line 13. The recursive call in line 11 invokes the function factorial with the argument i - 1. Thus, the recursive call supplies the function with a smaller (or simpler, if you prefer) argument.

The function permutation takes two int-typed parameters, m and n. The function calls the recursive function factorial twice—once with the argument m and once with the argument m - n. The function permutation returns the ratio of the two calls to the function factorial.

The function combination also takes two int-typed parameters, m and n. The function calls the function permutation and passes it the arguments m and n. The function also calls the function factorial and passes it the argument n. The function combination returns the ratio of the values returned by the functions permutation and factorial.

The function main declares the int-typed variable m and n. The function uses two do-while loops to prompt you for integer values. The output statement in the first loop prompts you to enter an integer between MIN and MAX. The statement in line 33 stores your input in variable m. The while clause of the do-while loop validates your input. The clause determines if your input is less than MIN or greater than MAX. If this condition is true, the loop iterates again.

The output statement in the second do-while loop prompts you to enter an integer between m and MAX. The statement in line 39 saves your input in variable n. The while clause validates your input. The clause determines if your input is less than MIN or greater than m. If this condition is true, the loop iterates again.

The output statement in lines 42 and 43 displays the permutations of the values in variables m and n. The statement calls the function permutation and passes it the argument m and n. The output statement in lines 44 and 45 displays the combinations of the values in variables m and n. The statement calls function combination and passes it the argument m and n.

Passing Pointers to Dynamic Structures

Implementing a binary tree requires functions that—at the very least—insert, search, delete, and traverse the tree. All these functions access the binary tree through the pointer of its *root*. Interestingly, operations such as tree insertion and deletion may affect the root itself. In such cases, the address of the root node changes. Consequently, you need to pass a reference to the pointer of the root node. Using a reference to a pointer guarantees that you maintain an updated address of the tree root.

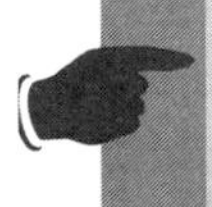

New Term: The *binary tree* is among the popular dynamic data structures. Such structures enable you to build ordered collections of data without prior knowledge of the number of data items. The basic building block for a binary tree is a *node*. Every node in a binary tree is the *root* of all subtrees below it. Terminal nodes are the roots of empty subtrees. The binary tree has a special node that is the root of all other nodes. Each node has a *field* (used as a sorting key), optional additional data (called *non-key data*), and two pointers to establish a link with other tree nodes. Dynamic memory allocation enables you to create space for each node and to set up the links between the various nodes dynamically. To learn more about binary tree structure, consult a textbook on data structure.

DO | **DON'T**

DO declare the parameters handling critical pointers to a data structure using the reference to these pointers. This declaration ensures that the addresses of these parameters are updated outside the scope of the function.

DON'T assume that when a function alters the address of a nonreference pointer parameter, the change also affects the address of the argument.

Let's look at an example that inserts and displays dynamic data in a binary tree. Listing 10.7 shows the source code for the program ADVFUN7.CPP. The program supplies its own set of data (a list of names), inserts the data in a binary tree, and then displays the data in ascending order.

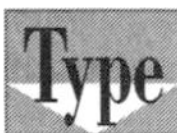

Listing 10.7. Source code for the program ADVFUN7.CPP.

```
// C++ program that passes parameter to dynamic data

#include <iostream.h>
#include <string.h>
```

continues

Listing 10.7. continued

```

const unsigned MAX = 30;

typedef struct node* nodeptr;

struct node {
   char value[MAX+1];
   nodeptr left;
   nodeptr right;
};

void insert(nodeptr& root, const char* item)
// Recursively insert element in binary tree
{
  if (!root)  {
    root = new node;
    strncpy(root->value, item, MAX);
    root->left = NULL;
    root->right = NULL;
  }
  else {
    if (strcmp(item, root->value) < 0)
      insert(root->left, item);
    else
      insert(root->right, item);
  }
}

void showTree(nodeptr& root)
{
  if (!root)
    return;

  showTree(root->left);
  cout << root->value << "\n";
  showTree(root->right);
}

main()
{
  char *names[] = { "Virginia", "California", "Maine", "Michigan",
                    "New York", "Florida", "Ohio", "Illinois",
                    "Alaska", "Arizona", "Oregon", "Vermont",
                    "Maryland", "Delaware", "NULL" };
  nodeptr treeRoot = NULL;
  int i = 0;

  // insert the names in the binary tree
  while (strcmp(names[i], "NULL") != 0)
```

```
54:      insert(treeRoot, names[i++]);
55:
56:    showTree(treeRoot);
57:    return 0;
58: }
```

Here is a sample session with the program in Listing 10.7:

```
Alaska
Arizona
California
Delaware
Florida
Illinois
Maine
Maryland
Michigan
New York
Ohio
Oregon
Vermont
Virginia
```

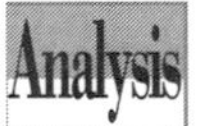

The program in Listing 10.7 declares the global constant `MAX` to specify the maximum number of characters stored by each node in the binary tree. The declaration in line 8 defines the pointer-type `nodeptr` based on the structure node. The program defines the structure `node` in lines 10 through 14. The structure contains the member `value` (which stores a string), the pointer to the left node, `left`, and the pointer to the right node, `right`. Both pointers have the `nodeptr` type.

The program declares the recursive function `insert` in order to insert a string in the binary tree. The function has two parameters: `root` and `item`. The parameter `root` is a reference to a `nodeptr`-typed pointer. This parameter keeps track of the various nodes of the binary tree and updates their addresses as needed. This update occurs when the binary tree inserts a data item.

The `if` statement in line 19 determines whether or not the parameter root is `NULL`. If this condition is true, the function executes the statement in lines 20 through 23. The statement in line 20 allocates a new node by employing the operator `new`. In line 21, the statement uses the function `strncpy` to copy up to `MAX` characters from the parameter `item` to the member `value`. The statements in lines 22 and 23 assign `NULL`s to the left and right node pointers of the newly created node. The statements in line 20 to 24 not only affect the actual root of the tree, but also alter the pointers to the various nodes. The condition in the `if` statement helps to end the recursive calls.

The `else` clause in line 25 handles the case when the parameter root is not `NULL`. The `if` statement in line 26 determines if the string accessed by pointer `item` is less than the string in the `value` member of the currently accessed tree node. If this condition is true, the function makes a recursive call passing the argument `root->left` and `item`. This call inserts the new string in the left subtree, whose root is the current node. Otherwise, the function makes a recursive call passing the argument `root->right` and `item`. This call inserts the new string in the right subtree, whose root is the current node.

The recursive function `showTree` traverses, in order, the nodes of the tree and subtree whose root is the reference parameter root. The function quickly exits if the current value of the parameter root is `NULL`. This condition indicates that the argument for parameter `root` is a terminal node. Therefore, this condition ends the recursive call. If the argument for parameter `root` is not `NULL`, the function makes a recursive call passing the argument `root->left`. This call allows the function to visit the left subtree whose root is the current node. Once the left subtree of the current node is visited, the function displays the string stored in the member value of the current node. Then the function makes another recursive call, this time passing the argument `root->right`. This call allows the function to visit the right subtree whose root is the current node. Once the right subtree of the current node is visited, the function exits.

The function `main` declares an array of pointers to the internal data, shown in lines 45 through 48. The function also declares the variable `treeRoot` as the root of the binary tree. The declaration of this variable also initializes the variable to `NULL`. The function also declares the `int`-typed variable `i` and initializes it with 0.

The function `main` uses the `while` loop in line 53 to insert the strings in the list of state names. The loop iterates until the current name matches the string `"NULL"`. This string is a special name that we use to track the end of the list. If you modify the program and add more state names, be sure to make the string `"NULL"` the last item in the list. The statement in line 54 calls the function `insert` to insert the element `names[i]` in the binary tree whose root is the pointer `treeRoot`.

The statement in line 56 calls the function `showTree` and supplies it the argument `treeRoot`. The call to this recursive function displays the names of the states in ascending order.

Pointers to Functions

The program compilation process translates the names of variables into memory addresses where data are stored and retrieved. Pointers to addresses can also access these addresses. This translation step holds true for variables and functions alike. The compiler translates the name of a function into the address of executable code. C++ extends the strategy of manipulating variables by using pointers to include functions.

Syntax

A Pointer to a Function

The general syntax for declaring a pointer to a function is

```
returnType (*functionPointer)(<list of parameters>);
```

This form tells the compiler that the *functionPointer* is a pointer to a function that has the *returnType* return type and a list of parameters.

Examples:

```
double (*fx)(int n);
void (*sort)(int* intArray, unsigned n);
unsigned (*search)(int searchKey, int* intArray, unsigned n);
```

The first identifier, `fx`, points to a function that returns a `double` and has a single `int`-typed parameter. The second identifier, `sort`, is a pointer to a function that returns a `void` type and takes two parameters: a pointer to `int` and an `unsigned`. The third identifier, `search`, is a pointer to a function that returns an `unsigned` and has three parameters: an `int`, a pointer to an `int`, and an `unsigned`.

Syntax

An Array of Function Pointers

C++ enables you to declare an array of function pointers. The general syntax is

```
returnType (*functionPointer[arraySize])(<list of parameters>);
```

Examples:

```
double (*fx[3])(int n);
void (*sort[MAX_SORT])(int* intArray, unsigned n);
unsigned (*search[MAX_SEARCH])(int searchKey,
                                int* intArray, unsigned n);
```

The first identifier, `fx`, points to an array of functions. Each member returns a `double` and has a single `int`-typed parameter. The second identifier, `sort`, is a pointer to an array of functions. Each member returns a `void` type and takes two parameters: a pointer to `int` and an `unsigned`. The third identifier, `search`, is a pointer to an array of functions. Each member returns an `unsigned` and has three parameters: an `int`, a pointer to an `int`, and an `unsigned`.

As with any pointer, you need to initialize a function pointer before using it. This step is very simple. You merely assign the bare name of a function to the function pointer.

Syntax

Initializing a Function Pointer

The general syntax for initializing a pointer to a function is

```
functionPointer = aFunction;
```

The assigned function must have the same return type and parameter list as the function pointer. Otherwise, the compiler flags an error.

Example:

```
void (*sort)(int* intArray, unsigned n);
sort = qsort;
```

Syntax

Assigning a Function to an Element

The general syntax for assigning a function to an element in an array of function pointers is

```
functionPointer[index] = aFunction;
```

Once you assign a function name to a function pointer, you can use the pointer to invoke its associated function. (Now it should be evident why the function pointer must have the same return type and parameter list as the accessed function.)

Example:

```
void (*sort[2])(int* intArray, unsigned n);
sort[0] = shellSort;
sort[1] = CombSort;
```

Syntax

The Function Pointer Expression

The general syntax for the expression that invokes function pointers is

```
(*functionPointer)(<argument list>);
(*functionPointer[index])(<argument list>);
```

Examples:

```
(*sort)(&intArray, n);
(*sort[0])(&intArray, n);
```

Let's look at an example. Listing 10.8 shows the source code for the program ADVFUN8.CPP. The program performs linearized regression on two observed variables: the independent variable *X*, and the dependent variable *Y*. The model that relates these two variables is

```
f(Y) = intercept + slope * g(X)
```

The function `f(Y)` transforms the data for the *Y* variable. The function `g(X)` transforms the data for the *X* variable. The functions `f(Y)` and `g(X)` can be linear, logarithmic, exponential, square root, square, or any other mathematical function. When both f(Y) = Y and g(X) = X, the model becomes this linear regression model:

```
Y = intercept + slope * X
```

10

The linearized regression (back to the general model) calculates the best values for the slope and intercept for the values of `f(Y)` and `g(X)`. The regression also provides the correlation coefficient statistic, which represents the percent (as a fractional number) of the `f(Y)` data that is explained by the variation in `g(X)`. A value of 1 represents a perfect fit, and 0 represents a total lack of any correlation between `f(Y)` and `g(X)` data.

Listing 10.8 performs linear regression and carries out the following tasks:

- Prompts you to enter the number of data. (Your input must be in the limit indicated by the program.)
- Prompts you to enter the observed values of *X* and *Y*.
- Prompts you to select the function that transforms the observations for variable *X*. (The program displays a small itemized menu that shows your options, indicating the linear, logarithmic, square, square root, and reciprocal functions.)
- Prompts you to select the function that transforms the observations for variable *Y*. (The program displays a small itemized menu that shows your options, indicating the linear, logarithmic, square, square root, and reciprocal functions.)
- Performs the regression calculations.
- Displays the intercept, slope, and correlation coefficient for the linearized regression.
- Prompts you to select another set of transformation functions. (If you choose to use another set of functions, the program resumes at step 3.)

Listing 10.8. Source code for the program ADVFUN8.CPP.

```
/*
   C++ program that uses pointers to functions to implement
   a linear regression program that supports temporary
   mathematical transformations.
*/

#include <iostream.h>
#include <math.h>

const unsigned MAX_SIZE = 100;

typedef double vector[MAX_SIZE];

struct regression {
   double Rsqr;
   double slope;
   double intercept;
};

// declare function pointer
double (*fx)(double);
double (*fy)(double);

// declare function prototypes
void initArray(double*, double*, unsigned);
double linear(double);
double sqr(double);
double reciprocal(double);
void calcRegression(double*, double*, unsigned, regression&,
                    double (*fx)(double), double (*fy)(double));
int select_transf(const char*);

main()
{
    char ans;
    unsigned count;
    vector x, y;
    regression stat;
    int trnsfx, trnsfy;

    do {
        cout << "Enter array size [2.."
             << MAX_SIZE << "] : ";
        cin >> count;
    } while (count <= 1 || count > MAX_SIZE);

    // initialize array
    initArray(x, y, count);
    // transform data
```

```
    do {
      // set the transformation functions
      trnsfx = select_transf("X");
      trnsfy = select_transf("Y");
      // set function pointer fx
      switch (trnsfx) {
       case 0 :
          fx = linear;
          break;
       case 1 :
          fx = log;
          break;
       case 2 :
          fx = sqrt;
          break;
       case 3 :
          fx = sqr;
          break;
       case 4 :
          fx = reciprocal;
          break;
       default :
          fx = linear;
          break;
      }
      // set function pointer fy
      switch (trnsfy) {
       case 0 :
          fy = linear;
          break;
       case 1 :
          fy = log;
          break;
       case 2 :
          fy = sqrt;
          break;
       case 3 :
          fy = sqr;
          break;
       case 4 :
          fy = reciprocal;
          break;
       default :
          fy = linear;
          break;
     }

     /*  call function with functional arguments
                                       |    |
                                       V    V */
```

continues

Listing 10.8. continued

```
     calcRegression(x, y, count, stat, fx, fy);

     cout << "\n\n"
          << "R-square = " << stat.Rsqr << "\n"
          << "Slope = " << stat.slope << "\n"
          << "Intercept = " << stat.intercept << "\n\n\n";
     cout << "Want to use other transformations? (Y/N) ";
     cin >> ans;
    } while (ans == 'Y' || ans == 'y');
  return 0;
}

void initArray(double* x, double* y, unsigned count)
// read data for array from the keyboard
{
    for (unsigned i = 0; i < count; i++, x++, y++) {
       cout << "X[" << i << "] : ";
       cin >> *x;
       cout << "Y[" << i << "] : ";
       cin >> *y;
   }
}

int select_transf(const char* var_name)
// select choice of transformation
{

   int choice = -1;
   cout << "\n";
   cout << "select transformation for variable " << var_name
        << "\n"
        << "0) No transformation\n"
        << "1) Logarithmic transformation\n"
        << "2) Square root transformation\n"
        << "3) Square  transformation\n"
        << "4) Reciprocal transformation\n";
   while (choice < 0 || choice > 4) {
      cout << "\nSelect choice by number : ";
      cin >> choice;
   }
   return choice;
}

double linear(double x)
{ return x; }

double sqr(double x)
{ return x * x; }

double reciprocal(double x)
```

```
{ return 1.0 / x; }

void calcRegression(double* x,
                    double* y,
                    unsigned count,
                    regression &stat,
                    double (*fx)(double),
                    double (*fy)(double))

{
     double meanx, meany, sdevx, sdevy;
     double sum = (double) count, sumx = 0, sumy = 0;
     double sumxx = 0, sumyy = 0, sumxy = 0;
     double xdata, ydata;

     for (unsigned i = 0; i < count; i++) {
         xdata = (*fx)(*(x+i));
         ydata = (*fy)(*(y+i));
         sumx += xdata;
         sumy += ydata;
         sumxx += sqr(xdata);
         sumyy += sqr(ydata);
         sumxy += xdata * ydata;
     }

     meanx = sumx / sum;
     meany = sumy / sum;
     sdevx = sqrt((sumxx - sqr(sumx) / sum)/(sum-1.0));
     sdevy = sqrt((sumyy - sqr(sumy) / sum)/(sum-1.0));
     stat.slope = (sumxy - meanx * meany * sum) /
                  sqr(sdevx)/(sum-1);
     stat.intercept = meany - stat.slope * meanx;
     stat.Rsqr = sqr(sdevx / sdevy * stat.slope);

}
```


Here is a sample session with the program in Listing 10.8:

```
Enter array size [2..100] : 5
X[0] : 10
Y[0] : 50
X[1] : 25
Y[1] : 78
X[2] : 30
Y[2] : 85
X[3] : 35
Y[3] : 95
X[4] : 100
Y[4] : 212
```

```
select transformation for variable X
0) No transformation
1) Logarithmic transformation
2) Square root transformation
3) Square  transformation
4) Reciprocal transformation

Select choice by number : 1

select transformation for variable Y
0) No transformation
1) Logarithmic transformation
2) Square root transformation
3) Square  transformation
4) Reciprocal transformation

Select choice by number : 1


R-square = 0.977011
Slope = 0.63039
Intercept = 2.37056


Want to use other transformations? (Y/N) y

select transformation for variable X
0) No transformation
1) Logarithmic transformation
2) Square root transformation
3) Square  transformation
4) Reciprocal transformation

Select choice by number : 0

select transformation for variable Y

0) No transformation
1) Logarithmic transformation
2) Square root transformation
3) Square  transformation
4) Reciprocal transformation

Select choice by number : 0


R-square = 0.999873
Slope = 1.79897
Intercept = 32.0412


Want to use other transformations? (Y/N) n
```

Analysis

The program in Listing 10.8 declares the global constant `MAX_SIZE`, which determines the maximum size of the arrays. The program also declares the type `vector` in line 12. In addition, the program defines the structure `regression` in lines 14 through 18. This structure stores the statistics of a regression. Lines 21 and 22 define the global function pointers `fx` and `fy`. Each pointer deals with a function that takes a `double`-typed argument and returns a `double`-typed value. The program uses these global pointers to store the mathematical transformations that you select.

The program also declares the functions `initArray`, `linear`, `sqr`, `reciprocal`, `calcRegression`, `select_transf`, and `main`. The function `initArray` prompts you to enter the data for the arrays `x` and `y`. The functions `linear`, `sqr`, and `reciprocal` are simple functions that provide the transformations for the data. These functions supplement the mathematical functions, such as `sqrt` and `log`, which are prototyped in the MATH.H header file. Each one of these functions has the same parameter and return type as the function pointers `fx` and `fy`.

10

The function `calcRegression` calculates the regression statistics based on the arrays passed by its array parameters `x` and `y`. The function uses the function pointer parameters `fx` and `fy` to transform the data in arrays `x` and `y`. The statements in lines 166 and 167 use the pointers `fx` and `fy` to transform the elements of arrays `x` and `y`, respectively.

The function `select_transf` prompts with a simple itemized menu to select the transformation functions by number. The function returns the value for the transformation code number that you select.

The function `main` declares the arrays `x` and `y`, using the type `vector`. The function also declares the structure `stat`, which stores the regression statistics. The function `main` prompts you to enter the number of data points that you want to process. Then, the function calls function `initArray` to obtain the data for the arrays `x` and `y`. Next, the function invokes the function `select_trans` twice, to select the transformation functions for the data in arrays `x` and `y`. The `switch` statement in line 55 examines the value in variable `trnsfx`, which contains the index of the transformation value for the array `x`. The various case labels assign the proper function to the pointer `fx`. Some of these functions, such as `log` and `sqrt`, are prototyped in the MATH.H header file. The `switch` statement in line 76 performs a similar task to assign the proper function to pointer `fy`.

The function `main` then calls the function `calcRegression` and passes the arguments `x`, `y`, `count`, `stat`, the function pointer `fx`, and the function pointer `fy`. The output statement in lines 102 through 105 displays the regression statistics for the current set of transformation functions. The statement in line 106 asks you if you wish to select another set of transformation functions. The statement in line 107 stores your input in variable `ans`. The `while` clause in line 108 determines if the program repeats the process of selecting the transformation functions and calculating the corresponding regression statistics.

Summary

Today's lesson presented simple C++ functions. You learned about the following topics:

- You can pass arrays as function arguments using pointers to the basic types. C++ enables you to declare array parameters using explicit pointer types or using the empty brackets. Such parameters enable you to write general-purpose functions that work with arrays of different sizes. In addition, these pointers access the array by using its address, instead of making a copy of the entire array.
- Passing strings as function arguments follows the same rules as passing arrays, because C++ strings are arrays of characters.
- Passing structures as function arguments enables you to shorten the parameter list by encapsulating various related information in C++ structures. C++ supports passing structures by value. Such parameters pass a copy of their arguments to the host function. Consequently, the changes made to the structure members do not affect the arguments outside the scope of the function.
- Passing reference parameters may use pointers or formal references. The formal references become aliases of their arguments. Any changes made to the parameters affect their arguments outside the function. You can declare a constant reference parameter to ensure that the function does not alter the arguments for the reference parameter. Accessing the members of a structured reference parameter uses the dot operator.
- Passing structures by pointer gives the host function the address of the structure. The pointer parameter needs to use the `->` operator to access the various members of the structure. You can use the `const` prefix with the pointer parameter to prevent the function from changing the members of the structure, which is accessed by the pointer parameters.
- Recursive functions are functions that obtain a result and/or perform a task by calling themselves. These recursive calls must be limited to avoid exhausting the memory resources of the computer. Consequently, every recursive function must examine a condition that determines the end of the recursion.

- Passing pointers to dynamic structures often requires passing the reference to the root or head pointers that manage such structures. Today's lesson illustrates how to create functions to insert data in a binary tree and display its data.
- Pointers to functions store the address of functions. Such pointers need to have the parameter list and return type defined, in order to access functions with the same prototype. Pointers to functions enable you to select which function you wish to invoke at runtime.

Q&A

Q How does using a reference parameter impact the design of a function, compared to a value parameter?

A The reference parameter can also update the argument (unless it is declared as a `const` parameter). Thus, the function can use reference parameters as an input data conduit and also as an output data conduit.

Q How can I distinguish between a pointer that passes an array of value and one used to pass back a value through its argument?

A You need to read the declaration of the function in context. However, you can use a reference parameter to declare a parameter that passes a value back to the caller.

Q What is the memory resource used in managing calls to recursive functions?

A The runtime system uses the stack to store intermediate values, including the ones generated by calls to recursive functions. As with other memory resources, stacks have a limited space. Consequently, recursive calls with long sequence or memory-consuming arguments drain the stack space and cause runtime errors.

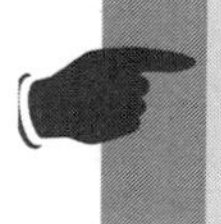

New Term: A *stack* is a memory location where information is inserted and removed on a last-in-first-out (LIFO) priority.

Workshop

The Workshop provides quiz questions to help you solidify your understanding of the material covered and exercises to provide you with experience in using what you've learned. Try to understand the quiz and exercise answers before continuing on to the next day's lesson. (Answers are provided in Appendix A, "Answers.")

Quiz

1. Can you use the conditional operator to write the recursive factorial function?
2. What is wrong with the following recursive function?

```
double factorial(int i)
{
  switch (i) {
    case 0:
    case 1:
         return 1;
         break;
    case 2:
         return 2;
         break;
    case 3:
         return 6;
         break;
    case 4:
         return 24;
         break;
    default:
         return double(i) * factorial(i-1);
  }
}
```

3. Convert the following recursive Fibonacci function (this function has the sequence Fib(0) = 0, Fib(1) = 1, Fib(2) = 1, Fib(3) = 2, Fib(4) = 3, and so on) into a nonrecursive version:

```
double Fibonacci(int n)
{
  if (n == 0)
    return 0;
  else if (n == 1 || n == 2)
    return 1;
  else
    return Fibonacci(n - 1) + Fibonacci(n - 2);
}
```

4. True or false? The two versions of the following functions are equivalent:

```
struct stringStruct {
     char source[MAX+1];
     char uprStr[MAX+1];
     char lwrStr[MAX+];
     char revStr[MAX+1];
};

void convertStr2(const char* str, stringStruct& s)
{
  strncpy(s.source, str, MAX);
  strncpy(s.uprStr, str, MAX);
  strncpy(s.lwrStr, str, MAX);
  strncpy(s.revStr, str, MAX);
  _strlwr(s.lwrStr);
  _strupr(s.uprStr);
  strrev(s.revStr);
}

void convertStr2(const char* str, stringStruct* s)
{
  strncpy(s->source, str, MAX);
  strncpy(s->uprStr, str, MAX);
  strncpy(s->lwrStr, str, MAX);
  strncpy(s->revStr, str, MAX);
  _strlwr(s->lwrStr);
  _strupr(s->uprStr);
  strrev(s->revStr);
}
```

Exercise

Create the program ADVFUN9.CPP from ADVFUN8.CPP by replacing the individual function pointers `fx` and `fy` with the array of function pointers `f`. In addition, replace the two function pointer parameters of function `calcRegression` with a parameter that is an array of function pointers.

Object-Oriented Programming and C++ Classes

WEEK 2

Classes provide C++ with object-oriented programming (OOP) constructs. Today's lesson, which marks an important milestone for learning C++, introduces you to building individual classes as well as class hierarchy. You learn about the following topics:

- The basics of object-oriented programming
- Declaring base classes
- Constructors
- Destructors
- Declaring a class hierarchy
- Virtual functions
- Friend functions
- Operators and friend operators

Basics of Object-Oriented Programming

We live in a world of objects. Each object has its attributes and operations. Some objects are more animated than others. You can categorize objects into classes. For example, a CASIO Data Bank watch is an object that belongs to the class of the CASIO Data Bank watches.

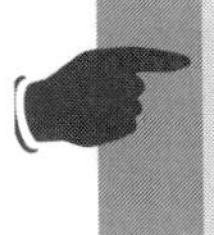

New Term: *Object-oriented programming (OOP)* uses the notions of real-world objects to develop applications.

You can also relate individual classes in a class hierarchy. The class of CASIO Data Bank watches is part of the watch class hierarchy. The basics of OOP include classes, objects, messages, methods, inheritance, and polymorphism.

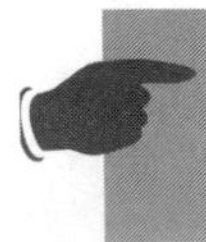

New Term: A `class` defines a category of objects. Each *object* is an instance of a class.

Classes and Objects

An object shares the same attributes and functionality of other objects in the same class. Typically, an object has a unique state, defined by the current values of its attributes. The functionality of a class determines the operations that are possible for the class instances. C++ calls the attributes of the class *data members* and calls the operations of the class *member functions*. Classes encapsulate data members and member functions.

Going back to the CASIO watch example, you can note that the buttons in the watch represent the member functions of the class of CASIO watches, whereas the display represents a data member. We can press certain buttons to edit the date and/or time. In OOP terms, the member functions alter the state of the object by changing its data members.

Messages and Methods

Object-oriented programming models the interaction with objects as events where messages are sent to an object or between objects. The object receiving a message responds by invoking the appropriate method (that's the member function in C++). C++ does not explicitly foster the notion of messages and methods as do other OOP languages, such as SmallTalk. However, we find it easier to discuss invoking member functions using the term "message." The terms *methods* and *member functions* are equivalent.

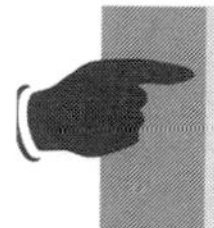

New Term: The *message* is **what** is done to an object. The *method* is **how** the object responds to the incoming message.

Inheritance

In object-oriented languages, you can derive a class from another one.

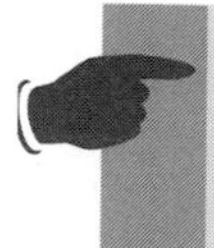

New Term: With *inheritance*, the derived class (also called the *descendant class*) inherits the data members and member functions of its *parent* and *ancestor classes*.

Deriving a class refines the parent class by appending new attributes and new operations. The derived class typically declares new data members and new member functions. In addition, the derived class can also override inherited member functions when the operations of these functions are not suitable for the derived class.

To apply the concept of inheritance to the CASIO Data Bank watch, consider the following possible scenario. Suppose that the watch manufacturer decides to create a CASIO Data Comm watch that offers the same features of the CASIO Data Bank plus a beeper! Rather than redesigning the new model (that is the new class, in OOP terms) from scratch, the CASIO engineers start with the existing design of the CASIO Data Bank and build on it. This process may well add new attributes and operations to the existing design and alter some existing operations to fit the new design. Thus, the CASIO Data Comm model inherits the attributes and the operations of the CASIO Data Bank model. In OOP terms, the class of CASIO Data Comm watches is a descendant of the class of CASIO Data Bank watches.

Polymorphism

The OOP feature of polymorphism allows the instances of different classes to react in a particular way to a message (or function invocation, in C++ terms). For example, in a hierarchy of graphical shapes (point, line, square, rectangle, circle, ellipse, and so on), each shape has a *Draw* function that is responsible for properly responding to a request to draw that shape.

New Term: *Polymorphism* enables the instances of different classes to respond to the same function in ways that are appropriate to each class.

Declaring Base Classes

C++ enables you to declare a class that encapsulates data members and member functions. These functions alter and/or retrieve the values of the data members as well as perform related tasks.

Syntax

A Base Class

The general syntax for declaring a base class is

```
class className
{
     private:
          <private data members>
          <private constructors>
          <private member functions>
     protected:
          <protected data members>
          <protected constructors>
          <protected member functions>
     public:
          <public data members>
          <public constructors>
          <public destructor>
          <public member functions>
};
```

Example:

```
class point
{
     protected:
          double x;
          double y;
     public:
          point(double xVal, double yVal);
          double getX();
          double getY();
          void assign(double xVal, double yVal);
          point& assign(point& pt);
};
```

The Sections of a Class

The previous syntax shows that the declaration involves the keyword `class`. C++ classes offer three levels of visibility for the various members (that is, both data members and member functions):

- The private section
- The protected section
- The public section

11

New Term: In the *private section*, only the member functions of the class can access the private members. In the *protected section*, only the member functions of the class and its descendant classes can access protected members. The *public section* specifies members that are visible to the member functions of the class, class instances, member functions of descendant classes, and their instances. Anything can access the public section.

The following rules apply to the various class sections:

1. The class sections can appear in any order.
2. The class sections may appear more than once.
3. If no class section is specified, the C++ compiler treats the members as protected.
4. You should avoid placing data members in the public section unless such a declaration significantly simplifies your design. Data members are typically placed in the protected section to allow their access by member functions of descendant classes.
5. Use member functions to set and/or query the values of data members. The members that set the data members assist in performing validation and updating other data members, if need be.
6. The class may have multiple constructors, which are typically located in the public section.
7. The class can have only one destructor, which must be declared in the public section.
8. The member functions (as well as the constructors and destructors) that have multiple statements are defined outside the class declaration. The definition may reside in the same file that declares the class.

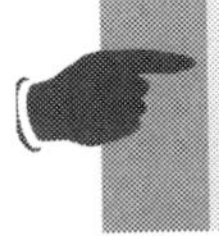

New Term: *Constructors* are special members that must have the same name as the host class. *Destructors* automatically remove class instances.

In software libraries, the definition of the member functions referred to in rule 8 typically resides in a separate source file (.H and .CPP files). When you define a member function, you must qualify the function name with the class name. The syntax of such a qualification involves using the class name followed by two colons (: :) and then the name of a function. For example, consider the following class:

```
class point
{
     protected:
          double x;
          double y;
     public:
          point(double xVal, double yVal);
          double getX();
          // other member functions
};
```

The definitions of the constructor and member functions are

```
point::point(double xVal, double yVal)
{
  // statements
}

double point::getX()
{
  // statements
}
```


After you declare a class, you can use the class name as a type identifier to declare class instances. The syntax resembles declaring variables.

Let's look at an example. Listing 11.1 shows the source code for the program CLASS1.CPP. The program prompts you to enter the length and width of a rectangle (which is an object). The program then displays the length, width, and area of the rectangle you specified.

Listing 11.1. Source code for the program CLASS1.CPP.

```
// C++ program that illustrates a class

#include <iostream.h>

class rectangle
{
  protected:
    double length;
    double width;
```

continues

Listing 11.1. continued

```
  public:
    rectangle() { assign(0, 0); }
    rectangle(double len, double wide) { assign(len, wide); }
    double getLength() { return length; }
    double getWidth() { return width; }
    double getArea() { return length * width; }
    void assign(double len, double wide);
};

void rectangle::assign(double len, double wide)
{
  length = len;
  width = wide;
}

main()
{
  rectangle rect;
  double len, wide;

  cout << "Enter length of rectangle : ";
  cin >> len;
  cout << "Enter width of rectangle : ";
  cin >> wide;
  rect.assign(len, wide);
  cout << "Rectangle length = " << rect.getLength() << "\n"
       << "          width  = " << rect.getWidth() << "\n"
       << "          area   = " << rect.getArea() << "\n";
  return 0;
}
```

Here is a sample session with the program in Listing 11.1:

```
Enter length of rectangle : 10
Enter width of rectangle : 12
Rectangle length = 10
          width  = 12
          area   = 120
```

The program in Listing 11.1 declares the class `rectangle`, which models a rectangle. The class has two `double`-typed data members, `length` and `width`, which store the dimensions of a rectangle. In addition, the class has two constructors: the default constructor and the nondefault constructor. The class also defines the member functions `getLength`, `getWidth`, `getArea`, and `assign`.

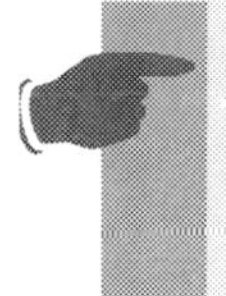

New Term: The *default constructor* creates an instance with 0 dimensions, and the *nondefault constructor* creates an instance with nonzero dimensions.

The function `getLength`, defined in the class declaration, simply returns the value in member `length`. The function `getWidth`, also defined in the class declaration, merely returns the value in member `width`. The function `getArea`, defined in the class declaration, simply returns the value of the result of multiplying the members `length` and `width`.

The member function `assign`, defined outside the class declaration, assigns the arguments for its parameters `len` and `wide` to the data members `length` and `width`, respectively. We simplify the implementation of this function by not checking for negative values.

The function `main` declares `rect` as the instance of class `rectangle` and declares the `double`-typed variables `len` and `wide`. The output statement in line 30 prompts you to enter the length of the rectangle. The statement in line 31 obtains your input and stores it in variable `len`. The output statement in line 32 prompts you to enter the width of the rectangle. The statement in line 33 obtains your input and stores it in variable `wide`.

The function `main` assigns the input values to the instance `rect` using the `assign` member function. In OOP terms, we can say that the function `main` sends the `assign` message to the object `rect`. The arguments of the message are variables `len` and `wide`. The object `rect` responds by invoking the method (the member function) `rectangle::assign(double, double)`.

The output statement in lines 35 through 37 displays the length, width, and area of the object `rect`. This statement sends the messages `getLength`, `getWidth`, and `getArea` to the object `rect`. In turn, the object `rect` invokes the appropriate methods (or member functions, if you prefer) to respond to each one of these messages.

Constructors

C++ constructors and destructors work automatically to guarantee the appropriate creation and removal of class instances.

Syntax

Constructors

The general syntax for constructors is

```
class className
{
     public:
          className(); // default constructor
          className(className& c); // copy constructor
          className(<parameter list>); // another constructor
};
```

Example:

```
class point
{
     protected:
          double x;
          double y;
     public:
          point();
          point(double xVal, double yVal);
          point(point& pt);
          double getX();
          double getY();
          void assign(double xVal, double yVal);
          point& assign(point& pt);
};
main()
{
  point p1;
  point p2(10, 20);
  point p3(p2);
  p1.assign(p2));
  cout << p1.getX() << " " << p1.getY() << "\n";
  cout << p2.getX() << " " << p2.getY() << "\n";
  cout << p3.getX() << " " << p3.getY() << "\n";
  return 0;
}
```

New Term: A *copy constructor* enables you to create class instances by copying the data from existing instances.

C++ has the following features and rules regarding constructors:

1. The name of the constructor must be identical to the name of its class.
2. You must not include any return type, not even `void`.

3. A class can have any number of constructors, including none. In the latter case, the compiler automatically creates one for that class.
4. The default constructor is the one that either has no parameters or possesses a parameter list where all the parameters use default arguments. Here are two examples:

```
// class use parameterless constructor
class point1
{
    protected:
         double x;
         double y;
    public:
         point1();
         // other member functions
};

// class use constructor with default arguments
class point2
{
    protected:
         double x;
         double y;
    public:
         point(double xVal = 0, double yVal = 0);
         // other member functions
};
```

5. The *copy constructor* enables you to create a class instance using an existing instance. Here is an example:

```
class point
{
    protected:
         double x;
         double y;
    public:
         point();
         point(double xVal, double yVal);
         point(point& pt);
         // other member functions
};
```

6. The declaration of a class instance (which includes function parameters and local instances) involves a constructor. Which constructor is called? The answer depends on how many constructors you have declared for the class and how you declared the class instance. For example, consider the following instances of the last version of the class `point`:

   ```
   point p1; // involves the default constructor
   point p2(1.1, 1.3); // uses the second constructor
   point p3(p2); // uses the copy constructor
   ```

   Because instance `p1` specifies no arguments, the compiler uses the default constructor. The instance `p2` specifies two floating-point arguments. Consequently, the compiler uses the second constructor. The instance `p3` has the instance `p2` as an argument. Therefore, the compiler uses the copy constructor to create instance `p3` from instance `p2`.

DO	DON'T

DO declare copy constructors, especially for classes that model dynamic data structures. These constructors perform what is called a *deep copy*, which includes the dynamic data. By default, the compiler creates what are called *shallow copy* constructors, which copy the data members only.

DON'T rely on the shallow copy constructor to copy instances for classes that have members that are pointers.

Destructors

C++ classes may contain destructors that automatically remove class instances.

Syntax

Destructors

The general syntax for destructors is

```
class className
{
     public:
          className(); // default constructor
          // other constructors
          ~className();
          // other member function
};
```

Example:

```
class String
{
     protected:
          char *str;
          int len;

     public:
          String();
          String(String& s);
          ~String();
          // other member functions
};
```

C++ has the following features and rules regarding destructors:

1. The name of the destructor must begin with a tilde (~). The rest of the destructor name must be identical to the name of its class.
2. You must not include any return type, not even `void`.
3. A class can have no more than one destructor. In addition, if you omit the destructor, the compiler automatically creates one for you.
4. The destructor cannot have any parameters.
5. The runtime system automatically invokes a class destructor when the instance of that class is out of scope, or when the instance is explicitly deleted.

Examples of Constructors and Destructors

Let's look at a program that typifies the use of constructors and destructors. Listing 11.2 contains the source code for the CLASS2.CPP program. The program performs the following tasks:

- Creates a dynamic array (the object)
- Assigns values to the elements of the dynamic array
- Displays the values in the dynamic array
- Removes the dynamic array

Type Listing 11.2. Source code for the CLASS2.CPP program.

```
// Program demonstrates constructors and destructors

#include <iostream.h>

const unsigned MIN_SIZE = 4;

class Array
{
   protected:
     double *dataPtr;
     unsigned size;

   public:
     Array(unsigned Size = MIN_SIZE);
     ~Array()
       { delete [] dataPtr; }
     unsigned getSize() const
       { return size; }
     void store(double x, unsigned index)
       { dataPtr[index] = x; }
     double recall(unsigned index)
       { return dataPtr[index]; }
};

Array::Array(unsigned Size)
{
  size = (Size < MIN_SIZE) ? MIN_SIZE : Size;
  dataPtr = new double[size];
}

main()
{
  Array Arr(10);
  double x;
  // assign data to array elements
  for (unsigned i = 0; i < Arr.getSize(); i++) {
    x = double(i);
    x = x * x - 5 * x + 10;
    Arr.store(x, i);
  }
  // display data in the array element
  cout << "Array Arr has the following values:\n\n";
  for (i = 0; i < Arr.getSize(); i++)
    cout << "Arr[" << i << "] = " << Arr.recall(i) << "\n";
  return 0;
}
```

Here is a sample session with the program in Listing 11.2:

```
Array Arr has the following values:
```

```
Arr[0] = 10
Arr[1] = 6
Arr[2] = 4
Arr[3] = 4
Arr[4] = 6
Arr[5] = 10
Arr[6] = 16
Arr[7] = 24
Arr[8] = 34
Arr[9] = 46
```

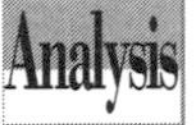

The program in Listing 11.2 declares the global constant `MIN_SIZE` in line 5, which specifies the minimum size of dynamic arrays. The program also declares the class `Array` in line 7. The class has two data members, `dataPtr` and `size`. The member `dataPtr` is the pointer to the array's dynamically allocated elements. The member `size` stores the number of elements in an instance of class `Array`.

The class declares a default constructor. (The constructor actually has a parameter with the default value `MIN_SIZE`.) The program defines the constructor in lines 25 through 29. The arguments for the parameter `Size` specify the number of array elements. The statement in line 27 assigns the greater value of parameter `Size` and the constant `MIN_SIZE` to the data member size. The statement in line 28 allocates the dynamic space for the array by using the operator `new`. The statement assigns the base address of the dynamic array to the member `dataPtr`.

The destructor `~Array` removes the dynamic space of the array by applying the operator `delete` to the member `dataPtr`.

The member function `getSize`, defined in the class declaration, returns the value in data member `size`.

The function `store`, defined in the class declaration, stores the value passed by parameter `x` at the element number specified by the parameter `index`. We simplify the implementation of this function by eliminating the out-of-range index check.

The function `recall`, defined in the class declaration, returns the value in the element specified by the parameter `index`. We simplify the implementation of this function by eliminating the out-of-range index check.

The function `main` declares the object `Arr` as an instance of class `Array`. The declaration, located in line 33, specifies that the instance has 10 elements. The function also declares the `double`-typed variable `x`. The `for` loop in lines 36 through 40 stores values in the instance `Arr`. The loop uses control variable `i` and iterates from 0 to `Arr.getSize()-1`, in increments of 1. The loop continuation condition sends the `getSize` message to instance `Arr` to obtain the number of elements in the array. The statements in lines 37 and 38 calculate the value to store in an element of instance `Arr`. The statement in line 39 sends the message `store` to instance `Arr` and passes the arguments `x` and `i`. The object `Arr` saves the value in variable `x` at the element number `i`.

The output statement in line 42 comments on the output of the `for` loop in lines 43 and 44. The loop uses the control variable `i` and iterates from 0 to `Arr.getSize()-1`, in increments of 1. The output statement in line 44 displays the element in instance `Arr` by sending the message `recall` to that instance. The message has the argument `i`.

Declaring a Class Hierarchy

The power of the OOP features of C++ comes from the fact that you can derive classes from existing ones. A descendant class inherits the members of its ancestor classes (that is, parent class, grandparent class, and so on) and can also override some of the inherited functions. Inheritance enables you to reuse code in descendant classes.

Syntax

A Derived Class

The general syntax for declaring a derived class is

```
class className : [public] parentClass
{
     <friend classes>

     private:
          <private data members>
          <private constructors>
          <private member functions>

     protected:
          <protected data members>
          <protected constructors>
          <protected member functions>

     public:
          <public data members>
          <public constructors>
          <public destructor>
          <public member functions>

          <friend functions and friend operators>
```

```
};
```

Example:

The following example shows the class `cRectangle` and its descendant, the class `cBox`:

```
class cRectangle
{
     protected:
          double length;
          double width;
     public:
          cRectangle(double len, double wide);
          double getLength() const;
          double getWidth(); const;
          double assign(double len, double wide);
          double calcArea();
};

class cBox : public cRectangle
{
     protected:
          double height;

     public:
          cBox(double len, double wide, double height);
          double getHeight() const;
          assign(double len, double wide, double height);
          double calcVolume();
};
```


The class lineage is indicated by a colon followed by the optional keyword `public` and then the name of the parent class. When you include the keyword `public`, you allow the instances of the descendant class to access the public members of the parent and other ancestor classes. By contrast, when you omit the keyword `public` or use the private keyword, you deprive the instance of the descendant class from accessing the members of the ancestor classes.

A descendant class inherits the data members of its ancestor classes. C++ has no mechanism for removing unwanted inherited data members—you are basically stuck with them. By contrast, C++ enables you to override inherited member functions. You will see more about this topic later in today's lesson. The descendant class declares new data members, new member functions, and overriding member functions. Again, you can place these members in the private, protected, or public sections, as you see fit in your class design.

DO | **DON'T**

DO reduce the number of constructors by using default argument parameters.

DO use member functions to access the values in the data members. These member functions enable you to control and validate the values in the data members.

DON'T declare all the constructors of a class protected unless you want to force the client programmers (that is, those programs that use the class) to use the class by declaring its descendants with public constructors.

DON'T declare the data members in the public section.

Let's look at an example that declares a small class hierarchy. Listing 11.3 shows the source code for the CLASS3.CPP program. This program declares classes that contain a hierarchy of two simple geometric shapes: a circle and a cylinder. The program requires no input. Instead, it uses internal data to create the geometric shapes and to display their dimensions, areas, and volume.

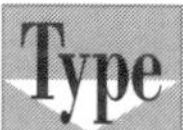

Listing 11.3. Source code for the CLASS3.CPP program.

```
// Program that demonstrates a small hierarchy of classes

#include <iostream.h>
#include <math.h>

const double pi = 4 * atan(1);

inline double sqr(double x)
{ return x * x; }

class cCircle
{
  protected:
    double radius;

  public:
    cCircle(double radiusVal = 0) : radius(radiusVal) {}
    void setRadius(double radiusVal)
      { radius = radiusVal; }
    double getRadius() const
```

```
        { return radius; }
      double area() const
        { return pi * sqr(radius); }
      void showData();
};

class cCylinder : public cCircle
{
  protected:
    double height;

  public:
     cCylinder(double heightVal = 0, double radiusVal = 0)
       : height(heightVal), cCircle(radiusVal) {}
     void setHeight(double heightVal)
       { height = heightVal; }
     double getHeight() const
       { return height; }
     double area() const
       { return 2 * cCircle::area() +
                2 * pi * radius * height; }
     void showData();
};

void cCircle::showData()
{
   cout << "Circle radius        = " << getRadius() << "\n"
        << "Circle area          = " << area() << "\n\n";
}

void cCylinder::showData()
{
   cout << "Cylinder radius      = " << getRadius() << "\n"
        << "Cylinder height      = " << getHeight() << "\n"
        << "Cylinder area        = " << area() << "\n\n";
}

main()
{
   cCircle Circle(1);
   cCylinder Cylinder(10, 1);

   Circle.showData();
   Cylinder.showData();
   return 0;
}
```

Here is a sample session with the program in Listing 11.3:

```
Circle radius       = 1
Circle area         = 3.14159

Cylinder radius     = 1
Cylinder height     = 10
Cylinder area       = 69.115
```

The program in Listing 11.3 declares the classes `cCircle` and `cCylinder`. The class `cCircle` models a circle, whereas the class `cCylinder` models a cylinder.

The `cCircle` class declares a single data member, `radius`, to store the radius of the circle. The class also declares a constructor and a number of member functions. The constructor assigns a value to the data member `radius` when you declare a class instance. Notice that the constructor uses a new syntax to initialize the member `radius`. The functions `setRadius` and `getRadius` serve to set and query the value in member `radius`, respectively. The function `area` returns the area of the circle. The function `showData` displays the radius and area of a class instance.

The class `cCylinder`, a descendant of `cCircle`, declares a single data member, `height`, to store the height of the cylinder. The class inherits the member radius needed to store the radius of the cylinder. The `cCylinder` class declares a constructor and a number of member functions. The constructor assigns values to the `radius` and `height` members when creating a class instance. Notice the use of a new syntax to initialize the members—member `height` is initialized, and member `radius` is initialized by invoking the constructor of class `cCircle` with the argument `radiusVal`. The functions `getHeight` and `setHeight` serve to set and query the value in member `height`, respectively. The class uses the inherited functions `setRadius` and `getRadius` to manipulate the inherited member `radius`. The function `area`, which overrides the inherited function `cCircle::area()`, returns the surface area of the cylinder. Notice that this function explicitly invokes the inherited function `cCircle::area()`. The function `showData` displays the radius, height, and area of a class instance.

We also would like to point out that the declarations of the functions `area`, `getHeight`, and `area` in lines 22, 37, and 39 end with the keyword `const`. Using the keyword `const` in this way tells the compiler that the member function cannot change any data member. This feature is aimed mainly at teams of programmers where the team manager sets the specifications for the class and determines which member functions can alter the values of data members.

The function `main` declares the instance `Circle`, of class `cCircle`, and assigns 1 to the circle's radius. In addition, the function also declares the instance `Cylinder`, of class

cCylinder, and assigns 10 and 1 to the circle's height and radius, respectively. The function then sends the showData message to the instances Circle and Cylinder. Each object responds to this message by invoking the appropriate member function.

Virtual Functions

As we mentioned previously, polymorphism is an important object-oriented programming feature. Consider the following simple classes and the function main:

```
#include <iostream.h>
class cA
{
     public:
          double A(double x) { return x * x; }
          double B(double x) { return A(x) / 2; }
};

class cB : public cA
{
     public:
          double A(double x) { return x * x * x; }
};

main()
{
     cB aB;
     cout << aB.B(3) << "\n";
     return 0;
}
```

Class cA contains functions A and B, where function B calls function A. Class cB, a descendant of class cA, inherits function B, but overrides function A. The intent here is to have the inherited function cA::B call function cB::A in order to support polymorphic behavior. What is the program output? The answer is 4.5 and not 13.5! Why? The answer lies in the fact that the compiler resolves the expression aB.B(3) by using the inherited function cA::B, which in turn calls function cA::A. Therefore, function cB:A is left out and the program fails to support polymorphic behavior.

C++ supports polymorphic behavior by offering virtual functions.

New Term: *Virtual functions*, which are bound at runtime, are declared by placing the keyword virtual before the function's return type.

Syntax

After you declare a function `virtual`, you can override it only with virtual functions in descendant classes. These overriding functions must have the same parameter list. Virtual functions can override nonvirtual functions in ancestor classes.

Virtual Functions

The general syntax for declaring virtual functions is

```
class className1
{
     // member functions
     virtual returnType functionName(<parameter list>);
};

class className2 : public className1
{
     // member functions
     virtual returnType functionName(<parameter list>);
};
```

Example:

This example shows how virtual functions can successfully implement polymorphic behavior in classes `cA` and `cB`:

```
#include <iostream.h>
class cA
{
     public:
          virtual double A(double x) { return x * x; }
          double B(double x) { return A(x) / 2; }
};

class cB : public cA
{
     public:
         virtual double A(double x) { return x * x * x; }
};

main()
{
     cB aB;
     cout << aB.B(3) << "\n";
     return 0;
}
```

This example displays 13.5, the correct result, because the call to the inherited function `cA::B` is resolved at runtime by calling `cB::A`.

DO	DON'T

DO use virtual functions when you have a callable function that implements a class-specific behavior. Declaring such a function as virtual ensures that it provides the correct response that is relevant to the associated class.

DON'T declare a member function as virtual by default. Virtual functions have some additional overhead.

Let's look at an example. Listing 11.4 shows the source code for the program CLASS4.CPP. The program creates a square and a rectangle and displays their dimensions and areas. No input is required.

Type **Listing 11.4. Source code for the program CLASS4.CPP.**

```
// Program that demonstrates virtual functions

#include <iostream.h>

class cSquare
{
  protected:
    double length;

  public:
    cSquare(double len) { length = len; }
    double getLength() { return length; }
    virtual double getWidth() { return length; }
    double getArea() { return getLength() * getWidth(); }
};

class cRectangle : public cSquare
{
  protected:
    double width;

  public:
    cRectangle(double len, double wide) :
       cSquare(len), width(wide) {}
    virtual double getWidth() { return width; }
};

main()
{
   cSquare square(10);
   cRectangle rectangle(10, 12);
```

continues

Listing 11.4. continued

```

    cout << "Square has length = " << square.getLength() << "\n"
         << "       and area   = " << square.getArea() << "\n";
    cout << "Rectangle has length = "
         << rectangle.getLength() << "\n"
         << "          and width  = "
         << rectangle.getWidth() << "\n"
         << "          and area   = "
         << rectangle.getArea() << "\n";
    return 0;
}
```

Here is a sample session with the program in Listing 11.4:

```
Square has length = 10
       and area   = 100
Rectangle has length = 10
          and width  = 12
          and area   = 120
```

The program in Listing 11.4 declares the classes `cSquare` and `cRectangle` to model squares and rectangles, respectively. The class `cSquare` declares a single data member, `length`, to store the length (and width) of the square. The class declares a constructor with the parameter `len`, which passes arguments to the member `length`. The class also declares the functions `getLength`, `getWidth`, and `getArea`. Both functions `getLength` and `getWidth` return the value in member `length`. Notice that the class declares function `getWidth` as `virtual`. The function `getArea` returns the area of the rectangle, calculated by calling the functions `getLength` and `getWidth`. We choose to invoke these functions rather than use the data member `length` in order to demonstrate how the virtual function `getWidth` works.

The program declares class `cRectangle` as a descendant of class `cSquare`. The class `cRectangle` declares the data member `width` and inherits the member `length`. These members enable the class to store the basic dimensions of a rectangle. The class constructor has the parameters `len` and `wide`, which pass values to the members `len` and `wide`. Notice that the constructor invokes the constructor `cSquare` and supplies it with the argument `len`. The constructor initializes the data member `width` with the value of parameter `wide`.

The class `cRectangle` declares the virtual function `getWidth`. This version returns the value in data member `width`. The class inherits the member functions `getLength` and `getArea` because their implementation is adequate for the `cRectangle`.

The function `main` declares the object `square` as an instance of class `cSquare`. The instance `square` has a length of 10. The function `main` also declares the object `rectangle` as an instance of class `cRectangle`. The instance `rectangle` has the length of 10 and the width of 12.

The output statement in lines 33 and 34 displays the length and area of the instance `square`. The statement sends the messages `getLength` and `getArea` to the preceding instance in order to obtain the sought values. The instance `square` invokes the function `getArea`, which in turn calls the functions `cSquare::getLength` and `cSquare::getWidth`.

The output statement in lines 35 through 40 displays the length, width, and area of the instance `rectangle`. The statement sends the messages `getLength`, `getWidth`, and `getArea` to this instance. The instance responds by calling the inherited function `cSquare::getLength`, the virtual function `cRectangle::getWidth`, and the inherited function `cSquare::getArea`. The latter function calls the inherited function `cSquare::getLength` and the virtual function `cRectangle::getWidth` to correctly calculate the area of the rectangle.

DO declare your destructor as virtual. This ensures polymorphic behavior in destroying class instances. In addition, we highly recommend that you declare a copy constructor and an assignment operator for each class.

DON'T forget that you can inherit virtual functions and destructors when appropriate for the descendant class. You need not declare shell functions and destructors that simply call the corresponding member of the parent class.

Rules for Virtual Functions

The rule for declaring a virtual function is "once virtual, always virtual." In other words, after you declare a function to be virtual in a class, any subclass that overrides the virtual function must do so using another virtual function (that has the same parameter list). The `virtual` declaration, while not mandatory for the descendant classes, is generally used to help the programmer identify the virtual functions in the descendant classes. At first, this rule seems to lock you in. This limitation is certainly true for object-oriented programming languages that support virtual functions but

not overloaded functions. In the case of C++, the work-around is interesting. You can declare nonvirtual and overloaded functions that have the same name as the virtual function, but bear a different parameter list. Moreover, you cannot inherit nonvirtual member functions that share the same name with a virtual function. Here is a simple example that illustrates the point:

```
#include <iostream.h>
class cA
{
  public:
    cA() {}
    virtual void foo(char c)
      { cout << "virtual cA::foo() returns " << c << '\n'; }
};

class cB : public cA
{
  public:
    cB() {}
    void foo(const char* s)
      { cout << "cB::foo() returns " << s << '\n'; }
    void foo(int i)
      { cout << "cB::foo() returns " << i << '\n'; }
    virtual void foo(char c)
      { cout << "virtual cB::foo() returns " << c << '\n'; }
};

class cC : public cB
{
  public:
    cC() {}
    void foo(const char* s)
      { cout << "cC::foo() returns " << s << '\n'; }
    void foo(double x)
      { cout << "cC::foo() returns " << x << '\n'; }
    virtual void foo(char c)
      { cout << "virtual cC::foo() returns " << c << '\n'; }
};

main()
{
  int n = 100;
  cA Aobj;
  cB Bobj;
  cC Cobj;

  Aobj.foo('A');
```

```
    Bobj.foo('B');
    Bobj.foo(10);
    Bobj.foo("Bobj");
    Cobj.foo('C');
    // if you uncomment the next statement, program does not compile
    // Cobj.foo(n);
    Cobj.foo(144.123);
    Cobj.foo("Cobj");
    return 0;
}
```

This code declares three classes—cA, cB, and cC—to form a linear hierarchy of classes. Class cA declares function foo(char) as virtual. Class cB also declares its own version of the virtual function foo(char). In addition, class cB declares the nonvirtual overloaded functions foo(const char* s) and foo(int). Class cC, the descendant of class cB, declares the virtual function foo(char) and the nonvirtual and overloaded functions foo(const char*) and foo(double). Notice that class cC must declare the foo(const char*) function if it needs the function because it cannot inherit the member function cB::foo(const char*). C++ supports a different function inheritance scheme when an overloaded function and virtual function are involved. The function main creates an instance for each of the three classes and involves the various versions of the member function foo.

Friend Functions

C++ allows member functions to access all the data members of a class. In addition, C++ grants the same privileged access to friend functions. The declaration of friend functions appears in the class and begins with the keyword friend. Other than using the special keyword, friend functions look very much like member functions, except they cannot return a reference to the befriended class because this requires returning the self-reference *this. However, when you define friend functions outside the declaration of their befriended class, you need not qualify the function names with the name of the class.

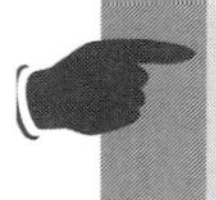

New Term: *Friend functions* are ordinary functions that have access to all data members of one or more classes.

Syntax

Friend Functions

The general form of friend functions is

```
class className
{
     public:
          className();
          // other constructors

          friend returnType friendFunction(<parameter list>);
};
```

Example:

```
class String
{
     protected:
          char *str;
          int len;

     public:
          String();
          ~String();
          // other member functions
          friend String& append(String& str1, String& str2);
          friend String& append(const char* str1, String& str2);
          friend String& append(String& str1, const char* str2);
};
```

Friend classes can accomplish tasks that are awkward, difficult, and even impossible with member functions.

Let's look at a simple example for using friend functions. Listing 11.5 contains the source code for the CLASS5.CPP program. This program internally creates two complex numbers, adds them, stores the result in another complex number, and then displays the operands and resulting complex numbers.

Type

Listing 11.5. Source code for the CLASS5.CPP program.

```
// Program that demonstrates friend functions

#include <iostream.h>

class Complex
{
   protected:
     double x;
```

```
      double y;

   public:
     Complex(double real = 0, double imag = 0);
     Complex(Complex& c) { assign(c); }
     void assign(Complex& c);
     double getReal() const { return x; }
     double getImag() const { return y; }
     friend Complex add(Complex& c1, Complex& c2);
};

Complex::Complex(double real, double imag)
{
  x = real;
  y = imag;
}

void Complex::assign(Complex& c)
{
  x = c.x;
  y = c.y;
}

Complex add(Complex& c1, Complex& c2)
{
  Complex result(c1);

  result.x += c2.x;
  result.y += c2.y;
  return result;
}

main()
{
  Complex c1(2, 3);
  Complex c2(5, 7);
  Complex c3;

  c3.assign(add(c1, c2));
  cout << "(" << c1.getReal() << " + i" << c1.getImag() << ")"
       << " + "
       << "(" << c2.getReal() << " + i" << c2.getImag() << ")"
       << " = "
       << "(" << c3.getReal() << " + i" << c3.getImag() << ")"
       << "\n\n";
  return 0;
}
```

Here is a sample session with the program in Listing 11.5:

```
(2 + i3) + (5 + i7) = (7 + i10)
```

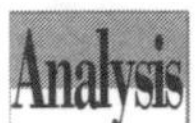

The program in Listing 11.5 declares the class `Complex`, which models complex numbers. This class declares two data members, two constructors, a friend function (the highlight of this example), and a set of member functions. The data members `x` and `y` store the real and imaginary components of a complex number, respectively.

The class has two constructors. The first constructor has two parameters (with default arguments) that enable you to build a class instance using the real and imaginary components of a complex number. Because the two parameters have default arguments, the constructor doubles up as the default constructor. The second constructor, `complex(complex&)`, is the copy constructor.

The `Complex` class declares three member functions. The function `assign` copies a class instance into another one. The functions `getReal` and `getImag` return the value stored in the members `real` and `imag`, respectively.

The `Complex` class declares the friend function `add` to add two complex numbers. To make the program short, we do not implement complementary friend functions that subtract, multiply, and divide class instances. What is so special about the friend function `add`? Why not use an ordinary member function to add a class instance? The following declaration of the alternate `add` member function answers these questions:

```
complex& add(complex& c)
```

This declaration states that the function treats the parameter `c` as a second operand. Here is how the member function `add` works:

```
complex c1(3, 4), c2(1.2, 4.5);
c1.add(c2); // adds c2 to c1
```

First, the member function `add` works as an increment and not as an addition function. Second, the targeted class instance is always the first operand. This is not a problem for operations like addition and multiplication, but it is a problem for subtraction and division. That is why the friend function `add` works better by giving you the freedom of choosing how to add the class instances.

The friend function `add` returns a class instance. The function creates a local instance of class `Complex` and returns that instance.

The function `main` uses the member function `assign` and the friend function `add` to perform basic complex operations. In addition, the function `main` invokes the

functions getReal and getImag with the various instances of class Complex to display the components of each instance.

Operators and Friend Operators

The last program used a member function and a friend function to implement complex math operations. The approach is typical in C and Pascal because these languages do not support user-defined operators. By contrast, C++ enables you to declare operators and friend operators. These operators include +, -, *, /, %, ==, !=, <=, <, >=, >, +=, -=, *=, /=, %=, [], (), <<, and >>. Consult a C++ language reference book for more details on the rules of using these operators. C++ treats operators and friend operators as special member functions and friend functions.

Syntax

Operators and Friend Operators

The general syntax for declaring operators and friend operators is

```
class className
{
     public:
          // constructors and destructor
          // member functions

          // unary operator
          returnType operator operatorSymbol(operand);
          // binary operator
          returnType operator operatorSymbol(firstOperand,
                                             secondOperand);
          // unary friend operator
          friend returnType operator operatorSymbol(operand);
          // binary operator
          friend returnType operator operatorSymbol(firstOperand,
                                                    secondOperand);
};
```

Example:

```
class String
{
     protected:
          char *str;
          int len;

     public:
          String();
          ~String();
```

```
        // other member functions
        // assignment operator
        String& operator =(String& s);
        String& operator +=(String& s);
        // concatenation operators
        friend String& operator +(String& s1, String& s2);
        friend String& operator +(const char* s1, String& s2);
        friend String& operator +(String& s1, const char* s2);
        // relational operators
        friend int operator >(String& s1, String& s2);
        friend int operator =>(String& s1, String& s2);
        friend int operator <(String& s1, String& s2);
        friend int operator <=(String& s1, String& s2);
        friend int operator ==(String& s1, String& s2);
        friend int operator !=(String& s1, String& s2);
};
```

The functions you write use the operators and friend operators just like predefined operators. Therefore, you can create operators to support the operations of classes that model, for example, complex numbers, strings, arrays, and matrices. These operators enable you to write expressions that are far more readable than expressions that use named functions.

Let's look at an example. Listing 11.6 contains the source code for the CLASS6.CPP program. We created this program by modifying and expanding Listing 11.5. The new program performs more additions and displays two sets of operands and results.

Type

Listing 11.6. Source code for the CLASS6.CPP program.

```
// Program that demonstrates operators and friend operators

#include <iostream.h>

class Complex
{
   protected:
     double x;
     double y;

   public:
     Complex(double real = 0, double imag = 0)
       { assign(real, imag); }
     Complex(Complex& c);
     void assign(double real = 0, double imag = 0);
     double getReal() const { return x; }
     double getImag() const { return y; }
     Complex& operator =(Complex& c);
     Complex& operator +=(Complex& c);
     friend Complex operator +(Complex& c1, Complex& c2);
```

```
     friend ostream& operator <<(ostream& os, Complex& c);
};

Complex::Complex(Complex& c)
{
  x = c.x;
  y = c.y;
}

void Complex::assign(double real, double imag)
{
  x = real;
  y = imag;
}

Complex& Complex::operator =(Complex& c)
{
  x = c.x;
  y = c.y;
  return *this;
}

Complex& Complex::operator +=(Complex& c)
{
  x += c.x;
  y += c.y;
  return *this;
}

Complex operator +(Complex& c1, Complex& c2)
{
  Complex result(c1);

  result.x += c2.x;
  result.y += c2.y;
  return result;
}

ostream& operator <<(ostream& os, Complex& c)
{
  os << "(" << c.x << " + i" << c.y << ")";
  return os;
}

main()
{
  Complex c1(3, 5);
  Complex c2(7, 5);
  Complex c3;
  Complex c4(2, 3);

```


continues

Listing 11.6. continued

```
    c3 = c1 + c2;
    cout << c1 << " + " << c2 << " = " << c3 << "\n";
    cout << c3 << " + " << c4 << " = ";
    c3 += c4;
    cout << c3 << "\n";
    return 0;
}
```

Here is a sample session with the program in Listing 11.6:

```
(3 + i5) + (7 + i5) = (10 + i10)
(10 + i10) + (2 + i3) = (12 + i13)
```

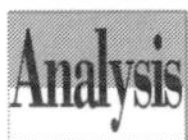

The new class `Complex` replaces the `assign(Complex&)` member function with the operator `=`. The class also replaces the friend function `add` with the friend operator `+`:

```
Complex& operator =(Complex& c);
friend Complex operator +(Complex& c1, Complex& c2);
```

The operator `=` has one parameter, a reference to an instance of class `Complex`, and also returns a reference to the same class. The friend operator `+` has two parameters (both are references to instances of class `Complex`) and yields a complex class type.

We also took the opportunity to add two new operators:

```
complex& operator +=(complex& c);
friend ostream& operator <<(ostream& os, complex& c);
```

The operator `+=` is a member of class `Complex`. It takes one parameter, a reference to an instance of class `Complex`, and yields a reference to the same class. The other new operator is the friend operator `<<`, which illustrates how to write a stream extractor operator for a class. The friend operator has two parameters: a reference to class `ostream` (the output stream class) and a reference to class `Complex`. The operator `<<` returns a reference to class `ostream`. This type of value enables you to chain stream output with other predefined types or other classes (assuming these classes have a friend operator `<<`). The definition of friend operator `<<` has two statements. The first one outputs strings and the data members of class `Complex` to the output stream parameter `os`. The friendship status of operator `<<` allows it to access the `real` and `imag` data members of its `Complex`-typed parameter `c`. The second statement in the operator definition returns the first parameter `os`.

The function `main` declares four instances of class `Complex`, `c1`, `c2`, `c3`, and `c4`. The instances `c1`, `c2`, and `c4` are created with nondefault values assigned to the data

members `real` and `imag`. The function tests use the operators `=`, `+`, `<<`, `+=`. The program illustrates that you can use operators and friend operators to write code that is more readable and supports a higher level of abstraction.

Summary

Today's lesson introduced you to C++ classes and discussed the following topics:

- The basics of object-oriented programming include classes, objects, messages, methods, inheritance, and polymorphism.
- You declare base classes to specify the various private, protected, and public members. C++ classes contain data members and member functions. The data members store the state of a class instance, and the member functions query and manipulate that state.
- Constructors and destructors support the automatic creation and removal of class instances. Constructors are special members that must have the same name as the host class. You may declare any number of constructors, or none at all. In the latter case, the compiler creates one for you. Each constructor enables you to create a class instance in a different way. There are two special kinds of constructors: the default constructor and the copy constructor. In contrast with constructors, C++ enables you to declare only one parameterless destructor. Destructors automatically remove class instances. The runtime system automatically invokes the constructor and destructor when a class instance comes into and goes out of its scope.
- Declaring a class hierarchy enables you to derive classes from existing ones. The descendant classes inherit the members of their ancestor classes. C++ classes are able to override inherited member functions by defining their own versions. If you override a nonvirtual function, you may declare the new version using a different parameter list. By contrast, you cannot alter the parameter list of an inherited virtual function.
- Virtual member functions enable your classes to support polymorphic behavior. Such behavior offers a response that is suitable for each class in a hierarchy. After you declare a function virtual, you can override it only with a virtual function in a descendant class. All versions of a virtual function in a class hierarchy must have the same signature.
- Friend functions are special nonmember functions that may access protected and private data members. These functions enable you to implement operations that are more flexible than those offered by member functions.

- ☐ Operators and friend operators enable you to support various operations, such as addition, assignment, and indexing. These operators enable you to offer a level of abstraction for your classes. In addition, they assist in making the expressions that manipulate class instances more readable and more intuitive.

Q&A

Q What happens if I declare the default, copy, and other constructors as protected?

A Client programs are unable to create instances of that class. However, client programs can use that class by declaring descendant classes with public constructors.

Q Can I use the constructor for typecasting?

A Yes, you can incorporate this kind of typecasting in the creation of a class instance. For example, if the class `Complex` has the constructor `Complex(double real, double imag)`, you can declare the instance `c` of class `Complex` as follows:

```
Complex c = Complex(1.7, 2.4);
```

Q Can I chain messages to an instance?

A Yes, you can as long as the chained messages invoke member functions that return a reference to the same class that receives the message. For example, if you have a class `String` with the following member functions

```
String& upperCase();
string& reverse();
String& mapChars(char find, char replace);
```

you can write the following statement for the instance of class `String` `s`:

```
s.upperCase().reverse().mapChar(' ', '+');
```

Q What happens if a class relies on the copy constructor, which is created by the compiler, to copy instances of a class that has pointers?

A These constructors perform a bit-by-bit copy. Consequently, the corresponding pointer members in both instances end up with the address to the same dynamic data. This kind of duplication is a recipe for trouble!

Q Can I create an array of instances?

A Yes, you can; however, the accompanying class must have a default constructor. The instantiation of the array uses the constructor mentioned previously.

Q Can I use a pointer to create an instance of class?

A Yes, you need to use the operators `new` and `delete` to allocate and deallocate the dynamic space for the instance. Here is an example using the class `Complex`:

```
Complex* pC;
pC = new Complex;
// manipulate the instance accessed by pointer pC
delete pC;
```

or

```
Complex* pC = new Complex;
// manipulate the instance accessed by pointer pC
delete pC;
```

Workshop

The Workshop provides quiz questions to help you solidify your understanding of the material covered and exercises to provide you with experience in using what you've learned. Try to understand the quiz and exercise answers before continuing on to the next day's lesson. Answers are provided in Appendix A, "Answers."

Quiz

1. Where is the error in the following class declaration?

```
class String {
        char *str;
        unsigned len;
        String();
        String(String& s);
        String(unsigned size, char = ' ');
        String(unsigned size);
        String& assign(String& s);
        ~String();
```

```
        unsigned getLen() const;
        char* getString();
        // other member functions
};
```

2. Where is the error in the following class declaration?

```
class String {
     protected:
       char *str;
       unsigned len;
     public:
       String();
       String(const char* s);
       String(String& s);
       String(unsigned size, char = ' ');
       String(unsigned size);
       ~String();
       // other member functions
};
```

3. True or false? The following statement, which creates the instance `s` based on the preceding declaration of class `String`, is correct:

```
s = String("Hello Borland C++");
```

4. Looking at the program CLASS6.CPP, if you change the declarations of the instances in function `main` to the following, will the program still compile?

```
Complex c1 = Complex(3, 5);
Complex c2 = Complex(7, 5);
Complex c3 = c1;
Complex c4 = Complex(2, 3);
```

Exercise

Create the program CLASS7.CPP from CLASS6.CPP by replacing the individual instances `c1` to `c4` with `c`, an array of instances.

12

Basic Stream File I/O

WEEK 2

Today's lesson introduces you to file I/O (input/output) operations using the C++ stream library. Although the STDIO.H library in C has been standardized by the ANSI C committee, the C++ stream library has not. You have a choice of using file I/O functions in the STDIO.H file or in the C++ stream library. Each of these two I/O libraries offers a lot of power and flexibility. Today's lesson presents basic and practical operations that enable you to read and write data to files. You learn about the following topics:

- Common stream I/O functions
- Sequential stream I/O for text
- Sequential stream I/O for binary data
- Random access stream I/O for binary data
- The new Borland C++ exception handling

To learn more about the C++ stream library, consult a C++ language reference book, such as Tom Swan's *C++ Primer* (Sams Publishing, 1992).

The C++ Stream Library

The C++ stream I/O library (also known as the iostream library) is made up of a hierarchy of classes that are declared in several header files. The IOSTREAM.H header file that we have used thus far is only one of these. Others include IO.H, ISTREAM.H, OSTREAM.H, IFSTREAM.H, OFSTREAM.H, and FSTREAM.H. The IO.H header file declares low-level classes and identifiers. The ISTREAM.H and OSTREAM.H files support the basic input and output stream classes. The IOSTREAM.H combines the operations of the classes in the previous two header files. Similarly, the IFSTREAM.H and OFSTREAM.H files support the basic file input and output stream classes. The FSTREAM.H file combines the operations of the classes in the previous two header files. There are additional stream library files that offer even more specialized stream I/O. The C++ ANSI committee will define the standard stream I/O library, and the committee's work will end any confusion regarding which classes and header files are part of the standard stream library and which ones are not.

Common Stream I/O Functions

In this section, we present stream I/O functions that are common to both sequential and random access I/O. These functions include `open`, `close`, `good`, and `fail`, in addition to the operator `!`.

The `open` function enables you to open a file stream for input, output, append, and both input and output. The function also permits you to specify whether the related I/O is binary or text.

Syntax

The *open* Function

The prototype for the `open` function is

```
void open(const char* filename,
          int mode,
          int m = filebuf::openprot);
```

The parameter `filename` specifies the name of the file to open. The parameter `mode` indicates the I/O mode. Here is a list of arguments for parameter `mode` that are exported by the IO.H header file:

`in`	Open stream for input.
`out`	Open stream for output.
`ate`	Set stream pointer to the end of the file.
`app`	Open stream for append mode.
`trunc`	Truncate file size to 0 if it already exists.
`nocreate`	Raise an error if the file does not already exist.
`noreplace`	Raise an error if the file already exists.
`binary`	Open in binary mode.

Examples:

```
// open stream for input
fstream f;
f.open("\\AUTOEXEC.BAT", ios::in);

// open stream for output
fstream f;
f.open("\\AUTOEXEC.OLD", ios:out);

// open stream for binary input and output
fstream f;
f.open("INCOME.DAT", ios::in ¦ ios::out ¦ ios::binary);
```

Note: The file stream classes offer constructors that include the action (and have the same parameters) of the function `open`.

The `close` function closes the stream and recuperates the resources involved. These resources include the memory buffer used in the stream I/O operations.

Syntax

The *close* Function

The prototype for the `close` function is

```
void close();
```

Example:

```
fstream f;
// open stream
f.open("\\AUTOEXEC.BAT", ios::in);
// process file
// now close stream
f.close();
```

The C++ stream library includes a set of basic functions that check the error status of a stream operation. These functions include the following:

1. The `good()` function returns a nonzero value if there is no error in a stream operation. The declaration of function `good` is

   ```
   int good();
   ```

2. The `fail()` function returns a nonzero value if there is an error in a stream operation. The declaration of function `fail` is

   ```
   int fail();
   ```

3. The overloaded operator `!` is applied to a stream instance to determine the error status.

The C++ stream libraries offer additional functions to set and query other aspects and types of stream errors.

Sequential Text Stream I/O

The functions and operators involved in sequential text I/O are simple. You have already been exposed to most of them in earlier lessons. The functions and operators include the following:

1. The stream extractor operator << writes strings and characters to a stream.
2. The stream inserter operator >> reads characters from a stream.
3. The `getline` function reads strings from a stream.

Syntax

The *getline* Function

The prototype for the function `getline` is

```
istream& getline(char* buffer,
                 int size,
                 char delimiter = '\n');

istream& getline(signed char* buffer,
                 int size,
                 char delimiter = '\n');

istream& getline(unsigned char* buffer,
                 int size,
                 char delimiter = '\n');
```

The parameter `buffer` is a pointer to the string receiving the characters from the stream. The parameter `size` specifies the maximum number of characters to read. The parameter `delimiter` specifies the delimiting character, which causes the string input to stop before reaching the number of characters specified by parameter `size`. The parameter delimiter has the default argument of `'\n'`.

Example:

```
fstream f;
char textLine[MAX];
f.open("\\CONFIG.SYS", ios::in);
while (!f.eof()) {
  f.getline(textLine, MAX);
  cout << textLine << "\n";
}
f.close();
```

Let's look at an example. Listing 12.1 shows the source code for the program IO1.CPP. The program performs the following tasks:

- Prompts you to enter the name of an input text file.
- Prompts you to enter the name of an output text file. (The program detects if the names of the input and output files are the same, and if so, reprompts you for a different output filename.)
- Reads the lines from the input files and removes any trailing spaces in these lines.
- Writes the lines to the output file and also to the standard output window.

Type

Listing 12.1. Source code for the IO1.CPP program.

```
// C++ program that demonstrates sequential file I/O

#include <iostream.h>
#include <fstream.h>
#include <string.h>

enum boolean { false, true };

const unsigned LINE_SIZE = 128;
const unsigned NAME_SIZE = 64;

void trimStr(char* s)
{
  int i = strlen(s) - 1;
  // locate the character where the trailing spaces begin
  while (i >= 0 && s[i] == ' ')
    i--;
  // truncate string
  s[i+1] = '\0';
}

void getInputFilename(char* inFile, fstream& f)
{
  boolean ok;

  do {
    ok = true;
    cout << "Enter input file : ";
    cin.getline(inFile, NAME_SIZE);
    f.open(inFile, ios::in);
    if (!f) {
      cout << "Cannot open file " << inFile << "\n\n";
      ok = false;
```

```
    }
  } while (!ok);

}

void getOutputFilename(char* outFile, const char* inFile,
                       fstream& f)
{
  boolean ok;

  do {
    ok = true;
    cout << "Enter output file : ";
    cin.getline(outFile, NAME_SIZE);
    if (stricmp(inFile, outFile) != 0) {
      f.open(outFile, ios::out);
      if (!f) {
        cout << "File " << outFile << " is invalid\n\n";
        ok = false;
      }
    }
    else {
      cout << "Input and output files must be different!\n";
      ok = false;
    }
  } while (!ok);
}

void processLines(fstream& fin, fstream& fout)
{
  char line[LINE_SIZE + 1];

  // loop to trim trailing spaces
  while (fin.getline(line, LINE_SIZE)) {
    trimStr(line);
    // write line to the output file
    fout << line << "\n";
    // echo updated line to the output window
    cout << line << "\n";
  }

}
main()
{

  fstream fin, fout;
  char inFile[NAME_SIZE + 1], outFile[NAME_SIZE + 1];

  getInputFilename(inFile, fin);
  getOutputFilename(outFile, inFile, fout);
```


continues

Listing 12.1. continued

```
84:    processLines(fin, fout);
85:    // close streams
86:    fin.close();
87:    fout.close();
88:    return 0;
89: }
```

Here is a sample session with the program in Listing 12.1:

```
Enter input file : sample.txt
Enter output file : sample.out
This is line 1
This is line 2
This is line 3
This is line 4
```

The program in Listing 12.1 declares no classes and instead focuses on using file streams to input and output text. The program declares the functions `trimStr`, `getInputFilename`, `getOutputFilename`, `processLines`, and `main`.

The function `trimStr` shaves the trailing spaces in the strings passed by parameter `s`. The function declares the local variable `i` and assigns it the index of the character just before the null terminator. The function uses the `while` loop in line 13 to perform a backward scan of the characters in string `s` for the first nonspace character. The statement at line 16 assigns the null terminator character to the character located right after the last nonspace character in the string `s`.

The function `getInputFilename` obtains the input filename and opens its corresponding input file stream. The parameter `inFile` passes the name of the input file to the function `caller`. The reference parameter `f` passes the opened input stream to the function `caller`. The function `getInputFilename` declares the local flag `ok`. The function uses the `do-while` loop in lines 26 through 35 to obtain a valid filename and to open that file for input. Line 27 contains the first statement inside the loop, which assigns the enumerated value `true` to the local variable `ok`. The output statement in line 28 prompts you for the input filename. The statement in line 29 calls the stream input function `getline` to obtain your input and to store it in the parameter `inFile`. The statement in line 30 opens the input file using the stream parameter `f`. The open statement uses the `ios::in` value to indicate that the stream is opened for text input. The `if` statement in line 31 determines whether or not the stream `f` is successfully opened. If not, the function executes the statements in lines 32 and 33. These statements display an error message and assign the enumerated value `false` to the local

variable ok. The loop's while clause in line 35 examines the condition !ok. The loop iterates until you supply it a valid filename, which must successfully be opened for input.

The function getOutputFilename complements the function getInputFilename and has three parameters. The parameter outFile passes the output filename of the function caller. The parameter inFile supplies the function with the input filename. The function uses this parameter to ensure that the input and output filenames are not the same. The parameter f passes the output stream to the function caller. The implementation of function getOutputFilename is very similar to that of function getInputFilename. The main difference is that the function getOutputFilename calls the function stricmp to compare the values in parameter inFile and outFile. The function uses the result of stricmp to determine whether the names of the input and output files are identical. If so, the function executes the statements in the else clause at lines 57 and 58. These statements display an error message and assign false to the local variable ok.

The function processLines reads the lines from the input file stream, trims them, and writes them to the output file stream. The parameters fin and fout pass the input and output file streams, respectively. The function declares the local string variable line and uses the while loop in lines 67 through 73 to process the text lines. The while clause contains the call to function getline, which reads the next line in the input stream fin and assigns the input line to variable line. The result of function getline causes the while loop to stop iterating when there are no more input lines. The first statement inside the loop, located at line 68, calls the function trimStr and passes it the argument line. This function call prunes any existing trailing spaces in the local variable line. The statement in line 70 writes the string in variable line to the output file stream. The statement in line 72 echoes the string in line to the standard output window. (We placed this statement in the program so that you can monitor the progress of the program.)

The function main declares the file streams fin and fout, and the string variables inFile and outFile. The statement in line 82 calls function getInputFilename and passes it the arguments inFile and fin. This call obtains the name of the input file and the input stream through the arguments inFile and fin, respectively. The statement in line 83 calls the function getOutputFilename and passes it the arguments outFile, inFile, and fout. This call obtains the name of the output file and the output stream through the arguments outFile and fout, respectively. The statement in line 84 calls function processLines and passes it the arguments fin and fout. This call processes the lines in the input file stream `fin` and writes the results to the output file stream `fout`. The statements in lines 86 and 87 close the input and output file streams, respectively.

Sequential Binary File Stream I/O

The C++ stream library offers the overloaded stream functions `write` and `read` for sequential binary file stream I/O. The function `write` sends multiple bytes to an output stream. This function can write any variable or instance to a stream.

Syntax

The *write* Function

The prototype for the overloaded function `write` is

```
ostream& write(const char* buff, int num);
ostream& write(const signed char* buff, int num);
ostream& write(const unsigned char* buff, int num);
```

The parameter `buff` is the pointer to the buffer that contains the data to be sent to the output stream. The parameter `num` indicates the number of bytes in the buffer that are sent to the stream.

Example:

```
const MAX = 80;
char buff[MAX+1] = "Hello World!";
int len = strlen(buffer) + 1;
fstream f;
f.open("CALC.DAT", ios::out ¦ ios::binary);
f.write((const unsigned char*)*len, sizeof(len));
f.write((const unsigned char*)buff, len);
f.close();
```

The function `read` receives multiple bytes from an input stream. This function can read any variable or can read from a stream.

Syntax

The *read* Function

The prototype for the overloaded function `read` is

```
istream& read(char* buff, int num);
istream& read(signed char* buff, int num);
istream& read(unsigned char* buff, int num);
```

The parameter `buff` is the pointer to the buffer that receives the data from the input stream. The parameter `num` indicates the number of bytes to read from the stream.

Example:

```
const MAX = 80;
char buff[MAX+1];
int len;
fstream f;
f.open("CALC.DAT", ios::in | ios::binary);
f.read((const unsigned char*)*len, sizeof(len));
f.read((const unsigned char*)buff, len);
f.close();
```

Let's look at an example that performs sequential binary stream I/O. Listing 12.2 shows the source code for the program IO2.CPP. The program declares a class that models dynamic numerical arrays. The stream I/O operations enable the program to read and write both the individual array elements and an entire array in binary files. The program creates the arrays `arr1`, `arr2`, and `arr3` and then performs the following tasks:

- Assigns values to the elements of array `arr1`. (This array has 10 elements.)
- Assigns values to the elements of array `arr3`. (This array has 20 elements.)
- Displays the values in array `arr1`.
- Writes the elements of array `arr1` to the file ARR1.DAT, one element at a time.
- Reads the elements of `arr1` from the file into the array `arr2`. (The array `arr2` has 10 elements—the same size as array `arr1`.)
- Displays the values in array `arr2`.
- Displays the values in array `arr3`.
- Writes the elements of array `arr3` to file ARR3.DAT in one swoop.
- Reads, in one swoop, the data in file ARR3.DAT and stores them in array `arr1`.
- Displays the values in array `arr1`. (The output shows that array `arr1` has the same size and data as array `arr3`.)

Listing 12.2. Source code for the IO2.CPP program.

```
/*
   C++ program that demonstrates sequential binary file I/O
*/

```

continues

Listing 12.2. continued

```
#include <iostream.h>
#include <fstream.h>

const unsigned MIN_SIZE = 10;
const double BAD_VALUE = -1.0e+30;
enum boolean { false, true };

class Array
{
   protected:
     double *dataPtr;
     unsigned size;
     double badIndex;

   public:
     Array(unsigned Size = MIN_SIZE);
     ~Array()
       { delete [] dataPtr; }
     unsigned getSize() const { return size; }
     double& operator [](unsigned index)
     { return (index < size) ? *(dataPtr + index) : badIndex; }
     boolean writeElem(fstream& os, unsigned index);
     boolean readElem(fstream& is, unsigned index);
     boolean writeArray(const char* filename);
     boolean readArray(const char* filename);
};

Array::Array(unsigned Size)
{
  size = (Size < MIN_SIZE) ? MIN_SIZE : Size;
  badIndex = BAD_VALUE;
  dataPtr = new double[size];
}

boolean Array::writeElem(fstream& os, unsigned index)
{
   if (index < size) {
     os.write((unsigned char*)(dataPtr + index), sizeof(double));
     return (os.good()) ? true : false;
   }
   else
     return false;
}

boolean Array::readElem(fstream& is, unsigned index)
{
   if (index < size) {
     is.read((unsigned char*)(dataPtr + index), sizeof(double));
     return (is.good()) ? true : false;
```

```
   }
   else
     return false;
}

boolean Array::writeArray(const char* filename)
{
   fstream f(filename, ios::out | ios::binary);

   if (f.fail())
     return false;
   f.write((unsigned char*) &size, sizeof(size));
   f.write((unsigned char*)dataPtr, size * sizeof(double));
   f.close();
   return (f.good()) ? true : false;
}

boolean Array::readArray(const char* filename)
{
   fstream f(filename, ios::in | ios::binary);
   unsigned sz;

   if (f.fail())
     return false;
   f.read((unsigned char*) &sz, sizeof(sz));
   // need to expand the array
   if (sz != size) {
     delete [] dataPtr;
     dataPtr = new double[sz];
     size = sz;
   }
   f.read((unsigned char*)dataPtr, size * sizeof(double));
   f.close();
   return (f.good()) ? true : false;
}

main()
{
  const unsigned SIZE1 = 10;
  const unsigned SIZE2 = 20;
  char* filename1 = "array1.dat";
  char* filename2 = "array3.dat";
  Array arr1(SIZE1), arr2(SIZE1), arr3(SIZE2);
  fstream f(filename1, ios::out | ios::binary);

  // assign values to array arr1
  for (unsigned i = 0; i < arr1.getSize(); i++)
    arr1[i] = 10 * i;

  // assign values to array arr3
```


continues

Listing 12.2. continued

```
  for (i = 0; i < SIZE2; i++)
    arr3[i] = i;

  cout << "Array arr1 has the following values:\n";
  for (i = 0; i < arr1.getSize(); i++)
    cout << arr1[i] << "  ";
  cout << "\n\n";

  // write elements of array arr1 to the stream
  for (i = 0; i < arr1.getSize(); i++)
    arr1.writeElem(f, i);
  f.close();

  // reopen the stream for input
  f.open(filename1, ios::in | ios::binary);

  for (i = 0; i < arr1.getSize(); i++)
    arr2.readElem(f, i);
  f.close();

  // display the elements of array arr2
  cout << "Array arr2 has the following values:\n";
  for (i = 0; i < arr2.getSize(); i++)
    cout << arr2[i] << "  ";
  cout << "\n\n";

  // display the elements of array arr3
  cout << "Array arr3 has the following values:\n";
  for (i = 0; i < arr3.getSize(); i++)
    cout << arr3[i] << "  ";
  cout << "\n\n";

  // write the array arr3 to file ARRAY3.DAT
  arr3.writeArray(filename2);
  // read the array arr1 from file ARRAY3.DAT
  arr1.readArray(filename2);

    // display the elements of array arr1
  cout << "Array arr1 now has the following values:\n";
  for (i = 0; i < arr1.getSize(); i++)
    cout << arr1[i] << "  ";
  cout << "\n\n";
  return 0;
}
```

Here is a sample session with the program in Listing 12.2:

```
Array arr1 has the following values:
0  10  20  30  40  50  60  70  80  90

Array arr2 has the following values:
0  10  20  30  40  50  60  70  80  90

Array arr3 has the following values:
0  1  2  3  4  5  6  7  8  9  10  11  12  13  14  15  16  17  18  19

Array arr1 now has the following values:
0  1  2  3  4  5  6  7  8  9  10  11  12  13  14  15  16  17  18  19
```

The program in Listing 12.2 declares a version of class `Array` that resembles the one in Day 11, Listing 11.2. The main difference is that here we use the operator `[]` to replace both the member functions `store` and `recall`. This operator checks for valid indices and returns the value in member `badIndex` if the argument is out of range. In addition to operator `[]`, we added the member functions `writeElem`, `readElem`, `writeArray`, and `readArray` to perform sequential binary file stream I/O.

The function `writeElem`, defined in lines 39 through 47, writes a single array element to an output stream. The parameter `os` represents the output stream. The parameter `index` specifies the array element to write. The function `writeElem` yields true if the argument for the index is valid and if the stream output proceeds without any error. After `writeElem` writes an array element, the internal stream pointer advances to the next location.

The function `readElem`, defined in lines 49 through 57, reads a single array element from an input stream. The parameter `is` represents the input stream. The parameter index specifies the array element to read. The function `readElem` returns true if the argument for the index is valid and if the stream input proceeds without any error. After the `readElem` reads an array element, the internal stream pointer advances to the next location.

The functions `writeElem` and `readElem` permit the same class instance to write and read data elements, respectively, from multiple streams.

The function `writeArray`, defined in lines 59 through 69, writes the entire elements of the array to a binary file. The parameter `filename` specifies the name of the output file. The function opens an output stream and writes the value of the data member `size` and then writes the elements of the dynamic array. The `writeArray` function returns true if it successfully writes the array to the stream. Otherwise, it yields false. The function opens a local output stream by using the stream function `open` and supplying it with the filename and I/O mode arguments. The I/O mode argument is the expression `ios::out | ios::binary`, which specifies that the stream is opened for binary output only. The function makes two calls to the stream function `write`—the first to write the data member `size`, and the second to write the elements of the dynamic array.

The function `readArray`, defined in lines 71 through 88, reads the entire elements of the array from a binary file. The parameter `filename` specifies the name of the input file. The function opens an input stream and reads the value of the data member `size` and then reads the elements of the dynamic array. The `readArray` function returns true if it successfully reads the array to the stream. Otherwise, the function yields false. The function opens a local input stream by using the stream function `open` and supplying it the filename and I/O mode arguments. The I/O mode argument is the expression `ios::in | ios::binary`, which specifies that the stream is opened for binary input only. The function makes two calls to the stream function `read`—the first to read the data member `size`, and the second to read the elements of the dynamic array. Another feature of function `readArray` is that it resizes the instance of class `Array` to accommodate the data from the binary file. This means that a dynamic array accessed by the class instance may either shrink or expand, depending on the size of the array stored on file.

The member functions in Listing 12.2 indicate that the program performs two types of sequential binary stream I/O. The first type of I/O, implemented in functions `readElem` and `writeElem`, involves items that have the same data type. The second type of I/O, implemented in the functions `readArray` and `writeArray`, involves items that have different data types.

In Listing 12.2, the function `main` performs the following relevant tasks:

- Declares, in line 96, three instances of class `Array`, namely, `arr1`, `arr2`, and `arr3`. (The first two instances have the same dynamic array size, specified by the constant `SIZE1`, whereas instance `arr3` has a larger size, specified by the constant `SIZE2`.)
- Declares, in line 97, the file stream `f` and opens it (using a stream constructor) to access file ARR1.DAT in binary output mode.
- Uses the `for` loops in lines 100 and 104 to arbitrarily assign values to the instance `arr1` and `arr3`, respectively.
- Displays the elements of instance `arr1` using the `for` loop in line 108.

- Writes the elements of array arr1 to the output file stream f, using the for loop in line 113 to send the writeElem message to instance arr1 and to supply the message with the output file stream f and the loop control variable i.
- Closes the output file stream by sending the close message to the output file stream f.
- Opens, in line 118, the file stream f to access the data file ARR1.DAT. (This time, the message open specifies a binary input mode.)
- Reads the elements of instance arr2 (which has not yet been assigned any values) from the input file stream f, using the for loop in line 120 to send the message readElem to instance arr2 and to supply the message with the arguments f, the file stream, and i, the loop control variable.
- Closes the input file stream, in line 122, by sending the message close to the input file stream f.
- Displays the elements of instance arr2 using the for loop in line 126. (These elements match those of instance arr1.)
- Displays the elements of instance arr3 by using the for loop in line 132.
- Writes the entire instance arr3 by sending the message writeArray to instance arr3. (The message writeArray has the filename argument of ARR3.DAT.)
- Reads the array in file ARR3.DAT into instance arr1, sending the message readArray to instance arr1 and supplying the message with the filename argument of ARR3.DAT.
- Displays the new elements of instance arr1 using the for loop in line 143.

Random Access File Stream I/O

Random access file stream operations also use the stream functions read and write that were presented in the preceding section. The stream library offers a number of stream-seeking functions to enable you to move the stream pointer to any valid location. The function seekg is one of such functions.

Syntax

The *seekg* Function

The prototype for the overloaded function `seekg` is

```
istream& seekg(long pos);
istream& seekg(long pos, seek_dir dir);
```

The parameter *pos* in the first version specifies the absolute byte position in the stream. In the second version, the parameter *pos* specifies a relative offset, based on the argument for parameter *dir*. Here are the arguments for the latter parameter:

`ios::beg`	From the beginning of the file
`ios::cur`	From the current position of the file
`ios::end`	From the end of the file

Example:

```
const BLOCK_SIZE = 80;
char buff[BLOCK_SIZE] = "Hello World!";
fstream f("CALC.DAT", ios::in ¦ ios::out ¦ ios::binary);
f.seekg(3 * BLOCK_SIZE); // seek block # 4
f.read((const unsigned char*)buff, BLOCK_SIZE);
cout << buff <<< "\n";
f.close();
```

New Term: A *virtual array* is a disk-based array that stores fixed-size strings on disk.

Let's look at an example that uses random access file stream I/O. Listing 12.3 shows the source code for the program IO3.CPP and implements a virtual array. The program performs the following tasks:

- Uses an internal list of names to create a virtual array object.
- Displays the elements in the unordered virtual array object.
- Prompts you to enter a character and press the Return key.
- Sorts the elements of the virtual array object; this process requires random access I/O.
- Displays the elements in the sorted virtual array object.

Listing 12.3. Source code for the IO3.CPP program.

```
/*
   C++ program that demonstrates random-access binary file I/O
*/

#include <iostream.h>
#include <fstream.h>
#include <stdlib.h>
#include <string.h>

const unsigned MIN_SIZE = 5;
const unsigned STR_SIZE = 31;
const double BAD_VALUE = -1.0e+30;
enum boolean { false, true };

class VmArray
{
   protected:
     fstream f;
     unsigned size;
     double badIndex;

   public:
     VmArray(unsigned Size, const char* filename);
     ~VmArray()
       { f.close(); }
     unsigned getSize() const
       { return size; }
     boolean writeElem(const char* str, unsigned index);
     boolean readElem(char* str, unsigned index);
     void Combsort();
};

VmArray::VmArray(unsigned Size, const char* filename)
{
  char s[STR_SIZE+1];
  size = (Size < MIN_SIZE) ? MIN_SIZE : Size;
  badIndex = BAD_VALUE;
  f.open(filename, ios::in | ios::out | ios::binary);
  if (f.good()) {
    // fill the file stream with empty strings
    strcpy(s, "");;
    f.seekg(0);
    for (unsigned i = 0; i < size; i++)
      f.write((unsigned char*)s, sizeof(s));
  }
}

```

continues

Listing 12.3. continued

```
boolean VmArray::writeElem(const char* str, unsigned index)
{
   if (index < size) {
     f.seekg(index * (STR_SIZE+1));
     f.write((unsigned char*)str, (STR_SIZE+1));
     return (f.good()) ? true : false;
   }
   else
     return false;
}

boolean VmArray::readElem(char* str, unsigned index)
{
   if (index < size) {
     f.seekg(index * (STR_SIZE+1));
     f.read((unsigned char*)str, (STR_SIZE+1));
     return (f.good()) ? true : false;
   }
   else
     return false;
}

void VmArray::Combsort()
{
   unsigned i, j, gap = size;
   boolean inOrder;
   char strI[STR_SIZE+1], strJ[STR_SIZE+1];

   do {
     gap = (gap * 8) / 11;
     if (gap < 1)
       gap = 1;
     inOrder = true;
     for (i = 0, j = gap; i < (size - gap); i++, j++) {
       readElem(strI, i);
       readElem(strJ, j);
       if (strcmp(strI, strJ) > 0) {
         inOrder = false;
         writeElem(strI, j);
         writeElem(strJ, i);
       }
     }
   } while (!(inOrder && gap == 1));
}

main()
{
  char* data[] = { "Michigan", "California", "Virginia", "Maine",
                   "New York", "Florida", "Nevada", "Alaska",
                   "Ohio", "Maryland" };
```

```
  VmArray arr(10, "arr.dat");
  char str[STR_SIZE+1];
  char c;

  // assign values to array arr
  for (unsigned i = 0; i < arr.getSize(); i++) {
    strcpy(str, data[i]);
    arr.writeElem(str, i);
  }
  // display unordered array
  cout << "Unsorted arrays is:\n";
  for (i = 0; i < arr.getSize(); i++) {
    arr.readElem(str, i);
    cout << str << "\n";
  }
  // pause
  cout << "\nPress any key and then Return to sort the array...";
  cin >> c;
  // sort the array
  arr.Combsort();
  // display sorted array
  cout << "Sorted arrays is:\n";
  for (i = 0; i < arr.getSize(); i++) {
    arr.readElem(str, i);
    cout << str << "\n";
  }
  return 0;
}
```


Here is a sample session with the program in Listing 12.3:

```
Unsorted arrays is:
Michigan
California
Virginia
Maine
New York
Florida
Nevada
Alaska
Ohio
Maryland

Press any key and then Return to sort the array...d
Sorted arrays is:
Alaska
California
Florida
Maine
Maryland
```

```
Michigan
Nevada
New York
Ohio
Virginia
```

The program in Listing 12.3 declares the class `VmArray`. This class models a disk-based dynamic array that stores all its elements in a random access binary file. Notice that the class declares an instance of class `fstream` and that there is no pointer to a dynamic array. The class declares a constructor, a destructor, and a number of member functions.

The class constructor has two parameters, namely, `Size` and `filename`. The parameter `Size` specifies the size of the virtual array. The parameter `filename` names the binary file that stores the elements of a class instance. The constructor opens the stream `f` using the stream function `open` and supplies it the argument of parameter `filename` and the I/O mode expression `ios::in ¦ ios::out ¦ ios::binary`. This expression specifies that the stream is opened for binary input and output mode (that is, random access mode). If the constructor successfully opens the file stream, it proceeds to fill the file with zeros. The class destructor performs the simple task of closing the file stream `f`.

The functions `writeElem` and `readElem` support the random access of array elements. These functions use the stream function `seekg` to position the stream pointer at the appropriate array element. The `writeElem` then calls the stream function `write` to store an array element (supplied by the parameter `str`). By contrast, the function `readElem` calls the stream function `read` to retrieve an array element (returned by the parameter `str`). Both functions return Boolean results that indicate the success of the I/O operation.

The `VmArray` class also declares the `Combsort` function to sort the elements of the virtual array. This function uses the `readElem` and `writeElem` member functions to access and swap the array elements.

The function `main` performs the following relevant tasks:

- Declares the instance `arr`, of class `VmArray`. (This instance stores 10 strings in the binary file ARR.DAT.)
- Assigns random values to the elements of instance `arr`, using the `for` loop in lines 103 through 106, to assign strings accessed by `data[i]` to the variable `str` and then to write the value in `str` to the instance `arr` by sending it the message `writeElem`. (The arguments for the message `writeElem` are the string variable, `str` and the loop control variable, `i`.)

- Displays the unsorted elements of instance `arr` using the `for` loop in line 109. (The statement in line 110 sends the message `readElem` to the instance `arr` to obtain an element in the virtual array.)
- Sorts the array by sending the message `Combsort` to the instance `arr`.
- Displays the sorted elements of instance `arr` using the `for` loop in line 120. (The statement in line 121 sends the message `readElem` to the instance `arr` to obtain an element in the virtual array.)

Exception Handling

The evolution of the C++ language has resulted in language extensions, some of which still await the approval by the ANSI Standard Committee for C++. One of these new extensions is a set of extensions that allow C++ programs to offer a more sophisticated mechanism for triggering, identifying, and dealing with runtime errors. This section offers you a brief introduction to the syntax of exception handling and provides you with an example.

The proposed exception mechanism revolves around placing the statements that might generate a runtime error in a special block, the `try` block. This block is followed by one or more `catch` blocks that identify and handle the errors generated in the try block.

12

Syntax

The *try* and *catch* Blocks

The syntax for the `try` and `catch` blocks is

```
try {
  // place code that may generate an exception
}
catch(T1 [X1]) {
  // handle exception type T1
}
[catch(T2 [X2]) {
  // handle exception type T2
}]
[other catch blocks]
[catch(...) {
  // handle remaining types of exceptions
}]
```

The types *T1* and *T2* are structures or classes that support user-defined exceptions. The parameter *X1* can have the type *T1*, *T1*&, const *T1*, and const *T1*&. The parameter *X2* can have the same variations for type *T2*. The last catch block uses the ellipsis (three dots) to indicate that it is a catch-all block.

```
try {
  // open stream for input
  fstream f;
  f.myOpen("CALC.TXT", ios::in);
}
catch(TFileError e) {
  cout << "Cannot open file for input\n"
}
```

The preceding example has a try block that attempts to open the file CALC.TXT using a user-defined member function myOpen. This function *throws* (that is, generates) an exception of the type TFileError (a user-defined exception type). The catch block handles the TFileError exception type by displaying an error message.

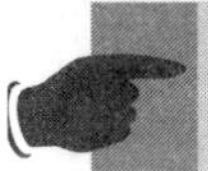

New Term: An *exception* is runtime error.

New Term: To *throw* an exception means to generate a runtime error.

Borland C++ enables you to define your own exception types, using structures or classes. An exception type can be an empty structure or class if you only need the name of the structure or class type. In case you want to provide more information related to the nature of the exception, the exception type may include data members and member functions that support manipulating the exception state.

Once you define the exception type, you can then declare normal functions and member functions of class to throw these exceptions.

Syntax

The Declaration of Exceptions Thrown by a Function

The syntax for declaring functions that can or cannot throw exceptions is

```
[returnType] functionName([parameterList]) throw();
```

The preceding syntax declares that the function `functionName` should *not* throw an exception.

```
[returnType] functionName([parameterList]);
```

The preceding syntax declares that the function *`functionName`* can throw any type of exceptions.

```
[returnType] functionName([parameterList])
   throw(exceptionTypeList)
```

The preceding syntax declares that the function *`functionName`* can only throw an exception in the comma-delimited exception type list, *`exceptionTypeList`*.

Examples:

```
void calc() throw();
void parse();
void input() throw(TFileErr, TMemoryErr);
```

The declaration of function `calc` states that the function cannot throw any kind of exception. By contrast, the declaration of function `parse` states that the function can throw any kind of exception. The declaration of function `input` states that the function can only throw the exceptions of type `TFileErr`, `TMemoryErr`, or their descendant classes. This function *throws* an exception of type `TFileError` (a user-defined exception type). The catch block handles the `TFileError` exception type by displaying an error message.

Borland C++ requires that you declare the `throw` clause in both the declaration and the definition of a function and a member function.

The last component of handling exceptions deals with throwing them. Borland C++ supplies the keyword `throw`, which throws an exception.

Syntax

The *throw* Keyword

The syntax for the `throw` keyword is

```
throw(exceptionInstance);
```

The exceptionInstance is an instance of an exception structure or class.

Example:

```
class TFileErr
{};

// declare an exception instance
TFileErr BadIO;
```

```
void input()
  throw(TFileErr)
{
  MyStream f;
  try {
    if (!f.MyOpen("calc.dat"))
       throw(badIO);
    // process input
  }
  catch(TFileErr e) {
    cout << "Failed to open file CALC.DAT\n";
  }
}
```

The preceding function throws the exception instance `BadIO` (an instance of the exception type class `TFileErr`).

Let's look at an example. Listing 12.4 shows the source code for the program IOERR1.CPP. This program is derived from program IO2.CPP in Listing 12.2. The program IOERR1.CPP performs the same tasks as program IO2.CPP and additionally attempts to access array elements at the out-of-range indices of 100, 1000, and 10000.

Listing 12.4. Source code for the IOERR1.CPP program.

```
/*
  C++ program that demonstrates sequential binary file I/O
*/

#include <iostream.h>
#include <fstream.h>

const unsigned MIN_SIZE = 10;
const double BAD_VALUE = -1.0e+30;
enum boolean { false, true };

class TErrIO
{};

class TErrIndex
{};

class Array
{
    protected:
      double *dataPtr;
      unsigned size;
      double badIndex;
      TErrIO ErrIO;
      TErrIndex ErrIndex;
```

```
     public:
       Array(unsigned Size = MIN_SIZE);
       ~Array()
           { delete [] dataPtr; }
       unsigned getSize() const { return size; }
       double& operator [](unsigned index)
       { return (index < size) ? *(dataPtr + index) : badIndex; }
       void writeElem(fstream& os, unsigned index)
            throw(TErrIO, TErrIndex);
       void readElem(fstream& is, unsigned index)
            throw(TErrIO, TErrIndex);
       void writeArray(const char* filename)
            throw(TErrIO);
       void readArray(const char* filename)
            throw(TErrIO);
};

Array::Array(unsigned Size)
{
  size = (Size < MIN_SIZE) ? MIN_SIZE : Size;
  badIndex = BAD_VALUE;
  dataPtr = new double[size];
}

void Array::writeElem(fstream& os, unsigned index)
  throw(TErrIO, TErrIndex)
{
    if (index < size) {
      os.write((unsigned char*)(dataPtr + index), sizeof(double));
      if(!os.good())
          throw(ErrIO);
    }
    else
      throw(ErrIndex);
}

void Array::readElem(fstream& is, unsigned index)
  throw(TErrIO, TErrIndex)
{
    if (index < size) {
      is.read((unsigned char*)(dataPtr + index), sizeof(double));
      if (!is.good())
          throw(ErrIO);
    }
    else
      throw(ErrIndex);
}

```

12

continues

Listing 12.4. continued

```
void Array::writeArray(const char* filename)
  throw(TErrIO)
{
    fstream f(filename, ios::out | ios::binary);

    if (f.fail())
      throw(ErrIO);
    f.write((unsigned char*) &size, sizeof(size));
    f.write((unsigned char*)dataPtr, size * sizeof(double));
    f.close();
    if (!f.good())
      throw(ErrIO);
}

void Array::readArray(const char* filename)
  throw(TErrIO)
{
    fstream f(filename, ios::in | ios::binary);
    unsigned sz;

    if (f.fail())
      throw(ErrIO);
    f.read((unsigned char*) &sz, sizeof(sz));
    // need to expand the array
    if (sz != size) {
      delete [] dataPtr;
      dataPtr = new double[sz];
      size = sz;
    }
    f.read((unsigned char*)dataPtr, size * sizeof(double));
    f.close();
    if (!f.good())
      throw(ErrIO);
}

main()
{
  const unsigned SIZE1 = 10;
  const unsigned SIZE2 = 20;
  char* filename1 = "array1.dat";
  char* filename2 = "array3.dat";
  int hiIndex = 10;
  Array arr1(SIZE1), arr2(SIZE1), arr3(SIZE2);
  fstream f(filename1, ios::out | ios::binary);

  // assign values to array arr1
  for (unsigned i = 0; i < arr1.getSize(); i++)
     arr1[i] = 10 * i;

```

```
   // assign values to array arr3
   for (i = 0; i < SIZE2; i++)
      arr3[i] = i;

   cout << "Array arr1 has the following values:\n";
   for (i = 0; i < arr1.getSize(); i++)
      cout << arr1[i] << "  ";
   cout << "\n\n";

   try {
      // write elements of array arr1 to the stream
      for (i = 0; i < arr1.getSize(); i++)
          arr1.writeElem(f, i);
   }
   catch(TErrIO e) {
      cout << "Bad stream output\n";
   }
   catch(TErrIndex e) {
      cout << "Error in writing element " << i << "\n";
   }
   f.close();

   // reopen the stream for input
   f.open(filename1, ios::in ¦ ios::binary);

   try {
      for (i = 0; i < arr1.getSize(); i++)
          arr2.readElem(f, i);
   }
   catch(TErrIO e) {
      cout << "Bad stream output\n";
   }
   catch(TErrIndex e) {
      cout << "Error in writing element " << i << "\n";
   }
   f.close();

   // display the elements of array arr2
   cout << "Array arr2 has the following values:\n";
   for (i = 0; i < arr2.getSize(); i++)
      cout << arr2[i] << "  ";
   cout << "\n\n";

   // display the elements of array arr3
   cout << "Array arr3 has the following values:\n";
   for (i = 0; i < arr3.getSize(); i++)
      cout << arr3[i] << "  ";
   cout << "\n\n";

   // write the array arr3 to file ARRAY3.DAT
```


continues

Listing 12.4. continued

```
   try {
      arr3.writeArray(filename2);
   }
   catch(TErrIO e) {
      cout << "Cannot write the entire array\n";
   }

   try {
      // read the array arr1 from file ARRAY3.DAT
      arr1.readArray(filename2);
   }
   catch(TErrIO e) {
      cout << "Cannot read the entire array\n";
   }

   // display the elements of array arr1
   cout << "Array arr1 now has the following values:\n";
   for (i = 0; i < arr1.getSize(); i++)
      cout << arr1[i] << "  ";
   cout << "\n\n";

   // reopen the stream for input
   f.open(filename1, ios::in | ios::binary);

   for (i = 0; i < 3; i++) {
      hiIndex *= 10;
      // attempt to read an element at index hiIndex
      try {
          arr1.readElem(f, hiIndex);
          cout << "Element at index " << hiIndex << " = "
                 << arr1[hiIndex] << "\n";
      }
      catch(TErrIndex) {
          cout << "Failed to read element at index "
               << hiIndex << "\n";
      }
   }
   f.close();
   return 0;
}
```

Here is a sample session with the program in Listing 12.4:

```
Array arr1 has the following values:
0  10  20  30  40  50  60  70  80  90

Array arr2 has the following values:
0  10  20  30  40  50  60  70  80  90
```

```
Array arr3 has the following values:
0  1  2  3  4  5  6  7  8  9  10  11  12  13  14  15  16  17  18  19

Array arr1 now has the following values:
0  1  2  3  4  5  6  7  8  9  10  11  12  13  14  15  16  17  18  19

Failed to read element at index 100
Failed to read element at index 1000
Failed to read element at index 10000
```

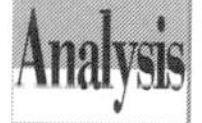

Because the program in Listing 12.4 is similar to the one in Listing 12.2, we will focus here on the differences in the code. First, you will notice that lines 12 and 15 declare the exception types `TErrIO` and `TErrIndex`. The class `TErrIO` supports file I/O exceptions. The class `TErrIndex` supports out-of-range index exceptions involved in storing or recalling an array element from a file. Both exception classes have no members, because the program only needs the name of the classes.

The class `Array` declares two new data members, `ErrIO` and `ErrIndex`, at lines 24 and 25, respectively. These data members are instances of the exception classes `TErrIO` and `TErrIndex`.

The class `Array` has different declarations for the member functions `writeElem`, `readElem`, `writeArray`, and `readArray`. First, all of these functions have the `void` return type, instead of the type `boolean`. Second, each of these member functions has a throw clause that states the kinds of exception that function can throw. The member functions `writeElem` and `readElem` can throw the `TErrIO` and `TErrIndex` exceptions. The member function `writeArray` and `readArray` can only throw the `TErrIO` exception.

The definitions of the preceding member functions are also different from those in program IO2.CPP. Let's look at member functions `writeElem` and `writeArray`—the other two are similar to these functions. The member function `writeElem` throws the member `ErrIndex` (an instance of class `TErrIndex`) at line 60, when the argument for the parameter `index` is not less than the value in the data member `size`. The function also throws the member `ErrIO` (an instance of class `TErrIO`) at line 57, when the expression `os.good()` is false.

The member function `writeArray` throws the member `ErrIO` at lines 81 and 86 when a stream I/O error is detected by the `if` statements at lines 80 and 85.

The function `main` uses several pairs of `try` and `catch` blocks to conduct various stream I/O operations. The code in most of these `try` blocks executes without a hitch. We inserted the statements at lines 195 through 211 to explicitly test the handling of generated exceptions by attempting to access an out-of-range element from the input

stream `f`. The `for` loop at line 198 performs three attempts to access an element at indices 100, 1000, and 10000—all of which are out of range. The loop uses the variable `hiIndex` to access the array element stored in the stream object `f`. Line 202 contains the call to function `readElem` that uses the out-of-range index of variable `hiIndex`. The stream input statement is inside the `try` block in lines 201 to 205. Lines 206 to 209 contain the `catch` block that handles the `TErrIndex` exception type. The block displays an error message.

Summary

Today's lesson gave you a brief introduction to the C++ stream I/O library and discussed the following topics:

- Common stream functions include `open`, `close`, `good`, `fail`, and the operator `!`. The function `open` opens a file for stream I/O and supports alternate and multiple I/O modes. The function `close` shuts down a file stream. The functions `good` and `fail` indicate the success or failure, respectively, of a stream I/O operation.
- C++ enables you to perform sequential stream I/O for text, using the operators << and >> as well as the stream function `getline`. The operator << is able to write characters and strings (as well as the other predefined data types). The operator >> is suitable for obtaining characters. The function `getline` enables your applications to read strings from the keyboard or from a text file.
- Sequential stream I/O for binary data uses the stream functions `write` and `read` to write and read data from any kind of variables.
- Random access stream I/O for binary data uses the `seekg` function in conjunction with the functions `read` and `write`. The `seekg` function enables you to move the stream pointer to either absolute or relative byte locations in the stream.
- Exception handling involves declaring exception types, declaring lists of exceptions that various function can throw, throwing the exceptions, and using the `try` and `catch` blocks to detect and manage the exceptions. The Borland C++ 4.5 compiler supports new keywords that relate to the exceptions mechanism.

Q&A

Q How can I emulate the random access of lines in a text file?

A First, read the lines in the file as text, obtain the length of the lines (plus the two characters for the end of each line), and store the cumulative length in a special array. (Call it `lineIndex`.) This array stores the byte location where each line starts. The last array element should store the size of the file. To access line number `i`, use the `seek` or `seekg` function to locate the offset value in `lineIndex[i]`. The size of line number `i` is equal to `lineIndex[i+1]-lineIndex[i]`.

Q How do I write a general-purpose routine to copy between an input and an output file stream?

A You need to use the stream function `gcount()` to obtain the number of bytes actually read in the last unformatted stream input. The following is the function `copyStream`:

```
void copyStream(fstream& fin, fstream& fout,
               unsigned char* buffer, int buffSize)
{
  int n;
  while (fin.read(buffer, buffSize) {
    n = fin.gcount();
    fout.write(buffer, n);
  }
}
```


Q Why declare data members in classes that support exceptions?

A These data members help the catch blocks to pass information related to the cause and state that lead to the exception. The simplest example is that the exception class has a string-typed data member that passes the error message text.

Q Can I include nested try and catch blocks in a catch block?

A Yes. You can implement a nested exception handler inside a `catch` block. The nested handler enables you to deal with new errors than may spring from dealing with current ones.

Workshop

The Workshop provides quiz questions to help you solidify your understanding of the material covered and exercises to provide you with experience in using what you've learned. Try to understand the quiz and exercise answers before continuing on to the next day's lesson. (Answers are provided in Appendix A, "Answers.")

Quiz

1. True or false? The stream I/O functions `read` and `write` are able to correctly read and write any data type.
2. True or false? The stream I/O functions `read` and `write` are able to correctly read and write any data type, as long as the type has no pointer members.
3. True or false? The `seek` and `seekg` functions expand the file when you supply them an index that is one byte beyond the current end of file.
4. True or false? The arguments of the functions `seek` and `seekg` require no range checking.

Exercise

Create the program IO4.CPP by modifying the program IO3.CPP. The class `VmArray` in IO4.CPP should have the function `binSearch`, which conducts a binary search on the members of the sorted array. Add a loop at the end of the function `main` to search in the array `arr`, using the unordered data of the initializing list. (The members of this list are accessed using the pointer data.)

The C++ *string* Class

WEEK 2

On Day 9, we covered strings and the functions in STRING.H that work with them. Borland C++ 4.5 provides a more powerful method of dealing with strings, the `string` class. This class conforms to the preliminary string class from the ANSI C++ committee and is prototyped in the header file CSTRING.H.

Note: ANSI is American National Standards Institute. ANSI is developing a standard for the C++ language.

C style strings are powerful but require control of many low-level items such as allocation sizes and pointer offsets. The C++ `string` class is designed to increase the power available above that of C strings, but without need for low-level concerns.

At the end of today's lesson, you will be familiar with the following:

- Benefits of the C++ `string` class
- I/O with the C++ `string` class
- Comparing strings
- Searching for "tokens"
- Controlling how string class comparisons are done
- Searching for substrings inside of larger strings
- Mixed operations with C/C++ style strings and the `string` class

Benefits of the C++ *string* Class

The programmer can design a class that inherits from the `string` class. The newly designed class can use all the power of the `string` class, as well as whatever else needs to be added.

The result is an object-oriented program design, one that is easier to write and easier to maintain. The following shows how the C++ `string` class provides solutions to C string difficulties.

C String Difficulty	C++ `string` Class Solution

C string functions have obscure names, which makes it difficult to find the function you want.	Operators such as `!=` or `=` are used when possible. When function names are used, they sound like what they do, for instance:
	`strcmp  versus  ==`
	`strcpy  versus  =`
	`strstr  versus  find`
	`strlwr  versus  to_lower`

No variable or function reports the allocated size of a C string. When copying to a string, the programmer must remember the allocated size or allocate a new string large enough to hold the string or strings that he wishes to store.	The C++ `string` class handles allocations and knows the allowed size. Operations are checked against the current size, and the allocated size is increased when necessary.
When allocating memory for a string, an additional byte must be allocated for the terminating `'\0'` character. Forgetting to do this is a common error.	String terminating characters are automatically provided.
Comparisons using C-style strings must be done with a call to a function such as `strcmp`. A frequent error is for the programmer to use logical operators such as `==` or `<` for C strings, receiving a result which tells of the relationship between the address of the strings in memory rather than of the strings themselves.	Source code to compare C++ strings can be written just as if comparing integers, because familiar comparison operators `==`, `!=`, `>=` and `>=` are provided. An explicit function call is not needed to do a comparison.

C String Difficulty	C++ `string` Class Solution
Parsing strings into words or finding substrings in C-style strings involves many lines of code with calls to functions such as `strtok`, the use of which are complicated and detail-intensive.	This work and the consequent debugging are now unnecessary. Powerful functions are in the `string` class to do such common tasks. For instance, reading the next word (token) from the keyboard, a file, or from another string is done with a call to `read_token`. It can be set to skip leading spaces or leave them in the string.
When an allocation error is made, other memory outside the string array is altered. When that memory is a critical area, it often will cause the program to crash or the computer to lock up.	Exception handling is done by the class. It traps allocation failures and errors, terminating the program safely.

The *string* Class Header File CSTRING.H

The `string` class uses three other classes. Those classes are as follows:

`TStringRef` The `string` class uses this class in reserving and managing memory. Normally the programmer need not access or use anything from this class. The string class is declared a friend within `TStringRef`. The `string` class declares `TStringRef` as a friend as well.

`TSubString` This is a class that handles the operations on substrings. Both the `string` and `TSubString` classes declare each other as friends. Many of the operations done with a `string` class actually are performed by `TSubString`.

`TReference` A base class used in copy and access operations, `TReference` is shown in the header file REF.H.

Note: All programs that use the `string` class must include the header file CSTRING.H.

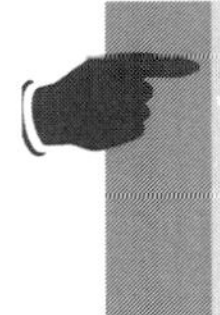

New Term: NPOS is used as a value to indicate that no position is specified. It is declared as follows:

```
const size_t NPOS = size_t(-1);
```

Constructors and Copy Constructors

What follows is a list of the public constructors for the `string` class that can be used to create a new `string` object instance:

```
string();
string( const string& s);
string( const string& s,  size_t startIndex,
        size_t numChars = NPOS);

string( const char   *cp);
string( const char   *cp, size_t startIndex,
        size_t numChars = NPOS);

string( char          c);
string( char          c,  size_t numChars);
string( signed char   c);
string( signed char   c,  size_t numChars);
string( unsigned char c);
string( unsigned char c,  size_t numChars);

string( const TSubString& ss);

string copy() const; // Note: There are other copy() functions below

string&     operator = (const string& s);
TSubString& operator = (const string& s);
```

The following constructor is only valid for Windows applications. It creates a string object that is loaded directly from the application's string resources:

```
string( HINSTANCE instance, UINT id, int numChars = 255);
```

Comparing

As stated earlier, the `string` class provides easier methods of comparison than the `strcmp` style functions. The following are the comparison operators defined by the `string` class:

```
friend int operator == ( const string& s1, const string& s2 );
friend int operator == ( const string& s,  const char   *cp );
```

13

```
friend int operator == ( const char   *cp, const string& s );
       int operator == ( const char   *cp );
       int operator == ( const string& s );

friend int operator != ( const string& s1, const string& s2 );
friend int operator != ( const string& s,  const char   *cp );
friend int operator != ( const char   *cp, const string& s );
       int operator != ( const char   *cp );
       int operator != ( const string& s );

friend int operator >  ( const string& s1, const string& s2 );
friend int operator >  ( const string& s,  const char   *cp );
friend int operator >  ( const char   *cp, const string& s );

friend int operator <  ( const string& s1, const string& s2 );
friend int operator <  ( const string& s,  const char   *cp );
friend int operator <  ( const char   *cp, const string& s );


friend int operator <= ( const string& s1, const string& s2 );
friend int operator <= ( const string& s,  const char   *cp );
friend int operator <= ( const char   *cp, const string& s );


friend int operator >= ( const string& s1, const string& s2 );
friend int operator >= ( const string& s,  const char   *cp );
friend int operator >= ( const char   *cp, const string& s );

int compare ( const string& s) const;
int compare ( const string& s, size_t startIndex,
                         size_t numChars = NPOS ) const;
```

Concatenating Strings

The `string` class provides simpler methods of concatenating strings than using the `strcat` style of functions. Several of these are implemented as operators, whereas others are implemented with the `append` member function for adding on to the end of a string and the `prepend` member function for adding on to the beginning of a string:

```
friend string operator + (  const string& s, const char *cp );

       string& operator += ( const string& s );
       string& operator += ( const char   *cp );

       string& append( const string& s );
       string& append( const string&& s, size_t startIndex,
                       size_t numChars = NPOS );

       string& prepend( const string& s );
       string& prepend( const string& s, size_t startIndex,
                        size_t numChars = NPOS )
```

```
        string& prepend( const char *cp );
        string& prepend( const char *cp, size_t startIndex,
                         size_t numChars = NPOS );
```

Inserting Characters into a String

The insert member function enables you to insert other strings into the middle of a string object:

```
string& insert( size_t startInsertAt, const string& s );
string& insert( size_t startInsertAt, const string& s,
                size_t startFrom, size_t numChars = NPOS );
```

Removing Characters from Within a String

There are two member functions for removing characters from within a string. The replace member function replaces characters in a string with the contents of another string. The strip member function removes characters from either the beginning, the ending, or both sides of a string.

```
string& replace( size_t removeFrom, size_t removeCount,
                 const string& s );
string& replace( size_t removeFrom, size_t removeCount,
                 const string& s,   size_t startReplacePosition,
                 size_t replaceCount = NPOS );

TSubString strip( StripType s = Trailing, char c = ' ' );

// Note: strip uses this enum which is defined within the class
//       enum StripType { Leading, Trailing, Both };
//
//       The programmer accesses it as one of
//         string::Leading  string::Trailing  string::Both
```

13

Addressing Individual Characters in a String

When dealing with regular C string arrays, it's possible to manipulate single characters within the string by using the array operators []. The C++ string object defines the bracket operators to perform the same function, as well as supplying parentheses operators.

Note in the following that these operators return a reference to the specified character rather than just the character itself. This means that you can assign new characters to that position in the string in the same way you would with a C string array.

In addition to the bracket and parentheses operators, get_at and put_at are provided for a more primitive method of getting and changing characters in a string object.

```
char& operator [] ( size_t index ); // Note: [] and () both
char& operator () ( size_t index ); //       do the same thing

char operator  [] ( size_t index ) const;
char operator  () ( size_t index ) const;

char get_at( size_t index ) const;
void put_at( size_t index, char c ) const;
```

Getting a Substring from Within a String

The `string` class provides methods for obtaining substrings from a string. There are two sets of these functions, ones that return results that can be modified and ones that can only be examined. For a result that can be examined, but won't be modified, see the following:

```
const TSubString operator()( size_t startIndex, size_t numChars );

const TSubString substring( const char *cp ) const;
const TSubString substring( const char *cp, size_t start ) const;
```

For a copy that can be both examined and modified, see this:

```
string substr( size_t startIndex ) const;
string substr( size_t startIndex, size_t numChars ) const;

TSubString substring( const char *cp );
TSubString substring( const char *cp, size_t startIndex );
```

Searching Within a String

One of the more useful features of the `string` class are its member functions that enable you to search the contents of a string. The basic member functions are `find_first_of`, `find_first_not_of`, `find_last_of`, and `find_last_not_of`. One of the most powerful searching functions, however, is in the overloaded parentheses operators, which allow you to supply a regular expression as the search parameter.

```
const TSubString operator()( const TRegexp& pattern ) const;
const TSubString operator()( const TRegexp& pattern,
                             size_t startIndex );

size_t find_first_of     ( const string& s ) const;
size_t find_first_of     ( const string& s, size_t startIndex ) const;
size_t find_first_not_of ( const string& s ) const;
size_t find_first_not_of ( const string& s, size_t startIndex ) const;
size_t find_last_of      ( const string& s ) const;
size_t find_last_of      ( const string& s, size_t startIndex ) const;
size_t find_last_not_of  ( const string& s ) const;
size_t find_last_not_of  ( const string& s, size_t startIndex );
```

Reading the Length

In order to get the length of a C-style string, you use the `strlen` function. The `string` class supplies the `length` member function to obtain the length of the string:

```
size_t length() const;
```

Copying to a C-Style String

Though using the `string` class is very useful, it may still be necessary to use a C-style string array from time to time. The `copy` member function copies the contents of a `string` object into a standard character array.

```
size_t copy( char *cb, size_t numChars );
size_t copy( char *cb, size_t numChars, size_t startIndex );
```

Reading and Setting Parameters for a Single String

A number of internal parameters affect how the `string` class acts. The `reserve` member function alternately sets or returns the number of characters reserved for the string; `hash` returns a hash value that can be used during sorting. The `is_null` member function can be used to inquire as to whether or not the string is empty, and `resize` can either contract or expand a string, appending spaces as necessary.

```
size_t   reserve();
void     reserve( size_t numChars );
unsigned hash() const;
int      is_null() const;
void     resize( size_t numChars );
```

13

I/O Operations

There are a number of functions for getting strings to interact with input and output streams. Some of these are member functions of the `string` class (`read_token`, `read_file`, `read_string`, `read_line`, and `read_to_delim`), whereas others are just globally declared (`operator >>`, `operator <<`, and `getline`).

```
istream& read_token( istream& is );
istream& read_file( istream& is );
istream& read_string( istream& is );
istream& read_line( istream& is );
istream& read_to_delim( istream& is, char delim = '\n' );

ostream& operator << ( ostream& os, const string& s );
istream& operator >> ( istream& is, string& s );
```

```
istream& getline( istream& is, string& s );
istream& getline( istream& is, string& s, char c ); **check**
```

Character Set Conversion

Several functions are available for manipulating such things as the case or the character set of a string. The case manipulators are `to_lower` and `to_upper`. There are two versions of these functions: member functions and globally declared functions. The globally declared functions return a copy of the converted string, whereas the member functions modify the string itself.

```
string to_lower( const string &s );
string to_upper( const string &s );

void to_lower();
void to_upper();
```

In the Windows environment, the string can be represented in either the ANSI character set or an OEM character set. The `ansi_to_oem` and `oem_to_ansi` member functions convert the string between the two sets.

```
void _RTLENTRY ansi_to_oem();
void _RTLENTRY oem_to_ansi();
```

Reading and Setting Parameters for the Whole Class

The following member functions set internal parameters that affect all `string` objects as opposed to just a particular instance. Most of the parameters affect such things as how searches are undertaken and the initial space reserved for characters when strings are created.

```
static int    set_case_sensitive ( int onOff = 1 );
static int    set_paranoid_check ( int onOff = 1 );
static int    skip_whitespace    ( int onOff = 1 );
static size_t initial_capacity   ( size_t numChars = 63 );
static size_t resize_increment   ( size_t numChars = 64 );
static size_t max_waste          ( size_t numChars = 63 );

static int    get_case_sensitive_flag();
static int    get_paranoid_check_flag();
static int    get_skip_whitespace_flag();
static size_t get_initial_capacity();
static size_t get_resize_increment();
static size_t get_max_waste();
```

Protected Items (Accessible Only in an Inherited Class)

The following member functions are declared as `protected`, which means that they can only be accessed from friends or from derived classes.

```
int  valid_element  ( size_t pos ) const;
int  valid_index    ( size_t pos ) const;

void assert_element ( size_t pos ) const;
void assert_index   ( size_t pos ) const;

string( const string& s, const char *cb );

void cow();    // Note: "cow" = "copy on write"
```

Syntax

Declaring a String

You can declare variables of `string` class type (called "instances of the class" or class instances). You can also declare pointers or references to a class instance. Any of these can be initialized in the same statement that declares the variable. A string can be declared with an optional initial value:

```
string Str1;
string Str2 = "String 2";
string Str3("String 3");
```

A string pointer or reference can also be allocated with an optional initial value:

```
string *pStr4 = new string;
string *pStr5 = new string("String 5");
string *pStr6;
string &rStr7 = * new string("String Reference");

pStr6 = new string("A New String Is Constructed");
```

`Str1`, `Str2`, and `Str3` are strings. `Str1` has not been given an initial value so it begins as an empty string (as ""). `Str2` is set to a value, but the initialization is done with an assignment statement on the same line; it also begins life as an empty string, but that is immediately changed. `Str3` takes advantage of the class constructor argument to set the initial value without the additional step of assigning it.

The `pStr4`, `pStr5`, and `pStr6` are not strings. They are pointers to strings; they each can hold the address of a string.

The `pStr4` and `pStr5` are each assigned the address of a string by a call to the function `new`. The string to which `pStr4` points is empty, and the one to which `pStr5` points contains "String 5".

13

The pStr6 begins as pointing to nothing in particular. The assignment statement creates a string with new, initializes it to the given value, and places the address into pStr6.

Bug Busters

Be careful to not use items such as pStr6 until they have been assigned a valid address. Forgetting this is a common programming mistake that can be difficult to track down. Always check that all pointers have been initialized before being used.

The rStr7 is a reference to a string. It can be thought of as a pointer to a string, which can be handled in source code as if it were a string.

When new is called to initialize pStr7, a * is placed before it. As new returns a pointer and a reference is treated as an actual string, the * indicates to use the item at the address contained in the pointer.

Reading and Comparing Strings

In C, to copy the contents of one string to another, one places the addresses of the source and destination C strings as calling arguments to the strcpy() function. The string class defines an = operator, so you need only do an assignment, just as is done with an integer.

Syntax

Assigning Strings

You can assign one string to another using the equals sign (=):

Example:

```
string string_1 = "First String";
string string_2 = "Second String";

string_2 = string_1;
```

This places the characters "First String" into string_2. The old contents of string_2 are lost.

As was the case with an assignment statement, the class provides familiar operators for use in doing comparisons. Operators such as == and < free you from calling and interpreting the results of the strcmp function used for C-style strings. For cases where you would like to save the comparison results, a strcmp-like function is available that returns the same kind of positive integer, zero, or negative integer. The name is a bit easier to remember than strcmp. It's called compare.

Syntax

Comparing Strings

Strings can be compared directly as if comparing an integer. Old-style strings can also be compared to C++ strings in this fashion.

The following comparison operators are supplied for strings:

```
==  <=  >=  <  >  !=
```

Examples:

```
char oldstyle[] = "OLD STYLE STRING";
string newstyle = "new style string";

if (oldstyle < newstyle)
  cout << "oldstyle is lower in value than newstyle" << endl;
```

The message will be displayed because capital letters have smaller values than lowercase letters. The line

```
int compare(const string &compareTo);
```

returns a positive value if the string is greater than compareTo, and a negative value if it is less. If the two strings are equal, zero is returned. Although using < > and == to compare strings is easy, compare provides a value that can be saved for use later.

Another version of the same function enables you to say at what position from the start of the string the comparison should start, and to specify a maximum number of characters to compare. Although these extra features are more specialized, it is not uncommon to need them.

```
int compare(const string& s,
            size_t startIndex, size_t numChars = NPOS);
```

The familiar cin >>, getline, and cout << syntax works well with C++ strings. Because the streams classes also handle file I/O, this works with disk files as well.

Syntax

Reading and Writing Strings

Normal iostreams functions are provided for the C++ string class. The cin, cout, and file I/O are supported.

Examples:

```
string textLine;

cin >> textLine;    // Get input from stdin.
// If "the word" is entered, textLine will become "the"

getline(cin, textLine);
// If "the word" is entered, textLine will become "the word"


ifstream inputFile;
ostream outputFile;

inputFile.open("FileName.Txt");
outputFile.open("FileName.Out");

getline(inputFile, textLine);
// textLine now contains the first line from the file

outputFile << textLine << endl;
// the string is now stored in the output disk file
```

Just as with C style strings, a C++ string can be addressed as if it were an array with an index within square brackets. You readers who have migrated from BASIC or FORTRAN may be pleased to learn that parentheses may also be used.

Examining Individual Characters

C++ strings can be accessed as arrays just as is done with C strings. Remember that the first element is `stringName[0]`. If the value contained in `stringVar` is "0123456789", then `cout << stringVar[7];` will print a 7 to the screen.

For those of you whose first love was FORTRAN or another language that uses parentheses for array subscripts, you can use them as well: `cout << stringVar(7);` would also print a 7.

This example is a small program using some of the syntax mentioned above. References are used so that the code is more readable.

Three references to string are created. The program reads strings from the keyboard and reports on how they compare. Entering a string of `end` ends the program. Because comparison defaults to being case-sensitive, a value of `END` will not end the program.

Listing 13.1 contains a program that reads and compares C++ `string` class strings.

Type

Listing 13.1. Source code for the program CSTRING1.CPP.

```
#include <iostream.h>
#include <cstring.h>

int main()
  {
  int result;

  string &s1 = * new string; // create 2 references to string
  string &s2 = * new string;
  string message;            // create an instance of a string

  while (1)     // run this loop forever
    {
    cout << "Enter two lines of text, \"end\" to end program\n";
    getline(cin, s1);    // read a line into s1 from the keyboard

    if (s1 == "end")     // If ending the program is requested
      break;             // break out of the loop

    getline(cin, s2);    // read a line into s2

    if (s2 == "end")     // If ending the program is requested
      break;             // break out of the loop

    result = s1.compare(s2); // get and save comparison result

    if (result == 0)         // save what we've found in "message"
      message = "The strings are equal";
    else if (result > 0)
      message = "The first string is greater";
    else
      message = "The second string is greater";

    cout << message << endl << endl; // report the result
    }

 delete &s1;  // References are handled in source code as if they
 delete &s2;  // were actual items. This is why the '&' operator
 return 0;           // is used to get their address for use by
 }                   // delete.
```

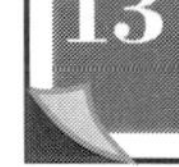

The following shows a sample session with the example program:

```
Enter two lines of text, "end" to end program
this
that
```

```
The first string is greater

Enter two lines of text, "end" to end program
that
this
The second string is greater

Enter two lines of text, "end" to end program
those
those
The strings are equal

Enter two lines of text, "end" to end program
end
```

In lines 8, 9, and 10, the string reference variables `s1`, `s2`, and the string variable `message` are declared, and instances of two of them are allocated by the call to `new`. The `*` in front of the `new` is said to "dereference the pointer." This means that it refers to the value at the address returned by `new` rather than the address itself. By using reference variables instead of pointers, the variables can be used in the following source lines without the special handling needed when using pointers.

On each of lines 15 and 20, a full line of text is read into a string. Remember that the `getline` function removes the end of line character from the input.

On line 22, a string is compared to another with only the `==` operator. With C-style strings, a call to `strcmp` would have been necessary. Line 25 uses the `string` class `compare` member function to return a value that will be tested on lines 27 and 29. Because it is done this way, the computer only examines the variable `result` instead of doing a second full-string comparison.

Assigning a new value to a string class item need not call `strcpy` or `strdup`. Lines 28, 30, and 32 show `message` being assigned a value with a simple assignment statement.

Lines 37 through 39 discard the strings that we have allocated. Although this program will end and the memory be recovered by the operating system, in a true application program memory management is of great concern, and objects that have been allocated should be discarded when they are no longer of use. The string variable `message` is not deleted because it was not created with `new`. When `main` ends, `message` will automatically be destroyed by the compiler's code.

String Search, Substitution, and File I/O

The `string` class provides powerful tools for searching within strings and substituting parts of strings (substrings). CSTRING2.CPP manipulates the text in a file, substituting alternative text for words and placing this new text in an output file. Listing 13.2 contains the source code for the program CSTRING2.CPP.

Listing 13.2. Source code for the program CSTRING2.CPP.

```
#include <fstream.h>
#include <cstring.h>

const short True = 1;
const short False = 0;

string    toFind;
string    replaceWith;
char      lineBuf[81];
ifstream  inFile;
ofstream  outFile;

short GetFindReplace()
  {
  char caseFlag;

  cout << "Enter the word to find: ";
  cin >> toFind;

  cout << endl << "Enter replacement word: ";
  cin >> replaceWith;

  while (1)
    {
    cout  << "Case sensitive [Y/N]? ";
    cin >> caseFlag;
    caseFlag = toupper(caseFlag);

    if ((caseFlag == 'Y') || (caseFlag == 'N'))
      {
      string::set_case_sensitive(caseFlag == 'Y');
      break;
      }
    }

```


continues

Listing 13.2. continued

```
  return (toFind != replaceWith) ? True : False;
  } // end GetFindReplace()

short ProcessFile()
  {
  short  findLen;      // Number of characters to find
  size_t foundPos;     // Position in string where found
  string buffer;       // Holds a line of input data from the file
  short  startPos;     // Position in string to start search
  short  replaced;     // Set to True if replacement has been done
  short  numFound = 0; // Number of replacements that were made

  inFile.open("\\BC45\\README.TXT");
  outFile.open("README.NEW");
  findLen = toFind.length();     // get # char's in string to find
  buffer.skip_whitespace(False); // don't skip leading spaces

  while (inFile)                 // while data left in input file
    {
    getline(inFile, buffer);     // read one line
    replaced = False;            // init flag and position
    startPos = 0;

    do
      {
      foundPos = buffer.find(toFind, startPos);

      if (foundPos != NPOS)      // if a match is found
        {
        buffer.replace(foundPos, findLen, replaceWith);
        ++numFound;
        replaced = True;
        startPos = foundPos + replaceWith.length();
        }
      } while (foundPos != NPOS);

    outFile << buffer << endl;   // copy line to the output file

    if (replaced)
      cout << buffer << endl;    // show modified lines on screen
    }

  inFile.close();
  outFile.close();
  cout << endl;
  return numFound;
  } // end ProcessFile()
```

```
84: int main()
85:   {
86:   if (GetFindReplace())
87:     cout << ProcessFile() << " words were replaced\n";
88:   else
89:     cout << "Error: Find and Replace words are the same\n";
90:
91:   return 0;
92:   }
```

The following is an example session with the CSTRING2 application:

```
Enter the word to find: important

Enter replacement word: unimportant
Case sensitive [Y/N]? y
  This README file contains unimportant information about
  Borland C++.

1 words were replaced
```

This program uses the C++ string class to take the README.TXT file, which came with Borland C++ 4.5, and to create a new file, README.NEW, in which it has substituted some words. When run, it asks for the word to find, the word to replace it, and whether the search is to be case-sensitive.

Constants are declared for `True` and `False` to make the program more readable.

Note: Windows declares `#define` macros for `TRUE` and `FALSE` in its header file WINDOWS.H. If you declare constants with these names, they will be replaced with 1 and 0 respectively and could generate an error. `True` and `False` are used here instead of `TRUE` and `FALSE` to avoid this.

The main program is small. It calls `GetFindReplace` on line 86, and if the user's input is valid calls `ProcessFile` on line 87, printing out the number of changes that were made. If the find and replace words are the same, no substitutions would be made, so `GetFindReplace` returns `False`, the program prints an error message, and ends.

`GetFindReplace`, starting on line 13, uses two instances of the C++ `string` class, `toFind` and `replaceWith`. The `string` class provides overloaded `input` >> and `output` >> operators, so values to and from the console are handled on lines 18 and 21 just as is done with C-style strings. On line 31, the case-sensitive flag for the string class is adjusted to control what kind of comparisons are to be made. In line 36, the function returns True if the two words compare differently.

Syntax

Case Sensitivity

The following is a member function of the `string` class. It sets how comparisons will be done.

```
static string::set_case_sensitive(int tf = 1);
```

The calling argument defaults to true. If called with a 0 or false value, this causes all comparisons to ignore uppercase versus lowercase.

Example:

```
string s1("THIS IS A STRING")
string s2("this is a string")

string::set_case_sensitive(0);

if (s1 == s2)
  cout << "the strings are equal\n"; /* this is printed */

string::set_case_sensitive();

if (s1 != s2)
  cout << "the strings are not equal\n"; /* this is printed */
```

Note: There is only one case-sensitive flag for the entire string class. When you change it, *all* instances of the class will have their style of comparisons changed.

If `GetFindReplace` returns `True`, then on line 87 `main` calls `ProcessFile` and prints the returned count of replaced words. That function opens the README.TXT file in the \BC45 directory and creates a README.NEW file in the current directory to receive the program output. On line 50, the `ProcessFile` function uses the `length` member function to have `toFind` report how many characters long the string is.

Sams Learning Center SAMS PUBLISHING

Syntax

Number of Characters in a String

Each `string` class variable has a member function called `length` that reports the length of the string in characters. The return value is an `unsigned`. The name `size_t` is defined by the language standards groups, so that it can be set to whatever is appropriate for the current machine. With Borland C++ 4.5, `size_t` is defined as an `unsigned`. The `stringVar.length();` returns the same value as `strlen(stringVar.c_str());`.

The loop that starts on line 53 and ends on line 76 is where the real work of `ProcessFile` is done. With each pass through the loop, a line of text is read from the input file into the string variable `buffer` (line 55).

Because the string class skip-whitespace flag was cleared on line 51, leading spaces are preserved. The variable `replaced` acts as a detector to remember if any words have been replaced on a line and is set to `False`. The `startPos` is the starting position for searching the line, and is set to the beginning of the line (to zero).

Syntax

Searching Within a String

The following `string` member functions search for a match with the `toFind` string. The return value is the index of where the match occurred, or `NPOS` if no match is found.

```
size_t find(const string &toFind);
size_t find(const string &toFind, size_t startAt);
```

The second version of the function specifies that, instead of beginning at the start of the string, the search will begin at position `startAt` in the string. Remember that the first character of an array in C or C++ is array index zero. Because of that, if `startAt` were 2, then the third character is where the search would begin.

13

The `do-while` loop from lines 59 through 70 processes a single line of text from the input file. Starting in character position `startPos`, it searches the string for a match with the `toFind` string. If successful, the `find` function returns the starting character position in `buffer` of the matching characters. In line 63, the position found is compared against the predefined symbol `NPOS`, whose value is used to indicate no position in the string matches the search string.

Lines 64 through 69 only execute if a match is found. The call to `replace` causes `findLen` characters beginning at position `foundPos` to be deleted and the contents of the string `replaceWith` to be inserted in their place.

Syntax

String Class I/O

The getline member functions using the C++ string class are declared for input and output file streams. The >> and << input and output operators are also provided for file operations with this class:

```
istream &getline(istream &is, string &s);
ostream &getline(istream &is, string &s);
operators >> and <<
```

Syntax

Controlling Whether Spaces are Skipped

The following two functions enable you to modify the skip-whitespace flag internal to the string class:

```
static int skip_whitespace(int skip = 1);
static int get_skip_whitespace_flag();
```

The skip_whitespace determines if whitespace will be skipped during read operations. The default value is to skip spaces and tabs on input operations such as getline, >>, and read_token. By calling get_skip_whitespace, you can read what the current setting of the flag is.

Example:

```
string   myString;
ifstream myFile("\\BC45\\DOC\\UTILS.TXT");

myString.skip_whitespace(0);
getline(myFile, myString);
```

The string myString will contain "   UTILS.TXT"

The string myString would have been "UTILS.TXT" had skip_whitespace not been called. There is only one whitespace setting for the entire string class. Any call to skip_whitespace changes the setting for all.

Syntax

Changing Part of a C++ String

The replace function, a member function of the C++ string class, is overloaded to have two forms:

```
string &replace(size_t       startPos,
                size_t       deleteLen,
                const string &replaceWith);
```

```
string &replace(size_t        startPos,
                size_t        deleteLength,
                const string &replaceWith,
                size_t        replaceFrom,
                size_t        replaceLength);
```

The first form will search the string, starting at the index given in `startPos`, until it finds a match to the string `replaceWith`. It will then delete `deleteLen` characters from the string, and insert the characters from `replaceWith` in that position.

If the string to be modified is too short to remove the requested number of characters, then the characters from `startPos` to the end of the string are removed.

The second form adds two additional arguments, `replaceFrom` and `replaceLength`. The `replaceLength` indicates how many characters from the replacement string will be inserted into the modified one.

For instance, `"Steven Smith"` could be searched for and `"Steven"` replaced with `"George"` from the string `"George Jones"`.

The `replaceFrom` argument specifies the starting position in the replacement string to begin in substituting characters. If there are no `replaceLength` characters in the replacement string, the number found in the string is used.

The `replaceLength` can be given the value `NPOS` and will use all remaining characters in the string if that value is given.

For instance, the following two lines perform the same function:

```
replace(startPos, deleteLen, replaceWith, 0, NPOS);
replace(startPos, deleteLen, replaceWith);
```

Line 72 executes independently of having done any replacements and writes the possibly altered string to the new file. Lines 74 and 75 detect whether any replacements have been done and, if so, writes the changed string to the console.

Lines 78 through 81 perform the clean-up actions of closing files and returning the number of replacements that have been made.

There are more useful functions in the `string` class.

Other C++ *string* Class Functions

The following `append` member function adds characters to the end of a string:

```
?string &append(const string &fromStr);
```

This places the characters from `fromStr` to the end of the string.

Example:

```
string firstString("ABC");
string secondString("DEF");

firstString.append(secondString); // firstString is now "ABCDEF"
```

Note that another way to append characters to the end of a string is to use the `+=` operator. The same appending operations could have been done with the following:

```
firstString += secondString;
```

Often it will be necessary to just pass a `string` object as if it were a C-style string array. The `string` class provides the `c_str` member function, which simply returns a `const char*` to a C-style version of the string.

The `contains` member function is used to determine whether or not a particular substring can be found in a `string` object:

```
int contains(const char *cStyleStr);
```

The member function returns either 1 or 0 if `cStyleStr` is or is not found in the string.

Once you've determined that a substring exists within a `string` object, it can be useful to determine where in that string the substring can be found. This is done with the `find_first_of` function:

```
size_t find_first_of(const string &s);
size_t find_first_of(const string &s, size_t startAt);
```

These return the position of the first character found in the string, which is one of the characters in the string `s` passed to the function. The second overloaded form starts the search at `startAt`. If nothing is found, these return `NPOS`.

In addition to finding the first position in a string at which another string begins, it is also possible to find the first position which isn't a part of another string. This is done with the `find_first_not_of` member function:

```
xsize_t find_first_not_of(const string &s);
size_t find_first_not_of(const string &s, size_t startAt);
```

These return the first character *not* in the calling argument or `NPOS` if nothing is found.

The `find_last_of` and `find_last_not_of` member functions are very similar to their `find_first` equivalents, only they search starting at the end of the string and work backward.

```
size_t find_last_of(const string &s);
size_t find_last_of(const string &s, size_t startAt);
size_t find_last_not_of(const string &s);
size_t find_last_not_of(const string &s, size_t startAt);
```

These are called in exactly the same manner as the corresponding `find_first` type functions, and they return the same type of information, except that they work backward.

When you want to delete characters from a string, you use the `remove` member function.

```
string &remove(size_t startAt);
string &remove(size_t startAt, size_t howMany);
```

These delete `howMany` characters from a string starting at position `startAt`. The version with only one argument removes all the remaining characters in the string. The `stringVar.remove(4);` statement is the same as `stringVar[4] = '\0';`.

Summary

This chapter presented the C++ string class. This class handles allocation and manipulation of strings without need for the low-level issues necessary when working with C-style strings.

When declaring a string variable, the initial value can be placed in parentheses immediately after (as in `string myStr("Init Value");`). When you assign a new value to it, any necessary size adjustment is handled for you.

Simple comparison operators can be used with this class. There is no need to call functions such as `strcmp` or `strncmp`.

Q&A

Q Can I get the value of a character in a string the way I can do it in C?

A Yes, and in the same way. If `strC` is a C-style array and `strCpp` is a C++ string class and both are set to `"ABC"`, then both `strC[1]` and `strCpp[1]` are equal to the character `'B'`.

Q What happens if I assign a `char` to a string index that is beyond the end of an array?

A In C, when you write to a character that is past the end of an array, the character is stored in the position where it would have been, had the array been large enough. If that memory contains critical information, then the computer could lock up, but only after it has run further, destroying the symptoms of where the problem occurred.

With a C++ string when you write past the end of the array, the over-write is detected and the exception handling system is called. If running a DOS program, the program ends with an "Abnormal program termination" error. If you were stepping through the program with Turbo Debugger, the error would be displayed at the line where it occurred, not somewhere else.

Q What happens if I copy to a string and the size is larger than has been allocated?

A The C++ string class detects that and expands the array to fit. Were you using C-style strings, a DOS Abnormal Termination would be presented or an equivalent complaint would be shown by Windows. If debugging, Turbo Debugger would stop at the line where the problem occurred, telling you of the problem.

Q I found a function that operates on C-style strings and that does what I want. How can I use it with C++ string class items?

A Use the `c_str` function. For instance, if `strCpp` is a C++ string, then `strlen(strCpp.c_str());` will find the length of the string.

Workshop

The Workshop provides quiz questions to help you solidify your understanding of the material covered and exercises to provide you with experience in using what you've learned. Try to understand the quiz and exercise answers before continuing on to the next day's lesson. (Answers are provided in Appendix A, "Answers.")

Quiz

1. What header file must be included to use the C++ string class?
2. How is a C++ string class variable declared?

3. How do you compare a string to a C-style string?
4. What string class function will find and replace text in one call?
5. To read the second character in a string, what array index is used?
6. Declare a string named `myString` with an initial value of "12".
7. Assuming that you have two string class variables, `s1` and `s2`, and that `s1` contains "11" and that `s2` contains "2112", what is the result of the following code lines?
   a. `s1 + s2;`
   b. `s2.contains(s1);`
   c. `s1 > s2`
   d. `s2.find(s1, 0);`

Exercises

1. Write a line of code that declares a C-style string of value "12", and another that declares a C++ string class variable with the same value.
2. Write a function that accepts a reference to a string as its calling argument and writes that string to the computer screen.
3. Modify the function written for Exercise 2 to perform a loop, writing all the characters from the string, one per pass through the loop, and to return the size of the string.
4. Write a line of code that uses the function `strrev`, which reverses the characters in a C-style string, to reverse the characters contained in a C++ string class variable.

   Hint: If `myCStr` is a C-style string, `strrev(myCStr);` would do this.

Programming Windows with OWL 2.5

WEEK
2

ObjectWindows version 2.5 (or OWL 2.5) is included with Borland C++ 4.5. It is a C++ library that shortens the time and effort needed to develop a Windows program. OWL uses a feature of the C++ language called templates. Today, you will learn about the following:

- Templates
- OWL and basic Windows issues
- Hungarian notation
- The basic structure of OWL
- Windows messages and OWL
- Developing a real OWL program, complete with resources, menus, screen writing

Templates

It's common for a language to have many functions that do the same thing, but for different data types. Wouldn't it be nice if you could tell the compiler, "Here's what I want to do; you figure out how to do it"? C++ has a feature that can do this. It's called a template.

Note: AT&T, the original developers of C++, originally added templates to version 2.0 of the C++ specification. That specification is currently at version 3.0 and this is the version used by Borland C++ 4.5.

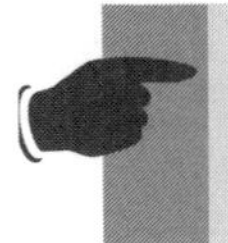

New Term: A *template* is a method for telling the compiler the algorithm to use for performing a function.

The compiler handles the details of the function for whatever data type is used. Both global functions and classes can be programmed as templates.

When programming a template, you provide a name to use as the symbol for the unknown data type and write the code using that symbol.

Here is a function defined as a template:

```
// return the lowest of 3 values
template <class T> const T& Low(const T& a, const T& b, const T& c)
  {
  if (a < b)
    {
    if (a < c)
        return a;
    }
  else if (b < c)
    return b;
  return c;
  }
```

The first line of the function is what identifies it as a template. (See Figure 14.1.)

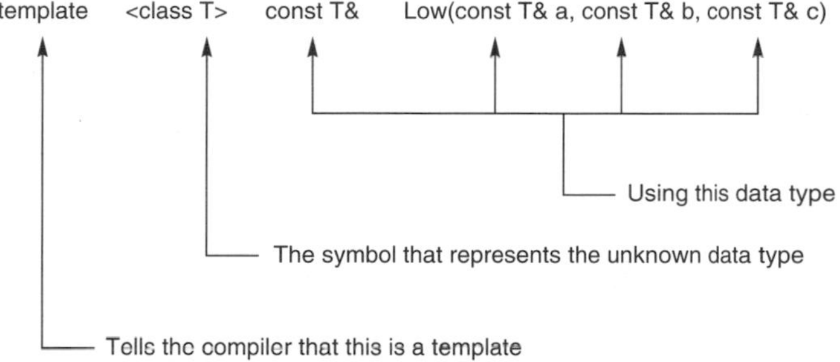

Figure 14.1. *A template function's declaration.*

The word `template` in the function definition is followed by the characters `<class`, then a symbol to use for the type that this is a template for, and then by a `>`. Although a single character is most often used for the symbol, it can be any legal C++ name.

This template function is used as any other function would be. For instance, this returns the lowest of three C++ string items.

```
string s1("6543");
string s2("5432");
string s3("4321"),
cout << Low(s1, s2, s3) << endl;
```

Although use of the word `class` is required when defining a template, templates are not limited to having classes as arguments. They can be used as fundamental data types also. For instance, `Low(1, 2, 3);` uses integers and is a valid call of the `Low` function.

A class can be defined in terms of templates. The syntax for doing this is the same as with the preceding function, but some changes are required when declaring instances of the class, as follows:

```
template <class TypeSymbol> class ArrayType
   {
protected:
   TypeSymbol *items;
   int        numItems;
public:
   ArrayType(const TypeSymbol& firstItem);
   ~ArrayType();
   int AddItem(TypeSymbol& toAdd);
   TypeSymbol& operator [] (int index);
   }
ArrayType<int> iArray(1);
```

When you declare an instance of this class, the compiler must know what data type is to be used with this class. The declaration for `iArray` shows this, as the angle brackets enclose the type to use, as follows:

```
ArrayType<int> iArray(1);
```

Listing 14.1 is an example of using templates. It implements a template class that can hold up to five items, gives them values, and prints them to the screen. Versions of the class are used for float and integer types. It also uses a template function that is not in a class. That function reports the size of the data type.

Listing 14.1. An example that uses templates.

```
#include <iostream.h>


const int True = 1;
const int False = 0;


template <class X> class ArrayType
   {
protected:
  int maxItems; // maximum number of items this will hold
  int numItems; // number of items it is holding now
  X  *items;    // array of items

public:
  ArrayType(int capacity);
  ~ArrayType()       { delete [] items; }

  int InRange(int n) { return((n >= 0) && (n < numItems)); }
```

```
  int Capacity()     { return maxItems; }
  int AddItem(X& toAdd);
  X& operator [] (int index) { return items[index]; }
  }


template <class X> ArrayType<X>::ArrayType(int capacity)
  {
  maxItems = capacity;
  items = new X[capacity];
  numItems = 0;
  } // end ArrayType::ArrayType()


template <class a> int ArrayType<a>::AddItem(a& toAdd)
  {
  if (numItems < maxItems)
    {
    items[numItems++] = toAdd;
    return True;
    }

  return False;
  } // end ArrayType::AddItem()


template <class SomeType> size_t Size(const SomeType&)
  {
  return sizeof(SomeType);
  } // end Size()


template <class D, class X> void Report(const char *s, D& d, X& x)
  {
  cout << endl << s << "has space for " << d.Capacity()
       << " items.  Each item uses " << Size(x) << " bytes.\n";

  for (int i = 0; d.InRange(i); i++)
    cout << "\t" << s << "[" << i << "] " << d[i] << endl;
  } // end Report()


int main()
  {
  int               iVal;
  float             fVal;
  ArrayType <int>   iArray(3);
  ArrayType <float> fArray(5);

```


continues

Listing 14.1. continued

```
69:   for (iVal = 0, fVal = 0.0; iVal < 10; ++iVal, fVal += 1.11)
70:     {
71:     iArray.AddItem(iVal);
72:     fArray.AddItem(fVal);
73:     }
74:
75:   Report("iArray: ", iArray, iArray[0]);
76:   Report("fArray: ", fArray, fArray[0]);
77:
78:   return 0;
79:   }
```

When you run this example, the results are as follows:

```
iArray: has space for 3 items. Each item uses 2 bytes.
        iArray: [0] 0
        iArray: [1] 1
        iArray: [2] 2

fArray: has space for 5 items. Each item uses 4 bytes.
        fArray: [0] 0
        fArray: [1] 1.11
        fArray: [2] 2.22
        fArray: [3] 3.33
        fArray: [4] 4.44
```

Beginning with line 8, the template class is defined. The symbol `X` is declared to be used for the type and is used within the body of the definition wherever the type name is needed.

The `X` is only valid within the block to which the `template` word refers. It is not related to what is used in other blocks. In line 34, a is used as the symbol for the type, and although the `AddItem()` function with which it is used is a member of the `ArrayType` class that uses an `X` in its template, there is no confusion. The compiler is content to use a for the function block.

The inline functions `InRange()`, `Capacity()`, operator `[]`, and `~ArrayType()` don't need a separate `template` word applied to them, because they are contained in the same one that is used for the class.

Both `ArrayType()` (line 26) and `AddItem()` (line 34) need `template` in their definition, because the lines of code for them are not located within the class and are not covered by the class use of the word `template`.

Line 46 has a template function that is neither a class nor a class member. The syntax of C++ still requires the word `class` in the function header. `SomeType` is used as the type symbol, but `X` or any other valid C++ name would have worked as well. The calling argument to `Size()` is described as a type without a variable name applied to it. Unlike C, C++ does not require that a variable name be placed there; the `Size()` function only needs to know the type, not an actual variable.

The function `Report()` (line 52) has an interesting variation on the template system. Two dummy type names are provided, and both types are used by the function. When called from lines 75 and 76, the function makes calls to `Capacity()` and `InRange()`. If the data type for the `d` calling argument in `Report()` did not have functions with those names, an error would be generated.

The `main()` function is in line 62. In lines 66 and 67 it declares two instances of `ArrayType`, one that will hold up to three items of type `int` and one that will hold up to three items of type `float`.

Between lines 69 and 73, the items in the two classes are initialized. Ten initializations are done for each, relying on the `AddItem()` function to detect and ignore initializations following those that have already filled the class to capacity.

Lines 75 and 76 call the `Report()` function to tell some things about the classes. `Report()` uses the `Capacity()` member function of the class to print the maximum number of items it can hold. It also calls `Size()` (line 55) to show the number of bytes used for each member.

Lines 57 through 59 then perform a `for` loop to display the data members of each class, stopping when the `InRange()` function returns False.

This example is a bit contrived in order to illustrate using templates. For a strong container class that you can use for general arrays, the `TArrayAsVector` class (which is part of the Borland C++ 4.5 class library) is a better choice.

OWL and Windows Issues

Although using OWL means that you need not worry about many of the details of Windows, you still need some knowledge of how Windows does things and especially of some of the symbols used in Windows programs.

Under DOS, there can only be one program running at a time (with the exception of TSR programs, such as Print). That program owns the screen, keyboard, and mouse. Under Windows, several programs can be running at a time, and normally each one has screen, keyboard and mouse I/O capability. To force these programs to cooperate, Windows enforces strict conditions on program structure, handling each task almost as if it were a function in a larger application of which Windows itself is the main program.

Windows administers a communication channel called the message loop, which acts as a type of "party line" by which it communicates to all the executing tasks. When a task writes to the screen or the user provides some keyboard or mouse input, Windows gathers up the information and calls a function in whichever task it has decided should receive the appropriate message.

The complexity of having independently executing functions for each of your program's screen windows, along with a main program that never calls any of them directly, is what OWL addresses. The problem is that no interface library can totally hide what is underneath. Windows uses an extensive set of macros that substitute for data types and other items. Table 14.1 is a list of some of the more important ones. You might want to put a bookmark on this page so that you can refer back to it.

Table 14.1. Some common Windows MACRO names.

Macro	Meaning	Equivalent
`TRUE`	Used for function return values	1
`FALSE`	Used for function return values	0
`NULL`	A null pointer, as in the C language	0
`UINT`	An unsigned 16-bit integer value	`unsigned int`
`BYTE`	An unsigned 8-bit value	`unsigned char`
`WORD`	An unsigned 16-bit value	`unsigned short`
`DWORD`	An unsigned 32-bit value	`unsigned long`
`LONG`	A signed 32-bit value	`long`
`VOID`	As a function return, it means that it returns nothing; as a pointer, it means that the data type it points to is not specified	`void`
`LPSTR`	Long pointer to a string	`char far *`

Type	Meaning	Equivalent
`HANDLE`	A generic handle to some form of Windows item	
`HWND`	A handle to a window	
`PASCAL`	Specifies that the function it applies to uses a calling method common in Windows	
`WPARAM`	A word parameter, used to define a data type as a calling argument to a function; defined as a `UINT`	
`LPARAM`	A long parameter, used to define a data type as a calling argument to a function; defined as a `LONG LRESULT`, used to define the data type a function returns	
`HINSTANCE`	Handle to the instance or copy of the program that is currently running	

Hungarian Notation

Microsoft has been developing Windows since the early 1980s. At its inception, the ANSI standard for C compilers did not exist and type-checking was minimal. Microsoft programmers adopted a naming convention for variables that had the data type indicated as the first few characters of the variable name. It was called "Hungarian notation," because its inventor was from Hungary.

With the introduction of the ANSI C standard with its stronger type checking, and especially with C++, a strongly typed language, Hungarian notation is no longer needed; still, it is not uncommon.

In a variable name such as `lpszFilename`, the `lpsz` means long pointer to zero-terminated string. Many programmers feel confident that they would know a variable called `Filename` is a string without having to add `lpsz` to the name. However, because Windows documentation uses Hungarian notation, it is important to have some feel for what the leading characters in the names are. Nonetheless, your program will run as well without them as with them.

The Basic Structure of OWL

OWL has groups of classes, each of which addresses a certain phase of Windows programming. The structure uses multiple inheritance to allow classes to encapsulate those combinations of functionality they need.

Event Handling, *TEventHandler*

The programmer does little with this directly. The functions it provides are available in many of the other program groups because of C++ inheritance. It manages the messages that constantly flow in a Windows program.

Streamable or Persistent Objects, *TStreamableBase*

This is actually part of the regular class library and not an OWL class. It allows a class to be viewed as a stream and saved to memory or disk for later use in the current run of the program, or at another time that the program is run. This is exotic for small programs but is of great value in more advanced programs, such as those using the document-view architecture.

Module Management—*TModule* and *TApplication*

`TModule` and `TApplication` are in the module management group. `TModule` is responsible for loading and unloading DLLs, while `TApplication` is responsible for initializing the program, managing it while it runs, and handling the tasks that are needed when the program ends.

Window Management, *TWindow*

`TWindow` is the base window class and inherits from `TEventHandler` and `TStreamableBase`. There are various kinds of windows that you might want to use in your program, and they all build on `TWindow`.

- `TFrameWindow` is a simple framed window with menu capability.
- `TDecoratedFrame` adds abilities to use other items, such as status bars and tool bars.

- TMDIFrame, TMDIChild and TDecoratedMDIFrame are Multiple Document Interface (MDI) classes used to present multiple windows in a single application.

Other functional groups are provided for the graphics, menu handling, dialog boxes, printing, and exception handling.

A Sample OWL Program

Our first OWL program only displays a window with a title. You have to press Alt+F4 or click the system menu and select Close to end it.

This program has two elements: a class to manage the window and a class to manage the application.

A class called MainApp is derived from TApplication, the class that manages the startup, the continuing message handling, and the ending tasks. TApplication has a virtual function called InitMainWindow(). In MainApp we overload that function and provide our own. Within the function, we make a call setting the main window to a frame window with our window title.

Windows applications do not normally start with a function called main(). Instead they use a function that is declared as follows:

```
int PASCAL WinMain(HINSTANCE hInstance, HINSTANCE hPrevInstance,
LPSTR lpszCmdLine, int cmdShow);
```

OWL allows a main() function similar to what you're used to with other C and C++ programs, as follows:

```
int OwlMain(int argc, char *argv[]);
```

For those with a taste for antacids, WinMain() can be used instead of OwlMain() in an OWL program.

Note: On the first day, when EasyWin was described, it was mentioned that when a so-called real Window program was created, the EasyWin flag needed to be turned off in the IDE's option screens. Since OWL applications are considered real Windows, you will need to access the IDE's TargetExpert by clicking the right mouse button and selecting the option from the pop-up menu. A dialog box will appear with a list box titled Target Type. You need to select the Application [.exe] item in this list box and then click the OK button.

Listing 14.2. FIRST.CPP, a first OWL program.

```
1:  #include <owl\framewin.h>
2:  #include <owl\applicat.h>
3:
4:  class MainApp : public TApplication
5:     {
6:  public:
7:     MainApp() : TApplication() {}
8:     void InitMainWindow();       // overload TApplication function
9:     };
10:
11: void MainApp::InitMainWindow()
12:    {
13:    SetMainWindow(new TFrameWindow(0, "First OWL Program"));
14:    }
15:
16: int OwlMain(int, char **)
17:    {
18:    return MainApp().Run();
19:    }
```

Figure 14.2 shows what the first OWL program does.

Figure 14.2. *The minimalist OWL program.*

`OwlMain` begins in line 16. It calls the `Run()` function, and OWL's default processing does the rest. (`Run()` is a function within `TApplication`.)

The "magic" of how this operates is hidden in how the classes are set up. `MainApp` calls the constructor for `TApplication` on line 7, inside of its own constructor. That triggers default processing for all maintenance functions except the `InitMainWindow()` function, which we have overloaded by declaring a member function of the same name in line 8.

In line 13, the `InitMainWindow()` function calls `SetMainWindow()` to allocate a `TFrameWindow` and link the application with this window object. The same line allocates the `TFrameWindow` by calling `new` for it and passes the window caption to it in the constructor call.

The two header files that are included are for `TFrameWindow` (framewin.H) and `TApplication` (applicat.H). A Windows program should have a .DEF file to tell the linker what to do with the segments and stack. Borland C++ supplies one for us, \BC45\LIB\DEFAULT.DEF, and that was used for this program. It should be added to the list in your project file.

Windows Messages and OWL

The Windows system calls the function in your program that it has logged as the handling function for an open window. Several calling arguments are passed to the function, one of which is called the message. The other calling parameters are `WPARAM` and an `LPARAM`. What they mean varies depending upon what the message was.

Messages are all named with `#define` macros. Two of the more common ones are:

> `WM_CHAR`, which reports a normal key is pressed. `WPARAM` argument contains the value of the key. `LPARAM` argument contains the number of time it has been pressed in the lower 16 bits, and has an array of bit flags in the upper 16 bits to indicate other data about the keyboard.
>
> `WM_SIZE`, which says window size has changed. `WPARAM` argument contains a value defining the type of size change, minimized into an icon for instance. `LPARAM` argument has the new width in the lower 16 bits and the new height in the upper 16 bits.

OWL provides two macros and an array of functions that know about Windows messages. When an event occurs for which Windows calls the OWL window procedure, OWL parses the information from the calling arguments and calls any function you may have provided to handle that event. You know the name to use for the function because it is derived from the name of the message, for instance:

Windows Message	Event-handler Function Name
`WM_CHAR`	`void EvChar(UINT key, UINT repeat, UINT flags);`
`WM_SIZE`	`void EvSize(UINT sizeType, TSize& newSize);` `TSize` is a structure with an `x` and a `y` member called `cx` and `cy`, respectively. It holds the new dimensions of the window.

In the OWL handlers, the other calling parameters are said to be "cracked"—broken down into more easily understood parameters and not buried into the middle of a parameter value. The cracking of messages avoids many common code bugs. OWL's handling of the repetitive overhead needed by each message avoids many more bugs.

The way you tell OWL that you have supplied an event handler is done with two macros and a declaration. Within your class derived from `TWindow`, you declare the function itself. Also within the class definition, you place a macro to tell it that the overloading of functions is being done. In a typical class definition, those lines would look like this:

```
class BaseWindow : public TWindow
  {
protected:
  void EvChar(UINT key, UINT repeatCount, UINT flags);
    :
public:
    :
  DECLARE_RESPONSE_TABLE(BaseWindow);
  };
```

Later in the code, you define the response table with one entry for each function that you need, for instance:

```
DEFINE_RESPONSE_TABLE1(BaseWindow, TWindow)
  EV_WM_CHAR,
  EV_WM_SIZE,
END_RESPONSE_TABLE;
```

The macro used here is `DEFINE_RESPONSE_TABLE1` because there is only one immediate class from which `BaseWindow` inherits. Were there to be two classes, then `DEFINE_RESPONSE_TABLE2` would be used and the second class would also be listed as an argument to the macro. Macros are available for up to three inherited classes.

The Windows message name has `EV_` placed in front of it to help in the macro parsing, but otherwise it is the same name as the message.

A helpful feature of the Borland C++ IDE is that if the cursor is placed on a name such as `EvChar` and Ctrl+F1 is pressed, the online Help will display the function, its calling arguments, and an explanation of what each argument means.

A Real OWL Program: Resources, Menus, Screen Writing

A demo that only puts a window on the screen is not very useful. Menus and screen writing have been added to our next example. It demonstrates techniques for handling normal Windows messages and messages from menus.

Menus are a feature that you can add to a window. The Windows system runs them for you, returning a number corresponding to the user selection. The message that Windows sends in response to a menu selection is `WM_COMMAND`, with the `WPARAM` parameter set to the value of the selected item. Because the selections in a menu that we create would not be part of the operating system, OWL has no built-in detection for them. What it does have is an `EV_COMMAND` macro that enables us to specify response functions for nonstandard events.

There are three source files involved in adding a menu to an application. The source file for the program is involved, but we also need a resource file.

Resources are predefined items that will be added to the executable as a last step. As the program is already compiled and linked when they are added, this arrangement enables resources to be more easily changed—a great advantage when changing a menu from English to German, for instance. Because a resource file normally has the file extension .RC, they are often called RC files.

The third file involved is a header file listing the macros used for menu selections, along with their number equivalents. By including the same header file in the source code and the RC file, any changes in the selection numbers will track through to the C++ compilation as well as to the resource compiler's handling of the RC file. As you did with DEFAULT.DEF, add the name REAL.RC to the IDE project file list. Listing 14.3 shows a resource file.

Type

Listing 14.3. REAL.RC, a resource file.

```
#include "real.rh"

MENU_1 MENU
  {
  POPUP "&File"
    {
```

continues

Listing 14.3. continued

```
7:        MENUITEM "&Clear", CM_CLEAR
8:        MENUITEM "E&xit",  CM_FILEEXIT
9:        }
10:
11:     MENUITEM "&About",  CM_ABOUT
12:     }
```

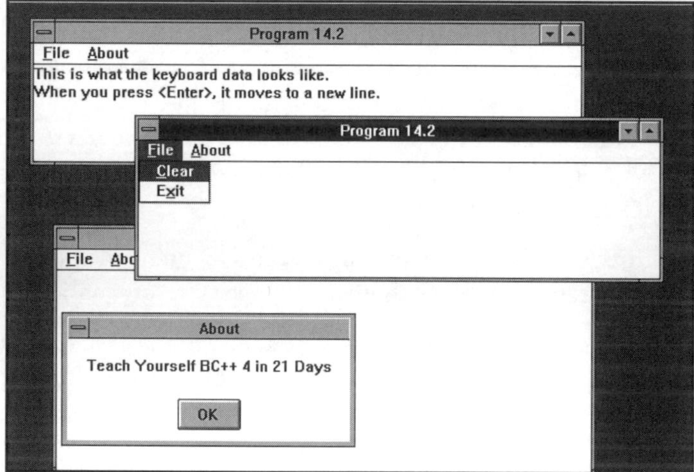

Figure 14.3. *From REAL.RC, a resource file.*

Later you will use Resource Workshop to create RC files containing menus and other items. For now, there is little value in using that tool unless you have some feel for what is being created with it, so this text file is what we will use instead.

On line 3, the `MENU_1` item is not referenced in the header file or the source file. With the available information, the resource compiler will make it a text string. We take advantage of this name string in the program when we load a menu identified as "MENU_1".

Line 5 starts defining a pop-up menu. A pop-up is a menu that when selected opens to display more menu selections. It does not return a value, although the newly shown selections often do. The pop-up first item in the menu is given the name "&File". The '&' character flags the 'F' as special. In the menu it will be shown underlined, and pressing Alt+F will cause it to be selected.

The pop-up contains two menu items on lines 7 and 8. A menu item does return a value to the program. In this case the displayed names for the menu items are "Clear" and "Exit," with the 'C' and 'x' underlined. Alt+C and Alt+X can be used to select these items when the pop-up is opened. If Clear is selected, `CM_CLEAR` is returned. The following header file assigns the number 1125 to `CM_CLEAR`, but the program doesn't care what that number is. All it cares about is if it receives a message with the `WPARAM` set equal to whatever the macro `CM_CLEAR` stands for.

On line 9, the curly brace after "E&xit" ends the pop-up. Following that on line 10 is another menu item selection for About. If selected, the value `CM_ABOUT` will be sent to the program, which will display an About box that tells the name of the program.

When the program is running, OWL doesn't have any knowledge of what the `CM_CLEAR`, `CM_FILEEXIT` or `CM_ABOUT` values accompanying a `WM_COMMAND` message are, so it ignores them. We can change this with additions to the response table, which tells OWL what to do with those messages.

Along with predefined messages such as `WM_SIZE` and `WM_CHAR`, we can use the `EV_COMMAND` macro to say that we have a command message that we want OWL to handle. It is used as follows:

```
DEFINE_RESPONSE_TABLE1(BaseWindow, TWindow)
  EV_WM_CHAR,
  EV_WM_SIZE,
  EV_COMMAND( CM_ABOUT, CmAbout),
END_RESPONSE_TABLE;
```

The function is expected to take no parameters and return no value—in other words, `void CmAbout();` OWL programmers commonly use a certain way of naming such functions, and if you follow that convention, your code will be more understandable to others, and you will be getting used to the same kind of naming that is used in the documentation that came with Borland C++. To name the function, delete any underscores and capitalize the first letter of each word. For example, `CM_ABOUT` becomes `CmAbout()`. Windows event handlers drop the `WM_` entirely and put `Ev` at the beginning of the name; thus `WM_CHAR` becomes `EvChar`. Remember that event handlers usually take some parameters. When you use one, look it up in the online Help to check that you have the arguments correct.

REAL.CPP writes what you have typed to the screen. OWL provides an entire class, called `TEdit`, which can edit and capture your input far better than REAL.CPP does. This and other controls will be covered in later chapters. This example's writing to the screen is meant to illustrate how one paints a window under Windows—which is very different than under DOS.

14

Windows uses an item called a *device context*, also called a DC. A DC is a structure containing information about a device such as a screen, a printer, or a block of memory. You can write to anything for which you have asked Windows to provide a DC. Windows only has a limited number of DC blocks, so they are handled by requesting one, using it, and then calling Windows to free it for other uses. Forgetting to release DCs can result in Windows apparently stopping. With OWL, you needn't worry unless requesting a DC yourself. OWL automatically checks out a DC when it's time to paint the screen and returns it afterward. OWL expands upon this by placing the device context into a class called `TDC` along with functions that use DCs. Those functions already know what device you are writing to when you call them. Listing 14.4 shows a header file.

Type

Listing 14.4. REAL.RH, a header file.

```
#define CM_CLEAR    1125
#define CM_FILEEXIT 1126
#define CM_ABOUT    1127
```

REAL.RH does not get listed in the compiler's project file. The compiler will discover what header files are used by itself.

Listing 14.5 shows a program that uses a menu, accepts keyboard input, and writes the input to the screen.

Type

Listing 14.5. REAL.CPP, a real OWL program.

```
#include <owl\framewin.h>
#include <owl\applicat.h>
#include <owl\dc.h>
#include <mem.h>

#pragma hdrstop

#include "real.rh"

const int maxLines = 25;
const int maxWidth = 80;
const int maxData = maxLines * (maxWidth + 1);

class BaseWindow : public TWindow
  {
protected:
  int   currentLine;         // line being typed in now
  int   lineLen[maxLines];   // length of each line
  char *linePtrs[maxLines];  // string for each line
  BOOL  isMinimized;         // TRUE if window is an icon
  TSize windowSize;          // structure with size in pixels

```

```
  void EvChar(UINT key, UINT repeatCount, UINT flags);
  void Paint(TDC& dc, BOOL, TRect&);
  void EvSize(UINT sizeType, TSize& size);

  void CmAbout();
  void CmClear();

  // Menu choice, end the program
  void CmFileExit() { PostQuitMessage(0); }

public:
  BaseWindow(TWindow *parent = 0);
  ~BaseWindow() {}
  DECLARE_RESPONSE_TABLE(BaseWindow); // says we'll have a
  };                                  // response table

DEFINE_RESPONSE_TABLE1(BaseWindow, TWindow)
  EV_WM_CHAR,
  EV_WM_SIZE,
  EV_COMMAND( CM_ABOUT,    CmAbout),
  EV_COMMAND( CM_FILEEXIT, CmFileExit),
  EV_COMMAND( CM_CLEAR,    CmClear),
END_RESPONSE_TABLE;

class MyApp : public TApplication
  {
public:
  MyApp() : TApplication() {}

  void InitMainWindow();
  };

BaseWindow::BaseWindow(TWindow *parent)
  {
  int lineNum;

  Init(parent, 0, 0);
  linePtrs[0] = new char[maxData]; // allocate edit buffer
  lineLen[0] = currentLine = 0;

  // apportion the buffer out to the line pointer array
  for (lineNum = 1; lineNum < maxLines; ++lineNum)
    {
    linePtrs[lineNum] = linePtrs[lineNum - 1] + maxWidth;
    lineLen[lineNum] = 0;
    }
  }

// Menu choice, display an About box, use a message box to do it
void BaseWindow::CmAbout()
```

continues

Listing 14.5. continued

```
  {
  MessageBox("Teach Yourself BC++ 4.5 in 21 Days", "About");
  }

// Menu choice, clear the display
void BaseWindow::CmClear()
  {
  for (int lineNum = 0; lineNum < maxLines; ++lineNum)
     lineLen[lineNum] = 0;    // empty all lines

  currentLine = 0;            // move back to top line
  Invalidate();               // window is invalid, repaint
  }

// this is called whenever the window changes size
void BaseWindow::EvSize(UINT sizeType, TSize& size)
  {
  if (sizeType == SIZE_MINIMIZED) // if shrunk to icon
     isMinimized = TRUE;
  else
     {
     windowSize = size;             // save window size
     isMinimized = FALSE;
     }
  }

// called when time to update (paint) the screen
void BaseWindow::Paint(TDC& dc, BOOL, TRect&)
  {
  int   lineNum;          // line number to write
  int   yPos;             // vertical position on screen
  int   displayedLines;   // number of linePtrs in this window
  TSize textSize;         // used to get char height in pixels

  if (isMinimized)        // don't write to an icon
     return;

  // get char sizes so that height is saved
  textSize = dc.GetTextExtent("W", 1);
  displayedLines = windowSize.cy / textSize.cy;

  if (displayedLines > maxLines)
     displayedLines = maxLines;

  for (lineNum = yPos = 0; lineNum < displayedLines; ++lineNum)
     {
     if (lineLen[lineNum] > 0)  // if any text on the line
        dc.TextOut(0, yPos, linePtrs[lineNum], lineLen[lineNum]);

     yPos += textSize.cy;   // adjust screen line position
```

```
      }
   }

// called when a normal key is pressed
void BaseWindow::EvChar(UINT key, UINT repeatCount, UINT)
   {
   BOOL invalidDisplay = FALSE;
   BOOL eraseBackground = FALSE;

   while (repeatCount--)
      {
      if ((key >= ' ') && (key <= '~')) // if a printable key
         {
         if (currentLine >= maxLines) // if buffer full
            {
            MessageBeep(-1);           //   complain
            break;
            }
         else                         // else
            {                          //   add char
            linePtrs[currentLine][lineLen[currentLine]] = (char)
                    key;

            if (++lineLen[currentLine] >= maxWidth)
              ++currentLine;

            invalidDisplay = TRUE;
            }
         }
      else if (key == '\b')  // rubout, delete char
         {
         if (currentLine >= maxLines)
            break;
         else if (lineLen[currentLine] == 0)
            {
            if (currentLine > 0)
              --currentLine;
            }
         else
            --lineLen[currentLine];

         invalidDisplay = eraseBackground = TRUE;
         }
      else if (key == '\r') // if carriage return (Enter key)
         ++currentLine;
      }

   if (currentLine >= maxLines)
      currentLine = maxLines - 1;

```

continues

Listing 14.5. continued

```
172:   if (invalidDisplay)             // if buffer has changed
173:      Invalidate(eraseBackground); //   force window repaint
174:    }
175:
176: void MyApp::InitMainWindow()
177:   {
178:   SetMainWindow(new TFrameWindow(0, "Program 14.2",
179:                                  new BaseWindow()));
180:   GetMainWindow()->AssignMenu("MENU_1");
181:   }
182:
183:
184: int OwlMain(int, char **)
185:   {
186:   return MyApp().Run();
187:   }
```

Before running this application, you may wish to get a feel for how it looks by examining Figure 14.2 and Figure 14.3. Three instances of this program are shown on the screen, one each for an About box displayed, data typed in, and the pop-up menu opened.

As with the first program, this begins in `OwlMain()`. Line 186 calls the constructor for `MyApp`, and then calls `Run()`.

The constructor is declared on line 52. It in turn calls the constructor for `TApplication`. Line 54 has a function called `InitMainWindow()` that overloads the virtual function of the same name in the inherited class.

`TApplication`'s constructor calls `InitMainWindow()` (lines 176 through 181). That function makes two calls to `new`, creating a base window and then a frame window to handle the items on the base window's borders. The `GetMainWindow()` call on the next line assigns the menu to the main window. From then on, the application runs on its own, with Windows driving it by way of messages about menu selections and keyboard events.

The response table on lines 39 through 45 declared response functions for a character being entered, a window size change, and any of the three menu selections. Also, `BaseWindow`'s inheritance chain includes a virtual function called `Paint()`, which we've overloaded.

The data in the `BaseWindow` class is for keyboard input. Such input causes `EvChar()` on line 127 to be called. The calling arguments are the value of the key, the number of times it has been entered since we were last called, and a flags variable that we don't

use. The repeat count is important because a long process such as saving a disk file could allow the keyboard to insert several keys into the keyboard buffer.

This function passes through a loop as many times as the repeat count directs, adding keys to the keyboard buffer. When a line is full, it skips to the next line and begins entering there. If the buffer is full, it beeps at you (line 138).

If the user presses the backspace button, it deletes the last character entered (if one exists). The end of the function calls `Invalidate()`, a function that tells Windows that the whole window must be updated. The `eraseBackground` variable is only set to `TRUE` if a character is deleted. This minimizes screen blinking.

In response to the `Invalidate()` call, Windows sends the window procedure a message to paint the window. In the process, it sets things up and calls `Paint()`.

`Paint()` gets the text size. Fonts in Windows are often of variable width, but the measurement we are interested in is the vertical, which doesn't vary. We also calculate the number of displayable lines. It's a waste of time to paint more than that, because additional lines won't be placed on the screen.

A loop starting on line 118 passes through each line, writing any data in it to the screen. Note that `linePtrs[lineNum]` is an array of characters, not a string. No `'\0'` has been placed at the end. It relies on the `lineLen` array to handle how long the string is.

Note the `TDC` argument to `Paint()`. That is the device context we are to use in writing the screen. OWL has assigned it and will delete it after our function ends.

If you grab the corner of the window with the mouse cursor and resize it, `EvSize()` from line 88 will be called. If the application is minimized (shrunk to an icon), it merely sets a flag and returns. If it is not minimized, it captures the window dimensions into the `TSize` structure called `windowSize` for later use by the `Paint()` function.

Menu operation is straightforward. Select any menu item and OWL calls the corresponding function. The `CMClear()` function (starting on line 78) sets the line length for all strings to zero and moves the current line number to point at the first line (`linePtrs[0]`). It then invalidates the window so that `Paint()` will be called. When called with no arguments, `Invalidate()` defaults to `TRUE` so the background will also be erased.

`CmAbout` calls a message box, a built-in Windows function, to show the name of the book.

`CmFileExit()` on line 31 calls a true Windows function, `PostQuitMessage()`. This function ends the program, and the return value (which Windows ignores in version 3.1) is the function argument.

Summary

Today's lesson introduced you to C++ templates and Borland's ObjectWindows application framework/class library and discussed the following topics:

- C++ templates can be used with functions and classes to work with any kind of data type. You define a template with "generic" arguments and use a template giving specific arguments. The compiler generates code appropriate to the actual argument types.
- Creating an instance of a template class requires that you specify the type(s) as part of the class name.
- Windows requires special programming techniques because it allows multiple programs to run at the same time (unlike DOS).
- Windows communicates with programs via messages, and programs receive and process these messages in their message loop.
- Windows defines several shorthand names for common types of variables.
- Hungarian notation is a style of naming variables to indicate the type of data they hold and help in preventing bugs caused by mixing incompatible types. It's somewhat old-fashioned, as Borland C++ implements very strong C++ type checking, but Windows still uses some of its notations.
- OWL consists of groups of classes used to represent Windows structures, including event handling, module management, and window management.
- OWL processes Windows messages by executing the appropriate functions found in a window object's response table. OWL also "cracks" the parameters that Windows sends into more meaningful values.
- Adding a menu to a window requires that you create a menu resource, tell OWL to load it, and process the menu items using the EV_COMMAND macro.

Q&A

Q Can I use templates with my own structures and classes, or am I limited to using C++'s built-in types?

A Templates can use any type, for example:

```
template <class T> const T& Dump(const T& objectToDump);

int a = 100;

struct {
  int p;
  long q;
  double r;
} b;

Dump(a);
Dump(b);
```

Q Can I create a template with more than one type?

A Yes. Just separate the types with commas, For example:

```
template <class Form, class Printer> class SpecialFormPrinter
{
  ...
};

InsuranceFormLaserPrinter = new SpecialFormPrinter<InsuranceForm,
LaserPrinter>;
```

Q I have a DOS program I'd like to port to Windows. Do I have to rewrite it to use Windows techniques like message loops?

A Yes. It won't be a Windows program if it doesn't follow Windows' rules. However, you can use Borland C++'s EasyWin library, which lets you use DOS-style input and output functions. The result is a Windows program that looks like a DOS program.

Q The shorthand type names like DWORD and LPCSTR are confusing; can't I just use the normal C++ types?

A Yes, you can, but you have to make sure you do everything exactly the same. For example, everywhere you would normally use LPCSTR, make sure you use `const char far *`. Although learning the types takes some time, it's usually worth the extra effort, if only in saving the time it takes to type!

Q What function in my program is called first?

A DOS programs start at the `main()` function, which has arguments for the command-line parameters. Windows instead looks for a `WinMain()` function, with several arguments for instance handles, command-line parameters, and main window sizes. OWL simplifies it by providing an `OwlMain()` function that takes the same parameters as `main()` does.

Q Do I have to use a resource editor like Resource Workshop to create my resources?

A No. Resource files (with a .RC extension) are text files, so you can create and edit them with any text editor. However, Resource Workshop greatly simplifies editing resources, especially graphical ones.

Workshop

The Workshop provides quiz questions to help you solidify your understanding of the material covered and exercises to provide you with experience in using what you've learned. Try to understand the answers before continuing on to the next day's lesson. Answers are provided in Appendix A, "Answers."

Quiz

1. True or false? Templates let you use any type, including your own classes, without ever having to provide any extra code.
2. True or false? The underlying types of Windows types like WORD and UINT will never change.
3. True or false? Even though an OWL program is quite different from a program written in C, it's still a normal Windows program.

Exercise

Create the program REAL2.CPP by using the `TWindow::MessageBox` function to display a message when the user types an invalid key.

WEEK 2 IN REVIEW

8 9 10 11 12 13 14

As you end the second week of learning to program with Borland C++ 4.5, let's look at an enhanced version of the number-guessing game. Listing R2.1 shows the source code for the GAME2.CPP program. Although this version interacts with you in the same way GAME1.CPP does, it uses a class and an enumerated type.

Listing R2.1. Source code for program GAME2.CPP.

```
#include <stdlib.h>
#include <iostream.h>
#include <time.h>

enum boolean { false, true };

// declare a global random number generating function
int random(int maxVal)
{ return rand() % maxVal; }

class game
{
  protected:
    int n;
    int m;
    int MaxIter;
    int iter;
    boolean ok;
    void prompt();
    void examineInput();

  public:
    game();
    void play();
}

game::game()
{
  MaxIter = 11;
  iter = 0;
  ok = true;

  // reseed random-number generator
  srand((unsigned)time(NULL));
  n = random(1001);
  m = -1;
}

void game::prompt()
```

```
{
  cout << "Enter a number between 0 and 1000 : ";
  cin >> m;
  ok = (m < 0) ? false : true;
}

void game::examineInput()
{
  // is the user's guess higher?
  if (m > n)
    cout << "Enter a lower guess\n\n";
  else if (m < n)
    cout << "Enter a higher guess\n\n";
  else
    cout << "You guessed it! Congratulations.";
}

void game::play()
{
  // loop to obtain the other guesses
  while (m != n && iter < MaxIter && ok) {
    prompt();
    iter++;
    examineInput();
  }
  // did the user guess the secret number
  if (iter >= MaxIter || ok == 0)
    cout << "The secret number is " << n << "\n";
}

main()
{
  game g;

  g.play();
  return 0;
}
```

Here is a sample session with the program in Listing R2.1:

```
Enter a number between 0 and 1000 : 500
Enter a lower guess

Enter a number between 0 and 1000 : 250
Enter a higher guess

Enter a number between 0 and 1000 : -1
Enter a higher guess

The secret number is 324
```

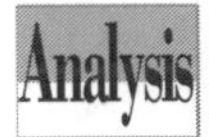

The program in Listing R2.1 declares the enumerated type `boolean` to model Boolean values. The program also declares the class `game`, which models the number-guessing game. The class has a number of data members, including the Boolean variable `ok`. In addition, the class declares the protected member functions `prompt` and `examineInput`, and the public constructor and member function `play`.

The constructor initializes the data members and reseeds the random-number generator. The member function `prompt`, defined in lines 39 through 44, prompts you for input, obtains your input, and assigns a true/false value to the variable `ok`, based on your input.

The function `examineInput`, defined in lines 46 through 55, compares your guess (stored in the data member `m`) with the secret number (stored in the data member `n`) and displays the appropriate message.

The member function `play`, defined in lines 57 through 68, contains the `while` loop that plays the game. The loop statements invoke the member functions `prompt` and `examineInput` and also increment the data member `iter`. In addition, the function contains the `if` statement that displays the secret number if you fail to guess it or if you quit the game.

The function `main` declares the instance `g` of class `game` and sends the message `play` to that instance.

WEEK 3

AT A GLANCE

15

16

17

18

19

20

21

This last week presents topics that cover more aspects of creating Windows applications using various classes in the OWL library. You will learn how to create scrolling windows. You will learn about using static text controls, edit controls, pushbuttons, check boxes, radio buttons, group controls, list boxes, scroll bars, combo boxes, dialog boxes, and OWL-compliant windows. These controls make up most of the visual controls that are common to Windows applications. The chapters in this week include nontrivial applications that illustrate the various features of these essential and common controls.

Basic Windows

WEEK

3

The most relevant aspect of the Windows environment, as the name suggests, is the use of windows. Windows are the holders of information. The application is responsible for maintaining information when you resize, move, or use existing scroll bars. In today's lesson, you learn about the following:

- Creating read-only text windows
- Scrolling through text using scroll bars
- Changing the scroll bar metrics (units, line size, page size, and ranges)
- Optimizing the `Paint` member function

Creating a Read-Only Text Window

In Day 14, we presented a number of menu-driven OWL applications. However, these programs did not display any information inside their windows. In this section, we present an OWL application that displays read-only text in its windows. The basic notion of the application is similar to that of the read-only online Help windows.

The purpose of the program is to demonstrate how to display text and maintain that text after one or more of the following has occurred:

- Resizing the window
- Minimizing, restoring, or maximizing the window
- Moving a window or dialog box over the text area

The main tools to implement the application's features are the member functions `TDC::TextOut` and `TWindow::Paint`. The function `TDC::TextOut` draws a character string on the specified display. The text appears in the currently selected font and at the specified window coordinates.

Syntax

The *TextOut* Function

The declarations for the overloaded `TDC` member function `TextOut` are

```
BOOL TextOut(int x, int y, const char far* str, int count = -1);
BOOL TextOut(const TPoint& p, const char far* str, int count = -1);
```

The `x` and `y` parameters identify the window location where the first character appears. The `str` parameter points to the string to be displayed in the window. The `count`

parameter indicates the leading number of characters of `str` to display. The argument for the last parameter is usually the size of the displayed string argument. Note that this has a default of 1, which means to display all the characters of `str`. In the second version of the function `TextOut`, the `x` and `y` parameters are replaced by a reference to a `TPoint` structure. The function returns a nonzero value when successful and zero when it fails.

Examples:

```
char s[81] = "Hello";
string str("Guten Tag!");
TPoint pt(10, 20);
TextOut(20, 10, s);
TextOut(pt, str.c_str());
```

As expected, the function `TDC::TextOut` displays text once. This means that altering the viewing area of the window or moving another window over the displayed text erases that text. What is needed is a mechanism that updates the display of text in the window. Enter the member function `TWindow::Paint`. This function enables you to display and maintain the contents of a window (both text and graphics). The versatility of the function `TWindow::Paint` comes from the fact that it responds to a `WM_PAINT` message whenever Windows determines that the window needs repainting. This repainting feature includes the initial creation of the window. Consequently, the versatility of `TWindow::Paint` includes setting the initial display as well as maintaining it.

Note: You need to declare your own version of the `Paint` member function in your derived window class. The code you place inside your version of the `Paint` function determines what information appears, remains, and disappears.

In the case of this OWL application, the same information is displayed from start to finish. The general form of the `Paint` member function is

```
void MyWindow::Paint(TDC& dc, BOOL erase, TRect& rect)
{
   // declarations

   // statements using the TextOut member function
   // e.g.
   //      dc.TextOut(x, y, s, strlen(s));
}
```

The parameter `dc` that is passed to the `Paint` member function is referred to as the device context, and it's the link to the display of the window. The `dc.TextOut` function can be used as needed to place text on the window. Interestingly, if you come across a C-coded Windows application that uses the `TextOut` API function, you note that a similar text output requires initializing the device-context object and then promptly releasing it once it has finished its task. These steps are automatically performed by the `TWindow::EvPaint` function, which in turn calls the `Paint` function.

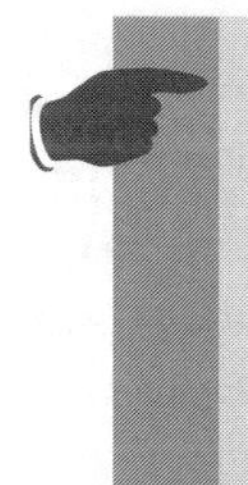

New Term: A *device context* (or DC for short) is the place in which all output goes. Anything that needs to be painted, such as text or graphics, must go onto DCs. These DCs can directly represent physical pixels on the screen, or they can be *memory DCs*. These memory DCs are typically used as temporary space in which to create such things as bitmaps before actually putting them on the screen by copying to another DC.

Let's now look at the code for the OWL application. Listing 15.1 contains the script for the resource file WINDOW1.RC. This resource file defines a menu with a single menu item, Exit, to exit the application. Listing 15.2 shows the source code for the WINDOW1.CPP program.

Create the directory WINDOW1 as a subdirectory of \BC45\BC21DAY and store all the project's files in the new directory. The project's IDE file should contain the files WINDOW1.CPP and WINDOW1.RC.

Compile and run the application. Notice that the lines of text appear when the window is created. Alter the window by resizing it, minimizing it, and then restoring it to normal. The lines of text are always visible (or at least a portion of them) as long as the upper-left portion of the screen is not obscured by another window. You can also click the left mouse button to display a message box. Drag that message box over the text lines and release the mouse. Then, drag the message box away from the text location. What do you see? The text lines reappear; `Paint` is constantly at work.

Listing 15.1. Script code for WINDOW1.RC.

```
#include <windows.h>
#include <owl\window.rh>

EXITMENU MENU LOADONCALL MOVEABLE PURE DISCARDABLE
BEGIN
   MENUITEM "E&xit", CM_EXIT
END
```

Type Listing 15.2. Source code for WINDOW1.CPP.

```
#include <owl\applicat.h>
#include <owl\dc.h>
#include <owl\framewin.h>
#include <owl\window.h>
#include <owl\window.rh>
#include <stdio.h>

const MAX_LINES = 30;

class TMyWindow : public TWindow
{
public:
   TMyWindow(TWindow* parent = 0);

protected:
   BOOL CanClose();

   void CmExit();
   void EvLButtonDown(UINT, TPoint &);

   void Paint(TDC &, BOOL, TRect &);

   DECLARE_RESPONSE_TABLE(TMyWindow);
};
DEFINE_RESPONSE_TABLE1(TMyWindow, TWindow)
   EV_WM_LBUTTONDOWN,
   EV_COMMAND(CM_EXIT, CmExit),
END_RESPONSE_TABLE;

class TMyApp : public TApplication
{
public:
   TMyApp() : TApplication() {}

   void InitMainWindow()
      {
      SetMainWindow(new TFrameWindow(  0,
                           "A Simple Read-Only Text Window",
                           new TMyWindow ));
      GetMainWindow()->AssignMenu("EXITMENU");
      }
};

TMyWindow::TMyWindow(TWindow* parent)
{
   Init(parent, 0, 0);
}

```

continues

Listing 15.2. continued

```
49: BOOL TMyWindow::CanClose()
50: {
51:    return IDYES == MessageBox("Want to close this application?",
52:                               "Query",
53:                               MB_YESNO ¦ MB_ICONQUESTION );
54: }
55:
56: void TMyWindow::CmExit()
57: {
58:    SendMessage(WM_CLOSE);
59: }
60:
61: void TMyWindow::EvLButtonDown(UINT, TPoint &)
62: {
63:    MessageBox( "You clicked the left button!",
64:                "Mouse Click Event",
65:                MB_OK );
66: }
67:
68: void TMyWindow::Paint(TDC& dc, BOOL /*erase*/, TRect& /*rect*/)
69: {
70:    char s[81];
71:    BOOL ok = TRUE;
72:    int y = 0;
73:
74:    for (int i = 0; i < MAX_LINES && ok; ++i)
75:       {
76:       sprintf(s, "This is line number %d", i);
77:       ok = dc.TextOut(0, y, s);
78:       y += dc.GetTextExtent(s, lstrlen(s)).cy;
79:       }
80: }
81:
82: int OwlMain(int, char *[])
83: {
84:    return TMyApp().Run();
85: }
```

Listing 15.2 shows the source code for the WINDOW1.CPP program file. The part of the program that is relevant to this application is the `TMyWindow` class and its member functions, declared on lines 10 through 28. The window class declares a constructor and three member functions, namely `EvLButtonDown`, `CmClose`, and `Paint`. The constructor creates a window on line 37 with the title `"A Simple Read-Only Text Window"` that has default size and location, and that uses the EXITMENU menu resource.

Figure 15.1 shows a sample session with the program WINDOW1.EXE.

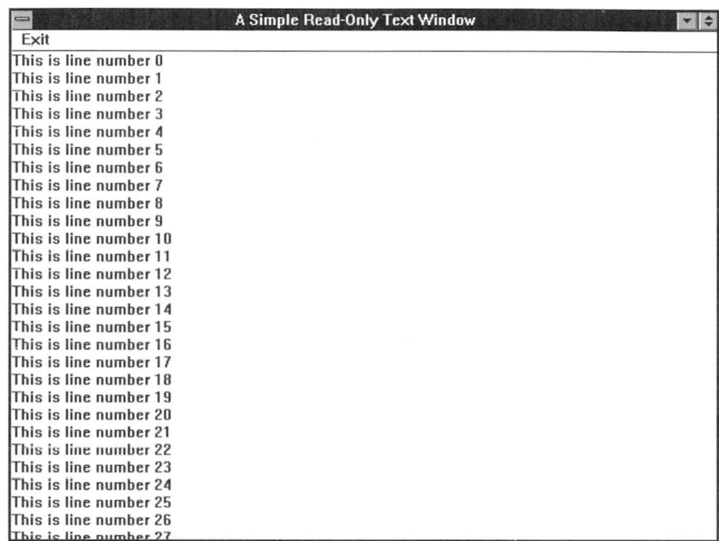

Figure 15.1. *A sample session with the program WINDOW1.EXE.*

The main point of interest is the `Paint` function that starts on line 68. The function declares the constant `MAX_LINES`, the string variable `s`, and the `BOOL`-typed variable `ok`. The `Paint` function displays the lines using the `for` loop on lines 74 through 79. Each loop iteration executes two statements. The first statement calls the `sprintf` function (prototyped in the STDIO.H header file) to create the image of a formatted output and store it in the variable `s`. The next statement calls the `dc`'s `TextOut` member function, which places the formatted output on the window. Notice the first two arguments of the `TextOut` function. They are 0 (for parameter `X`) and `y`. These values result in displaying the text, starting with the left margin of the window. The next function called is the `dc`'s `GetTextExtent` member function. This is used to determine the height of the text and any line spacing and to use that information by adding it to the `y` variable so that the next time through the loop, the next line is placed appropriately below the previous line.

Scrolling Through Text

One of the versatile features of windows is the ability to scroll information, if that information cannot be contained in the current viewing portion of the window. The scroll bars are the visual components of a window that assist in scrolling through the window's contents. Recall that a window can have a vertical scroll bar, horizontal scroll bar, or both. A scroll bar has an arrow box at each end and a scroll thumb. The arrow boxes enable you to scroll the window's contents to either end or to either side. In today's lesson, you learn about scrolling windows that contain text drawn using device-context objects.

New Term: The *scroll thumb* serves two purposes. First, it shows where you are relative to the entire width or length of the viewed information. Second, when you drag the thumb with the mouse, you can move to a specific portion of the viewed information.

The scrolling effect that we mentioned at the beginning of today's lesson is supported by a visual interface and an internal "engine." You can easily include the visual scroll bars in a window by incorporating the `WS_VSCROLL` and `WS_HSCROLL` styles in the `Attr.Style` member data from the window's constructor. For example, to create a window with both vertical and horizontal scroll bars, use the following statement:

```
// both vertical and horizontal scroll bars
Attr.Style |= WS_VSCROLL | WS_HSCROLL;
```

The `WS_VSCROLL` and `WS_HSCROLL` constants add the visual aspect of the scroll bars. The functionality is supported by overriding the `EvVScroll`, `EvHScroll`, and `EvSize` functions, then adjusting your Paint function to take advantage of any scrolling changes. OWL provides an integrated class that does just this, called `TScroller`. An object of this class, when assigned the `TWindow`'s `Scroller` member function, provides scrolling by working with the `TWindow` class to automatically sense the setting of the scroll bars and adjust the window's viewport accordingly.

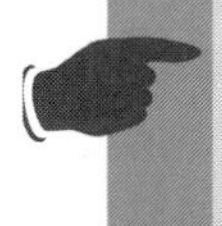

New Term: The *viewport* is that portion of the window that is visible at any one time. It is possible to paint on a window outside of the visible portion, but that will be *clipped* from view. By adjusting the viewport's origin, the clipped region will change, and offsets within the window will be adjusted accordingly. For example, given a standard window, when a string of text is drawn at (10,10), the text will appear offset down and to the right of the upper left-hand corner of the window. By adjusting the viewport origin to begin at (10,10), drawing that same text at the same location will now make it appear in the upper left-hand corner.

The constructor for the `TScroller` class looks like this:

```
TScroller(TWindow* window, int xUnit, int yUnit,
         long xRange, long yRange);
```

The `window` parameter is a pointer to the window for which the `TScroller` object is being created. The `xUnit` and `yUnit` parameters specify how many device units to scroll in each direction. In the case of textual information, this is usually going to be the size of a single character, so that scrolling goes by lines. Note, however, that since most fonts in Windows are variable (each of the characters are of differing widths), the horizontal unit tends to be the average width of all the characters. Finally, the xRange and yRange parameters specify how many scrolling positions exist. For example, a yRange of 20 would mean that the down arrow on the scroll bar could be pressed 20 times.

It would be an easy thing to add an additional include file at the top,

```
#include <owl\scroller.h>
```

and the following two lines to the constructor of the `TMyWindow` class from the last example:

```
Attr.Style |= WS_VSCROLL | WS_HSCROLL;
Scroller = new TScroller(7, 16, 20, MAX_LINES - 1);
```

If you add those two lines and recompile, you'll find your window now has scroll bars on its bottom and right side, and you can scroll to the right 20 columns and down as many lines as are drawn (minus one, so at least one of the lines stays on the screen). The two more interesting functions of the `TScroller` class are the `VScroll` and `HScroll` member functions.

Syntax

Manually Scrolling with *TScroller*

The declarations of `TScroller`'s `VScroll` and `HScroll` member functions are

```
void VScroll(UINT scrollEvent, int thumbPos);
void HScroll(UINT scrollEvent, int thumbPos);
```

The `scrollEvent` specifies the scrolling request. Table 15.1 shows the predefined constants for the various scrolling requests. The `thumbPos` parameter specifies the position of the thumb box when the argument for `scrollEvent` is either `SB_THUMBPOSITION` or `SB_THUMBTRACK`.

Examples:

```
Scroller->VScroll(SB_LINEDOWN, 0);
Scroller->HScroll(SB_THUMBPOSITION, 23);
```

Table 15.1. Predefined constants for vertical scrolling requests.

Value	Meaning
SB_BOTTOM	Scroll to the bottom
SB_ENDSCROLL	End scroll
SB_LINEDOWN	Scroll one line down
SB_LINEUP	Scroll one line up
SB_PAGEDOWN	Scroll one page down
SB_PAGEUP	Scroll one page up
SB_THUMBPOSITION	Scroll to the nPos position
SB_THUMBTRACK	Drag the scroll thumb box to the nPos position
SB_TOP	Scroll to the top

In the preceding short example, the 7 and 16 are approximations of a character's width and height. They will work when using the default font on most standard VGA screens, but you will run into problems when you try to use different fonts or when you run on screens that use a smaller font (like an 800×600 or 1024×768 screen). The solution to this is to figure out the size of the font beforehand and set the scroll units accordingly.

A Scrolling Window

This section presents a program that defines general scrollable windows. WINDOW2.EXE has two main menu items, Exit and Char Sets. The second menu item is a pop-up menu that has three selections: Set 1, Set 2, and Set 3. These options produce text lines that have a different line spacing and different maximum number of lines. The text fonts are the same for all three sets. Initially, the client area of the application window is clear. Therefore, you must select one of the three character sets. The application also supports the cursor movement keys to scroll the text. The <Home> and <End> keys scroll vertically to the top and bottom, respectively. Similarly, the <PgUp> and <PgDn> keys scroll one page up and down. The up and down arrow keys scroll one line at a time. The left and right arrow keys scroll horizontally by pages.

This program illustrates two main aspects of scrolling windows:

1. Declaring a scrolling window class with additional member functions that manage the assignment, access, and use of scrolling-related data.
2. Using assigned values to control vertical scrolling, and relying on the current window metrics to control the horizontal scrolling.

Let's look at the code for the general text scroller window application. Listings 15.3 and 15.4 show the header file WINDOW2.H and the resource file WINDOW2.RC, respectively. Listing 15.5 contains the source code for the WINDOW2.CPP program.

Create the directory WINDOW2 as a subdirectory of \BC45\BC21DAY and store all the project's files in the new directory. The project should contain the files WINDOW2.CPP and WINDOW2.RC.

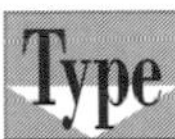

Listing 15.3. Source code for WINDOW2.H.

```
#define  CM_HEIGHT8     (WM_USER + 100)
#define  CM_HEIGHT10    (WM_USER + 101)
#define  CM_HEIGHT14    (WM_USER + 102)
#define  CM_HEIGHT20    (WM_USER + 103)
#define  CM_HEIGHT26    (WM_USER + 104)
```

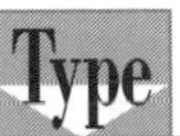

Listing 15.4. Script code for WINDOW2.RC.

```
#include <windows.h>
#include <owl\window.rh>
#include "window2.h"

EXITMENU MENU LOADONCALL MOVEABLE PURE DISCARDABLE
BEGIN
   MENUITEM "E&xit", CM_EXIT
   POPUP "&Char Heights"
   BEGIN
      MENUITEM "&8", CM_HEIGHT8
      MENUITEM "1&0", CM_HEIGHT10
      MENUITEM "1&4", CM_HEIGHT14
      MENUITEM "&20", CM_HEIGHT20
      MENUITEM "2&6", CM_HEIGHT26
   END
END
```

Listing 15.5. Source code for WINDOW2.CPP.

```
#include <owl\applicat.h>
#include <owl\dc.h>
#include <owl\framewin.h>
#include <owl\scroller.h>
#include <owl\window.h>
#include <owl\window.rh>
#include <stdio.h>

#include "window2.h"

const MAX_LINES = 30;

class TMyWindow : public TWindow
{
public:
   TMyWindow(TWindow* parent = 0);
   ~TMyWindow();

protected:
   virtual void SetupWindow();

   BOOL CanClose();

   void CmExit();
   void CmHeight8();
   void CmHeight10();
   void CmHeight14();
   void CmHeight20();
   void CmHeight26();
   void EvKeyDown(UINT, UINT, UINT);
   void EvLButtonDown(UINT, TPoint &);

   void Paint(TDC &, BOOL, TRect &);

private:
   TFont* pFont;

   void NewFont(int);

   DECLARE_RESPONSE_TABLE(TMyWindow);
};
DEFINE_RESPONSE_TABLE1(TMyWindow, TWindow)
   EV_WM_KEYDOWN,
   EV_WM_LBUTTONDOWN,
   EV_COMMAND(CM_EXIT, CmExit),
   EV_COMMAND(CM_HEIGHT8, CmHeight8),
   EV_COMMAND(CM_HEIGHT10, CmHeight10),
   EV_COMMAND(CM_HEIGHT14, CmHeight14),
```

```
   EV_COMMAND(CM_HEIGHT20, CmHeight20),
   EV_COMMAND(CM_HEIGHT26, CmHeight26),
END_RESPONSE_TABLE;

class TMyApp : public TApplication
{
public:
   TMyApp() : TApplication() {}

   void InitMainWindow()
      {
      SetMainWindow(new TFrameWindow(  0,
                            "A Simple Read-Only Text Window",
                            new TMyWindow ));
      GetMainWindow()->AssignMenu("EXITMENU");
      }
};

TMyWindow::TMyWindow(TWindow* parent)
{
   Init(parent, 0, 0);
   Attr.Style |= WS_VSCROLL | WS_HSCROLL;    // Add scroll bars
   pFont = NULL;
}

TMyWindow::~TMyWindow()
{
   if (pFont)
      delete pFont;
}

void TMyWindow::SetupWindow()
{
   TWindow::SetupWindow();

   // Set up the scroller and font.  Note that
   // dummy values of 7 and 16 are used for the
   // scroll bar's units, but they'll be reset
   // as soon as the font is set.
   //
   Scroller = new TScroller(this, 7, 16, 20, MAX_LINES - 1);
   NowFont(8);                                // Initialize our font
}

BOOL TMyWindow::CanClose()
{
   return IDYES == MessageBox("Want to close this application?",
                              "Query",
                              MB_YESNO | MB_ICONQUESTION );
}
```

continues

Listing 15.5. continued

```
void TMyWindow::CmExit()
{
   SendMessage(WM_CLOSE);
}

void TMyWindow::CmHeight8()
{
   NewFont(8);
}

void TMyWindow::CmHeight10()
{
   NewFont(10);
}

void TMyWindow::CmHeight14()
{
   NewFont(14);
}

void TMyWindow::CmHeight20()
{
   NewFont(20);
}

void TMyWindow::CmHeight26()
{
   NewFont(26);
}

void TMyWindow::EvKeyDown( UINT key,
                           UINT /*repeatCount*/,
                           UINT /*flags*/ )
{
   if (Scroller)        // Can't scroll if it ain't there!
      switch (key)
         {
         case VK_HOME:
            Scroller->VScroll(SB_TOP, 0);
            break;
         case VK_END:
            Scroller->VScroll(SB_BOTTOM, 0);
            break;
         case VK_PRIOR:
            Scroller->VScroll(SB_PAGEUP, 0);
            break;
         case VK_NEXT:
            Scroller->VScroll(SB_PAGEDOWN, 0);
            break;
```

```
         case VK_UP:
            Scroller->VScroll(SB_LINEUP, 0);
            break;
         case VK_DOWN:
            Scroller->VScroll(SB_LINEDOWN, 0);
            break;
         }
}

void TMyWindow::EvLButtonDown(UINT, TPoint &)
{
   MessageBox( "You clicked the left button!",
               "Mouse Click Event",
               MB_OK );
}

void TMyWindow::Paint(TDC& dc, BOOL /*erase*/, TRect& /*rect*/)
{
   char s[81];
   BOOL ok = TRUE;
   int y = 0;

   for (int i = 0; i < MAX_LINES && ok; ++i)
      {
      if (pFont)
         dc.SelectObject(*pFont);
      sprintf(s, "This is line number %d", i);
      ok = dc.TextOut(0, y, s);
      y += dc.GetTextExtent(s, lstrlen(s)).cy;
      if (pFont)
         dc.RestoreFont();
      }
}

void TMyWindow::NewFont(int nHeight)
{
   if (pFont)
      delete pFont;
   pFont = new TFont("Arial", nHeight);

   // Now reset the scroller's units
   if (pFont && Scroller)
      {
      TClientDC dc(*this);
      TEXTMETRIC tm;

      dc.SelectObject(*pFont);
      dc.GetTextMetrics(tm);
      dc.RestoreFont();

```

continues

Listing 15.5. continued

```
        Scroller->SetUnits(  tm.tmAveCharWidth,
                             tm.tmHeight + tm.tmExternalLeading );

        Invalidate();
        }
}

int OwlMain(int, char *[])
{
   return TMyApp().Run();
}
```

Figure 15.2 shows a sample session with the program WINDOW2.EXE.

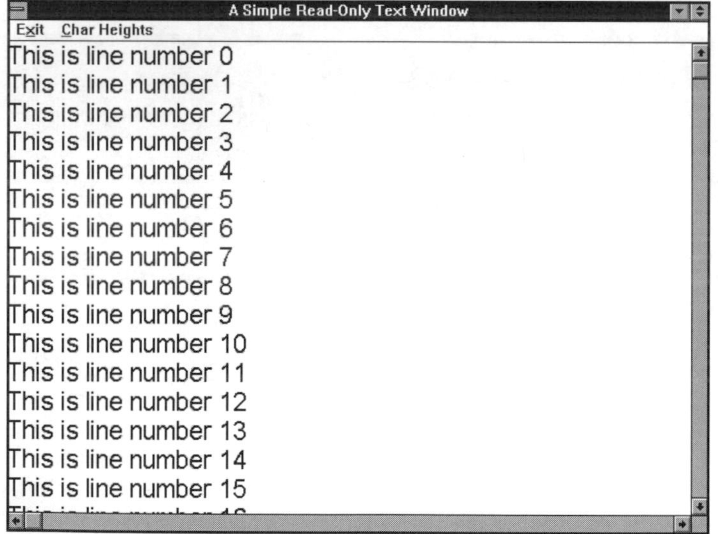

Figure 15.2. *A sample session with the program WINDOW2.EXE.*

Analysis

This program is very similar to the first one presented in this chapter. The major differences are the addition of the scroll bars on the right and bottom of the window and the new menu item allowing the user to change the font as it is displayed on the screen.

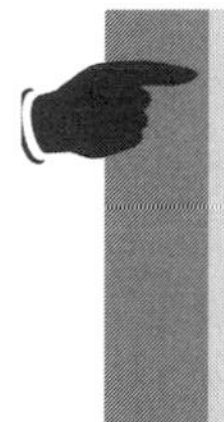

New Term: A *font* is a description of the type of characters used to display text. This description includes what the characters look like, called the *typeface*, as well as their size, referred to as their *point size*. Some common typefaces are *Arial* and *Times New Roman*, both of which come with Windows. Also, such things as italics and bold characters are described by fonts.

The `TMyWindow` class on lines 13 through 51 declares a new data member and a new function member, both private, for use in displaying using different point-sized fonts:

- The `pFont` member on line 36 stores a pointer to the font used to display the text. This variable is preset to `NULL` in the class's constructor on line 71 and initialized in the `SetupWindow` function on line 90. It is then reset by the user via the menus.
- The `NewFont` function starting on line 183 is used to change the font. It takes an integer value that is used as the point size, and it then creates a `TFont` object, assigning it to the `pFont` data member.
- The `Paint` function starting on line 165 first selects the `pFont` object into the device context before writing to the window. After it's done, it reselects the original font back into the window.

Note: When dealing with windows and selecting objects into device contexts like fonts or text colors, it's always a good idea to make sure you leave the DC in the same condition as when you found it. If you change the font, make sure you change it back to whatever it might have been before you messed with it.

Note that the `pFont` is only preset to `NULL` in the constructor, but the real initialization occurs in the `SetupWindow` member function. This is a very important distinction, as creating the font requires the existence of a window.

The *SetupWindow* Member Function

Although the `TWindow` class has the usual constructor where things can get initialized as in any other class, it also has the member function `SetupWindow` for all initializations that rely on an actual window to be there. The `SetupWindow` function looks like this:

```
void SetupWindow(void);
```

When the `TWindow` class is first created, all that exists is the interface object or C++ object. For many initializations, an actual interface element or Windows object (a window) may need to exist. During the course of the window's initialization, the `SetupWindow` will be called. This function does the actual creation of the Windows object to which the C++ object is to be connected. That is why it's vitally important for any derived versions of `SetupWindow` to call the parent's version. Until the actual `TWindow::SetupWindow` function is called, there will be no Windows object.

This program enables the user to use the keyboard to scroll the window. It does this through a single member function `EvKeyDown` starting on line 130. In this function is a switch statement that checks for the keys on the keypad. For each of these, it sends the `Scroller` object the appropriate command (refer to Table 15.1) to scroll the window. The `Scroller` object is closely tied to the `TWindow` object, of which `TMyWindow` is directly descended, so it handles all the dirty work of changing the scroll bars and telling the window to update itself, which then calls Paint to paint the right portions of the screen.

In order to let the user change the font, the "Char Heights" pop-up menu item has been added with various selections enabling the user to select specific point sizes for the fonts. The program responds to these menu selections through the various `CmHeight`*`XX`* member functions on lines 105 through 128. These functions serve only to call the `NewFont` member function with the appropriate point size, as specified by the user.

Finally, the `NewFont` member function, starting on line 183, handles the creation of the fonts used in painting the window:

- First, it checks to see if the `pFont` data member has been set yet. If so, it deletes the old one in preparation for replacing the old one with a new version, which it does immediately. It allocates a new `TFont` object with the typeface *Arial* and a point size of `nHeight`.

Note: Although it is safe to delete a `NULL` pointer in Borland C++ 4.5, it's still a good idea to check first, because not all compilers are as safe.

- Assuming the `Scroller` object exists and the creation of `pFont` succeeded, the function proceeds to set the `Scroller` with new values to let it know how big the characters are now. To do this, it first gets a device context from the window and selects the new `pFont` into it. The font's attributes are placed into the `TEXTMETRIC` object and that information is used in the `TScroller`'s `SetUnits` function.
- Finally, because the font we use to paint the window has changed, we need to tell the window to update itself with the new font. This is done with the `Invalidate` function, which tells the window that its contents are no longer valid and need repainting. Windows will automatically tell the window to repaint itself, at which time the `Paint` function will be entered.

Summary

Today's lesson discussed the mechanics of creating windows that show fixed and scrollable text. The lesson included the following topics:

- Read-only text windows that display information are the basis of help screens.
- You can write text in a window using the versatile `TDC::TextOut` member function.
- Scrollable windows can be created with vertical and horizontal scroll bars. These windows scroll using either the mouse or the cursor control keys. The classes of scrollable windows use the `TScroller` class assigned to the `TWindow`'s `Scroller` data member, as well as other functions to manage the text metrics.

Q&A

Q Is the member function `Paint` needed to maintain windows with visual controls such as command buttons?

A No. You need only to write the function `Paint` to maintain windows that draw text and graphics. In the case of windows with controls, you need not declare your own version of function `Paint`.

Workshop

The Workshop provides quiz questions to help you solidify your understanding of the material covered and exercises to provide you with experience in using what you've learned. Try to understand the quiz and exercise answers before continuing on to the next day's lesson. Answers are provided in Appendix A, "Answers."

Quiz

1. True or false? The member function `Paint` redraws the window only when needed.
2. True or false? The `TWindow::Scroller` data member offers default scrolling features.
3. True or false? Omitting the `EvKeyDown` member function in program WINDOW2.CPP disables the vertical scrolling feature altogether.

Exercise

Experiment with modifying the WINDOW2.CPP program by adding cases to the `EvKeyDown` function that will allow the window to scroll horizontally in response to the right arrow and left arrow keys being pressed. In addition, you can experiment with adding more `CmHeight`*`XX`* member functions and the corresponding menu selections.

16

OWL Controls

WEEK

3

Interacting with Windows applications often involves dialog boxes that contain various types of controls, such as the list box, the edit control (also called edit box), and the pushbutton. These controls can be included in windows or, more frequently, in dialog boxes. Today's lesson and the next three look at the controls as they appear in windows and focus on the basic properties of these controls. Day 20 presents dialog boxes and views how the controls work with these boxes. Today, you learn about the following topics:

- The `TControl` object
- Static text control
- Edit control
- Pushbutton control

Understanding the various controls and mastering how they behave and interact enables you to implement highly interactive Windows applications. Today's lesson and the two that follow discuss the constructors and relevant member functions for the control classes.

The *TControl* Object

To learn about OWL controls, it's best to start with the `TControl` object. This object is the base from which all other control objects are derived. Note that you will never have any need to create a `TControl` object directly, but a discussion of it here helps you to understand the control objects derived from it.

The `TControl` object is derived from the `TWindow` class, which means that it has much of the same functionality as the `TWindow` class. This is actually a direct mapping of the Windows environment where controls are, indeed, just specialized child windows. Because the `TControl` class is meant merely as a common base class for the rest of the control classes, the only public function is the constructor.

Syntax

The *TControl* Constructor

The constructor of the `TControl` class is

```
TControl(TWindow*         parent,
         int              id,
         const char far* title,
         int              x,
```

```
        int             y,
        int             w,
        int             h,
        TModule*        module = 0);
```

The parent parameter is a pointer to the parent window in which the control will be placed. The id represents the control's ID, which is used in communication between the parent window and the control itself (more on this later, when specific controls are discussed). Next comes the title of the control. This parameter isn't always displayed by the particular control created, but it's always set. The four parameters x, y, w, and h describe the position and size of the control to be created. Finally, the module parameter specifies the DLL with which the control is associated. This has a default value of 0, and you will rarely find a need to override that.

16

You will see the parameters to this class duplicated again and again in the various control classes derived from TControl. Added on to these standard parameters will be other parameters specific to the particular class being created.

The Static Text Control

The static text control provides a window or a dialog box with static text. The TStatic class implements the static text control. Let's look at the class constructor and members.

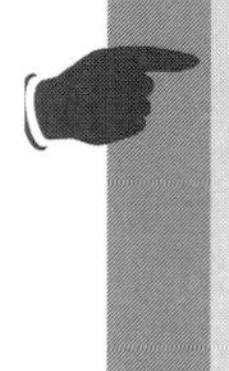

New Term: *Static text* is text that the application user cannot easily and readily change. Static text does not necessarily mean text etched in stone! In fact, static text controls allow your OWL applications to alter the text at any time, or you can still specify that the text be permanent and unchangeable. The choice is ultimately yours.

The TStatic class, a descendant of TControl (which, in turn, is descended from TWindow), offers static text that is defined by a display area, text to display, and text attributes. Of these three components, you can alter only the displayed text during runtime.

Syntax

The *TStatic* Constructor

The constructor of the `TStatic` control is

```
TStatic(TWindow*         parent,
        int              id,
        const char far *title,
        int              x,
        int              y,
        int              w,
        int              h,
        UINT             textLen = 0,
        TModule*         module = 0 );
```

Example:

```
pText = new TStatic(this, -1, "Sample Text", 10, 10, 75, 25);
pText->Attr.Style &=~SS_LEFT;
pText->Attr.Style |=SS_SIMPLE;
```

The `parent` parameter specifies the parent window into which the static control will be placed. The `id` is used to give the static control a unique identifier. A control's ID is typically used when the control needs to send notification messages to its parent window or the static text needs to be changed by the application. In the case of a static control, this is a very rare occasion, so the `id` parameter is usually set to -1. The `title` sets an initial text string that will appear within the control. The next four parameters—`x`, `y`, `w`, and `h`—describe the location and size of the control as it will appear within its parent window. The `textLen` parameter is used for advanced transfer and streaming capabilities, and the `module` pointer is used for specifying the DLL with which the static control is associated. Note that these last two both have default values of 0, and you will rarely find a need to override that.

In addition to the usual `WS_CHILD` and `WS_VISIBLE` styles that go along with all controls, static controls have their own special set of `SS_`*`XXX`* styles, as shown in Table 16.1. Note that the `TStatic` class automatically includes the `SS_LEFT` style.

Table 16.1. Values for static text styles.

Value	Meaning
`SS_BLACKFRAME`	Designates a box with a frame drawn with the color matching that of the window frame (black, in the default Windows color scheme).

Value	Meaning
SS_BLACKRECT	Specifies a rectangle filled with the color matching that of the window frame (black, in the default Windows color scheme).
SS_CENTER	Centers the static text characters; text is wrappable.
SS_GRAYFRAME	Specifies a box with a frame that has the same color as the screen background (gray, in the default Windows color scheme).
SS_GRAYRECT	Selects a rectangle filled with the same color as the screen background (gray, in the default Windows color scheme).
SS_ICON	Specifies an icon that is to be displayed in the control. The text is interpreted as the resource name of the icon. (Note that the width and height of the control are ignored as the icon is automatically sized.)
SS_LEFT	Indicates left-justified text; text is wrappable.
SS_LEFTNOWORDWRAP	Indicates left-justified text that cannot be wrapped.
SS_NOPREFIX	Specifies that the ampersand character (&) in the static text string should not be a hot key designator character, but rather part of the static text character.
SS_RIGHT	Selects right-justified text that is wrappable.
SS_SIMPLE	Indicates that the static text characters cannot be altered at runtime and that the static text is displayed on a single line with line breaks ignored.
SS_WHITEFRAME	Specifies a box with a frame that has the same color as the window background (white, in the default Windows color scheme).
SS_WHITERECT	Selects a rectangle filled with the same color as the window background (white, in the default Windows color scheme).

The string accessed by the `title` pointer in the constructor may include the ampersand (`&`) character to visually specify a hot key to actually support the hot key your application needs to load accelerator keys. The hot-key character appears as an underlined character. The ampersand should be placed before the hot key character. If the string contains more than one ampersand character, only the last occurrence is effective. The other occurrences of the ampersand are not displayed and are ignored. To display the `&` character, you need to specify the `SS_NOPREFIX` style. The price you pay for using this style is the inability to display a hot key character.

Now, let's focus on the component of the static text control that you can change during runtime, namely, the text itself. If you specify the `SS_SIMPLE` style in the control's `Attr.Style` data member, you cannot alter its text. In this sense, the instance of `TStatic` is, indeed, etched in stone. The `TStatic` class enables you to set, query, and clear the characters of the static text using the `GetTextLen`, `GetText`, `SetText`, and `Clear` functions.

Syntax

The *GetTextLen* Function

The parameterless `GetTextLen` member function returns the length of the control's text:

```
int GetTextLen()
```

Example:

```
int nLen = pText->GetTextLen();
```

Syntax

The *GetText* Function

The `GetText` member function enables you to access the static text characters. The declaration of the function is

```
int GetText(char far* text, int maxChars);
```

The `text` parameter is a pointer to the string that receives a copy of the static text characters. The `maxChars` parameter specifies the maximum number of static text characters to copy. The function result returns the actual number of characters copied to the string accessed by the pointer `text`.

Example:

```
char s[128];
pText->GetText(s, sizeof(s) - 1);
```

Syntax

The *SetText* Function

The `SetText` member function overwrites the current static text characters with those of a new string. The declaration of the function is

```
void SetText(const char far* str);
```

The `str` parameter is the pointer to the new text for the control. If the new text is an empty string, the `SetText` function call simply clears the text in the static text control instance.

Example:

```
pText->SetText("New Text");
```

Syntax

The *Clear* Function

The `Clear` member function is simply a wrapper that passes an empty string to the `SetText` member function. The declaration of the function is

```
void Clear();
```

Its existence is there to make code look a little cleaner by enabling you to call the `Clear` function rather than `SetText("");`.

The Edit Control

The ObjectWindows Library offers the `TEdit` class that implements an edit control. You have encountered this control in some of the earlier programs that use the input dialog box. The edit control enables the user to type in and edit the text in the input dialog box. In this section, we discuss the functionality of class `TEdit` in more detail, because implementing customized text editors in your OWL application requires you to become quite familiar with the `TEdit` member functions.

The *TEdit* Class

The `TEdit` class is derived from the `TStatic` class and implements a versatile edit control that supports single-line and multiline text, as well as the ability to cut, paste, copy, delete, and clear text. The edit control can also undo the last text changes and exchange text with the Clipboard.

Syntax

The *TEdit* Constructor

The declaration of the TEdit constructor is

```
TEdit(TWindow*          parent,
      int               id,
      const char far* text,
      int               x,
      int               y,
      int               w,
      int               h,
      UINT              textLen = 0,
      BOOL              multiline = FALSE,
      TModule*          module = 0 );
```

The parameters to the first constructor are almost identical to the ones for the TStatic constructor. The only difference is the addition of a multiline parameter. This tells whether the edit control should have more than one input line, like a text editor. Unlike the TStatic control, however, it never makes sense to use an invalid number in the id parameter of the TEdit control, as the TEdit control will need to send notification messages back to its parent window.

The second constructor is identical in usage to the second constructor for the TStatic control. It is used to associate a C++ class object with a control loaded with a dialog resource.

Example:

```
const IDE_INPUT = 101;
pInput = new TEdit(this, IDE_INPUT, "", 10, 10, 100, 25);
```

The TEdit control also has its own set of special styles, ES_*XXX*, that can be used to modify its behavior (see Table 16.2). When you create a TEdit object, the ES_LEFT and ES_AUTOHSCROLL are automatically added in. If the multiline parameter is set, then the ES_MULTILINE and ES_AUTOVSCROLL are also automatically set.

Table 16.2. Values for edit control styles.

Value	Meaning
ES_AUTOHSCROLL	Allows the text to automatically scroll to the right by 10 characters when the user enters a character at the end of the line; when the user presses the Enter key, text scrolls back to the left.

Value	Meaning
ES_AUTOVSCROLL	Permits the text to scroll up by one page when the user presses the Enter key on the last visible line.
ES_CENTER	Centers the text in a multiline edit control.
ES_LEFT	Justifies the text to the left.
ES_LOWERCASE	Converts into lowercase all the letters that the user types.
ES_MULTILINE	Specifies a multiline edit control that recognizes line breaks (designated by the sequence of carriage return and line feed characters).
ES_NOHIDESEL	By default, hides the selected text when it loses focus and shows the selection when it gains focus again; prevents edit control from restoring the selected text.
ES_OEMCONVERT	Converts the entered text from the Windows character set to the OEM character set and back again. This is useful for controls that receive filenames.
ES_PASSWORD	Displays all characters as asterisks (*) as they are typed. Note that this only affects the display; what the user types is stored accurately in the control.
ES_READONLY	Prevents the user from modifying the contents of the control, although it is still possible to select text in the control.
ES_RIGHT	Justifies the text to the right in multiline edit controls.
ES_UPPERCASE	Converts into uppercase all the letters that the user types.
ES_WANTRETURN	Normally, the Enter key will click the default button. When this style is set in an edit control, however, pressing Enter while editing text will insert a new line. This applies only to multiline edit controls

Clipboard-Related Editing Functions

The `TEdit` class includes a set of member functions that handle Clipboard-related text editing commands. These commands are available in typical menu options: Cut, Copy, Paste, Clear, Undo, and Delete. Table 16.3 shows the `TEdit` member functions and their purpose. These functions work with the Clipboard in the `CF_TEXT` format.

Table 16.3. TEdit member functions that support Clipboard-related editing menu commands.

Member Function	Purpose
`CanUndo`	Returns whether or not an undo operation is possible at the moment. It's used to enable and disable the Undo menu item accordingly.
`Cut`	Deletes the current selection in the edit control and copies the text to the Clipboard.
`Copy`	Copies the current selection to the Clipboard.
`Paste`	Inserts the text from the Clipboard to the current cursor position in the edit control.
`Clear`	Deletes the current selection; does not affect the Clipboard.
`Undo`	Undoes the last change made to the text of the edit control.

Query of Edit Controls

The `TEdit` class has a family of text query member functions. These functions enable you to retrieve either the entire control text or parts of it, or they permit you to obtain information on the text statistics (number of lines, length of lines, and so on). Two of these functions are inherited directly from the `TStatic` class. They are `GetTextLen` and `GetText`. They are used to retrieve the contents of edit controls and are declared and used in the same way as they are in the `TStatic` class.

Because edit controls allow for both multiple lines and user manipulation, additional functions are used to get text from different lines and for manipulating the selection.

Syntax

'The *GetNumLines* Function

The `GetNumLines` member function returns the number of lines in the edit control. The declaration is

```
int GetNumLines() const;
```

Example:

```
nLineCount = pEdit->GetNumLines();
```

Note: In the case of multiline edit controls, you should take into account the characters involved in either the soft or hard line breaks.

Hard line breaks use pairs of carriage return and line feed characters ("\r\n") at the end of each line. Soft line breaks use two carriage returns and a line feed at line breaks ("\r\r\n").

This information is relevant when you are counting the number of characters to process.

Syntax

The *GetLineFromPos* Function

The `GetLineFromPos` member function returns the line number of a specified character index. Its declaration is

```
int GetLineFromPos(UINT charPos) const;
```

If the `charPos` argument is -1, then the function will return either of these two values:

- If there is selected text, the function yields the line number where the first selected character is located.
- If there is no selected text, the function returns the line number where the caret is, where character insertion occurs.

Example:

```
nLineNum = pEdit->GetLineFromPos(-1);
```

Syntax

The *GetLineIndex* Function

The `GetLineIndex` member function returns the character index of a specific line. The character index is also the size of the text in the edit control up to the specified line number. Its declaration is

```
UINT GetLineIndex(int lineNumber) const;
```

The `lineNumber` parameter specifies the line index. If it is -1, it represents the current line as represented by the caret, which marks the user's current position. The function returns the number of characters from the first line through to the specified line. If the argument of `lineNumber` is greater than the actual number of lines, the function will return -1.

Example:

```
nCharIndex = pEdit->GetLineIndex(-1);
```

Syntax

The *GetLineLength* Function

The `GetLineLength` member function returns the length of a line for a specific line number. Its declaration is

```
int GetLineLength(int lineNumber) const;
```

The `lineNumber` parameter specifies the line number from which to get the length. If `lineNumber` is -1, then the function will return one of the following:

- If no text is selected, the length of the current line is returned.
- If text is selected, the length of the line, minus the length of the currently selected text, is returned.

Example:

```
nLen = pEdit->GetLineLength(1);
```

Syntax

The *GetSelection* Function

The `GetSelection` member function returns the starting and ending character positions of the selected text. The starting character position is the index of the first selected character. The ending position is the index of the first character *after* the selected text. The declaration of the function is

```
void GetSelection(UINT& startPos, UINT& endPos) const;
```

The function fills in the passed `startPos` and `endPos` with the corresponding selection locations. If these two values are equal, there is no selected text, because both UINTs are the character indices to the current position.

Example:

```
pEdit->GetSelection(start, end);
```

Syntax

The *GetLine* Function

The `GetLine` member function returns a line from a multiline edit control. Its declaration is

```
BOOL GetLine(char far* str, int strSize, int lineNumber) const;
```

The `str` parameter points to a buffer that is to receive the text of the line; `strSize` is the number of characters to receive; and `lineNumber` is the line to retrieve. If there is a problem copying the line or if the line is longer than `strSize`, the function will return `FALSE`. Otherwise it will return `TRUE`.

Example:

```
char s[128];
pEdit->GetLine(s, sizeof(s) - 1, 22);
```

Altering the Edit Controls

Let's now focus on the member functions of `TEdit` that alter the edit control text. The operations of these member functions include writing new text to the control, selecting text, and replacing the selected text:

- The `SetText` member function that is inherited from the parent `TStatic` class acts in the same manner; it overwrites the current edit control characters with those of a new string.
- The `SetSelection` member function defines a block of characters as the new selected text.
- The `Insert` member function replaces the selected text with new characters.

Syntax

The *SetSelection* Function

The declaration of the `SetSelection` function is

```
BOOL SetSelection(UINT startPos, UINT endPos);
```

The `startPos` and `endPos` parameters define the range of characters that make up the new selected text. If the starting and ending positions are 0 and -1 respectively, the entire text in the edit control is selected. If `startPos` is -1, any selection is removed. The current position is placed at the greater of the two parameters.

Example:

```
pEdit->SetSelection(0, -1);
```

Syntax

The *Insert* Function

The declaration of the `Insert` function is

```
void Insert(const char far* str);
```

The `str` parameter is the pointer to the new selected text that replaces the current selection. If there is no selected text, the function simply inserts the text accessed by `str` at the current insertion point.

Example:

```
pEdit->Insert("New Text");
```

Note: You can use the `Insert` function to delete parts of the edit control text by first selecting that part and then replacing it with an empty string.

The Pushbutton Control

The pushbutton control is perhaps psychologically the most powerful control (you never hear about the nuclear list box or the nuclear check box). In a sense, the pushbutton control represents the fundamental notion of a control—you click on the control and something happens. The rest of today's lesson focuses on the aspects of the class `TButton` that deal with the pushbutton controls.

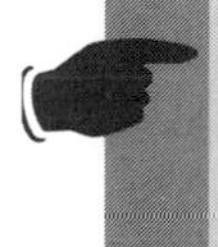

New Term: There are basically two types of pushbutton controls: *default buttons* and *nondefault buttons*. Default buttons have slightly thicker edges than nondefault buttons. Pressing the Enter key is equivalent to clicking the default button in a dialog box. There can be only one default button in a dialog box. You can select a new default button by pressing the Tab key. This feature works only when the buttons are in a dialog box. If a nondialog box window owns a pushbutton control, it can only visually display a default button—the functionality is not supported.

16

The *TButton* Class

The `TButton` class, a descendant of `TControl`, doesn't declare any public member functions other than its constructors.

Syntax

The *TButton* Constructor

The declaration for the `TButton` constructor is

```
TButton(TWindow*        parent,
        int             id,
        const char far* text,
        int             X,
        int             Y,
        int             W,
        int             H,
        BOOL            isDefault = FALSE,
        TModule*        module = 0 );
TButton(TWindow* parent, int resourceId, TModule* module = 0);
```

The first seven parameters to this function should be relatively familiar to you now, as they're identical to the ones in both the `TStatic` and `TEdit` controls. In fact, you'll find that most of these controls are descendants of the `TControl` class; the parameters will be virtually the same across the control classes. In this case, the difference is the addition of an `isDefault` parameter. This parameter specifies whether or not the button is default.

Examples:

```
pOk = new TButton(this, IDOK, "&OK", 10, 10, 50, 25, TRUE);
pCancel = new TButton(this, IDCANCEL, "&Cancel", 70, 10, 50, 25);
```

Handling Button Messages

When you click a button, the control sends the BN_CLICKED notification message to its parent window. The parent window responds to this message by invoking a message response member function based on the ID of the button. For example, if you have a button that was created with an ID of IDB_EXIT, the message handler function is

```
// Other declarations
void HandleExitBtn();
// Other declarations

DEFINE_RESPONSE_TABLE1(TMyWindow, TWindow)
   // Other possible message mapping macros
   EV_BN_CLICKED(IDB_EXIT, HandleExitBtn),
   // Other possible message mapping macros
END_RESPONSE_TABLE;
```

This example shows that the message map macro EV_BN_CLICKED is used to map the IDB_EXIT notification message with the HandleExitBtn member function.

Manipulating Buttons

You can disable and enable a button by using the EnableWindow function, which is inherited from the TWindow ancestor. A disabled button has a faded gray caption and does not respond to mouse clicks or keyboard input. The TWindow::EnableWindow function enables you to enable or disable a button. The function accepts a single argument, a Boolean argument that specifies whether the button is enabled (when the argument is TRUE) or disabled (when the argument is FALSE). Sample calls to the EnableWindow member function are

```
pOk->EnableWindow(FALSE);
pCalculate->EnableWindow(TRUE);
```

You can query the enabled state of a button by using the Boolean IsWindowEnabled function, which takes no arguments. A sample call to IsWindowEnabled is

```
// Toggle the enabled state of a button
pButton->EnableWindow(!pButton->IsWindowEnabled());
```

You can also hide and show a button using the ShowWindow function. The function takes one argument, either the SW_HIDE constant to hide the button or the SW_SHOW constant to show the button. Other constant values are defined for this function, but the SW_HIDE and SW_SHOW are the only two that apply to pushbuttons. The Boolean

IsWindowVisible function queries the visibility of a button. This function takes no arguments. A sample call to the ShowWindow and IsWindowVisible functions is

```
// Toggle the visibility of a button
pButton->ShowWindow(pButton->IsWindowVisible() ? SW_HIDE : SW_SHOW);
```

16

Mr. Calculator

Let's look at an application that uses static text, single-line edit controls, multiline edit controls, and pushbuttons—Mr. Calculator. This nontrivial application implements a floating-point calculator that uses edit controls instead of buttons. This type of interface is somewhat visually inferior to the typical button-populated calculator Windows applications. However, this interface can support more mathematical functions without requiring the addition of the buttons for those extra functions. In Mr. Calculator, the calculator is made up of the following controls:

- Two edit controls for the first and second operands to accept integers, floating-point numbers, and the names of single-letter variables, *A* to *Z*.
- One edit control for the operator supports the calculator's four basic math operations and the exponentiation (using a caret, ^).
- One edit control displays the result of the math operation.
- One edit control displays any error messages.
- One multiline edit control enables you to store a number in the Result edit control in one of 26 single-letter variables, *A* to *Z*. The multiline edit displays the current values stored in these variables and enables you to view and edit these numbers. You can use the vertical scroll bar to inspect the values in the different variables.
- Multiple static text controls serve to label the various edit controls. Of particular interest is the static control for the Error Message box. If you click the accompanying static text, the Error Message is cleared of any text.
- A menu has the single Exit option.
- A pushbutton with the caption "Calc" performs the operation specified in the Operator edit control, using the operands in the operand edit controls.
- A pushbutton with the caption "Store" stores the contents of the result edit control in the currently selected line of the multiline edit control.
- A pushbutton with the caption "Exit" exits the application.

The program supports the following special features for the Store button control:

- The Store pushbutton is disabled if the application attempts to execute an invalid operator. This feature illustrates an example of disabling a pushbutton when a certain condition arises (in this case, a specific calculation error).
- The Store pushbutton is enabled if you click the Error Message static text. The same button is enabled when you successfully execute a math operation.

The calculator application demonstrates the following tasks:

- Using single-line edit controls for simple input
- Using a multiline edit control to view and edit information
- Accessing and editing line-oriented text
- Simulating static text that responds to mouse clicks
- Using pushbuttons
- Disabling and enabling pushbuttons

Create the directory MRCALC as a subdirectory of \BC45\BC21DAY and store all the project's files in the new directory. The project's .IDE file should contain the files MRCALC.CPP and MRCALC.RC.

First, compile and run the application to get a good sense for how the calculator application works. Experiment with typing different numeric operands and the supported operators and click the Calc button. Each time, the result appears in the Result box, overwriting the previous result. Try dividing a number by zero to experiment with the error handling features.

Using the single-letter variables is easy. All these variables are initialized with 0. Therefore, the first step to using them is to store a nonzero value. Perform an operation and then click inside the Variables edit box. Select the first line that contains the variable *A*. Now click the Store button and watch the number in the Result box appear in the first line of the Variables edit box. The name of the variable and the colon and space characters that follow reappear with the new text line. Now replace the contents of the Operand1 edit box with the variable *A*, and then click the Calc button. The Result edit box displays the result of the latest operation.

Listing 16.1 shows the source code for the MRCALC.H header file. The header file declares the command constants for the menu item and the various controls. Listing 16.2 contains the script for the MRCALC.RC resource file. Listing 16.3 contains the source code for the MRCALC.CPP program file.

Listing 16.1. Source code for the MRCALC.H header file.

```
#define IDB_CALC      101
#dcfine IDB_STORE     102
#define IDB_EXIT      103
#define IDE_OPERAND1 104
#define IDE_OPERATOR 105
#define IDE_OPERAND2 106
#define IDE_RESULT   107
#define IDE_ERRMSG   108
#define IDE_VARIABLE 109
```

Listing 16.2. Script for the MRCALC.RC resource file.

```
#include <windows.h>
#include <owl\window.rh>

EXITMENU MENU LOADONCALL MOVEABLE PURE DISCARDABLE
BEGIN
   MENUITEM "E&xit", CM_EXIT
END
```

Listing 16.3. Source code for the MRCALC.CPP program file.

```
#include <ctype.h>
#include <math.h>
#include <stdio.h>
#include <owl\applicat.h>
#include <owl\button.h>
#include <owl\edit.h>
#include <owl\framewin.h>
#include <owl\static.h>
#include <owl\window.h>
#include <owl\window.rh>

#include "mrcalc.h"

class TCalcWindow : public TWindow
{
public:
   TCalcWindow(TWindow* parent = 0);
   ~TCalcWindow();

protected:
```

continues

Listing 16.3. continued

```
   virtual void SetupWindow();
   virtual void EvLButtonDown(UINT modKeys, TPoint &point);

   void CmCalc();
   void CmStore();
   void CmExit();

private:
   TStatic  *ErrMsgLabel;
   TEdit    *Operand1, *Operator, *Operand2, *Result,
            *ErrMsg, *Variable;
   TButton  *Store;

   double get_number(TEdit* edit);
   double get_var(int line);
   void put_var(double val);

   DECLARE_RESPONSE_TABLE(TCalcWindow);
};
DEFINE_RESPONSE_TABLE1(TCalcWindow, TWindow)
   EV_WM_LBUTTONDOWN,
   EV_COMMAND(CM_EXIT, CmExit),
   EV_BN_CLICKED(IDB_CALC, CmCalc),
   EV_BN_CLICKED(IDB_STORE, CmStore),
   EV_BN_CLICKED(IDB_EXIT, CmExit),
END_RESPONSE_TABLE;

TCalcWindow::TCalcWindow(TWindow* parent)
{
   Init(parent, 0, 0);

   int   wlblspacing = 40,
         hlblspacing = 5,
         wlbl = 100,
         hlbl = 20,
         wbox = 100,
         hbox = 30,
         wboxspacing = 40,
         hboxspacing = 40,
         wbtn = 80,
         hbtn = 30,
         wbtnspacing = 30;
   int   wlongbox = 4 * (wbox + wboxspacing);
   int   wvarbox = 2 * wbox,
         hvarbox = 3 * hbox;
   int   x0 = 20, y0 = 30;
   int   x, y;

   // First, create the labels for the edit text boxes.
   //
   x = x0;
```

```
    y = y0;
    new TStatic(this, -1, "Operand1", x, y, wlbl, hlbl);
    x += wlbl + wlblspacing;
    new TStatic(this, -1, "Operator", x, y, wlbl, hlbl);
    x += wlbl + wlblspacing;
    new TStatic(this, -1, "Operand2", x, y, wlbl, hlbl);
    x += wlbl + wlblspacing;
    new TStatic(this, -1, "Result", x, y, wlbl, hlbl);
    x += wlbl + wlblspacing;

    // Now create the edit text boxes
    //
    x = x0;
    y += hlbl + hlblspacing;
    if (NULL != (Operand1 = new TEdit(this, IDE_OPERAND1, "",
                                       x, y, wbox, hbox)))
       Operand1->Attr.Style |= ES_UPPERCASE;
    x += wbox + wboxspacing;
    if (NULL != (Operator = new TEdit(this, IDE_OPERATOR, "",
                                       x, y, wbox, hbox)))
       Operator->Attr.Style |= ES_UPPERCASE;
    x += wbox + wboxspacing;
    if (NULL != (Operand2 = new TEdit(this, IDE_OPERAND2, "",
                                       x, y, wbox, hbox)))
       Operand2->Attr.Style |= ES_UPPERCASE;
    x += wbox + wboxspacing;
    Result = new TEdit(this, IDE_RESULT, "", x, y, wbox, hbox);
    x += wbox + wboxspacing;

    // Now create the label and box for the error message
    //
    x = x0;
    y += hbox + hboxspacing;
    ErrMsgLabel = new TStatic( this, -1, "Error Message", x, y,
                               wlbl, hlbl );
    y += hlbl + hlblspacing;
    ErrMsg = new TEdit(this, IDE_ERRMSG, "", x, y, wlongbox, hbox);

    // Create the label and box for the single-letter
    // variable selection
    //
    y += hbox + hboxspacing;
    new TStatic(this, -1, "Variables", x, y, wlbl, hlbl);
    y += hlbl + hlblspacing;
    char str[6 * ('Z' - 'A' + 1) + 1];
    char *p = str;
    for (char ch = 'A'; ch <= 'Z'; ++ch)
       p += sprintf(p, "%c: 0\r\n", ch);
    Variable = new TEdit(this, IDE_VARIABLE, str, x, y,
                         wvarbox, hvarbox, 0, TRUE );
```

continues

Listing 16.3. continued

```

   // Finally create some buttons
   //
   x += wvarbox + wbtnspacing;
   new TButton(this, IDB_CALC, "Calc", x, y, wbtn, hbtn);
   x += wbtn + wbtnspacing;
   Store = new TButton(this, IDB_STORE, "Store", x, y, wbtn, hbtn);
   x += wbtn + wbtnspacing;
   new TButton(this, IDB_EXIT, "Exit", x, y, wbtn, hbtn);
}

TCalcWindow::~TCalcWindow()
{
}

void TCalcWindow::SetupWindow()
{
   TWindow::SetupWindow();    // Initialize the visual element

   // Keep the users out of the destination areas.
   //
   if (Result)
      Result->SetReadOnly(TRUE);
   if (ErrMsg)
      ErrMsg->SetReadOnly(TRUE);
   if (Variable)
      Variable->SetReadOnly(TRUE);
}

void TCalcWindow::EvLButtonDown(UINT /*modKeys*/, TPoint& point)
{
   if (      ErrMsgLabel
         && (ErrMsgLabel->HWindow == ChildWindowFromPoint(point)) )
      {
      if (ErrMsg)
         ErrMsg->Clear();
      if (Store)
         Store->EnableWindow(TRUE);
      }
}

double TCalcWindow::get_number(TEdit *edit)
{
   double rslt;
   char *str;
   int size;

   if (edit)
      {
      str = new char[size = edit->GetWindowTextLength() + 1];
```

```
        if (str)
            {
            edit->GetWindowText(str, size);
            if (isalpha(str[0]))
                rslt = get_var(tolower(str[0]) - 'a');
            else
                rslt = atof(str);
            delete str;
            }
        }
    return rslt;
}

double TCalcWindow::get_var(int line)
{
    double rslt = 0;

    if (Variable)
        {
        int size = Variable->GetLineLength(line) + 1;
        char *str = new char[size];
        if (str)
            {
            Variable->GetLine(str, size, line);
            rslt = atof(str + 3);        // Don't want first 3 chars
            delete str;
            }
        }
    return rslt;
}

void TCalcWindow::put_var(double var)
{
    if (Variable)
        {
        UINT start, end;
        Variable->GetSelection(start, end);
        if (start != end)
            Variable->SetSelection(start, start);
        int line = Variable->GetLineFromPos(-1);
        int size = Variable->GetLineLength(line) + 1;
        char *str = new char[size];
        if (str)
            {
            Variable->GetLine(str, size, line);
            sprintf(str, "%c: %g", str[0], var);
            start = Variable->GetLineIndex(-1);
            end = start + Variable->GetLineLength(-1);
            Variable->SetSelection(start, end);
            Variable->Insert(str);
```

continues

Listing 16.3. continued

```
            delete str;
            }
         }

}

void TCalcWindow::CmCalc()
{
   double x, y, z = 0;
   char   *str, *err = NULL;
   int    size;

   x = get_number(Operand1);
   y = get_number(Operand2);

   if (Operator)
      {
      str = new char[size = Operator->GetWindowTextLength() + 1];
      if (str)
         {
         Operator->GetWindowText(str, size);
         if (str[1] != '\0')
            err = "Invalid operator";
         else
            switch (str[0])
               {
               case '+':
                  z = x + y;
                  break;
               case '-':
                  z = x - y;
                  break;
               case '*':
                  z = x * y;
                  break;
               case '/':
                  if (y)
                     z = x / y;
                  else
                     err = "Division by zero error";
                  break;
               case '^':
                  if (x > 0)
                     z = exp(y * log(x));
                  else
                     err = "Can't raise power of negative numbers";
                  break;
               default:
                  err = "Invalid operator";
                  break;
```

```
               }
            if (ErrMsg)
               if (!err)
                  ErrMsg->Clear();
               else
                  ErrMsg->SetWindowText(err);
            if (Store)
               Store->EnableWindow(!err);
            if (!err && Result)
               {
               char dest[81];
               sprintf(dest, "%g", z);
               Result->SetWindowText(dest);
               }
         delete str;
         }
      }
}

void TCalcWindow::CmStore()
{
   if (Result)
      {
      int size = Result->GetWindowTextLength() + 1;
      char *str = new char[size];
      if (str)
         {
         Result->GetWindowText(str, size);
         put_var(atof(str));
         delete str;
         }
      }
}

void TCalcWindow::CmExit()
{
   SendMessage(WM_CLOSE);
}

class TCalcApp : public TApplication
{
public:
   TCalcApp() : TApplication()
      { nCmdShow = SW_SHOWMAXIMIZED; }

   void InitMainWindow()
      {
      SetMainWindow(new TFrameWindow(  0,
                                 "Mr. Calculator",
```

continues

Listing 16.3. continued

```
321:                                  new TCalcWindow ));
322:          GetMainWindow()->AssignMenu("EXITMENU");
323:          }
324: };
325:
326: int OwlMain(int, char *[])
327: {
328:     return TCalcApp().Run();
329: }
330:
```

Figure 16.1 shows a sample session with the Mr. Calculator program.

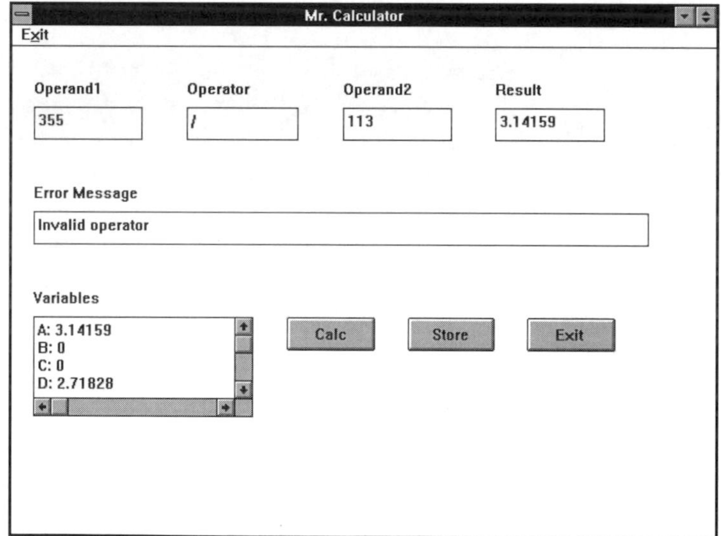

Figure 16.1. *A sample session with MRCALC.EXE.*

The program in Listing 16.3 contains a number of data members in the `TCalcWindow` class, each of which is a pointer to a control class. These are the `TStatic`, `TEdit`, and `TButton` controls declared on lines 29 through 32. In general, there is no real need to keep track of these controls because OWL will automatically take care of deleting these controls when their corresponding Windows elements are destroyed. However, if you may have some need to access them during the duration of their existence, you will need a pointer in order to affect them.

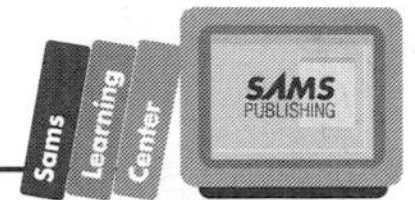

Note that as the operand and operator edit boxes are created on lines 82 through 96, they are given the style of `ES_UPPERCASE`. This style results in automatically converting into uppercase the single-letter variable names that you type in these edit controls.

Usually, such controls as `TButton` and especially `TStatic` can be created without bothering to keep a pointer to them; a button will automatically send notifications to its parent and, because static text controls are usually used as labels, there is rarely a need to keep track of them. In this case, however, you need to keep track of the Store button so you can enable and disable it according to error conditions, and you also need to keep track of the Error Message label so you can tell when the user has clicked it, at which point you need to clear the error message and re-enable the Store button.

16

In the constructor of `TCalcWindow` are a number of declarations between lines 52 and 57. These are used when placing the controls as they are created. The declarations define the various widths and heights of the controls as well as the space in between them. As the controls are created, the local variables `x` and `y` are updated to the location of the next control.

In the `SetupWindow` member function of `TCalcWindow` starting on line 37, the `Result`, `ErrMsg`, and `Variable` edit controls are set to read-only by calling the `TEdit::SetReadOnly` member function. This is done to prevent the user from modifying the parts of the screen that should be updated only by the program itself. The user can still place the caret in these edit controls, even select text and scroll around in them, but Windows will prevent the user from changing any of the contents.

The `Variable` edit box is created on lines 110 through 121 somewhat differently from the other edit boxes. First, a somewhat elaborate initializing string is made up for it. This string consists of 26 letters (`'A'` through `'Z'`), each followed by a colon, a space, the number 0, and finally the characters `"\r\n"`. This makes up the format of the list box and will be changed dynamically later by the user pressing the Store button.

Secondly, the `Variable` edit box constructor receives two extra parameters on lines 120 through 121. The first of the two extra parameters, 0, is the same as the default parameter that is used whenever the constructor is called without passing anything for that argument. The next parameter, however, is the one stating that you want a multiline edit control. This automatically sets the control to allowing for multiple lines, as well as adding the horizontal and vertical scroll bars.

The `EvLButtonDown` member function starting on line 151 performs a simple task. It checks whether or not the mouse click occurs in the rectangle occupied by the error message static text control. If this condition is true, the function performs the following tasks:

- Uses the `ChildWindowFromPoint` function starting on line 154 to determine in which window the mouse was clicked, then checks that against the window of `ErrMsgLabel`
- Clears the error message box by invoking the function `Clear` on line 157
- Enables the Store button by invoking the function `EnableWindow` on line 159

Because you will have two edit boxes from which you will want to get either a number or a value associated with a variable, it makes sense to have only one function that performs this action and is called for each edit box. This is the purpose of the `get_number` private member function starting on line 163. Its single parameter is a pointer to a `TEdit` object. From this, the function obtains the text that's stored in that edit box on line 174. If the first character in that edit box is an alphabetic character (checked through the ANSI C function `isalpha` on line 175), then the private `get_var` function is called on line 176; otherwise the contents are converted to a floating point number with the `atof` function on line 178.

The `get_var` function starting on line 185 is used to obtain the value associated with a specific variable in the Variable edit control. Given a line number, it gets the text from that line in the edit control, then passes that line, skipping the first three characters (the variable letter, the colon, and the space), to the `atof` function for conversion to a floating point number.

The `put_var` function starting on line 203 changes a variable in the Variable edit box. It does so with the following steps:

- You check for a selection in the `Variable` edit box on lines 208 and 209. If there is one, you remove that selection and set the current insertion point to the beginning of the selection.
- Using the `GetLineFromPos` function, you get the line of the insertion point on line 211.
- After creating a string large enough to hold the line, you get the line and then change it to include the new value on lines 212 through 217.
- By passing -1 to the `GetLineIndex` function on line 218, you obtain the character location of the start of the current line. Adding the length of the line, you get the start of the next line.
- Using the `SetSelection` function on line 220, you select the current line. Then you `Insert` the new string on line 221, replacing the current selection.

The CmCalc member function starting on line 228 responds to the notification message emitted by the Calc button. You told the window to have the function called by using the EV_BN_CLICKED macro during the TCalcWindow's response table declaration on line 43. The function performs the following tasks:

- Obtains the two operands from the Operand1 and Operand2 edit boxes with the get_number private member function on lines 234 and 235.
- Copies the text in the Operator edit box into the local variable str on line 242.
- Determines and performs the requested operation by using a switch statement on lines 246 through 272, checking the first character of the string for the supported operators +, –, *, / and ^ (power).
- If at any time an error is detected, the err local variable is set to a string describing the error, and at the end on line 273, if this variable is non-NULL, its value is placed in the Error Message edit box, and the Store button is disabled.

The CmStore member function starting on line 291 stores the contents of the Result box in a single-letter variable. The function first obtains the string from the Result edit box by calling the GetWindowText function on line 299. Then, the function invokes the private member function put_var on line 300 to actually store the result string at the current insertion point in the Variables edit box.

The CmExit member function starting on line 306 responds to the notification message of both the Exit button and the Exit menu item. It sends a WM_CLOSE message to the window, which effectively terminates the program.

Summary

Today's lesson looked at the static text, edit box, and pushbutton controls. Using these and other controls animates the Windows applications and provides a more consistent user interface. You learned about the following topics:

- You can create static text controls and manipulate their text at runtime.
- Single-line and multiline edit box controls enable you to type in and edit the text in the input dialog box.

In Day 17, we will present the grouped controls, the classes for group, check box, and radio controls. These controls are used to fine-tune the execution of a specified task, such as searching and replacing text in a text editor.

Q&A

Q How do I create a string for a multiline static text control?

A You build a multiline string, such as `"This is\r\na multiline"` (notice the embedded `\r\n` characters, which break the line) and pass it as the third argument to the `TStatic` class's constructor.

Q Why does program MRCALC.CPP use local variables such as `x` and `y` to specify the location of a control? Why not replace these variables with numeric constants?

A Using variables, such as `x` and `y`, enables you to specify the location of the controls relative to one another. This method enables you to shift controls very easily. By contrast, using numeric constants specifies the absolute values for the control locations. Shifting controls, in this case, means plugging in a new set of numbers.

Q What do .RC resource files compile into?

A The .RC resource files are compiled into .RES files. Also, you should note that the Resource Workshop is quite capable of saving your various dialog boxes and other resources in an .RES file as well as an .RC file. This precompiled file could then be included in your .IDE file instead of the .RC.

Workshop

The Workshop provides quiz questions to help you solidify your understanding of the material covered and exercises to provide you with experience in using what you've learned. Try to understand the quiz and exercise answers before continuing on to the next day's lesson. Answers are provided in Appendix A, "Answers."

Quiz

1. True or false? The text for all static text controls are unchangeable.
2. True or false? The `SS_CENTER` style centers each line of a multiline static text control.
3. True or false? A static text control needs an accompanying pointer for access only when the program needs to set or query the text in the control.

4. True or false? Every edit control needs an accompanying pointer for access.
5. True or false? The API Windows function `EnableWindow` can disable any control.
6. True or false? The Windows messages emitted by a pushbutton can be mapped using the `EV_COMMAND` map.

Exercises

1. Experiment with the program MRCALC.CPP to add trigonometric functions, inverse trigonometric functions, hyperbolic functions, and inverse hyperbolic functions.
2. Experiment with a copy of the program MRCALC.CPP by changing values assigned to the constants that specify the size and spacing of the various controls.

Grouped Controls

Windows supports check box and radio button controls that act as software switches. These controls appear in typical Search and Replace dialog boxes and influence certain aspects of the text search or replacement. These aspects include the scope, direction, and case-sensitivity of searching or replacing text. In today's lesson, you learn about the following topics:

- The check box control
- The radio button control
- The group control

Today's lesson also shows you how to respond to the messages emitted by these controls as well as how to use the `ForEach` iterators to manipulate the check box and radio button controls.

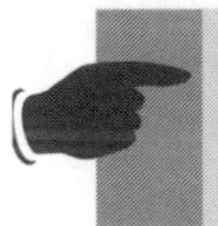

New Term: The *group box control* is a special control that visually and logically groups the check box and radio button controls.

The Check Box Control

The check box control is a special button that toggles a check mark. The control instances appear with a small rectangular button and a title that appears, by default, to the right side of the square. When you click the square, you toggle the control's check mark. Think of the check box as a binary digit that can be either set or cleared. The instances of a check box can appear inside or outside a group box and are not mutually exclusive—toggling any check box does not affect the check state of other check boxes.

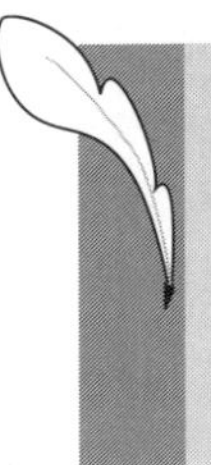

Note: Placing check boxes inside groups (inside a dialog box) serves two purposes. First, the group box provides a visual grouping that clarifies the purpose of the check boxes to the application user. Second, you can streamline the notification messages emitted by the check boxes in a group to detect any change in the checked state of the check boxes.

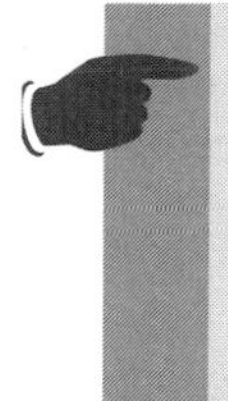

New Term: Windows enables you to specify a check box that can have one of three states: checked, unchecked, and *grayed*. The grayed state fills the control's rectangular button with a gray color. This third state can serve to indicate that the check box control is in an indeterminate (or "don't care") state.

The *TCheckBox* Class

The ObjectWindows Library offers the `TCheckBox` class, a descendant of `TButton`, as the class that provides the instances of check box controls. Day 16 introduces you to the `TButton` class and discusses the aspects of that class that are related to the pushbutton controls. Because check boxes are really just specialized buttons, much of what applies to buttons also applies to check boxes. By deriving the `TCheckBox` class from the `TButton` class, we ensure that `TCheckBox` inherits much of the parent's functionality. The check box styles shown in Table 17.1 indicate that there are two basic modes for managing the check state of a check box control: automatic and nonautomatic (manual, if you prefer). In automatic mode (specified by `BS_AUTOCHECKBOX` and `BS_AUTO3STATE`), Windows toggles the check state when you click the control. In manual mode, your application code is responsible for managing the check state of the check box.

17

Table 17.1. Check box control styles.

Style	Meaning
`BS_CHECKBOX`	Specifies a check box with the title to the right of the rectangular button.
`BS_AUTOCHECKBOX`	Same as `BS_CHECKBOX`, except the button is automatically toggled when you click it. This is the default setting for the `TCheckBox` class.
`BS_3STATE`	Same as `BS_CHECKBOX`, except that the control has three states: checked, unchecked, and grayed.
`BS_AUTO3STATE`	Same as `BS_3STATE`, except the button is automatically toggled when you click it.
`BS_LEFTTEXT`	Sets the control's title to the left of the button. Note that this is the only style that can be ORed into the style.

The TCheckBox class provides member functions to set and query the state of the check box. The GetCheck member function returns a state of the check box control and is declared as follows:

```
UINT GetCheck() const;
```

The function returns a UINT-typed value that represents the check state. A value of BF_UNCHECKED indicates that the control is not checked. A value of BF_CHECKED signals that the control is checked. A value of BF_GRAYED indicates that the control is in an indeterminate state. The latter value is valid for the BS_3STATE and BS_AUTO3STATE styles.

The SetCheck member function enables you to set the check state of a check box control. The declaration of the SetCheck function is

```
void SetCheck(UINT check);
```

The check parameter specifies the new state of the check box control and should be one of the BF_*XXX* values.

Responding to Check Box Messages

Because check boxes are descendants of TButton with a BS_CHECKBOX or BS_AUTOCHECKBOX style, your OWL application responds to the messages emitted by check boxes in a manner similar to the pushbuttons. The EV_BN_CLICKED macro maps the message sent by the check box control with the member function that responds to that message.

The Radio Button Control

Radio buttons typically enable you to select an option from two or more options. This kind of control comes with a circular button and a title that appears, by default, to the right of the button. When you check a radio button, a tiny, filled circle appears inside the circular button. Radio buttons need to be placed in group boxes that visually and logically group them. In each group of radio buttons, only one button can be selected. Therefore, radio buttons are mutually exclusive.

The *TRadioButton* Class

OWL applications use the TRadioButton class, a descendant of TCheckBox, to create radio button controls by specifying BS_RADIOBUTTON or BS_AUTORADIOBUTTON.

Table 17.2 contains the radio button styles. The constructor creates a radio button with the `BS_AUTORADIOBUTTON` style. Like the check box controls, the radio buttons use the `GetCheck` and `SetCheck` member functions to query and set the state. Unlike the check box, the radio button has only two states: checked and unchecked.

Table 17.2. Radio button control styles.

Style	Meaning
`BS_RADIOBUTTON`	Specifies a radio button with the title to the right of the circular button.
`BS_AUTORADIOBUTTON`	Same as `BS_RADIOBUTTON`, except the button is automatically toggled when you click it. This is the default style for the `TRadioButton` class.
`BS_LEFTTEXT`	Sets the control's title to the left of the button. This is the only style that can be ORed into the style.

The radio button controls send the same type of notification messages to their parent windows as do the check box controls. Handling these messages for radio buttons is identical to that of check box and pushbutton controls.

The Group Control

The group box control encloses radio buttons and check boxes. The group box performs the following tasks:

- Visually groups radio buttons or check boxes, which makes relating these controls to each other clearer for the application user, by placing a box around them. Note that you don't necessarily need controls in a box to get the visual effect.
- Logically groups multiple radio buttons so that when you select one radio button, the other buttons in the same group are automatically deselected.

New Term: The group box control is a special type of control known as a *container control*.

You can code your OWL application so that the controls inside a group box notify the parent of the group box that you have changed the state of its controls.

The *TGroupBox* Class

Your OWL applications can create group boxes with the `TGroupBox` class, descended from `TControl`. This automatically creates the visual element and provides access via its `SelectionChanged` member function. The declaration of the `SelectionChanged` function is

```
void SelectionChanged(int controlId);
```

When an item in the group is changed, this function gets called. By default, the `SelectionChanged` function checks the `TGroupBox`'s `NotifyParent` data member. If it's `TRUE`, then the function notifies the parent window of the group box that one of its selections has changed by sending it a child-ID-based message. By deriving your own version of `TGroupBox` and redefining `SelectionChanged`, you can handle selection changes from the group box itself.

The Widget Selection Application

Here's a short application that demonstrates a possible use for the controls introduced in this chapter. The program shows a sample order form for the World-Wide Widget Weilders company. On it, the user can select one each of Type A, Type B, and Type C widgets. For each of those widget types, there are several different models from which the user can choose. In each case, the different models are disabled so long as the widget type is not checked.

This program illustrates the following:

- The basic use of check box controls
- The basic use of radio buttons
- Responding to check box notification messages
- Overriding a group box to keep track of changes in radio button selections
- Making initial radio button selections

Listing 17.1 contains the source code for the WIDGETS.H header file. Listing 17.2 shows the source code for the WIDGETS.CPP program file. Create the directory WIDGETS as a subdirectory of \BC45\BC21DAY and store all the project's files in the new directory. The project's .IDE file should contain the file WIDGETS.CPP.

Listing 17.1. Source code for the WIDGETS.H header file.

```
#define IDC_TYPEA       101
#define IDC_TYPEB       102
#define IDC_TYPEC       103
#define IDR_ETCHED      104
#define IDR_POLISHED    105
#define IDR_WOODGRAIN   106
#define IDR_VARNISHED   107
#define IDR_ENGRAVED    108
#define IDR_MEDIOCRE    109
#define IDR_DELUXE      110
#define IDG_TYPEA       111
#define IDG_TYPEB       112
#define IDG_TYPEC       113
```

Listing 17.2. Source code for the WIDGETS.CPP program file.

```
#include <stdio.h>
#include <owl\applicat.h>
#include <owl\button.h>
#include <owl\checkbox.h>
#include <owl\framewin.h>
#include <owl\groupbox.h>
#include <owl\radiobut.h>
#include <owl\window.h>
#include <owl\window.rh>

#include "widgets.h"

class TMyGroup : public TGroupBox
{
public:
   TMyGroup(TWindow*       parent,
            int            id,
            const char far* text,
            int X, int Y, int W, int H,
            TModule*        module = 0 )
      : TGroupBox(parent, id, text, X, Y, W, H, module), cur(-1)
      { }

   LPCSTR GetCurCheck();

   virtual void SelectionChanged(int controlId)
      { TGroupBox::SelectionChanged(cur = controlId); }

```

continues

Listing 17.2. continued

```
private:
    int cur;
};

LPCSTR TMyGroup::GetCurCheck()
{
    TWindow* w = Parent->ChildWithId(cur);
    return w ? w->Title : NULL;
}

class TWidgetWindow : public TWindow
{
public:
    TWidgetWindow(TWindow* parent = 0);

protected:
    virtual void SetupWindow();

    void EnableGroupA(BOOL enable);
    void EnableGroupB(BOOL enable);
    void EnableGroupC(BOOL enable);

    BOOL BuildStr( LPSTR str,
                   LPCSTR name,
                   TCheckBox* check,
                   TMyGroup* group );

    void CmDone();
    void CmCancel();
    void CmTypeA();
    void CmTypeB();
    void CmTypeC();
private:
    TCheckBox      *TypeA, *TypeB, *TypeC;
    TMyGroup       *GroupA, *GroupB, *GroupC;
    TRadioButton   *Etched, *Polished,
                   *WoodGrain, *Varnished, *Engraved,
                   *Mediocre, *Deluxe;

  DECLARE_RESPONSE_TABLE(TWidgetWindow);
};
DEFINE_RESPONSE_TABLE1(TWidgetWindow, TWindow)
    EV_BN_CLICKED(IDOK, CmDone),
    EV_BN_CLICKED(IDCANCEL, CmCancel),
    EV_BN_CLICKED(IDC_TYPEA, CmTypeA),
    EV_BN_CLICKED(IDC_TYPEB, CmTypeB),
    EV_BN_CLICKED(IDC_TYPEC, CmTypeC),
END_RESPONSE_TABLE;
```

```
TWidgetWindow::TWidgetWindow(TWindow* parent)
{
   Init(parent, 0, 0);

   new TButton(this, IDOK, "Done", 175, 350, 100, 30);
   new TButton(this, IDCANCEL, "Cancel", 400, 350, 100, 30);

   TypeA = new TCheckBox(this, IDC_TYPEA, "Type A",
                                      70, 40, 100, 20);
   GroupA = new TMyGroup(this, IDG_TYPEA, NULL,
                                      192, 15, 280, 75);
   Etched = new TRadioButton(this, IDR_ETCHED, "Etched",
                                      203, 42, 100, 20, GroupA);
   Polished = new TRadioButton(this, IDR_POLISHED, "Polished",
                                      332, 42, 100, 20, GroupA);

   TypeB = new TCheckBox(this, IDC_TYPEB, "Type B",
                                      70, 153, 100, 20);
   GroupB = new TMyGroup(this, IDG_TYPEB, NULL,
                                      192, 123, 280, 75);
   WoodGrain = new TRadioButton(this, IDR_WOODGRAIN, "Wood-Grain",
                                      203, 138, 100, 20, GroupB);
   Varnished = new TRadioButton(this, IDR_VARNISHED, "Varnished",
                                      332, 138, 100, 20, GroupB);
   Engraved = new TRadioButton(this, IDR_ENGRAVED, "Engraved",
                                      203, 172, 100, 20, GroupB);

   TypeC = new TCheckBox(this, IDC_TYPEC, "Type C",
                                      70, 272, 100, 20);
   GroupC = new TMyGroup(this, IDG_TYPEC, NULL,
                                      192, 247, 280, 75);
   Mediocre = new TRadioButton(this, IDR_MEDIOCRE, "Mediocre",
                                      203, 273, 100, 20, GroupC);
   Deluxe = new TRadioButton(this, IDR_DELUXE, "Deluxe",
                                      332, 273, 100, 20, GroupC);
}

void TWidgetWindow::SetupWindow()
{
   TWindow::SetupWindow();    // Initialize the visual element

   EnableGroupA(FALSE);
   EnableGroupB(FALSE);
   EnableGroupC(FALSE);
}

void TWidgetWindow::EnableGroupA(BOOL enable)
{
   if (Etched)
      Etched->EnableWindow(enable);
```

17

continues

Listing 17.2. continued

```
   if (Polished)
      Polished->EnableWindow(enable);
}

void TWidgetWindow::EnableGroupB(BOOL enable)
{
   if (WoodGrain)
      WoodGrain->EnableWindow(enable);
   if (Varnished)
      Varnished->EnableWindow(enable);
   if (Engraved)
      Engraved->EnableWindow(enable);
}

void TWidgetWindow::EnableGroupC(BOOL enable)
{
   if (Mediocre)
      Mediocre->EnableWindow(enable);
   if (Deluxe)
      Deluxe->EnableWindow(enable);
}

BOOL TWidgetWindow::BuildStr( LPSTR str,
                              LPCSTR name,
                              TCheckBox* check,
                              TMyGroup* group )
{
   BOOL rslt = FALSE;
   if (str && check && check->GetCheck())
      {
      rslt = TRUE;
      LPCSTR groupname;

      str += lstrlen(str);    // point to end of str
      sprintf(str, "\n   %s: ", name);
      if (group && (NULL != (groupname = group->GetCurCheck())))
         strcat(str, groupname);
      }
   return rslt;
}


void TWidgetWindow::CmDone()
{
   char           str[256] = "";
   int            sels = 0;

   strcpy(str, "You have selected the following:");
   sels += BuildStr(str, "Widget A", TypeA, GroupA);
   sels += BuildStr(str, "Widget B", TypeB, GroupB);
```

```
   sels += BuildStr(str, "Widget C", TypeC, GroupC);
   if (!sels)
      strcat(str, "\n   << No selections >>");
   MessageBox(str, "Widget Selection", MB_OK);
   SendMessage(WM_CLOSE);
}

void TWidgetWindow::CmCancel()
{
   SendMessage(WM_CLOSE);
}

void TWidgetWindow::CmTypeA()
{
   if (TypeA)
      EnableGroupA(TypeA->GetCheck());
   if (GroupA && !GroupA->GetCurCheck() && Etched)
      Etched->Check();
}

void TWidgetWindow::CmTypeB()
{
   if (TypeB)
      EnableGroupB(TypeB->GetCheck());
   if (GroupB && !GroupB->GetCurCheck() && WoodGrain)
      WoodGrain->Check();
}

void TWidgetWindow::CmTypeC()
{
   if (TypeC)
      EnableGroupC(TypeC->GetCheck());
   if (GroupC && !GroupC->GetCurCheck() && Mediocre)
      Mediocre->Check();
}


class TWidgetApp : public TApplication
{
public:
   TWidgetApp() : TApplication()
      { nCmdShow = SW_SHOWMAXIMIZED; }

   void InitMainWindow()
      {
      SetMainWindow(new TFrameWindow(  0,
                                 "World-Wide Widget Weilders",
                                 new TWidgetWindow ));
      }
};

```

continues

Listing 17.2. continued

```
229: int OwlMain(int, char *[])
230: {
231:     return TWidgetApp().Run();
232: }
```

Figure 17.1 shows a sample session with the WIDGETS.EXE program.

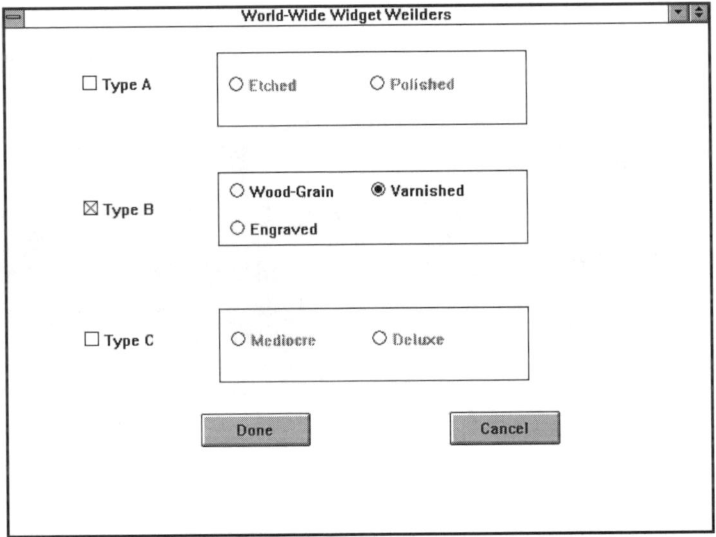

Figure 17.1. *A sample session with program WIDGETS.EXE.*

The program starts off on line 13 by declaring a descendant of `TGroupBox` called `TMyGroup`. The purpose of this is to keep track of the selections made by the controls contained within it. The class initializes its `cur` data member to –1 in the constructor on line 21. This signifies that no control has yet been selected inside the group. This value is changed in the overridden `SelectionChanged` member function on line 27. This function, as described earlier, is called whenever a control inside the group is selected. Our version of the function simply passes the single parameter along to the parent's version of the function while assigning the value of that parameter to our `cur` data member. Finally, the `TMyGroup` class defines the `GetCurCheck` member function starting on line 33. This function uses the parent window's `ChildWithId` function to obtain a `TWindow` pointer to the control with the ID recorded in `cur`. If a control was found, then its `Title` data member is returned.

The main window `TWidgetWindow` is then declared, starting on line 39. As usual, there is a constructor and a `SetupWindow` member function. The constructor creates all the various controls that are to appear on the screen, starting on line 78: three check boxes, each with a group next to it, then between two and three radio buttons inside that group. At the bottom of the window are two buttons, "Done" and "Cancel." The `SetupWindow` member function that starts on line 115, after calling its parent's version of the function, makes calls to three functions to initially disable the various groups of radio buttons.

Next are the helper functions `EnableGroupA`, `EnableGroupB`, and `EnableGroupC` on lines 124 through 148. These are used to enable and disable whole groups of controls via `TWindow`'s `EnableWindow` member function. They each take a single `BOOL`-typed `enable` parameter that determines whether the controls are to be enabled or disabled. This parameter is passed directly on to the individual control's `EnableWindow` function.

The two functions `CmDone` and `CmCancel` on lines 170 through 188 come next. They respond to the two buttons "Done" and "Cancel," respectively. In both cases, they send the `WM_CLOSE` message to the main window in order to shut the application down, but the `CmDone` function first creates and displays a message box informing the user of the selections made. It builds this string by doing the following:

- First, it fills in the `str` variable on line 175 with an initial string, letting the user know what information follows.
- Next, the `BuildStr` member function (discussed next) is called for each of the three check boxes and group boxes on lines 176 through 178. The return values of these calls are added to the `sels` variable and `BuildStr` modifies `str`.
- After filling up the string with results of the user's selections, the `sels` variable is checked. If it's still 0, then nothing was selected, and the `str` variable is filled to reflect that on lines 179 and 180. This bit of code works because `TRUE` is defined to be 1 and `FALSE` to be 0. So, when the `BOOL` return values from multiple calls to `BuildStr` are added together in `sels`, we're checking to see if any of the return values were `TRUE` without actually caring about which one.
- The `str` variable is then sent to the `MessageBox` function on line 181 for display to the user.
- Finally, the `WM_CLOSE` message is sent to the window via the `SendMessage` function on line 182 to effectively terminate the window and, thus, the program.

The `BuildStr` member function, starting on line 150, works by taking a destination string in its `str` parameter, the name of the check box to be reported to the user in the `name` parameter, and the pointers to the check box and group box controls in the `check` and `group` parameters, respectively. The function does the following things:

- First, it checks on line 156 to make sure it received valid `str` and `check` parameters. It's always a good idea to check parameters before trying to use them to help prevent unwanted bugs in the program. In the same statement, it also calls `check`'s `GetCheck` function. If that returns `TRUE`, then the check box has been checked, and we need to start filling in the `str` parameter.
- In order to keep from overwriting the previous contents of the `str` parameter, `str` is made to point at its end by adding the value obtained from the `lstrlen` function on line 161.
- The name of the check box is printed into the `str`, along with some formatting characters on line 162.
- If we have a valid `group` parameter and we're able to get the title of its selected radio button, then that title is concatenated to the `str` parameter on line 164.
- Finally, the result of whether or not anything was actually added to `str` is returned on line 166.

The last functions of interest are the `CmTypeA`, `CmTypeB`, and `CmTypeC` member functions on lines 190 through 212. These each respond, in turn, to the Type A, Type B, and Type C check boxes respectively. In each one, first the appropriate `EnableGroupX` is called with the check box's check state to either enable or disable the appropriate group's radio buttons. Then, the function attempts to find out the title of the currently selected radio button. If this value isn't set, then we know this is the first time the check box has been set, so we initialize the radio buttons by setting the first one with its `Check` member function.

Summary

Today's lesson discussed the special switch controls: group box, check box, and radio button. You learned about the following:

- Check box and radio button controls act as software switches.
- You can set and query the check state for the check box and radio button controls.

- ☐ Notification messages can be sent by these controls to their parent window.
- ☐ Group box controls enclose radio buttons and check boxes.
- ☐ Switch controls can be selectively manipulated.

Day 18 presents the scroll bar, list box, and combo box controls. These controls are value selectors because they enable you to select from a list or range of values.

Q&A

Q The check box has the states `BF_UNCHECKED`, `BF_CHECKED`, and `BF_GRAYED`. What can I use the third state for?

A You can use the `BF_GRAYED` state as a "don't care" or as an undetermined state.

Q Does it make any difference if I place check box controls in a group control?

A Placing check box controls in a group control affects the logical grouping of such controls as the user sees it. Consequently, this can enhance the interface for the user.

Workshop

The Workshop provides quiz questions to help you solidify your understanding of the material covered and exercises to provide you with experience in using what you've learned. Try to understand the quiz and exercise answers before continuing on to the next day's lesson. Answers are provided in Appendix A, "Answers."

Quiz

1. True or false? A check box can replace any two radio buttons in a group control.
2. True or false? You should use radio buttons in a group control when you have three or more options.
3. True or false? A set of check boxes parallels the bits in a byte or word.
4. True or false? Radio buttons, in a group control, are mutually nonexclusive.

Exercise

Expand on program WIDGETS.CPP by adding more widget types and more design types for each widget.

List Box Controls

WEEK

3

List box controls are input tools that conveniently provide you with the items to choose. This feature makes list box controls popular because they absolve you from remembering the list members—especially when computer programs expect exact spelling. Experience with DOS programs has shown that the various DOS utilities that display lists of files and directories are far easier and friendlier to use than their counterparts that assume the user knows all the names of the files and directories. Using list box controls has gradually become a routine method for retrieving information. Today's lesson discusses the single-selection and multiple-selection list boxes. You will learn about the following topics:

- The list box control
- Handling single-selection list boxes
- Handling multiple-selection list boxes

The List Box Control

List boxes typically are framed and include a vertical scroll bar. When you select an item by clicking it, the selection is highlighted. Microsoft suggests the following guidelines for making a selection:

- Use a single mouse click to select a new or an additional item. A separate button control retrieves the selected item.
- Use a double-click as a shortcut for selecting an item and retrieving it.

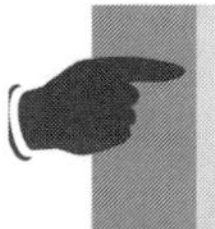

New Term: The *list box* is an input control that permits the application user to select from a list of items.

A list box control supports multiple selections only if you specify the multiple-selection style when you create the control. Making multiple selections is convenient when you want to process the selected items in a similar manner. For example, selecting multiple files for deletion speeds up the process and reduces the effort you have to make.

The *TListBox* Class

The Borland ObjectWindows Library offers the `TListBox` class, a descendant of `TControl`, to implement list box controls. The `TListBox` class has a set of member

functions that enable you to easily manipulate and query both the contents of the list box and the selected item. As with many other classes in OWL, the class `TListBox` uses a default constructor to create list box instances.

Syntax

The *TListBox* Constructor

The declaration of the `TListBox` constructor is

```
TListBox(TWindow* parent,
         int      Id,
         int      x,
         int      y,
         int      w,
         int      h,
         TModule* module = 0 );
```

You will notice that the `TListBox` class constructor looks very much like the other controls descended from `TControl` (such as `TEdit`, `TButton`, and so on). You specify the control's parent window, its control ID, and its dimensions within that window.

Example:

```
TListBox* pList = new TListBox(this, IDL_FILES, 10, 10, 75, 250);
```

18

Along with the regular `WS_XXX` styles, the list box makes use of the special `LBS_XXX` styles (see Table 18.1). The `TListBox` class, by default, sets the `LBS_STANDARD` style. This is equivalent to the `WS_BORDER`, `WS_VSCROLL`, `LBS_SORT`, and `LBS_NOTIFY` styles. You can remove the `LBS_SORT` style from the list box controls to maintain a list of items that is not automatically sorted. Such a list enables you to maintain items in a chronological fashion. You can also use this type of list to maintain the items sorted in descending order. Of course, you are responsible for maintaining the list items in that order. Removing the `WS_VSCROLL` style gives you a list box without the vertical scroll bar. The next section presents a demonstration program that uses this type of list box to implement the synchronized scrolling of multiple list boxes.

Table 18.1. List box control styles.

Style	Meaning
`LBS_DISABLENOSCROLL`	Specifies that the list box is to always have a scroll bar that is gray when there is nothing to scroll. Normally, the scroll bar disappears when not needed.
`LBS_EXTENDEDSEL`	Allows the extension of multiple-selections in the list box by using the Shift key.

continues

Table 18.1. continued

Style	Meaning
`LBS_HASSTRINGS`	Used in owner-drawn list boxes to have the control maintain a copy of the strings added.
`LBS_MULTICOLUMN`	Designates a multicolumn list box that scrolls horizontally.
`LBS_MULTIPLESEL`	Supports multiple selections in a list box.
`LBS_NOINTEGRALHEIGHT`	Suppresses showing parts of an item.
`LBS_NOREDRAW`	Prevents the list box from being updated when the selection is changed (you can use the `SetRedraw` member function to change this at will).
`LBS_NOTIFY`	Notifies the parent window when you click or double-click in the list box.
`LBS_OWNERDRAWFIXED`	Used to specify an owner-drawn list box (a list box for which the application is responsible for drawing, instead of the automatic Windows functions). Specifies that the list box items all will be the same height.
`LBS_OWNERDRAWVARIABLE`	Specifies an owner-drawn list box that contains items of differing heights.
`LBS_SORT`	Specifies that the items inserted in the list box be automatically sorted in ascending alphanumeric order.
`LBS_STANDARD`	Sets the `WS_BORDER`, `WS_VSCROLL`, `LBS_SORT`, and `LBS_NOTIFY` styles.
`LBS_USETABSTOPS`	Allows the tab character to be expanded within the list box control.
`LBS_WANTKEYBOARDINPUT`	Permits the list box owner to receive `WM_VKEYTOITEM` or `WM_CHARTOITEM` messages when a key is pressed while the list box has the focus (allows the application to manipulate the items in the list box).

The `TListBox` class enables you to refer to the items in a list box by index. The index of the first item is 0. The `TListBox` class offers the following member functions to set and query ordinary and selected list members:

- The `AddString` member function adds a string to the list box.
- The `DeleteString` member function removes a list member from a specified position.
- The parameterless `ClearList` member function clears the list of strings in the list box control in one swoop. This function serves to reset the contents of a list box before building up a new list.
- The `FindExactString` and `FindString` member functions perform case-insensitive searches for items in the list box. The first searches the list box for an exact match to a string, whereas the second searches for a list box entry that begins with a string.
- The parameterless `GetCount` member function returns the number of items in the list box. The function returns a negative number if there is an error.
- The parameterless `GetSelIndex` member function returns the position of the selected item in a single-selection list box. If there is no selected item, the function yields a negative value. This function is aimed at single-selection list boxes only.
- The `GetSel` member function returns the selection state of a list box item, specified by an index.
- The parameterless `GetSelCount` member function returns the number of selected items in the list box. For single-selection list boxes, the number will be either 0 or 1.
- The `GetSelIndexes` member function returns the number and positions of the selected items in a multiple-selection list box.
- The `GetString` member function obtains an item in a list box by specifying its index.
- The `GetStringLen` member function returns the length of a list item specified by its position in the list.
- The `GetTopIndex` member function returns the index of the first visible list box item.

- The `InsertString` member function inserts a string in a list box.
- The `SetSelString` member function selects a list box item that matches a search string.
- The `SetSelItemRange` member function enables you to select a range of items in one call.
- The `SetSelIndex` member function chooses a list item as the new selection in a single-selection list box.
- The `SetSel` member function makes or clears a selection in a multiple-selection list box.
- The `SetTopIndex` member function selects the list box entry that becomes the first visible item in the list box control.
- The `DirectoryList` member function is a special member function that enables you to automatically insert filenames in a list box.

Note: Many of the `TListBox` functions return either `LB_ERR` or `LB_ERRSPACE`. It should be noted that both of these values are negative, so just checking a return value to see if it's less than 0 is often enough.

Syntax

The *AddString* Function

The declaration of the `AddString` member function is

```
int AddString(const char far* str);
```

The `str` parameter is the pointer to the added string. The function returns the position of the added string in the control. If there is any error in adding the string, the function yields an `LB_ERR` or `LB_ERRSPACE` value (out-of-memory error). If the `LBS_SORT` style is set, the string is inserted so that the list order is maintained. If the `LBS_SORT` style is not set, the added string is inserted at the end of the list.

Example:

```
pList->AddString("MS-DOS");
```

Syntax

The *DeleteString* Function

The declaration of the DeleteString member function is

```
int DeleteString(int index);
```

The index parameter specifies the position of the item to delete. The function returns the number of remaining list members. If errors occur, DeleteString yields the value LB_ERR.

Example:

```
pList->DeleteString(0); //Deletes item 0
```

Syntax

The *FindExactString* and *FindString* Functions

The declarations of the FindExactString and FindString functions are

```
int FindExactString(const char far* str, int searchIndex) const;
int FindString(const char far* str, int searchIndex) const;
```

In both cases, the searchIndex parameter specifies the index of the first list box member to be searched, and the str parameter is the pointer to the searched string. The functions search the *entire* list, beginning with position searchIndex and resuming at the beginning of the list, if needed. The search stops when either a list member matches the search string or the entire list is searched. Passing an argument of –1 to searchIndex forces the functions to start searching from the beginning. The functions return the position of the matching list item, or they yield the LB_ERR value if no match is found or when an error occurs.

The difference between the two functions is that, although FindExactString looks for an exact match of the parameter str to an entry in the list box, FindString will stop as soon as it finds an entry that *begins* with str.

Example:

```
int msdos = pList->FindString("MS-DOS", -1);
int anti = pList->FindString("anti", -1);
```

Note: The interesting search method used by FindExactString and FindString enables you to speed up the search by specifying a position that comes closely before the most likely location for a match. For example, if you happen to know where the first item starting with an s is located, and you're searching for something that begins with the same character, you can specify that initial index in an attempt to speed up the search.

The beauty of this method is that if you specify a position that is *actually* beyond that of the string you seek, you cannot miss finding that string because the function resumes searching at the beginning of the list. Another benefit of `FindExactString` and `FindString` is their ability to find duplicate strings.

Syntax

The *GetSel* Function

The declaration of the function `GetSel` is

```
BOOL GetSel(int index) const;
```

The `index` parameter specifies the index of the queried list box item. The function returns a `TRUE` if the item is selected, `FALSE` if the item is not selected.

Example:

```
pList->SetSel(0, !pList->GetSel(0)); //toggles sel state of item 0
```

Syntax

The *GetSelIndexes* Function

The declaration of the `GetSelIndexes` function is

```
int GetSelIndexes(int* indexes, int maxCount) const;
```

The `maxCount` parameter specifies the size of the array accessed by the `indexes` pointer. The `indexes` parameter is the pointer to an array of integers that stores the positions of the selected items. The function returns the current number of selections. The function yields `LB_ERR` with single-selection list boxes.

Example:

```
int num_items = pList->GetSelCount();
int* items = new int[num_items];
pList->GetSelIndexes(items, num_items);
```

Syntax

The *GetString* Function

The declaration for the `GetString` function is

```
int GetString(char far* str, int index) const;
```

The `index` parameter specifies the index of the retrieved item. The first list box item has the index of 0. The `str` parameter points to a buffer that receives the retrieved item.

You are responsible for ensuring that the buffer has enough space for the retrieved item (for example, using GetStringLen when allocating a receiving buffer). The function returns the number of characters retrieved from the list box.

Example:

```
char* s = NULL;
int size = pList->GetStringLen(ix);
if ((size > 0) && (NULL != (s = new char[size + 1])))
   pList->GetString(s, ix);
```

Syntax

The *GetStringLen* Function

The declaration of the GetStringLen function is

```
int GetStringLen(int index) const;
```

The parameter index specifies the index of the target list item. The function returns the length of the target item, or the LB_ERR result if an error occurs.

Example:

See GetString's example.

18

Syntax

The *InsertString* Function

The declaration of the InsertString function is

```
int InsertString(const char far* str, int index);
```

The index parameter specifies the requested insertion position. The str parameter is the pointer to the inserted string. The function returns the actual insertion position, or it yields the LB_ERR value if an error occurs. If the argument for index is –1, the string is simply appended to the end of the list.

Example:

```
pList->InsertString("Windows", 0);
```

Warning: In general, do not use the InsertString member function with list boxes that have the LBS_SORT style set. Using this function with ordered list boxes will most likely corrupt the sort order of the list.

Syntax

The *SetSelString* Function

The declaration of the SetSelString function is

```
int SetSelString(const char far* str, int searchIndex);
```

The parameters and search mechanism of SetSelString are identical to those of FindString. The difference is that SetSelString selects the list box item that matches the string accessed by parameter str.

Example:

```
int ix = pList->SetSelString("MS-DOS", -1);
```

Syntax

The *SetSelItemRange* Function

The declaration of the SetSelItemRange function is

```
int SetSelItemRange(BOOL select, int first, int last);
```

The select parameter acts as a switch used to select or deselect the range of list box items defined by parameters of first and last. The number returned is the number of items actually selected between and including first and last.

Example:

```
pList->SetSelItemRange(TRUE, 0, 10);
```

Syntax

The *SetSelIndex* Function

The declaration of the SetSelIndex function is

```
int SetSelIndex(int index);
```

The parameter index specifies the position of the new selection. To clear a list box from any selection, pass a –1 argument as the select parameter. The function returns LB_ERR if an error occurs. This is used for single-selection list boxes.

Example:

```
pList-SetSelIndex(-1);      // clear current selection
```

Syntax

The *SetSel* Function

The declaration of the `SetSel` function is

```
int SetSel(int index, BOOL select);
```

The `index` parameter specifies the list box item to either select, if select is `TRUE`, or deselect, if `select` is `FALSE`. The function returns `LB_ERR` if an error occurs. The function result serves only to flag a selection/deselection error. You can use the `SetSel` function to toggle the selection of multiple items in a multiple-selection list box, one at a time.

Example:

```
pList->SetSel(0, TRUE);      // select first item in list
```

Syntax

The *SetTopIndex* Function

The declaration of the function `SetTopIndex` is

```
int SetTopIndex(int index);
```

The `index` parameter specifies the index of the list box item that becomes the first visible item. This selection scrolls the list box, unless item `index` is already the first visible item. The function returns `LB_ERR` if an error occurs. Otherwise, the result is meaningless.

Example:

```
pList->SetTopIndex(10);
```

Syntax

The *DirectoryList* Function

The declaration of the `DirectoryList` function is

```
int DirectoryList(UINT attrs, const char far* fileSpec);
```

The `attrs` parameter specifies the combination of attributes, as shown in Table 18.2. The table also shows the equivalent file attribute constants that are declared in the DOS.H header file. The `fileSpec` parameter is the pointer to the filename specification, such as `*.*`, `L*.EXE`, or `A???.CPP`. The return value is the number of files added to the list box.

Example:

```
int numFiles = pList->DirectoryList(DDL_ARCHIVE, "CTL*.CPP");
```

Table 18.2. Attributes for the attrs parameter in the TListbox::DirectoryList member function.

Attribute Value	Equivalent Constant in DOS.H Header File	Meaning
DDL_READWRITE	FA_NORMAL or _A_NORMAL	File can be used for input and output.
DDL_READONLY	FA_RDONLY or _A_RDONLY	File is read only.
DDL_HIDDEN	FA_HIDDEN or _A_HIDDEN	File is hidden.
DDL_SYSTEM	FA_SYSTEM or _A_SYSTEM	File is system file.
DDL_DIRECTORY	FA_DIREC or _A_SUBDIR	Name indicated by parameter fileSpec also supplies the directory.
DDL_ARCHIVE	FA_ARCH or _A_ARCH	File has the archive bit set.
DDL_POSTMSGS		Posts messages to the application instead of sending them directly to the list box.
DDL_DRIVES		Includes all the drives that match the filename supplied by fileSpec.
DDL_EXCLUSIVE		Exclusive flag (prevents normal files from being included with specified files).

Note that in the preceding table, there are two constants defined in the DOS.H header file for each item. The first is the value defined by Borland. The second is the one defined for the Microsoft compiler. Borland defines these to help with compatibility, to make programs more easily portable between the two compilers.

Responding to List Box Notification Messages

The list box control emits various types of messages, as shown in Table 18.3. The table also shows the message-mapping macros that are associated with the various command

and notification messages. Each type of command or notification message requires a separate member function declared in the control's parent window class.

Table 18.3. List box notification messages.

Message	Macro	Meaning
`WM_COMMAND`	`EV_COMMAND`	A Windows command message.
`LBN_DBLCLK`	`EV_LBN_DBLCLK`	A list item is selected with a mouse double-click.
`LBN_ERRSPACE`	`EV_LBN_ERRSPACE`	The list box cannot allocate more dynamic memory to accommodate new list items.
`LBN_KILLFOCUS`	`EV_LBN_KILLFOCUS`	The list box has lost focus.
`LBN_SELCHANGE`	`EV_LBN_SELCHANGE`	A list item is selected with a mouse click.
`LBN_SETFOCUS`	`EV_LBN_SETFOCUS`	The list box has gained focus.

The List Manipulation Tester

The next program demonstrates how to set and query normal and selected strings, and how to set and query the current selection in a single-selection list box—a simple list manipulation tester. This program focuses on illustrating how to use most of the `TListBox` member functions presented earlier in this section. The program contains the following controls, which offer the indicated test features:

- A list box control.
- A String Box edit control that enables you to type in and retrieve a list member.
- An Index Box edit control that enables you to key in and retrieve the position of the current selection.
- An Add String pushbutton to add the contents of the String Box to the list box (the program does not enable you to add duplicate names, and, if you attempt to do so, the program displays a warning message).
- A Delete String pushbutton to delete the current selection in the list box (the program automatically selects another list member).

- The Get Selected String pushbutton that copies the current list selection to the String Box.
- The Set Selected String pushbutton that overwrites the current selection with the string in the String Box.
- The Get Selected Index pushbutton that writes the position of the current selection in the Index Box.
- The Set Selected Index pushbutton that uses the integer value in the Index Box as the position of the new list box selection.
- The Get String button that copies the string whose position appears in the Index Box into the String Box.
- The Exit pushbutton.

These controls exercise various aspects of manipulating a sorted list box and its members. The program is coded to retain a current selection and to prevent the insertion of duplicate names.

Listings 18.1, 18.2, and 18.3 show the header file CTLLST.H, the script for the CTLLST.RC resource file, and the source code for the CTLLST.CPP program file, respectively. The resource file contains a single-item menu resource.

Create the directory CTLLST as a subdirectory of BC45\BC21DAY and store all the project's files in the new directory. The project's IDE file should contain the files CTLLST.CPP and the CTLLST.RC.

Compile and run the program. When the program starts running, it places a set of names in the list box. Experiment with the various pushbutton controls to add, delete, and obtain strings. The program is straightforward and easy to run.

Listing 18.1. Source code for the CTLLST.H header file.

```
#define IDL_STRINGS      101
#define IDE_STRING       102
#define IDE_INDEX        103
#define IDB_ADD          104
#define IDB_DEL          105
#define IDB_GETSELSTR    106
#define IDB_SETSELSTR    107
#define IDB_GETSELIDX    108
#define IDB_SETSELIDX    109
#define IDB_GETSTR       110
#define IDB_EXIT         111
```

Listing 18.2. Script for the CTLLST.RC resource file.

```
#include <windows.h>
#include <owl\window.rh>

EXITMENU MENU LOADONCALL MOVEABLE PURE DISCARDABLE
BEGIN
   MENUITEM "E&xit", CM_EXIT
END
```

Listing 18.3. Source code for the CTLLST.CPP program file.

```
#include <stdio.h>
#include <windows.h>
#include <owl\applicat.h>
#include <owl\button.h>
#include <owl\edit.h>
#include <owl\framewin.h>
#include <owl\listbox.h>
#include <owl\static.h>
#include <owl\window.h>
#include <owl\window.rh>

#include "ctllst1.h"

class TMyWindow : public TWindow
{
public:
   TMyWindow(TWindow* parent = 0);
   virtual ~TMyWindow();

protected:
   virtual void SetupWindow();

   void CbAdd();
   void CbDel();
   void CbGetSelStr();
   void CbSetSelStr();
   void CbGetSelIdx();
   void CbSetSelIdx();
   void CbGetStr();
   void CmExit();

private:
   TListBox* list;
   TEdit* strbox,* idxbox;
```


continues

Listing 18.3. continued

```

    DECLARE_RESPONSE_TABLE(TMyWindow);
};
DEFINE_RESPONSE_TABLE1(TMyWindow, TWindow)
    EV_COMMAND(CM_EXIT, CmExit),
    EV_BN_CLICKED(IDB_ADD, CbAdd),
    EV_BN_CLICKED(IDB_DEL, CbDel),
    EV_BN_CLICKED(IDB_GETSELSTR, CbGetSelStr),
    EV_BN_CLICKED(IDB_SETSELSTR, CbSetSelStr),
    EV_BN_CLICKED(IDB_GETSELIDX, CbGetSelIdx),
    EV_BN_CLICKED(IDB_SETSELIDX, CbSetSelIdx),
    EV_BN_CLICKED(IDB_GETSTR, CbGetStr),
    EV_BN_CLICKED(IDB_EXIT, CmExit),
END_RESPONSE_TABLE;

TMyWindow::TMyWindow(TWindow* parent)
{
    Init(parent, 0, 0);

    int   lowvspacing = 5,
          hivspacing = 25,
          hspacing = 50,
          wctl = 150,
          hctl = 30,
          x0 = 30,
          y0 = 50,
          y1;
    int   wbox = 2 * wctl + hspacing;
    int   hlist = hctl + lowvspacing + 4 * (hctl + hivspacing);

    int   x = x0, y = y0;

    // Create the listbox and its label
    //
    new TStatic(this, -1, "List Box", x, y, wctl, hctl);
    y += hctl + lowvspacing;
    list = new TListBox(this, IDL_STRINGS, x, y, wctl, hlist);

    // Create the edit boxes and their labels
    //
    x += wctl + hspacing;
    y = y0;
    new TStatic(this, -1, "String Box", x, y, wctl, hctl);
    y += hctl + lowvspacing;
    strbox = new TEdit(this, IDE_STRING, "", x, y, wbox, hctl);
    y += hctl + hivspacing;
    new TStatic(this, -1, "Index Box", x, y, wctl, hctl);
    y += hctl + lowvspacing;
    idxbox = new TEdit(this, IDE_INDEX, "", x, y, wbox, hctl);

```

```
    // Create first column of buttons
    //
    y1 = y += hctl + hivspacing;
    new TButton(this, IDB_ADD, "Add String", x, y, wctl, hctl);
    y += hctl + hivspacing;
    new TButton(this, IDB_DEL, "Delete String", x, y, wctl, hctl);
    y += hctl + hivspacing;
    new TButton(this, IDB_GETSELSTR, "Get Selected String", x, y,
                wctl, hctl);
    y += hctl + hivspacing;
    new TButton(this, IDB_SETSELSTR, "Set Selected String", x, y,
                wctl, hctl);

    // Create the second column of buttons
    y = y1;
    x += wctl + hspacing;
    new TButton(this, IDB_GETSELIDX, "Get Selected Index", x, y,
                wctl, hctl);
    y += hctl + hivspacing;
    new TButton(this, IDB_SETSELIDX, "Set Selected Index", x, y,
                wctl, hctl);
    y += hctl + hivspacing;
    new TButton(this, IDB_GETSTR, "Get String by Index", x, y, wctl,
                hctl);
    y += hctl + hivspacing;
    new TButton(this, IDB_EXIT, "Exit", x, y, wctl, hctl);
}

TMyWindow::~TMyWindow()
{
}

void TMyWindow::SetupWindow()
{
    TWindow::SetupWindow();    // Initialize the visual element

    // Initialize the list box with some data and
    // select the second item
    //
    if (list)
        {
        list->AddString("Keith");
        list->AddString("Kevin");
        list->AddString("Ingrid");
        list->AddString("Roger");
        list->AddString("Rick");
        list->AddString("Beth");
        list->AddString("Kate");
        list->AddString("James");
        list->SetSelIndex(1);
```

18

continues

Listing 18.3. continued

```
        }
}

void TMyWindow::CbAdd()
{
    if (strbox && list)
        {
        char *str;
        int size = strbox->GetWindowTextLength() + 1;
        if ((size > 1) && (NULL != (str = new char[size])))
            {
            strbox->GetWindowText(str, size);
            if (list->FindExactString(str, -1) >= 0)
                MessageBox("Cannot add duplicate names", "Bad Data");
            else
                {
                int ix = list->AddString(str);
                list->SetSelIndex(ix);
                }
            delete str;
            }
        }
}

void TMyWindow::CbDel()
{
    if (list)
        {
        int ix = list->GetSelIndex();
        list->DeleteString(ix);
        list->SetSelIndex((ix > 0) ? (ix - 1) : 0);
        }
}

void TMyWindow::CbGetSelStr()
{
    if (list && strbox)
        {
        char *str;
        int ix = list->GetSelIndex();
        if (ix >= 0)
            {
            if (NULL != (str = new char[list->GetStringLen(ix) + 1]))
                {
                list->GetString(str, ix);
                strbox->SetWindowText(str);
                delete str;
                }
            }
```

```
      }
}

void TMyWindow::CbSetSelStr()
{
   if (list && strbox)
      {
      int ix = list->GetSelIndex();

      char *str;
      int size = strbox->GetWindowTextLength() + 1;
      if ((size > 1) && (NULL != (str = new char[size])))
         {
         strbox->GetWindowText(str, size);
         if (list->FindExactString(str, -1) >= 0)
            MessageBox("Cannot add duplicate names", "Bad Data");
         else
            {
            list->DeleteString(ix);
            ix = list->AddString(str);
            list->SetSelIndex(ix);
            }
         delete str;
         }
      }
}

void TMyWindow::CbGetSelIdx()
{
   if (list && idxbox)
      {
      char str[15];
      sprintf(str, "%d", list->GetSelIndex());
      idxbox->SetWindowText(str);
      }
}

void TMyWindow::CbSetSelIdx()
{
   if (list && idxbox)
      {
      char *str;
      int size = idxbox->GetWindowTextLength() + 1;
      if ((size > 1) && (NULL != (str = new char[size])))
         {
         idxbox->GetWindowText(str, size);
         list->SetSelIndex(atoi(str));
         delete str;
         }
      }
```

continues

Listing 18.3. continued

```
}

void TMyWindow::CbGetStr()
{
   if (list && idxbox && strbox)
      {
      char *str;
      int ix = -1;
      int size = idxbox->GetWindowTextLength() + 1;
      if ((size > 1) && (NULL != (str = new char[size])))
         {
         idxbox->GetWindowText(str, size);
         ix = atoi(str);
         delete str;
         }
      if ((ix >= 0) && (NULL != (str = new char[list
       ->GetStringLen(ix) + 1])))
         {
         list->GetString(str, ix);
         strbox->SetWindowText(str);
         delete str;
         }
      }
}


void TMyWindow::CmExit()
{
   SendMessage(WM_CLOSE);
}

class TListApp : public TApplication
{
public:
   TListApp() : TApplication()
      { nCmdShow = SW_SHOWMAXIMIZED; }

   void InitMainWindow()
      {
      SetMainWindow(new TFrameWindow(  0,
                           "Simple List Box Tester Application",
                           new TMyWindow ));
      GetMainWindow()->AssignMenu("EXITMENU");
      }
};

int OwlMain(int, char *[])
{
   return TListApp().Run();
}
```

Figure 18.1 shows a sample session with the CTLLST.EXE application.

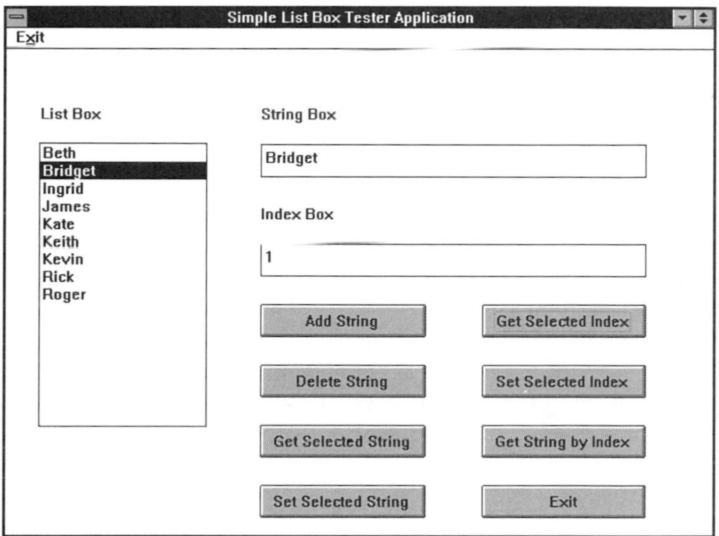

Figure 18.1. *A sample session with the CTLLST.EXE application.*

18

The program in Listing 18.3 declares the window class `TMyWindow`, starting on line 14, which contains a number of data members that are pointers to the controls owned by the main window. The class also declares a `SetupWindow` member function and several member functions that respond to the notification messages emitted by the various pushbutton controls.

The `TMyWindow` constructor, starting on line 50, performs the creation of all the controls in the window. It makes use of the control classes' default settings, which include an automatic scroll bar on the list box when it gets enough entries, as well as automatic sorting of the listbox. Then the `SetupWindow` member function initializes the listbox, starting on line 112.

The member function `CbAdd`, starting on line 133, adds the string of the String Box in the list box control. The function performs the following tasks:

- Ensures that the list box and edit box were created properly on line 135.
- If the String Box edit control isn't empty, the function creates room for copying the contents of the edit control and then places those contents in the `str` variable on lines 137 through 141.

- Verifies that the added string does not already exist in the list box, using the `FindExactString` function on line 142 to detect an attempt to add duplicate strings, and complains with a message box on line 143 if a duplicate is found.
- Adds the string in `str` to the list box and assigns the position of the string to the local variable `ix` using the `AddString` function on line 146.
- Makes the added string the current selection by invoking the `SetSelIndex` function with the argument `ix` on line 147.

The member function `CbDel`, starting on line 154, deletes the current selection by carrying out the following tasks:

- After ensuring the `list` pointer was created properly on line 156, it obtains the position of the current selection by invoking the `GetSelIndex` function on line 158, and stores the selection position in the local variable `ix`.
- Deletes the selection by calling the `DeleteString` function and supplying it the argument `ix` on line 159.
- Selects another list item on line 160 as the new selection at position `ix - 1` (if the variable `ix` already contains 0, the new first list item becomes the new selection).

The member function `CbGetSelStr` starting on line 164 copies the current selection to the String Box edit control. The function performs the following tasks:

- Creates room for and copies the contents of the list box's current selection using the `GetSelIndex`, `GetStringLen`, and `GetString` functions on lines 168 through 174.
- Overwrites the contents of the String Box with the characters retrieved from the list box on line 175.

The member function `CbSetSelStr`, starting on line 182, overwrites the current selection with the string in the String Box edit control. Because the list maintains sorted items, the replacement string likely has a different position from the original selection. The function performs the following tasks:

- Obtains the position of the current selection, using the `GetSelIndex` function, and assigns that value to the local variable `ix` on line 186.
- Copies the text in the String Box to the newly allocated `str` variable on line 192.

- Verifies that the string in `str` does not already exist in the list box, using the `FindExactString` function on line 193, displaying a message box if the string already exists on line 194.
- If the string is new to the list, the function uses the `DeleteString` function to delete the current selection on line 197, uses the `AddString` function to add the string on line 198, and then uses `SetSelIndex` to select the added string on line 199.

If the string has a matching list item, the function displays a message informing you that you cannot add duplicate strings in the list box. This warning also appears if you attempt to overwrite the current selection with the same string.

The member function `CbGetSelIdx`, starting on line 206, writes the position of the current selection to the Index Box edit box on line 212. The function uses the `GetSelIndex` function to obtain the sought position on line 211.

The member function `CbSetSelIdx`, starting on line 216, reads the value in the Index Box edit control and uses that value to set the new current selection. The function uses the `SetSelIndex` function to make the new selection on line 225.

18

The member function `CbGetStr`, starting on line 231, enables you to retrieve the list item whose position appears in the Index Box edit control. The function performs the following tasks:

- Copies the characters of the Index Box to an allocated string in the `str` data member on line 240.
- Converts the string in `str` to the `int`-typed local variable `ix` on line 241.
- Copies the characters of the list item at position `ix` to a reallocated `str` on line 246.
- Writes the characters of `str` to the String Box edit control on line 247.

Handling Multiple-Selection Lists

This section demonstrates the use of multiple-selection lists and focuses on getting and setting the selection strings and their indexes. There are two modes for making multiple selections in a list box. These modes depend on whether or not you set the `LBS_EXTENDEDSEL` style when you create a `TListBox` instance. Setting this style enables you to quickly extend the range of selected items by holding down the Shift key and clicking the mouse. The disadvantage for this style is that you are committed to selecting blocks of contiguous items in the list box manually (that is, using the mouse or cursor keys). Using the `SetSel` or `SetSelItemRange` member functions, you can make your program select noncontiguous items. However, this approach requires extra effort on behalf of the application user and a few extra controls. By contrast, if you do not set the `LBS_EXTENDEDSEL` style, you can make dispersed selections easily by clicking the mouse button on the individual items that you want to select. The disadvantage of this selection mode is that you must click every item to select it, including neighboring items. Choose the selection mode that you feel best meets the user-interface requirements for your OWL applications.

The Multiple-Selection List Tester

Figure 18.2 shows a sample session with the XFERLIST.EXE application—a program that demonstrates how to query multiple selections in a list box—and also shows the controls used by that application. The controls used by the test program and the operations they support are the following:

- Two multiple-selection list boxes that have the `LBS_MULTIPLESEL` style selected, but not the `LBS_EXTENDEDSEL` style.
- Two pushbuttons, one with the caption "<--" and the other with the caption "-->", that transfer the selected items of one list box to the other.
- Static text controls that label the list boxes.

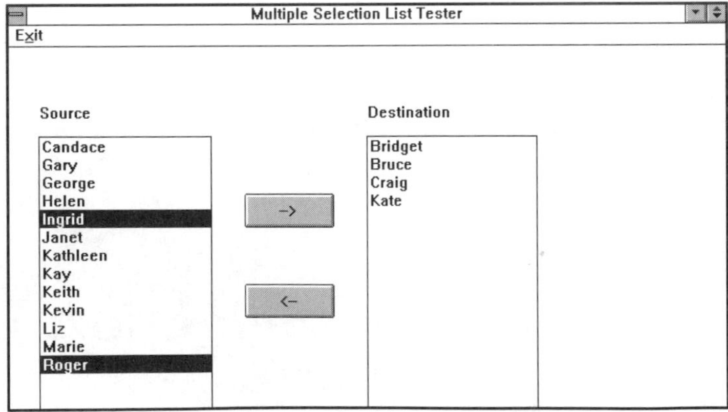

Figure 18.2. *A sample session with the XFERLIST.EXE application.*

The multiple-selection list tester application basically enables the user to transfer the contents of one list box to the other and back again. Listings 18.4, 18.5, and 18.6 contain the source code for the XFERLIST.H, XFERLIST.RC, and XFERLIST.CPP files, respectively.

Create the directory XFERLIST as a subdirectory of \BC45\BC21DAY and store all the project's files in the new directory. As before, the project's IDE file should contain the files XFERLIST.CPP and XFERLIST.RC.

Compile and run the program. The application initializes the list box with many names. Select a few list items in the Source list box and click the -- > pushbutton. The selected strings appear in the Destination list box and disappear from the Source list box. Now select on a few names in the Destination list box and click the <-- pushbutton. The names move over to the Source list box. When you have finished experimenting with the program, click the Exit menu item or press the Alt+X keys.

Type

Listing 18.4. Source code for the XFERLIST.H header file.

```
#define IDL_SRC    101
#define IDL_DST    102
#define IDB_TOSRC 103
#define IDB_TODST 104
```

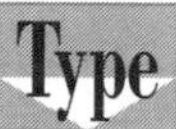

Listing 18.5. Script for the XFERLIST.RC resource file.

```
#include <windows.h>
#include <owl\window.rh>

EXITMENU MENU LOADONCALL MOVEABLE PURE DISCARDABLE
BEGIN
   MENUITEM "E&xit", CM_EXIT
END
```

Listing 18.6. Source code for the XFERLIST.CPP program file.

```
#include <windows.h>
#include <owl\applicat.h>
#include <owl\button.h>
#include <owl\framewin.h>
#include <owl\listbox.h>
```

continues

Listin 18.6. continued

```
#include <owl\static.h>
#include <owl\window.h>
#include <owl\window.rh>

#include "xferlist.h"

class TMyWindow : public TWindow
{
public:
   TMyWindow(TWindow* parent = 0);
   virtual ~TMyWindow();

protected:
   virtual void SetupWindow();

   void CbToDst();
   void CbToSrc();
   void CmExit();

private:
   TListBox *src, *dst;

   void MoveSels(TListBox* src, TListBox* dst);

   DECLARE_RESPONSE_TABLE(TMyWindow);
};
DEFINE_RESPONSE_TABLE1(TMyWindow, TWindow)
   EV_COMMAND(CM_EXIT, CmExit),
   EV_BN_CLICKED(IDB_TODST, CbToDst),
   EV_BN_CLICKED(IDB_TOSRC, CbToSrc),
END_RESPONSE_TABLE;

TMyWindow::TMyWindow(TWindow* parent)
{
   Init(parent, 0, 0);

   int   wbtn = 80,
         hbtn = 30,
         wlist = 150,
         hlist = 250,
         wspace = 30,
         hspace = 50,
         x0 = 30,
         y0 = 50;
   int   x = x0, y = y0;

   new TStatic(this, -1, "Source", x, y, wlist, hbtn);
   y += hbtn;
   if (NULL != (src = new TListBox(this, IDL_SRC, x, y, wlist,
   hlist)))
```

```
      src->Attr.Style |= LBS_MULTIPLESEL;

   x += wlist + wspace;
   y += hspace;
   new TButton(this, IDB_TODST, "-->", x, y, wbtn, hbtn);
   y += hbtn + hspace;
   new TButton(this, IDB_TOSRC, "<--", x, y, wbtn, hbtn);

   x += wbtn + wspace;
   y = y0;
   new TStatic(this, -1, "Destination", x, y, wlist, hbtn);
   y += hbtn;
   if (NULL != (dst = new TListBox(this, IDL_DST, x, y, wlist,
                                   hlist)))
      dst->Attr.Style |= LBS_MULTIPLESEL;
}

TMyWindow::~TMyWindow()
{
}

void TMyWindow::SetupWindow()
{
   static char* names[] =
      {  "Keith", "Bruce", "Kevin", "Bridget", "Kate",
         "Kay", "Roger", "Marie", "Kathleen", "Liz",
         "Ingrid", "Craig", "George", "Janet", "Gary",
         "Helen", "Candace",
         NULL };

   TWindow::SetupWindow();

   if (src)
      for (int ix = 0; names[ix]; ++ix)
         src->AddString(names[ix]);
}

void TMyWindow::MoveSels(TListBox* src, TListBox* dst)
{
   if (src && dst)
      {
      int* sels, numsels = src->GetSelCount();
      if ((numsels > 0) && (NULL != (sels = new int[numsels])))
         {
         int ix;

         src->GetSelIndexes(sels, numsels);
         for (ix = 0; ix < numsels; ++ix)
            {
            char *str;
```


continues

Listing 18.6. continued

```
            int size = src->GetStringLen(sels[ix]) + 1;
            if ((size > 1) && (NULL != (str = new char[size])))
               {
               src->GetString(str, sels[ix]);
               dst->AddString(str);
               delete str;
               }
            }
         for (ix = numsels - 1; ix >= 0; --ix)
            src->DeleteString(sels[ix]);

         delete sels;
         }
      }
}

void TMyWindow::CbToDst()
{
   MoveSels(src, dst);
}

void TMyWindow::CbToSrc()
{
   MoveSels(dst, src);
}

void TMyWindow::CmExit()
{
   SendMessage(WM_CLOSE);
}

class TXferApp : public TApplication
{
public:
   TXferApp() : TApplication()
      { nCmdShow = SW_SHOWMAXIMIZED; }

   void InitMainWindow()
      {
      SetMainWindow(new TFrameWindow(  0,
                           "Multiple Selection List Tester",
                           new TMyWindow ));
      GetMainWindow()->AssignMenu("EXITMENU");
      }
};

int OwlMain(int, char *[])
{
   return TXferApp().Run();
}
```

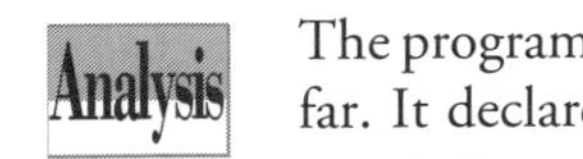

The program in Listing 18.6 works similarly to the other programs presented so far. It declares an application class `TXferApp` on line 135 and a window class `TMyWindow` on line 12. The window class creates a number of controls in its constructor and then does its initialization in the `SetupWindow` member function.

The `TMyWindow` window class declares two data members, `src` and `dst`, on line 26, which are pointers to class objects of type `TListBox`. These are used to access the source and destination list boxes after they are created. When they are created in the constructor on lines 54 through 55 and 67 through 68, their `Attr.Style` members are modified to include the `LBS_MULTIPLESEL` style, enabling the list boxes to allow multiple selections.

The function `MoveSels`, starting on line 91, is the main workhorse of the program. It does the following:

- It takes two parameters, the source list box `src` and the destination list box `dst`.
- After making sure it was given valid `TListBox` pointers, it obtains the number of selections from the source list box on line 95 and creates an array to hold those indexes on line 96. Then, it retrieves those indexes and stores them in the newly created `sels` array on line 100.
- The function then iterates through the list of selections on lines 101 through 111 and gets a string for each entry with the `GetString` function on line 107. It then adds this string to the destination list box with the `AddString` function on line 108.
- Finally, the function iterates through the list of selections again, this time backwards, and deletes them from the source list box with the `DeleteString` function on lines 112 and 113.

Note that when the `MoveSels` function deletes the selections from the source list box, it does so in reverse order. The reason for this is that, as the function deletes an entry, every item after the now-deleted one in the list box has its index decreased by one. If the function were to delete the strings forwards, then all but the first selection would be incorrect, because the retrieved list became out of synch with the list box itself.

The two functions that respond to the buttons, `CbToDst` on line 120 and `CbToSrc` on line 125, both call the `MoveSels` function, and they both pass the same arguments. But they each pass them in a different order. By doing this, you can use the `MoveSels` function for both buttons, but have it move the selections between opposite list boxes as the parameters are switched.

Summary

Today's lesson presented the list box control, which enables an application user to choose from a collection of values. You learned about the following topics:

- The single-selection list box control provides you with a list of items from which to select. This kind of list box enables you to select only one item at a time.
- The multiple-selection list box permits you to select multiple items in a list box for collective processing. Setting the `LBS_EXTENDEDSEL` style when you create the list box enables you to quickly extend the range of selected items by holding down the Shift key and clicking the mouse.

Q&A

Q Can the argument for the `fileSpec` parameter in function `TListBox::DirectoryList` contain multiple wildcards, such as `"*.CPP *.H"`?

A No, the argument list for `fileSpec` is limited to one filename wildcard.

Q Does OWL support intercepting the messages related to the movement of the thumb box in a list box control?

A No. Windows doesn't send any messages for OWL to intercept.

Q What is the general approach to implementing a program with two list boxes that scroll simultaneously?

A The general approach is to create the two list boxes with hidden scroll bars and then add a scroll bar control (see Day 19). The list boxes then are made to scroll in synch with the scroll bar control, because you can handle the messages emitted by this control and scroll the lists accordingly. You cannot intercept the messages sent by the scroll bars that are part of the list box itself.

Q Should I use `InsertString` in a list box created with the `LBS_SORT` style?

A No, you shouldn't because the `LBS_SORT` style maintains the list box items in order. Using `InsertString` corrupts the order in the list box. Instead, use the `AddString` member function.

Workshop

The Workshop provides quiz questions to help you solidify your understanding of the material covered and exercises to provide you with experience in using what you've learned. Try to understand the quiz and exercise answers before continuing on to the next day's lesson. Answers are provided in Appendix A, "Answers."

Quiz

1. True or false? The list box notification message `LBN_SETFOCUS` is suitable for optional initializing related to selecting a list box control.
2. True or false? The list box notification message `LBN_KILLFOCUS` is suitable for optional validation after you deselect a list box control.
3. True or false? The list box enables you to detect only the final selection, using the `LBN_KILLFOCUS` notification.
4. True or false? You should use `LBN_SELCHANGE` with a special flag to detect mouse double-clicks on a list box item.
5. True or false? `LBS_STANDARD` creates a list box control with unordered items.

Exercise

Modify the XFERLIST program to initialize the source list box with a directory listing, and then have it enable and disable the appropriate push buttons depending upon whether or not there is anything selected in the corresponding list boxes.

Scroll Bars and Combo Boxes

WEEK 3

Day 18 presented list box controls. Today's lesson presents two somewhat similar controls: the scroll bar and the combo box. The scroll bar control enables you to select a numeric value quickly, usually in a wide range of values. The combo box control combines the edit control and the list box, enabling the user to select a value from the list box component or to enter a new value in the edit control part. You will learn about the following topics:

- The scroll bar control
- The combo box control in its various styles

The Scroll Bar Control

Windows allows the scroll bar to exist as a separate control, as well as to be incorporated in windows, lists, and combo boxes. The scroll bar control appears and behaves much like the scroll bar of a window. The control has a thumb box that keeps track of the current value; the thumb box moves, either by single lines or by pages, when the user clicks it. This thumb box mechanism is supported by the `EvVScroll` or `EvHScroll` member functions. In addition, the scroll bar responds to cursor control keys, such as Home, End, PageUp, and PageDown. This feature is supported by the `EvKeyDown` member function. The main purpose of the scroll bar control is to enable you to quickly and efficiently select an integer value in a predefined range of values. Windows, for example, uses scroll bars to fine-tune the color palette, the keyboard rate, and the mouse sensitivity.

The *TScrollBar* Class

The ObjectWindows Library offers the `TScrollBar` class, a descendant of `TControl`, as the class that models the scroll bar controls. The `TScrollBar` class declares a class constructor and a number of member functions to set and query the control's current position and range of values.

The class constructor appears similar to all the other classes derived from `TControl`.

Syntax

The *TScrollBar* Constructor

The declaration of the `TScrollBar` constructor is

```
TScrollBar( TWindow* parent,
            int id,
            int x,
            int y,
```

```
                int w,
                int h,
                BOOL isHScrollBar,
                TModule* module = 0 );
```

As with the other control class constructors, parent refers to the parent window that contains the control, and id is the identifier used in differentiating the control from others. The x, y, w, and h parameters describe the location and size of the scroll bar control. The isHScrollBar parameter is used to specify in which direction the scroll bar will be. If the parameter is TRUE, the scroll bar will extend horizontally; FALSE will mean a vertical scroll bar.

Note that type of scroll bar that appears will be the same regardless of the values specified in the w and h parameters. If you specify a width and height for a vertical scroll bar, but specify TRUE for the isHScrollBar parameter, you'll end up with a very oddly shaped horizontal scroll bar. For this reason, the constructor will automatically set either the width or height of the control if the appropriate parameter is set to 0. For example, when creating a horizontal scroll bar, specifying 0 for the h parameter will give the control a standard height.

There are several styles, described in Table 19.1, that can be used to control the display of the scroll bar with respect to the rectangle you define in the constructor. Only two of them, the SBS_HORZ and SBS_VERT styles, are automatically set, depending upon the state of the isHScrollBar parameter.

Example:

```
TScrollBar* pThermometer = TScrollBar( this,
                                       IDSB_THERMOMETER,
                                       10, 10, 180, 0,
                                       TRUE );
```

Table 19.1. SBS_XXX styles for the scroll bar control.

Value	Meaning
SBS_BOTTOMALIGN	Specifies a style used with SBS_HORZ to align the bottom of the scroll bar with the bottom edge of the rectangle specified in the TScrollBar constructor.
SBS_HORZ	Specifies a horizontal scroll bar whose location, width, and height are specified by the parameters in the constructor, if neither SBS_BOTTOMALIGN nor SBS_TOPALIGN.

continues

Table 19.1. continued

Value	Meaning
SBS_LEFTALIGN	Specifies a style used with the SBS_VERT to align the left edge of the scroll bar with the left edge of the rectangle specified in the constructor.
SBS_RIGHTALIGN	Specifies a style used with SBS_VERT to align the right edge of the scroll bar with the right edge of the rectangle specified in the constructor.
SBS_SIZEBOX	Specifies a size box whose location, width, and height are specified by the parameters in the constructor, if neither one of the next two SBS_*XXX* styles is specified.
SBS_SIZEBOXBOTTOMRIGHTALIGN	Specifies a style used with SBS_SIZEBOX to align the lower-right corner of the size box with the lower-right corner of the rectangle specified in the constructor.
SBS_SIZEBOXTOPLEFTALIGN	Specifies a style used with the SBS_SIZEBOX style to align the upper-left corner of the size box with the upper-left corner of the rectangle specified in the constructor.
SBS_TOPALIGN	Specifies a style used with SBS_HORZ to align the top of the scroll bar with the top edge of the rectangle specified in the constructor.
SBS_VERT	Specifies a vertical scroll bar whose location, width, and height are specified by the parameters in the constructor, if neither SBS_RIGHTALIGN nor SBS_LEFTALIGN is specified.

The TScrollBar class declares a number of member functions. The following are some of the more useful functions:

- The first member function that you will most likely use after creating a TScrollBar instance is SetRange. This function enables you to set the range of values for the scroll bar.
- The GetRange member function enables you to query the current range of values for the scroll bar.
- The parameterless GetPosition member function returns the current position of the thumb box.
- The SetPosition member function moves the thumb box to the specified position. You are responsible for ensuring that the new thumb position is within the current scroll bar range.

Syntax

The *SetRange* Function

The declaration of the SetRange function is

```
void SetRange(int min, int max);
```

The arguments for the min and max parameters designate the new range of values for the scroll bar control.

Example:

```
pThermometer->SetRange(32,212);      // Freezing to boiling
```

Syntax

The *GetRange* Function

The declaration of the GetRange function is

```
void GetRange(int& min, int& max) const;
```

The parameters min and max are filled in by the GetRange member function with the minimum and maximum of the current range values for the scroll bar control.

Example:

```
int freezing, boiling;
pThermometer->GetRange(freezing, boiling);
```

Syntax

The *SetPosition* Function

The declaration of the member function `SetPosition` is

```
void SetPosition(int thumbPos);
```

The parameter `thumbPos` specifies the new thumb box position.

Example:

```
pThermometer->SetPosition(72);     // a comfortable temp
```

Responding to Scroll Bar Notification Messages

There are several methods by which a program can handle scroll bar notifications. The first is by creating a descendant class of the `TScrollBar` class, then overriding the various member functions that are called in response to the `SB_XXX` notification messages as listed in Day 15's lesson. The following table associates the notification messages with their corresponding `TScrollBar` member functions:

Table 19.2. `SBS_XXX` and `TScrollBar` member functions.

Notification Message	`TScrollBar` member function
SB_LINEUP	SBLineUp
SB_LINEDOWN	SBLineDown
SB_PAGEUP	SBPageUp
SB_PAGEDOWN	SBPageDown
SB_THUMBPOSITION	SBThumbPosition
SB_THUMBTRACK	SBThumbTrack
SB_TOP	SBTop
SB_BOTTOM	SBBottom

One must remember, however, that when overriding a descendant class's version of a response function, the parent's version must be called first. It is that version that keeps the scroll bar updated. Consider the following example:

```
void TMyScrollBar::SBTop()
{
   TScrollBar::SBTop();      // Make sure our parent gets a chance
   sndPlaySound("TOP.WAV", SND_ASYNC);    // Play a sound
}
```

Another method of responding to scroll bar notification messages is by intercepting the `EvHScroll` or `EvVScroll` member functions in the scroll bar's parent class. There, you can interrogate the scroll bar as to its current position and then act accordingly.

```
void TMyWindow::EvVScroll(UINT code, UINT pos, HWND hwnd)
{
   TWindow::EvVScroll(code, pos, hwnd);  // Give our parent a chance
   int newpos = scrollbar->GetPosition(); // get the updated position
   switch (code)
      {
      case SB_TOP:
         sndPlaySound("TOP.WAV", SND_ASYNC);
         break;
      }
}
```

Finally, if one uses the `EV_CHILD_NOTIFY_ALL_CODES` macro when defining the response table to assign a function response to the scroll bar's ID, the assigned function will be called for all notification messages coming from the scroll bar. The response function looks and acts similarly to the `EvXScroll` functions, but in this case it isn't necessary to call the parent's version of the function.

```
DEFINE_RESPONSE_TABLE1(TMyWindow, TWindow)
   EV_CHILD_NOTIFY_ALL_CODES(IDSC_THERMOMETER, EvScrollBar),
END_RESPONSE_TABLE;

void TMyWindow::EvScrollBar(UINT code)
{
   switch (code)
      {
      case SB_TOP:
         sndPlaySound("TOP.WAV", SND_ASYNC);
         break;
      }
}
```

The Countdown Timer

The countdown timer application contains the following controls:

- A timer scroll bar control that has a default range of 0 to 60 seconds

- Two static text controls that label the range of values for the timer scroll bar
- A static text control to show the current setting of the scroll bar
- Start and Exit buttons

You can set the number of seconds by using the scroll bar. When you move the scroll bar thumb box, the current thumb position appears in a static box. To trigger the countdown process, click the Start button. During the countdown, the application decrements the number of seconds in the edit box and moves the scroll bar's thumb box upward. When the countdown ends, the program sounds a beep and restores the scroll bar to its starting value.

The countdown timer application illustrates the following scroll bar manipulations:

- Setting and altering the scroll bar range of values
- Moving and changing the scroll bar thumb box position (the program illustrates how these tasks are performed internally or with the mouse)
- Using the scroll bar to supply a value

Listing 19.1 shows the source code for the COUNTDN.H header file. Listing 19.2 shows the source code for the COUNTDN.CPP program file.

Type

Listing 19.1. Source code for the COUNTDN.H header file.

```
#define IDB_START    101
#define IDB_EXIT     102
#define IDS_STATUS   103
#define IDSC_TIMER   104
```

Type

Listing 19.2. Source code for the COUNTDN.CPP program file.

```
#include <stdio.h>
#include <windows.h>
#include <owl\applicat.h>
#include <owl\button.h>
#include <owl\framewin.h>
#include <owl\scrollba.h>
#include <owl\static.h>
#include <owl\window.h>
#include <owl\window.rh>

```

```
#include "countdn.h"

class TMyWindow : public TWindow
{
public:
   TMyWindow(TWindow* parent = 0);

protected:
   virtual void SetupWindow();

   void EvTimerBar(UINT code);
   void CbStart();
   void CbExit();

private:
   TScrollBar*  timerbar;
   TStatic*     status;

   DECLARE_RESPONSE_TABLE(TMyWindow);
};
DEFINE_RESPONSE_TABLE1(TMyWindow, TWindow)
   EV_CHILD_NOTIFY_ALL_CODES(IDSC_TIMER, EvTimerBar),
   EV_BN_CLICKED(IDB_START, CbStart),
   EV_BN_CLICKED(IDB_EXIT, CbExit),
END_RESPONSE_TABLE;

TMyWindow::TMyWindow(TWindow* parent)
{
   Init(parent, 0, 0);

   TStatic *st = new TStatic(this, -1, "Countdown: ",
                                                    50, 50, 150, 30);
   if (st)
      {
      st->Attr.Style &= ~SS_LEFT;
      st->Attr.Style |= SS_RIGHT;
      }
   status = new TStatic(this, IDS_STATUS, "", 200, 50, 100, 30);
   new TButton(this, IDB_START, "Start", 50, 135, 60, 40);
   new TButton(this, IDB_EXIT, "Exit", 130, 135, 60, 40);
   timerbar = new TScrollBar(this, IDSC_TIMER,
                                             300, 100, 0, 150, FALSE);
   new TStatic(this, -1, "0", 330, 100, 80, 20);
   new TStatic(this, -1, "60", 330, 230, 80, 20);
}

void TMyWindow::SetupWindow()
{
   TWindow::SetupWindow();    // Initialize the visual element

```


continues

Listing 19.2. continued

```
   if (timerbar)
      {
      timerbar->SetRange(0, 60);
      timerbar->SetPosition(15);
      EvTimerBar(SB_THUMBPOSITION);
      }
}

void TMyWindow::EvTimerBar(UINT /*code*/)
{
   if (status)
      {
      char text[25];
      sprintf(text, "%d", timerbar ? timerbar->GetPosition() : 0);
      status->SetText(text);
      }
}

void DelaySecs(DWORD dwSecs)
{
   DWORD dwTime = GetTickCount() + (dwSecs * 1000L);
   while (GetTickCount() < dwTime)
      /* Just wait a while. */;
}

void TMyWindow::CbStart()
{
   if (timerbar)
      {
      // First, let the user know that we're stopping the
      // system for a time.
      //
      ::SetCursor(::LoadCursor(NULL, IDC_WAIT));

      int start = timerbar->GetPosition();
      for (int ix = start - 1; ix >= 0; --ix)
         {
         timerbar->SetPosition(ix);
         EvTimerBar(SB_THUMBPOSITION);
         DelaySecs(1);
         }
      timerbar->SetPosition(start);
      EvTimerBar(SB_THUMBPOSITION);
      }
}

void TMyWindow::CbExit()
{
```

```
    SendMessage(WM_CLOSE);
}

class TCountDownApp : public TApplication
{
public:
    TCountDownApp() : TApplication()
      { nCmdShow = SW_SHOWMAXIMIZED; }

    void InitMainWindow()
      {
      SetMainWindow(new TFrameWindow(  0,
                                   "Count Down Timer",
                                   new TMyWindow ));
      }
};

int OwlMain(int, char *[])
{
    return TCountDownApp().Run();
}
```

Figure 19.1 shows a sample session with the COUNTDN.EXE application.

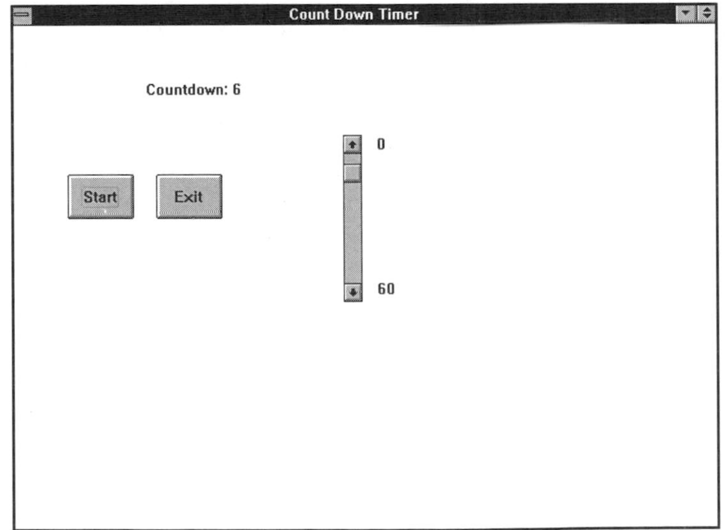

Figure 19.1. *A sample session with the COUNTDN.EXE application.*

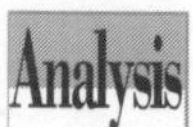

The interesting parts of the program in Listing 19.2 start on line 92 with `TMyWindow`'s constructor, where it creates the "Countdown" static text control. Normally, that control would just be created, but in order to make a better appearance on the screen, we change its style on lines 45 and 46 so that it's right-aligned. This means that we can then create another static text box just to its right on line 48, into which we will be able to place the current position of the scroll bar.

Next, in the `SetupWindow` member function starting on line 57, we first make sure to call the parent's version to create the actual visual elements. After making sure we were able to create the `timerbar` object, its range and position are initialized on lines 63 and 64, and the `EvTimerBar` member function is called with the parameter `SB_THUMBPOSITION` on line 65. Although `EvTimerBar` doesn't actually make use of the parameter it has passed, we should be sure that we send an accurate value, just in case some future version of this program *does* make use of the parameter.

The `EvTimerBar` member function that starts on line 69 responds to any notification message that might be sent by the scroll bar, as well as the various times it's called explicitly by the program itself. Its sole purpose at this point is to keep the `status` static text box updated with the current position of the scrollbar.

The next function is the nonmember function `DelaySecs` starting on line 79. This simply sits on its laurels for the number of seconds specified in the `dwSecs` parameter. It does this by calling the Windows `GetTickCount` function. This function returns the number of milliseconds elapsed since Windows was started. By multiplying `dwSecs` by `1000L` and then adding that to the result of the `GetTickCount` call on line 81, we get the end time. From there, all that's needed is a small loop that keeps calling the `GetTickCount` function so long as its result is less than the end time.

It's the `CbStart` function that provides the real meat of the program, starting on line 86. After ensuring on line 88 that we have a valid pointer to the `timerbar` object, we set the cursor to the hourglass on line 93. Because we'll be delaying the entire Windows system for the duration of the countdown, it's polite to let the user know that we're taking over for a while by changing the cursor to the hourglass. As soon as we exit the loop and go back to Windows, the cursor will automatically be changed back to the regular arrow. Note the use of the scope modifier on the calls to `SetCursor` and `LoadCursor`. This is used to make sure we get the original Windows functions instead of the `TWindow` member functions, which behave slightly differently.

Then on line 95 we initialize the `start` variable with the current position of the scroll bar and start a countdown to 0 from there. As we count down, we set the scroll bar's position, update the static text box, and then call the `DelaySecs` function on lines 98 through 100. Once the loop is finished, we reset the scroll bar to its original position on line 102 and update the static text control on line 103.

The Combo Box Control

Windows supports the combo box control, which combines an edit box with a list box. Thus, a combo box enables you either to select an item in the list box component (or part, if you prefer) or to type in your own input. In a sense, the list box part of the combo box contains convenient or frequently used selections. A combo box, unlike a list box, does not confine you to choosing items in the list box. There are three kinds of combo boxes: simple, drop-down, and drop-down list.

New Term: The *simple combo box* includes the edit box and the list box that are always displayed. The *drop-down combo box* differs from the simple type by the fact that the list box appears only when you click the down scroll arrow. The *drop-down list combo box* provides a drop-down list that appears when you click the down scroll arrow. There is no edit box in this kind of combo box.

Syntax

The *TComboBox* Class

OWL offers the `TComboBox` class, a descendant of `TListBox`, to support the combo box controls. The `TComboBox` class declares a constructor and a rich set of member functions to support both the edit control components, in addition to all the inherited list box member functions.

The declaration of the constructor is

```
TComboBox( TWindow* parent,
           int      id,
           int x, int y, int w, in h,
           DWORD    style,
           UINT     textLen,
           TModule* module = 0 );
```

The new parameters to this control class are the `style` and `textLen` parameters. The `TComboBox` control is the only control class whose constructor takes a parameter for specifying the style. This is because it is the one class in which you will most often want to modify the style. These styles are described in Table 19.3, and only the `CBS_SORT` and `CBS_AUTOHSCROLL` styles are set automatically; anything else you might want must be passed via the `style` parameter. The `textLen` parameter works similarly to the one sent to the `TEdit` class from Day 16. When the combo box has an edit box at the top, this parameter specifies the text length for that box.

Example:

```
pcb = new TComboBox(this, 101, 10, 10, 100, 150, CBS_DROPDOWN, 0);
```

The `style` parameter may include either `CBS_SIMPLE` for a simple combo box, `CBS_DROPDOWN` for a drop-down combo box, or `CBS_DROPDOWNLIST` for a drop-down list combo box.

Table 19.3. Combo box control styles.

Style	Meaning
`CBS_AUTOHSCROLL`	Automatically scrolls the text in the edit control to the right when you enter a character at the end of the line (removing this style limits the text to the characters that fit inside the rectangular boundary of the edit control).
`CBS_DISABLENOSCROLL`	Causes the scroll bar of the dropped-down list box portion of the combo box to simply become disabled and gray when scrolling is not allowed. By default, the scroll bar disappears.
`CBS_DROPDOWN`	Specifies a drop-down combo box.
`CBS_DROPDOWNLIST`	Specifies a drop-down list combo box.
`CBS_HASSTRINGS`	When used with an owner-drawn combo box, it causes the strings added to the combo box to be copied internally by the standard Windows routines. This is always the case when Windows does the drawing of the combo box.
`CBS_NOINTEGRALHEIGHT`	Tells the combo box that its drop-down list box portion need not be truncated to fit the height of its items; partial displays of items may be displayed.
`CBS_OEMCONVERT`	Allows Windows to convert the character sets as appropriate (useful for filenames).
`CBS_OWNERDRAWFIXED`	Creates an owner-drawn combo box; the programmer must create routines to display the items in the combo box. All items in the drop-down list box portion will be the same height.

Style	Meaning
`CBS_OWNERDRAWVARIABLE`	Exactly the same as `CBS_OWNERDRAWFIXED`, except the display items may be of differing heights.
`CBS_SIMPLE`	Specifies a simple combo box.
`CBS_SORT`	Automatically sorts the items in the list box.

The `TComboBox` class declares member functions to manage the edit box component and overrides member functions to manage the list box components. Most of these functions are similar to the corresponding members of the `TEdit` and `TListBox` classes.

In addition to the inherited `TListBox` member functions, the `TComboBox` class declares some extra member functions to handle the drop-down specifics of the combo box control. Among these are the following:

- The parameterless `ShowList` and `HideList` functions to drop down and roll up the combo box, respectively. Note that these are just wrapper functions that call the version of the `ShowList` function that takes a `BOOL` parameter, `ShowList` passing `TRUE`, and `HideList` passing `FALSE`.
- The `GetDroppedControlRect` member function to obtain the size of the dropped-down control.
- The parameterless `GetDroppedState` member function that returns a `BOOL` to tell whether the combo box is currently dropped down.
- The pair of member functions `GetExtendedUI` and `SetExtendedUI` that get and set the extended user interface for the combo box.

Syntax

The *GetDroppedControlRect* Function

The declaration of the `GetDroppedControlRect` function is

```
void GetDroppedControlRect(TRect& Rect) const;
```

When this function is called, the `Rect` parameter is filled with the screen coordinates of the dropped-down list box.

Example:

```
TRect rct;
pcb->GetDroppedControlRect(rct);
```

Although the TComboBox class isn't directly derived from the TEdit class, it has member functions to manipulate the edit control that comes as part of the combo box:

- The parameterless GetTextLen member function that returns an integer specifying the length of the text in the edit box.
- The GetText and SetText member functions for modifying the edit text.
- The GetEditSel and SetEditSel member functions that allow the manipulation of the starting and ending character position (that is, the index of the first selected character and the index of the first selected character that is not in the selected text).
- The parameterless Clear member function that clears the selected text.

Syntax

The *GetText* Function

The declaration of the GetText function is

```
int GetText(char far *str, int maxChars) const;
```

The parameter str is a pointer to a buffer into which GetText will copy the contents of the edit box, and maxChars is the maximum number of characters to copy (the size of the input buffer).

Example:

```
int len = pcb->GetTextLen() + 1;
char* str = new char[len];
if (str)
   pcb->GetText(str, len);
```

Responding to Combo Box Notification Messages

The combo box control emits various types of messages, shown in Table 19.4. The table also shows the message-mapping macros that are associated with the various command and notification messages. Each type of command or notification message requires a separate member function declared in the control's parent window class.

Table 19.4. Combo box notification messages.

Message	Macro	Meaning
CBN_CLOSEUP	EV_CBN_CLOSEUP	The combo box has been closed up.
CBN_DBLCLK	EV_CBN_DBLCLK	A combo item is selected with a mouse double-click.
CBN_DROPDOWN	EV_CBN_DROPDOWN	The combo box has been dropped down.
CBN_EDITCHANGE	EV_CBN_EDITCHANGE	The contents of the edit box are changed.
CBN_EDITUPDATE	EV_CBN_EDITUPDATE	The contents of the edit box are updated.
CBN_ERRSPACE	EV_CBN_ERRSPACE	The combo box cannot allocate more dynamic memory to accommodate new list items.
CBN_KILLFOCUS	EV_CBN_KILLFOCUS	The combo box has lost focus.
CBN_SELCHANGE	EV_CBN_SELCHANGE	A combo item is selected or deselected with a mouse click.
CBN_SELENDCANCEL	EV_CBN_SELENDCANCEL	The user has just selected an item and then selected another control or closed the window.
CBN_SELENDOK	EV_CBN_SELENDOK	The user has just clicked a list item or selected an item and closed the list. This is sent before every CBN_SELCHANGE message.
CBN_SETFOCUS	EV_CBN_SETFOCUS	The combo box has gained focus.

Combo Boxes as History List Boxes

A combo box can also be a history list box. History list boxes typically follow these rules of operation:

- The combo list box removes the `CBS_SORT` style to insert the list items in a chronological fashion. New items are inserted at position 0, pushing the older items farther down the list. The oldest item is the one at the bottom of the list.
- History boxes usually have a limit on the number of items you can insert, to prevent bleeding memory. This conservation scheme requires that oldest list items be removed after the number of list items reaches a maximum limit.
- If the edit control contains a string that does not have an exact match in the accompanying list box, the edit control string is inserted as a new member at position 0.
- If the edit control contains a string that has an exact match in the accompanying list box, the matching list member is moved to position 0, the top of the list. Of course, this process involves first deleting the matching list member from its current position and then reinserting it at position 0.

A history list box is really a combo box that manipulates its edit control and list box items in a certain way. There is no need to derive a descendant of `TComboBox` to add new member functions; although, if you use a history list box enough, it might make sense to create a descendant class that automates the functionality. Furthermore, for additional functionality, the descendent class could save the history list to disk for future invocations of the program.

The Son of Mister Calculator Application

Let us present an updated version of the calculator application, Son of Mister Calculator. This new version adds functionality to Day 16's version by using history combo boxes for the operands and result, instead of the standard edit boxes, and using a simple combo box that contains the list of supported operators and functions. Figure 19.2 shows a sample session with the CALCJR.EXE application and indicates the controls that are used.

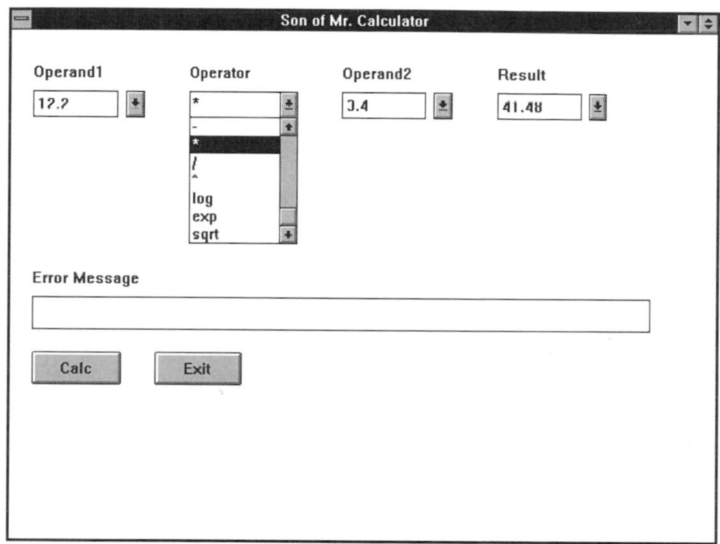

Figure 19.2. *A sample session with the CALCJR.EXE application.*

Compile and run the program. Experiment with entering and executing numbers and operators or functions. Notice that combo boxes for the operands and the result fill in their accompanying list boxes in a chronological order. The Operand and Result combo boxes remember the last 30 different operands you entered. In a way, the Result combo box acts as temporary memory.

Listing 19.3 shows the source code for the CALCJR.H header file. Listing 19.4 contains the source code for the CALCJR.CPP program file. The resource file defines the accelerator keys and menu resources.

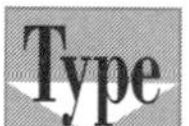

Listing 19.3. Source code for the CALCJR.H header file.

```
#define IDB_CALC      101
#define IDB_EXIT      102
#define IDC_OPERAND1  103
#define IDC_OPERATOR  104
#define IDC_OPERAND2  105
#define IDC_RESULT    106
#define IDE_ERRMSG    107
```

Listing 19.4. Source code for the CALCJR.CPP program file.

```
#include <ctype.h>
#include <math.h>
#include <stdio.h>
#include <owl\applicat.h>
#include <owl\button.h>
#include <owl\combobox.h>
#include <owl\edit.h>
#include <owl\framewin.h>
#include <owl\static.h>
#include <owl\window.h>
#include <owl\window.rh>

#include "calcjr.h"

class THistoryBox : public TComboBox
{
public:
   THistoryBox(TWindow* parent,
               int      id,
               int x, int y, int w, int h,
               UINT     textLen,
               int      historyLen,
               TModule* module = 0);

   void EvKillFocus(HWND);

private:
   int history;

   DECLARE_RESPONSE_TABLE(THistoryBox);
};
DEFINE_RESPONSE_TABLE1(THistoryBox, TComboBox)
   EV_WM_KILLFOCUS,
END_RESPONSE_TABLE;

THistoryBox::THistoryBox(  TWindow* parent,
                           int id,
                           int x, int y, int w, int h,
                           UINT textLen,
                           int historyLen,
                           TModule* module )
   : TComboBox(parent, id, x, y, w, h, CBS_DROPDOWN, textLen,
               module)
{
   Attr.Style &= ~CBS_SORT;      // We don't want to sort
   history = historyLen;
}

```

```
void THistoryBox::EvKillFocus(HWND)
{
   int len = GetTextLen() + 1;
   char *str = new char[len];
   if (str)
      {
      GetText(str, len);
      int ix = FindExactString(str, -1);
      if (ix < 0)
         {
         InsertString(str, 0);
         while (GetCount() >= history)
            DeleteString(GetCount() - 1);
         }
      else if (ix > 0)
         {
         DeleteString(ix);
         InsertString(str, 0);
         SetSelIndex(0);
         }
      delete str;
      }
}

class TCalcJrWindow : public TWindow
{
public:
   TCalcJrWindow(TWindow* parent = 0);

protected:
   virtual void SetupWindow();

   void CmCalc();
   void CmExit();

private:
   TComboBox*   Operator;
   THistoryBox* Operand1, *Operand2, *Result;
   TEdit*       ErrMsg;

   DECLARE_RESPONSE_TABLE(TCalcJrWindow);
};
DEFINE_RESPONSE_TABLE1(TCalcJrWindow, TWindow)
   EV_BN_CLICKED(IDB_CALC, CmCalc),
   EV_BN_CLICKED(IDB_EXIT, CmExit),
END_RESPONSE_TABLE;

TCalcJrWindow::TCalcJrWindow(TWindow* parent)
{
   Init(parent, 0, 0);

```


continues

Listing 19.4. continued

```
    new TStatic(this, -1, "Operand1", 20, 30, 100, 20);
    new TStatic(this, -1, "Operator", 160, 30, 100, 20);
    new TStatic(this, -1, "Operand2", 300, 30, 100, 20);
    new TStatic(this, -1, "Result", 440, 30, 100, 20);

    Operand1 = new THistoryBox(this, IDC_OPERAND1, 20, 55, 100, 150,
                                                  0, 30);
    Operator = new TComboBox(this, IDC_OPERATOR, 160, 55, 100, 150,
                                                  CBS_DROPDOWNLIST, 0);
    if (Operator)
       Operator->Attr.Style &= ~CBS_SORT;
    Operand2 = new THistoryBox(this, IDC_OPERAND2, 300, 55, 100,
                                                  150, 0, 30);
    Result = new THistoryBox(this, IDC_RESULT, 440, 55, 100, 150,
                                                  0, 30);

    new TStatic(this, -1, "Error Message", 20, 215, 100, 20);
    ErrMsg = new TEdit(this, IDE_ERRMSG, "", 20, 240, 560, 30);

    new TButton(this, IDB_CALC, "Calc", 20, 290, 80, 30);
    new TButton(this, IDB_EXIT, "Exit", 130, 290, 80, 30);
}

void TCalcJrWindow::SetupWindow()
{
    TWindow::SetupWindow();    // Initialize the visual element

    // Fill up out Operator combo box with a variety
    // of operators for our user's computational pleasure.
    //
    if (Operator)
       {
       static char* p[] =
          { "+", "-", "*", "/", "^", "log", "exp", "sqrt", NULL };
       for (int ix = 0; p[ix]; ++ix)
          Operator->AddString(p[ix]);
       }

    // Keep the users out of the error box.
    //
    if (ErrMsg)
       ErrMsg->SetReadOnly(TRUE);
}

double get_number(TComboBox* numbox)
{
    double rslt = 0;         // default to 0
    char* str;
```

```
   int size;

   if (numbox)
      {
      str = new char[size = numbox->GetTextLen() + 1];
      if (str)
         {
         numbox->GetText(str, size);
         rslt = atof(str);
         delete str;
         }
      }
   return rslt;
}

void TCalcJrWindow::CmCalc()
{
   double x, y, z = 0;

   x = get_number(Operand1);
   y = get_number(Operand2);

   if (Operator)
      {
      int   ix = Operator->GetSelIndex();
      if (ix >= 0)
         {
         char* err = NULL;

         switch (ix)
            {
            case 0:      // + operator
               z = x + y;
               break;
            case 1:      // - operator
               z = x - y;
               break;
            case 2:      // * operator
               z = x * y;
               break;
            case 3:      // / operator
               if (y)
                  z = x / y;
               else
                  err = "Can't divide by zero.";
               break;
            case 4:      // ^ operator
               if (x > 0)
                  z = exp(y * log(x));
               else
                  err = "Need positive number to raise power.";
```

19

continues

Listing 19.4. continued

```
               break;
            case 5:     // log function
               if (x > 0)
                  z = log(x);
               else
                  err = "Need positive number for log.";
               break;
            case 6:     // exp function
               if (x < 230)
                  z = exp(x);
               else
                  err = "Need a smaller number for exp.";
               break;
            case 7:     // sqrt function
               if (x >= 0)
                  z = sqrt(x);
               else
                  err = "Can't do sqrt of negative number.";
               break;
            default:
               err = "Unknown operator";
               break;
            }

         if (ErrMsg)
            if (!err)
               ErrMsg->Clear();
            else
               ErrMsg->SetWindowText(err);
         if (!err && Result)
            {
            char dest[81];
            sprintf(dest, "%g", z);
            Result->SetWindowText(dest);
            Result->EvKillFocus(NULL);    // Force history addition
            }
         }
      }
}

void TCalcJrWindow::CmExit()
{
   SendMessage(WM_CLOSE);
}

class TCalcJrApp : public TApplication
{
public:
```

```
246:    TCalcJrApp() : TApplication()
247:       { nCmdShow = SW_SHOWMAXIMIZED; }
248:
249:    void InitMainWindow()
250:       {
251:       SetMainWindow(new TFrameWindow(  0,
252:                            "Son of Mr. Calculator",
253:                            new TCalcJrWindow ));
254:       }
255: };
256:
257: int OwlMain(int, char *[])
258: {
259:    return TCalcJrApp().Run();
260: }
```

Analysis The program in Listing 19.4 begins by declaring, starting on line 15, a descendant of `TComboBox` called `THistoryBox`. This descendant declares its constructor, a single member function, and a single data member. The constructor specifies the `CBS_DROPDOWN` style when calling the parent `TComboBox` constructor on line 42, then turns off the `CBS_SORT` style and initializes the `history` member data with the `historyLen` parameter on lines 44 and 45.

The `EvKillFocus` member function of `THistoryBox` that starts on line 48 is called in response to the `WM_KILLFOCUS` Windows message. At this time, the function inserts the string of the edit control part in the list box part. This insertion occurs only if the string is not already in the list box part. In this case, the string is inserted at index 0 and becomes the new top-of-the-list item. If the targeted string is already in the list box part, the function deletes the existing item in the list box and reinserts it at index 0. Thus, the targeted string appears to have moved up to the top of the list box part.

The `TCalcJrWindow`'s constructor that starts on line 95 does the usual creation of controls. The `SetupWindow` member function then initializes the Operator combo box by filling its list box component with the supported operators and functions on lines 129 through 135.

The `get_number` function, starting on line 143, is used, as in Day 16, to obtain a `double` value from a control. This time, it receives a `TComboBox` pointer, gets the contents of its edit box, then uses the `atof` function to obtain the `double` value that is returned.

The Calc button causes the `CmCalc` member function, starting on line 162, to be called. This is the function that does all the following work of the application:

- Retrieves the values from the Operand1 and Operand2 combo boxes and places their values in the `x` and `y` variables, respectively, on lines 166 and 167.
- Obtains the index of the selected operator in the Operator combo box on line 171.
- If something is actually selected, a `switch` statement is used to determine the requested operation or math function, then the `case` statement performs the requested task and assigns the result to variable `z`, or sets the `err` pointer to an appropriate error string.
- Sets the Error Message edit box if an error occurred or clears that same edit box if no error was detected on lines 222 through 226.
- If no error occurred, displays the result of the operation or function evaluation in the edit control box of the Result combo box, then calls its `EvKillFocus` function directly to have that value inserted into its list box component on lines 227 through 233.

Summary

Today's lesson presented the scroll bar and combo box controls. These controls share the common factor of being input objects. You learned about the following topics:

- The scroll bar control enables you to select quickly from a wide range of integers.
- There are various types of combo box controls: simple, drop-down, and drop-down list.
- You can make a history list box out of a drop-down combo box.

Q&A

Q Do the scroll bars strictly select integers?

A Yes. However, these integers can be indexes to arrays, items in list box controls, and other integer codes to various attributes such as colors. Therefore, in a sense, the scroll bar can be used to select nonintegers.

Q Can I create a scroll bar control with an excluded sub-range of values?

A No. You may want to use a list box control instead and have that control list the value numbers.

Workshop

The Workshop provides quiz questions to help you solidify your understanding of the material covered and exercises to provide you with experience in using what you've learned. Try to understand the quiz and exercise answers before continuing on to the next day's lesson. Answers are provided in Appendix A, "Answers."

Quiz

1. True or false? If you do not include the `CBS_AUTOHSCROLL` style in creating a combo list box, you limit the text to the characters that fit inside the rectangular boundary of the edit control.
2. True or false? You can handle the `CBN_SELCHANGE` notification message to monitor every keystroke in the edit control of a combo box.
3. True or false? Setting `CBS_SORT` creates a combo box whose list box items are sorted and unique.
4. True or false? To emulate a history list box, a combo box must be created without the `CBS_SORT` style.
5. True or false? A history list may have duplicate items.
6. True or false? COUNTDN.CPP demonstrates how to implement a two-way connection between the current value of a scroll bar control and the numeric value in a text box.
7. True or false? The range of values for a scroll bar control are fixed when you create the control.

Exercise

Modify the CALCJR.CPP program by adding a Variables multiline box and a Store pushbutton.

Dialog Boxes

WEEK 3

Dialog boxes are special child windows that contain controls serving to display information or to input data. Windows applications use dialog boxes to exchange information with the user. Today's lesson looks at the modal and modeless dialog boxes supported by Windows.

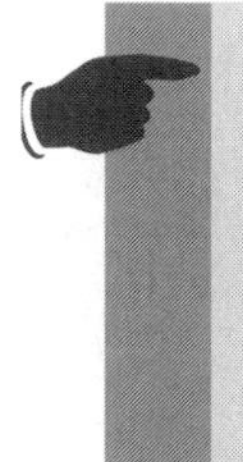

New Term: *Modal dialog boxes* require you to close them before you can proceed any further with the application because they are meant to perform a critical exchange of data. In fact, modal dialog boxes disable their parent windows while they have the focus. *Modeless dialog boxes* do not need to be closed to continue using the application. You need merely to click on another of the application's windows to continue.

Today you learn about the following topics:

- Constructing instances of the class `TDialog`
- Executing a modal dialog box
- Transferring control data
- Transferring data for modal dialog boxes
- Transferring data for modeless dialog boxes

Constructing Dialog Boxes

OWL declares the `TDialog` class to support both modeless and modal dialog boxes. The `TDialog` class, a descendant of `TWindow`, has a class constructor and a number of member functions, including the `Create` and `Execute` functions. The `TDialog` constructor is declared as follows:

```
TDialog(TWindow* parent, TResId resId, TModule* module = 0);
```

The `parent` parameter is a pointer to the parent window. The `resId` parameter describes the dialog box's resource name or ID. The `module` parameter, which is normally left out of calls to the constructor, can be used to specify different locations from which to load the resource (for example, loading from a separate DLL).

The TResId class is a method used by OWL to encapsulate the different ways that a resource can be named in an application's resources. For example, one could specify a dialog template as having either a number or a name. The useful TResId class has three overloaded constructors. The first one, the default constructor, takes no arguments and initializes the class to a 0 value. The other two constructors look like this:

```
TResId(LPCSTR resString);
TResId(int resNum);
```

This means that you can easily create a TResId by simply passing the appropriate value for the constructor. Also, if you use it as a temporary object, you can have TDialog constructors that look something like this:

```
TDialog* errdlg = new TDialog(this, "ErrorDlg");
TDialog* newdlg = new TDialog(this, 101);
```

Note: Using resources to define dialog boxes and their controls enables you to define the location, dimensions, style, and caption of a control outside the Windows application source code. Thus, you can change the resource file, recompile it, and then incorporate it in the .EXE application file without recompiling the source file itself. This approach enables you to develop different resource versions with varying colors, styles, and even languages while maintaining a single copy of the application code. Furthermore, this approach does away with the need to write all that complicated code for creating and placing controls in the constructor of a TWindow class.

20

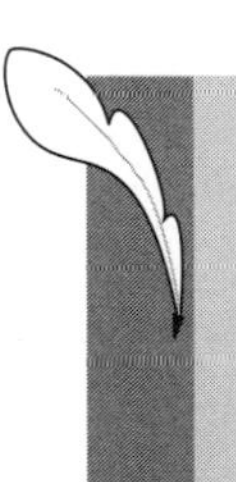

Note: The Borland C++ package includes the Resource Workshop, which enables you to create dialog boxes by drawing the controls in the dialog boxes. The Resource Workshop creates .RC resource files that are then bound in your Windows applications. If you are a novice Windows programmer, first learn about the .RC file and its script. Using the Resource Workshop is very easy and intuitive. Knowing about the .RC resource script makes working with the output of the Resource Workshop even easier.

Creating Dialog Boxes

Typically, modal dialog boxes are created and removed more frequently than modeless dialog boxes and much more frequently than windows. Executing modal dialog boxes involves the following steps:

1. Create a dialog box object by using `TDialog` constructor.
2. Call the `Execute` member function, declared in the class `TDialog`, to bring up the dialog box. Typically, dialog boxes contain the OK and Cancel pushbuttons, with the OK button as the default button. The OK and Cancel buttons have the predefined IDs of `IDOK` and `IDCANCEL`, respectively. You may use pushbutton controls with different captions than OK and Cancel. However, you should still use the `IDOK` and `IDCANCEL` with these renamed buttons. Using these IDs enables you to take advantage of the automatic response to `IDOK` and `IDCANCEL` provided by the `CmOk` and `CmCancel` member functions defined in the `TDialog` class. Clicking OK or pressing the Enter key usually signals your acceptance of the current (that is, the default or edited) data in the dialog box. By contrast, clicking the Cancel button signals your dissatisfaction with the current data. The declaration of the `Execute` function is this:

   ```
   int Execute();
   ```

   The function returns an integer that represents the outcome. This is typically the value of a pushbutton ID, like `IDOK` and `IDCANCEL`.
3. Compare the result of the `Execute` function with `IDOK` (or, less frequently, `IDCANCEL`). The outcome of this comparison determines the steps to take. Such steps usually involve accessing data that you entered in the dialog box controls.

Creating modeless dialog boxes takes only a little more effort. First, they must be created on the heap with a call to `new`. Then its `Create` and `ShowWindow` member functions must be called, for example,

```
TDialog* pdlg = new TDialog(this, "My Dialog");
pdlg -> Create();
pdlg -> ShowWindow(SW_SHOW);
```

The dialog object will be deleted automatically when the dialog box is closed. This can, of course, cause problems if you attempt to use the dialog pointer after the dialog is closed.

Like the `TWindow` class, from which much of `TDialog`'s functionality is inherited, the `SetupWindow`, `CanClose`, and `Destroy` member functions support the execution of both modal and modeless dialog boxes. The `SetupWindow` member function serves to initialize the dialog box and its controls. The declaration of the `SetupWindow` function is as follows:

```
virtual void SetupWindow();
```

Typically, the `SetupWindow` function initializes the controls of the dialog box. This initialization usually involves copying data from buffers or data members.

The `CanClose` function is called whenever the user presses the OK button. The declaration of the `CanClose` function is this:

```
virtual BOOL CanClose();
```

The `CanClose` acts to copy data from the dialog-box controls to data members or buffers after deciding whether or not it's okay to close the dialog. This function returns either `TRUE` or `FALSE`, depending upon whether or not the user is allowed to close the dialog box, given the data entered.

The `Destroy` member function handles the closing of the dialog box. The declaration of the `Destroy` is this:

```
virtual void Destroy(int retValue = IDCANCEL);
```

The `Destroy` function serves to clean up before the dialog box is closed, which may involve closing data files, for example. Usually, the last statement in the `Destroy` member function definition is a call to the `Destroy` function of its parent class.

The next example is a simple OWL program that uses a dialog box defined in resource files. It also uses resource files to create alternate forms of the same dialog box; the first uses modern English and the second uses old English. The application is simple and is made up of an empty window with a single menu item, Exit. When you click the Exit menu item (or press the Alt+X keys), you get a dialog box that asks you whether or not you want to exit the application. The dialog box has a title, a message, and the two buttons (in fact, we purposely made it to resemble the dialog boxes spawned by the `MessageBox` function). The program alternates between the two versions of the dialog box. When you first click the Exit menu, you get the modern English version (with OK and Cancel buttons), shown in Figure 20.1. If you click the Cancel button and then click the Exit menu again, you get the old English version of the dialog box (with Yea and Nay buttons), shown in Figure 20.2. Every time you select the Cancel or Nay button and then click the Exit menu, you toggle between the two versions of the dialog box. To exit the application, click the OK or Yea button, depending on the current dialog box version.

Listing 20.1 shows the DIALOG1.RC resource file. Listing 20.2 shows the source code for the DIALOG1.CPP program.

Listing 20.1. Script for the DIALOG1.RC resource file.

```
#include <windows.h>
#include <owl\window.rh>

EXITMENU MENU LOADONCALL MOVEABLE PURE DISCARDABLE
BEGIN
  MENUITEM "E&xit", CM_EXIT
END

ModernEnglish DIALOG DISCARDABLE LOADONCALL PURE MOVEABLE 20, 50,
  200, 100
STYLE WS_POPUP | DS_MODALFRAME
CAPTION "Message"
BEGIN
   CTEXT "Exit the application?", -1, 10, 10, 170, 15
   DEFPUSHBUTTON "OK", IDOK, 20, 50, 70, 15, WS_VISIBLE | WS_TABSTOP
   PUSHBUTTON "Cancel", IDCANCEL, 110, 50, 70, 15, WS_VISIBLE |
     WS_TABSTOP
END

OldeEnglish DIALOG DISCARDABLE LOADONCALL PURE MOVEABLE 20, 50, 200,
  100
STYLE WS_POPUP | DS_MODALFRAME
CAPTION "Message"
BEGIN
   CTEXT "Leavest thou now?", -1, 10, 10, 170, 15
   DEFPUSHBUTTON "Yea", IDOK, 20, 50, 70, 15, WS_VISIBLE |
     WS_TABSTOP
   PUSHBUTTON "Nay", IDCANCEL, 110, 50, 70, 15, WS_VISIBLE |
     WS_TABSTOP
END
```

Type

Listing 20.2. Source code for the DIALOG1.CPP program file.

```
#include <windows.h>
#include <owl\applicat.h>
#include <owl\dialog.h>
#include <owl\framewin.h>
#include <owl\window.h>
#include <owl\window.rh>

class TMyWindow : public TWindow
{
```

```
public:
   TMyWindow(TWindow* parent = 0);

   virtual BOOL CanClose();

protected:
   void CmExit();

   DECLARE_RESPONSE_TABLE(TMyWindow);
};
DEFINE_RESPONSE_TABLE1(TMyWindow, TWindow)
   EV_COMMAND(CM_EXIT, CmExit),
END_RESPONSE_TABLE;

TMyWindow::TMyWindow(TWindow* parent)
   : TWindow(parent)
{
}

BOOL TMyWindow::CanClose()
{
   static BOOL bFlag = FALSE;

   bFlag = !bFlag;
   if (bFlag)
      return TDialog(this, "ModernEnglish").Execute() == IDOK;
   else
      return TDialog(this, "OldeEnglish").Execute() == IDOK;
}

void TMyWindow::CmExit()
{
   SendMessage(WM_CLOSE);
}

class TDialogApp : public TApplication
{
public:
   TDialogApp() : TApplication()
      { nCmdShow = SW_SHOWMAXIMIZED; }

   void InitMainWindow()
      {
      SetMainWindow(new TFrameWindow(  0,
                            "Simple Dialog Box Tester Application",
                            new TMyWindow ));
      GetMainWindow()->AssignMenu("EXITMENU");
      }
};

```

continues

Listing 20.2. continued

```
int OwlMain(int, char *[])
{
    return TDialogApp().Run();
}
```

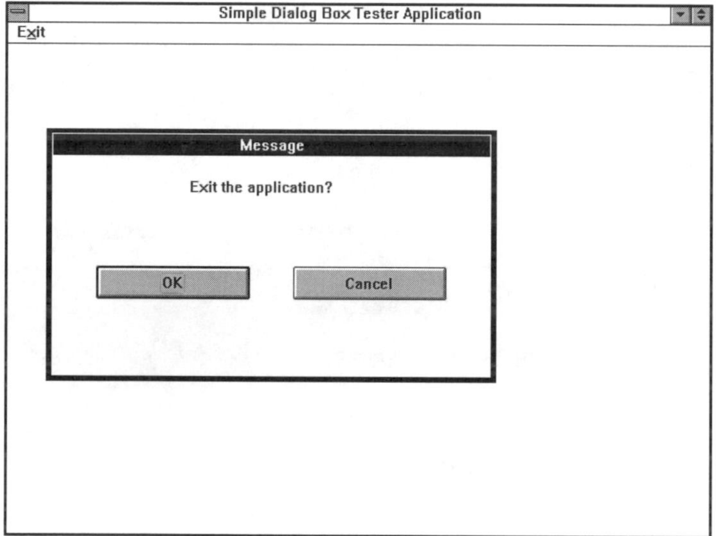

Figure 20.1. *A sample session with the DIALOG1.EXE application showing the dialog box with modern English wording.*

Listing 20.1 shows the script for the DIALOG1.RC resource file, which defines the following resources:

- The menu resource, `EXITMENU`, which displays a single menu with the single item Exit.
- The dialog-box resource starting on line 9, `ModernEnglish`, which has a defined style, caption, and list of child controls. The specified style indicates that the dialog box is a modal pop-up child window. The caption specified on line 11 is the string `Message`. The dialog box contains three controls: a centered static text (for the dialog box message), a default OK pushbutton, and an ordinary Cancel button. The OK button has the resource ID of the predefined `IDOK` constant, and the Cancel button has the resource ID of the predefined `IDCANCEL` constant.

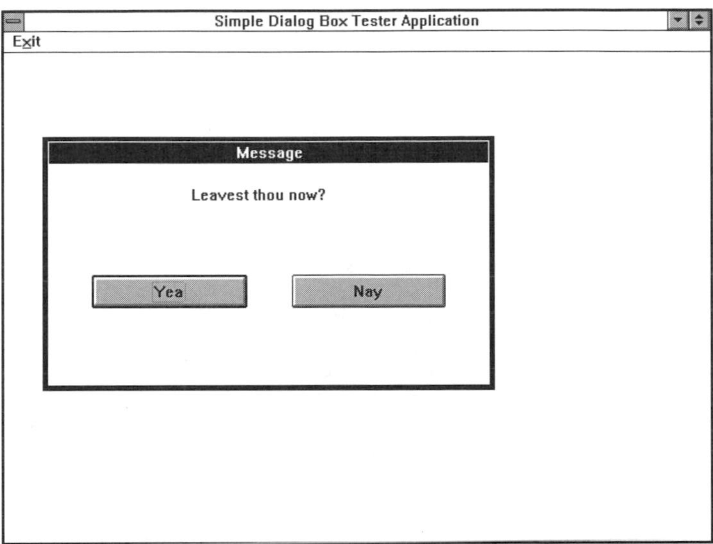

Figure 20.2. *A sample session with the DIALOG1.EXE application showing the dialog box with the old English wording.*

- The dialog-box resource starting on line 18, `OldeEnglish`, which is similar to the `ModernEnglish` dialog-box resource, except that it uses an old English wording. The Yea button has the resource ID of the predefined `IDOK` constant. The Nay button has the resource ID of the predefined `IDCANCEL` constant. These buttons are examples of exit buttons with atypical captions.

The `CTEXT` keyword specifies centered text. The `DEFPUSHBUTTON` keyword enables you to define any control and requires the caption, ID, location, dimensions, and control style of the control. The `PUSHBUTTON` definition is identical to the `DEFPUSHBUTTON` keyword's definition, but it describes an ordinary button instead of a default pushbutton.

Up until now, you've been creating resources by manually creating the .RC file. When making dialog boxes, it's far easier to use the Resource Workshop. This provides an easy interface by which dialog boxes can be painted on the screen exactly the way you want them to appear when your application is run.

Listing 20.2 shows the source code for the DIALOG1.CPP program file. The source code declares two classes: an application class starting on line 45 and a window class starting on line 8. The application uses the standard `TDialog` class; it does not derive a specialized descendant because no additional dialog box functionality is required.

The most relevant member function is `CanClose` starting on line 29, which responds to the user's request to close the window (triggered by the `CmExit` function on line 40, which in turn is triggered by the Exit menu choice). The function uses the Boolean static local variable, `bFlag`, to toggle between the two dialog-box resources `ModernEnglish` and `OldeEnglish`. The new English dialog box is invoked in the following statement:

```
return TDialog(this, "ModernEnglish").Execute() == IDOK;
```

The dialog-box object is executed using the `Execute` function, disabling the parent window until you click either pushbutton control. The value returned by the `Execute` member function is compared with the `IDOK` constant, and the result is returned to the caller to let it know what the user selected, and whether or not to close the application window.

The instance of the old English version of the dialog box is similarly created, as shown in the following statement:

```
return TDialog(this, "OldeEnglish").Execute() == IDOK;
```

Connecting OWL Objects with Windows Controls

Up until now, the constructors for the various controls you've learned all have had the same general look of the constructor of the `TControl` class from which they're all descendants.

```
TControl( TWindow* parent,
          int id,
          const char far* title,
          int x,
          int y,
          int w,
          int h,
          TModule* module = 0 );
```

Occasionally, there have been additional parameters after the `h` and before the module parameters, as the various controls needed. These all assume that the controls needed to be created from scratch, including their positions in their parent window.

When creating a dialog box from a resource file, however, these controls will be created automatically from the resource script at the same time as the dialog box. In order to have access to the controls from an OWL object, there is a second constructor for each control class that enables you to create an object that has a direct correspondence with the actual Windows control.

The following are the constructors for creating the various controls:

```
TStatic( TWindow* parent, int resourceId, UINT textLen = 0,
         TModule* module = 0);
TEdit( TWindow* parent, int resourceId, UINT textLen = 0,
       TModule* module = 0 );
TButton(TWindow* parent, int resourceId, TModule* module = 0);
TCheckBox( TWindow* parent, int resourceId, TGroupBox* group = 0,
           TModule* module = 0 );
TRadioButton( TWindow* parent, int resourceId, TGroupBox* group = 0,
              TModule* module = 0 );
TGroupBox(TWindow* parent, int resourceId, TModule* module = 0);
TListBox(TWindow* parent, int resourceId, TModule* module = 0);
TComboBox( TWindow* parent, int resourceId, UINT textLen = 0,
           TModule* module = 0 );
TScrollBar(TWindow* parent, int resourceId, TModule* module = 0);
```

The control objects, as with the full versions, should be created in a dialog's constructor. The following is an example of creating an OWL object to interface with a window's Cancel button:

```
cancel = new TButton(this, IDCANCEL);
```

Transferring Control Data

Dialog boxes serve mainly as pop-up windows to request input from the application user. This input often includes a variety of settings that use radio buttons, check boxes, and edit boxes. Because dialog boxes are frequently created, it makes sense to preserve the latest values in the dialog's controls for the next time it appears. The Search and Replace dialog boxes that are found in many Windows editors are typical examples. These dialog boxes remember the settings of all or some of their controls from the last time the dialog box was executed. You can also use the transfer mechanism as an easy way to set and retrieve data in the dialog for simple initialization and retrieval purposes.

20

To implement this feature in dialog boxes, you need a data transfer mechanism between the dialog box and a buffer. This buffer is usually a data member of the parent window. Therefore, the first step in supporting data transfer is to define a transfer buffer type. The buffer declares the data fields to buffer the controls that transfer their data. These controls typically include the edit box, list box, combo box, scroll bar, check box, and radio button. The static text, group box, and pushbutton controls usually have no data to transfer and therefore do not enter in the declaration of the data transfer buffer type, because OWL has them disabled by default. A sample data buffer type that includes a single instance of each allowable control is this:

```
struct TAppTransferBuffer
{
   char EditBox[MaxEditLen];
   TListBoxData ListBoxData;
   TComboBoxData ComboBoxData;
   TScrollBarData ScrollBarData;
   UINT CheckBox;
   UINT RadioButton;
};
```

The buffer structure needs only to include the controls that actually transfer data. You do not need to declare the fields of the buffer structure in any particular order, so long as the controls they match are created in the same order. This sample buffer type includes three special classes that transfer data between dialog boxes and list boxes, combo boxes, and scroll bars. You will see more about these classes later in this section.

Let's look at the various members of the data transfer buffer type:

- The `EditBox` member assists in moving data between the edit control and the data buffer. The data member defines a character array that should be equal to or greater than the number of characters in the edit control.
- The `ListBoxData` member helps to transfer data between a list box control and the data buffer. The `ListBoxData` is an instance of the `TListBoxData` class that OWL provides for keeping track of the contents of a list box, including any selections.
- The `ComboBoxData` member helps to move data between a combo box control and the data buffer. The `ComboBoxData` is an instance of the `TComboBoxData` class. This, too, is provided by OWL to keep track of the contents and state of a combo box.
- The `ScrollBarData` member is an instance of the `TScrollBarData` class that assists in transferring data between a scroll bar control and the data buffer.
- The `CheckBox` member stores the current check state of a check box in a `UINT` type.
- The `RadioButton` member stores the current check state of a radio button in a `UINT` type.

Data Transfer for Modal Dialog Boxes

The next application is a simple example of transferring data between the controls of a modal dialog box and a buffer. It creates a typical dialog box that is used in replacing characters in a text editor. The dialog box contains the following controls:

- Find edit box
- Replace edit box
- Scope group box that contains the Global and Selected Text radio button controls
- Case-Sensitive check box
- The Whole Word check box
- The OK pushbutton control
- The Cancel pushbutton control

The application has a main menu with the Exit and Dialog menu items. To invoke the dialog box, click the Dialog menu item or press the Alt+D keys. When you invoke the dialog box for the first time, the controls have the following initial values and states:

- The Find edit box contains the string DOS.
- The Replace edit box has the string Windows.
- The Global radio button is checked.
- The Case-Sensitive check box is checked.
- The Whole Word check box is checked.

Type new strings in the edit box and alter the check states of the radio buttons and check boxes. Now, click the OK button (or press the Alt+O keys) to close the dialog box. Invoke the Dialog menu item again to pop up the dialog box. Notice that the controls of the dialog box have the same values and states as when you last closed the dialog box.

Listing 20.3 shows the source code for the DIALOG2.H header file. Listing 20.4 contains the script for the DIALOG2.RC resource file. Listing 20.5 shows the source code for the DIALOG2.CPP program file.

Listing 20.3. Source code for the DIALOG2.H header file.

```
#define CM_DIALOG (WM_USER + 100)

#define IDE_FIND        101
#define IDE_REPLACE     102
#define IDR_GLOBAL      103
#define IDR_SELTEXT     104
#define IDC_CASE        105
#define IDC_WHOLEWORD   106
```

Type

Listing 20.4. Script for the DIALOG2.RC resource file.

```
#include <windows.h>
#include <owl\window.rh>
#include "dialog2.h"

Search DIALOG DISCARDABLE LOADONCALL PURE MOVEABLE 10, 10, 200, 150
STYLE DS_MODALFRAME | WS_POPUP | WS_VISIBLE | WS_CAPTION |
  WS_SYSMENU
CAPTION "Controls Demo"
BEGIN
  LTEXT "Find", -1, 20, 10, 100, 15, NOT WS_GROUP
   EDITTEXT IDE_FIND, 20, 25, 100, 15
   LTEXT "Replace", -1, 20, 45, 100, 15, NOT WS_GROUP
   EDITTEXT IDE_REPLACE, 20, 60, 100, 15
   GROUPBOX " Scope ", -1, 20, 80, 90, 50, BS_GROUPBOX
   RADIOBUTTON "Global", IDR_GLOBAL, 30, 90, 50, 15,
      BS_AUTORADIOBUTTON
   RADIOBUTTON "Selected Text", IDR_SELTEXT, 30, 105, 60, 15,
       BS_AUTORADIOBUTTON
   CHECKBOX "Case Sensitive", IDC_CASE, 20, 130, 80, 15,
      BS_AUTOCHECKBOX |
       WS_TABSTOP
   CHECKBOX "Whole Word", IDC_WHOLEWORD, 100, 130, 80, 15,
      BS_AUTOCHECKBOX
       | WS_TABSTOP
   DEFPUSHBUTTON "&OK", IDOK, 120, 90, 30, 20
   PUSHBUTTON "&Cancel", IDCANCEL, 160, 90, 30, 20
END

MainMenu MENU LOADONCALL MOVEABLE PURE DISCARDABLE
BEGIN
```

```
   MENUITEM "E&xit", CM_EXIT
   MENUITEM "&Dialog", CM_DIALOG
END
```

Type Listing 20.5. Source code for the DIALOG2.CPP program file.

```
#include <cstring.h>
#include <windows.h>
#include <owl\applicat.h>
#include <owl\checkbox.h>
#include <owl\dialog.h>
#include <owl\edit.h>
#include <owl\framewin.h>
#include <owl\radiobut.h>
#include <owl\window.h>
#include <owl\window.rh>

#include "dialog2.h"

const MaxEditLen = 30;

struct TTransferBuffer
{
   char find[MaxEditLen];
   char replace[MaxEditLen];
   UINT global, seltext, csensitive, wholeword;
};

class TSearchDialog : public TDialog
{
public:
   TSearchDialog( TWindow* parent,
                  TTransferBuffer* xfer,
                  TModule* module = 0);

};

TSearchDialog::TSearchDialog( TWindow* parent,
                              TTransferBuffer* xfer,
                              TModule* module)
   : TDialog(parent, "Search", module)
{
   new TEdit(this, IDE_FIND, MaxEditLen);
   new TEdit(this, IDE_REPLACE, MaxEditLen);
   new TRadioButton(this, IDR_GLOBAL);
   new TRadioButton(this, IDR_SELTEXT);
   new TCheckBox(this, IDC_CASE);
```

20

continues

Listing 20.5. continued

```
   new TCheckBox(this, IDC_WHOLEWORD);
   SetTransferBuffer(xfer);
}

class TMyWindow : public TWindow
{
public:
   TMyWindow(TWindow* parent = 0);

protected:
   void CmExit();
   void CmDialog();

private:
   TTransferBuffer xfer;

   DECLARE_RESPONSE_TABLE(TMyWindow);
};
DEFINE_RESPONSE_TABLE1(TMyWindow, TWindow)
   EV_COMMAND(CM_EXIT, CmExit),
   EV_COMMAND(CM_DIALOG, CmDialog),
END_RESPONSE_TABLE;

TMyWindow::TMyWindow(TWindow* parent)
   : TWindow(parent)
{
   memset(&xfer, 0, sizeof(xfer));
   lstrcpy(xfer.find, "DOS");
   lstrcpy(xfer.replace, "Replace");
   xfer.global = BF_CHECKED;
   xfer.csensitive = BF_CHECKED;
   xfer.wholeword = BF_CHECKED;
}

void TMyWindow::CmExit()
{
   SendMessage(WM_CLOSE);
}

void TMyWindow::CmDialog()
{
   if (TSearchDialog(this, &xfer).Execute() == IDOK)
     {
      string msg("Find String: ");
      msg += xfer.find;
      msg += "\n\nReplace String: ";
      msg += xfer.replace;
      MessageBox(msg.c_str(), "Dialog Box Data");
      }
```

```
}

class TDialogApp : public TApplication
{
public:
   TDialogApp() : TApplication()
      { nCmdShow = SW_SHOWMAXIMIZED; }

   void InitMainWindow()
      {
      SetMainWindow(new TFrameWindow(  0,
                                "Modal Dialog Box Data Transfer Tester",
                                new TMyWindow ));
      GetMainWindow()->AssignMenu("MainMenu");
      }
};

int OwlMain(int, char *[])
{
   return TDialogApp().Run();
}
```

Figure 20.3 shows a sample session with the DIALOG2.EXE application.

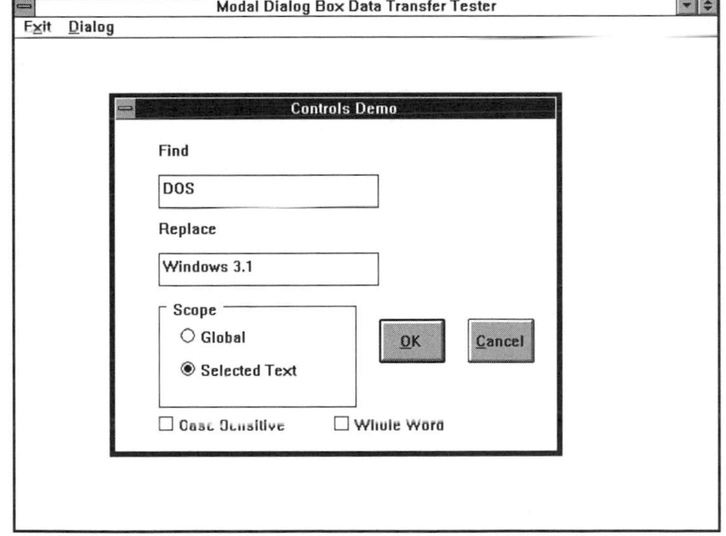

Figure 20.3. *A sample session with the DIALOG2.EXE application.*

Listing 20.4 contains the script for the DIALOG2.RC resource file. This file defines the resources for the menu and the dialog box, including its controls. In the dialog box resource definition, the OK and Cancel pushbuttons have the predefined `IDOK` and `IDCANCEL` IDs, respectively.

Listing 20.5 shows the source code for the DIALOG2.CPP program file. The program declares the data transfer type `TTransferBuffer` starting on line 16 and includes members for the edit boxes, radio buttons, and check boxes.

The application declares the `TSearchDialog` class starting on line 23 as a descendant of the `TDialog` class. You'll notice that it doesn't have any member data, and the only function declared is its constructor. This constructor starts on line 32 and, in turn, does nothing more than create some OWL interface objects to be associated with the various controls created from the dialog resource. Then the constructor makes a call to the `SetTransferBuffer` function on line 43, passing the `xfer` parameter along. OWL will take over from here and automatically perform all the transfers between `xfer` and the actual controls.

The `TMyWindow` class starting on line 43 declares its constructor, two functions to respond to the menu, and a data member of type `TTransferBuffer`. This data member is initialized in the constructor, first with a call to the `memset` function on line 68. This call fills the `xfer` data member with zeros. We recommend that you systematically call the `memset` function to perform a basic initialization of buffers and structures before assigning specific values to them. Then the `xfer`'s data members are set to some initial values. Another way to ensure an empty structure is to provide it with a default constructor that clears all the data members.

The `CmDialog` function starting on line 81, which responds to the Dialog menu item, creates a modal dialog of type `TSearchDialog` on line 83, passing the `xfer` data member as a parameter. If the user presses the OK button to exit this dialog, it will return `IDOK`, and the `CmDialog` function will then build and display a message string that reflects the current Find and Replace text on lines 85 through 89.

Transferring Data for Modeless Dialog Boxes

The method of transferring data from modeless dialog boxes is almost the same as that used for modal dialog boxes. The main difference is that the mechanism that automatically transfers the data between the controls, and the transfer buffer is only called when the dialog window is modal. The programmer needs to make the call

explicitly in the case of a modeless dialog box. This can be done by overriding the `CloseWindow` member function in the dialog's descendant class:

```
void TMyDialog::CloseWindow(int retValue)
{
   TransferData(tdGetData);
   TDialog::CloseWindow(retValue);
}
```

At this point, all the control data will be transferred to the buffer that was sent to the `SetTransferBuffer` in the dialog's constructor.

Another possible action might be to have a Send button in the dialog with a response function that looks similar to this:

```
void TMyDialog::CmSend()
{
   TransferData(tdGetData);
   Parent->HandleMessage(WM_COMMAND, IDB_SEND);
}
```

Then, in the dialog parent's window class, add a member function to handle the Send button in the same way you did this for the dialog class. This function will be called automatically when the dialog simulates the press of the Send button via the call to its parent's `HandleMessage` function.

Summary

Today's lesson presented you with powerful dialog boxes that serve as input tools. You learned about the following topics:

- You can construct instances of class `TDialog` to create modeless or modal dialog boxes.
- You can construct instances of the various control classes that give access to the controls created automatically from the dialog resource.
- Modal dialog boxes are executed with the `Execute` member function.
- The basics of transferring control data include declaring the data transfer buffer type, declaring the buffer, creating the controls in a sequence that matches their buffers, and establishing the buffer link with the `SetTransferBuffer` member function.
- The first step in supporting data transfer is to define a transfer buffer type. You can transfer data for modal dialog boxes and modeless dialog boxes.

Q&A

Q Does OWL support specialized dialog boxes?

A Yes. OWL has a set of classes that implement dialog boxes for selecting files, selecting colors, selecting fonts, printing, and searching/replacing text. The classes that model these dialog boxes are all descendants of the class `TDialog` and bring up the common dialogs.

Q Is the data transfer buffer necessary for modeless dialog boxes?

A Not always. You can have an application that pops up multiple modeless dialog boxes and have them communicate with each other directly, without the need of a data transfer buffer.

Workshop

The Workshop provides quiz questions to help you solidify your understanding of the material covered and exercises to provide you with experience in using what you've learned. Try to understand the quiz and exercise answers before continuing on to the next day's lesson. Answers are provided in Appendix A, "Answers."

Quiz

1. True or false? You must compile all the .RC files into .RES before or during the creation of the application.
2. True or false? The OK and Cancel buttons in a dialog box are optional.
3. True or false? You can create a dialog box with buttons labeled Yes and No.
4. True or false? Nested dialog boxes are not allowed by Windows.
5. True or false? Dialog boxes must always have a nondialog window parent.

Exercises

1. Create a version of the MrCalc application (from previous chapters) that uses a dialog box as a stand-alone window.
2. Use the Resource Workshop to create the dialog-box resource for the DIALOG2 program.

MDI Windows

WEEK 3

The Multiple Document Interface (MDI) is a standard Windows interface used by many popular Windows applications and utilities, such as the Windows Program Manager, the Windows File Manager, and even the Borland C++ IDE. The MDI interface is also part of the Common User Access (CUA) standard set by IBM. Each MDI-compliant application enables you to open child windows for file-specific tasks such as editing text, managing a database, or working with a spreadsheet. In this chapter, you will learn the following topics on managing MDI windows and objects:

- The basic features and components of an MDI-compliant application
- Basics of building an MDI-compliant application
- The class `TMDIFrame`
- The class `TMDIClient`
- Building MDI client windows
- The class `TMDIChild`
- Building MDI child windows
- Managing messages in an MDI-compliant application

The MDI Application Features and Components

An MDI-compliant application is made up of the following objects:

- The visible **MDI frame window** that contains all other MDI objects. The MDI frame window is an instance of the class `TMDIFrame` or its descendants. Each MDI application has one MDI frame window.
- The invisible **MDI client window** that performs underlying management of the MDI child windows that are dynamically created and removed. The MDI client window is an instance of the class `TMDIClient`. Each MDI application has one MDI client window.
- The dynamic and visible **MDI child window**. An MDI application dynamically creates and removes multiple instances of MDI child windows. An MDI child window is an instance of `TMDIChild` or its descendant. These windows are located, moved, resized, maximized, and minimized inside the

area defined by the MDI frame window. At any given time (and while there is at least one MDI child window), there is only one active MDI child window.

When you maximize an MDI child window, it occupies the area defined by the client area of the MDI frame window. When you minimize an MDI child window, the icon of that window appears at the bottom area of the MDI frame window.

Note: The MDI frame window has a menu that manipulates the MDI child windows and their contents. The MDI child windows cannot have a menu, but they may contain controls. In any other respect, you can think of an MDI child window as an instance of `TFrameWindow` or its descendants.

Basics of Building an MDI Application

Before we discuss in more detail the creation of the various components that make up an MDI application, let's focus on the basic strategy involved. In the last section, you learned that the basic ingredients for an MDI application are the `TMDIFrame`, `TMDIClient`, and `TMDIChild` (or a `TMDIChild` descendant) classes. The `TMDIFrame` class supports the following tasks:

- The creation and handling of the MDI client window
- The creation and handling of the MDI child windows
- Managing menus

The `TMDIClient` class focuses on the underlying management of MDI child windows. The `TMDIChild` class offers the functionality for the MDI child windows.

At this stage you might ask, Do I typically derive descendants for all three classes to create MDI applications? The answer is no. You normally need to derive descendants only for the `TMDIFrame` and `TMDIChild` classes. The functionality of the `TMDIClient` class is adequate for most MDI-compliant applications.

The *TMDIFrame* Class

ObjectWindows offers the TMDIFrame class, a descendant of TFrameWindow, to implement the MDI frame window of an MDI application. The declaration of the TMDIFrame class is as follows:

```
class _OWLCLASS TMDIFrame : virtual public TFrameWindow {
  public:
    TMDIFrame(const char far* title,
              TResId          menuResId,
              TMDIClient&     clientWnd = *new TMDIClient,
              TModule*        module = 0);


    TMDIFrame(HWND hWindow, HWND clientHWnd, TModule* module = 0);

    //
    // override virtual functions defined by TFrameWindow
    //
    BOOL         SetMenu(HMENU);
    TMDIClient*  GetClientWindow();

    //
    // find & return the child menu of an MDI frame's (or anyone's) menu
    // bar.
    //
    static HMENU FindChildMenu(HMENU);

  protected:
    //
    // call ::DefFrameProc() instead of ::DefWindowProc()
    //
    LRESULT DefWindowProc(UINT message, WPARAM wParam, LPARAM lParam);

  private:
    //
    // hidden to prevent accidental copying or assignment
    //
    TMDIFrame(const TMDIFrame&);
    TMDIFrame& operator=(const TMDIFrame&);

  DECLARE_RESPONSE_TABLE(TMDIFrame);
  DECLARE_STREAMABLE(_OWLCLASS, TMDIFrame, 1);
};
```

The TMDIFrame class has public, protected, and private members. The MDI frame window class has three constructors, one of which is private. The first constructor creates a class instance by specifying the title, associated menu resource ID, and

reference to the associated MDI client window. The second constructor creates a class instance from an existing non-OWL window. The third constructor, which is declared private, creates an instance of class `TMDIFrame` using another existing instance.

The class `TMDIFrame` declares the public member functions `SetMenu`, `GetClientWindow`, and `FindChildMenu`. The function `SetMenu` looks for the MDI submenu in the new menu bar and updates member `ChildMenuPos` if the menu is found. The function searches for the MDI submenu in the menu bar and updates the position in the MDI window's top-level menu of the child window submenu. The function `GetClientWindow` returns a pointer to the associated MDI client window. The function `FindChildMenu` searches for the child menu of an MDI frame's menu bar.

The class `TMDIFrame` declares the single protected member function `DefWindowProc`. This function overrides the inherited function `TWindow::DefWindowProc` and invokes the Windows API function `DefFrameProc`. The API function provides the default processing for any incoming Windows message that is not handled by the MDI frame window.

Building MDI Frame Windows

The usual approach for creating the objects that make up an ObjectWindows application starts with creating the application instance and then its main window instance. In the case of an MDI-compliant application, the application's main window is typically a descendant of class `TMDIFrame`. The `InitMainWindow` member function of the application class creates this window. Looking at the first two `TMDIFrame` constructors, you can tell that creating the main MDI window involves a title and menu resource—there is no pointer to a parent window because MDI frame windows have no parent windows. The MDI frame window, unlike most descendants of class `TWindow`, must have a menu associated with it. This menu typically includes the items shown in Table 21.1, needed to manipulate the MDI children. In addition, the menu of the MDI frame window is dynamically and automatically updated to include the current MDI children.

The constructor of the descendant of `TMDIFrame` (call it the application frame class) can, in many cases, simply invoke the parent class constructor. This invocation occurs if the steps taken by the parent class are adequate for creating the MDI frame window instance. In the case where you want to modify the behavior of the application frame class, you need to include the required statements. Such statements might assign initial values to data members declared in the application frame class.

The `SetupWindow` member function invokes the `InitClientWindow` to create the `TMDIClient` instance. You can modify the `SetupWindow` function to, for example, automatically create the first child MDI window.

The *TMDIClient* Class

ObjectWindows offers the `TMDIClient` class, a descendant of `TWindow`, to implement the invisible MDI client window. The declaration of the `TMDIClient` class is as follows:

```
class _OWLCLASS TMDIClient : public virtual TWindow {
  public:
    LPCLIENTCREATESTRUCT  ClientAttr;

    TMDIClient(TModule* module = 0);
   ~TMDIClient();

    virtual BOOL CloseChildren();

    TMDIChild* GetActiveMDIChild();

    //
    // member functions to arrange the MDI children
    //
    virtual void ArrangeIcons();
    virtual void CascadeChildren();
    virtual void TileChildren(int tile = MDITILE_VERTICAL);

    //
    // override member functions defined by TWindow
    //
    BOOL PreProcessMsg(MSG& msg);
    BOOL Create();

    virtual TWindow* CreateChild();

    //
    // constructs a new MDI child window object. By default, constructs
    // an instance of TWindow as an MDI child window object
    //
    // will almost always be overridden by derived classes to construct
    // an instance of a user-defined TWindow derived class as an MDI
    // child window object
    //
    virtual TMDIChild* InitChild();
```

```
  protected:
    char far* GetClassName();

    //
    // menu command handlers & enabler
    //
    void CmCreateChild()
           { CreateChild(); }  // CM_CREATECHILD
    void CmTileChildren()
           { TileChildren(); }  // CM_TILECHILDREN
    void CmTileChildrenHoriz()
           { TileChildren(MDITILE_HORIZONTAL); }  // CM_TILECHILDREN
    void CmCascadeChildren()
           { CascadeChildren(); }  // CM_CASCADECHILDREN
    void CmArrangeIcons()
           { ArrangeIcons(); }  // CM_ARRANGEICONS
    void CmCloseChildren()
           { CloseChildren(); }  // CM_CLOSECHILDREN
    void CmChildActionEnable(TCommandEnabler& commandEnabler);

    LRESULT EvMDICreate(MDICREATESTRUCT far& createStruct);

  private:
    friend class TMDIFrame;
    TMDIClient(HWND hWnd, TModule*   module = 0);

    //
    // hidden to prevent accidental copying or assignment
    //
    TMDIClient(const TMDIClient&);
    TMDIClient& operator =(const TMDIClient&);

  DECLARE_RESPONSE_TABLE(TMDIClient);
  DECLARE_STREAMABLE(_OWLCLASS, TMDIClient, 1);
};
```

The class `TMDIClient` declares a public constructor and destructor. The MDI client class declares a number of member functions that handle Windows and menu command messages for activating an MDI child window; arranging the MDI child icons; cascading and tiling MDI children; closing MDI children; and creating an MDI child window. These message response functions use sibling member functions. Table 21.1 shows the predefined menu ID constants and the `TMDIClient` member functions that respond to them.

21

Table 21.1. The predefined menu command messages for manipulating MDI children.

Action	Menu ID Constant	Responding TMDIClient Member Function
Tile	CM_TILECHILDREN	CmTileChildren
Tile Horizon	CM_TILECHILDRENHORIZ	CmTileChildrenHoriz
Cascade	CM_CASCASDECHILDREN	CmCascadeChildren
Arrange Icons	CM_ARRANGEICONS	CmArrangeIcons
Close All	CM_CLOSECHILDREN	CmCloseChildren

There are a number of member functions in the class `TMDIClient` that you may want to modify when you create class descendants. The list of such member functions includes `CreateChild`, `SetupWindow`, `CanClose`, and `CloseChildren`. These functions enable you to modify how to create, set up, and close MDI children.

The MDI Child Window Class

The class `TMDIChild` models the basic operations of all MDI child windows. The declaration for the class `TMDIChild` is as follows:

```
class _OWLCLASS TMDIChild : virtual public TFrameWindow {
  public:
    TMDIChild(TMDIClient&     parent,
              const char far* title = 0,
              TWindow*        clientWnd = 0,
              BOOL            shrinkToClient = FALSE,
              TModule*        module = 0);

    TMDIChild(HWND hWnd, TModule* module = 0);

   ~TMDIChild() {}

    //
    // override method defined by TWindow
    //
    BOOL PreProcessMsg(MSG& msg);

  protected:
    void Destroy(int retVal = 0);
    void PerformCreate(int menuOrId);
```

```
    LRESULT DefWindowProc(UINT msg, WPARAM wParam, LPARAM lParam);
    void EvMDIActivate(HWND hWndActivated,
                       HWND hWndDeactivated);

  private:
    //
    // hidden to prevent accidental copying or assignment
    //
    TMDIChild(const TMDIChild&);
    TMDIChild& operator =(const TMDIChild&);

  DECLARE_RESPONSE_TABLE(TMDIChild);
  DECLARE_STREAMABLE(_OWLCLASS, TMDIChild, 1);
};
```

The class `TMDIChild` declares three constructors (one of which is private) and a destructor. The first constructor enables you to create a class instance by specifying the parent MDI client window, MDI child window title, the client window, and whether or not the MDI child window shrinks to fit the client area. The second constructor creates a class instance using an existing non-OWL MDI child window. The third constructor, which is declared private, creates a `TMDIChild` class instance using an existing instance.

The MDI child window class declares the single public member function `PreProcessMsg`. This function preprocesses the Windows messages sent to the MDI child windows. The class `TMDIChild` offers a set of protected functions that create, destroy, and activate MDI child windows. In addition, the class provides its own version of function `DefWindowProc` to handle default Windows message processing.

Building MDI Child Windows

Building MDI child windows is very similar to building application windows in the programs presented earlier. The differences are as follows:

- An MDI child window cannot have its own menu. The menu of the MDI frame window is the one that manipulates the currently active MDI child window or all of the MDI children.

21

Note: The keyboard handler must not be enabled. It actually causes the reverse effect in the MDI children and antagonizes the proper operations of the MDI application.

- An MDI child window can have controls—this is unusual but certainly allowed.

Managing MDI Messages

The message loop directs the command messages first to the active MDI child window to allow it to respond. If that window does not respond, the message is then sent to the parent MDI frame window. Of course, the active MDI child window responds to the notification messages sent by its controls, just as any window or dialog box would.

Simple Text Viewer

Let's look at a simple MDI-compliant application. Because MDI applications are frequently used as text viewer and text editors, we present the next application that emulates a simple text viewer. We say "emulates" because the application actually displays random text, instead of text that you can retrieve from a file. This approach keeps the program simple and helps you to focus on implementing the various MDI objects. Figure 21.1 shows a sample session with the MDI1.EXE program. The MDI application has a simple menu containing the Exit and MDI Children items.

Compile and run the application. Experiment with creating MDI children. Notice that the text in odd-numbered MDI child windows is static, whereas the text in even-numbered windows can be edited. We implemented this feature to illustrate how to create a simple form of text viewer and text editor (with no Save option, to keep the example short). Try to tile, cascade, maximize, and minimize these windows. Also test closing individual MDI child windows as well as closing all of the MDI children.

Let's examine the code that implements this simple MDI application. Listing 21.1 shows the contents of the MDI1.DEF definition file. Listing 21.2 shows the source code for the MDI1.H header file. This file declares the command message constants and a control ID constant. Listing 21.3 contains the script for the MDI1.RC resource file. The file defines the menu resource required by the MDI frame window. The menu has two menu items, Exit and MDI Children. The latter menu item is a pop-up menu with several options. The commands, except the option Count Children, use predefined command message constants. Listing 21.4 shows the source code for the MDI1.CPP program file.

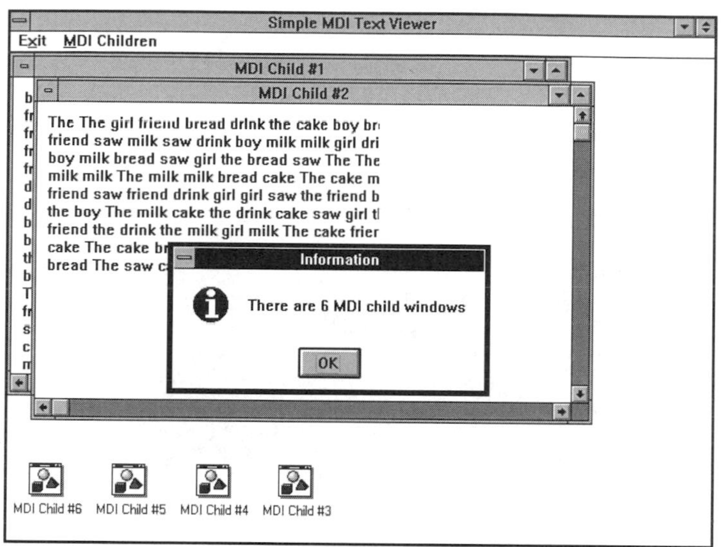

Figure 21.1. *A sample session with the MDI1.EXE program.*

Listing 21.1. The contents of the MDI1.DEF definition file.

```
NAME          MDI1
DESCRIPTION   'An OWL Windows Application'
EXETYPE       WINDOWS
CODE          PRELOAD MOVEABLE DISCARDABLE
DATA          PRELOAD MOVEABLE MULTIPLE
HEAPSIZE      1024
STACKSIZE     8192
```

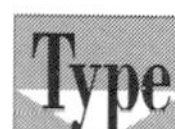

Listing 21.2. The source code for the MDI1.H header file.

```
#define CM_COUNTCHILDREN 101
#define ID_TEXT_EDIT     102
#define IDM_COMMANDS     400
```

Listing 21.3. The script for the MDI1.RC resource file.

```
#include <windows.h>
#include <owl\window.rh>
#include <owl\mdi.rh>
#include "mdi1.h"
IDM_COMMANDS MENU LOADONCALL MOVEABLE PURE DISCARDABLE
BEGIN
  MENUITEM "E&xit", CM_EXIT
  POPUP "&MDI Children"
  BEGIN
    MENUITEM  "C&reate", CM_CREATECHILD
    MENUITEM  "&Cascade", CM_CASCADECHILDREN
    MENUITEM  "&Tile", CM_TILECHILDREN
    MENUITEM  "Arrange &Icons", CM_ARRANGEICONS
    MENUITEM  "C&lose All", CM_CLOSECHILDREN
    MENUITEM  "C&ount Children", CM_COUNTCHILDREN
  END
END
```

Listing 21.4. The source code for the MDI1.CPP program file.

```
/*
  Program to illustrate simple MDI windows
*/
#include <owl\mdi.rh>
#include <owl\applicat.h>
#include <owl\framewin.h>
#include <owl\mdi.h>
#include <owl\static.h>
#include <owl\edit.h>
#include <owl\scroller.h>
#include "mdi1.h"
#include <stdio.h>
#include <string.h>

const MaxWords = 100;
const WordsPerLine = 12;
const NumWords = 10;
char* Words[NumWords] = { "The ", "friend ", "saw ", "the ",
                "girl ", "drink ", "milk ", "boy ",
                "cake ", "bread " };

BOOL ExpressClose = FALSE;
int NumMDIChild = 0;
int HighMDIindex = 0;

```

```
class TWinApp : public TApplication
{
public:
  TWinApp() : TApplication() {}

protected:
  virtual void InitMainWindow();
};

class TAppMDIChild : public TMDIChild
{
public:
  // pointer to the edit box control
  TEdit* TextBox;
  TStatic* TextTxt;

  TAppMDIChild(TMDIClient& parent, int ChildNum);

protected:

  // handle closing the MDI child window
  virtual BOOL CanClose();
};

class TAppMDIClient : public TMDIClient
{
public:

  TAppMDIClient() : TMDIClient() {}

 protected:

  // create a new child
  virtual TMDIChild* InitChild();

  // close all MDI children
  virtual BOOL CloseChildren();

  // handle the command for counting the MDI children
  void CMCountChildren();

  // handle closing the MDI frame window
  virtual BOOL CanClose();

  // declare response table
  DECLARE_RESPONSE_TABLE(TAppMDIClient);
};

DEFINE_RESPONSE_TABLE1(TAppMDIClient, TMDIClient)
  EV_COMMAND(CM_COUNTCHILDREN, CMCountChildren),
```


continues

Listing 21.4. continued

```
END_RESPONSE_TABLE;

TAppMDIChild::TAppMDIChild(TMDIClient& parent, int ChildNum)
  : TMDIChild(parent),
     TFrameWindow(&parent),
     TWindow(&parent)
{
  char s[1024];

  // set the scrollers in the window
  Attr.Style |= WS_VSCROLL | WS_HSCROLL;
  // create the TScroller instance
  Scroller = new TScroller(this, 200, 15, 10, 50);

  // set MDI child window title
  sprintf(s, "%s%i", "MDI Child #", ChildNum);
  Title = _fstrdup(s);

  // randomize the seed for the random-number generator
  randomize();

  // assign a null string to the variable s
  strcpy(s, "");
  // build the list of random words
  for (int i = 0; i < MaxWords; i++) {
      if (i > 0 && i % WordsPerLine == 0)
         strcat(s, "\r\n");
      strcat(s, Words[random(NumWords)]);
  }
  // create a static text object in the child window if the
  // ChildNum variable stores an odd number. Otherwise,
  // create an edit box control
  if (ChildNum % 2 == 0) {
     // create the edit box
     TextBox = new TEdit(this, ID_TEXT_EDIT, s,
              10, 10, 300, 400, 0, TRUE);
     // remove borders and scroll bars
     TextBox->Attr.Style &= ~WS_BORDER;
     TextBox->Attr.Style &= ~WS_VSCROLL;
     TextBox->Attr.Style &= ~WS_HSCROLL;
  }
  else
     // create static text
     TextTxt = new TStatic(this, -1, s, 10, 10, 300, 400,
                           strlen(s));
}

BOOL TAppMDIChild::CanClose()
{
  // return TRUE if the ExpressClose member of the
```

```
  // parent MDI frame window is TRUE
  if (ExpressClose == TRUE) {
    NumMDIChild--;
    return TRUE;
  }
  else
    // prompt the user and return the prompt result
     if (MessageBox("Close this MDI window?",
         "Query", MB_YESNO | MB_ICONQUESTION) == IDYES) {
      NumMDIChild--;
      return TRUE;
    }
    else
      return FALSE;
}

TMDIChild* TAppMDIClient::InitChild()
{
  ++NumMDIChild;
  return new TAppMDIChild(*this, ++HighMDIindex);
}

BOOL TAppMDIClient::CloseChildren()
{
  BOOL result;
  // set the ExpressClose flag
  ExpressClose = TRUE;
  // invoke the parent class CloseChildren() member function
  result = TMDIClient::CloseChildren();
  // clear the ExpressClose flag
  ExpressClose = FALSE;
  NumMDIChild = 0;
  HighMDIindex = 0;
  return result;
}

//  display a message box that shows the number of children
void TAppMDIClient::CMCountChildren()
{
  char msgStr[81];

  sprintf(msgStr, "There are %i MDI child windows", NumMDIChild);
  MessageBox(msgStr, "Information", MB_OK | MB_ICONINFORMATION);
}

BOOL TAppMDIClient::CanClose()
{
  return MessageBox("Close this application?", "Query",
                    MB_YESNO | MB_ICONQUESTION) == IDYES;
}

```

continues

Listing 21.4. continued

```
177: void TWinApp::InitMainWindow()
178: {
179:   MainWindow = new TMDIFrame("Simple MDI Text Viewer",
180:                         TResId(IDM_COMMANDS),
181:                         *new TAppMDIClient);
182: }
183:
184: int OwlMain(int /* argc */, char** /*argv[] */)
185: {
186:   TWinApp app;
187:   return app.Run();
188: }
189:
```

The program in Listing 21.4 declares a set of global constants used in generating the random text in each MDI child window. The global array of pointer `Words` contains the program's somewhat restricted vocabulary. The listing also declares the global variables `ExpressClose`, `NumMDIChild`, and `HighMDIindex`. These variables provide a simple solution for sharing information between the descendants of branched-out OWL classes. The variable `ExpressClose` assists in closing all of the child MDI windows in one swoop. The variable `NumMDIChild` maintains the actual number of MDI child windows. The variable `HighMDIindex` stores the index of the last MDI child window created.

The program listing declares three classes: the application class, `TWinApp`, in line 26; the MDI client class, `TAppMDIClient`, in line 50; and the MDI child window class, `TAppMDIChild`, in line 35. We will discuss these classes in order.

The code for the application class looks very much like the ones in previous programs, with one exception. The `InitMainWindow` member function, defined in lines 177 to 182, creates an instance of the stock MDI frame class, `TMDIFrame`. The `TMDIFrame` constructor call has the following arguments: title of the application; the name of the menu resource, `COMMANDS`; and the pointer to the dynamically allocated instances of `TAppMDIClient`.

The `TAppMDIClient` class declares a constructor and a group of protected member functions. The member functions are as follows:

1. The member function `InitChild` (defined in lines 142 to 146) initializes an MDI child window. The function increments the global variable `NumMDIChild` and then returns a dynamically allocated instance of `TAppMDIChild`. The arguments of creating this instance are `*this` (a reference

to the object itself) and `++HighMDIindex`. The second argument pre-increments the global variable `HighMDIindex`, which keeps track of the highest index for an MDI child window.

2. The member function `CloseChildren` (defined in lines 148 to 160) alters the behavior of the inherited `CloseChildren` function. The new version performs the following tasks:

    - Assigns `TRUE` to the global variable `ExpressClose` (see line 152).
    - Invokes the parent class version of `CloseChildren` and stores the result of that function call in the local variable result.
    - Assigns `FALSE` to the variable `ExpressClose` in line 156.
    - Assigns 0 to the global variable `NumMDIChild` in line 157.
    - Assigns 0 to the global variable `HighMDIindex` in line 157. This task resets the value in variable `HighMDIindex` when you close all of the MDI child windows.
    - Returns the value stored in the variable result.

3. The member function `CMCountChildren` (defined in lines 163 to 168) responds to the Windows command message `CM_COUNTCHILDREN` generated by the menu option Count Children. The function displays the number of MDI child windows in a message dialog box. The function first builds the string `msgStr` to contain the formatted image of the global variable `NumMDIChild`. Then, the function invokes the member function `MessageBox` to display the sought information.

4. The virtual member function `CanClose` (defined in lines 171 to 175) prompts you to confirm closing the MDI-compliant application.

The MDI child window class, `TAppMDIChild`, declares the `TextBox` and `TextTxt` data members, a constructor, and the `CanClose` member function. The member `TextBox` is the pointer to the `TEdit` instance created to store the random text in one kind of the MDI child windows. The member `TextTxt` is the pointer to the `TStatic` instance created to store random text in the other kind of MDI child windows.

The `TAppMDIChild` constructor (defined in lines 78 to 121) performs a variety of tasks, as follows:

- Sets the window style to include the vertical and horizontal scroll bars (see line 86).

- Creates an instance of `TScroller` to animate the window's scroll bars (see line 88).
- Sets the window title to include the MDI child window number, using the statements in lines 91 and 92.
- Randomizes the seed for the random-number generator function, `random`.
- Creates the random text and stores it in the local string variable `s`. This task uses the `for` loop in lines 100 to 104.
- If the MDI child window number is even, creates a multiline instance of `TEdit` in lines 110 and 111. This instance contains a copy of the text stored in variable `s`. In addition, the constructor disables the border, vertical scroll bar, and horizontal scroll bar styles (see the statements in lines 113 to 115). These scroll bars are not needed because the MDI child window itself has scroll bars. In the case of an odd-numbered MDI child window number, the constructor creates static text using the characters in variable `s` (see the statement in lines 119 and 120).

The `CanClose` member function regulates closing an MDI child window. When you close such a window using the Close option in its own system menu, the function requires your confirmation. If the request to close comes from the Close All menu command in the parent window, the MDI child window closes without confirmation. The function decrements the global variable `NumMDIChild` in two cases: first, when the global variable `ExpressClose` is `TRUE`; and second, when the function `MessageBox`, which prompts you to confirm closing the window, returns `IDYES`.

Revised Text Viewer

Let's expand on the MDI1.EXE program to illustrate other aspects of managing MDI windows. The next application also creates MDI children that contain edit box controls with random text. However, each MDI child window has the following additional controls:

- An ->UpperCase pushbutton control that converts the text in the MDI child window into uppercase.
- A ->LowerCase pushbutton control that converts the text in the MDI child window into lowercase.
- A Can Close check box. Using this box replaces using the confirmation dialog box that appears when you want to close the MDI child window. The

check box enables you to predetermine whether or not the MDI child window can be closed.

The application menu adds a new pop-up menu item, Current MDI Child. This menu item has options that work on the current MDI child window. The commands enable you to clear, convert to uppercase, convert to lowercase, or rewrite the characters in the MDI child window. The new pop-up menu shows how you can manipulate MDI children with custom menus.

Compile and run the application. Create a few MDI children and use their pushbutton controls to toggle the case of characters in these windows. Also use the Current MDI Child commands to further manipulate the text in the currently active MDI child window. Try to close the MDI children with the Can Close check box marked and unmarked. Only the MDI children with the Can Close control checked close individually. Use the Close All option in the MDI Children pop-up menu and watch all of the MDI children close, regardless of the check state of the Can Close control. Figure 21.2 shows a sample session with the MDI2.EXE program.

Listing 21.5 shows the contents of the MDI2.DEF definition file. Listing 21.6 shows the source code for the MDI2.H header file. The file contains the constants for the menu commands and the control IDs. Listing 21.7 contains the script for the MDI2.RC resource file and shows the resource for the expanded menu. Listing 21.8 contains the source code for the MDI2.CPP program file.

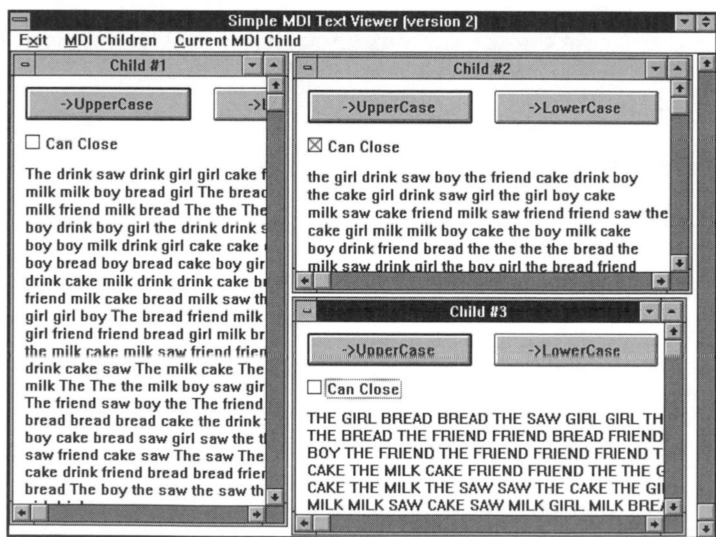

Figure 21.2. *A sample session with the MDI2.EXE program.*

Listing 21.5. The contents of the MDI2.DEF definition file.

```
NAME          MDI2
DESCRIPTION   'An OWL Windows Application'
EXETYPE       WINDOWS
CODE          PRELOAD MOVEABLE DISCARDABLE
DATA          PRELOAD MOVEABLE MULTIPLE
HEAPSIZE      1024
STACKSIZE     8192
```

Listing 21.6. The source code for the MDI2.H header file.

```
#define CM_COUNTCHILDREN 101
#define CM_CLEAR         102
#define CM_UPPERCASE     103
#define CM_LOWERCASE     104
#define CM_RESET         105
#define ID_TEXT_EDIT     106
#define ID_CANCLOSE_CHK  107
#define ID_UPPERCASE_BTN 108
#define ID_LOWERCASE_BTN 109
#define IDM_COMMANDS     400
```

Listing 21.7. The script for the MDI2.RC resource file.

```
#include <windows.h>
#include <owl\window.rh>
#include <owl\mdi.rh>
#include "mdi2.h"
IDM_COMMANDS MENU LOADONCALL MOVEABLE PURE DISCARDABLE
BEGIN
  MENUITEM "E&xit", CM_EXIT
  POPUP "&MDI Children"
  BEGIN
    MENUITEM  "C&reate", CM_CREATECHILD
    MENUITEM  "&Cascade", CM_CASCADECHILDREN
    MENUITEM  "&Tile", CM_TILECHILDREN
    MENUITEM  "Arrange &Icons", CM_ARRANGEICONS
    MENUITEM  "C&lose All", CM_CLOSECHILDREN
    MENUITEM  "C&ount Children", CM_COUNTCHILDREN
  END
  POPUP "&Current MDI Child"
  BEGIN
    MENUITEM  "&Clear", CM_CLEAR
    MENUITEM  "&Uppercase", CM_UPPERCASE
```

```
    MENUITEM  "&Lowercase", CM_LOWERCASE
    MENUITEM  "&Reset", CM_RESET
  END
END
```

Listing 21.8. The source code for the MDI2.CPP program file.

```
/*
  Program to demonstrate MDI windows with controls
*/
#include <owl\mdi.rh>
#include <owl\applicat.h>
#include <owl\framewin.h>
#include <owl\button.h>
#include <owl\edit.h>
#include <owl\checkbox.h>
#include <owl\scroller.h>
#include <owl\mdi.h>
#include "mdi2.h"
#include <stdio.h>
#include <string.h>

// declare constants for sizing and spacing the controls
// in the MDI child window
const Wbtn = 50 * 3;
const Hbtn = 30;
const BtnHorzSpacing = 20;
const BtnVertSpacing = 10;
const Wchk = 200 * 3;
const Hchk = 20;
const ChkVertSpacing = 10;
const Wbox = 400 * 3;
const Hbox = 200 * 3;

// declare the constants for the random text that appears
// in the MDI child window
const MaxWords = 200;
const WordsPerLine = 10;
const NumWords = 10;
const BufferSize = 1024;
char AppBuffer[BufferSize];
char* Words[NumWords] = { "The ", "friend ", "saw ", "the ",
                "girl ", "drink ", "milk ", "boy ",
                "cake ", "bread " };


BOOL ExpressClose = FALSE;
int NumMDIChild = 0;
```

continues

Listing 21.8. continued

```
int HighMDIindex = 0;

class TWinApp : public TApplication
{
public:
  TWinApp() : TApplication() {}

protected:
  virtual void InitMainWindow();
};

class TAppMDIChild : public TMDIChild
{
public:


  TAppMDIChild(TMDIClient& parent, int ChildNum);

protected:

  TEdit* TextBox;
  TCheckBox* CanCloseChk;

  // handle the UpperCase button
  void HandleUpperCaseBtn()
    { CMUpperCase(); }

  // handle the LowerCase button
  void HandleLowerCaseBtn()
    { CMLowerCase(); }

  // handle clear the active MDI child
  void CMClear()
    { TextBox->Clear(); }

  // handle converting the text of the active
  // MDI child to uppercase
  void CMUpperCase();

  // handle converting the text of the active
  // MDI child to lowercase
  void CMLowerCase();

  // handle resetting the text of the active MDI child
  void CMReset();

  // reset the text in an MDI child window
  void InitText();

```

```
    // handle closing the MDI child window
    virtual BOOL CanClose();

    // declare response table
    DECLARE_RESPONSE_TABLE(TAppMDIChild);
};

DEFINE_RESPONSE_TABLE1(TAppMDIChild, TMDIChild)
  EV_COMMAND(ID_UPPERCASE_BTN, HandleUpperCaseBtn),
  EV_COMMAND(ID_LOWERCASE_BTN, HandleLowerCaseBtn),
  EV_COMMAND(CM_CLEAR, CMClear),
  EV_COMMAND(CM_UPPERCASE, CMUpperCase),
  EV_COMMAND(CM_LOWERCASE, CMLowerCase),
  EV_COMMAND(CM_RESET, CMReset),
END_RESPONSE_TABLE;

class TAppMDIClient : public TMDIClient
{
public:

 TAppMDIClient() : TMDIClient() {}

 protected:

  // create a new child
  virtual TMDIChild* InitChild();

  // close all MDI children
  virtual BOOL CloseChildren();

  // handle the command for counting the MDI children
  void CMCountChildren();

  // handle closing the MDI frame window
  virtual BOOL CanClose();

  // declare response table
  DECLARE_RESPONSE_TABLE(TAppMDIClient);
};

DEFINE_RESPONSE_TABLE1(TAppMDIClient, TMDIClient)
  EV_COMMAND(CM_COUNTCHILDREN, CMCountChildren),
END_RESPONSE_TABLE;

TAppMDIChild::TAppMDIChild(TMDIClient& parent, int ChildNum)
  : TMDIChild(parent),
    TFrameWindow(&parent),
    TWindow(&parent)
{
  char s[41];
  int x0 = 10;
```

continues

Listing 21.8. continued

```
  int y0 = 10;
  int x = x0;
  int y = y0;

  // set the scrollers in the window
  Attr.Style |= WS_VSCROLL | WS_HSCROLL;
  // create the TScroller instance
  Scroller = new TScroller(this, 200, 15, 10, 50);

  // set MDI child window title
  sprintf(s, "%s%i", "Child #", ChildNum);
  Title = _fstrdup(s);

  // create the push button controls
  new TButton(this, ID_UPPERCASE_BTN, "->UpperCase",
              x, y, Wbtn, Hbtn, TRUE);
  x += Wbtn + BtnHorzSpacing;
  new TButton(this, ID_LOWERCASE_BTN, "->LowerCase",
              x, y, Wbtn, Hbtn, FALSE);

  x = x0;
  y += Hbtn + BtnVertSpacing;
  CanCloseChk = new TCheckBox(this, ID_CANCLOSE_CHK, "Can Close",
                              x, y, Wchk, Hchk, NULL);
  y += Hchk + ChkVertSpacing;
  InitText();
  // create the edit box
  TextBox = new TEdit(this, ID_TEXT_EDIT, AppBuffer,
                      x, y, Wbox, Hbox, 0, TRUE);
  // remove borders and scroll bars
  TextBox->Attr.Style &= ~WS_BORDER;
  TextBox->Attr.Style &= ~WS_VSCROLL;
  TextBox->Attr.Style &= ~WS_HSCROLL;
}

void TAppMDIChild::CMUpperCase()
{
  TextBox->GetText(AppBuffer, BufferSize);
  strupr(AppBuffer);
  TextBox->SetText(AppBuffer);
}

void TAppMDIChild::CMLowerCase()
{
  TextBox->GetText(AppBuffer, BufferSize);
  strlwr(AppBuffer);
  TextBox->SetText(AppBuffer);
}

```

```
void TAppMDIChild::CMReset()
{
  InitText();
  TextBox->SetText(AppBuffer);
}

BOOL TAppMDIChild::CanClose()
{
  // return TRUE if the ExpressClose member of the
  // parent MDI frame window is TRUE
  if (ExpressClose == TRUE) {
    NumMDIChild--;
    return TRUE;
  }
  else
  // do not close the MDi child window if the Can Close is
  // not checked
  if (CanCloseChk->GetCheck() == BF_UNCHECKED)
    return FALSE;
  else {
    NumMDIChild--;
     return TRUE;
  }
}

void TAppMDIChild::InitText()
{
  // randomize the seed for the random-number generator
  randomize();

  // assign a null string to the buffer
  AppBuffer[0] = '\0';
  // build the list of random words
  for (int i = 0;
       i < MaxWords && strlen(AppBuffer) <= (BufferSize - 10);
       i++) {
    if (i > 0 && i % WordsPerLine == 0)
      strcat(AppBuffer, "\r\n");
    strcat(AppBuffer, Words[random(NumWords)]);
  }
}

TMDIChild* TAppMDIClient::InitChild()
{
  ++NumMDIChild;
  return new TAppMDIChild(*this, ++HighMDIindex);
}

BOOL TAppMDIClient::CloseChildren()
{
  BOOL result;
```

continues

Listing 21.8. continued

```
  // set the ExpressClose flag
  ExpressClose = TRUE;
  // invoke the parent class CloseChildren() member function
  result = TMDIClient::CloseChildren();
  // clear the ExpressClose flag
  ExpressClose = FALSE;
  NumMDIChild = 0;
  HighMDIindex = 0;
  return result;
}

//  display a message box that shows the number of children
void TAppMDIClient::CMCountChildren()
{
  char msgStr[81];

  sprintf(msgStr, "There are %i MDI children", NumMDIChild);
  MessageBox(msgStr, "Information", MB_OK | MB_ICONINFORMATION);
}

BOOL TAppMDIClient::CanClose()
{
  return MessageBox("Close this application?",
             "Query", MB_YESNO | MB_ICONQUESTION) == IDYES;
}

void TWinApp::InitMainWindow()
{
  MainWindow = new TMDIFrame("Simple MDI Text Viewer (version 2)",
                    TResId(IDM_COMMANDS),
                    *new TAppMDIClient);
}

int OwlMain(int /* argc */, char** /*argv[] */)
{
  TWinApp app;
  return app.Run();
}
```

Analysis The program in Listing 21.8 declares two sets of constants. The first set is used for sizing and spacing the controls of each MDI child window. The second set of constants is used to manage the random text. The program also declares variable `AppBuffer` as a single 1KB text buffer. We chose to make the buffer global instead of a class data member mainly to reduce the buffer space—the application classes need only one shared buffer at any time. The program listing also declares the

global variables `ExpressClose`, `NumMDIChild`, and `HighMDIindex`—another set of components carried over from the program in file MDI1.CPP.

The new application maintains the same three classes described in the last program. However, the MDI child class has different members in this program. The new members manage the response to the control notification messages as well as the Current MDI Child menu command messages.

The `TAppMDIChild` constructor (defined in lines 135 to 175) performs the following tasks:

- Sets the window style to include the vertical and horizontal scroll bars, using the statement in line 147.
- Creates an instance of `TScroller` to animate the window's scroll bars, using the statement in line 149.
- Sets the window title to include the MDI child window number using the statements in lines 152 and 153.
- Creates the ->LowerCase and ->UpperCase pushbutton controls using the statements in lines 156 to 160.
- Creates the Can Close check box control using the statements in lines 162 to 165.
- Calls the `InitText` member function to generate random text in the application buffer `AppBuffer`.
- Creates a multiline instance of `TEdit` in statement located in lines 169 and 170. This instance contains a copy of the text stored in the application buffer.
- Disables the border, vertical scroll bar, and horizontal scroll bar styles of the edit control. This task uses the statements in lines 172 to 174.

The member function `CMUpperCase` (defined in 177 lines to 182) responds to the command message emitted by the `UpperCase` command. The function copies the text in the MDI child window to the application's buffer, converts the characters in the buffer to uppercase, and then writes the buffer back to the MDI child window.

The member function `CMLowerCase` (defined in lines 184 to 189) responds to the command message emitted by the Lowercase command. The function performs similar steps to those in `CMUpperCase`—except the text is converted into lowercase.

The member function `CanClose` (defined in lines 197 to 214) responds to the `WM_CLOSE` message emitted by the Close option in the system menu available in each MDI child window. If the MDI frame window's `ExpressClose` variable is `TRUE`, the function decrements the global variable `NumMDIChild` and then returns `TRUE`. Otherwise, the function returns `FALSE` if the Can Close check box is unchecked, or it decrements the global variable `NumMDIChild` and then returns `FALSE` if the control is not checked.

The member function `InitText` (defined in lines 233 to 237) is an auxiliary routine that fills the application buffer with random text. The function creates up to `MaxWords` words or enough that the buffer limit is closely reached (within 10 bytes). Checking the number of characters in the buffer ensures that the program does not corrupt the memory while attempting to add `MaxWords` words to the buffer.

The member functions `HandleUpperCaseBtn` and `HandleLowerCase` respond to the notification messages sent by the pushbuttons of an MDI child window. These functions perform the same tasks of `CMUpperCase` and `CMLowerCase`, respectively. Therefore, the notification response functions call their respective command-message response member functions.

The member function `CMClear` (defined in lines 74 and 75) responds to the command message emitted by the Clear command in the Current MDI Child menu item. The function simply invokes the `TextBox->Clear()` function call.

The member function `CMReset` (defined in lines 191 to 195) responds to the command message emitted by the Reset command in the Current MDI Child menu item. The function calls the `InitText` member function to create a new batch of random text and then copies the buffer's text to the edit control of the MDI child window.

Note: The Current MDI Child pop-up menu has four options that manipulate the currently active MDI child window. The command messages emitted by these options are handled by the MDI child window instances and not the MDI frame instance—which is what a window instance normally does regarding its own menu commands. This order of handling the command messages is preferred and makes use of the fact that the menu-based messages do reach the currently active MDI child window first. You can rewrite the program such that the functions `CMClear`, `CMUpperCase`, `CMLowerCase`, and `CMReset` appear as member functions of class `TAppMDIFrame`.

Summary

This chapter presented the Multiple Document Interface (MDI), which is an interface standard in Windows. The chapter discussed the following subjects:

- The basic features and components of an MDI-compliant application. These components include the MDI frame window, the invisible MDI client window, and the dynamically created MDI child windows.
- Basics of building an MDI application.
- The `TMDIFrame` class, which manages the MDI client window, the MDI child windows, and the execution of the menu commands.
- Building MDI frame windows as objects that are owned by the application and that own the MDI client window.
- The `TMDIClient` class, which owns the MDI child windows.
- Building MDI child windows as an instance of a `TWindow` descendant and using customized client windows.
- Managing messages in an MDI-compliant application. The currently active MDI child window has a higher priority for handling menu-based command message than its parent, the MDI frame window.

Q&A

Q Should each MDI child window have an ID?

A Yes. Associating each MDI child window with an ID gives you more control over managing these windows, especially if they vary in relevance. Thus, you can use the ID to exclude special MDI child windows from collective operations.

Q Can I hide MDI child windows?

A Yes, you can use the inherited member function `Twindow::ShowWindow` to show and hide one MDI child window or more.

Workshop

The Workshop provides quiz questions to help you solidify your understanding of the material covered and exercises to provide you with experience in using what you've learned. Try to understand the quiz and exercise answers before continuing on to the bonus chapters. Answers are provided in Appendix A, "Answers."

Quiz

1. True or false? MDI child windows can have their own menus.
2. True or false? MDI child windows can be moved outside the area of the frame window.
3. True or false? The MFC library supports nested MDI child windows.
4. True or false? This is the last quiz question in this book!

Exercises

1. Experiment with the expanding vocabulary of programs MDI1.EXE and MDI2.EXE.
2. Add a control that inserts the date and time in MDI child windows of program MDI1.EXE.

WEEK 3 IN REVIEW

15 16 17 18 19 20 21

You have come to the end of your last week of learning to program and to create Windows applications using Borland C++. Among other things, you have learned how to create scrolling windows and how to use static text controls, edit controls, pushbuttons, check boxes, radio buttons, group controls, list boxes, combo boxes, dialog boxes, and OWL-compliant windows. You will best review what you have learned by examining the information and the listings presented in the seven extra-credit chapters.

Extra Credit Bonus

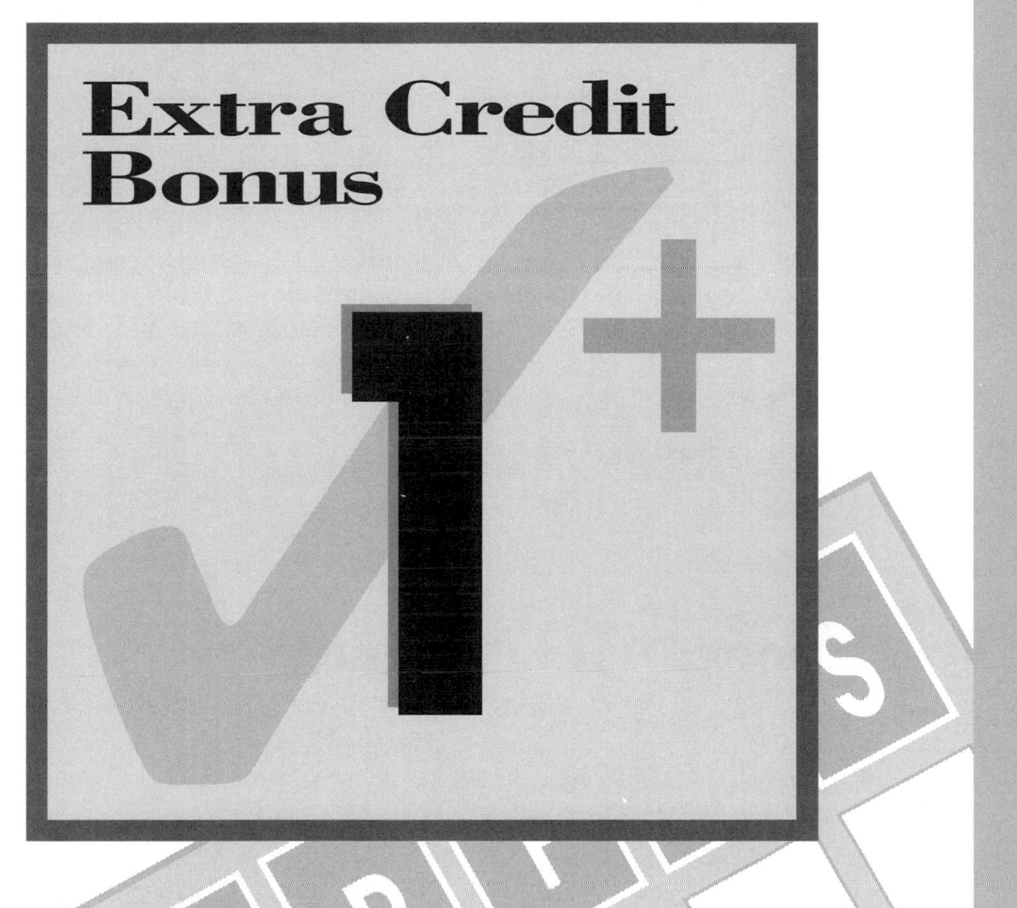

Debugging

No matter how well you may try to write a program, and no matter how good at writing programs you ever become, you will always make mistakes and cause bugs to appear in your program. The easiest bugs to locate and fix are those caught by the compiler as it shows you your syntax and other related errors. However, it is quite possible to have a program compile flawlessly, even without any warnings, and still fail in some miserable ways. When a program fails, a debugger can be the best tool for figuring out what went wrong. In today's lesson, you learn about the following:

- The integrated debugger commands
- How to debug a simple program
- Other debugging tools

The Integrated Debugger

Built into the Integrated Development Environment (IDE) are several debugging functions. You can use these to stop a running program in the middle of its execution, to view the values of variables and member data, and to watch how programming constructs are executed on a line-by-line basis.

In the IDE's top-level menu are two submenus that can be used in debugging. The first is the Debug menu. This menu provides a number of commands that control the execution of programs and enable you to view individual variables and structures. The second menu is the View menu. Inside this menu are, among other items, commands to open various debugging windows.

The Debug Menu

The principal commands for debugging are located in the Debug menu. These are the commands that enable you to execute your program on a line-by-line basis, to set breakpoints, and evaluate individual expressions.

New Term: A *breakpoint* is a point in a program at which execution will stop or break. Once a breakpoint is set, you can go ahead and let the program run. When the line of code where the breakpoint is set is reached, the program will pause, and the debugger will come up with the specified line highlighted. At this point, you can evaluate expressions and execute the code one line at a time.

- The `Run` command starts a program's execution. If the source code has changed and the program isn't already in a suspended state of execution, the IDE goes through the rebuild process, compiling and linking as necessary.
- The `Step over` command is used to *single-step* through the program code on a line-by-line basis. Each time you select `Step over`, the highlighted line is executed. If that line contains a function call, the function is called, and when it returns, the debugger will stop again on the next line.
- If you wish to actually go into the function instead of skipping over it, you can use the `Trace into` command. This is the same as stepping over lines of code, except that this will follow into function calls, enabling you to step through them. If there is no function call, the trace acts exactly like a step. Note, however, that some function calls aren't as visible as others. For example, when an object is created, its constructor function will be called, even if there doesn't appear to be any direct call to that function.
- The `Toggle breakpoint` command sets or clears a breakpoint on the line of code with the cursor. If the program is executing freely when it reaches this line of code (you aren't stepping or tracing through the code), then the program will pause and the debugger will come up with the cursor on this line of code.
- If your program is paused and you move the cursor around, or perhaps you look at some other files, you might lose track of the line of code at which the program was paused. In this case, you can use the `Find execution point` command to place the cursor on the current line of executing code.
- Sometimes, you might have started a program running, and then later decided that you need to pause the program, but you didn't set any breakpoints. You can use the `Pause program` command to pause the program at its current execution point. At this point, you will be able to evaluate expressions and look at various global variables. Unfortunately, you will not always be able to locate the current execution point in the code. Also, you may not always be able to use the `Pause program` command to stop the program if, say, it's in an infinite loop. In these cases, you can sometimes use the Ctrl+Alt+SysRq key sequence to pause the program and return to the debugger.
- The `Terminate program` command stops the program's execution and then resets it to the beginning. This means that the next time you might try to run or step into the program, it will be at the beginning.

- There is a window in the debugger called the Watch window. When you use the `Add watch...` command, you are given a dialog box, shown in Figure X1.1, that enables you to add an expression. This expression will be placed in the Watch window and will be updated as the program continues execution. The watch expressions are excellent ways to see how certain variables change over the course of the program.

Figure X1.1. *The dialog from which a watch expression may be added.*

- Figure X1.2 shows the dialog box that is brought up when you select the `Add breakpoint...` command. This sets a breakpoint on the current line in the same way as `Toggle breakpoint`, except that you are allowed to add some parameters to the breakpoint. For example, you can have the debugger break out only when a certain condition is true (for example, a variable being equal to a certain value).

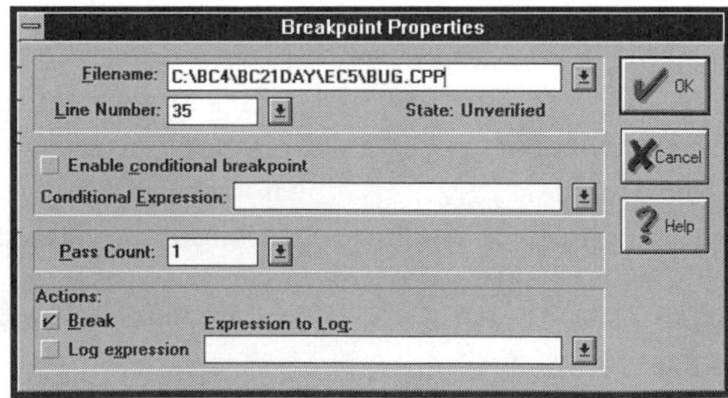

Figure X1.2. *The dialog on which breakpoint properties may be modified.*

- The `Evaluate/Modify...` command opens a dialog box that enables you to enter expressions and see what they evaluate to. It also enables you to change the value of certain variables by first evaluating them and then changing their contents.

- The `Inspect...` command yields a window for each item you inspect. This window is customized to the type of variable being inspected. For example, if you're looking at a variable, you get simple information showing the name of the variable, its location in memory, and its value. Classes, on the other hand, display all the same data in addition to their member data, their values, and the locations and names of their member functions. Figure X1.3 shows a sample inspection window.

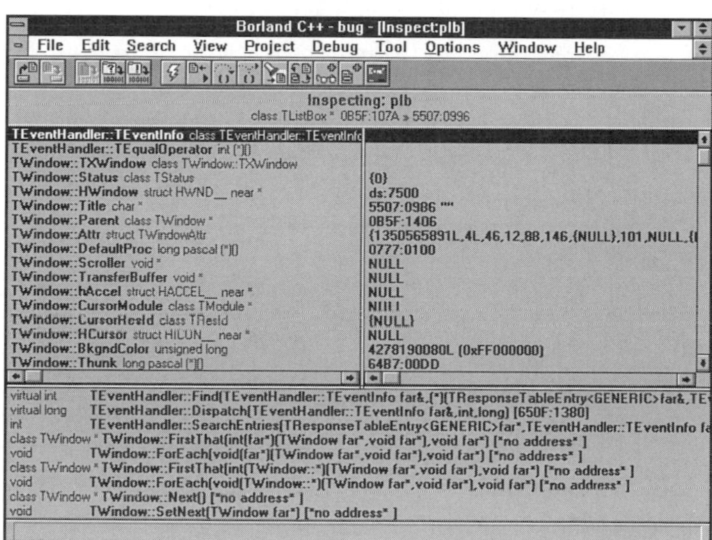

Figure X1.3. *A sample session in the IDE's debugger with an inspection window.*

- Finally, the `Load symbol table...` command enables you to load a symbol table when you try to debug something like a DLL. In this case, the symbol table for the application you debug will be loaded automatically, but you will have to load the DLL's symbols by hand.

The View Menu

The View menu contains commands that bring up different windows. One section of that menu enables you to bring up windows associated with debugging. These are the Watch, Breakpoint, Call Stack, Register, and Event Log windows.

- The Watch window shows a list of expressions you've entered and their evaluation. As the program runs and the variables mentioned in the expressions change, so will the evaluations.
- The Breakpoint window shows a list of all the breakpoints set in the program. Also, when you double-click a breakpoint entry in this window, you are allowed to bring up the breakpoint properties window, enabling you to modify the breakpoint's settings.
- When you've stopped in the middle of a program, it's often helpful to see where you've come from. For example, if you find yourself in a function that could be called by any of a number of other locations, it would be useful to know which particular function called the current function and, in turn, who called that. This progression of calls is in the Call Stack window, along with the parameters of the functions for which debugging information is available.
- Although you are using C++ here, the machine itself actually deals on a much lower level, with machine code and assembly language. Basic to this lower level are registers that act like a limited set of variables for assembly language. Occasionally, it is useful to be able to view the contents of those registers during the execution of a program, and these are displayed in the Registers window. Note, however, that this is usually not very useful unless you know how your program works on the lower-level translated assembly language.
- The Event Log window displays a list of such things as when breakpoints were reached, or debugging information is displayed by the program (with the Windows `OutputDebugString` function).

In addition to all these menu commands, there is also the `Locate function...` command found under the Search menu. This brings up a dialog box that prompts you to enter a function name. The IDE's debugger will then attempt to find the requested function and place the cursor at that point. In order for the debugger to find the function, it must be listed in the loaded debugging information.

Debugging a Program

When debugging a program, you must first make sure that debugging information is included when the program is compiled and built. With that done, you'll be able to step through the program a line at a time, view the contents of variables as you go, set breakpoints, and so on.

Unfortunately, the standard libraries (the runtime library, the class library, and the Object Windows Library) don't come with debugging information included in them by default. Because of this, you won't be able to step or trace into its code, just as you won't be able to step or trace into the internal Windows code. You can, however, rebuild the Borland libraries to include debugging information if you have the source code. The class library and OWL source code is included with the standard Borland package, but the runtime library source code is available only on the CD version or at an extra cost.

The best way to learn how to debug a program is to sit down and do it. To start, type in and compile the program in Listings X1.1 and X1.2. You'll notice that it compiles with no warnings or errors, but if you try to run it and select the Dialog menu item, you'll get either a GP fault or, barring that, an hourglass that doesn't go away. In any case, the program certainly isn't doing what you would want it to do.

Listing X1.1. Script for the BUG.RC resource file.

```
#include <windows.h>
#include <owl\window.rh>

TheDialog DIALOG 6, 15, 207, 111
STYLE DS_MODALFRAME | WS_POPUP | WS_VISIBLE | WS_CAPTION |
         WS_SYSMENU
CAPTION "Dialog of the Century"
FONT 8, "MS Sans Serif"
BEGIN
   LISTBOX 101, 27, 8, 49, 88, LBS_STANDARD | WS_TABSTOP
   DEFPUSHBUTTON "OK", IDOK, 148, 6, 50, 14
   PUSHBUTTON "Cancel", IDCANCEL, 148, 24, 50, 14
END

MainMenu MENU LOADONCALL MOVEABLE PURE DISCARDABLE
BEGIN
   MENUITEM "E&xit", CM_EXIT
   MENUITEM "&Dialog", 100
END
```

Type

Listing X1.2. Source code for the BUG.CPP program file.

```
#include <stdio.h>
#include <windows.h>
#include <owl\applicat.h>
#include <owl\dialog.h>
#include <owl\framewin.h>
#include <owl\listbox.h>
#include <owl\window.h>
#include <owl\window.rh>

class TMyDialog : public TDialog
{
public:
   TMyDialog(TWindow* parent, TModule* module = 0);

   void SetupWindow();

private:
   TListBox* numbers;
};

TMyDialog::TMyDialog(TWindow* parent, TModule* module)
   : TDialog(parent, "TheDialog", module)
{
}

void fill_lb(TListBox* plb, int count)
{
   for (int ix = 0; ix < count; ++count)
      {
      char str[25];
      sprintf(str, "%d", ix + 1);
      plb->AddString(str);
      }
}

void TMyDialog::SetupWindow()
{
   fill_lb(numbers, 20);
}

class TMyWindow : public TWindow
{
public:
   TMyWindow(TWindow* parent = 0);

protected:
   void CmExit();
   void CmDialog();
```

```
49:
50: private:
51:    DECLARE_RESPONSE_TABLE(TMyWindow);
52: };
53: DEFINE_RESPONSE_TABLE1(TMyWindow, TWindow)
54:    EV_COMMAND(CM_EXIT, CmExit),
55:    EV_COMMAND(100, CmDialog),
56: END_RESPONSE_TABLE;
57:
58: TMyWindow::TMyWindow(TWindow* parent)
59:    : TWindow(parent)
60: {
61: }
62:
63: void TMyWindow::CmExit()
64: {
65:    SendMessage(WM_CLOSE);
66: }
67:
68: void TMyWindow::CmDialog()
69: {
70:    TMyDialog(this).Execute();
71: }
72:
73: class TDialogApp : public TApplication
74: {
75: public:
76:    TDialogApp() : TApplication()
77:       { nCmdShow = SW_SHOWMAXIMIZED; }
78:
79:    void InitMainWindow()
80:       {
81:       SetMainWindow(new TFrameWindow(  0,
82:                               "Dialog Testers, Inc.",
83:                               new TMyWindow ));
84:       GetMainWindow()->AssignMenu("MainMenu");
85:       }
86: };
87:
88: int OwlMain(int, char *[])
89: {
90:    return TDialogApp().Run();
91: }
```

Analysis

If you run the program from the IDE, and then select the Dialog menu item, you are likely to get a dialog box that comes up entitled Unhandled Exception, with the message that a General Protection Exception occurred in BUG.CPP on line 32. By clicking OK, the IDE will come back up and place you on line 32 of the BUG.CPP file.

New Term: A *general protection violation* or *general protection fault* occurs when some code attempts to read or write to a part of memory that it isn't allowed. In C++, this usually means that a pointer is used that hasn't been initialized or is still pointing at memory that has been deleted and no longer exists. When running under the IDE, a general protection fault, which is Windows terminology, is reported as a general protection *exception* in keeping with C++ terminology.

Line 32 of BUG.CPP contains the following code:

```
plb->AddString(str);
```

So, remembering that a general protection exception usually has something to do with accessing memory that is off limits, you might think that the `str` variable is probably at fault, because it's a pointer. The only problem with that theory is that `str` is really a pointer to a local area of memory that's just been set up. We know that it still exists because it's still in scope.

The only other pointer here is the `plb` parameter. Considering, however, that we're just calling one of its member functions, how could it possibly be the problem? Let's take a look at the function it is calling, `AddString`. This function is declared in the `TListBox` class in the following manner:

```
virtual int AddString(const char far* str);
```

Note that the function is declared as virtual. This means that when the code to call it is compiled, a direct call to the member function isn't generated; rather, code to look up the location of the function is generated. The reason is that, since a derived class could have written its own version of the function, the base class will need to be able to access that new function, without necessarily knowing where this function resides. So, when the pointer is used to call `AddString`, it really does use `plb` as a pointer, by looking up the function's address in the virtual table.

New Term: The *virtual table* is a list of pointers to virtual functions. Each class has a virtual table associated with it, in which all the virtual functions have their addresses listed. Along with each object is a *virtual table pointer*, which points to the virtual table for the appropriate class. When some code attempts to call a virtual function, the generated assembly code first looks up the virtual table, then the virtual function's address, then actually calls the function.

The only possibility at this point is the `plb` parameter. This pointer appears to be invalid for some reason. The next step is to see who gave us this pointer. Let's go into the View menu and select Call Stack. A window comes up showing the current function `fill_lb` at the top. The next function down is `TMyDialog::SetupWindow`. Double-click that next line to position the cursor at the place where the `fill_lb` function was called.

We are now placed directly into the middle of the `SetupWindow` function on the following line:

```
fill_lb(numbers, 20);
```

It appears that the `numbers` member data is invalid, because that's the parameter that becomes `plb` in the `fill_lb` function. If you take a look around, you'll notice that we forgot to set `numbers` to anything. It's declared in the class, but nobody ever assigns it any value. Oops! This must be fixed before we can continue trying to run the program. Obviously, we needed to initialize `numbers` in the constructor to connect with the listbox interface element in the dialog box we load from the resource. Go up to the constructor and add the following line:

```
numbers = new TListBox(this, 101, module);
```

Now if you take a look at the Debug menu, you'll notice that the Run item is grayed out. This is because you've changed the file and trying to continue running would make little sense. So use the Terminate program option to stop the program and then rebuild and run the application.

This time when you select the Dialog menu item, you get an hourglass that seems to hang around forever. After a while you may be getting the idea that something is wrong. The only way to stop the program now is to do the "three fingered salute" and press the Ctrl+Alt+Del keys. Windows will give you a choice of going back and waiting a little longer, or of ending the program, or of rebooting Windows. Because waiting a little longer for the program to do something looks a little hopeless and restarting Windows seems a bit drastic, let's end the program. In this case, when you get back to the IDE, the program will already have been terminated, and there will be no reason to use the Terminate program menu item.

In finding this problem, we're going to have to look at a bit of code to help narrow down where the problem might be. We know the bug occurs after we select the Dialog menu option but before the dialog actually makes it up onto the screen. At times like this, it's a good idea to set breakpoints on some likely areas and run through the code, one line at a time, to see what happens.

Position the cursor on the `TMyWindow::CmDialog` function and select Toggle breakpoint from the Debug menu (or press Ctrl+F8). Note how the line changes color to reflect the state of the breakpoint. Now set breakpoints on the `TMyDialog` constructor and its `SetupWindow` function, and then run the program.

When you select the Dialog menu item now, you are returned to the IDE with the cursor on the line where you set the breakpoint, the line where `TMyWindow::CmDialog` is declared. Select the `Step over` command in the Debug menu. The screen flashes to the application and then flashes back to the source code, with the cursor on the next line, where the dialog is actually created and executed. This line looks okay, so let's step over it as well.

Now we're looking at the `TMyDialog` constructor. Looking at the code, there doesn't seem to be anything out of the ordinary. Here we run into the nonlinearity of Windows. If you simply keep stepping, you'll end up running through the constructor and then back to the `TMyWindow::CmDialog` function. We know we have a breakpoint on the next bit of code we want to look at, so it's a good idea to just continue running from here.

When next we break into the source code, we're on the `TMyDialog::SetupWindow` function. There's only one function call in here, and it's something we wrote, so there's probably good reason to suspect that that might have inadvertently caused a problem in there. So let's use the Trace function in the Debug menu now. Your first trace takes you onto the call to `fill_lb`, and your next trace takes you right inside it.

Inside here you will see a `for` loop. It might be a good idea to walk through that one step at a time, watching the relevant variables `plb`, `count`, `ix`, and `str`. Place the cursor on each of these variables and select the Add Watch item from the Debug menu. We're not particularly interested in any fancy displays right now, so just click OK on the resultant Watch Properties dialog box. You may notice that some of the values are weird or possibly even undefined, but that's okay for right now. We're not really in the function yet, so the debugger hasn't had a chance to figure out what those values are. Also, because the `str` variable hasn't even been declared yet, it will be listed as undefined until we get where it is declared, at which point the Watch window will get synchronized properly.

Step over the beginning of the function. The cursor is placed on the first line of the `for` loop, and the `count` variable shows up as the number 20 in the watch window. This is good. We specified 20 when we called this function. Step again and see that the `ix` variable is now set to 0 and the `str` variable is now recognized.

Notice how `str` is uninitialized at this point, showing random data. Stepping once more will fill `str` with what should be more reasonable data. Note, however, that the

data isn't in a very readable format. It would be better if we could see it as a string. If you double click the data item, you will bring back the Watch Properties dialog box. If you take a look in the Display As section, you will see a radio button marked String. Select this item and then click OK. When you get back to the Watch window, you'll see a string containing something a little more akin to what you expected.

Stepping again calls the `AddString` member function and brings us back to the line with the `sprintf`. Let's take another look at the Watch window and see how things are doing.

Wait a minute!

Why is `count` now 21, and why `ix` is still 0? Let's take a look at that `for` loop again:

```
for (int ix = 0; ix < count; ++count)
```

Oops, again! Incrementing the limit instead of the counter is a common mistake. No wonder the program seemed to have stopped. It was never leaving the loop and was trying to keep filling the list box with ever increasing numbers. Okay, let's fix that by changing the line to

```
for (int ix = 0; ix < count; ++ix)
```

Now terminate the application, remove the breakpoints, rebuild, and start over again. When you select the Dialog menu item now, you at least get the dialog box up on the screen. Unfortunately, the list box appears to be completely empty.

The question here comes down to figuring out from where the failure is coming. We know that the pointer to the list box is valid; otherwise we would have had another general protection exception. So the problem must be somewhere with the portion that's adding the string. So set a breakpoint on the line that reads

```
plb->AddString(str);
```

Start the program and select the Dialog menu item. When you reach the breakpoint, take a closer look at the `plb` parameter. Place the cursor over the `plb` variable and select the Inspect item from the Debug menu.

Looking at the inspection window, we can clearly see that, although we were obviously capable of creating the class object, it doesn't appear to be hooked up to the actual Windows interface item. The `TWindow::HWindow` data member is `NULL`, and the `TWindow::Attr` data member is mostly empty, except for the 101 that we passed to it earlier.

If you remember, the `SetupWindow` function is the location where class objects get associated with their Windows counterparts. Taking a look at the `TMyDialog`'s version of the function, we can see that we forgot to call the parent's version of the `SetupWindow` function. Without that call, the actual work never gets done that connects the class with the interface element. To fix this, simply change the function to look like this:

```
void TMyDialog::SetupWindow()
{
   TDialog::SetupWindow();
   fill_lb(numbers, 20);
}
```

Now, when you next compile and run the program, you'll see a fully functional, if boring, application that enables you to bring up a dialog with a listbox containing the numbers 1 to 20.

Other Debugging Tools

Along with the integrated debugger included in the IDE, a number of other tools are useful in finding and fixing problems with your applications. The first are the stand-alone versions of the debugger. There are two different ones: one for when you need to debug an MS-DOS program and another for Windows. The advantages of the stand-alone debuggers over the IDE include the following:

- They have the capability to view the CPU window, a lower-level listing of the code in its generated assembly language. Sometimes it's necessary to follow program execution in the generated assembly language in order to find out exactly what is going wrong.
- They allow for hardware debugging. This lets the debugger use the computer's built-in debugging capabilities to put breakpoints on changes in memory as well as execution of code.
- By allowing you to use a secondary, monochrome monitor, the stand-alone debuggers can reduce the annoyance of having the screen flicker every time you step or trace through your program.

Another useful program is WinSight. This program can display a listing of all the windows currently registered with Windows, whether those windows are visible or not. You can even see the hierarchy of the windows—which windows are children of which others. From there, you can select one or more windows and watch the messages received by them.

Finally, one of the most useful programs is WinSpector. Normally, whenever you run your application from outside the IDE, general-protection (GP) faults will simply display a nasty error window and terminate your program. If you have WinSpector running when that GP fault occurs, WinSpector will record the location in your application that caused the GP fault. WinSpector will also attempt to figure out what other sections of your application had been executed immediately prior to the fault occurring, by performing a stack trace. The results of this can then be run through the DFA program to match up the memory locations with the debugging information of your program. The final results can often tell you exactly what line in your application's source code died and what functions had been called before.

Summary

Today's lesson presented a short tutorial on some of the debugging techniques provided by the IDE. You learned about the following subjects:

- The debugging commands available in the Integrated Development Environment
- Examples of some of the more common programming mistakes
- Some of the techniques used to track down and exterminate bugs

Q&A

Q Do my watches need to be limited to variables?

A No. You may supply whole expressions, such as `(count + 1) * 2`.

Q If I set a breakpoint on a line of code, do I have to stop there every single time the program comes to that line?

A No. You may set up conditions on the breakpoint so that, for example, if you are in the middle of a loop, the debugger will break in only when the iterator is equal to a certain value.

Visual Programming

Many PC users who worked with DOS applications have come to appreciate Windows applications. Windows (along with the Apple Macintosh) has popularized the graphical user interface (GUI). This interface is simpler to use and is more compatible across diverse applications than the character-based user interface of MS-DOS and PC-DOS. Also, software vendors such as Microsoft and Borland have shaped the development of programming for the masses by incorporating visual programming tools in their software-development packages. Although visual programming did exist in the 1980s, it was restricted to special university projects. This chapter looks at the visual programming aspects of Borland C++ 4.5 that are signficantly supported by the Resource Workshop. Resource Workshop is a utility that employs visual tools to help you create resources that can be used by all Windows-compliant programming languages, not just Borland C++. In this extra-credit chapter, you will learn about the following topics:

- General functions of the Resource Workshop
- Types of resources supported by the Resource Workshop
- Resource files
- Creating menu resources
- Creating accelerator resources
- Creating icon resources
- Creating a bare-bones dialog-box resource
- Creating resources for a dialog box with nontrivial interfaces
- Creating a fully-functioning dialog box

Resource Workshop Overview

Resources are special ingredients of Windows applications. Using resources, you can modify messages, menus, and icons, and even use different human languages without having to change the source code, recompile it, or relink it. Thus, for example, you can employ resources in different human languages with the same source code. This kind of flexibility requires that resources have their own C-like *script* language. The preceding chapter showed you how to use resource scripts to define menus. You can develop resources by typing their script in .RC and .DLG files, in a manner that is typical of any programming language.

The Resource Workshop is a powerful tool that enables you to develop resources using visual programming techniques. In other words, you can "draw" the resources you need using a mouse, visual tools, and a set of menus and dialog boxes. The Resource Workshop then translates your drawings into the proper resource files, such as the script resource .RC files.

This chapter does not discuss the Resource Workshop from *A* to *Z*. Instead, it serves to illustrate how to use this graphical tool in creating significant (and generally visual) ingredients of Windows programs.

Types of Resources

The Resource Workshop supports the following kinds of resources:

- Accelerators
- Bitmaps
- Cursors
- Dialog boxes
- Fonts
- Icons
- Menus
- String tables
- User-defined and rcdata resources
- VERSIONINFO

These resources are briefly defined in the following subsections.

Accelerators

Accelerators are basically "hot keys" that enable you to invoke a command without first choosing its parent menus and options. Accelerators offer a quick and direct way to perform a task and are very useful for invoking nested commands.

Bitmaps

Bitmaps are binary representations of a graphical image. The popular Windows controls—such as pushbuttons, radio buttons, and scroll bars—use bitmaps. The Resource Workshop enables you to create bitmaps using the Paint editor. This editor supports the drawing, coloring, and editing of bitmaps.

Cursors

Cursors are special small bitmaps, 32×32 pixels in size. A cursor displays the location of the mouse on the screen. Windows supports using different cursor shapes to signal various tasks. For example, the hourglass cursor indicates that a Windows application is busy processing data. The Resource Workshop enables you to create cursors with the Paint editor.

Dialog Boxes

Dialog boxes are special windows that interact with the application user. Typically, dialog boxes prompt you to enter or confirm current data. The Resource Workshop supports creating dialog-box resources and visually drawing their controls. This feature is the highlight of this chapter.

Fonts

Fonts are special bitmaps that represent the various typographic characters that appear in a window or that are printed. The Resource Workshop enables you to edit existing fonts and to create your own fonts.

Icons

Icons are special bitmaps, each being 16×32, 32×32, or 64×64 (for high-resolution devices) pixels in size. Windows uses icons to represent minimized windows, and it supports inserting icons in windows and dialog boxes to incorporate small visual images.

Menus

Menus are resources that offer selections and options for the diverse operations of a Windows application. Because menus are resources, you can create different menu

resources in different human languages. This enables you to distribute your applications to various countries.

String Tables

String tables are resources that contain text for various messages, prompts, and descriptions. Like menu resources, you can create different string tables in different human languages to support multinational versions of your software. This requires that you avoid imbedding string literals in your source code and instead rely completely on the string table resources.

User-Defined and *rcdata* Resources

The user-defined and `rcdata` resources support special information that is incorporated into the executable files. This kind of information provides read-only data used by the host program to initialize itself.

VERSIONINFO

The VERSIONINFO resource is a special version-stamper resource for Windows 3.1 .EXE, .DLL, and .DRV files.

Resource Files

The Resource Workshop works with the following kinds of resource files:

- The resource script files with .RC extensions. These text files contain resource statements, which define various kinds of resources, such as menus, accelerators, string tables, and dialog boxes.
- The binary .RES files, which contain compiled resources. The Resource Workshop can read and produce either .RC or .RES files. In other words, you can ask the Resource Workshop to read a .RES, decompile it, and then create a corresponding .RC file that you can edit.
- The bitmapped resource files .BMP, .ICO, .CUR, and .FON, which contain bitmaps, icons, cursors, and fonts resources. The Resource Workshop also supports font resource files with the .FNT extension.
- The dialog-box script resource files, with the extension .DLG. Typically, these files contain resource script for reusable dialog boxes. You can include

the .DLG files (and also other .RC files) in an .RC file using the special directive `#rcinclude`.

- The executable .EXE and dynamic-link library .DLL files, which contain executable code bound together with compiled resources. The Resource Workshop enables you to read resources in .EXE and .DLL files, decompile them, edit them, and then save the new resources back to the .EXE and .DLL binary files.
- The device driver files, with the extension .DRV, which are special .DLL files. As with ordinary .DLL files, the Resource Workshop enables you to edit the resources in a .DRV file.

Creating Menu Resources

Let's look at a hands-on example that illustrates the creation of a menu resource. Listing X2.1 presents the resource file AMENU.RC as a map for creating the same resource using the Resource Workshop. This file declares the `LONGMENU` and `SHORTMENU` menu resources. You can think of these menus as novice and expert menus, respectively.

Listing X2.1. The script for the AMENU.RC resource file.

```
#include <windows.h>
#include <owl\window.rh>
#include "amenu.h"
LONGMENU MENU LOADONCALL MOVEABLE PURE DISCARDABLE
BEGIN
  POPUP "&File"
  BEGIN
    MENUITEM "&New", CM_FILENEW, GRAYED
    MENUITEM "&Open", CM_FILEOPEN, GRAYED
    MENUITEM "&Save", CM_FILESAVE, GRAYED
    MENUITEM "Save&As", CM_FILESAVEAS, GRAYED
    MENUITEM SEPARATOR
    MENUITEM "Short &Menus", CM_SHORTMENU
    MENUITEM SEPARATOR
    MENUITEM "E&xit", CM_EXIT
  END
  POPUP "&Edit"
  BEGIN
    MENUITEM "&Undo", CM_EDITUNDO, GRAYED
    MENUITEM SEPARATOR
    MENUITEM "C&ut", CM_EDITCUT
    MENUITEM "C&opy", CM_EDITCOPY
```

```
    MENUITEM "&Paste", CM_EDITPASTE
    MENUITEM "&Delete", CM_EDITDELETE, GRAYED
    MENUITEM "&Clear", CM_EDITCLEAR, GRAYED
  END
  MENUITEM "&Help", CM_HELP, HELP
END
SHORTMENU MENU LOADONCALL MOVEABLE PURE DISCARDABLE
BEGIN
  POPUP "&File"
  BEGIN
    MENUITEM "&Open", CM_FILEOPEN, GRAYED
    MENUITEM "Save&As", CM_FILESAVEAS, GRAYED
    MENUITEM SEPARATOR
    MENUITEM "&Long Menus", CM_LONGMENU
    MENUITEM SEPARATOR
    MENUITEM "E&xit", CM_EXIT
  END
  POPUP "&Edit"
  BEGIN
    MENUITEM "C&ut", CM_EDITCUT
    MENUITEM "C&opy", CM_EDITCOPY
    MENUITEM "&Paste", CM_EDITPASTE
  END
  MENUITEM "&Help", CM_HELP, HELP
END
```

Let's proceed with creating the menu resource using the Resource Workshop. First, you need to load the Borland C++ IDE and create the new project RWMENU1 with the files RWMENU1.DEF, RWMENU1.CPP, and RWMENU1.RC. Listing X2.5 shows the contents of the RWMENU1.DEF definition file. Listing X2.6 contains the source code for the RWMENU1.CPP implementation file. Let's examine the process of creating the menu resources. The general steps are as follows:

1. Invoke the Resource Workshop option from the Tool menu. The Resource Workshop displays a window with a menu, a status bar, and a client area. The client area contains an empty resource window, as shown in Figure X2.1. The resource window has two panes. The first pane lists the current resources. The second pane is the preview pane, which shows the contents of the currently selected resource in the first pane.

2. Choose the Resource menu and invoke the New… command. This option brings up the New Resource dialog box, shown in Figure X2.2, which enables you to choose a new resource. Scroll down through the resource-type list box until you find MENU. Click the OK pushbutton in the New Resource dialog box.

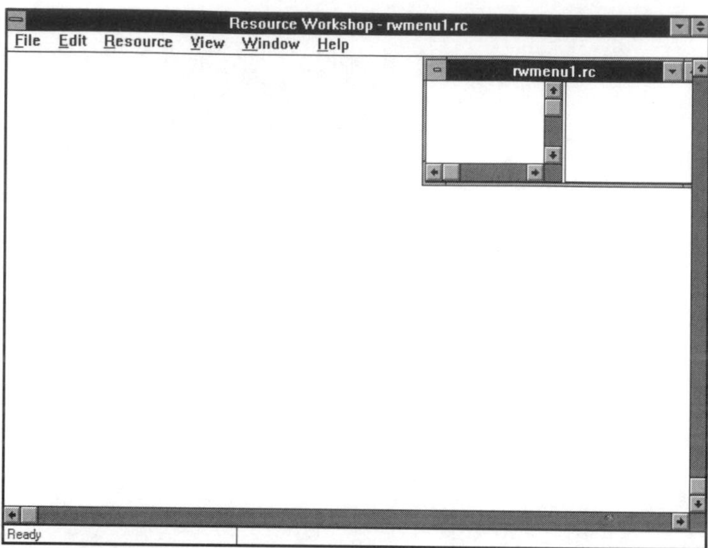

Figure X2.1. *The Resource Workshop showing an empty resource window.*

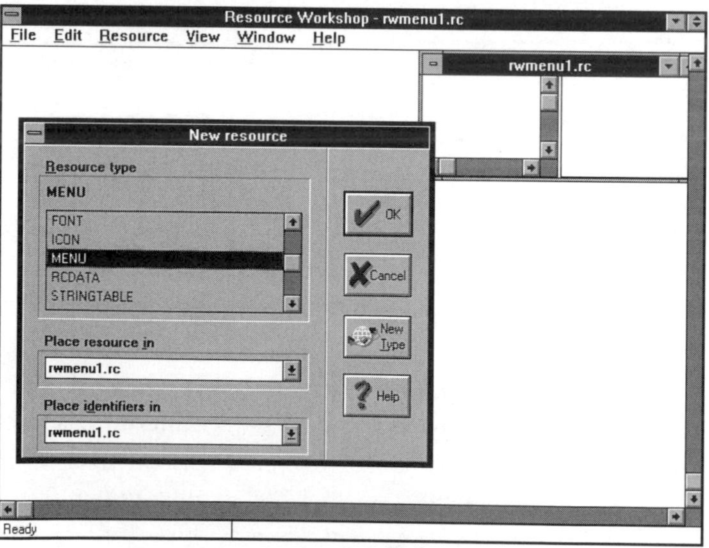

Figure X2.2. *A sample session with the New Resource dialog box.*

3. The Resource Workshop invokes the MENU:MENU_1 dialog box, as shown in Figure X2.3. The caption of the dialog box incorporates the

default name of the new menu resource. The dialog box is made up of three panes: the attribute pane, the outline pane, and the test menu pane. The attribute pane contains the following groups of controls:

- The set of edit boxes labeled Item Text, Item Help, and Item ID. These controls enable you to enter the caption of a menu item, its corresponding one-line help text (which appears in the status bar when you select the item), and the identifier for the new menu item, respectively.
- The diamond-shaped item-type radio buttons: Pop-up, Menu Item, and Separator. If the Pop-up control is enabled, the other two buttons are disabled, and vice versa. The last two controls, when enabled, allow you to select between creating a menu item or a separator.
- The Checked check box and the diamond-shaped initial-state radio buttons: Enabled, Disabled, and Grayed. These controls enable you to specify the initial state of a menu item.
- The diamond-shaped Break-before radio buttons: No break, Menu bar break, Menu break, and Help break. Use the last radio button to display the Help menu to the right edge of the menu bar.
- The modifiers check boxes: Alt, Shift, Control, and Invert menu item. These check boxes enable you to fine-tune the hot keys that respond to the commands.
- The Key edit box and the key-type radio buttons: ASCII and Virtual Key. These controls enable you to associate hot keys with commands.

4. Type in the menu items for the `LONGMENU` resource (which is currently being created as the resource menu `MENU_1`) using the following tasks in their appropriate sequence (Listing X2.1 should guide your input and selections):

   - To add a new pop-up item as a menu, move to the bottom of the menu outline and then invoke the Menu menu and select the New pop-up item option. The hot-key combination for this option is Ctrl+P.
   - To add a new menu item, invoke the Menu menu and select the New menu item option. The hot key for this option is the Insert key.
   - To insert a selector, first insert a new menu item, click the Menu Item radio button in the item-type control group, and then press Enter. You can also use the Ctrl+S keys as hot keys for inserting a separator.

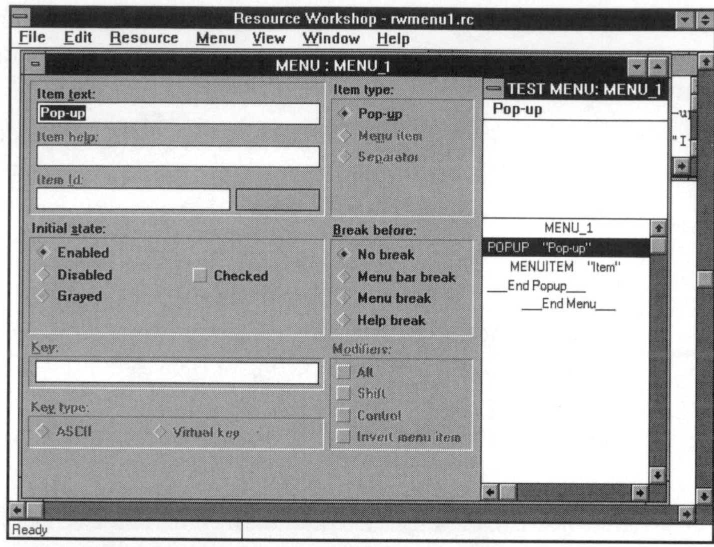

Figure X2.3. *The MENU:MENU_1 dialog box, which creates the menu resource.*

- ☐ To insert the Help menu, move to the end of the outline and press the Insert key to insert an unnested menu item.
- ☐ To make a menu item gray, click the Grayed radio button in the initial-state control group.
- ☐ Each menu item requires a caption. Place the `&` character before the hot-key character if any. Use the same hot keys as shown in Listing X2.1.
- ☐ Each command requires an ID. Enter `CM_XXXX` ID in the Item Id edit box. Use the same `CM_XXXX` constants as in Listing X2.1.
- ☐ The menu Menu also has options that spawn standard file, edit, and help selections (including standard options).

5. Repeat steps 2 through 4 to create the `SHORTMENU` menu resource (which is initially created as the resource menu `MENU_2`). Use the Listing X2.1 as a guide for your input. Keep in mind that the two menu resources have a few `CM_XXXX` identifiers in common. Make sure that these common `CM_XXXX` identifiers have the same values.

6. Rename the resources `MENU_1` and `MENU_2` as `LONGMENU` and `SHORTMENU`, respectively. This task involves using the Identifiers... option in the Resource menu. The Resource Workshop displays the Identifiers dialog box, shown in Figure X2.4, which enables you to select a resource, rename it, and renumber it. Select each of the menu resources MENU_1 and MENU_2 and click the Rename pushbutton. The Resource Workshop displays a simple input dialog box that enables you to enter the new name for the currently selected resource. Click the Change pushbutton in the Identifiers dialog box to assign numbers 101 and 102 to the menu resources `LONGMENU` and `SHORTMENU`.

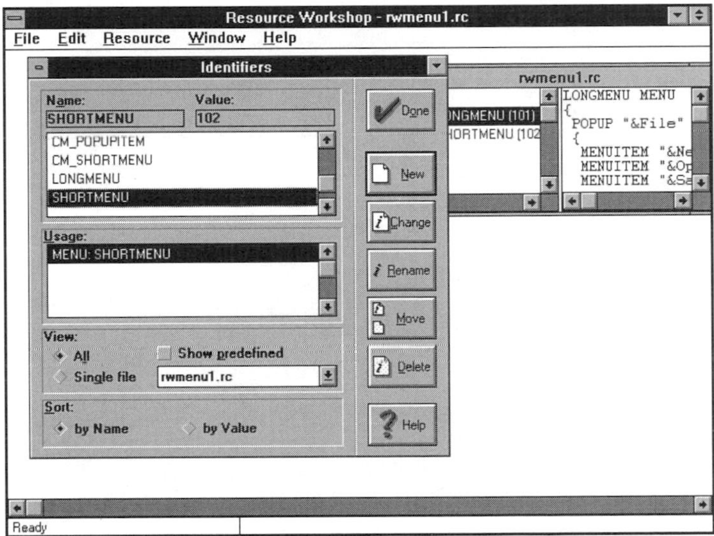

Figure X2.4. *A sample session with the Identifiers dialog box.*

7. Renumber the value of the identifier `CM_SHORTMENU`, changing its value from 1 to 9 (or any other integer that does not duplicate the values of the other `CM_XXXX` identifiers). Use the Identifier dialog box for this task.

The Resource Workshop produces the resource file RWMENU1.RC, shown in Listing X2.2.

Listing X2.2. The script for the resource file RWMENU1.RC, which is generated by the Resource Workshop.

```
/*****************************************************************


RWMENU1.RC

produced by Borland Resource Workshop


*****************************************************************/

#define LONGMENU        101
#define SHORTMENU       102
#define CM_LONGMENU     1
#define CM_POPUPITEM    101
#define CM_HELP         8
#define CM_EDITCLEAR    7
#define CM_EDITDELETE   6
#define CM_EDITPASTE    5
#define CM_EDITCOPY     4
#define CM_EDITCUT      3
#define CM_EDITUNDO     105
#define CM_EXIT         2
#define CM_SHORTMENU    1
#define CM_FILESAVEAS   104
#define CM_FILESAVE     103
#define CM_FILENEW      101
#define CM_FILEOPEN     102

LONGMENU MENU
{
 POPUP "&File"
 {
  MENUITEM "&New", CM_FILENEW, GRAYED
  MENUITEM "&Open", CM_FILEOPEN, GRAYED
  MENUITEM "&Save", CM_FILESAVE, GRAYED
  MENUITEM "Save&As", CM_FILESAVEAS, GRAYED
  MENUITEM SEPARATOR
  MENUITEM "Short &Menus", CM_SHORTMENU
  MENUITEM SEPARATOR
  MENUITEM "E&xit", CM_EXIT
 }

 POPUP "&Edit"
 {
  MENUITEM "&Undo", CM_EDITUNDO, GRAYED
  MENUITEM SEPARATOR
```

```
47:     MENUITEM "C&ut", CM_EDITCUT
48:     MENUITEM "C&opy", CM_EDITCOPY
49:     MENUITEM "&Paste", CM_EDITPASTE
50:     MENUITEM "&Delete", CM_EDITDELETE, GRAYED
51:     MENUITEM "&Clear", CM_EDITCLEAR, GRAYED
52:    }
53:
54:   MENUITEM "&Help", CM_HELP
55:  }
56:
57:
58:  SHORTMENU MENU
59:  {
60:   POPUP "&File"
61:    {
62:     MENUITEM "&Open", CM_FILEOPEN, GRAYED
63:     MENUITEM "Save&AS", CM_FILESAVEAS, GRAYED
64:     MENUITEM SEPARATOR
65:     MENUITEM "&Long Menus", CM_LONGMENU
66:     MENUITEM SEPARATOR
67:     MENUITEM "E&xit", CM_EXIT
68:    }
69:
70:   POPUP "&Edit"
71:    {
72:     MENUITEM "C&ut", CM_EDITCUT
73:     MENUITEM "C&opy", CM_EDITCOPY
74:     MENUITEM "&Paste", CM_EDITPASTE
75:    }
76:
77:   MENUITEM "&Help", CM_HELP
78:  }
```

Analysis Notice that Listing X2.2 includes the definitions of the `CM_XXXX` constant (in line 22) and other resource identifiers. The resource script in Listing X2.2 resembles that in Listing X2.1, except that the keywords `BEGIN` and `END` (in Listing X2.1) are replaced with the open and close brace.

Now, let's focus on editing the projects files. The first task involves creating the empty header file RWMENU1.H and moving the set of `#define` statements from the resource file RWMENU1.RC to that header file. In addition, you need to delete the definition of the identifier `CM_EXIT` because the program needs to use Windows' own definition found in the resource header file WINDOW.H. Listing X2.3 shows the resulting source code for the RWMENU1.H header file.

Listing X2.3. The source code for the RWMENU1.H header file.

```
#define LONGMENU          101
#define SHORTMENU         102
#define CM_LONGMENU       1
#define CM_POPUPITEM      101
#define CM_HELP           8
#define CM_EDITCLEAR      7
#define CM_EDITDELETE     6
#define CM_EDITPASTE      5
#define CM_EDITCOPY       4
#define CM_EDITCUT        3
#define CM_EDITUNDO       105
#define CM_SHORTMENU      9
#define CM_FILESAVEAS     104
#define CM_FILESAVE       103
#define CM_FILENEW        101
#define CM_FILEOPEN       102
```

Let's work on the resource file RWMEMU1.RC. After removing the set of `#define` statements, you need to insert the following `#include` statements:

```
#include <windows.h>
#include <owl\window.rh>
#include "rwmenu1.h"
```

These statements enable the resource file to access the proper definitions of the various identifiers. Listing X2.4 shows the script for the edited RWMENU1.RC resource file.

Listing X2.4. The script for the RWMENU1.RC resource file.

```
#include <windows.h>
#include <owl\window.rh>
#include "rwmenu1.h"
LONGMENU MENU
{
 POPUP "&File"
 {
  MENUITEM "&New", CM_FILENEW, GRAYED
  MENUITEM "&Open", CM_FILEOPEN, GRAYED
  MENUITEM "&Save", CM_FILESAVE, GRAYED
  MENUITEM "Save&As", CM_FILESAVEAS, GRAYED
```

```
    MENUITEM SEPARATOR
    MENUITEM "Short &Menus", CM_SHORTMENU
    MENUITEM SEPARATOR
    MENUITEM "E&xit", CM_EXIT
  }
  POPUP "&Edit"
  {
    MENUITEM "&Undo", CM_EDITUNDO, GRAYED
    MENUITEM SEPARATOR
    MENUITEM "C&ut", CM_EDITCUT
    MENUITEM "C&opy", CM_EDITCOPY
    MENUITEM "&Paste", CM_EDITPASTE
    MENUITEM "&Delete", CM_EDITDELETE, GRAYED
    MENUITEM "&Clear", CM_EDITCLEAR, GRAYED
  }
  MENUITEM "&Help", CM_HELP
}

SHORTMENU MENU
{
  POPUP "&File"
  {
    MENUITEM "&Open", CM_FILEOPEN, GRAYED
    MENUITEM "Save&AS", CM_FILESAVEAS, GRAYED
    MENUITEM SEPARATOR
    MENUITEM "&Long Menus", CM_LONGMENU
    MENUITEM SEPARATOR
    MENUITEM "E&xit", CM_EXIT
  }
  POPUP "&Edit"
  {
    MENUITEM "C&ut", CM_EDITCUT
    MENUITEM "C&opy", CM_EDITCOPY
    MENUITEM "&Paste", CM_EDITPASTE
  }
  MENUITEM "&Help", CM_HELP
}
```

Listing X2.5 shows the contents of the RWMENU1.DEF definition file. This file is typical of the .DEF files presented in earlier chapters

Listing X2.5. The contents of the RWMENU1.DEF definition file.

```
NAME          RwMenu1
DESCRIPTION   'An OWL Windows Application'
EXETYPE       WINDOWS
CODE          PRELOAD MOVEABLE DISCARDABLE
DATA          PRELOAD MOVEABLE MULTIPLE
HEAPSIZE      1024
STACKSIZE     8192
```

Listing X2.6 shows the source code for the RWMENU1.CPP implementation file. This program loads the menu resources `LONGMENU` and `SHORTMENU`. The program starts with the `LONGMENU` resource and enables you to switch between the `SHORTMENU` and `LONGMENU` resources using menu commands. Figure X2.5 shows a sample session with the program RWMENU1.EXE while the long menu is loaded. Figure X2.6 shows a sample session with the program RWMENU1.EXE while the short menu is loaded.

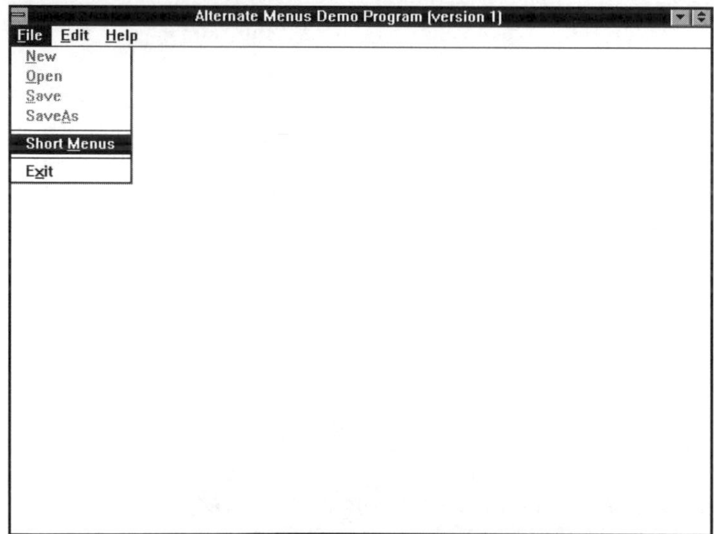

Figure X2.5. *A sample session with the program RWMENU1.EXE while the long menu is loaded.*

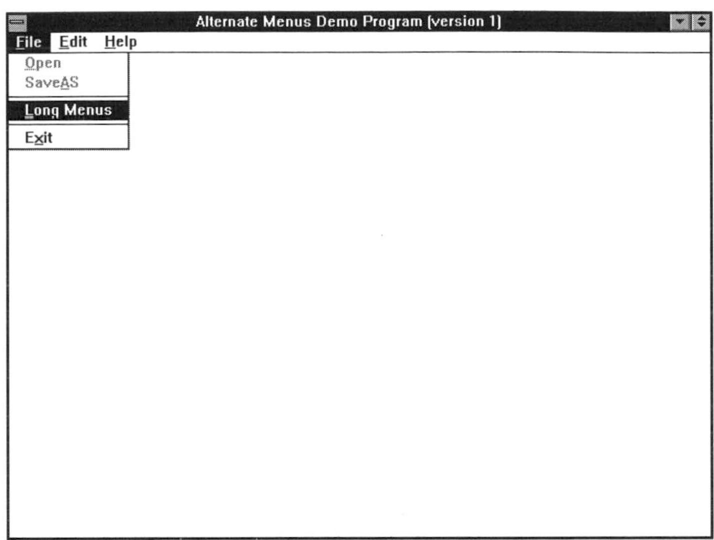

Figure X2.6. *A sample session with the program RWMENU1.EXE while the short menu is loaded.*

Type Listing X2.6. The source code for the RWMENU1.CPP implementation file.

```
/*
  Program that uses alternate menus with minimal response
*/

#include <owl\applicat.h>
#include <owl\framewin.h>
#include "rwmenu1.h"

// declare the custom application class as
// a subclass of TApplication

class TWinApp : public TApplication
{
public:
  TWinApp() : TApplication() {}

protected:
  virtual void InitMainWindow();
};

```

continues

Listing X2.6. continued

```
// expand the functionality of TWindow by deriving class
// TMainWindow
class TMainWindow : public TWindow
{
 public:
   TMainWindow()
     : TWindow(0, 0, 0)
     { LongMenuSelected = TRUE; }

 protected:

   BOOL LongMenuSelected;

   // handle clicking the left mouse button
   void EvLButtonDown(UINT, TPoint&);

   // handle clicking the right mouse button
   void EvRButtonDown(UINT, TPoint&);

   // handle the long menu
   void CMLongMenu();

   // handle the short menu
   void CMShortMenu();

   // handle the help menu
    void CMHelp();

   // handle the Edit Copy menu
   void CMEditCopy();

   // handle the Edit Cut menu
   void CMEditCut();

   // handle the Edit Paste
   void CMEditPaste();

   // display a message "Feature not implemented"
   void notImplemented();

   // handle confirming closing the window
   virtual BOOL CanClose();

   // declare the response table
   DECLARE_RESPONSE_TABLE(TMainWindow);

};
```

```
DEFINE_RESPONSE_TABLE1(TMainWindow, TWindow)
  EV_WM_LBUTTONDOWN,
  EV_WM_RBUTTONDOWN,
  EV_COMMAND(CM_LONGMENU, CMLongMenu),
  EV_COMMAND(CM_SHORTMENU, CMShortMenu),
  EV_COMMAND(CM_HELP, CMHelp),
  EV_COMMAND(CM_EDITCOPY, CMEditCopy),
  EV_COMMAND(CM_EDITCUT, CMEditCut),
  EV_COMMAND(CM_EDITPASTE, CMEditPaste),
END_RESPONSE_TABLE;

void TMainWindow::EvLButtonDown(UINT, TPoint&)
{
  MessageBox("You clicked the left mouse!", "Mouse Event",
             MB_OK | MB_ICONEXCLAMATION);
}

void TMainWindow::EvRButtonDown(UINT, TPoint&)
{
  if (LongMenuSelected)
    CMShortMenu();
  else
    CMLongMenu();
}

void TMainWindow::CMLongMenu()
{
  GetApplication()->MainWindow->AssignMenu(TResID(LONGMENU));
  LongMenuSelected = TRUE;
  MessageBox("The long menu is now active", "Menu Change",
           MB_OK | MB_ICONINFORMATION);
}

// assign the short menu
void TMainWindow::CMShortMenu()
{
  GetApplication()->MainWindow->AssignMenu(TResID(SHORTMENU));
  LongMenuSelected = FALSE;
  MessageBox("The short menu is now active", "Menu Change",
           MB_OK | MB_ICONINFORMATION);}

void TMainWindow::CMEditCut()
{
  notImplemented();
}

void TMainWindow::CMEditCopy()
{
  notImplemented();
}

```

continues

Listing X2.6. continued

```
void TMainWindow::CMEditPaste()
{
  notImplemented();
}

void TMainWindow::CMHelp()
{
  MessageBox(
   "This a sample online help (that leaves more to be desired)",
   "Help", MB_OK | MB_ICONINFORMATION);
}

void TMainWindow::notImplemented()
{
  MessageBox("This feature is not implemented",
           "Information", MB_OK | MB_ICONEXCLAMATION);
}

BOOL TMainWindow::CanClose()
{
  return MessageBox("Want to close this application?",
               "Query", MB_YESNO | MB_ICONQUESTION) == IDYES;
}

void TWinApp::InitMainWindow()
{
  MainWindow = new TFrameWindow(0,
                  "Alternate Menus Demo Program (version 1)",
                      new TMainWindow);
  // load the menu resource
  MainWindow->AssignMenu(TResID(LONGMENU));
}

int OwlMain(int /* argc */, char** /*argv[] */)
{
  TWinApp app;
  return app.Run();
}
```

Creating Accelerator Resources

Let's look at modifying the preceding project to offer accelerators for the Exit, Cut, Copy, and Paste commands. This new program offers the accelerators Alt+X, Ctrl+X, Ctrl+C, and Ctrl+V for the preceding commands, respectively. In addition, the

program has extended menu text for these commands to remind you of the accelerator keys (that is, the hot keys).

You can create the files of the new RWMENU2 from those of RMMENU1. Use the files RWMENU1.IDE, RMENU1.DEF, RMENU1.H, RMENU1.RC, and RMENU1.CPP to create the files RWMENU2.IDE, RMENU2.DEF, RMENU2.H, RMENU2.RC, and RMENU2.CPP, respectively. You need to set up the project by making the following changes:

1. In file RMENU2.DEF, change the project name from RwMenu1 to RwMenu2.
2. In files RMENU2.RC and RWMENU2.CPP, change the name of the header file RWMENU1.H to RWMENU2.H.
3. Delete the files for the target RWMENU1 in the project file RWMENU2.IDE, and then insert the new target RWMENU2.

The preceding steps prepare the files for editing. Load the Resource Workshop by double-clicking the RWMENU2.RC node in the Project window. The Resource Workshop will load the resources in file RWMENU2.RC.

The Resource Workshop utility permits you to insert accelerators in two ways. First, you can create a new accelerator resource that is not explicitly connected with any menu resource. Second, you can incorporate the accelerator resources with the menu. This seems the logical route for the task at hand. For each of the two menu resources, perform the following tasks:

1. Select the targeted menu resource to bring up the MENU dialog box.
2. Select one of the targeted commands (Exit, Cut, Copy, or Paste).
3. Click the Item text edit box and expand the menu text by first adding a few spaces and then typing in the characters for the corresponding accelerator keys. This action enables the menu text to show the associated accelerator keys.
4. Press the Tab key until you select the Key edit box.
5. The dialog box switches into accelerator-input mode and replaces the outline pane with a message pane. This message tells you to enter the accelerator key you want and then press Esc when you are done.
6. Enter the accelerator keys for the currently selected option. Press Esc when you are done.

7. Repeat steps 2 through 6 for the other targeted commands.
8. Invoke the Save project option in the menu File.

The RWMENU2.RC file now contains two accelerator resources, LONGMENU and SHORTMENU. These resources have the same accelerator keys. In addition, the resource file contains modified menu text for the targeted commands.

Compile and run the program RWMENU2.EXE. Press the Ctrl+X, Ctrl+C, or Ctrl+V keys. Notice that the program responds by displaying the message dialog box that tells you that the invoked feature is not implemented. These accelerator keys work with either long or short menu versions. To exit the program, press the Alt+X keys. The program offers a message dialog box to confirm the request to exit.

Listing X2.7 shows the contents of the RWMENU2.DEF definition file. Listing X2.8 shows the source code for the RWMENU2.H header file. Listing X2.9 shows the script of the RWMENU2.RC resource file. Listing X2.10 shows the source code for the RWMENU3.CPP implementation file. Figure X2.7 shows a sample session with the RWMENU2.EXE program.

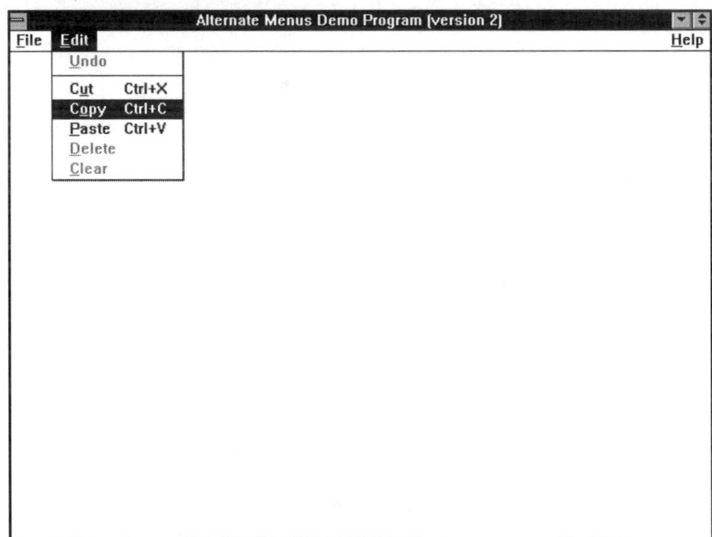

Figure X2.7. *A sample session with the RWMENU2.EXE program.*

Listing X2.7. The contents of the RWMENU2.DEF definition file.

```
NAME          RwMenu2
DESCRIPTION   'An OWL Windows Application'
EXETYPE       WINDOWS
CODE          PRELOAD MOVEABLE DISCARDABLE
DATA          PRELOAD MOVEABLE MULTIPLE
HEAPSIZE      1024
STACKSIZE     8192
```

Listing X2.8. The source code for the RWMENU2.H header file.

```
#define LONGMENU          101
#define SHORTMENU         102
#define CM_LONGMENU       1
#define CM_POPUPITEM      101
#define CM_HELP           8
#define CM_EDITCLEAR      7
#define CM_EDITDELETE     6
#define CM_EDITPASTE      5
#define CM_EDITCOPY       4
#define CM_EDITCUT        3
#define CM_EDITUNDO       105
#define CM_SHORTMENU      9
#define CM_FILENEW        106
#define CM_FILESAVEAS     104
#define CM_FILESAVE       103
#define CM_FILEOPEN       102
```

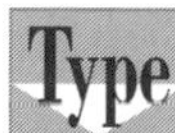

Listing X2.9. The script of the RWMENU2.RC resource file.

```
#include <windows.h>
#include <owl\window.rh>
#include "rwmenu2.h"

LONGMENU MENU
{
 POPUP "&File"
 {
  MENUITEM "&New", CM_FILENEW, GRAYED
  MENUITEM "&Open", CM_FILEOPEN, GRAYED
```

continues

Listing X2.9. continued

```
    MENUITEM "&Save", CM_FILESAVE, GRAYED
    MENUITEM "Save&As", CM_FILESAVEAS, GRAYED
    MENUITEM SEPARATOR
    MENUITEM "Short &Menus", CM_SHORTMENU
    MENUITEM SEPARATOR
    MENUITEM "E&xit    ALT+X", CM_EXIT
  }

  POPUP "&Edit"
  {
    MENUITEM "&Undo", CM_EDITUNDO, GRAYED
    MENUITEM SEPARATOR
    MENUITEM "C&ut       CTRL+X", CM_EDITCUT
    MENUITEM "C&opy    CTRL+C", CM_EDITCOPY
    MENUITEM "&Paste   CTRL+V", CM_EDITPASTE
    MENUITEM "&Delete", CM_EDITDELETE, GRAYED
    MENUITEM "&Clear", CM_EDITCLEAR, GRAYED
  }

  MENUITEM "&Help", CM_HELP, HELP
}


SHORTMENU MENU
{
  POPUP "&File"
  {
    MENUITEM "&Open", CM_FILEOPEN, GRAYED
    MENUITEM "Save&AS", CM_FILESAVEAS, GRAYED
    MENUITEM SEPARATOR
    MENUITEM "&Long Menus", CM_LONGMENU
    MENUITEM SEPARATOR
    MENUITEM "E&xit   ALT+X", CM_EXIT
  }

  POPUP "&Edit"
  {
    MENUITEM "C&ut       CTRL+X", CM_EDITCUT
    MENUITEM "C&opy    CTRL+C", CM_EDITCOPY
    MENUITEM "&Paste   CTRL+V", CM_EDITPASTE
  }

  MENUITEM "&Help", CM_HELP, HELP
}



LONGMENU ACCELERATORS
{
```

```
  "^X", CM_EDITCUT
  "^C", CM_EDITCOPY
  "^V", CM_EDITPASTE
  "x", CM_EXIT, ASCII, ALT
}

SHORTMENU ACCELERATORS
{
  "x", CM_EXIT, ASCII, ALT
  "^X", CM_EDITCUT
  "^C", CM_EDITCOPY
  "^V", CM_EDITPASTE, ASCII
}
```

Type

Listing X2.10. The source code for the RWMENU2.CPP implementation file.

```
/*
  Program which uses alternate menus with minimal response
*/

#include <owl\applicat.h>
#include <owl\framewin.h>
#include "rwmenu2.h"

// declare the custom application class as
// a subclass of TApplication
class TWinApp : public TApplication
{
public:
  TWinApp() : TApplication() {}

protected:
  virtual void InitMainWindow();
};

// expand the functionality of TWindow by deriving
// class TMainWindow
class TMainWindow : public TWindow
{
 public:
   TMainWindow()
     : TWindow(0, 0, 0)
     { LongMenuSelected = TRUE; }

 protected:

```

continues

Listing X2.10. continued

```
    BOOL LongMenuSelected;

    // handle clicking the left mouse button
    void EvLButtonDown(UINT, TPoint&);

    // handle clicking the right mouse button
    void EvRButtonDown(UINT, TPoint&);

    // handle the long menu
    void CMLongMenu();

    // handle the short menu
    void CMShortMenu();

    // handle the help menu
     void CMHelp();

    // handle the Edit Copy menu
    void CMEditCopy();

    // handle the Edit Cut menu
    void CMEditCut();

    // handle the Edit Paste
    void CMEditPaste();

    // display a message "Feature not implemented"
    void notImplemented();

    // handle confirming closing the window
    virtual BOOL CanClose();

    // declare the response table
    DECLARE_RESPONSE_TABLE(TMainWindow);

};

DEFINE_RESPONSE_TABLE1(TMainWindow, TWindow)
  EV_WM_LBUTTONDOWN,
  EV_WM_RBUTTONDOWN,
  EV_COMMAND(CM_LONGMENU, CMLongMenu),
  EV_COMMAND(CM_SHORTMENU, CMShortMenu),
  EV_COMMAND(CM_HELP, CMHelp),
  EV_COMMAND(CM_EDITCOPY, CMEditCopy),
  EV_COMMAND(CM_EDITCUT, CMEditCut),
  EV_COMMAND(CM_EDITPASTE, CMEditPaste),
END_RESPONSE_TABLE;
```

```
void TMainWindow::EvLButtonDown(UINT, TPoint&)
{
  MessageBox("You clicked the left mouse!", "Mouse Event",
             MB_OK | MB_ICONEXCLAMATION);
}

void TMainWindow::EvRButtonDown(UINT, TPoint&)
{
  if (LongMenuSelected)
    CMShortMenu();
  else
    CMLongMenu();
}

void TMainWindow::CMLongMenu()
{
  GetApplication()->MainWindow->AssignMenu(TResID(LONGMENU));
  GetApplication()->MainWindow->Attr.AccelTable =
                                            TResID(LONGMENU);
  LongMenuSelected = TRUE;
  MessageBox("The long menu is now active", "Menu Change",
           MB_OK | MB_ICONINFORMATION);
}

// assign the short menu
void TMainWindow::CMShortMenu()
{
  GetApplication()->MainWindow->AssignMenu(TResID(SHORTMENU));
  GetApplication()->MainWindow->Attr.AccelTable =
                                              TResID(SHORTMENU);
  LongMenuSelected = FALSE;
  MessageBox("The short menu is now active", "Menu Change",
           MB_OK | MB_ICONINFORMATION);}

void TMainWindow::CMEditCut()
{
  notImplemented();
}

void TMainWindow::CMEditCopy()
{
  notImplemented();
}

void TMainWindow::CMEditPaste()
{
  notImplemented();
}

void TMainWindow::CMHelp()
{
```

continues

Listing X2.10. continued

```
    MessageBox(
     "This a sample online help (that leaves more to be desired)",
     "Help", MB_OK | MB_ICONINFORMATION);
}

void TMainWindow::notImplemented()
{
  MessageBox("This feature is not implemented",
             "Information", MB_OK | MB_ICONEXCLAMATION);
}

BOOL TMainWindow::CanClose()
{
  return MessageBox("Want to close this application?",
                 "Query", MB_YESNO | MB_ICONQUESTION) == IDYES;
}

void TWinApp::InitMainWindow()
{
  MainWindow = new TFrameWindow(0,
                "Alternate Menus Demo Program (version 2)",
                new TMainWindow);
  // load the menu resource
  MainWindow->AssignMenu(TResID(LONGMENU));
  MainWindow->Attr.AccelTable = TResID(LONGMENU);
}

int OwlMain(int /* argc */, char** /*argv[] */)
{
  TWinApp app;
  return app.Run();
}
```

The header file RWMENU2.H has the same declarations as the file RWMENU1.H because the menu systems in the projects RWMENU1 and RWMENU2 are the same. The resource file RWMENU2.RC differs from the file RWMENU1.RC in the following ways:

1. The new resource file includes the header file RWMENU2.H, instead of the file RWMENU1.H.
2. The commands Exit, Cut, Copy, and Paste in the new resource file have extended menu text.
3. The `LONGMENU` accelerators resource defines the accelerator keys for the commands `CM_EDITCUT`, `CM_EDITCOPY`, `CM_EDITPASTE`, and `CM_EXIT`.

4. The `SHORTMENU` accelerators resource defines the accelerator keys for the commands `CM_EDITCUT`, `CM_EDITCOPY`, `CM_EDITPASTE`, and `CM_EXIT`.

The implementation file RWMENU2.CPP contains the C++ source code for the program. The statements in this file are similar to those in the file RWMENU1.CPP. The relevant differences between the two implementation files are as follows:

1. The statement at line 96 in member function `CMLongMenu` is new. This statement loads the accelerator-key resource `LONGMENU`. This statement keeps the selection of the menu and the accelerators resource in sync with each other.

2. The statement at line 107 in member function `CMShortMenu` is new. This statement loads the accelerator-key resource `SHORTMENU`. This statement keeps the selection of the menu and the accelerators resource in sync with each other.

3. The statement at line 149 in the member function `InitMainWindow` has a different window title.

4. The statement at line 154 in the member function `InitMainWindow` is new. The function `LoadAccelerators` loads the accelerator-key resource `LONGMENU`.

Creating Icon Resources

The Resource Workshop enables you to create icon resources using the following steps:

1. Select the New... command in the Resource menu. This command brings up the New resource dialog box.

2. Choose the ICON item in the Resource-type list box of the New resource dialog box.

3. Click the OK button in the New resource dialog box.

4. The Resource Workshop displays a message box asking you whether you want to create the resource in readable source or binary form. To create the icon resource in source form, click the Source pushbutton. To create the icon resource in binary form, click the Binary pushbutton control. The remaining steps focus on the binary form.

5. The Resource Workshop displays the New File Resource dialog box (see Figure X2.8), which enables you to select the following items:

- ☐ The resource filename.
- ☐ The resource file type. Select the .RC file type.
- ☐ The filename that contains the reference to the resource you are creating.
- ☐ The host drive and directory.

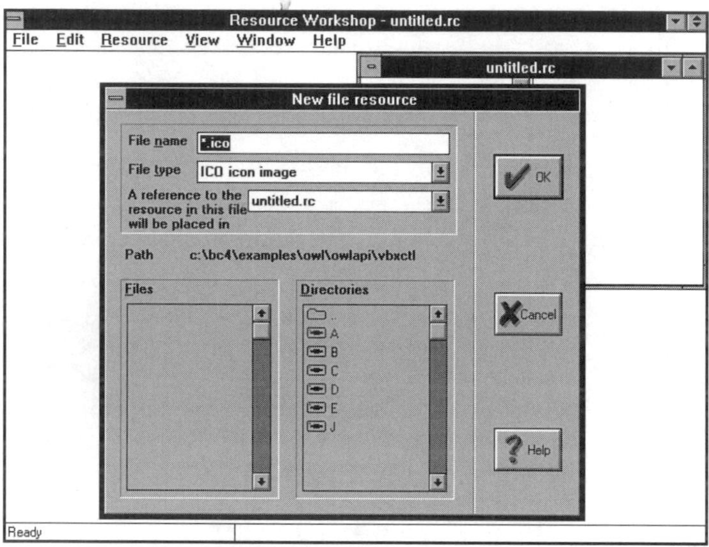

Figure X2.8. *A sample session with Resource Workshop showing the New file resource dialog box.*

6. When you finish working with the New file resource dialog box, click its OK pushbutton.
7. The Resource Workshop displays a relatively small New icon image dialog box, which contains two sets of radio buttons. The first set enables you to specify the size of the icon (a choice between 32×32, 32×16, or 64×64 pixels). The normal size is 32×32 pixels. The set of radio buttons enables you to choose a palette of 2, 8, 16, or 256 colors. (The latter option may be disabled for your system). Select the size and color settings, then click the OK pushbutton.
8. The Resource Workshop displays the Paint editor. Figure X2.9 shows a sample session with the Paint editor. The editor has two panes. The edit pane is located to the left and displays the icon at different zoom levels.

From the View menu, you can use the Zoom In, Zoom Out, and Actual Size commands to magnify the icon, demagnify the icon, or view the icon in its actual size. The preview pane, which is located to the right, always shows the icon in its actual size. Initially, the Resource Workshop displays the Colors and Tools palettes in the preview pane. The Colors palette displays the available colors and enables you to select the foreground and background colors. To select the foreground color, move the mouse over the color you want to select and click the left mouse button. To select the background color, move the mouse over the color you want to select and click the right mouse button. The Colors palette displays the following color-selection indicators:

- The letters FG appear inside the foreground color.
- The letters BK appear inside the background color.
- The letters BF appear inside the color that is both the foreground and background colors.

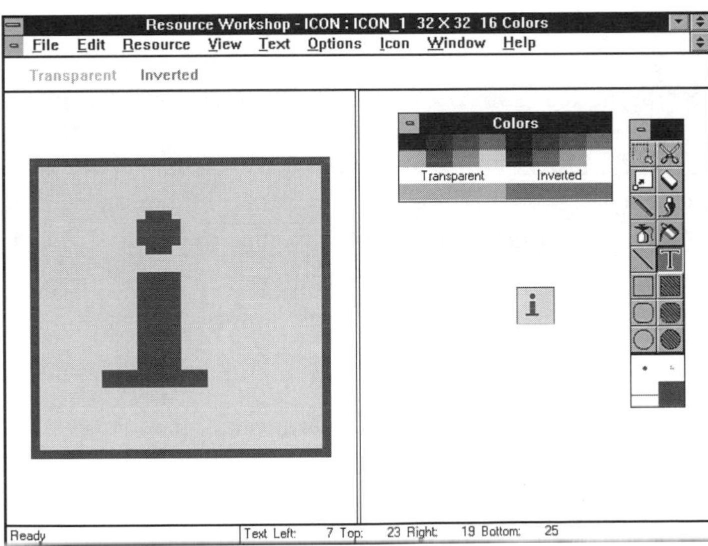

Figure X2.9. *A sample session with the Paint editor.*

The Tools palette resembles those in Paintbrush and includes the following:

- Tools to cut and move bitmaps.
- A tool to erase bitmaps.

- Tools to draw pixels, lines, empty rectangles (both sharp and rounded-edge rectangles), empty circles, full rectangles (both sharp and rounded-edge rectangles), and full circles.
- Airbrush, paintbrush, and paint-can tools.
- A tool to enter text.
- A zoom tool.

9. Draw the icon using the various colors and tools.
10. Save the icon by saving the project.

Creating Dialog-Box Resources

The ability of the Resource Workshop to create dialog boxes containing various controls represents an important aspect of visual programming. Although creating menus and accelerator resources involves working with special dialog boxes, creating dialog box resources involves the actual drawing of the controls pasted onto the dialog box.

To create a new dialog box resource in the Resource Workshop, you begin as with any new resource—by selecting the command New... from the Resource menu. Then you select the DIALOG resource type from Resource-type list box in the New resource dialog box. After you click the OK pushbutton of this dialog box, the Resource Workshop brings up the DialogExpert dialog box. This dialog box enables you to select one of the following kinds of dialog-box resources:

- Windows dialog box with standard buttons at the bottom
- Windows dialog box with standard buttons near the right edge
- Borland dialog box with standard buttons at the bottom
- Borland dialog box with standard buttons near the right edge
- Child dialog box with no buttons
- Standard window with no buttons

When you click the OK button of the DialogExpert dialog box, the Resource Workshop brings up the Dialog editor. Figure X2.10 shows a sample session with the Dialog editor.

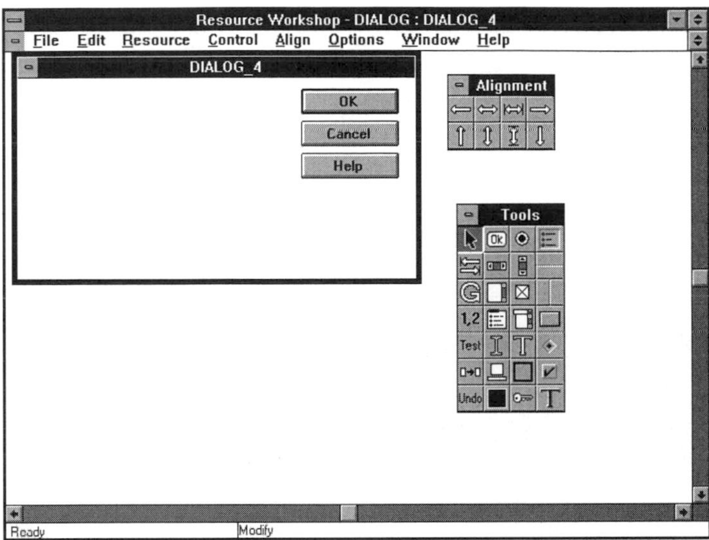

Figure X2.10. *A sample session with the Dialog editor.*

The Dialog editor displays the dialog-box resource in its initial state (this includes the default buttons, location, and size) along with the Alignment palette and the Tools palette. You can move and resize the dialog box using the mouse to accommodate the required size and location.

To rename a resource dialog box (or any other resource), use the Rename... command in the Resource menu. This option brings up an input dialog box that enables you to enter the new resource name.

The Tools Palette

The Tools palette offers the tools to draw and manage the various controls in the dialog-box resource. The Tools palette supports the following controls:

- Windows static text
- Borland static text
- Iconic static control
- Black frame static (text) control
- Black rectangle static (text) control

- Windows pushbutton
- Borland pushbutton
- Edit text control
- Group box
- Check box
- Radio button
- Vertical scroll bar
- Horizontal scroll bar
- List box
- Combo box
- Custom controls
- Vertical dip
- Horizontal dip

Other tools enable you to manage the creating of the dialog-box resources by supporting the following operations:

- Setting the tab order of the controls
- Enabling and disabling tabbing to a control
- Group selection and shading
- Duplicating controls
- Undoing the last action
- Testing the dialog box

Using the Dialog editor is fairly intuitive.

The Alignment Palette

The Alignment palette contains a set of tools that enable you to align the controls in the dialog box. In order to align multiple controls, you need to select them. This process involves clicking each of the controls while holding down the Shift key. This process creates a red selection frame that defines metrics for the aligned controls. The Alignment tools support the following operations:

- Aligning the selected controls so their left sides are on the left side of the selection frame.
- Aligning the selected controls so their right sides are on the left side of the selection frame.
- Aligning the selected controls so their horizontal centers are in the center of the selection frame.
- Moving the selection frame horizontally to center it in the dialog box. This operation maintains the relative position of the selected controls in the frame.
- Aligning the selected controls so their tops are at the top of the selection frame.
- Aligning the selected controls so their bottoms are at the bottom of the selection frame.
- Aligning the selected controls so their vertical centers are in the center of the selection frame.
- Moving the selection frame vertically to center it in the dialog box. This operation maintains the relative position of the selected controls in the framc.

Creating a Bare-Bones Dialog-Box Resource

Let's look at a simple program that brings up bare-bones dialog boxes. The next project, RWDLG1, implements a simple Windows program that responds to the left and right mouse clicks by displaying custom message dialog boxes created by the Resource Workshop.

First, let's peek at the listings to make setting up the project a bit easier. Listing X2.11 shows the contents of the RWDLG1.DEF definition file. Listing X2.12 shows the source code for the RWDLG1.H header file. Listing X2.13 shows the script of the RWDLG1.RC resource file. Listing X2.14 shows the source code for the RWDLG1.CPP implementation file.

Prepare the files RWDLG1.DEF, RWDLG1.H, and RWDLG1.CPP by typing the contents shown in their respective listings. By contrast, type only the `#include` directive and the menu resource in the RWDLG1.RC; do not type the dialog-box resources. Create the new RWDLG1 project and include the preceding files. Now you are ready to invoke the Resource Workshop.

Use the Resource Workshop to create the resource `IDD_LCKICK_DLG`. (This resource starts out with the default name `DIALOG_1`, which you need to change.) Create a Windows dialog box with the buttons located near the bottom edge. The Dialog editor brings up the initial dialog box with the default set of buttons OK, Cancel, and Help. Delete the latter two, first by clicking them with the mouse and then pressing the Delete key. You can use the Shift key to obtain multiple selections that can be deleted in one swoop.

Create the new dialog box with the Modal frame, Pop-up, Visible, Caption, and System menu styles. The caption of the dialog box is Mouse Event. The dialog box has two controls, as follows:

1. The OK pushbutton, which the Resource Workshop inserts by default.
2. The static text control, which features the centered text "You clicked the left button!"

Figure X2.11 shows a session with the Dialog editor while the `IDD_LCLICK_DLG` dialog-box resource is created.

Now create the other dialog-box resource, `IDD_RCLICK_DLG`, in a manner similar to the resource `IDD_LCLICK_DLG`. The second dialog box differs from the first in its name and in the static text message. When you are done, save both new dialog-box resources (by saving the project). Compile and run the program. Click in the client window area with the left or right mouse buttons. Observe how the program displays the dialog boxes you created in the Resource Workshop. Figure X2.12 shows a sample session with the RWDLG1.EXE program.

Listing X2.11. The contents of the RWDLG1.DEF definition file.

```
NAME         RwDlg1
DESCRIPTION  'An OWL Windows Application'
EXETYPE      WINDOWS
CODE         PRELOAD MOVEABLE DISCARDABLE
DATA         PRELOAD MOVEABLE MULTIPLE
HEAPSIZE     1024
STACKSIZE    8192
```

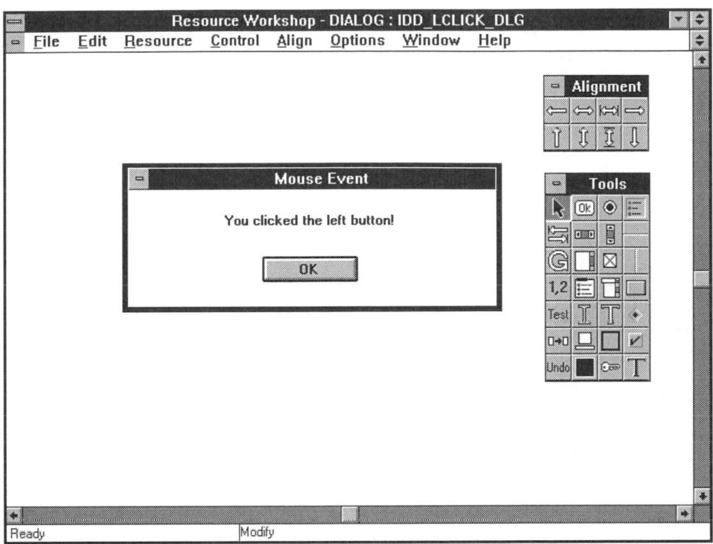

Figure X2.11. *A session with the Dialog editor while creating the IDD_LCLICK_DLG dialog-box resource.*

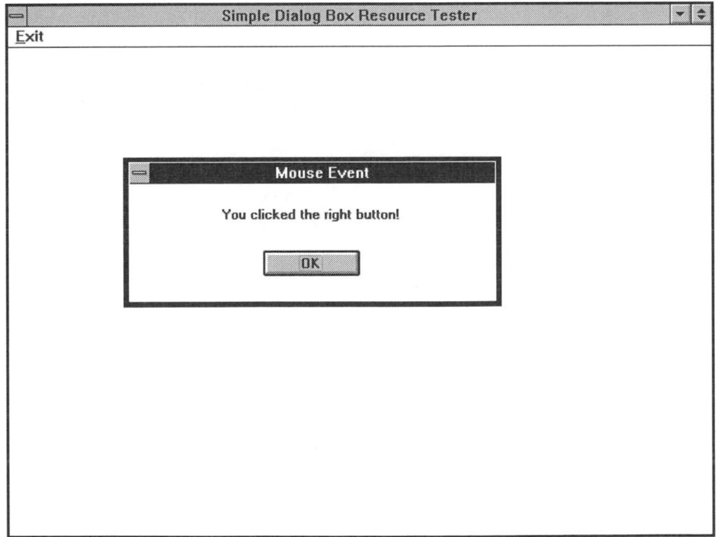

Figure X2.12. *A sample session with the RWDLG1.EXE program.*

Listing X2.12. The source code for the RWDLG1.H header file.

```
#define IDD_LCLICK_DLG  100
#define IDD_RCLICK_DLG  101
#define EXITMENU        102
```

Listing X2.13. The script of the RWDLG1.RC resource file.

```
#include <windows.h>
#include <owl\window.rh>
#include "rwdlg1.h"

IDD_LCLICK_DLG DIALOG 63, 76, 191, 65
STYLE DS_MODALFRAME ¦ WS_POPUP ¦ WS_VISIBLE ¦
      WS_CAPTION ¦ WS_SYSMENU
CAPTION "Mouse Event"
FONT 8, "MS Sans Serif"
{
 DEFPUSHBUTTON "OK", IDOK, 70, 37, 50, 14
 CTEXT "You clicked the left button!", -1, 18, 13, 154, 10
}

IDD_RCLICK_DLG DIALOG 63, 76, 191, 65
STYLE DS_MODALFRAME ¦ WS_POPUP ¦ WS_VISIBLE ¦
      WS_CAPTION ¦ WS_SYSMENU
CAPTION "Mouse Event"
FONT 8, "MS Sans Serif"
{
 DEFPUSHBUTTON "OK", IDOK, 70, 37, 50, 14
 CTEXT "You clicked the right button!", -1, 18, 13, 154, 10
}

EXITMENU MENU
{
 MENUITEM "&Exit", CM_EXIT
}
```

Listing X2.14. The source code for the RWDLG1.CPP implementation file.

```
/*
  Program that tests simple dialog resources
*/

#include <owl\applicat.h>
#include <owl\framewin.h>
```

```
#include <owl\dialog.h>
#include "rwdlg1.h"

// declare the custom application class as
// a subclass of TApplication

class TWinApp : public TApplication
{
public:
  TWinApp() : TApplication() {}

protected:
  virtual void InitMainWindow();
};

// expand the functionality of TWindow by deriving
// class TMainWindow
class TMainWindow : public TWindow
{
 public:
   TMainWindow() : TWindow(0, 0, 0) {}

 protected:

   // handle clicking the left mouse button
   void EvLButtonDown(UINT, TPoint&);

   // handlc clicking the right mouse button
   void EvRButtonDown(UINT, TPoint&);

   // handle confirming closing the window
   virtual BOOL CanClose();

   // declare the response table
   DECLARE_RESPONSE_TABLE(TMainWindow);

};

DEFINE_RESPONSE_TABLE1(TMainWindow, TWindow)
  EV_WM_LBUTTONDOWN,
  EV_WM_RBUTTONDOWN,
END_RESPONSE_TABLE;

void TMainWindow::EvLButtonDown(UINT, TPoint&)
{
  TDialog* pDlg = new TDialog(this, TResID(IDD_LCLICK_DLG));

  pDlg->Execute();
}

```

continues

Listing X2.14. continued

```
void TMainWindow::EvRButtonDown(UINT, TPoint&)
{
  TDialog* pDlg = new TDialog(this, TResID(IDD_RCLICK_DLG));

  pDlg->Execute();
}

BOOL TMainWindow::CanClose()
{
  return MessageBox("Want to close this application?",
                    "Query", MB_YESNO | MB_ICONQUESTION) == IDYES;
}

void TWinApp::InitMainWindow()
{
  MainWindow = new TFrameWindow(0,
                          "Simple Dialog Box Resource Tester",
                          new TMainWindow);
  // load the menu resource
  MainWindow->AssignMenu(TResID(EXITMENU));
}

int OwlMain(int /* argc */, char** /*argv[] */)
{
  TWinApp app;
  return app.Run();
}
```

Listing X2.13 shows the script for the resource file RWDLG1.RC. This file contains the script for the two dialog-box resources, `IDD_LCLICK_DLG` and `IDD_RCLICK_DLG`. The coordinates, widths, and heights of the two dialog boxes and their controls may not match. (In Listing X2.13, they do.) To make them match, you can edit the resource script to duplicate the locations and dimensions of the dialog boxes and their controls. This little trick enables you to smooth the visual design of dialog boxes and their controls.

The implementation source code in Listing X2.14 is simple. The main window class, `TMainWindow`, responds to the left and right mouse clicks using the member functions `EvLButtonDown` and `EvRButtonDown`, respectively. The member function `EvLButtonDown` creates a dialog box using the OWL class `TDialog` and the resource `IDD_LCLICK_DLG`. To invoke the dialog box, the member function sends the C++ message `Execute` (which invokes a modal dialog box) to the dialog-box object, accessed using the local pointer `pDlg`. The member function `EvRButtonDown` performs a similar task to invoke the dialog-box resource `IDD_RCLICK_DLG`.

Creating Dialog-Box Resources with Basic Controls

Let's look at another example of a dialog-box resource. The next project, RWDLG2, creates and displays a dialog box that represents a *dummy* simple calculator. We say dummy because the implementation program does not *animate* the custom dialog-box class. This means that clicking the buttons of the calculator does not perform the anticipated operations. (What a letdown!) This does not mean that the calculator dialog box is doing absolutely nothing. The dialog box is reacting minimally by emulating the button-down action when you click a button. You can also enter, edit, and select text in the edit box control that emulates the calculator's display. Figure X2.13 shows a sample session with the RWDLG2.EXE program. As the figure shows, the calculator dialog box has the digits, decimal, clear, change of sign, basic math operations, and Close buttons. (The latter button is really the OK button appearing with a different caption.) To close the dialog box, click the Close button.

First, let's peek at the listings to make setting up the project a bit easier. Listing X2.15 shows the contents of the RWDLG2.DEF definition file. Listing X2.16 contains the source code for the RWDLG2.H header file. Listing X2.17 contains the script of the RWDLG2.RC resource file. Listing X2.18 contains the source code for the RWDLG2.CPP implementation file.

Prepare the files RWDLG2.DEF, RWDLG2.H, and RWDLG2.CPP by typing the contents shown in their respective listings. By contrast, type only the `#include` directive and the menu resource in the RWDLG2.RC; do not type the dialog-box resources. Create the new RWDLG2 project and include the preceding files. Now you are ready to invoke the Resource Workshop.

Use the Resource Workshop to create the resource `IDD_CALC_DLG`. (This resource starts out with the default name `DIALOG_1`, which you need to change.) Create a Windows dialog box with the buttons located near the bottom edge. The Dialog edit brings up the initial dialog box with the default set of buttons OK, Cancel, and Help. Delete the latter two by clicking them with the mouse and then pressing the Delete key.

Create the new dialog box with the Modal frame, Pop-up, Visible, Caption, and System menu styles. The caption of the dialog box is Dummy Calculator. The dialog box has the following sets of controls:

1. The Close pushbutton, which is really the OK button renamed. This button is the default pushbutton.

2. The edit box control with the text "Major Malfunction!" This control has the style options Tab stop, Border, and Automatic horizontal scroll.
3. The pushbutton controls for the digits and operators. Make each of these buttons ordinary pushbuttons (and not the default pushbutton). Use the identifiers in the file RWDLG2.H for the various controls. For example, the digit button 1 has the identifier `IDC_1`.

The process of creating the above controls involves selecting them from the Tools palette and then drawing them. Because there are many pushbutton controls, you can use the Copy and Paste commands (in the Edit menu) to create these controls. You will probably need to use the Alignment palette to align the rows and columns of the buttons. Figure X2.13 shows a session with the Dialog editor while creating the `IDD_LCLICK_DLG` dialog box resource. The figure shows the configuration and location of the various controls. When you are done, save the new dialog-box resource (by saving the project). Compile and run the program. Click the Calc menu to bring up the calculator resource dialog box. Click the digit and operators pushbuttons and observe how they simulate pushing these buttons down. You can also type and edit text in the edit text control. When you are done, click the Close pushbutton to close the dialog box. Figure X2.14 shows a sample session with the RWDLG2.EXE program.

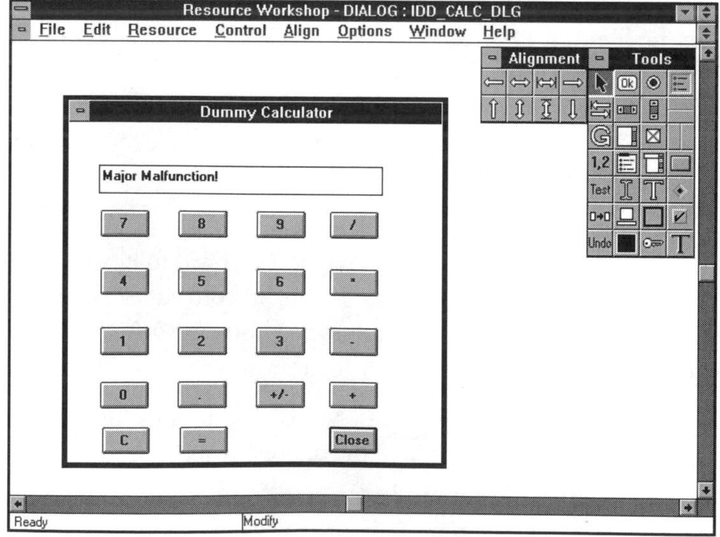

Figure X2.13. *A sample session with the Dialog editor while creating the calculator dialog-box resource.*

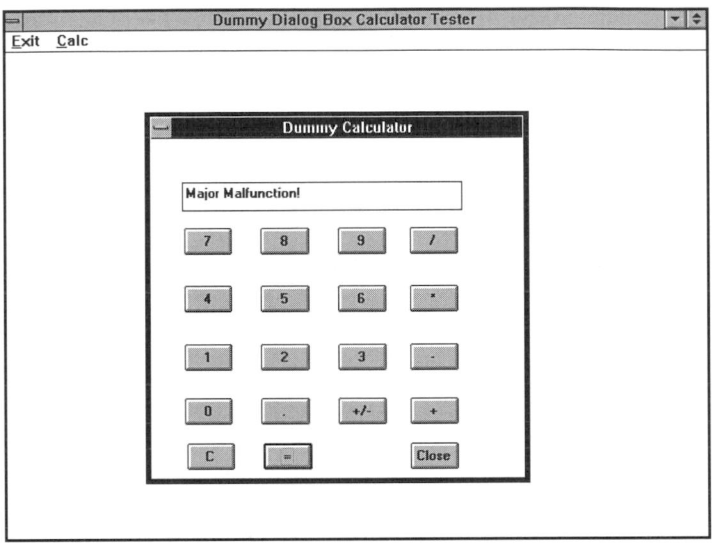

Figure X2.14. *A sample session with the RWDLG2.EXE program.*

Listing X2.15. The contents of the RWDLG2.DEF definition file.

```
NAME            RwDlg2
DESCRIPTION     'An OWL Windows Application'
EXETYPE         WINDOWS
CODE            PRELOAD MOVEABLE DISCARDABLE
DATA            PRELOAD MOVEABLE MULTIPLE
HEAPSIZE        1024
STACKSIZE       8192
```

Listing X2.16. The source code for the RWDLG2.H header file.

```
#define IDC_0               100
#define IDC_1               101
#define IDC_2               102
#define IDC_3               103
#define IDC_4               104
#define IDC_5               105
#define IDC_6               106
#define IDC_7               107
```

continues

Listing X2.16. continued

```
#define IDC_8                108
#define IDC_9                109
#define IDC_CLEAR            110
#define IDC_ADD              111
#define IDC_CHS              112
#define IDC_DOT              113
#define IDC_SUB              114
#define IDC_MUL              115
#define IDC_DIV              116
#define IDC_EQL              117
#define IDC_EDIT1            118
#define CM_CALC              200
#define EXITMENU             201
#define IDD_CALC_DLG         202
```

Listing X2.17. The script of the RWDLG2.RC resource file.

```
#include <windows.h>
#include <owl\window.rh>
#include "rwdlg2.h"

IDD_CALC_DLG DIALOG 6, 15, 194, 189
STYLE DS_MODALFRAME | WS_POPUP | WS_VISIBLE | WS_CAPTION |
      WS_SYSMENU
CAPTION "Dummy Calculator"
FONT 8, "MS Sans Serif"
{
 DEFPUSHBUTTON "Close", IDOK, 135, 169, 25, 15
 PUSHBUTTON "7", IDC_7, 17, 49, 25, 15
 PUSHBUTTON "8", IDC_8, 57, 49, 25, 15
 PUSHBUTTON "9", IDC_9, 97, 49, 25, 15
 PUSHBUTTON "/", IDC_DIV, 135, 49, 25, 15
 PUSHBUTTON "4", IDC_4, 17, 81, 25, 15
 PUSHBUTTON "5", IDC_5, 57, 81, 25, 15
 PUSHBUTTON "6", IDC_6, 97, 81, 25, 15
 PUSHBUTTON "*", IDC_MUL, 135, 81, 25, 15
 PUSHBUTTON "1", IDC_1, 17, 114, 25, 15
 PUSHBUTTON "2", IDC_2, 57, 114, 25, 15
 PUSHBUTTON "3", IDC_3, 97, 114, 25, 15
 PUSHBUTTON "-", IDC_SUB, 135, 114, 25, 15
 PUSHBUTTON "0", IDC_0, 17, 144, 25, 15
 PUSHBUTTON ".", IDC_DOT, 57, 144, 25, 15
 PUSHBUTTON "+/-", IDC_CHS, 97, 144, 25, 15
 PUSHBUTTON "+", IDC_ADD, 135, 144, 25, 15
 PUSHBUTTON "C", IDC_CLEAR, 18, 169, 25, 15
 PUSHBUTTON "=", IDC_EQL, 58, 169, 25, 15
 CONTROL "Major Malfunction!", IDC_EDIT1, "EDIT",
```

```
          ES_AUTOHSCROLL | WS_BORDER | WS_TABSTOP,
          16, 24, 146, 16
}

EXITMENU MENU
{
 MENUITEM "&Exit", CM_EXIT
 MENUITEM "&Calc", CM_CALC
}
```

Listing X2.18. The source code for the RWDLG2.CPP implementation file.

```
/*
  Program that tests simple dialog resources
*/

#include <owl\applicat.h>
#include <owl\framewin.h>
#include <owl\dialog.h>
#include "rwdlg2.h"

// declare the custom application class as
// a subclass of TApplication

class TWinApp : public TApplication
{
public:
  TWinApp() : TApplication() {}

protected:
  virtual void InitMainWindow();
};

// expand the functionality of TWindow by deriving
//  class TMainWindow
class TMainWindow : public TWindow
{
 public:
   TMainWindow() : TWindow(0, 0, 0) {}

 protected:

   // handle the Calc menu
   void CMCalc();

   // handle confirming closing the window
   virtual BOOL CanClose();

```

continues

Listing X2.18. continued

```
    // declare the response table
    DECLARE_RESPONSE_TABLE(TMainWindow);

};

DEFINE_RESPONSE_TABLE1(TMainWindow, TWindow)
  EV_COMMAND(CM_CALC, CMCalc),
END_RESPONSE_TABLE;

void TMainWindow::CMCalc()
{
  TDialog* pDlg = new TDialog(this, TResID(IDD_CALC_DLG));

  pDlg->Execute();
}

BOOL TMainWindow::CanClose()
{
  return MessageBox("Want to close this application?",
            "Query", MB_YESNO ¦ MB_ICONQUESTION) == IDYES;
}

void TWinApp::InitMainWindow()
{
  MainWindow = new TFrameWindow(0,
                     "Dummy Dialog Box Calculator Tester",
                     new TMainWindow);
  // load the menu resource
  MainWindow->AssignMenu(TResID(EXITMENU));
}

int OwlMain(int /* argc */, char** /*argv[] */)
{
  TWinApp app;
  return app.Run();
}
```

Listing X2.16 shows the RWDLG2.H header file, which contains the definitions of the identifiers for the dialog box, its controls, and the menu resources.

Listing X2.17 contains the RWDLG2.RC resource file, which contains the dialog box and menu resources. The dialog-box resource shows that there is one default pushbutton with the label Close and the ID `OK`. The other pushbutton controls are declared as nondefault controls and have the appropriate labels and IDs.

Listing X2.18 shows the source code for the implementation file RWDLG2.CPP. The file declares the application class, `TWinApp`, and the main window class, `TMainWindow`. The most relevant member function of the latter class is the function `CMCalc`, which responds to the `CM_CALC` Windows command message sent by the menu `Calc`. The function creates a dynamic instance of the dialog class `TDialog` and specifies the dialog-box resource `IDD_CALC_DLG`. The function then invokes this dialog box by sending the C++ message `Execute` to the dialog-box instance (accessed using the local pointer `pDlg`).

Creating Dialog-Box Resources with Grouped Controls

Let's look at an example of a dialog-box resource that contains grouped controls—group boxes, check boxes, and radio buttons. The next project, RWDLG3, creates resource dialog boxes for typical Find and Replace dialog boxes. Such dialog boxes are available in typical Windows text editors, including the IDE's editor. The Find dialog box that is implemented in project RWDLG3 contains the following controls:

- The edit text control, which holds the search string
- The static text control, which labels the edit control
- The Options group box, which contains the following check boxes:
    - The Whole Word check box
    - The Case Sensitive check box
    - The Prompt check box
- The Directions group box, which contains the following radio buttons:
    - The Forward radio button
    - The Backward radio button
    - The Entire radio button
- The Find Next pushbutton (which is the OK button renamed)
- The Cancel pushbutton
- The Help button

The Replace dialog box has these controls plus the following ones:

- The edit text control, to enter the replacement string
- The static text control, which labels the preceding control
- The Replace pushbutton
- The Replace All pushbutton

Let's look at the listings to make setting up the project a bit easier. Listing X2.19 shows the contents of the RWDLG3.DEF definition file. Listing X2.20 shows the source code for the RWDLG3.H header file. Listing X2.21 shows the script of the RWDLG3.RC resource file. Listing X2.22 shows the source code for the RWDLG3.CPP implementation file.

Prepare the files RWDLG3.DEF, RWDLG3.H, and RWDLG3.CPP by typing the contents shown in their respective listings. By contrast, type in only the `#include` directive and the menu resource in the RWDLG3.RC; do not type the dialog-box resources. Create the new RWDLG3 project and include the above files. Now you are ready to invoke the Resource Workshop.

Use the Resource Workshop to create the resource `IDD_FIND_DLG`. (This resource starts out with the default name `DIALOG_1`, which you need to change.) Create a Windows dialog box with the buttons located near the bottom edge. The Dialog edit brings up the initial dialog box with the default set of buttons OK, Cancel, and Help. Select the OK button and make its caption Find Next.

Create the new Find dialog box with the Modal frame, Pop-up, Visible, Caption, and System menu styles. The caption of the dialog box is Find. The dialog box has controls that were mentioned earlier. Figure X2.15 shows a sample session with the Dialog editor while creating the Find dialog box. Use this figure to guide you in placing the various controls.

The process of creating the preceding controls involves selecting them from the Tools palette and then drawing them. You can use the Copy and Paste commands (in the Edit menu) to create additional check boxes and radio buttons. You will most likely need to use the Alignment palette to align each set of these controls in the same column. Use the default setting for the group boxes, check boxes, and radio buttons. In the case of the latter two kinds of controls, the default setting enables automatic checking and selection of the controls.

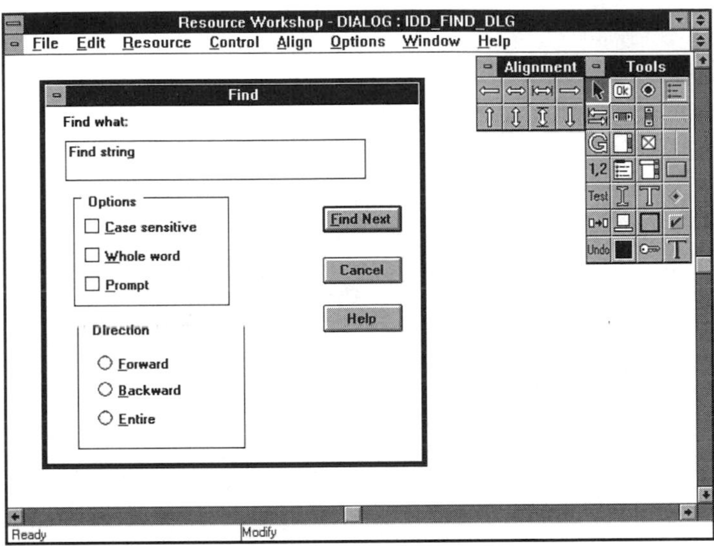

Figure X2.15. *A sample session with the Dialog editor while creating the Find dialog box.*

When you are finished with the Find dialog box, close the Dialog editor and move on to create the Replace dialog-box resource. This new resource has the ID of `IDD_REPLACE_DLG` and the caption Replace. Make this new dialog box a Borland-style dialog box, with the Modal frame, Pop-up, Visible, Caption, and System menu styles. The dialog box has controls that were mentioned earlier. Figure X2.16 shows a sample session with the Dialog editor while creating the Replace dialog box. Use this figure to guide you in placing the various controls. Include the Borland dips inside the dialog box and inside the group boxes.

When you are done, save the dialog-box resources (by saving the project). Compile and run the program. Invoke the Find... command in the Search menu to bring up the Find dialog box. Experiment with clicking the check boxes, radio buttons, and Find Next button. Notice that the dialog box selects only one radio button at a time. Also, type text in the edit box control. When you are done, click the Cancel pushbutton to close the dialog box. Invoke the Replace... command to bring up the Replace dialog box. Experiment with this Borland-style dialog box as you did with the Find dialog box. When you are done, click the Cancel pushbutton to close the dialog box. Figures X2.17 and X2.18 show sessions with the RWDLG3.EXE program.

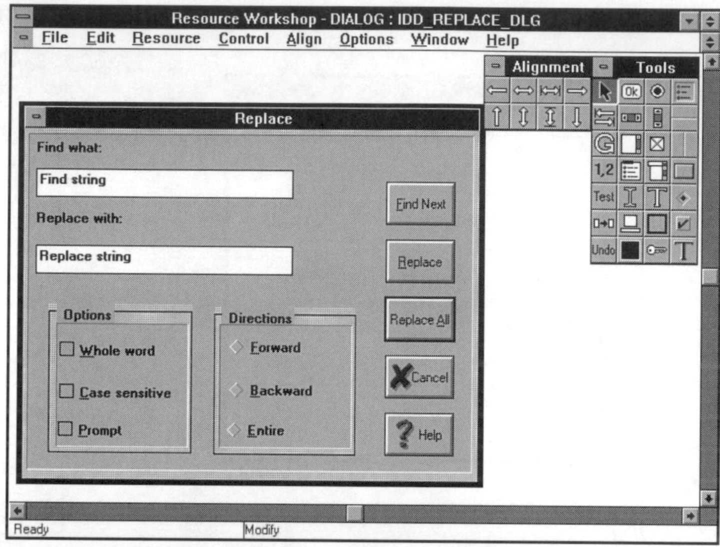

Figure X2.16. *A sample session with the Dialog editor while creating the Replace dialog box.*

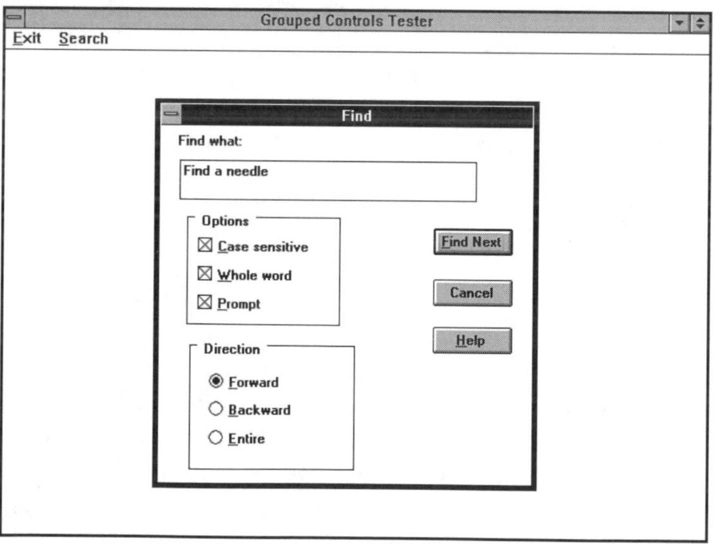

Figure X2.17. *A sample session with the RWDLG3.EXE program showing the Find dialog box.*

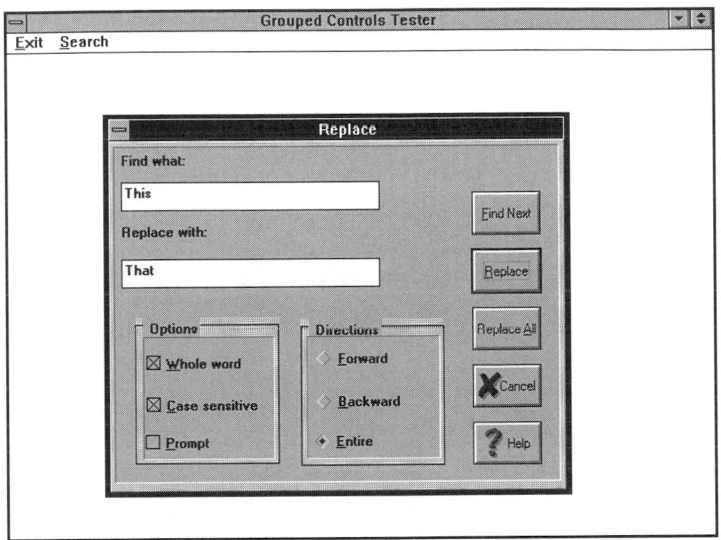

Figure X2.18. *A sample session with the RWDLG3.EXE program showing the Replace dialog box.*

Listing X2.19. The contents of the RWDLG3.DEF definition file.

```
NAME          RwMenu3
DESCRIPTION   'An OWL Windows Application'
EXETYPE       WINDOWS
CODE          PRELOAD MOVEABLE DISCARDABLE
DATA          PRELOAD MOVEABLE MULTIPLE
HEAPSIZE      1024
STACKSIZE     8192
```

Listing X2.20. The source code for the RWDLG3.H header file.

```
#define IDC_FIND_BOX        100
#define IDC_OPTIONS_GRP     101
#define IDC_WHOLE_CHK       102
#define IDC_CASE_CHK        103
#define IDC_REPLACE_BOX     104
#define IDC_UP_RBT          105
```

continues

Listing X2.20. continued

```
#define IDC_FIND_BTN         106
#define IDC_REPLACE_BTN      107
#define IDC_WHOLEWORD_CHK    108
#define IDC_CASESENSE_CHK    109
#define IDC_CHECKBOX2        110
#define IDC_DIRECTION_GRP    111
#define IDC_PROMPT_CHK       112
#define IDC_DOWN_RBT         113
#define IDC_ALL_RBT          114
#define IDC_DIRECTIONS_GRP   115
#define IDC_REPLACEALL_BTN   116
#define CM_FIND              10
#define CM_REPLACE           11
#define EXITMENU             200
#define IDD_FIND_DLG         301
#define IDD_REPLACE_DLG      302
```

Listing X2.21. The script of the RWDLG3.RC resource file.

```
#include <windows.h>
#include <owl\window.rh>
#include "rwdlg3.h"

EXITMENU MENU
{
 MENUITEM "&Exit", CM_EXIT
 POPUP "&Search"
 {
   MENUITEM "&Find...", CM_FIND
   MENUITEM "&Replace...", CM_REPLACE
 }
}

IDD_FIND_DLG DIALOG 21, -129, 194, 199
STYLE DS_MODALFRAME | WS_POPUP | WS_VISIBLE |
      WS_CAPTION | WS_SYSMENU
CAPTION "Find"
FONT 8, "MS Sans Serif"
{
 CONTROL "Find string", IDC_FIND_BOX, "EDIT", ES_AUTOHSCROLL |
         WS_BORDER | WS_TABSTOP, 10, 19, 155, 22
 LTEXT "Find what:", -1, 9, 4, 51, 13
 DEFPUSHBUTTON "&Find Next", IDC_FIND_BTN, 143, 56, 41, 15
 PUSHBUTTON "Cancel", IDCANCEL, 143, 84, 41, 15
 PUSHBUTTON "&Help", IDHELP, 143, 111, 41, 15
 GROUPBOX " Options ", IDC_OPTIONS_GRP, 14, 47, 80, 64,
          BS_GROUPBOX
```

```
 CHECKBOX "&Whole word", IDC_WHOLEWORD_CHK, 20, 76, 60, 12,
           BS_AUTOCHECKBOX | WS_TABSTOP
 CHECKBOX "&Prompt", IDC_PROMPT_CHK, 20, 92, 60, 12,
           BS_AUTOCHECKBOX | WS_TABSTOP
 CHECKBOX "&Case sensitive", IDC_CHECKBOX2, 20, 60, 60, 12,
           BS_AUTOCHECKBOX | WS_TABSTOP
 GROUPBOX " Direction ", IDC_DIRECTION_GRP, 16, 118, 86, 73,
          BS_GROUPBOX
 CONTROL "&Forward", IDC_DOWN_RBT, "BUTTON", BS_AUTORADIOBUTTON,
          26, 135, 50, 15
 CONTROL "&Backward", IDC_DOWN_RBT, "BUTTON", BS_AUTORADIOBUTTON,
          26, 150, 50, 15
 CONTROL "&Entire", IDC_ALL_RBT, "BUTTON", BS_AUTORADIOBUTTON,
          26, 166, 50, 15
}

IDD_REPLACE_DLG DIALOG 6, 15, 236, 195
STYLE DS_MODALFRAME | WS_POPUP | WS_VISIBLE |
      WS_CAPTION | WS_SYSMENU
CLASS "bordlg"
CAPTION "Replace"
FONT 8, "MS Sans Serif"
{
 CONTROL "Replace &All", IDC_REPLACEALL_BTN, "BorBtn",
         BS_DEFPUSHBUTTON | WS_CHILD | WS_VISIBLE | WS_TABSTOP,
         187, 92, 37, 25
 CONTROL "", IDCANCEL, "BorBtn", BS_PUSHBUTTON | WS_CHILD |
         WS_VISIBLE | WS_TABSTOP, 187, 124, 37, 25
 CONTROL "", IDHELP, "BorBtn", BS_PUSHBUTTON | WS_CHILD |
         WS_VISIBLE | WS_TABSTOP, 187, 156, 37, 25
 CONTROL "&Find Next", IDC_FIND_BTN, "BorBtn", BS_PUSHBUTTON |
         WS_CHILD | WS_VISIBLE | WS_TABSTOP, 187, 28, 37, 25
 CONTROL "&Replace", IDC_REPLACE_BTN, "BorBtn", BS_PUSHBUTTON |
         WS_CHILD | WS_VISIBLE | WS_TABSTOP, 187, 60, 37, 25
 CONTROL "Find what:", -1, "BorStatic", SS_LEFT | WS_CHILD |
         WS_VISIBLE | WS_GROUP, 6, 7, 73, 10
 CONTROL "Replace with:", -1, "BorStatic", SS_LEFT | WS_CHILD |
          WS_VISIBLE | WS_GROUP, 6, 46, 73, 10
 CONTROL "Find string", IDC_FIND_BOX, "EDIT", ES_AUTOHSCROLL |
         WS_BORDER | WS_TABSTOP, 6, 23, 133, 16
 CONTROL "Replace string", IDC_REPLACE_BOX, "EDIT",
         ES_AUTOHSCROLL | WS_BORDER | WS_TABSTOP, 6, 65, 133, 16
 GROUPBOX " Options", IDC_OPTIONS_GRP, 13, 98, 74, 82, BS_GROUPBOX
 CHECKBOX "&Whole word", IDC_WHOLE_CHK, 19, 117, 61, 12,
          BS_AUTOCHECKBOX | WS_TABSTOP
 CHECKBOX "&Case sensitive", IDC_CASE_CHK, 19, 140, 61, 12,
           BS_AUTOCHECKBOX | WS_TABSTOP
 CHECKBOX "&Prompt", IDC_PROMPT_CHK, 18, 161, 61, 12,
          BS_AUTOCHECKBOX | WS_TABSTOP
 GROUPBOX " Directions", IDC_DIRECTIONS_GRP, 98, 99, 74, 82,
          BS_GROUPBOX
```

continues

Listing X2.21. continued

```
 CONTROL "&Forward", IDC_DOWN_RBT, "BorRadio",
         BS_AUTORADIOBUTTON | WS_CHILD | WS_VISIBLE | WS_TABSTOP,
         106, 115, 59, 12
 CONTROL "&Backward", IDC_UP_RBT, "BorRadio", BS_AUTORADIOBUTTON |
         WS_CHILD | WS_VISIBLE | WS_TABSTOP, 106, 139, 59, 12
 CONTROL "&Entire", IDC_ALL_RBT, "BorRadio", BS_AUTORADIOBUTTON |
         WS_CHILD | WS_VISIBLE | WS_TABSTOP, 105, 161, 59, 12
 CONTROL "", -1, "BorShade", BSS_GROUP | BSS_CAPTION | BSS_LEFT |
         WS_CHILD | WS_VISIBLE, 2, 3, 231, 187
 CONTROL "", -1, "BorShade", BSS_GROUP | BSS_CAPTION | BSS_LEFT |
         WS_CHILD | WS_VISIBLE, 17, 108, 68, 69
 CONTROL "", -1, "BorShade", BSS_GROUP | BSS_CAPTION | BSS_LEFT |
         WS_CHILD | WS_VISIBLE, 101, 108, 69, 69
}
```

Type

Listing X2.22. The source code for the RWDLG3.CPP implementation file.

```
/*
  Program that tests dialog resources with grouped controls
*/

#include <owl\applicat.h>
#include <owl\framewin.h>
#include <owl\dialog.h>
#include "rwdlg3.h"

// declare the custom application class as
// a subclass of TApplication

class TWinApp : public TApplication
{
public:
  TWinApp() : TApplication() {}

protected:
  virtual void InitMainWindow();
};

// expand the functionality of TWindow by deriving class
// TMainWindow
class TMainWindow : public TWindow
{
 public:
   TMainWindow() : TWindow(0, 0, 0) {}

```

```
 protected:

   // handle the Find command
   void CMFind();

   // handle the Replace command
   void CMReplace();

   // handle confirming closing the window
   virtual BOOL CanClose();

   // declare the response table
   DECLARE_RESPONSE_TABLE(TMainWindow);

};

DEFINE_RESPONSE_TABLE1(TMainWindow, TWindow)
  EV_COMMAND(CM_FIND, CMFind),
  EV_COMMAND(CM_REPLACE, CMReplace),
END_RESPONSE_TABLE;

void TMainWindow::CMFind()
{
  TDialog* pDlg = new TDialog(this, TResID(IDD_FIND_DLG));

  pDlg->Execute();
}

void TMainWindow::CMReplace()
{
  TDialog* pDlg = new TDialog(this, TResID(IDD_REPLACE_DLG));

  pDlg->Execute();
}

BOOL TMainWindow::CanClose()
{
  return MessageBox("Want to close this application?",
                    "Query", MB_YESNO | MB_ICONQUESTION) == IDYES;
}

void TWinApp::InitMainWindow()
{
  MainWindow = new TFrameWindow(0,
                    "Grouped Controls Tester",
                    new TMainWindow);
  // load the menu resource
  MainWindow->AssignMenu(TResID(EXITMENU));
EnableVWCC(); // enable Borland controls
}
```

continues

Listing X2.22. continued

```
78:  int OwlMain(int /* argc */, char** /*argv[] */)
79:  {
80:    TWinApp app;
81:    return app.Run();
82:  }
```

Listing X2.20 shows the RWDLG3.H header file, which contains the definitions of the identifiers for the dialog box, its controls, and the menu resources.

Listing X2.21 contains the RWDLG3.RC resource file, which contains the dialog-box and menu resources. The dialog-box resource `IDD_FIND_DLG` contains the resource statements for the various controls. The dialog-box resource `IDD_REPLACE_DLG` is similar to the `IDD_FIND_DLG` dialog-box resource. Notice the following new declarations in the `IDD_REPLACE_DLG` dialog-box resources:

1. The `CLASS "borldlg"` statement specifies that the dialog box is a Borland-style dialog box.
2. The static text controls are of the type `BorStatic`.
3. The pushbutton controls are of the type `BorBtn`.
4. The radio button controls are of type `BorRadio`.

These `BorXXXX` control types support the various Borland controls.

Listing X2.22 shows the source code for the implementation file RWDLG3.CPP. The file declares the application class, `TWinApp`, and the main window class, `TMainWindow`. The most relevant member functions of the latter class are `CMFind` and `CMReplace`, which respond, respectively, to the `CM_FIND` and `CM_REPLACE` Windows command messages sent by the commands Find… and Replace….

The member function `CMFind` (defined in lines 49 to 54) creates a dynamic instance of the dialog class `TDialog` and specifies the dialog-box resource `IDD_FIND_DLG`. The function then invokes this dialog box by sending the C++ message `Execute` to the dialog-box instance (accessed using the local pointer `pDlg`).

The member function `CMReplace` (defined in lines 56 to 61) creates a dynamic instance of the dialog class `TDialog` and specifies the dialog-box resource `IDD_REPLACE_DLG`. The function then invokes this dialog box by sending the C++ message `Execute` to the dialog-box instance (accessed using the local pointer `pDlg`).

Creating a Fully Operational Dialog Box

The mock dialog boxes that we presented in the preceding two sections lack the interaction you expect from dialog boxes. If you have grown somewhat disappointed (or just completely bored), we have some good news for you—this section presents a simple, yet fully functional dialog box.

The next project, RWDLG4, presents a dialog box that supports a command-line, oriented floating-point calculator that contains the following controls:

- The Operand 1 edit box, in which you type the first operand.
- The Operator edit box, in which you type an operator. The program supports the operators +, –, /, *, and ^ (raising to powers).
- The Operand 2 edit box, in which you type the second operand.
- The Result edit box, which displays the results of a mathematical operation. This control has the read-only style.
- The Error Message edit box, which displays any error messages. This control has the read-only style.
- The Calc pushbutton, which executes the sought operation using the operands you have entered in the two operands edit boxes.
- The Exit pushbutton, which closes the dialog box.
- A set of static text controls, which label the preceding edit-box controls.

Create the project file and the calculator resource dialog box (with an ID of `IDD_CALC_DLG`) in a manner similar to the steps mentioned in the preceding two sections. Figure X2.19 shows a sample session with the RWMENU4.EXE program. Use this figure to guide you in creating the calculator dialog-box resource.

Compile and run the program. Click the Calc menu to invoke the operational command-oriented calculator dialog box. Enter valid operands and the operator in their respective edit boxes and click the Calc pushbutton. Observe the result in the read-only Result edit box. If you enter an invalid operator or attempt to divide by zero, the dialog box displays an error message in the read-only Error Message edit box. When you are finished experimenting with the calculator dialog box, click the Exit button.

Listing X2.23 shows the contents of the RWDLG4.DEF definition file. Listing X2.24 shows the source code for the RWDLG4.H header file. Listing X2.25 shows the script of the RWDLG4.RC resource file. Listing X2.26 shows the source code for the RWDLG4.CPP implementation file.

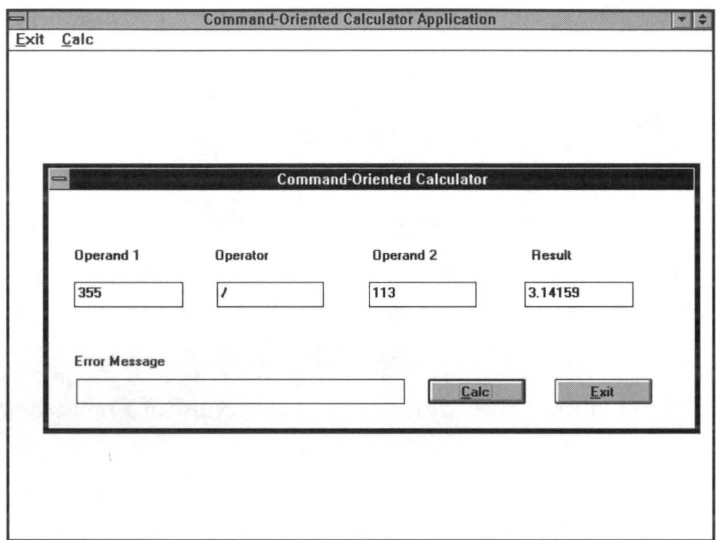

Figure X2.19. *A sample session with the RWDLG4.EXE program.*

Listing X2.23. The contents of the RWDLG4.DEF definition file.

```
NAME         RwDlg4
DESCRIPTION  'An OWL Windows Application'
EXETYPE      WINDOWS
CODE         PRELOAD MOVEABLE DISCARDABLE
DATA         PRELOAD MOVEABLE MULTIPLE
HEAPSIZE     1024
STACKSIZE    8192
```

Listing X2.24. The source code for the RWDLG4.H header file.

```
#define IDC_OPERAND1_BOX 100
#define IDC_OPERATOR_BOX 101
#define IDC_OPERAND2_BOX 102
#define IDC_RESULT_BOX   103
#define IDC_ERRMSG_BOX   104
#define IDC_CALC_BTN     105
#define CM_CALC          110
#define EXITMENU         201
#define IDD_CALC_DLG     202
```

Listing X2.25. The script of the RWDLG4.RC resource file.

```
#include <windows.h>
#include <owl\window.rh>
#include "rwdlg4.h"

EXITMENU MENU
{
 MENUITEM "&Exit", CM_EXIT
 MENUITEM "&Calc", CM_CALC
}

IDD_CALC_DLG DIALOG 20, 100, 335, 133
STYLE DS_MODALFRAME | WS_POPUP | WS_VISIBLE | WS_CAPTION |
      WS_SYSMENU
CAPTION "Command-Oriented Calculator"
FONT 8, "MS Sans Serif"
{
 DEFPUSHBUTTON "&Calc", IDC_CALC_BTN, 197, 105, 50, 14
 PUSHBUTTON "&Exit", IDOK, 262, 105, 50, 14
 LTEXT "Operand 1", -1, 13, 32, 58, 13
 LTEXT "Operator", -1, 85, 32, 58, 13
 LTEXT "Operand 2", -1, 168, 32, 58, 13
 LTEXT "Result", -1, 250, 32, 58, 13
 EDITTEXT IDC_OPERAND1_BOX, 13, 51, 56, 14
 EDITTEXT IDC_OPERATOR_BOX, 86, 51, 56, 14
 EDITTEXT IDC_OPERAND2_BOX, 166, 51, 56, 14
 EDITTEXT IDC_RESULT_BOX, 247, 51, 56, 14, ES_READONLY |
          WS_BORDER | WS_TABSTOP
 LTEXT "Error Message", -1, 13, 91, 74, 14
 EDITTEXT IDC_ERRMSG_BOX, 14, 105, 171, 14, ES_READONLY |
          WS_BORDER | WS_TABSTOP
}
```

Listing X2.26. The source code for the RWDLG4.CPP implementation file.

```
/*
  Program to test the resources for the static text, edit box,
  and pushbutton controls.
  The program uses these controls to implement a command-line
  oriented calculator application (COCA)
*/

#include <owl\applicat.h>
#include <owl\framewin.h>
#include <owl\dialog.h>
#include <owl\window.rh>
#include "rwdlg4.h"
#include <stdlib.h>
#include <stdio.h>
#include <math.h>
#include <string.h>

const MaxEditLen = 40;

// declare the custom application class as
// a subclass of TApplication
class TWinApp : public TApplication
{
public:
  TWinApp() : TApplication() {}

protected:
  virtual void InitMainWindow();
};

// expand the functionality of TWindow by
// deriving class TMainWindow
class TMainWindow : public TWindow
{
public:

  TMainWindow() : TWindow(0, 0, 0) {}

protected:
  //--------------- member functions ----------------

  // handle Calc command
  void CMCalc();

  void CMExit()
    { Parent->SendMessage(WM_CLOSE); }

```

```
  // handle closing the window
  virtual BOOL CanClose();

  // declare the message map macro
  DECLARE_RESPONSE_TABLE(TMainWindow);

};

class TCalcDialog : public TDialog
{
public:

  TCalcDialog(TWindow* parent, TResID resID) :
     TWindow(0, 0, 0), TDialog(parent, resID) {}

protected:

  // math error flag
  BOOL InError;

  //------------------- member functions -------------------

  // handle the calculation
  void HandleCalcBtn();

  // declare the message map macro
  DECLARE_RESPONSE_TABLE(TCalcDialog);
};

DEFINE_RESPONSE_TABLE1(TMainWindow, TWindow)
  EV_COMMAND(CM_CALC, CMCalc),
END_RESPONSE_TABLE;


DEFINE_RESPONSE_TABLE1(TCalcDialog, TDialog)
  EV_COMMAND(IDC_CALC_BTN, HandleCalcBtn),
END_RESPONSE_TABLE;

void TCalcDialog::HandleCalcBtn()
{
  double x, y, z;
  char opStr[MaxEditLen+1];
  char s[MaxEditLen+1];

  // obtain the string in the Operand1 edit box
  GetDlgItemText(IDC_OPERAND1_BOX, s, MaxEditLen);
  // convert the string in the edit box
  x = atof(s);

```

continues

Listing X2.26. continued

```
   // obtain the string in the Operand2 edit box
   GetDlgItemText(IDC_OPERAND2_BOX, s, MaxEditLen);
   // convert the string in the edit box
   y = atof(s);

   // obtain the string in the Operator edit box
   GetDlgItemText(IDC_OPERATOR_BOX, opStr, MaxEditLen);

   // clear the error message box
   SetDlgItemText(IDC_ERRMSG_BOX, "");
   InError = FALSE;

   // determine the requested operation
   if (strcmp(opStr, "+") == 0)
     z = x + y;
   else if (strcmp(opStr, "-") == 0)
     z = x - y;
   else if (strcmp(opStr, "*") == 0)
     z = x * y;
   else if (strcmp(opStr, "/") == 0) {
     if (y != 0)
          z = x / y;
     else {
       z = 0;
       InError = TRUE;
       SetDlgItemText(IDC_ERRMSG_BOX, "Division-by-zero error");
     }
   }
   else if (strcmp(opStr, "^") == 0) {
     if (x > 0)
       z = exp(y * log(x));
     else {
       InError = TRUE;
          SetDlgItemText(IDC_ERRMSG_BOX,
            "Cannot raise the power of a negative number");
     }
   }
   else {
     InError = TRUE;
     SetDlgItemText(IDC_ERRMSG_BOX, "Invalid operator");
   }
   // display the result if no error has occurred
   if (!InError) {
     sprintf(s, "%g", z);
     SetDlgItemText(IDC_RESULT_BOX, s);
   }
 }
```

```
void TMainWindow::CMCalc()
{
  TCalcDialog* pDlg = new TCalcDialog(this, TResID(IDD_CALC_DLG));
  pDlg->Execute();
}

BOOL TMainWindow::CanClose()
{
  return MessageBox("Want to close this application?",
                    "Query", MB_YESNO ¦ MB_ICONQUESTION) == IDYES;
}

void TWinApp::InitMainWindow()
{
  MainWindow = new TFrameWindow(0,
          "Command-Oriented Calculator Application",
          new TMainWindow);
  // load the menu resource
  MainWindow->AssignMenu(TResID(EXITMENU));
  // enable the keyboard handler
  MainWindow->EnableKBHandler();
}

int OwlMain(int /* argc */, char** /*argv[] */)
{
  TWinApp app;
  return app.Run();
}
```

Analysis Listing X2.25 contains the script of the RWDLG4.RC resource file. This resource file defines the `IDD_CALC_DLG` dialog-box resource. This resource is a Windows dialog-box resource that contains `LTEXT`, `EDITTEXT`, `DEFPUSHBUTTON`, and `PUSHBUTTON` statements.

Listing X2.26 shows the source code for the RWDLG4.CPP implementation file. This file declares the application class, `TWinApp`; the main window class, `TMainWindow`; and the calculator dialog-box class, `TCalcDialog`.

The *TMainWindow* Class

The class `TMainWindow` declares a constructor and a set of member functions. The most relevant member function is `CMCalc`. This function creates a dynamic instance of the class `TCalcDialog` and specifies the dialog-box resource `IDD_CALC_DLG`. The function pops up the dialog box by sending the C++ message `Execute` to the dialog-box instance. The function accesses this instance using the local pointer `pDlg`.

The *TCalcDialog* Class

The class TCalcDialog, which is a descendant of the class TDialog, supports the operations of the calculator dialog box. The class declares a constructor, the data member InError, and the member function HandleCalcBtn. The constructor creates the dialog-box instance by invoking the ancestors' constructors (both classes TDialog and TWindow). The member function HandleCalcBtn responds to the command message sent by the Calc pushbutton. The member function performs the following tasks:

- Obtains the first operand from the Operand 1 edit box. This task involves the function GetDlgItemText, which obtains the text from the targeted dialog-box control. The arguments for calling the function GetDlgItemText are IDC_OPERAND1_BOX, s, and MaxEditLen. The function HandleCalcBtn also uses the function atof to convert the contents of variable s into a double-typed number, and stores that number in the local variable x.

- Obtains the second operand in a manner identical to the first one. The function stores the actual (numeric) second operand in variable y.

- Copies the text in the Operator edit box into the local variable opStr. This task also uses the function GetDlgItemText and specifies the control ID of IDC_OPERATOR_BOX.

- Clears the error-message text box and sets the InError data member to FALSE. Clearing the error-message edit box involves the function SetDlgItemText, which sets the text for the targeted dialog-box control. The arguments for calling the function SetDlgItemText are IDC_ERRMSG_BOX and the empty literal string.

- Determines the requested operation by using a series of if and if-else statements. The operators supported are +, –, *, /, and ^ (power). If the function detects an error, it sets the InError data member to TRUE and displays a message in the error-message box.

- Displays the result in the Result box if the InError data member is FALSE. The function first converts the result from double to a string and then writes to the Result box using the function SetDlgItemText. The arguments for calling function SetDlgItemText are IDC_RESULT_BOX and the local string variable s.

Summary

This extra-credit chapter discussed visual programming using Resource Workshop. You learned the following:

- An overview of Resource Workshop and its support for visual programming techniques in creating various resources.
- The Resource Workshop supports accelerator, bitmap, cursor, dialog-box, font, icon, menu, string-table, user-defined, rcdata, and VERSIONINFO resources.
- The Resource Workshop works with various kinds of files, including the .RC and .DLG script resource files; the .RES compiled resource files; the .BMP, .ICO, .CUR, .FON, and .FNT bitmapped resource files; and the .EXE, .DLL, .DRV binary files, which contain bound resources.
- The Resource Workshop supports creating menu resources using commands and a special dialog box that enables you to define each menu item and fine-tune its appearance and operations.
- The Resource Workshop enables you to create accelerator resources that are either closely associated with a menu resource or more independent. These resources differ only in the steps used to create them. The final script is of the same nature.
- The Resource Workshop enables you to create and edit icon resources using the Paint editor. This editor contains Colors and Tools palettes, which enable you to select different drawing colors and tools.
- The chapter showed you how to create a message dialog-box resource and use it to respond to the left and right mouse-button clicks. The example used the custom message dialog box in place of the standard message dialog box.
- The chapter showed you how to create resources for dialog boxes with nontrivial interfaces. These interfaces include pushbuttons, edit boxes, grouped boxes, check boxes, and radio buttons. The chapter illustrated these controls in creating dialog-boxes resources for a simple calculator, a Find dialog box, and a Replace dialog box.

- The chapter showed you how to create a fully-functioning dialog-box resource. The example offered an operational command-oriented calculator that supports the four basic math operations as well as exponentiation. The example demonstrated the use of a dialog-box class to animate the calculator dialog-box resource.

Q&A

Q How can I fine-tune the location and dimensions of related controls?

A The Resource Workshop provides the alignment tools for this task. Another way to fine-tune the location and dimensions of related controls is by massaging the numbers for the coordinates and dimensions that appear in the .RC file. This action enables you to create sets of controls that are perfectly aligned and have the exact dimensions you specify.

Q Does the Resource Workshop support custom Visual Basic controls (also called VBX controls)?

A Yes. The Resource Workshop enables you to install VBX controls, adding them to the palette.

Q How can I access and manipulate the text of an edit box defined in a resource file?

A Use the function `GetDlgItem` to obtain the address of a control defined in a dialog-box resource. This function works with all controls and not just edit boxes. To store and recall text in an edit box, use the function `SetDlgItemText` and `GetDlgItemText`.

Exercises

1. Use the Workshop Resource to create a dialog box with two sets of grouped controls. The first set offers the choice between the MM/DD/YY, DD/MM/YY, and YY/MM/DD time formats. The second group offers the choice between AM/PM and 24-hour time format.
2. Modify the resources of the RWDLG4.EXE program to replace the edit boxes for the operands, the operator, and the result with combo boxes that act as history list boxes (which store the most recent input).

Using the Application Expert

The AppExpert utility is a versatile tool that helps you create project source code files quickly and systematically. The utility generates functioning skeleton-code that you can customize to meet the needs of your Windows applications. Thus, rather than starting from scratch or from adapting similar existing code, you can rely on the AppExpert utility to do much of the systematic work for you, freeing you to concentrate on implementing the code that supports your application's special features. It's like having a consultant inside Borland C++! A guide to using the AppExpert along with the ClassExpert utility (which is covered in extra-credit chapter X5, "Using the ClassExpert") is worthy of a small book—there is a lot to learn. This chapter focuses on the following topics:

- Using the AppExpert utility
- Examining the different source code output that is generated by selecting various project options in AppExpert

Note: The listings generated by AppExpert were edited to better fit the pages in this book.

Using the AppExpert Utility

To use the AppExpert utility, invoke the AppExpert option in the Project menu. The IDE brings up the project file-selection dialog box. This dialog box is very similar to the Open A File dialog box. Select an .IDE filename or type in the name of a new .IDE file and then click the OK button. If you type in the name of a new .IDE file, the AppExpert utility creates a new project file. On the other hand, if you choose an existing .IDE file, the AppExpert utility merely adds the new target to that project file. Next, the AppExpert utility displays the AppExpert Application Generation Options dialog box (called the AppExpert dialog box for short), as shown in Figure X3.1. This dialog box has three topics: Application, Main Window, and MDI Child/View.

Note: It is important to know that the AppExpert dialog box hides and shows different controls based on the currently selected topic or subtopic.

The Application Topic

Figure X3.1 shows the options of the Application topic. You will be working with these options in this chapter and the following chapter to generate projects with the AppExpert utility. The options of the Application topic are as follows:

- The choice between an application that supports SDI or MDI child windows, or one that supports a dialog client
- The use of document and view classes in the text editor
- The inclusion of a toolbar
- The inclusion of a status line
- The support for the drag-and-drop feature
- The support for printing and print-previewing features

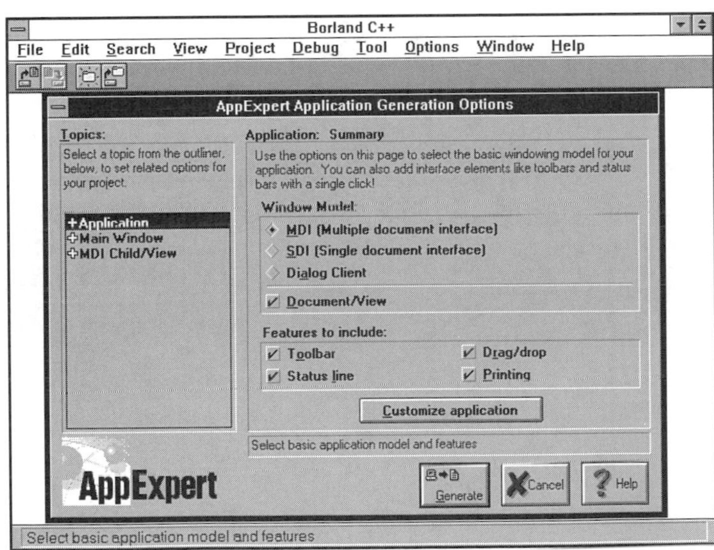

Figure X3.1. *The AppExpert Application Generation Options dialog box.*

If you click the + sign located to the left of the Application topic (or double-click the Application topic itself), you expand the Application subtopics. Figure X3.2 shows the options offered by the Application subtopics:

- Basic Options
- OLE 2 Options

- Code Gen Control
- Admin Options

The Basic Options Subtopic

Figure X3.2 shows the options offered by the Basic Options subtopic. The option choices include the following:

- The name of the target
- The base directory for the target
- The option to provide online help with its corresponding help file
- The application's startup state
- The control styles

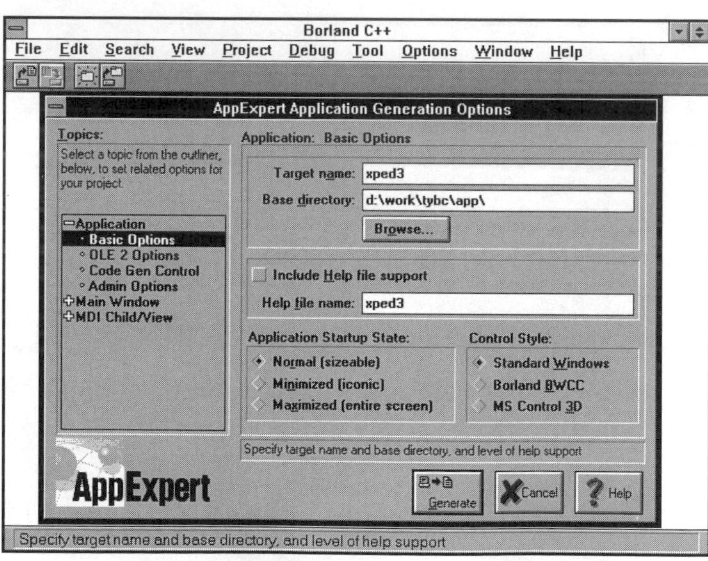

Figure X3.2. *The AppExpert dialog box showing the Basic Options subtopic in the Application topic.*

The dialog box offers three edit box controls for you to enter the preceding information. In addition, the dialog box shows a Browse pushbutton, which enables you to invoke a dialog box for selecting a new base directory. As for the help file, the AppExpert dialog box contains a check box that enables you to either support or prevent the creation of the help file.

The radio buttons for setting the startup options allow you to have the application automatically minimized or maximized when it starts up, or to start up in the normal manner. The radio buttons for the control styles default to the standard Windows setting, which shows a white background on dialog boxes. The BWCC style refers to Borland's set of "chiseled steel" dialogs with the mottled background and controls with a more three-dimensional appearance. The MS Control 3D appearance is used in standard Microsoft applications.

The OLE 2 Options Subtopic

The OLE 2 options offered by the Application Generator are shown in figure X3.3. They include the following:

- Whether or not an application is an OLE 2 container
- Whether or not an application is an OLE 2 server, and whether it's an EXE or a DLL server
- Whether or not the application should be automated
- The server ID to be used in registering the application

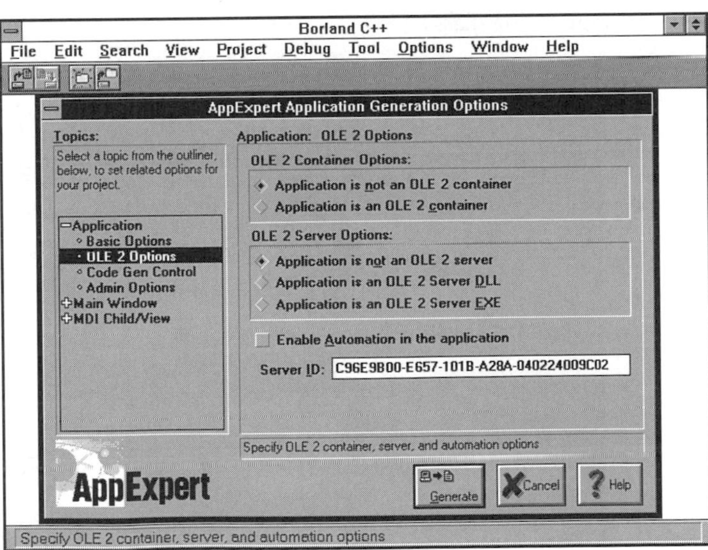

Figure X3.3. *The AppExpert dialog box showing the OLE 2 Options subtopic in the Application topic.*

The first option is obvious; an application either is or isn't an OLE 2 container. With the server, however, an application may have the OLE 2 server routines reside in either an EXE or a DLL, and the application generator will handle both cases. The automation routines allow one application to be controlled from another. Finally, the server ID is a unique number, guaranteed to be different from all other IDs that might exist. OLE 2 is described in more detail in the extra-credit chapter 7 ("OLE 2").

The Code Gen Control Subtopic

The Code Gen Control subtopic offers the options shown in Figure X3.4. When you select this subtopic, the AppExpert dialog box displays the target name and the base directory. In addition, the dialog box offers edit-box controls to select the following:

- The source directory
- The header directory
- The main source file
- The main header file
- The application class
- The About dialog class

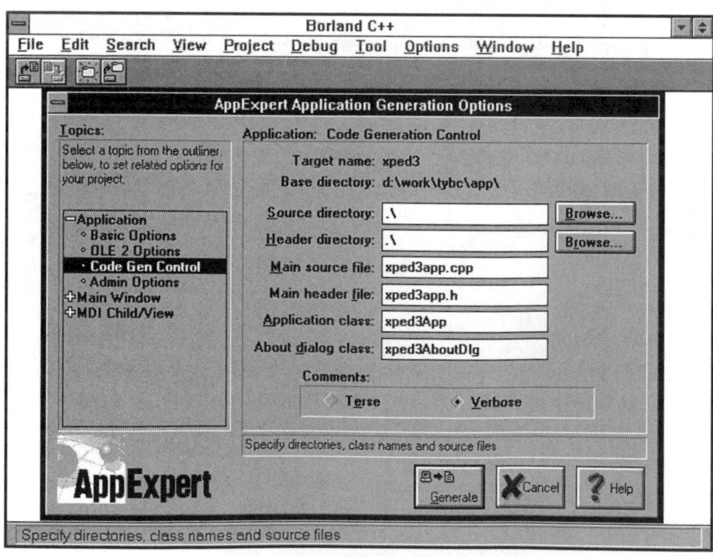

Figure X3.4. *The AppExpert dialog box showing the Code Generation Control subtopic.*

The dialog box offers browse buttons for the preceding source and header directory options. In addition, the dialog box presents a frame with two radio buttons that enable you to select between verbose or terse comments. The default setting enables verbose comments.

The Admin Options Subtopic

The Admin Options subtopic, shown in Figure X3.5, handles the administrative side of the project. The AppExpert dialog box provides you with edit-box controls to enter the following information:

- The version number. The default is 1.0.
- The copyright notice. The dialog box offers a default wording for the copyright notice.
- The description. The default description is the target name.
- The name of the target author.
- The name of the company.

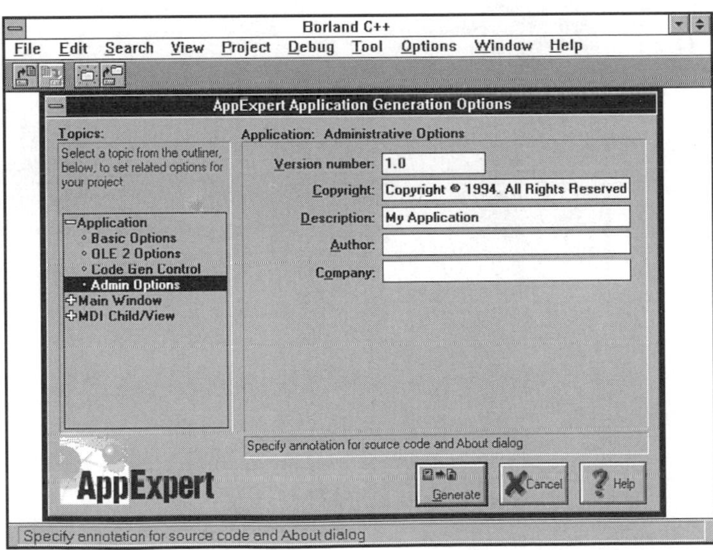

Figure X3.5. *The AppExpert dialog box showing the Administration Options subtopic.*

The Main Window Topic

The Main Window topic alters the AppExpert dialog box (see Figure X3.6) to offer you options that set the window title and background. The dialog box also presents a Set Background Color pushbutton for altering the background color.

The Main Window topic has the following subtopics:

- Basic Options
- SDI Client
- MDI Client
- Dialog Client

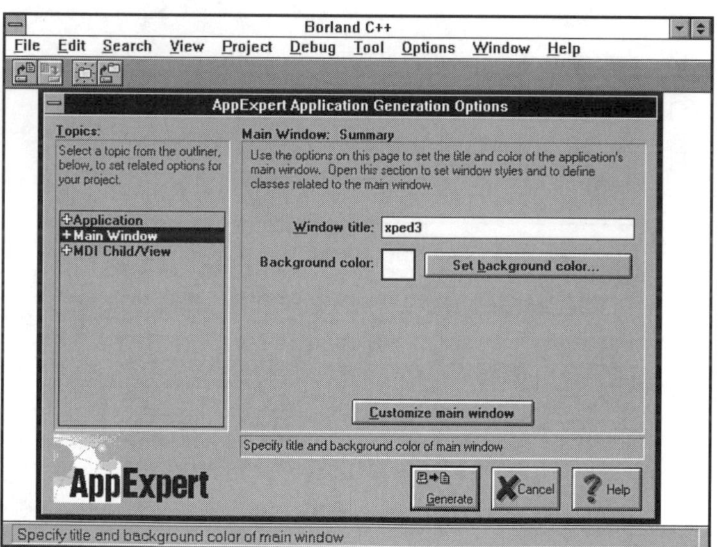

Figure X3.6. *The AppExpert dialog box showing the Main Window topic.*

The Basic Options Subtopic

The Basic Options subtopic in the Main Window topic permits you to select the window style. Figure X3.7 shows the options offered by this subtopic, as follows:

- Caption: Creates a single thin border and a title bar that can display a caption.
- Border: Creates a single thin border that has no title bar.

- Max box: Adds a maximize button to the right side of the title bar that belongs to the application's main window.
- Min box: Adds a minimize button to the right side of the title bar that belongs to the application's main window.
- Vertical scroll: Includes a vertical scroll on the right side of the main window.
- Horizontal scroll: Includes a horizontal scroll on the bottom of the main window.
- System menu: Includes the system-menu button located to the left side of the title bar in the main window. The Caption option must be selected to make this option available.
- Visible: Makes the main window visible.
- Disabled: Disables the main window.
- Thick frame: Displays the main window as a dialog box, with a double border. Consequently, you cannot resize the main window.
- Clip siblings: Protects the sibling windows of the main window.
- Clip children: Ensures that the main window is not painted over by the child windows.

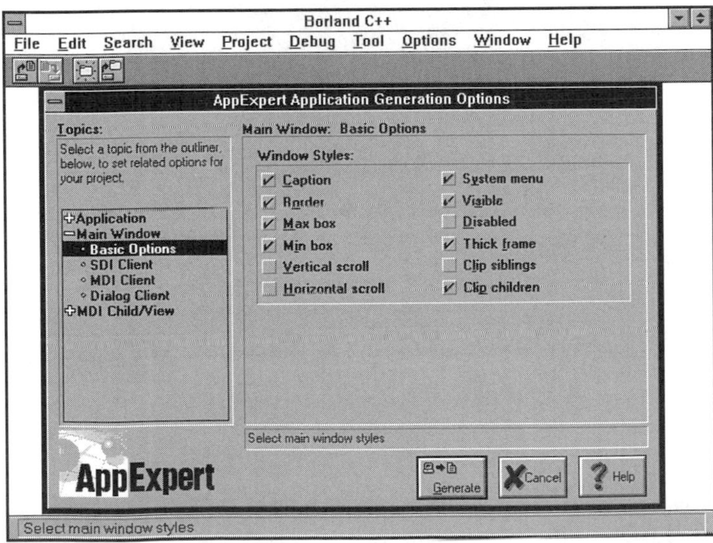

Figure X3.7. *The AppExpert dialog box showing the Basic Options subtopic in the Main Window topic.*

The SDI Client Subtopic

The SDI Client subtopic offers options that define the class, which in turn models the client area of an SDI-compliant main window. These options are effective only if you select the Single Document Interface option in the opening AppExpert dialog box. Figure X3.8 shows the AppExpert dialog box displaying the SDI Client subtopic with the following options:

- The drop-down combo box that enables you to select the Client/View class.
- The drop-down combo box that permits you to select the Document class.
- The three edit boxes to enter the file-type filters. These controls accept the file description, filters, and default extensions.
- An edit box allowing you to set the name of the SDI view class.
- Two edit boxes to set the names of the header file and the source file for the SDI class.

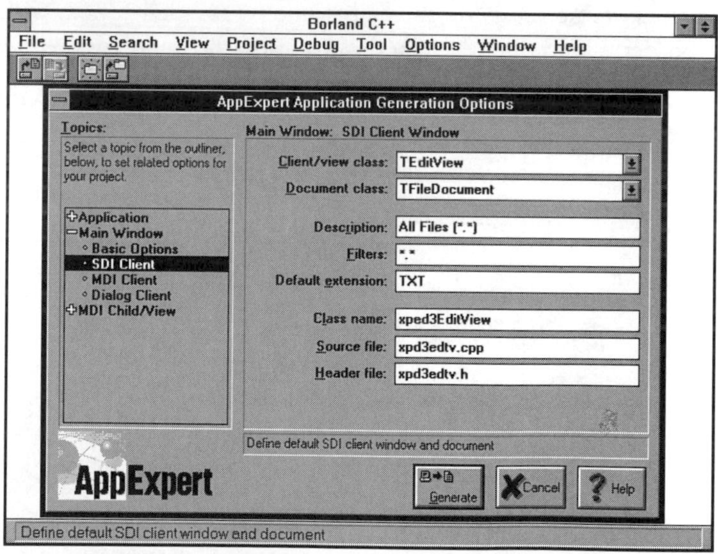

Figure X3.8. *The AppExpert dialog box showing the SDI Client subtopic.*

The MDI Client Subtopic

The MDI Client subtopic offers options to define the class that models the client area of an MDI-compliant frame window. These options are effective only if you select the

Multiple Document Interface option in the opening AppExpert dialog box. Figure X3.9 shows the AppExpert dialog box displaying the MDI Client subtopic with the following options:

- The name of the MDI client window class
- The source (which we are calling *implementation* in this book because we mean *source* in a broad sense) filename
- The header filename

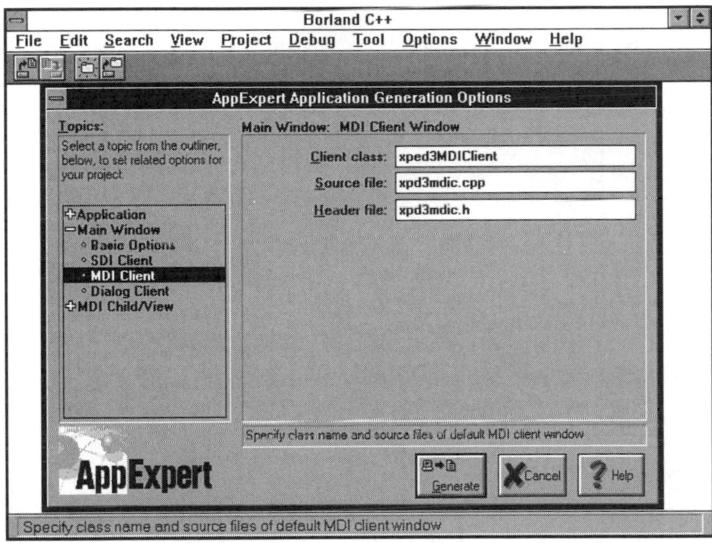

Figure X3.9. *The AppExpert dialog box showing the MDI Client subtopic.*

The Dialog Client Subtopic

The Dialog Client subtopic offers options to define the class that models the client area of a dialog frame window. You can select the resource ID of the dialog to load, and you can select whether to include a menu bar. These options are effective only if you select the Dialog Client option in the opening AppExpert dialog box. Figure X3.10 shows the AppExpert dialog box displaying the MDI Client subtopic with the following options:

- The name of the MDI client window class
- The source (which we are calling implementation in this book, because we mean source in a broad sense) filename

- The header filename
- The resource ID of the dialog box to load into the client
- Whether or not to include a menu bar in the frame

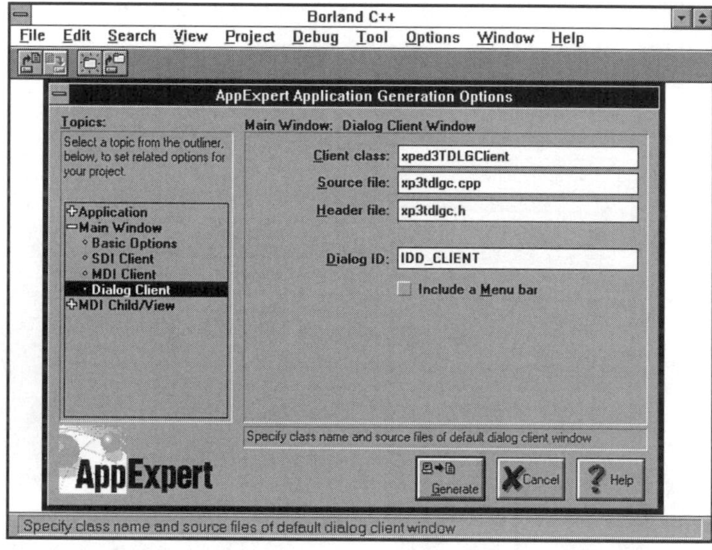

Figure X3.10. *The AppExpert dialog box showing the MDI Client subtopic.*

The MDI Child/View Topic

The MDI Child/View topic, shown in Figure X3.11, has options that enable you to specify the following:

- The name of the MDI child-window class
- The source file that contains the implementation of the MDI child-window class
- The header file that contains the declaration of the MDI child-window class

The AppExpert dialog box offers the Customize child and view pushbutton control, which simply invokes the Basic Options subtopic that is discussed next.

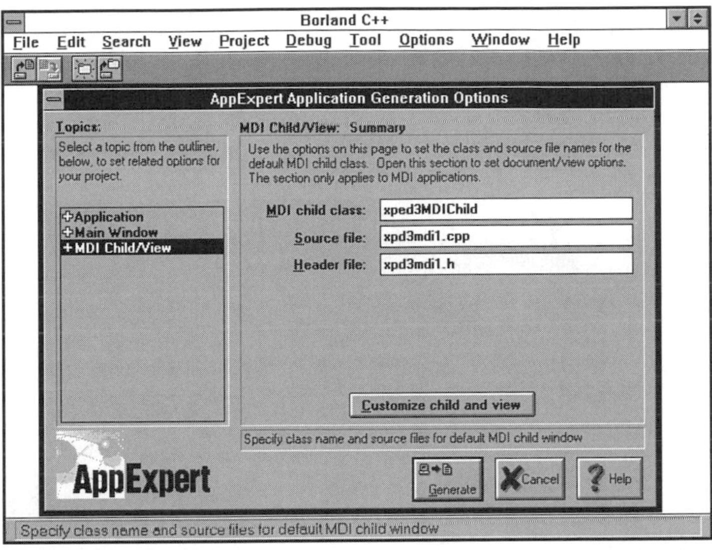

Figure X3.11. *The AppExpert dialog box showing the MDI Child/View topic.*

The Basic Options Subtopic

The Basic Options subtopic offers options to define the class that models the client area of an MDI child window. These options are effective only if you select the Multiple Document Interface option in the opening AppExpert dialog box. Figure X3.12 shows the AppExpert dialog box displaying the Basic Options subtopic with the following options:

- The drop-down combo box that enables you to select the MDI Client/view class.
- The drop-down combo box that enables you to select the Document class.
- The three edit boxes to enter the file-type filters. These controls accept the file description, filters, and default extensions.
- The class name, header file, and source file.

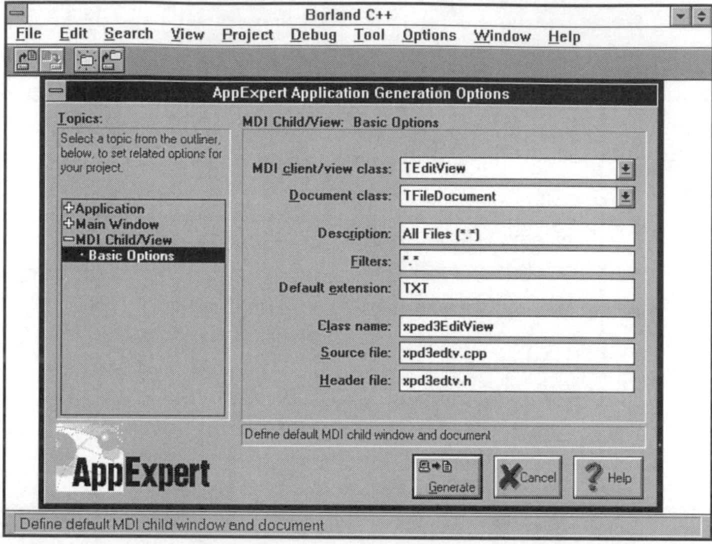

Figure X3.12. *The AppExpert dialog box showing the Basic Options subtopic in the MDI Child/View topic.*

Studying the AppExpert Output

The preceding section indicates that the AppExpert utility offers many options that determine the kind of source code files to generate. In the next sections, we present two different versions of SDI-compliant projects generated by altering the AppExpert options. In the next extra-credit chapter, we present three different versions of MDI-compliant projects created by changing the AppExpert options. Because the total number of possible source-code listings is rather large, we will focus on a selection of source-code files generated by AppExpert. Table X3.1 shows the SDI-compliant text-editor projects that we generate using AppExpert, as well as the options influencing them.

Note: Although the AppExpert creates a sizable amount of source code very quickly, you should nonetheless study the output. Acquainting yourself with the output enables you to quickly and efficiently customize the AppExpert output. This approach shortens the overall process of developing your applications. By contrast, not becoming familiar with the emitted source code will cost you extra time in debugging your programs.

The ideal study of the source-code files generated by AppExpert would include varying each of the AppExpert options, one at a time, and covering all of the possible combinations. Because the total number of these combinations is relatively large, we will examine the output source-code that is generated by sometimes changing two options at a time. In addition, we will select a total of five output cases in both this chapter and in the next one. In each case, the AppExpert generates a minimally functioning text editor. Please do not interpret the words *minimally functioning* to mean that it's a real dud. In fact, the generated text editors offer an acceptable level of operations, because the various OWL classes used in these editors support these operations. We would like to point out that working with all the different combinations is a good independent exercise. We suggest that you experiment with these various combinations to see what kind of program each combination generates.

Note: Keep in mind the following points regarding the source-code files presented both in this chapter and in the next one:

1. The projects of Table X3.1 are generated by changing only the options in the opening AppExpert dialog box. The other settings of AppExpert use the default values. Changing these settings would lead to an even greater variation in the different kinds of project files generated by AppExpert.
2. Use a separate directory for each project.
3. The output source code listings have been edited to fit the page layout of this book, as well as to shorten the listings.

Table X3.1. The various projects generated by AppExpert for this chapter's case studies.

Project	SDI?	Doc/ View?	Toolbar?	Status?	Drag/ Drop?	Print?
XPED1	Yes	No	No	No	No	No
XPED2	Yes	No	Yes	Yes	No	No

The XPED1 Project

The first project, the ground-zero project, is XPED1. This project generates an SDI-compliant text editor with no toolbar, no status line, no drag-and-drop feature support, and no printing-related features. In other words, the XPED1 project is the simplest text editor generated by AppExpert.

When you invoke the AppExpert utility from the IDE Project menu, select the SDI option and turn off the other options in the opening dialog box of AppExpert. In addition, select the Code Gen Control subtopic (in the Application topic of the AppExpert dialog box) to make the application and dialog box class names `XpEd1App` and `XpEd1AboutDlg`, respectively. The utility generates the following set of files.

Filename	Size	Description
`applsdi.ico`	1,086	Application icon
`xpd1edtf.cpp`	1,125	`TEditFile` descendent class source
`xpd1edtf.h`	1,000	`TEditFile` descendent class header
`xped1.apx`	19,711	AppExpert reference file
`xped1.dsw`	206	Borland IDE Desktop file
`xped1.ide`	27,524	IDE project file
`xped1abd.cpp`	4,928	About box source
`xped1abd.h`	1,470	About box header
`xped1app.cpp`	4,507	Main application source
`xped1app.def`	499	Application definition file
`xped1app.h`	1,546	Main application header
`xped1app.rc`	13,359	Resource source
`xped1app.rh`	4,402	Resource header

The preceding files contain an icon, header, definition, resource header, resource, implementation, and IDE files. Let's look at the .DEF, .H, .RH, .RC, and .CPP files. Listing X3.1 shows the contents of the XPED1APP.DEF definition file. The .DEF definition files for the other projects are very similar and differ mainly in the name of the project. Because showing the other .DEF files will not reveal any significant new information, the XPED1APP.DEF serves here as a representative sample for the other XPED*x*APP.DEF files.

Build the XPED1 project and experiment with its text-editing features.

Listing X3.1. The contents of the XPED1APP.DEF definition file.

```
;-----------------------------------------------
;    Project xped1
;
;   Copyright _ 1994. All Rights Reserved.
;
;   SUBSYSTEM:    xped1.exe Module  Defintion File
;   FILE:         xped1app.def
;   AUTHOR:
;
;-----------------------------------------------

NAME xped1

DESCRIPTION 'xped1 Application - Copyright 1994. All Rights Reserved.'
EXETYPE     WINDOWS
CODE        PRELOAD MOVEABLE DISCARDABLE
DATA        PRELOAD MOVEABLE
HEAPSIZE    4096
STACKSIZE   8192
```

Listing X3.2. The source code for the XPED1APP.RH resource header file.

```
//#if !defined(__xped1app_rh)              // Sentry use file
➥only if it's not already included.
//#define __xped1app_rh

/*   Project xped1

    Copyright _ 1994. All Rights Reserved.

    SUBSYSTEM:    xped1.exe Application
    FILE:         xped1app.h
    AUTHOR:


    OVERVIEW
    ========
    Constant definitions for all resources defined in xped1app.rc.
*/


//
// IDHELP BorButton for BWCC dialogs.
//
```

continues

Listing X3.2. continued

```
#define IDHELP                          998             // Id of help button


//
// Application specific definitions:
//
#define IDI_SDIAPPLICATION              1001            // Application icon

#define SDI_MENU                        100             // Menu resource
➥ID and Accelerator IDs

//
// CM_FILEnnnn commands (include\owl\editfile.rh except for
➥CM_FILEPRINTPREVIEW)
//
#define CM_FILENEW                      24331           // SDI New
#define CM_FILEOPEN                     24332           // SDI Open
#define CM_FILECLOSE                    24339
#define CM_FILESAVE                     24333
#define CM_FILESAVEAS                   24334


//
// Window commands (include\owl\ window.rh)
//
#define CM_EXIT                         24310


//
// CM_EDITnnnn commands (include\owl\ window.rh)
//
#define CM_EDITUNDO                     24321
#define CM_EDITCUT                      24322
#define CM_EDITCOPY                     24323
#define CM_EDITPASTE                    24324
#define CM_EDITDELETE                   24325
#define CM_EDITCLEAR                    24326
#define CM_EDITADD                      24327
#define CM_EDITEDIT                     24328


//
// Search menu commands (include\owl\editsear.rh)
//
#define CM_EDITFIND                     24351
#define CM_EDITREPLACE                  24352
#define CM_EDITFINDNEXT                 24353


```

```
//
// Help menu commands.
//
#define CM_HELPABOUT              2009
//
// About Dialogs
//
#define IDD_ABOUT                22000
#define IDC_VERSION              22001
#define IDC_COPYRIGHT            22002
#define IDC_DEBUG                22003
//
// OWL defined strings
//
// Statusbar
#define IDS_MODES                32530
#define IDS_MODESOFF             32531
// EditFile
#define IDS_UNTITLED             32550
#define IDS_UNABLEREAD           32551
#define IDS_UNABLEWRITE          32552
#define IDS_FILECHANGED          32553
#define IDS_FILEFILTER           32554
// EditSearch
#define IDS_CANNOTFIND           32540
//
// General & application exception messages (include\owl\except.rh)
//
#define IDS_UNKNOWNEXCEPTION     32767
#define IDS_OWLEXCEPTION         32766
#define IDS_OKTORESUME           32765
#define IDS_UNHANDLEDXMSG        32764
#define IDS_UNKNOWNERROR         32763
#define IDS_NOAPP                32762
#define IDS_OUTOFMEMORY          32761
#define IDS_INVALIDMODULE        32760
#define IDS_INVALIDMAINWINDOW    32759
#define IDS_VBXLIBRARYFAIL       32758
//
// Owl 1 compatibility messages
```

continues

Listing X3.2. continued

```
//
#define IDS_INVALIDWINDOW       32756
#define IDS_INVALIDCHILDWINDOW  32755
#define IDS_INVALIDCLIENTWINDOW 32754

//
// TXWindow messages
//
#define IDS_CLASSREGISTERFAIL   32749
#define IDS_CHILDREGISTERFAIL   32748
#define IDS_WINDOWCREATEFAIL    32747
#define IDS_WINDOWEXECUTEFAIL   32746
#define IDS_CHILDCREATEFAIL     32745

#define IDS_MENUFAILURE         32744
#define IDS_VALIDATORSYNTAX     32743
#define IDS_PRINTERERROR        32742

#define IDS_LAYOUTINCOMPLETE    32741
#define IDS_LAYOUTBADRELWIN     32740

//
// TXGdi messages
//
#define IDS_GDIFAILURE          32739
#define IDS_GDIALLOCFAIL        32738
#define IDS_GDICREATEFAIL       32737
#define IDS_GDIRESLOADFAIL      32736
#define IDS_GDIFILEREADFAIL     32735
#define IDS_GDIDELETEFAIL       32734
#define IDS_GDIDESTROYFAIL      32733
#define IDS_INVALIDDIBHANDLE    32732


// TInputDialog DIALOG resource (include\owl\inputdia.rh)
#define IDD_INPUTDIALOG         32514
#define ID_PROMPT               4091
#define ID_INPUT                4090


// TSlider bitmaps (horizontal and vertical)
(include\owl\slider.rh)
#define IDB_HSLIDERTHUMB        32000
#define IDB_VSLIDERTHUMB        32001


// Validation messages (include\owl\validate.rh)
#define IDS_VALPXPCONFORM       32520
#define IDS_VALINVALIDCHAR      32521
```

```
168: #define IDS_VALNOTINRANGE       32522
169: #define IDS_VALNOTINLIST        32523
170:
171:
172: //#endif          // __xped1app_rh sentry.
```

Listing X3.2 shows the source code for the XPED1APP.RH resource header file. The file contains the definitions of constants used to manage the following menu commands and resources:

- The File menu options (lines 32 to 39)
- The Edit menu options (lines 48 to 66)
- The Help menu options (lines 69 to 72)
- The About dialog box (lines 75 to 81)
- The edit file messages (lines 93 to 98)
- The general and application exception messages (lines 104 to 116)
- The GDI exception messages (lines 141 to 151)
- The input dialog box resources (lines 154 to 157)
- The slider bitmaps (lines 160 and 162)
- The validation messages (lines 165 to 169)

Listing X3.3. The source code for the XPED1APP.H header file.

```
#if !defined(__xped1app_h)              // Sentry, use file only if it's not already included.
#define __xped1app_h

/*  Project xped1

    Copyright _ 1994. All Rights Reserved.

    SUBSYSTEM:    xped1.exe Application
    FILE:         xped1app.h
    AUTHOR:


    OVERVIEW
    ========
    Class definition for XpEd1App (TApplication).
```

continues

Listing X3.3. continued

```
*/


#include <owl\owlpch.h>
#pragma hdrstop


#include "xped1app.rh"            // Definition of all resources.


//
// FrameWindow must be derived to override Paint for Preview and Print.
//
//{{TDecoratedFrame = SDIDecFrame}}
class SDIDecFrame : public TDecoratedFrame {
public:
    SDIDecFrame (TWindow *parent, const char far *title, TWindow *clientWnd, bool trackMenuSelection = false, TModule *module = 0);
    ~SDIDecFrame ();
};    //{{SDIDecFrame}}


//{{TApplication = XpEd1App}}
class XpEd1App : public TApplication {
private:

public:
    XpEd1App ();
    virtual ~XpEd1App ();

    TOpenSaveDialog::TData FileData;                    // Data to control open/saveas standard dialog.
    void OpenFile (const char *fileName = 0);
//{{XpEd1AppVIRTUAL_BEGIN}}
public:
    virtual void InitMainWindow();
//{{XpEd1AppVIRTUAL_END}}

//{{XpEd1AppRSP_TBL_BEGIN}}
protected:
    void CmFileNew ();
    void CmFileOpen ();
    void CmFileClose ();
    void CmHelpAbout ();
//{{XpEd1AppRSP_TBL_END}}
DECLARE_RESPONSE_TABLE(XpEd1App);
```

```
60: };    //{{XpEd1App}}
61:
62:
63: #endif                                        // __xped1app_h sentry.
```

Analysis Listing X3.3 shows the source code for the XPED1APP.H header file. This file declares the text-editor application class `XpEd1App` as a descendent of `TApplication`. The class has public, protected, and private members. The public members include the constructor, destructor, and member function `InitMainWindow`. The protected members include the `CmXXXX` functions that respond to various menu commands. Note the data member `FileData` (declared in line 45), an instance of class `TOpenSaveDialog::TData`, which stores the data for the File Open and File Save dialog boxes.

Type **Listing X3.4. The source code for the XPED1ABD.H header file.**

```
#if !defined(__xped1abd_h)              // Sentry, use file only
➥if it's not already included.
#define __xped1abd_h

/*  Project xped1

    Copyright _ 1994. All Rights Reserved.

    SUBSYSTEM:    xped1.exe Application
    FILE:         xped1abd.h
    AUTHOR:


    OVERVIEW
    ========
    Class definition for XpEd1AboutDlg (TDialog).
*/


#include <owl\owlpch.h>
#pragma hdrstop

#include "xped1app.rh"                  // Definition of all resources.


//{{TDialog = XpEd1AboutDlg}}
class XpEd1AboutDlg : public TDialog {
public:
    XpEd1AboutDlg (TWindow *parent, TResId resId = IDD_ABOUT,
➥TModule*module = 0);
```

continues

Listing X3.4. continued

```
    virtual ~XpEd1AboutDlg ();

//{{XpEd1AboutDlgVIRTUAL_BEGIN}}
public:
    void SetupWindow ();
//{{XpEd1AboutDlgVIRTUAL_END}}
};    //{{XpEd1AboutDlg}}


// Reading the VERSIONINFO resource.
class ProjectRCVersion {
public:
    ProjectRCVersion (TModule *module);
    virtual ~ProjectRCVersion ();

    bool GetProductName (LPSTR &prodName);
    bool GetProductVersion (LPSTR &prodVersion);
    bool GetCopyright (LPSTR &copyright);
    bool GetDebug (LPSTR &debug);

protected:
    LPBYTE      TransBlock;
    void FAR    *FVData;

private:
    // Don't allow this object to be copied.
    ProjectRCVersion (const ProjectRCVersion &);
    ProjectRCVersion & operator =(const ProjectRCVersion &);
};


#endif                                      // __xped1abd_h sentry.
```

Analysis

Listing X3.4. shows the source code for the XPED1ABD.H header file. This header file contains the declaration of the About dialog box class, `XpEd1AboutDlg`. This class is a descendant of the class `TDialog` and declares a constructor, destructor, and the member function `SetupWindow`. Because the other text-editor projects use the same kind of About dialog box, the file XPED1ABD.H is representative of the other XPED*x*ABD.H header files. These files differ only in the name of the dialog box class, which is derived from the project name.

Listing X3.5. The script for the XPED1APP.RC resource file.

```
 /*   Project xped1

    Copyright _ 1994. All Rights Reserved.

    SUBSYSTEM:    xped1.exe Application
    FILE:         xped1app.rc
    AUTHOR:


    OVERVIEW
    ========
    All resources defined here.
*/

#if !defined(WORKSHOP_INVOKED)
#include <windows.h>
#endif
#include "xped1app.rh"

SDI_MENU MENU
BEGIN
    POPUP "&File"
    BEGIN
        MENUITEM "&New", CM_FILENEW
        MENUITEM "&Open...", CM_FILEOPEN
        MENUITEM "&Close", CM_FILECLOSE
        MENUITEM SEPARATOR
        MENUITEM "&Save", CM_FILESAVE, GRAYED
        MENUITEM "Save &As...", CM_FILESAVEAS, GRAYED
        MENUITEM SEPARATOR
        MENUITEM "E&xit\tAlt+F4", CM_EXIT
    END

 MENUITEM SEPARATOR

    POPUP "&Edit"
    BEGIN
        MENUITEM "&Undo\tAlt+BkSp", CM_EDITUNDO, GRAYED
        MENUITEM SEPARATOR
        MENUITEM "Cu&t\tShift+Del", CM_EDITCUT, GRAYED
        MENUITEM "&Copy\tCtrl+Ins", CM_EDITCOPY, GRAYED
        MENUITEM "&Paste\tShift+Ins", CM_EDITPASTE, GRAYED
        MENUITEM SEPARATOR
        MENUITEM "Clear &All\tCtrl+Del", CM_EDITCLEAR, GRAYED
        MENUITEM "&Delete\tDel", CM_EDITDELETE, GRAYED
    END

    POPUP "&Search"
```

continues

Listing X3.5. continued

```
    BEGIN
        MENUITEM "&Find...", CM_EDITFIND, GRAYED
        MENUITEM "&Replace...", CM_EDITREPLACE, GRAYED
        MENUITEM "&Next\aF3", CM_EDITFINDNEXT, GRAYED
    END

 MENUITEM SEPARATOR

 MENUITEM SEPARATOR

 MENUITEM SEPARATOR


 MENUITEM SEPARATOR

    POPUP "&Help"
    BEGIN
        MENUITEM "&About...", CM_HELPABOUT
    END

END


// Accelerator table for short-cut to menu commands. (include\owl\editfile.rc)
SDI_MENU ACCELERATORS
BEGIN
  VK_DELETE, CM_EDITDELETE, VIRTKEY
  VK_DELETE, CM_EDITCUT, VIRTKEY, SHIFT
  VK_INSERT, CM_EDITCOPY, VIRTKEY, CONTROL
  VK_INSERT, CM_EDITPASTE, VIRTKEY, SHIFT
  VK_DELETE, CM_EDITCLEAR, VIRTKEY, CONTROL
  VK_BACK,   CM_EDITUNDO, VIRTKEY, ALT
  VK_F3,     CM_EDITFINDNEXT, VIRTKEY
END


//
// Table of help hints displayed in the status bar.
//
STRINGTABLE
BEGIN
    -1,                       "File/document operations"
    CM_FILENEW,               "Creates a new window"
    CM_FILEOPEN,              "Opens a window"
    CM_FILECLOSE,             "Close this document"
    CM_FILESAVE,              "Saves this document"
    CM_FILESAVEAS,            "Saves this document with a new name"
```

```
    CM_EXIT,                      "Quits XpEd1App and prompts to save
➥the documents"
    CM_EDITUNDO-1,                "Edit operations"
    CM_EDITUNDO,                  "Reverses the last operation"
    CM_EDITCUT,                   "Cuts the selection and puts it on
➥the Clipboard"
    CM_EDITCOPY,                  "Copies the selection and puts it on
➥the Clipboard"
    CM_EDITPASTE,                 "Inserts the clipboard contents at
➥the insertion point"
    CM_EDITDELETE,                "Deletes the selection"
    CM_EDITCLEAR,                 "Clear the document"
    CM_EDITADD,                   "Insert a new line"
    CM_EDITEDIT,                  "Edit the current line"
    CM_EDITFIND-1,                "Search/replace operations"
    CM_EDITFIND,                  "Finds the specified text"
    CM_EDITREPLACE,               "Finds the specified text and
➥changes it"
    CM_EDITFINDNEXT,              "Finds the next match"
    CM_HELPABOUT-1,               "Access About"
    CM_HELPABOUT,                 "About the xped1 application"
END


//
// OWL string table
//

// EditFile (include\owl\editfile.rc and include\owl\editsear.rc)
STRINGTABLE LOADONCALL MOVEABLE DISCARDABLE
BEGIN
    IDS_CANNOTFIND,                "Cannot find ""%s""."
    IDS_UNTITLED,                  "Document"
    IDS_UNABLEREAD,                "Unable to read file %s from disk."
    IDS_UNABLEWRITE,               "Unable to write file %s to disk."
    IDS_FILECHANGED,               "The text in the %s file has
➥changed.\n\nDo you want to save the changes?"
    IDS_FILEFILTER,                "Text files (*.TXT)¦*.TXT¦AllFiles
➥(*.*)¦*.*¦"
END


// Exception string resources (include\owl\except.rc)
STRINGTABLE LOADONCALL MOVEABLE DISCARDABLE
BEGIN
    IDS_OWLEXCEPTION,              "ObjectWindows Exception"
    IDS_UNHANDLEDXMSG,             "Unhandled Exception"
    IDS_OKTORESUME,                "OK to resume?"
    IDS_UNKNOWNEXCEPTION,          "Unknown exception"

    IDS_UNKNOWNERROR,              "Unknown error"
```

continues

Listing X3.5. continued

```
        IDS_NOAPP,                  "No application object"
        IDS_OUTOFMEMORY,            "Out of memory"
        IDS_INVALIDMODULE,          "Invalid module specified for
    ➥window"
        IDS_INVALIDMAINWINDOW,      "Invalid MainWindow"
        IDS_VBXLIBRARYFAIL,         "VBX Library init failure"

        IDS_INVALIDWINDOW,          "Invalid window %s"
        IDS_INVALIDCHILDWINDOW,     "Invalid child window %s"
        IDS_INVALIDCLIENTWINDOW,    "Invalid client window %s"

        IDS_CLASSREGISTERFAIL,      "Class registration fail for
    ➥window %s"
        IDS_CHILDREGISTERFAIL,      "Child class registration fail for
    ➥window %s"
        IDS_WINDOWCREATEFAIL,       "Create fail for window %s"
        IDS_WINDOWEXECUTEFAIL,      "Execute fail for window %s"
        IDS_CHILDCREATEFAIL,        "Child create fail for window %s"

        IDS_MENUFAILURE,            "Menu creation failure"
        IDS_VALIDATORSYNTAX,        "Validator syntax error"
        IDS_PRINTERERROR,           "Printer error"

        IDS_LAYOUTINCOMPLETE,       "Incomplete layout constraints
    ➥specified in window %s"
        IDS_LAYOUTBADRELWIN,        "Invalid relative window specified
    ➥in layout constraint in window %s"

        IDS_GDIFAILURE,             "GDI failure"
        IDS_GDIALLOCFAIL,           "GDI allocate failure"
        IDS_GDICREATEFAIL,          "GDI creation failure"
        IDS_GDIRESLOADFAIL,         "GDI resource load failure"
        IDS_GDIFILEREADFAIL,        "GDI file read failure"
        IDS_GDIDELETEFAIL,          "GDI object %X delete failure"
        IDS_GDIDESTROYFAIL,         "GDI object %X destroy failure"
        IDS_INVALIDDIBHANDLE,       "Invalid DIB handle %X"
   END


   // General Window's status bar messages. (include\owl\statusba.rc)
   STRINGTABLE
   BEGIN
        IDS_MODES                   "EXT¦CAPS¦NUM¦SCRL¦OVR¦REC"
        IDS_MODESOFF                "   ¦    ¦   ¦    ¦   ¦   "
        SC_SIZE,                    "Changes the size of the window"
        SC_MOVE,                    "Moves the window to another
    ➥position"
        SC_MINIMIZE,                "Reduces the window to an icon"
```

```
    SC_MAXIMIZE,                    "Enlarges the window to it maximum
➥size"
    SC_RESTORE,                     "Restores the window to its
➥previous size"
    SC_CLOSE,                       "Closes the window"
    SC_TASKLIST,                    "Opens task list"
    SC_NEXTWINDOW,                  "Switches to next window"
END


// Validator messages (include\owl\validate.rc)
STRINGTABLE LOADONCALL MOVEABLE DISCARDABLE
BEGIN
    IDS_VALPXPCONFORM              "Input does not conform to
➥picture:\n""%s"""
    IDS_VALINVALIDCHAR             "Invalid character in input"
    IDS_VALNOTINRANGE              "Value is not in the range %ld to
➥%ld."
    IDS_VALNOTINLIST               "Input is not in valid-list"
END


//
// Misc application definitions
//

// Application ICON
IDI_SDIAPPLICATION ICON "applsdi.ico"


// About box.
IDD_ABOUT DIALOG 12, 17, 204, 65
STYLE DS_MODALFRAME | WS_POPUP | WS_CAPTION | WS_SYSMENU
CAPTION "About xped1"
FONT 8, "MS Sans Serif"
BEGIN
    CTEXT "Version", IDC_VERSION, 2, 14, 200, 8, SS_NOPREFIX
    CTEXT "My Application", -1, 2, 4, 200, 8, SS_NOPREFIX
    CTEXT "", IDC_COPYRIGHT, 2, 27, 200, 17, SS_NOPREFIX
    RTEXT "", IDC_DEBUG, 136, 55, 66, 8, SS_NOPREFIX
    ICON IDI_SDIAPPLICATION, -1, 2, 2,  34, 34
    DEFPUSHBUTTON "OK", IDOK,  82, 48,  40, 14
END


// TInputDialog class dialog box.
IDD_INPUTDIALOG DIALOG 20, 24, 180, 64
STYLE WS_POPUP | WS_CAPTION | DS_SETFONT
FONT 8, "Helv"
BEGIN
    LTEXT "", ID_PROMPT, 10, 8, 160, 10, SS_NOPREFIX
```

continues

Listing X3.5. continued

```
    CONTROL "", ID_INPUT, "EDIT", WS_CHILD | WS_VISIBLE | WS_BORDER | WS_TABSTOP | ES_AUTOHSCROLL, 10, 20, 160, 12
    DEFPUSHBUTTON "&OK", IDOK, 47, 42, 40, 14
    PUSHBUTTON "&Cancel", IDCANCEL, 93, 42, 40, 14
END


// Horizontal slider thumb bitmap for TSlider and VSlider (include\owl\slider.rc)
IDB_HSLIDERTHUMB BITMAP PRELOAD MOVEABLE DISCARDABLE
BEGIN
     '42 4D 66 01 00 00 00 00 00 00 76 00 00 00 28 00'
     '00 00 12 00 00 00 14 00 00 00 01 00 04 00 00 00'
     '00 00 F0 00 00 00 00 00 00 00 00 00 00 00 00 00'
     '00 00 10 00 00 00 00 00 00 00 00 00 C0 00 00 C0'
     '00 00 00 C0 C0 00 C0 00 00 00 C0 00 C0 00 C0 C0'
     '00 00 C0 C0 C0 00 80 80 80 00 00 00 FF 00 00 FF'
     '00 00 00 FF FF 00 FF 00 00 00 FF 00 FF 00 FF FF'
     '00 00 FF FF FF 00 BB BB 0B BB BB BB B0 BB BB 00'
     '00 00 BB B0 80 BB BB BB 08 0B BB 00 00 00 BB 08'
     'F8 0B BB B0 87 70 BB 00 00 00 B0 8F F8 80 BB 08'
     '77 77 0B 00 00 00 08 F8 88 88 00 88 88 87 70 00'
     '00 00 0F F7 77 88 00 88 77 77 70 00 00 00 0F F8'
     '88 88 00 88 88 87 70 00 00 00 0F F7 77 88 00 88'
     '77 77 70 00 00 00 0F F8 88 88 00 88 88 87 70 00'
     '00 00 0F F7 77 88 00 88 77 77 70 00 00 00 0F F8'
     '88 88 00 88 88 87 70 00 00 00 0F F7 77 88 00 88'
     '77 77 70 00 00 00 0F F8 88 88 00 88 88 87 70 00'
     '00 00 0F F7 77 88 00 88 77 77 70 00 00 00 0F F8'
     '88 88 00 88 88 87 70 00 00 00 0F F7 77 88 00 88'
     '77 77 70 00 00 00 0F F8 88 88 00 88 88 87 70 00'
     '00 00 0F F7 77 78 00 88 77 77 70 00 00 00 0F FF'
     'FF FF 00 88 88 88 80 00 00 00 B0 00 00 00 BB 00'
     '00 00 0B 00 00 00'
END


// Vertical slider thumb bitmap for TSlider and HSlider (include\owl\slider.rc)
IDB_VSLIDERTHUMB BITMAP PRELOAD MOVEABLE DISCARDABLE
BEGIN
     '42 4D 2A 01 00 00 00 00 00 00 76 00 00 00 28 00'
     '00 00 28 00 00 00 09 00 00 00 01 00 04 00 00 00'
     '00 00 B4 00 00 00 00 00 00 00 00 00 00 00 00 00'
     '00 00 10 00 00 00 00 00 00 00 00 00 C0 00 00 C0'
     '00 00 00 C0 C0 00 C0 00 00 00 C0 00 C0 00 C0 C0'
     '00 00 C0 C0 C0 00 80 80 80 00 00 00 FF 00 00 FF'
     '00 00 00 FF FF 00 FF 00 00 00 FF 00 FF 00 FF FF'
     '00 00 FF FF FF 00 B0 00 00 00 00 00 00 00 00 0B'
```

```
        'B0 00 00 00 00 00 00 00 00 0B 0F 88 88 88 88 88'
        '88 88 88 80 08 88 88 88 88 88 88 88 88 80 0F 77'
        '77 77 77 77 77 77 77 80 08 77 77 77 77 77 77 77'
        '77 80 0F 77 FF FF FF FF FF FF F7 80 08 77 FF FF'
        'FF FF FF FF F7 80 0F 70 00 00 00 00 00 00 77 80'
        '08 70 00 00 00 00 00 00 77 80 0F 77 77 77 77 77'
        '77 77 77 80 08 77 77 77 77 77 77 77 77 80 0F 77'
        '77 77 77 77 77 77 77 80 08 77 77 77 77 77 77 77'
        '77 80 0F FF FF FF FF FF FF FF FF F0 08 88 88 88'
        '88 88 88 88 88 80 B0 00 00 00 00 00 00 00 00 0B'
        'B0 00 00 00 00 00 00 00 00 0B'
END


// Version info.
//
#if !defined(__DEBUG_)
// Non-Debug VERSIONINFO
1 VERSIONINFO LOADONCALL MOVEABLE
FILEVERSION 1, 0, 0, 0
PRODUCTVERSION 1, 0, 0, 0
FILEFLAGSMASK 0
FILEFLAGS VS_FFI_FILEFLAGSMASK
FILEOS VOS__WINDOWS16
FILETYPE VFT_APP
BEGIN
    BLOCK "StringFileInfo"
    BEGIN
        // Language type = U.S. English (0x0409) and Character
➥Set = Windows, Multilingual(0x04e4)
        BLOCK "040904E4"                          // Matches
➥ VarFileInfo Translation hex value.
        BEGIN
            VALUE "CompanyName", "\000"
            VALUE "FileDescription", "xped1 for Windows\000"
            VALUE "FileVersion", "1.0\000"
            VALUE "InternalName", "xped1\000"
            VALUE "LegalCopyright", "Copyright _ 1994. All Rights
➥Reserved.\000"
            VALUE "LegalTrademarks", "Windows (TM) is a trademark
➥of Microsoft Corporation\000"
            VALUE "OriginalFilename", "xped1.EXE\000"
            VALUE "ProductName", "xped1\000"
            VALUE "ProductVersion", "1.0\000"
        END
    END

    BLOCK "VarFileInfo"
    BEGIN
        VALUE "Translation", 0x0409, 0x04e4         // U.S.
➥English(0x0409) & Windows Multilingual(0x04e4) 1252
```

continues

Listing X3.5. continued

```
    END

END
#else

// Debug VERSIONINFO
1 VERSIONINFO LOADONCALL MOVEABLE
FILEVERSION 1, 0, 0, 0
PRODUCTVERSION 1, 0, 0, 0
FILEFLAGSMASK VS_FF_DEBUG ¦ VS_FF_PRERELEASE ¦ VS_FF_PATCHED ¦ VS_FF_PRIVATEBUILD ¦ VS_FF_SPECIALBUILD
FILEFLAGS VS_FFI_FILEFLAGSMASK
FILEOS VOS__WINDOWS16
FILETYPE VFT_APP
BEGIN
    BLOCK "StringFileInfo"
    BEGIN
        // Language type = U.S. English (0x0409) and Character Set =Windows, Multilingual(0x04e4)
        BLOCK "040904E4"                            // Matches VarFileInfo Translation hex value.
        BEGIN
            VALUE "CompanyName", "\000"
            VALUE "FileDescription", "xped1 for Windows\000"
            VALUE "FileVersion", "1.0\000"
            VALUE "InternalName", "xped1\000"
            VALUE "LegalCopyright", "Copyright _ 1994. All Rights Reserved.\000"
            VALUE "LegalTrademarks", "Windows (TM) is a trademark of Microsoft Corporation\000"
            VALUE "OriginalFilename", "xped1.EXE\000"
            VALUE "ProductName", "xped1\000"
            VALUE "ProductVersion", "1.0\000"
            VALUE "SpecialBuild", "Debug Version\000"
            VALUE "PrivateBuild", "Built by \000"
        END
    END

    BLOCK "VarFileInfo"
    BEGIN
        VALUE "Translation", 0x0409, 0x04e4        // U.S. English(0x0409) & Windows Multilingual(0x04e4) 1252
    END

END
#endif
```

Listing X3.5 contains the script for the XPED1APP.RC resource file. This file contains the definition of the various menu, accelerator, string, icon, and dialog box resources. The resource files for the other text-editor projects contain script that varies somewhat from the one in Listing X3.6. Because the variation is not major, we will not list the .RC files for the other text-editor projects. You are encouraged to browse through the other .RC files and compare them with file XPED1APP.RC.

Listing X3.6. The source code for the XPED1ABD.CPP implementation file.

```
/*  Project xped1

    Copyright 1994. All Rights Reserved.

    SUBSYSTEM:    xped1.exe Application
    FILE:         xped1abd.cpp
    AUTHOR:


    OVERVIEW
    ========
    Source file for implementation of XpEd1AboutDlg (TDialog).
*/


#include <owl\owlpch.h>
#pragma hdrstop

#if !defined(__FLAT__)
#include <ver.h>
#endif

#include "xped1app.h"
#include "xped1abd.h"


ProjectRCVersion::ProjectRCVersion (TModule *module)
{
    char    appFName[255];
    char    subBlockName[255];
    DWORD   fvHandle;
    UINT    vSize;

    FVData = 0;

    module->GetModuleFileName(appFName, sizeof(appFName));
    DWORD dwSize = ::GetFileVersionInfoSize(appFName, &fvHandle);
    if (dwSize) {
        FVData  = (void FAR *)new char[(UINT)dwSize];
```

Listing X3.6. continued

```
        if (::GetFileVersionInfo(appFName, fvHandle, dwSize,
➥ FVData)) {
            // Copy string to buffer so if the -dc compiler switch
➥(Put constant strings in code segments)
            // is on VerQueryValue will work under Win16. This
➥works around a problem in Microsoft's ver.dll
            // which writes to the string pointed to by
➥subBlockName.
            strcpy(subBlockName, "\\VarFileInfo\\Translation");
            if (!::VerQueryValue(FVData, subBlockName, (void FAR*
➥FAR*)&TransBlock, &vSize)) {
                delete FVData;
                FVData = 0;
            } else
                // Swap the words so wsprintf will print the
➥lang-charset in the correct format.
                *(DWORD *)TransBlock = MAKELONG(HIWORD(*(DWORD
➥*)TransBlock), LOWORD(*(DWORD *)TransBlock));
        }
    }
}


ProjectRCVersion::~ProjectRCVersion ()
{
    if (FVData)
        delete FVData;
}


bool ProjectRCVersion::GetProductName (LPSTR &prodName)
{
    UINT    vSize;
    char    subBlockName[255];

    wsprintf(subBlockName, "\\StringFileInfo\\%08lx\\%s", *(DWORD
➥*)TransBlock, (LPSTR)"ProductName");
    return FVData ? ::VerQueryValue(FVData, subBlockName, (void
➥FAR*FAR*)&prodName, &vSize) :  false;
}


bool ProjectRCVersion::GetProductVersion (LPSTR &prodVersion)
{
    UINT    vSize;
    char    subBlockName[255];

    wsprintf(subBlockName, "\\StringFileInfo\\%08lx\\%s", *(DWORD
➥*)TransBlock, (LPSTR)"ProductVersion");
```

```
    return FVData ? ::VerQueryValue(FVData, subBlockName, (void
➥FAR*FAR*)&prodVersion, &vSize) :  false;
}


bool ProjectRCVersion::GetCopyright (LPSTR &copyright)
{
    UINT    vSize;
    char    subBlockName[255];

    wsprintf(subBlockName, "\\StringFileInfo\\%08lx\\%s", *(DWORD
➥*)TransBlock, (LPSTR)"LegalCopyright");
    return FVData ? ::VerQueryValue(FVData, subBlockName, (void
➥FAR*FAR*)&copyright, &vSize) :  false;
}


bool ProjectRCVersion::GetDebug (LPSTR &debug)
{
    UINT    vSize;
    char    subBlockName[255];

    wsprintf(subBlockName, "\\StringFileInfo\\%08lx\\%s", *(DWORD
➥*)TransBlock, (LPSTR)"SpecialBuild");
    return FVData ? ::VerQueryValue(FVData, subBlockName, (void
➥FAR*FAR*)&debug, &vSize) :  false;
}


//{{XpEd1AboutDlg Implementation}}


//////////////////////////////////////////////////////////////
// XpEd1AboutDlg
// ==========
// Construction/Destruction handling.
XpEd1AboutDlg::XpEd1AboutDlg (TWindow *parent, TResId resId,
➥TModule *module)
    : TDialog(parent, resId, module)
{
    // INSERT>> Your constructor code here.
}


XpEd1AboutDlg::~XpEd1AboutDlg ()
{
    Destroy();

    // INSERT>> Your destructor code here.
}

```

Listing X3.6. continued

```

void XpEd1AboutDlg::SetupWindow ()
{
    LPSTR prodName = 0, prodVersion = 0, copyright = 0, debug = 0;

    // Get the static text  for the value  based on VERSIONINFO.
    TStatic *versionCtrl = new TStatic(this, IDC_VERSION, 255);
    TStatic *copyrightCtrl = new TStatic(this, IDC_COPYRIGHT, 255);
    TStatic *debugCtrl = new TStatic(this, IDC_DEBUG, 255);

    TDialog::SetupWindow();

    // Process the VERSIONINFO.
    ProjectRCVersion applVersion(GetModule());

    // Get the product name and product version  strings.
    if (applVersion.GetProductName(prodName) &&
➥applVersion.GetProductVersion(prodVersion)) {
        // IDC_VERSION is the product name and version number, the
➥initial value of IDC_VERSION is
        // the word Version (in whatever language) product name
➥VERSION product version.
        char    buffer[255];
        char    versionName[128];

        buffer[0] = '\0';
        versionName[0] = '\0';

        versionCtrl->GetText(versionName, sizeof(versionName));
        wsprintf(buffer, "%s %s %s", prodName, versionName,
➥prodVersion);

        versionCtrl->SetText(buffer);
    }

    //Get the legal copyright string.
    if (applVersion.GetCopyright(copyright))
        copyrightCtrl->SetText(copyright);

    // Only get the SpecialBuild text if the VERSIONINFO resource
➥is there.
    if (applVersion.GetDebug(debug))
        debugCtrl->SetText(debug);
}
```

Analysis Listing X3.6 shows the source code for the XPED1ABD.CPP implementation file. This file defines the class `XpEd1AboutDlg`, which implements the About dialog box. In addition, the file declares and defines the project resource version class, `ProjectRCVersion`. Let's briefly look at this class first. The class defines a constructor, destructor, a set of public member functions, and two protected data members. The class `ProjectRCVersion` supports operations that extract the information about the product name, version, and copyright.

The About dialog box class defines the following members:

1. The constructor (defined in lines 106 to 114) simply invokes the constructor of the parent class `TDialog`. The constructor has no executable statements and contains a comment that indicates where to place your code to support additional initialization.

2. The destructor (defined in lines 117 to 122) simply calls the inherited member function `Destroy`. The definition contains a comment that indicates where to place your code to support additional cleanup.

3. The member function `SetupWindow` (defined in lines 125 to 153) sets up the About dialog box by carrying out the following tasks:

   - ☐ Creates three static text control objects for the version, copyright, and debug information. The function assigns the addresses of these controls to the local pointers `versionCtrl`, `copyrightCtrl`, and `debugCtrl`. These objects are surrogate objects for the statics created in the dialog resource.

   - ☐ Invokes the `SetupWindow` member function of the parent dialog box class.

   - ☐ Creates the instance `applVersion` of the class `ProjectRCVersion`.

   - ☐ Calls `applVersion`'s `GetProductName` and `GetProductVersion` to obtain the product name and version. If successful in getting these, the function then sets the `versionCtrl` static text box with the names.

   - ☐ Calls `applVersion`'s `GetCopyright` to obtain the copyright information from the dialog box resource. If successful, it then sets the corresponding static text box.

   - ☐ Assigns the debug information to the debug static text control if `applVersion`'s `GetDebug` function returns a nonzero value.

Listing X3.7. The source code for the XPED1APP.CPP implementation file.

```
/*  Project xped1
    Copyright _ 1994. All Rights Reserved.
    SUBSYSTEM:    xped1.exe Application
    FILE:         xped1app.cpp
    AUTHOR:
    OVERVIEW
    ========
    Source file for implementation of XpEd1App (TApplication).
*/
#include <owl\owlpch.h>
#pragma hdrstop
#include "xped1app.h"
#include "xpd1edtf.h"                          // Definition of client class.
#include "xped1abd.h"                          // Definition of about dialog.
//{{XpEd1App Implementation}}
//
// Build a response table for all messages/commands handled
// by the application.
//
DEFINE_RESPONSE_TABLE1(XpEd1App, TApplication)
//{{XpEd1AppRSP_TBL_BEGIN}}
    EV_COMMAND(CM_FILENEW, CmFileNew),
    EV_COMMAND(CM_FILEOPEN, CmFileOpen),
    EV_COMMAND(CM_FILECLOSE, CmFileClose),
    EV_COMMAND(CM_HELPABOUT, CmHelpAbout),
//{{XpEd1AppRSP_TBL_END}}
END_RESPONSE_TABLE;
//////////////////////////////////////////////////////////
// XpEd1App
// =====
//
XpEd1App::XpEd1App () : TApplication("xped1")
```

```
{

    // Common file file flags and filters for Open/Save As dialogs.
➥Filename and directory are
    // computed in the member functions CmFileOpen, and
➥CmFileSaveAs.
     FileData.Flags = OFN_FILEMUSTEXIST ¦ OFN_HIDEREADONLY ¦
➥OFN_OVERWRITEPROMPT;
     FileData.SetFilter("All Files (*.*)¦*.*¦");

    // INSERT>> Your constructor code here.
}


XpEd1App::~XpEd1App ()
{
    // INSERT>> Your destructor code here.
}


//////////////////////////////////////////////////////////////
// XpEd1App
// =====
// Application intialization.
//
void XpEd1App::InitMainWindow ()
{
    if (nCmdShow != SW_HIDE)
        nCmdShow = (nCmdShow != SW_SHOWMINNOACTIVE) ? SW_SHOWNORMAL
➥:nCmdShow;

    SDIDecFrame *frame = new SDIDecFrame(0, GetName(),  0, false);

    //
    // Assign ICON w/ this application.
    //
    frame->SetIcon(this, IDI_SDIAPPLICATION);

    //
    // Menu associated with window and accelerator table associated
➥with table.
    //
    frame->AssignMenu(SDI_MENU);

    //
    // Associate with the accelerator table.
    //
    frame->Attr.AccelTable = SDI_MENU;


    SetMainWindow(frame);
```

continues

Listing X3.7. continued

```
    frame->SetMenuDescr(TMenuDescr(SDI_MENU));
}


//////////////////////////////////////////////////////////////////////
// XpEd1App
// ===========
// Menu File New command
void XpEd1App::CmFileNew ()
{
    xped1EditFile *client = TYPESAFE_DOWNCAST(GetMainWindow()->
➥GetClientWindow(), xped1EditFile);  // Client window for the frame.
    client->NewFile();
}


//////////////////////////////////////////////////////////////////////
// XpEd1App
// ===========
// Menu File Open command
void XpEd1App::CmFileOpen ()
{
    //
    // Display standard Open dialog box to select a file name.
    //
    *FileData.FileName = 0;

    xped1EditFile *client = TYPESAFE_DOWNCAST(GetMainWindow()->
➥GetClientWindow(), xped1EditFile);  // Client window for the frame.
     if (client->CanClose())
        if (TFileOpenDialog(GetMainWindow(), FileData).Execute()
➥== IDOK)
            OpenFile();
}


void XpEd1App::OpenFile (const char *fileName)
{
    if (fileName)
        strcpy(FileData.FileName, fileName);

    xped1EditFile *client = TYPESAFE_DOWNCAST(GetMainWindow()->
➥GetClientWindow(), xped1EditFile);  // Client window for the frame.
    client->ReplaceWith(FileData.FileName);
}


```

```
/////////////////////////////////////////////////////////////
// XpEd1App
// =====
// Menu File Close command
void XpEd1App::CmFileClose ()
{
    CmFileNew();
}


//{{SDIDecFrame Implementation}}


SDIDecFrame::SDIDecFrame (TWindow *parent, const char far *title, TWindow *clientWnd, bool trackMenuSelection, TModule *module)
    : TDecoratedFrame(parent, title, clientWnd == 0 ? new xped1EditFile(0, 0, 0) : clientWnd, trackMenuSelection, module)
{
    // INSERT>> Your constructor code here.

}


SDIDecFrame::~SDIDecFrame ()
{
    // INSERT>> Your destructor code here.

}


/////////////////////////////////////////////////////////////
// XpEd1App
// ==========
// Menu Help About xped1.exe command
void XpEd1App::CmHelpAbout ()
{
    //
    // Show the modal dialog.
    //
    XpEd1AboutDlg(MainWindow).Execute();
}
int OwlMain (int , char* [])
{
    try {
        XpEd1App    app;
        return app.Run();
    }
     catch (xmsg& x) {
        ::MessageBox(0, x.why().c_str(), "Exception", MB_OK);
```

continues

Listing X3.7. continued

```
184:      }
185:
186:       return -1;
187: }
```

Listing X3.7 shows the source code for the XPED1APP.CPP implementation file. The listing includes the XPED1ABD.H header file to access the definition of the application and About dialog box classes. In addition the listing contains the declaration of a class that models a decorated SDI window frame.

The listing contains the definition of the message-response table for the application class `XpEd1App`. The table includes a set of `EV_COMMAND` macros to map the various `CM_XXXX` commands with their respective `CmXXXX` member functions.

The listing contains the definitions of the following members:

1. The constructor (defined in lines 42 to55), which performs the following minimal initialization:

   - Assigns an expression of bitwise `ORed` `OFN_XXXX` constants to the `Flags` member of the data member `FileData`.

   - Calls the data member `FileData`'s `SetFilter` member function with a string literal argument that assigns the file-type filters to the member `FileData`.

   The preceding assignments initialize the data member `FileData` to prepare it for the dialog boxes that open and save files. The constructor contains a comment that indicates where to place statements for additional initialization.

2. The destructor (defined in lines 58 to 61) merely contains a comment that indicates where to place statements for application clean-up.

3. The member function `InitMainWindow` (defined in lines 64 to 95) initializes the main window by carrying out the following tasks:

   - Assigns a value to the inherited data member `nCmdShow` such that the window appears in its normal state.

   - Creates a new decorated SDI frame window by allocating an instance of class `SDIDecFrame`. The function assigns the address of this instance to the local pointer `frame`.

- Assigns the application's icon using the icon resource `IDI_SDIAPPLICATION`. This task involves calling the member function `SetIcon` of the SDI window accessed by the pointer `frame`.
- Assigns the application's menu using the menu resource SDI_MENU using the `frame`'s `AssignMenu` member function.
- Assigns the accelerator table `SDI_MENU` to the frame window.
- Uses the `SetMainWindow` member function to set the main window to `frame`.
- Set's the menu descriptor to the `SDI_MENU` resource.

4. The member function `CmFileNew` (defined in lines 98 to 106) responds to the New menu option by sending the C++ message `NewFile` to the window client area accessed by pointer `client`.
5. The member function `CmFileOpen` (defined in lines 109 to 124) responds to the Open menu option. The function contains nested `if` statements. The outer `if` statement sends the C++ message `CanClose` to the client area. If this message returns a nonzero value, the function `CmFileOpen` executes the nested `if` statement. This statement creates a dynamic instance of the class `TFileOpenDialog` and sends it the C++ message `Execute`. The `if` statement compares the result of the message with the predefined constant `IDOK`. If the two values match, the function invokes the member function `OpenFile`.
6. The member function `OpenFile` (defined in lines 127 to 134) performs two simple tasks. The first task assigns the string in the parameter `fileName` to the member `FileName` of data member `FileData`. The second task updates the title of the window with the name of the newly opened file. The function performs this task by sending the C++ message `ReplaceWith` to the window client area object. The argument of this message is the member `FileName` of the data member `FileData`.
7. The member function `CmFileClose` simply makes a call to `CmFileNew`. Because this is an SDI application, a file must be open at all times. Therefore, closing one file means that another needs to be opened immediately.
8. The listing offers the definition of class `SDIDecFrame`. This class, a descendent of class `TDecoratedFrame`, models the decorated SDI frame window. The AppExpert comments remind you that this class needs to override the member functions that support the printing and print-previewing features. The class declares a constructor and a dummy destructor.

9. The `XpEd1App`'s member function `CmHelpAbout` (defined in lines 165 to 175) responds to the Help|About menu option. The function creates a new instance of class `XpEd1AboutDlg` to invoke the About dialog box. The function invokes this modal dialog box by sending it the C++ message `Execute`.

Finally, the typical `OwlMain` is presented in which an `XpEd1App` object is created and run. Note that this is automatically enclosed in a `try/catch` block to keep exceptions from getting out of hand.

The XPED2 Project

The project XPED2 supports an SDI-compliant editor with a toolbar and a status line. When you invoke the AppExpert, check the options for the SDI window, the toolbar, and the status line. Uncheck all of the other options. In addition, select the Code Gen Control subtopic (in the Application topic of the AppExpert dialog box) to make the application and dialog box class names `XpEd2App` and `XpEd2AboutDlg`, respectively. Also select the Maximized window option in the Advanced Options subtopic. The AppExpert generates the following files:

Filename	Size	Description
`applsdi.ico`	1,086	Application icon
`copy.bmp`	358	Toolbar copy bitmap
`cut.bmp`	358	Toolbar cut bitmap
`find.bmp`	358	Toolbar find bitmap
`findnext.bmp`	358	Toolbar find next bitmap
`new.bmp`	358	Toolbar new bitmap
`open.bmp`	358	Toolbar open bitmap
`paste.bmp`	358	Toolbar paste bitmap
`print.bmp`	358	Toolbar print bitmap
`save.bmp`	358	Toolbar save bitmap
`undo.bmp`	358	Toolbar undo bitmap
`xpd2edtf.cpp`	1,125	`TEditFile` descendent class source
`xpd2edtf.h`	1,000	`TEditFile` descendent class header
`xped2.apx`	19,711	AppExpert reference file
`xped2.dsw`	236	Borland IDE Desktop file
`xped2.ide`	27,516	IDE project file
`xped2abd.cpp`	4,928	About box source
`xped2abd.h`	1,470	About box header
`xped2app.cpp`	5,959	Main application source

Filename	Size	Description
`xped2app.def`	499	Application definition file
`xped2app.h`	1,598	Main application header
`xped2app.rc`	13,793	Resource source
`xped2app.rh`	4,402	Resource header

The preceding list of files exceeds that of project XPED1 by several .BMP files because the toolbar buttons use these bitmaps.

Build the XPED2 project and experiment with its text-editing features. Due to limited space, we'll be focusing only on the header and implementation files which are fairly different from those in project XPED1. The files XPED2ABD.H and XPED2ABD.CPP are very similar to files XPED1ABD.H and XPED1ABD.CPP, respectively. The main differences are in the class names, which are derived from the project name. By contrast, the files XPED2APP.H and XPED2APP.CPP have more statements and declarations than the files XPED1APP.H and XPED1APP.CPP, respectively.

Listing X3.8. The source code for the XPED2APP.H header file.

```
#if !defined(__xped2app_h)              // Sentry, use file only if
➥it's not already included.
#define __xped2app_h

/*  Project xped2

    Copyright _ 1994. All Rights Reserved.

    SUBSYSTEM:    xped2.exe Application
    FILE:         xped2app.h
    AUTHOR:


    OVERVIEW
    ========
    Class definition for XpEd2App (TApplication).
*/


#include <owl\owlpch.h>
#pragma hdrstop


#include "xped2app.rh"            // Definition of all resources.

```

continues

Listing X3.8. continued

```

//
// FrameWindow must be derived to override Paint for Preview and Print.
//
//{{TDecoratedFrame = SDIDecFrame}}
class SDIDecFrame : public TDecoratedFrame {
public:
    SDIDecFrame (TWindow *parent, const char far *title, TWindow *clientWnd, bool trackMenuSelection = false, TModule *module = 0);
    ~SDIDecFrame ();
};    //{{SDIDecFrame}}


//{{TApplication = XpEd2App}}
class XpEd2App : public TApplication {
private:

    void SetupSpeedBar (TDecoratedFrame *frame);

public:
    XpEd2App ();
    virtual ~XpEd2App ();

    TOpenSaveDialog::TData FileData;                    // Data to control open/saveas standard dialog.
    void OpenFile (const char *fileName = 0);
//{{XpEd2AppVIRTUAL_BEGIN}}
public:
    virtual void InitMainWindow();
//{{XpEd2AppVIRTUAL_END}}

//{{XpEd2AppRSP_TBL_BEGIN}}
protected:
    void CmFileNew ();
    void CmFileOpen ();
    void CmFileClose ();
    void CmHelpAbout ();
//{{XpEd2AppRSP_TBL_END}}
DECLARE_RESPONSE_TABLE(XpEd2App);
};    //{{XpEd2App}}


#endif                                          // __xped2app_h sentry.
```

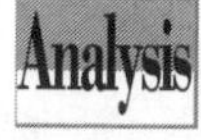

Listing X3.8 shows the source code for the XPED2APP.H header file. This file includes more nested header files than XPED1APP.H in order to support the status bar and the toolbar features. In addition, the XPED2APP.H header file declares the application class `XpEd2App` in line 38. This class is similar to the class `XpEd1App`, except it has the additional public member function `SetupSpeedBar`, located in line 41.

Listing X3.9. The source code for the XPED2PP.CPP implementation file.

```
/*  Project xped2

    Copyright 1994. All Rights Reserved.

    SUBSYSTEM:    xped2.exe Application
    FILE:         xped2app.cpp
    AUTHOR:


    OVERVIEW
    ========
    Source file for implementation of XpEd2App (TApplication).
*/


#include <owl\owlpch.h>
#pragma hdrstop


#include "xped2app.h"
#include "xpd2edtf.h"                              // Definition of clientclass.
#include "xped2abd.h"                              // Definition of about dialog.


//{{XpEd2App Implementation}}


//
// Build a response table for all messages/commands handled
// by the application.
//
DEFINE_RESPONSE_TABLE1(XpEd2App, TApplication)
//{{XpEd2AppRSP_TBL_BEGIN}}
    EV_COMMAND(CM_FILENEW, CmFileNew),
    EV_COMMAND(CM_FILEOPEN, CmFileOpen),
    EV_COMMAND(CM_FILECLOSE, CmFileClose),
    EV_COMMAND(CM_HELPABOUT, CmHelpAbout),
//{{XpEd2AppRSP_TBL_END}}
```

continues

Listing X3.9. continued

```
END_RESPONSE_TABLE;


//////////////////////////////////////////////////////////////
// XpEd2App
// =====
//
XpEd2App::XpEd2App () : TApplication("xped2")
{

    // Common file file flags and filters for Open/Save As dialogs.
➥Filename and directory are
    // computed in the member functions CmFileOpen, and
➥CmFileSaveAs.
    FileData.Flags = OFN_FILEMUSTEXIST ¦ OFN_HIDEREADONLY ¦
➥OFN_OVERWRITEPROMPT;
    FileData.SetFilter("All Files (*.*)¦*.*¦");

    // INSERT>> Your constructor code here.
}


XpEd2App::~XpEd2App ()
{
    // INSERT>> Your destructor code here.
}


void XpEd2App::SetupSpeedBar (TDecoratedFrame *frame)
{
    //
    // Create default toolbar New and associate toolbar buttons
➥with commands.
    //
    TControlBar* cb = new TControlBar(frame);
    cb->Insert(*new TButtonGadget(CM_FILENEW, CM_FILENEW));
    cb->Insert(*new TButtonGadget(CM_FILEOPEN, CM_FILEOPEN));
    cb->Insert(*new TButtonGadget(CM_FILESAVE, CM_FILESAVE));
    cb->Insert(*new TSeparatorGadget(6));
    cb->Insert(*new TButtonGadget(CM_EDITCUT, CM_EDITCUT));
    cb->Insert(*new TButtonGadget(CM_EDITCOPY, CM_EDITCOPY));
    cb->Insert(*new TButtonGadget(CM_EDITPASTE, CM_EDITPASTE));
    cb->Insert(*new TSeparatorGadget(6));
    cb->Insert(*new TButtonGadget(CM_EDITUNDO, CM_EDITUNDO));
    cb->Insert(*new TSeparatorGadget(6));
    cb->Insert(*new TButtonGadget(CM_EDITFIND, CM_EDITFIND));
    cb->Insert(*new TButtonGadget(CM_EDITFINDNEXT,
➥CM_EDITFINDNEXT));

```

```
    // Add fly-over help hints.
    cb->SetHintMode(TGadgetWindow::EnterHints);

    frame->Insert(*cb, TDecoratedFrame::Top);
}


//////////////////////////////////////////////////////////////
// XpEd2App
// =====
// Application  intialization.
//
void XpEd2App::InitMainWindow ()
{
    if (nCmdShow != SW_HIDE)
        nCmdShow = (nCmdShow != SW_SHOWMINNOACTIVE) ?
➥SW_SHOWMAXIMIZED:nCmdShow;

    SDIDecFrame *frame = new SDIDecFrame(0, GetName(),  0, true);

    //
    // Assign ICON w/ this application.
    //
    frame->SetIcon(this, IDI_SDIAPPLICATION);

    //
    // Menu associated with window and accelerator table associated
➥with table.
    //
    frame->AssignMenu(SDI_MENU);

    //
    // Associate with the accelerator table.
    //
    frame->Attr.AccelTable = SDI_MENU;

    SetupSpeedBar(frame);

    TStatusBar *sb = new TStatusBar(frame, TGadget::Recessed,
                                    TStatusBar::CapsLock        |
                                    TStatusBar::NumLock         |
                                    TStatusBar::ScrollLock      |
                                    TStatusBar::Overtype);
    frame->Insert(*sb, TDecoratedFrame::Bottom);

    SetMainWindow(frame);

    frame->SetMenuDescr(TMenuDescr(SDI_MENU));
}
```

continues

Listing X3.9. continued

```
///////////////////////////////////////////////////////////////
// XpEd2App
// ===========
// Menu File New command
void XpEd2App::CmFileNew ()
{
    xped2EditFile *client = TYPESAFE_DOWNCAST(GetMainWindow()->GetClientWindow(), xped2EditFile);  // Client window for the frame.
    client->NewFile();
}


///////////////////////////////////////////////////////////////
// XpEd2App
// ===========
// Menu File Open command
void XpEd2App::CmFileOpen ()
{
    //
    // Display standard Open dialog box to select a file name.
    //
    *FileData.FileName = 0;

    xped2EditFile *client = TYPESAFE_DOWNCAST(GetMainWindow()->GetClientWindow(), xped2EditFile);  // Client window for the frame.
     if (client->CanClose())
        if (TFileOpenDialog(GetMainWindow(), FileData).Execute() == IDOK)
            OpenFile();
}


void XpEd2App::OpenFile (const char *fileName)
{
    if (fileName)
        strcpy(FileData.FileName, fileName);

    xped2EditFile *client = TYPESAFE_DOWNCAST(GetMainWindow()->GetClientWindow(), xped2EditFile);  // Client window for the frame.
    client->ReplaceWith(FileData.FileName);
}


///////////////////////////////////////////////////////////////
// XpEd2App
// =====
// Menu File Close command
void XpEd2App::CmFileClose ()
{
```

```
    CmFileNew();
}


//{{SDIDecFrame Implementation}}


SDIDecFrame::SDIDecFrame (TWindow *parent, const char far *title,
➥TWindow *clientWnd, bool trackMenuSelection, TModule *module)
    : TDecoratedFrame(parent, title, clientWnd == 0 ? new
➥xped2EditFile(0, 0, 0) : clientWnd, trackMenuSelection, module)
{
    // INSERT>> Your constructor code here.

}


SDIDecFrame::~SDIDecFrame ()
{
    // INSERT>> Your destructor code here.

}


/////////////////////////////////////////////////////////////
// XpEd2App
// ===========
// Menu Help About xped2.exe command
void XpEd2App::CmHelpAbout ()
{
    //
    // Show the modal dialog.
    //
    XpEd2AboutDlg(MainWindow).Execute();
}
int OwlMain (int , char* [])
{
    try {
        XpEd2App     app;
        return  app.Run();
    }
    catch (xmsg& x) {
        ::MessageBox(0, x.why().c_str(), "Exception", MB_OK);
    }

    return -1;
}
```

Analysis Listing X3.9 contains the source code for the XPED2APP.CPP implementation file. The file contains the message-response table macro, the definition of the class `SDIDecFrame`, and the definition of the members of the class `XpEd2App`. The message-response macro table and definition of the class `SDIDecFrame` are similar to those in the file XPED1APP.CPP. The following application class member functions are new or different in the file XPED2APP.CPP:

1. The member function `SetupSpeedBar` (defined in lines 64 to 87) sets up the application's speed bar by carrying out these subsequent tasks:
   - Creates a new instance of the class `TControlBar` and assigns the address of that instance to the local pointer `cb`.
   - Inserts the bitmapped buttons in the speed bar by sending a sequence of the C++ message `Insert` to the instance accessed by pointer `cb`. Each message has the appropriate arguments needed to insert a specific bitmapped button. These messages also include the `CM_XXXX` identifiers for the buttons, defined in resource header file.
   - Includes fly-over help hints by sending the C++ message `SetHintMode` to the control bar accessed by pointer `cb`.
   - Sends the C++ message `Insert` to the object accessed by the pointer-type parameter `frame`. This parameter represents the SDI decorated frame window.
2. The member function `InitMainWindow` (defined in lines 90 to 129) initializes the main window by carrying out the following tasks:
   - Assigns a value to the inherited data member `nCmdShow` such that the window appears in its maximized state (as requested in the application setup of AppExpert).
   - Creates a new decorated SDI frame window by allocating an instance of the class `SDIDecFrame`. The function assigns the address of this instance to the local pointer `frame`.
   - Assigns the application's icon using the icon resource `IDI_SDIAPPLICATION`. This task involves sending the C++ message `SetIcon` to the SDI window accessed by the pointer `frame`.
   - Assigns the application's menu using the menu resource `SDI_MENU`. This task involves sending the C++ message `AssignMenu` to the SDI window accessed by the pointer `frame`.

- Assigns the accelerator table `SDI_MENU` to the frame window.
- Invokes the member function `SetupSpeedBar` to set up the tool bar. The argument for this member function is the local pointer `frame`.
- Creates a new instance of the class `TStatusBar`. The function assigns the address of the status bar object to the local pointer `sb`.
- Inserts the status bar in the SDI frame window. This task involves sending the C++ message `Insert` to the frame window. The arguments for this message are the speed bar object (represented by the expression `*sb`) and the `TDecoratedFrame::Bottom` value. This value locates the status bar at the bottom of the SDI frame window.
- Makes the pointer `frame` the main window.
- Sets the menu descriptor from the `SDI_MENU` resource.

The next extra-credit chapter looks at the MDI-compliant text editors generated by AppExpert.

Summary

This chapter introduced you to using the AppExpert utility and offered sample SDI-compliant text-editor applications generated by that utility. You learned about the following topics:

- Working with the AppExpert utility, which you invoke from inside the IDE.
- The Application topics in AppExpert, which enable you to make main selections about the kind of application you wish AppExpert to generate.
- The Main Window topics in AppExpert, which enable you to fine-tune the window styles and the SDI or MDI client windows.
- The MDI Child/View options in AppExpert, which enable you to control the creation of the MDI child windows.
- The XPED1 and XPED2 projects, which implement SDI-compliant, minimally functioning text editors generated by the AppExpert utility. The XPED1 project implements the simplest kind of text editor that you can create with the AppExpert utility. The XPED2 project supports an SDI-compliant editor that has a speed bar and a status line.

Q&A

Q How does the ClassExpert utility complement the source code generated by AppExpert?

A The ClassExpert enables you to fine-tune the source code of AppExpert by adding new classes and/or member functions that support custom operations of your program.

Q Can I customize the code generated by AppExpert without using ClassExpert?

A Yes. However, depending on how you manually customize the code, it may be difficult to use ClassExpert later for further customization.

Q How can I change the menus and other resources?

A Use the Workshop Resource utility.

Exercises

1. Use the AppExpert utility to create a text editor that supports the drag/drop and printing features. Compare the output code with the listings in this chapter.
2. Use the AppExpert utility to create a text editor that supports the speed bar, status line, drag/drop, and printing features. Compare the output code with the listings in this chapter.
3. Use the AppExpert utility to create a text editor that uses the document/view feature. Compare the output code with the listings in this chapter.

Generating MDI Applications with AppExpert

This extra-credit chapter complements the preceding one and examines the different versions of the MDI-compliant text editors generated by the AppExpert utility. You will learn about the following minimal MDI editors:

- An editor that contains the speed bar and the status line.
- An editor that supports the drag-and-drop and printing features.
- An editor that uses the document and view classes.

Note: The listings generated by AppExpert were edited to better fit the pages in this book.

Table X4.1 shows the various projects that create different versions of the MDI-compliant text editors.

Table X4.1. The various MDI-compliant projects generated by AppExpert for this chapter's case studies.

Project	MDI?	Doc/ View?	ToolBar?	Status	Drag Line?	Print? & Drop?
XPED3	Yes	No	Yes	Yes	No	No
XPED4	Yes	No	No	No	Yes	Yes
XPED5	Yes	Yes	No	No	No	No

The XPED3 Project

The XPED3 project creates an MDI-compliant text editor that contains the speed bar and the status line. When you invoke the AppExpert menu option, select the options for the MDI windows, the speed bar, and the status line. Clear the check marks for the remaining options. In addition, select the Code Gen Control subtopic (in the Application topic of the AppExpert dialog box) to make the application and dialog-box class names `XpEd3App` and `XpEd3AboutDlg`, respectively. The AppExpert utility generates the following files:

File Name	Size	Description
applmdi.ico	1,086	Application icon
copy.bmp	358	Toolbar "copy" bitmap
cut.bmp	358	Toolbar "cut" bitmap
find.bmp	358	Toolbar "find" bitmap
findnext.bmp	358	Toolbar "find next" bitmap
mdichild.ico	1,086	Child window icon
new.bmp	358	Toolbar "new" bitmap
open.bmp	358	Toolbar "open" bitmap
paste.bmp	358	Toolbar "paste" bitmap
print.bmp	358	Toolbar "print" bitmap
save.bmp	358	Toolbar "save" bitmap
undo.bmp	358	Toolbar "undo" bitmap
xpd3edtf.cpp	1,146	TEditFile descendent class source
xpd3edtf.h	1,000	TEditFile descendent class header
xpd3mdi1.cpp	972	TMDIChild descendent class source
xpd3mdi1.h	846	TMDIChild descendent class header
xpd3mdic.cpp	5,146	TMDIClient descendent class source
xpd3mdic.h	1,233	TMDIClient descendent class header
xped3.apx	30,467	AppExpert reference file
xped3.dsw	220	Borland IDE Desktop file
xped3.ide	28,522	IDE project file
xped3abd.cpp	4,928	About box source
xped3abd.h	1,470	About box header
xped3app.cpp	3,919	Main application source
xped3app.def	499	Application definition file
xped3app.h	1,182	Main application header
xped3app.rc	14,417	Resource source
xped3app.rh	4,726	Resource header

Build the XPED3 project and run the XPED3.EXE program. Experiment with this version of the text editor to develop a feel for the supported features. The preceding list of files shows the additional header and implementation files XPD3MDI1.H, XPD3MDI1.CPP, XPD3MDIC.H, and XPD3MDIC.CPP. Listing X4.1 shows the source code for the XPD3MDI1.H header file. This file contains the declaration of the MDI child window class `XPD3MDIChild`. The class is declared as a descendent of the class `TMDIChild` and includes a constructor and a destructor.

Listing X4.1. The source code for the XPD3MDI1.H header file.

```
#if !defined(__xpd3mdi1_h)              // Sentry, use file only if
➥it's not already included.
#define __xpd3mdi1_h

/*  Project xped3

    Copyright © 1995. All Rights Reserved.

    SUBSYSTEM:    xped3.exe Application
    FILE:         xpd3mdi1.h
    AUTHOR:


    OVERVIEW
    ========
     Class definition for xped3MDIChild (TMDIChild).
*/


#include <owl\owlpch.h>
#pragma hdrstop

#include "xped3app.rh"            // Definition of all resources.


//{{TMDIChild = xped3MDIChild}}
class  xped3MDIChild : public TMDIChild {
public:
    xped3MDIChild (TMDIClient &parent,  const char far *title,
➥TWindow *clientWnd,  bool shrinkToClient = false,  TModule*
➥module = 0);
    virtual ~ xped3MDIChild ();
};    //{{xped3MDIChild}}


#endif                                    // __xpd3mdi1_h sentry.
```

Listing X4.2. The source code for the XPD3MDI1.CPP implementation file.

```
/*  Project xped3

    Copyright © 1995. All Rights Reserved.

    SUBSYSTEM:    xped3.exe Application
    FILE:         xpd3mdi1.cpp
```

```
    AUTHOR:


    OVERVIEW
    ========
    Source file for implementation of xped3MDIChild (TMDIChild).
*/


#include <owl\owlpch.h>
#pragma hdrstop

#include "xped3app.h"
#include "xpd3edtf.h"
#include "xpd3mdi1.h"


//{{ xped3MDIChild Implementation}}


//////////////////////////////////////////////////////////////////
//  xped3MDIChild
// ==========
// Construction/Destruction handling.
      xped3MDIChild::xped3MDIChild (TMDIClient &parent, const char
➥far *title, TWindow *clientWnd,  bool shrinkToClient, TModule
➥*module)
    : TMDIChild (parent, title, clientWnd == 0 ? new
➥xped3EditFile(0, 0, 0) : clientWnd, shrinkToClient, module)
{
    // INSERT>> Your constructor code here.

}


xped3MDIChild::~xped3MDIChild ()
{
    Destroy();

    // INSERT>> Your destructor code here.

}
```

Analysis Listing X4.2 shows the source code for the XPD3MDI1.CPP implementation file. The listing contains the implementation for the constructor and destructor of the class `XPD3MDIChild`. The constructor invokes the constructor of the parent class. The destructor simply invokes the member function `Destroy` to remove the MDI child window. Both members include comments that indicate where to insert additional code.

Listing X4.3. The source code for the XPD3MDIC.H header file.

```
#if !defined(__xpd3mdic_h)              // Sentry, use file only if
➥it's not already included.
#define __xpd3mdic_h

/*  Project xped3

    Copyright © 1995. All Rights Reserved.

    SUBSYSTEM:    xped3.exe Application
    FILE:         xpd3mdic.h
    AUTHOR:


    OVERVIEW
    ========
     Class definition for xped3MDIClient (TMDIClient).
*/


#include <owl\owlpch.h>
#pragma hdrstop

#include "xped3app.rh"             // Definition of all resources.


//{{TMDIClient = xped3MDIClient}}
class  xped3MDIClient : public TMDIClient {
public:
    int                        ChildCount;                // Number of
➥child window created.

    xped3MDIClient(TModule* module = 0);
    virtual ~xped3MDIClient ();

    void OpenFile (const char *fileName = 0);

private:
    void LoadTextFile ();

//{{xped3MDIClientVIRTUAL_BEGIN}}
protected:
    virtual void SetupWindow ();
//{{xped3MDIClientVIRTUAL_END}}

//{{xped3MDIClientRSP_TBL_BEGIN}}
protected:
    void CmFileNew ();
    void CmFileOpen ();
```

```
47: //{{xped3MDIClientRSP_TBL_END}}
48: DECLARE_RESPONSE_TABLE(xped3MDIClient);
49: };    //{{xped3MDIClient}}
50:
51:
52: #endif                                          // __xpd3mdic_h sentry.
```

Listing X4.3 shows the source code for the XPD3MDIC.H implementation file. This file contains the declaration of the MDI client window `XPD3MDIClient`, as a descendent of the class `TMDIClient`. The class declares the following members:

1. The public data member `ChildCount` (declared in line 28), which stores the number of MDI child windows.
2. The constructor, declared in line 30.
3. The destructor, declared in line 31.
4. The member function OpenFile, declared in line 33.
5. The private member function `LoadTextFile`, declared in line 36.
6. The protected member function `SetupWindow`, declared in line 40.
7. The protected member functions `CmFileNew` and `CmFileOpen` (declared in lines 45 and 46), which handle menu commands.

Listing X4.4. The source code for the XPD3MDIC.CPP implementation file.

```
/*  Project xped3

    Copyright © 1995. All Rights Reserved.

    SUBSYSTEM:    xped3.exe Application
    FILE:         xpd3mdic.cpp
    AUTHOR:


    OVERVIEW
    ========
    Source file for implementation of xped3MDIClient (TMDIClient).
*/


#include <owl\owlpch.h>
#pragma hdrstop

```

continues

Listing X4.4. continued

```
#include <dir.h>

#include "xped3app.h"
#include "xpd3edtf.h"
#include "xpd3mdi1.h"
#include "xpd3mdic.h"


//{{ xped3MDIClient Implementation}}


//
// Build a response table for all messages/commands handled
// by xped3MDIClient derived from TMDIClient.
//
DEFINE_RESPONSE_TABLE1(xped3MDIClient, TMDIClient)
//{{xped3MDIClientRSP_TBL_BEGIN}}
    EV_COMMAND(CM_MDIFILENEW, CmFileNew),
    EV_COMMAND(CM_MDIFILEOPEN, CmFileOpen),
//{{xped3MDIClientRSP_TBL_END}}
END_RESPONSE_TABLE;


//////////////////////////////////////////////////////////
//  xped3MDIClient
//  ===========
// Construction/Destruction handling.
xped3MDIClient::xped3MDIClient (TModule* module)
 : TMDIClient (module)
{
    ChildCount = 0;

    // INSERT>> Your constructor code here.

}


xped3MDIClient::~xped3MDIClient ()
{
    Destroy();

    // INSERT>> Your destructor code here.

}


//////////////////////////////////////////////////////////
//  xped3MDIClient
//  ===========
```

```
// MDIClient site initialization.
void  xped3MDIClient::SetupWindow ()
{
    // Default SetUpWindow processing.
    TMDIClient::SetupWindow ();

    XpEd3App *theApp = TYPESAFE_DOWNCAST(GetApplication(),
➥XpEd3App);

    // Common file file flags and filters for Open/Save As dialogs.
➥Filename and directory are
    // computed in the member functions CmFileOpen, and
➥CmFileSaveAs.
    theApp->FileData.Flags = OFN_FILEMUSTEXIST ¦ OFN_HIDEREADONLY ¦
➥ OFN_OVERWRITEPROMPT;
    theApp->FileData.SetFilter("All Files (*.*)¦*.*¦");

}


//////////////////////////////////////////////////////////////
//  xped3MDIClient
// ===========
// Menu File New command
void  xped3MDIClient::CmFileNew ()
{
    char    title[255];

    // Generate a title for the MDI child window.
    wsprintf(title, "%d", ChildCount++);

    xped3MDIChild* child = new xped3MDIChild(*this, title, 0);

    // Associate ICON w/ this child window.
    child->SetIcon(GetApplication(), IDI_DOC);

    // If the current active MDI child is maximize then this one
➥should be also.
    xped3MDIChild *curChild = (xped3MDIChild
➥ *)GetActiveMDIChild();
    if (curChild && (curChild->GetWindowLong(GWL_STYLE) &
➥ WS_MAXIMIZE))
        child->Attr.Style ¦= WS_MAXIMIZE;

    child->Create();
}


void  xped3MDIClient::OpenFile (const char *fileName)
{
    XpEd3App *theApp = TYPESAFE_DOWNCAST(GetApplication(),
➥XpEd3App);
```

Listing X4.4. continued

```

    if (fileName)
        strcpy(theApp->FileData.FileName, fileName);

    //
    // Create a MDIChild window whose client is xped3EditFile.
    //
    xped3MDIChild* child = new xped3MDIChild(*this, "",  new
➥xped3EditFile(0, 0, 0, 0, 0, 0, 0,  theApp->FileData.FileName));

    // Associate ICON w/ this child window.
    child->SetIcon(GetApplication(), IDI_DOC);

    // If the current active MDI child is maximize then this one
➥should be also.
    xped3MDIChild *curChild = (xped3MDIChild *)GetActiveMDIChild();
    if (curChild && (curChild->GetWindowLong(GWL_STYLE) &
➥WS_MAXIMIZE))
         child->Attr.Style |= WS_MAXIMIZE;

    child->Create();

    LoadTextFile();
}


///////////////////////////////////////////////////////////////////
//  xped3MDIClient
// ===========
// Menu File Open command
void  xped3MDIClient::CmFileOpen ()
{
    XpEd3App *theApp = TYPESAFE_DOWNCAST(GetApplication(),
➥XpEd3App);

    //
    // Display standard Open dialog box to select a file name.
    //
    *(theApp->FileData.FileName) = 0;
    if (TFileOpenDialog(this, theApp->FileData).Execute() == IDOK)
        OpenFile();
}


// Used by ListBox client to read a text file into the list box.
void  xped3MDIClient::LoadTextFile ()
{
```

```
    char            buf[255+1];
    ifstream        *inStream;

    XpEd3App *theApp = TYPESAFE_DOWNCAST(GetApplication(),
➥XpEd3App);

    xped3MDIChild  *curChild = (xped3MDIChild
➥ *)GetActiveMDIChild();
    TListBox        *client = TYPESAFE_DOWNCAST( curChild->
➥GetClientWindow(), TListBox);

    // Only work if the client class is a TListBox.
    if (client) {
        client->ClearList();
        inStream = new  ifstream(theApp->FileData.FileName);
        while (inStream->good()) {
            inStream->getline(buf, sizeof(buf) - 1);
            if (inStream->good())
                client->AddString(buf);
        }

        // Return an error message if we had a stream error and
➥it wasn't the eof.
        if (inStream->bad() && !inStream->eof()) {
            string msgTemplate(*GetModule(), IDS_UNABLEREAD);
            char*  msg = new char[MAXPATH + msgTemplate.length()];
            wsprintf(msg, msgTemplate.c_str(), *(theApp->
➥FileData.FileName));
            MessageBox(msg, GetApplication()->GetName(),
➥MB_ICONEXCLAMATION ¦ MB_OK);
            delete msg;
        }

        delete inStream;
    }
}
```

Figure X4.1 shows a sample session with the XPED3.EXE application.

Listing X4.4 contains the source code for the XPD3MDIC.CPP implementation file. The listing contains the message-response table macros and the definitions of the various class members.

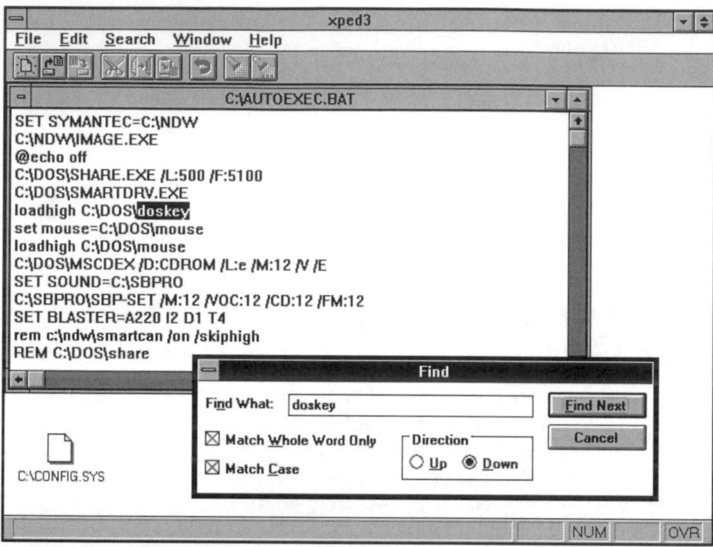

Figure X4.1. *A sample session with the XPED3.EXE application.*

The message-response table maps the messages for the support-menu commands. The class defines the following relevant members:

1. The constructor (defined in lines 42 to 53), which invokes the constructor of the parent class and assigns 0 to the data member `ChildCount`.
2. The destructor (defined in lines 56 to 62), which invokes the member function `Destroy`.
3. The member function `SetupWindow` (defined in lines 65 to 81), which initializes an MDI client window by performing the following tasks:
   - Invokes the `SetupWindow` of the parent class.
   - Assigns the bitwise ORed expression of `OFN_XXXX` constants to the `Flags` member of the application's data member `FileData`.
   - Calls FileData's function `SetFilter` to set the file-type filters used in the Open and Save File dialog boxes.
4. The member function `CmFileNew` (defined in lines 84 to 106), which creates a new MDI child window by performing the following tasks:
   - Generates the title of the new MDI child window.

- Creates a new MDI child window object and assigns its address to the local pointer `child`.
- Associates an icon with the MDI `child` window using the SetIcon member function.
- Maximizes the new MDI child window if the current MDI child window is also maximized.
- Creates the visible MDI child window.

5. The member function `OpenFile` (defined in lines 109 to 132), which creates a new MDI child window and loads the text from the filename specified by the parameter `fileName`. The tasks of this function resemble those of `CmFileNew`. The main difference is that this function supplies an xped3EditFile client window to the child and invokes the member function `LoadTextFile` after creating the MDI child window.
6. The member function `CmFileOpen` (defined in lines 135 to 149), which invokes the Open dialog box and then calls the member function `OpenFile` to process the selected file.
7. The member function `LoadTextFile` (defined in lines 152 to 184), which loads the text from the input file into the current MDI child window.

Listing X4.5. The source code for the XPED3APP.H header file.

```
#if !defined(__xped3app_h)              // Sentry, use file only if
➥it's not already included.
#define __xped3app_h

/*  Project xped3

    Copyright © 1995. All Rights Reserved.

    SUBSYSTEM:    xped3.exe Application
    FILE:         xped3app.h
    AUTHOR:


    OVERVIEW
    ========
    Class definition for XpEd3App (TApplication).
*/


```

continues

Listing X4.5. continued

```
#include <owl\owlpch.h>
#pragma hdrstop

#include "xpd3mdic.h"

#include "xped3app.rh"            // Definition of all resources.


//{{TApplication = XpEd3App}}
class XpEd3App : public TApplication {
private:

    void SetupSpeedBar (TDecoratedMDIFrame *frame);

public:
    XpEd3App ();
    virtual ~XpEd3App ();

    TOpenSaveDialog::TData  FileData;                    // Data to
➥control open/saveas standard dialog.

    xped3MDIClient  *mdiClient;

//{{XpEd3AppVIRTUAL_BEGIN}}
public:
    virtual void InitMainWindow();
//{{XpEd3AppVIRTUAL_END}}

//{{XpEd3AppRSP_TBL_BEGIN}}
protected:
    void CmHelpAbout ();
//{{XpEd3AppRSP_TBL_END}}
DECLARE_RESPONSE_TABLE(XpEd3App);
};    //{{XpEd3App}}


#endif                                    // __xped3app_h sentry.
```

Analysis

Listing X4.5 shows the source code for the XPED3APP.H header file.

This file contains the declaration of the application class `XpEd3App`. This declaration includes a constructor, a destructor, and the member functions `InitMainWindow`, `SetupSpeedBar`, and `CmHelpAbout`.

Type

Listing X4.6. The source code for the XPED3APP.CPP implementation file.

```
/*  Project xped3

    Copyright © 1995. All Rights Reserved.

    SUBSYSTEM:    xped3.exe Application
    FILE:         xped3app.cpp
    AUTHOR:


    OVERVIEW
    ========
    Source file for implementation of XpEd3App (TApplication).
*/


#include <owl\owlpch.h>
#pragma hdrstop

#include "xped3app.h"
#include "xpd3mdic.h"
#include "xped3abd.h"                          // Definition of about dialog.


//{{XpEd3App Implementation}}


//
// Build a response table for all messages/commands handled
// by the application.
//
DEFINE_RESPONSE_TABLE1(XpEd3App, TApplication)
//{{XpEd3AppRSP_TBL_BEGIN}}
    EV_COMMAND(CM_HELPABOUT, CmHelpAbout),
//{{XpEd3AppRSP_TBL_END}}
END_RESPONSE_TABLE;


//////////////////////////////////////////////////////////
// XpEd3App
// =====
//
XpEd3App::XpEd3App () : TApplication("xped3")
{

    // INSERT>> Your constructor code here.
}
```

continues

Listing X4.6. continued

```
XpEd3App::~XpEd3App ()
{
    // INSERT>> Your destructor code here.
}


void XpEd3App::SetupSpeedBar (TDecoratedMDIFrame *frame)
{
    //
    // Create default toolbar New and associate toolbar buttons with commands.
    //
    TControlBar* cb = new TControlBar(frame);
    cb->Insert(*new TButtonGadget(CM_MDIFILENEW, CM_MDIFILENEW));
    cb->Insert(*new TButtonGadget(CM_MDIFILEOPEN,  CM_MDIFILEOPEN));
    cb->Insert(*new TButtonGadget(CM_FILESAVE, CM_FILESAVE));
    cb->Insert(*new TSeparatorGadget(6));
    cb->Insert(*new TButtonGadget(CM_EDITCUT, CM_EDITCUT));
    cb->Insert(*new TButtonGadget(CM_EDITCOPY, CM_EDITCOPY));
    cb->Insert(*new TButtonGadget(CM_EDITPASTE, CM_EDITPASTE));
    cb->Insert(*new TSeparatorGadget(6));
    cb->Insert(*new TButtonGadget(CM_EDITUNDO, CM_EDITUNDO));
    cb->Insert(*new TSeparatorGadget(6));
    cb->Insert(*new TButtonGadget(CM_EDITFIND, CM_EDITFIND));
    cb->Insert(*new TButtonGadget(CM_EDITFINDNEXT, CM_EDITFINDNEXT));

    // Add fly-over help hints.
    cb->SetHintMode(TGadgetWindow::EnterHints);

    frame->Insert(*cb, TDecoratedFrame::Top);
}


/////////////////////////////////////////////////////////////////
// XpEd3App
// =====
// Application  intialization.
//
void XpEd3App::InitMainWindow ()
{
    if (nCmdShow != SW_HIDE)
        nCmdShow = (nCmdShow != SW_SHOWMINNOACTIVE) ?  SW_SHOWNORMAL :nCmdShow;

    mdiClient = new xped3MDIClient;
    TDecoratedMDIFrame* frame = new TDecoratedMDIFrame(Name, MDI_MENU, *mdiClient, true);
```

```

    // Set the client area to the application workspace color.
    frame->SetBkgndColor(::GetSysColor(COLOR_APPWORKSPACE));

    //
    // Assign ICON w/ this application.
    //
     frame->SetIcon(this, IDI_MDIAPPLICATION);

     //
     // Menu associated with window and accelerator table associated with table.
     //
     frame->AssignMenu(MDI_MENU);

     //
     // Associate with the accelerator table.
     //
     frame->Attr.AccelTable = MDI_MENU;

     SetupSpeedBar(frame);

     TStatusBar *sb = new TStatusBar(frame, TGadget::Recessed,
                                     TStatusBar::CapsLock       |
                                     TStatusBar::NumLock        |
                                     TStatusBar::ScrollLock     |
                                     TStatusBar::Overtype);
     frame->Insert(*sb, TDecoratedFrame::Bottom);

     SetMainWindow(frame);

     frame->SetMenuDescr(TMenuDescr(MDI_MENU));
}


//////////////////////////////////////////////////////////
// XpEd3App
// ==========
// Menu Help About xped3.exe command
void XpEd3App::CmHelpAbout ()
{
     //
     // Show the modal dialog.
     //
     XpEd3AboutDlg(MainWindow).Execute();
}
int OwlMain (int , char* [])
{
     try {
         XpEd3App    app;
         return app.Run();
```

continues

Listing X4.6. continued

```
143:     }
144:     catch (xmsg& x) {
145:         ::MessageBox(0, x.why().c_str(), "Exception", MB_OK);
146:     }
147:
148:      return -1;
149: }
```

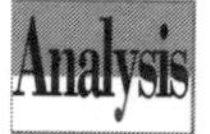

Listing X4.6 shows the source code for the XPED3APP.CPP implementation file. The listing contains the implementation for the constructor, the destructor, and the member functions `SetupSpeedBar`, `InitMainWindow`, and `CmHelpAbout`. The constructor (defined in lines 38 to 46) simply invokes the constructor of the parent class. The destructor (defined in lines 49 to 52) is a dummy member that contains no executable statements.

The XPED4 Project

The project XPED4 creates an MDI-compliant text editor that supports the drag-and-drop and printing features. When you invoke the AppExpert menu option, select the options for the MDI windows, the drag-and-drop feature, and the printing-related features. Clear the check marks for the other options. In addition, select the Code Gen Control subtopic (in the Application topic of the AppExpert dialog box) to make the application and dialog box class names `XpEd4App` and `XpEd4AboutDlg`, respectively. The AppExpert utility generates the following files.

File Name	Size	Description
applmdi.ico	1,086	Application icon
apxprev.cpp	9,416	Print preview source
apxprev.h	1,741	Print preview header
apxprint.cpp	5,148	Printout source
apxprint.h	1,258	Printout header
mdichild.ico	1,086	Child window icon
next.bmp	322	Print preview toolbar "next"
preview1.bmp	322	Print preview toolbar "one up"
preview2.bmp	322	Print preview toolbar "two up"
previous.bmp	322	Print preview toolbar "previous"

File Name	Size	Description
prexit.bmp	518	Print preview toolbar "done"
print.bmp	358	Print preview toolbar "print"
xpd4edtf.cpp	4,396	TEditFile descendent class source
xpd4edtf.h	1,234	TEditFile descendent class header
xpd4mdi1.cpp	972	TMDIChild descendent class source
xpd4mdi1.h	846	TMDIChild descendent class header
xpd4mdic.cpp	8,790	TMDIClient descendent class source
xpd4mdic.h	1,406	TMDIClient descendent class header
xped4.apx	42,882	AppExpert reference file
xped4.dsw	220	Borland IDE Desktop file
xped4.ide	29,520	IDE project file
xped4abd.cpp	4,928	About box source
xped4abd.h	1,470	About box header
xped4app.cpp	7,184	Main application source
xped4app.def	499	Application definition file
xped4app.h	2,269	Main application header
xped4app.rc	15,737	Resource source
xped4app.rh	5,968	Resource header

The XPED4 project files include a set of header and implementation files that are similar to those in project XPED3.

Build the XPED4 project and run the XPED4.EXE program. Experiment with this version of the text editor to develop a sense for the supported features.

Type **Listing X4.7. The source code for the APXPRINT.H header file.**

```
#if !defined(__apxprint_h)              // Sentry use file only if
➥it's not already included.
#define __apxprint_h

/*   Project xped4

    Copyright © 1995. All Rights Reserved.

    SUBSYSTEM:    xped4.exe Application
    FILE:         APXPrint.H
    AUTHOR:


    OVERVIEW
    ========
```

continues

Listing X4.7. continued

```
15:      Class definition for APXPrintOut (TPrintOut).
16: */
17:
18:
19: #include <owl\owlpch.h>
20: #pragma hdrstop
21:
22:
23: class APXPrintOut : public TPrintout {
24: public:
25:     APXPrintOut (TPrinter *printer, const char far *title,  TWindow*
   ➥ window,  bool scale =  true) : TPrintout(title)
26:       { Printer = printer;  Window = window;  Scale = scale;
   ➥MapMode = MM_ANISOTROPIC; }
27:
28:     void GetDialogInfo (int& minPage, int& maxPage,  int&
   ➥selFromPage, int& selToPage);
29:     void BeginPrinting ();
30:     void BeginPage (TRect &clientR);
31:     void PrintPage (int page, TRect& rect, unsigned flags);
32:     void EndPage ();
33:     void SetBanding (bool b)        { Banding = b; }
34:     bool HasPage (int pageNumber);
35:
36: protected:
37:     TWindow     *Window;
38:     bool        Scale;
39:     TPrinter    *Printer;
40:     int         MapMode;
41:
42:     int         PrevMode;
43:     TSize       OldVExt, OldWExt;
44:     TRect       OrgR;
45: };
46:
47:
48: #endif            // __apxprint_h sentry.
```

Analysis Listing X4.7 shows the source code for the APXPRINT.H header file. This file declares the class `APXPrintOut` (a descendant of the OWL class `TPrintout`) in line 23. The descendant class supports printing. The class declares a constructor and the member functions `GetDialogInfo`, `BeginPrinting`, `BeginPage`, `PrintPage`, `EndPage`, `SetBanding`, and `HasPage` in lines 24 to 34. The class also declares a set of protected data members, in lines 36 to 44, to manage the printing process. The header file contains the definition of the constructor, which calls the constructor of the parent class and then assigns the arguments of its parameters to the related data members. The

file APXPRINT.CPP contains the implementation for the member functions of the class `APXPrintOut`.

Listing X4.8. The source code for the APXPREV.H header file.

```
#if !defined(__apxprev_h)              // Sentry, use file only if
➥it's not already included.
#define __apxprev_h

/*   Project xped4

     Copyright © 1995. All Rights Reserved.

     SUBSYSTEM:    xped4.exe Application
     FILE:         APXPrev.H
     AUTHOR:


     OVERVIEW
     ========
     Class definition for PreviewWindow (Print Preview).
*/


#include <owl\owlpch.h>
#pragma hdrstop

#include "apxprint.h"
#include "xped4app.rh"


//{{TDecoratedFrame = PreviewWindow}}
class PreviewWindow : public TDecoratedFrame {
public:
     PreviewWindow (TWindow *parentWindow, TPrinter *printer,
➥TWindow* currWindow, const char far* title,  TLayoutWindow* client);
     ~PreviewWindow ();

     int              PageNumber;

     TWindow          *CurrWindow;
     TControlBar      *PreviewSpeedBar;
     TPreviewPage     *Page1;
     TPreviewPage     *Page2;
     TPrinter         *Printer;

     TPrintDC         *PrnDC;
```

continues

Listing X4.8. continued

```
41:     TSize           *PrintExtent;
42:     APXPrintOut     *Printout;
43:
44: private:
45:     TLayoutWindow   *Client;
46:
47:     void SpeedBarState ();
48:     void PPR_PreviousEnable (TCommandEnabler &tce);
49:     void PPR_NextEnable (TCommandEnabler &tce);
50:     void PPR_Previous ();
51:     void PPR_Next ();
52:     void PPR_OneUp ();
53:     void PPR_TwoUpEnable (TCommandEnabler &tce);
54:     void PPR_TwoUp ();
55:     void PPR_Done ();
56:     void CmPrintEnable (TCommandEnabler &tce);
57:     void CmPrint ();
58:
59: //{{PreviewWindowVIRTUAL_BEGIN}}
60: protected:
61:     virtual void SetupWindow ();
62: //{{PreviewWindowVIRTUAL_END}}
63:
64: //{{PreviewWindowRSP_TBL_BEGIN}}
65: protected:
66: //{{PreviewWindowRSP_TBL_END}}
67: DECLARE_RESPONSE_TABLE(PreviewWindow);
68: };    //{{PreviewWindow}}
69:
70:
71: #endif      // __apxprev_h sentry.
```

Analysis Listing X4.8 shows the source code for the APXPREV.H header file. The file declares the class `PreviewWindow` (a descendant of the class `TDecoratedFrame`) in line 27. The descendant class supports the print preview feature. The file APXPREV.CPP contains the implementation for the member functions of the class `PreviewWindow`. The class declares the following members:

1. The constructor in line 29.
2. The destructor in line 30.
3. The set of public members (in lines 32 to 42), which are mostly pointers to pages, control bars, printer devices, and printout objects.
4. The private member `Client` (in line 45), which is a pointer to the layout window class `TLayoutWindow`.

5. The private member function `SpeedBarState` in line 47.
6. The protected member functions `PPR_XXXX` (in lines 48 to 55), which respond to the speed bar buttons that support previewing the next and previous pages.
7. The protected member function `SetupWindow` in line 61.

Listing X4.9. The source code for the XPD4EDTF.H header file.

```
1: #if ! defined(__xpd4edtf_h)              // Sentry, use file only if
  ➥it's not already included.
2: #define __xpd4edtf_h
3:
4: /*  Project xped4
5:
6:     Copyright © 1995. All Rights Reserved.
7:
8:     SUBSYSTEM:    xped4.exe Application
9:     FILE:          xpd4edtf.h
10:     AUTHOR:
11:
12:
13:     OVERVIEW
14:     ========
15:      Class definition for xped4EditFile (TEditFile).
16: */
17:
18:
19: #include <owl\owlpch.h>
20: #pragma hdrstop
21:
22:
23: #include "xped4app.rh"            // Definition of all resources.
24:
25:
26: //{{TEditFile = xped4EditFile}}
27: class  xped4EditFile : public  TEditFile {
28: public:
29:     xped4EditFile (TWindow* parent = 0, int id = 0, const char far*
   ➥text = 0, int x = 0, int y = 0, int w = 0, int h = 0, const char
   ➥far* fileName = 0, TModule* module = 0);
30:     virtual ~ xped4EditFile ();
31:
32: //{{xped4EditFileVIRTUAL_BEGIN}}
33: public:
34:     virtual void Paint (TDC& dc,  bool erase, TRect& rect);
35:     virtual void SetupWindow ();
```

continues

Listing X4.9. continued

```
36: //{{xped4EditFileVIRTUAL_END}}
37: //{{xped4EditFileRSP_TBL_BEGIN}}
38: protected:
39:     void EvGetMinMaxInfo (MINMAXINFO far& minmaxinfo);
40: //{{xped4EditFileRSP_TBL_END}}
41: DECLARE_RESPONSE_TABLE(xped4EditFile);
42: };    //{{xped4EditFile}}
43:
44:
45: #endif                                        // __xpd4edtf_h sentry.
```

Listing X4.9 shows the source code for the XPD4EDTF.H header file. This file contains the declaration for the TEditFile descendent class, xped4EditFile. The declaration includes the following members:

1. The constructor, declared on lines 29.
2. The destructor, declared in line 30.
3. The public member function `Paint`, declared in line 34.
4. The protected member function `EvGetMinMaxInfo`, declared in line 39.

Listing X4.10. The source code for the XPD4EDTF.CPP implementation file.

```
/*  Project xped4

    Copyright _ 1994. All Rights Reserved.

    SUBSYSTEM:    xped4.exe Application
    FILE:          xpd4edtf.cpp
    AUTHOR:


    OVERVIEW
    ========
    Source file for implementation of xped4EditFile (TEditFile).
*/


#include <owl\owlpch.h>
#pragma hdrstop

#include "xped4app.h"
#include "xpd4edtf.h"
#include "xpd4edtf.h"
```

```
#include <stdio.h>


//{{ xped4EditFile Implementation}}


//
// Build a response table for all messages/commands handled
// by  xped4EditFile derived from  TEditFile.
//
DEFINE_RESPONSE_TABLE1(xped4EditFile, TEditFile)
//{{xped4EditFileRSP_TBL_BEGIN}}
    EV_WM_GETMINMAXINFO,
//{{xped4EditFileRSP_TBL_END}}
END_RESPONSE_TABLE;


//////////////////////////////////////////////////////////
//  xped4EditFile
// ==========
// Construction/Destruction handling.
xped4EditFile::xped4EditFile (TWindow* parent, int id, const char
➥far* text, int x, int y, int w, int h, const char far* fileName,
➥TModule* module)
    : TEditFile(parent, id, text, x, y, w, h, fileName, module)
 {
    // INSERT>> Your constructor code here.

}


xped4EditFile::~xped4EditFile ()
{
    Destroy();

    // INSERT>> Your destructor code here.

}


void xped4EditFile::SetupWindow ()
{
    TEditFile::SetupWindow();

    XpEd4App *theApp = TYPESAFE_DOWNCAST(GetApplication(),
➥XpEd4App);
    FileData = theApp->FileData;
}


```

continues

Listing X4.10. continued

```
//
// Paint routine for Window, Printer, and PrintPreview for an TEdit
➥client.
//
void xped4EditFile::Paint (TDC& dc, bool, TRect& rect)
{
    XpEd4App *theApp = TYPESAFE_DOWNCAST(GetApplication(),
➥XpEd4App);
    if (theApp) {
        // Only paint if we're printing and we have something to
➥paint, otherwise do nothing.
        if (theApp->Printing && theApp->Printer && !rect.IsEmpty()) {
            // Use pageSize to get the size of the window to render
➥into.  For a Window it's the client area,
            // for a printer it's the printer DC dimensions and for
➥print preview it's the layout window.
            TSize   pageSize(rect.right - rect.left,  rect.bottom -
➥rect.top);
            HFONT   hFont = (HFONT)GetWindowFont();
            TFont   font("Arial", -12);
            if (hFont == 0)
              dc.SelectObject(font);
            else
              dc.SelectObject(TFont(hFont));
            TEXTMETRIC  tm;
            int fHeight = (dc.GetTextMetrics(tm) == true) ?
➥tm.tmHeight + tm.tmExternalLeading : 10;
            // How many lines of this font can we fit on a page.
            int linesPerPage = MulDiv(pageSize.cy, 1, fHeight);
            if (linesPerPage) {
                TPrintDialog::TData &printerData =  theApp->Printer
➥->GetSetup();
                int maxPg = 1;
                 maxPg = ((GetNumLines() /  linesPerPage) + 1.0);
                 // Compute the number of pages to print.
                 printerData.MinPage = 1;
                 printerData.MaxPage = maxPg;
                 // Do the text stuff:
                 int     fromPage = printerData.FromPage ==
➥-1 ?  1 : printerData.FromPage;
```

```
                int     toPage = printerData.ToPage ==
➥-1 ?  1 : printerData.ToPage;
                char    buffer[255];
                int     currentPage = fromPage;

                while (currentPage <= toPage) {
                    int startLine = (currentPage - 1) *
➥ linesPerPage;
                    int lineIdx = 0;
                    while (lineIdx < linesPerPage) {
                        // If the string is no longer valid then
➥ there's nothing more to display.
                        if (!GetLine(buffer,  sizeof(buffer),
➥startLine + lineIdx))
                            break;
                        dc.TabbedTextOut(TPoint(0, lineIdx *
➥fHeight), buffer, strlen(buffer),  0, NULL, 0);
                        lineIdx++;
                    }
                    currentPage++;
                }
            }
        }
    }
}


void  xped4EditFile::EvGetMinMaxInfo (MINMAXINFO far& minmaxinfo)
{
    XpEd4App *theApp = TYPESAFE_DOWNCAST(GetApplication(),
➥XpEd4App);
    if (theApp) {
        if (theApp->Printing) {
            minmaxinfo.ptMaxSize = TPoint(32000, 32000);
            minmaxinfo.ptMaxTrackSize = TPoint(32000, 32000);
            return;
        }
    }
    TEditFile::EvGetMinMaxInfo(minmaxinfo);
}
```

Figure X4.2 shows a sample session with the XPED4.EXE application.

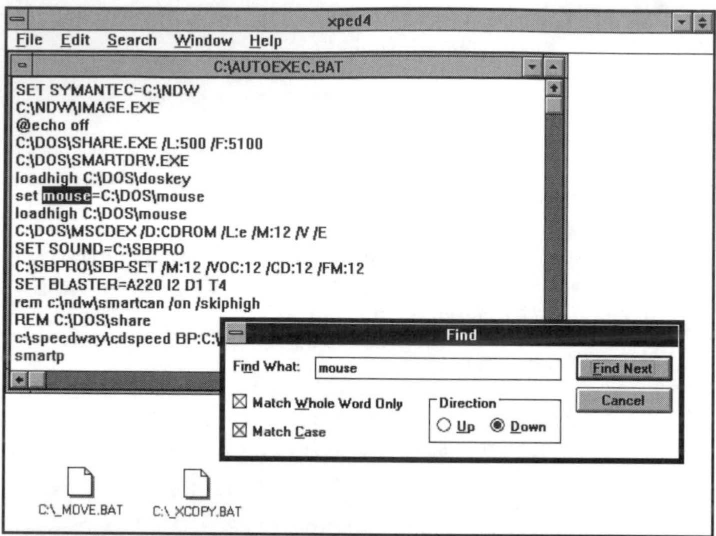

Figure X4.2. *A sample session with the XPED4.EXE application.*

Listing X4.10 shows the source code for the XPD4EDTF.CPP implementation file. The MDI child window class declares the following relevant members:

1. The constructor (defined in lines 40 to 49), which invokes the constructors of the parent class. The constructor contains comment-based placeholders for inserting additional class-initialization statements.
2. The destructor (defined in lines 52 to 58), which destroys the edit window (by calling the inherited member function `Destroy`).
3. The member function `Paint` (defined in lines 70 to 127), which performs the following tasks:
   - Declares the local pointer `theApp` (in line 75), which accesses the application object using the TYPESAFE_DOWNCAST (a macro that supports a safe form for typecasting of classes).
   - Determines whether the application is printing, whether there is a connected printer, and whether there is something to print. If these conditions are all true, the function performs the remaining tasks.
   - Declares `pageSize` (in line 81) as an instance of the class `TSize` and initializes it with the coordinates of the upper-left and lower-right corner of the parameter `rect`.

- Declares font handle, `hFont` (in lines 83 to 88), used in the client window. If the handle is 0, the function uses an Arial font when it later selects the font on lines 86 and 88.
- Declares the `TEXTMETRIC`-type variable `tm` in line 90.
- Declares the variable `fHeight` (in line 91) and assigns the font height to this variable.
- Declares the variable `linesPerPage` (in line 94) and assigns the number of lines per page to this variable.
- Declares the variables `fromPage` and `toPage` (in lines 107 and 108) and assigns values to these variables.
- Declares a local buffer to hold 255 characters in line 109.
- Starts a conditional `while` loop (in line 112) to print the range of selected pages. The loop performs these following tasks:
- Declares the variable `startLine` and assigns it a value based on the contents of variable `currentPage` and `linesPerPage`.
- Declares the variable `lineIdx` and initializes it to 0.
- Starts a nested `while` loop (in line 115) that obtains the currently printed line, and sends it to the printer. Each loop iteration increments the variable `lineIdx`.
- Increments the variable `currentPage`.

4. The member function `EvGetMinMaxInfo` (defined in lines 130 to 141), which returns the information about the window's maximum size and about the minimum and maximum tracking size if printing. The function passes this information using the `MINMAXINFO`-type reference parameter `minmaxinfo`.

Listing X4.11. The source code for the XPD4MDIC.H header file.

```
      #if !defined(__xpd4mdic_h)              // Sentry, use file
➥only if it's not already included.
#define __xpd4mdic_h

/*  Project xped4

    Copyright © 1995. All Rights Reserved.

```

continues

Listing X4.11. continued

```
    SUBSYSTEM:    xped4.exe Application
    FILE:         xpd4mdic.h
    AUTHOR:


    OVERVIEW
    ========
     Class definition for  xped4MDIClient (TMDIClient).
*/


#include <owl\owlpch.h>
#pragma hdrstop

#include "xped4app.rh"            // Definition of all resources.


//{{TMDIClient = xped4MDIClient}}
class xped4MDIClient : public TMDIClient {
public:
    int                     ChildCount;                    // Number of child window created.

    xped4MDIClient(TModule* module = 0);
    virtual ~xped4MDIClient ();

    void OpenFile (const char *fileName = 0);

private:
    void LoadTextFile ();

//{{xped4MDIClientVIRTUAL_BEGIN}}
protected:
    virtual void SetupWindow ();
//{{xped4MDIClientVIRTUAL_END}}

//{{xped4MDIClientRSP_TBL_BEGIN}}
protected:
    void CmFileNew ();
    void CmFileOpen ();
    void CmFilePrint ();
    void CmFilePrintSetup ();
    void CmFilePrintPreview ();
    void CmPrintEnable (TCommandEnabler &tce);
    void EvDropFiles (TDropInfo);
//{{xped4MDIClientRSP_TBL_END}}
DECLARE_RESPONSE_TABLE(xped4MDIClient);
};    //{{xped4MDIClient}}
```

```
55:
56:
57: #endif                                              // __xpd4mdic_h sentry.
```

Listing X4.11 shows the source code for the XPD4MDIC.H header file. This listing declares the the MDI client window class xped4MDIClient. This declaration is very similar to that of the class xped3MDIClient in file XPD3MDI1.H found in Listing X4.3. The main difference between the two classes is that the class xped4MDIClient declares the member functions `CmFilePrint`. `CmFilePrintSetup`, `CmFilePrintPreview`, `CmPrintEnable`, and `EvDropFiles` in lines 47 through 51.

Listing X4.12. The source code for the XPD4MDIC.CPP implementation file.

```
/*  Project xped4

    Copyright © 1995. All Rights Reserved.

    SUBSYSTEM:    xped4.exe Application
    FILE:         xpd4mdic.cpp
    AUTHOR:


    OVERVIEW
    ========
    Source file for implementation of  xped4MDIClient (TMDIClient).
*/


#include <owl\owlpch.h>
#pragma hdrstop

#include <dir.h>

#include "xped4app.h"
#include "xpd4edtf.h"
#include "xpd4mdi1.h"
#include "xpd4mdic.h"
#include "apxprint.h"
#include "apxprev.h"


//{{ xped4MDIClient Implementation}}


//
```

continues

Listing X4.12. continued

```
// Build a response table for all messages/commands handled
// by xped4MDIClient derived from TMDIClient.
//
DEFINE_RESPONSE_TABLE1(xped4MDIClient, TMDIClient)
//{{xped4MDIClientRSP_TBL_BEGIN}}
    EV_COMMAND(CM_MDIFILENEW, CmFileNew),
    EV_COMMAND(CM_MDIFILEOPEN, CmFileOpen),
    EV_COMMAND(CM_FILEPRINT, CmFilePrint),
    EV_COMMAND(CM_FILEPRINTERSETUP, CmFilePrintSetup),
    EV_COMMAND(CM_FILEPRINTPREVIEW, CmFilePrintPreview),
    EV_COMMAND_ENABLE(CM_FILEPRINT, CmPrintEnable),
    EV_COMMAND_ENABLE(CM_FILEPRINTERSETUP, CmPrintEnable),
    EV_COMMAND_ENABLE(CM_FILEPRINTPREVIEW, CmPrintEnable),
    EV_WM_DROPFILES,
//{{xped4MDIClientRSP_TBL_END}}
END_RESPONSE_TABLE;


//////////////////////////////////////////////////////////
//  xped4MDIClient
// ===========
// Construction/Destruction handling.
xped4MDIClient::xped4MDIClient (TModule* module)
 : TMDIClient (module)
{
    ChildCount = 0;

    // INSERT>> Your constructor code here.

}


xped4MDIClient::~xped4MDIClient ()
{
    Destroy();

    // INSERT>> Your destructor code here.

}


//////////////////////////////////////////////////////////
//  xped4MDIClient
// ===========
// MDIClient site initialization.
void  xped4MDIClient::SetupWindow ()
{
    // Default SetUpWindow processing.
    TMDIClient::SetupWindow ();
```

```

    XpEd4App *theApp = TYPESAFE_DOWNCAST(GetApplication(),
➥XpEd4App);

     // Common file file flags and filters for Open/Save As dialogs.
➥Filename and directory are
    // computed in the member functions CmFileOpen, and
➥CmFileSaveAs.
    theApp->FileData.Flags = OFN_FILEMUSTEXIST | OFN_HIDEREADONLY |
➥OFN_OVERWRITEPROMPT;
    theApp->FileData.SetFilter("All Files (*.*)|*.*|");

    // Accept files via drag/drop in the client window.
    DragAcceptFiles(true);
}


//////////////////////////////////////////////////////////////
//  xped4MDIClient
// ===========
// Menu File New command
void  xped4MDIClient::CmFileNew ()
{
    char    title[255];

    // Generate a title for the MDI child window.
    wsprintf(title, "%d", ChildCount++);

    xped4MDIChild * child = new xped4MDIChild(*this, title, 0);

    // Associate ICON w/ this child window.
    child->SetIcon(GetApplication(), IDI_DOC);

    // If the current active MDI child is maximize then this one
➥should be also.
    xped4MDIChild *curChild = (xped4MDIChild *)GetActiveMDIChild();
    if (curChild && (curChild->GetWindowLong(GWL_STYLE) &
➥WS_MAXIMIZE))
        child->Attr.Style |= WS_MAXIMIZE;

    child->Create();
}


void  xped4MDIClient::OpenFile (const char *fileName)
{
    XpEd4App *theApp = TYPESAFE_DOWNCAST(GetApplication(),
➥XpEd4App);

    if (fileName)
        strcpy(theApp->FileData.FileName, fileName);
```

Listing X4.12. continued

```

    //
    // Create a MDIChild window whose client is xped4EditFile.
    //
    xped4MDIChild* child = new xped4MDIChild(*this, "",  new
➥xped4EditFile(0, 0, 0, 0, 0, 0, 0,  theApp->FileData.FileName));

    // Associate ICON w/ this child window.
    child->SetIcon(GetApplication(), IDI_DOC);

    // If the current active MDI child is maximize then this one
➥should be also.
    xped4MDIChild *curChild = (xped4MDIChild *)GetActiveMDIChild();
    if (curChild && (curChild->GetWindowLong(GWL_STYLE) &
➥WS_MAXIMIZE))
        child->Attr.Style |= WS_MAXIMIZE;

    child->Create();

    LoadTextFile();
}


/////////////////////////////////////////////////////////////
// xped4MDIClient
// ===========
// Menu File Open command
void xped4MDIClient::CmFileOpen ()
{
    XpEd4App *theApp = TYPESAFE_DOWNCAST(GetApplication(),
➥XpEd4App);

    //
    // Display standard Open dialog box to select a file name.
    //
    *(theApp->FileData.FileName) = 0;
    if (TFileOpenDialog(this, theApp->FileData).Execute() == IDOK)
        OpenFile();
}


// Used by ListBox client to read a text file into the list box.
void xped4MDIClient::LoadTextFile ()
{
    char            buf[255+1];
    ifstream        *inStream;

    XpEd4App *theApp = TYPESAFE_DOWNCAST(GetApplication(),
➥XpEd4App);
```

```

    xped4MDIChild   *curChild = (xped4MDIChild *)GetActiveMDIChild();
    TListBox        *client = TYPESAFE_DOWNCAST( curChild->GetClientWindow(), TListBox);

    // Only work if the client class is a TListBox.
    if (client) {
        client->ClearList();
        inStream = new  ifstream(theApp->FileData.FileName);
        while (inStream->good()) {
            inStream->getline(buf, sizeof(buf) - 1);
            if (inStream->good())
                client->AddString(buf);
        }

        // Return an error message if we had a stream error and it wasn't the eof.
        if (inStream->bad() && !inStream->eof()) {
            string msgTemplate(*GetModule(), IDS_UNABLEREAD);
            char*  msg = new char[MAXPATH + msgTemplate.length()];
            wsprintf(msg, msgTemplate.c_str(), *(theApp->FileData.FileName));
            MessageBox(msg, GetApplication()->GetName(), MB_ICONEXCLAMATION | MB_OK);
            delete msg;
        }

        delete inStream;
    }
}


////////////////////////////////////////////////////////////
//  xped4MDIClient
// ==========
// Menu File Print command
void  xped4MDIClient::CmFilePrint ()
{
    //
    // Create Printer object if not already created.
    //
    XpEd4App *theApp = TYPESAFE_DOWNCAST(GetApplication(), XpEd4App);
    if (theApp) {
        if (!theApp->Printer)
            theApp->Printer = new TPrinter;

        //
        // Create Printout window and set characteristics.
        //
```

continues

Listing X4.12. continued

```
        APXPrintOut printout(theApp->Printer, Title,
➥GetActiveMDIChild()->GetClientWindow(), true);

        theApp-> Printing++;

        //
        // Bring up the Print dialog and print the document.
        //
        theApp->Printer->Print(GetWindowPtr(GetActiveWindow()),
➥printout,  true);

        theApp->Printing--;
    }
}


//////////////////////////////////////////////////////////////
//  xped4MDIClient
// ==========
// Menu File Print Setup command
void  xped4MDIClient::CmFilePrintSetup ()
{
    XpEd4App *theApp = TYPESAFE_DOWNCAST(GetApplication(),
➥XpEd4App);
    if (theApp) {
        if (!theApp->Printer)
            theApp->Printer = new TPrinter;

        //
        // Bring up the Print Setup dialog.
        //
        theApp->Printer->Setup(this);
    }
}


//////////////////////////////////////////////////////////////
//  xped4MDIClient
// ==========
// Menu File Print Preview command
void xped4MDIClient::CmFilePrintPreview ()
{
    XpEd4App *theApp = TYPESAFE_DOWNCAST(GetApplication(),
➥XpEd4App);
    if (theApp) {
        if (!theApp->Printer)
            theApp->Printer = new TPrinter;

        theApp-> Printing++;

```

```
        PreviewWindow *prevW = new PreviewWindow(Parent, theApp->Printer, GetActiveMDIChild()->GetClientWindow(), "Print Preview", new TLayoutWindow(0));
        prevW->Create();

        GetApplication()->BeginModal(GetApplication()->GetMainWindow());

        // We must destroy the preview window explicitly. Otherwise, the window will not be destroyed until
        // it's parent the MainWindow is destroyed.
        prevW->Destroy();
        delete prevW;

        theApp->Printing--;
    }
}


//////////////////////////////////////////////////////////////
//  xped4MDIClient
// ==========
// Menu enabler used by Print, Print Setup and Print Preview.
void xped4MDIClient::CmPrintEnable (TCommandEnabler &tce)
{
    if (GetActiveMDIChild()) {
        XpEd4App *theApp = TYPESAFE_DOWNCAST(GetApplication(), XpEd4App);
        if (theApp) {
            // If we have a Printer already created just test if all is okay.
            // Otherwise create a Printer object and make sure the printer
            // really exists and then delete the Printer object.
            if (!theApp->Printer) {
                theApp->Printer = new TPrinter;

                tce.Enable(theApp->Printer->GetSetup().Error == 0);
            } else
                tce.Enable(theApp->Printer->GetSetup().Error == 0);
        }
    } else
        tce.Enable(false);
}


void xped4MDIClient::EvDropFiles (TDropInfo)
{
    Parent->ForwardMessage();
}
```

Listing X4.12 shows the source code for the XPD4MDIC.CPP implementation file. The listing defines the following relevant members of the class xped4MDIClient:

1. The member function `SetupWindow` (defined in lines 74 to 92), which performs the following tasks to set up the MDI client window:
   - ☐ Invokes the `SetupWindow` of the parent class.
   - ☐ Assigns the bitwise ORed expression of `OFN_XXXX` constants to the `Flags` member of the application's data member `FileData`.
   - ☐ Calls the function `SetFilter` of the application's data member `FileData`. This function sets the file type filters used in the Open and Save file dialog boxes.
   - ☐ Accepts files via the dragging or dropping of a file in the client window. This task involves invoking the inherited member function `DragAcceptFiles`.
2. The member function `CmFilePrint` (defined in lines 198 to 226), which responds to the Print menu command. The function performs the following tasks:
   - ☐ Assigns the address of the application to the local pointer `theApp` using the TYPESAFE_DOWNCAST macro. The function performs the remaining tasks if the pointer `theApp` is not `NULL`.
   - ☐ Creates a printer object (if the pointer `theApp->Printer` is `NULL`) and assigns the address of that object to the application member `Printer`.
   - ☐ Creates the instance `printout` of the class `APXPrintOut` and assigns the printing characteristics.
   - ☐ Increments the application's member `Printing`.
   - ☐ Invokes the Print dialog box and prints the document. This task involves sending the C++ message `Print` to the printer object.
   - ☐ Decrements the application's member `Printing`.
3. The member function `CmFilePrintSetup` (defined in lines 229 to 245), which sets up the printer by performing the following tasks:
   - ☐ Assigns the address of the application to the local pointer `theApp` using the TYPESAFE_DOWNCAST macro. The function performs the remaining tasks if the pointer `theApp` is not `NULL`.

- Creates a printer object (if the pointer `theApp->Printer` is `NULL`) and assigns the address of that object to the application member `Printer`.
- Invokes the Print Setup dialog box by sending the application's Printer object's Setup member function.

4. The member function `CmFilePrintPreview` (defined in lines 248 to 273) responds to the Preview Menu option. The function performs the following tasks:

   - Assigns the address of the application to the local pointer `theApp` using the TYPESAFE_DOWNCAST macro. The function performs the remaining tasks if the pointer `theApp` is not `NULL`.
   - Creates a printer object (if the pointer `theApp->Printer` is `NULL`) and assigns the address of that object to the application member `Printer`.
   - Increment's the application's Printing member.
   - Creates the instance `prevW` of the class `PreviewWindow` and assigns the printing-preview aspects.
   - Creates the print-preview window by calling its Create member function.
   - Invokes the preview window by sending the C++ message `BeginModal` to the application object.
   - Destroys the preview window by sending it the C++ message `Destroy`.
   - Removes the dynamic instance of the preview window.
   - Decrements the application's member `Printing`.

The files XPED4APP.H and XPED4APP.CPP are very similar to the files XPED3APP.H and XPED3APP.CPP, respectively.

The XPED5 Project

The XPED5 project creates an MDI-compliant text editor that uses the document and view classes. The application contains no speed bar and no status line, does not support printing, and does not support the drag-and-drop feature. When you invoke the AppExpert menu option, select the options for the MDI windows and the Document/Views feature. Clear the check marks for the other options. In addition, select the Code Gen Control subtopic (in the Application topic of the AppExpert dialog box) to make the application and dialog-box class names `XpEd5App` and `XpEd5AboutDlg`, respectively. The AppExpert utility generates the following files. (The date and time stamps are for the files that we generated on one of our systems):

File Name	Size	Description
appldocv.ico	1,086	Application icon
mdichild.ico	1,086	Child window icon
xpd5edtv.cpp	801	TEditView descendent class source
xpd5edtv.h	772	TEditView descendent class header
xpd5mdi1.cpp	903	TMDIChild descendent class source
xpd5mdi1.h	846	TMDIChild descendent class header
xpd5mdic.cpp	1,349	TMDIClient descendent class source
xpd5mdic.h	1,184	TMDIClient descendent class header
xped5.apx	30,334	AppExpert reference file
xped5.dsw	220	Borland IDE Desktop file
xped5.ide	28,514	IDE project file
xped5abd.cpp	4,928	About box source
xped5abd.h	1,470	About box header
xped5app.cpp	3,389	Main application source
xped5app.def	499	Application definition file
xped5app.h	1,091	Main application header
xped5app.rc	17,185	Resource source
xped5app.rh	5,635	Resource header

The header file XPD5MDI1.H is very similar to the header file XPD3MDI1.H, and declares a constructor, a destructor, and the message response table. The implementation file XPD5MDI1.CPP is similar to the file XPD3MDI1.CPP.

Build the XPED5 project and run the XPED5.EXE program. Experiment with this version of the text editor to develop a sense for the supported features. Figure X4.3 shows a sample session with the XPED5.EXE application.

The header file XPD5MDI1.H is similar to the header file XPD3MDI1.H. The main difference is that file XPD5MDI1.H does not declare the functions `CmFileNew` and `CmFileOpen` as members of the MDI client window class.

The implementation file XPD5MDI1.CPP is similar to the implementation file XPD3MDI1.CPP. The main difference is that file XPD5MDI1.CPP does not define the functions `CmFileNew` and `CmFileOpen` and has no entries for these functions in the message response table.

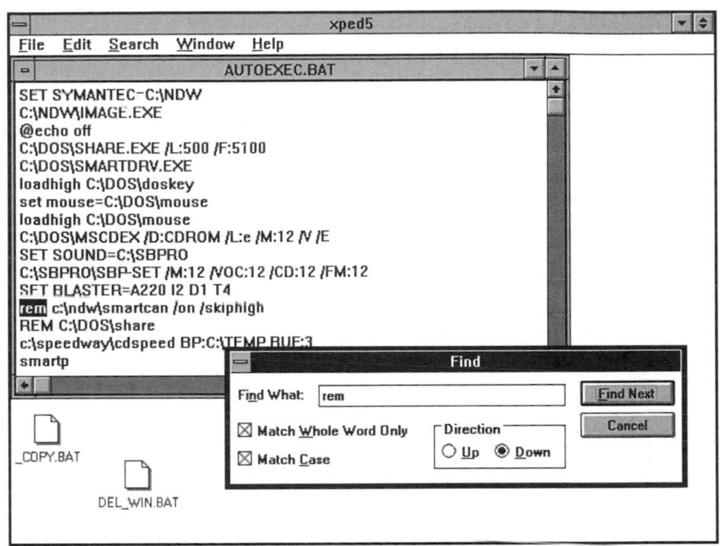

Figure X4.3. *A sample session with the XPED5.EXE application.*

Listing X4.13. The source code for the XPED5APP.H header file.

```
#if !defined(__xped5app_h)              // Sentry, use file only if
➥it's not already included.
#define __xped5app_h

/*  Project xped5

    Copyright © 1995. All Rights Reserved.

    SUBSYSTEM:    xped5.exe Application
    FILE:         xped5app.h
    AUTHOR:


    OVERVIEW
    ========
    Class definition for XpEd5App (TApplication).
*/


#include <owl\owlpch.h>
#pragma hdrstop

#include "xpd5mdic.h"
```

continues

Listing X4.13. continued

```

#include "xped5app.rh"                // Definition of all resources.


//{{TApplication = XpEd5App}}
class XpEd5App : public TApplication {
private:
public:
    XpEd5App ();
    virtual ~XpEd5App ();

    xped5MDIClient  *mdiClient;

//{{XpEd5AppVIRTUAL_BEGIN}}
public:
    virtual void InitMainWindow ();
//{{XpEd5AppVIRTUAL_END}}

//{{XpEd5AppRSP_TBL_BEGIN}}
protected:
    void EvNewView (TView& view);
    void EvCloseView (TView& view);
    void CmHelpAbout ();
//{{XpEd5AppRSP_TBL_END}}
DECLARE_RESPONSE_TABLE(XpEd5App);
};    //{{XpEd5App}}


#endif                                        // __xped5app_h sentry.
```

Listing X4.13 shows the source code for the XPED5APP.H header file. This file declares the application class XpEd5App. The class declaration includes the default constructor, the destructor, and the member functions `InitMainWindow`, `EvNewView`, `EvCloseView`, and `CmHelpAbout`. The last three member functions enable the application to handle creating a new view, closing a view, and responding to the Help menu option.

Listing X4.14. The source code for the XPED5APP.CPP implementation file.

```
/*  Project xped5

    Copyright © 1995. All Rights Reserved.

    SUBSYSTEM:    xped5.exe Application
    FILE:         xped5app.cpp
```

```
    AUTHOR:


    OVERVIEW
    ========
    Source file for implementation of XpEd5App (TApplication).
*/


#include <owl\owlpch.h>
#pragma hdrstop

#include "xped5app.h"
#include "xpd5mdic.h"
#include "xpd5mdi1.h"
#include "xpd5edtv.h"
#include "xped5abd.h"                        // Definition of about
➥dialog.


//{{XpEd5App Implementation}}



//{{DOC_VIEW}}
DEFINE_DOC_TEMPLATE_CLASS(TFileDocument,  xped5EditView, DocType1);
//{{DOC_VIEW_END}}

//{{DOC_MANAGER}}
DocType1 __dvt1("All Files (*.*)", "*.*", 0, "TXT",  dtAutoDelete ¦
➥dtUpdateDir);
//{{DOC_MANAGER_END}}


//
// Build a response table for all messages/commands handled
// by the application.
//
DEFINE_RESPONSE_TABLE1(XpEd5App, TApplication)
//{{XpEd5AppRSP_TBL_BEGIN}}
    EV_OWLVIEW(dnCreate, EvNewView),
    EV_OWLVIEW(dnClose,  EvCloseView),
    EV_COMMAND(CM_HELPABOUT, CmHelpAbout),
//{{XpEd5AppRSP_TBL_END}}
END_RESPONSE_TABLE;


//////////////////////////////////////////////////////////
// XpEd5App
// =====
//
```

continues

Listing X4.14. continued

```
XpEd5App::XpEd5App () : TApplication("xped5")
{
    SetDocManager(new TDocManager(dmMDI ¦ dmMenu, this));

    // INSERT>> Your constructor code here.
}


XpEd5App::~XpEd5App ()
{
    // INSERT>> Your destructor code here.
}


//////////////////////////////////////////////////////////
// XpEd5App
// =====
// Application  intialization.
//
void XpEd5App::InitMainWindow ()
{
    if (nCmdShow != SW_HIDE)
        nCmdShow = (nCmdShow != SW_SHOWMINNOACTIVE) ?
➥SW_SHOWNORMAL : nCmdShow;

    mdiClient = new xped5MDIClient(this);
    TDecoratedMDIFrame* frame = new TDecoratedMDIFrame(Name,
➥MDI_MENU, *mdiClient, false, this);

    nCmdShow = (nCmdShow != SW_SHOWMINNOACTIVE) ? SW_SHOWNORMAL :
➥nCmdShow;

    //
    // Assign ICON w/ this application.
    //
    frame->SetIcon(this, IDI_MDIAPPLICATION);

    //
    // Menu associated with window and accelerator table associated
➥with table.
    //
    frame->AssignMenu(MDI_MENU);

    //
    // Associate with the accelerator table.
    //
    frame->Attr.AccelTable = MDI_MENU;

```

```
     SetMainWindow(frame);

    frame->SetMenuDescr(TMenuDescr(MDI_MENU));

}


//////////////////////////////////////////////////////////////
// XpEd5App
// =====
// Response Table handlers:
//
void XpEd5App::EvNewView (TView& view)
{
    TMDIClient *mdiClient = TYPESAFE_DOWNCAST(GetMainWindow()->GetClientWindow(), TMDIClient);
    if (mdiClient) {
        xped5MDIChild* child = new xped5MDIChild(*mdiClient, 0, view.GetWindow());

        // Associate ICON w/ this child window.
        child->SetIcon(this, IDI_DOC);

        child->Create();
    }
}


void XpEd5App::EvCloseView (TView&)
{
}


//////////////////////////////////////////////////////////////
// XpEd5App
// ===========
// Menu Help About xped5.exe command
void XpEd5App::CmHelpAbout ()
{
    //
    // Show the modal dialog.
    //
     XpEd5AboutDlg(GetMainWindow()).Execute();
}


int OwlMain (int , char* [])
{
     try {
         XpEd5App    app;
        return app.Run();
```

continues

Listing X4.14. continued

```
150:     }
151:     catch (xmsg& x) {
152:         ::MessageBox(0, x.why().c_str(), "Exception", MB_OK);
153:     }
154:
155:     return -1;
156: }
```

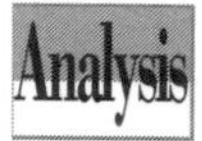

Listing X4.14 shows the source code for the XPED5APP.CPP implementation file. The listing defines the following class members:

1. The constructor (defined in lines 52 to 61), which invokes the constructor of the parent class and creates a new document manager object. The member performs the latter task by creating a new instance of the class TDocManager and passing it along to the SetDocManager function.
2. The destructor (defined in lines 64 to 67), which has no executable statements.
3. The member function `InitMainWindow` (defined in lines 70 to 105), which initializes the main window by carrying out the following tasks:
   - Assigns a value to the inherited data member nCmdShow such that the window appears in its normal state.
   - Creates a new decorated MDI frame window by allocating an instance of the class `TDecoratedMDIFrame`. The function assigns the address of this instance to the local pointer `frame`.
   - Assigns the application's icon using the icon resource `IDI_MDIAPPLICATION`. This task involves calling frame's member function SetIcon.
   - Assigns the application's menu using the menu resource `MDI_MENU`. This task involves sending the C++ message `AssignMenu` to the MDI window accessed by the pointer `frame`.
   - Assigns the accelerator table `MDI_MENU` to the `AccelTable` member of the `Attr` member.
   - Sets the main window to frame.
4. The member function `EvNewView` (defined in lines 108 to 124), which creates a new MDI child window by performing the following steps:

- Obtains the address of the MDI client window and assigns that address to the local pointer `mdiClient`.
- Creates a new instance of the class `xped5MDIChild` and assigns the address of this instance to the local pointer `child`. This task invokes linking the new MDI child window with the MDI client window using the pointer `mdiClient`.
- Sets the icon for the new MDI child window. This task sends the C++ message `SetIcon` to the new MDI child window.
- Creates the visible part of the MDI child window. This task involves sending the C++ message `Create` to the new MDI child window.

5. The member function `EvCloseView`, which has no executable statements.
6. The member function `CmHelpAbout` (defined in lines 132 to 142), which creates an instance of the class `XpEd5AboutDlg` (which models the modal About dialog box) and sends it the C++ message `Execute`.

Summary

This chapter presented the following MDI-compliant minimally functioning text editors, which are generated by the AppExpert utility:

- The XPED3 project, which implements an editor with a speed bar and a status line.
- The XPED4 project, which offers an editor that supports the printing-related and drag-and-drop features.
- The XPED5 project, which provides an editor that uses the document and view classes.

The chapter examined the difference and similarities between the header and implementation files for the preceding projects. The information presented should make you familiar with the source code generated by AppExpert. This familiarity is the key to efficiently customizing AppExpert-generated source-code files.

Q&A

Q Can I make AppExpert switch the source code of an application between SDI and MDI support?

A No; but you can ask AppExpert to generate the other version (for SDI or MDI support) of the program.

Q Does AppExpert generate source code that supports OLE 2.0?

A Yes. This is covered in a later Extra Credit chapter.

Q Does AppExpert generate source code that supports VBX (Visual basic) controls?

A No; but you can use OWL classes to support VBX controls.

Q Does AppExpert generate source code that supports ODBC (Open Database Connectivity)?

A No.

Exercises

1. Use the AppExpert utility to create an MDI-compliant text editor that uses document/views classes and supports the toolbar and status lines. Compare the resulting code with that of project XPED3.
2. Use the AppExpert utility to create an MDI-compliant text editor that uses document/views classes and supports the drag/drop and print features. Compare the resulting code with that of project XPED4.
3. Use the AppExpert utility to create an MDI-compliant text editor that uses document/views classes and supports the toolbar and status lines. Compare the resulting code with that of projects XPED3, XPED4, and XPED5.

Using the ClassExpert

The previous two chapters discussed using the AppExpert utility in generating various kinds of SDI and MDI editors. The ClassExpert utility complements AppExpert by enabling you to declare new member functions and classes. These additional items enable you to customize and fine-tune the classes generated by AppExpert. In this chapter, you will learn about the following topics:

- Invoking the ClassExpert utility.
- Adding new member functions to a class created by AppExpert.
- Adding a new class to the project created by AppExpert.

Invoking ClassExpert

To use the ClassExpert, invoke the ClassExpert menu option in the View menu selection. Figure X5.1 shows a sample session with the ClassExpert utility in a project created by AppExpert. The ClassExpert window contains three panes: the Classes pane, the Events pane, and the editor pane. The Classes pane lists the classes in the current project. If there are too many classes to fit in this pane, the ClassExpert window displays vertical scroll bars. The Events pane shows an outline of the various messages for the selected class in the Classes pane. These messages include command notifications, control notifications, virtual functions, and Windows messages. The thick + symbol indicates that an outline item is hiding subitems. The thick – symbol indicates that the item is expanded. The editor pane is supported by a BRIEF-like smart editor that enables you to enter, edit, and delete statements.

When you select a different class in the Class pane, the contents of the Events pane automatically change to reflect the events available for the newly selected class.

When you expand the outlines in the Events pane, you will notice check marks to the left of certain outline items. These check marks indicate that the event has a handler in the project's source code.

Note: The right mouse button offers versatile context-sensitive pop-up menus that enable you to perform various tasks. (The pop-up menus are so context-sensitive that they vary not only from one pane to another, but also between one type of selection and another in the same pane.)

In the following sections, we describe how to add new member functions and classes.

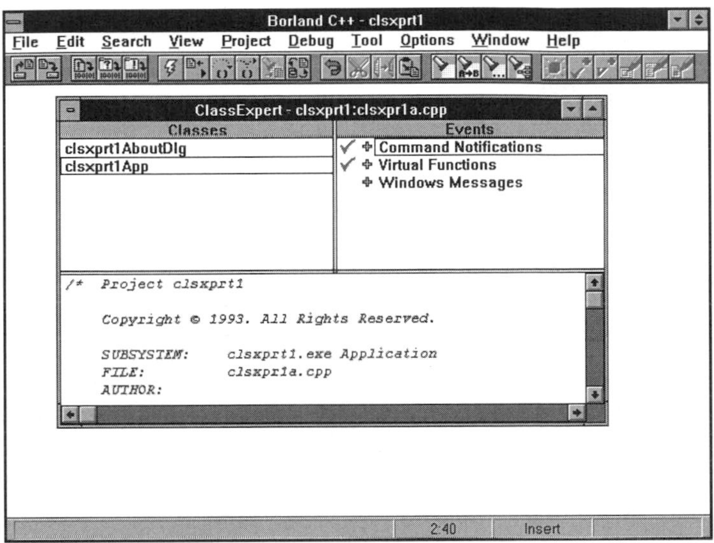

Figure X5.1. *A sample session with the ClassExpert utility.*

Note: The listings generated by AppExpert and ClassExpert were edited to better fit the pages in this book.

Adding New Member Functions

Let's look at an example of a simple SDI-compliant text editor (which is very similar to program XPED1.EXE in the extra-credit Chapter 3) with an additional menu. This menu supports the following features:

- Converting the selected text or the entire contents of the file (if there is no selected text) to lowercase characters.
- Converting the selected text or the entire contents of the file (if there is no selected text) to uppercase characters.
- Reversing the characters of the selected text or the entire contents of the file (if there is no selected text).
- Inserting the current date.

- Inserting the current time.
- Inserting the current date and time.

Each of the preceding features is supported by a menu option. Each menu option has an event-handler member function.

To create the application, follow these general steps:

1. Use the AppExpert to create the new editor CLSXPRT1.EXE as an SDI-compliant application with no speed bar, no status line, no support for drag-and-drop, and no printing-related features.
2. Use the Resource Workshop to add the menu selection Special and its nested menu options Lowercase, Uppercase, Reverse, Insert Date, Insert Time, and Insert Date/Time. (Consult Part II of the *Borland C++ User's Guide* manual to learn more about using this utility.) Use the identifiers `CM_LOWERCASE`, `CM_UPPERCASE`, `CM_REVERSE`, `CM_INSDATE`, `CM_INSTIME`, and `CM_INSDATETIME`, respectively, for the preceding menu options. Insert a separator menu item between the first three and last three menu options in the menu selection. The targeted menu resource is the one with the ID `SDI_MENU`. When you are finished adding the preceding menu items, save the updated resources.
3. Use the ClassExpert utility to add the member functions needed to handle the six new menu options. Click the Command Notifications item in the Events pane to expand that outline item.
4. Search for the `CM_LOWERCASE` identifier, which represents the commands for the new menu option Lowercase.
5. Click in the + symbol located to the left of the identifier `CM_LOWERCASE`. This action reveals two nested outline items: Command and Command Enable.
6. Select the Command outline and click the right mouse button to access the pop-up menu.
7. Select and invoke the Add Handler menu option. This option prompts a simple input dialog box, which requests that you type in the name of the handler member function. Enter `CmLowercase` and then click the OK button of the dialog box. The ClassExpert responds by creating the following:
    - The declaration of member function `CmLowercase` in the declaration of class `clsxprt1App` (located in the header file CLSXPR1A.H).

- The event response-table macro that links the command `CM_LOWERCASE` with the member function `CmLowercase` (located in the implementation file CLSXPR1A.CPP).
- The empty definition of member function `CmLowercase` (located in the implementation file CLSXPR1A.CPP).

8. Repeat steps 4 through 7 for the other `CM_XXXX` constants that handle the remaining new menu options. Specify the member functions `CmUppercase`, `CmInsertDate`, `CmInsertTime`, `CmInsertDateTime`, and `CmReverse` to handle the Windows commands `CM_UPPERCASE`, `CM_INSDATE`, `CM_INSTIME`, `CM_INSDATETIME`, and `CM_REVERSE`, respectively.
9. Add the header files STDIO.H, STRING.H, and DOS.H, along with the statements for the member function `CmXXXX` in file CLSXPR1A.CPP. (More about these statements later.)

Listing X5.1 shows the contents of the CLSXPR1A.DEF definition file. Listing X5.2 contains the source code for the CLSXPR1A.H header file. Listing X5.3 contains the source code for the CLSXPR1A.RH header file. Listing X5.4 shows the script of the CLSXPR1A.RC resource file. Listing X5.5 contains the source code for the CLSXPR1A.CPP implementation file.

Type

Listing X5.1. The contents of the CLSXPR1A.DEF definition file.

```
;-----------------------------------------------
;   Main clsxprt1
;
;   Copyright © 1993. All Rights Reserved.
;
;   SUBSYSTEM:    clsxprt1.exe Module Definition File
;   FILE:         clsxpr1a.def
;   AUTHOR:
;
;-----------------------------------------------
NAME clsxprt1
DESCRIPTION 'clsxprt1 Application - Copyright © 1993. All Rights
             Reserved.'
EXETYPE     WINDOWS
CODE        PRELOAD MOVEABLE DISCARDABLE
DATA        PRELOAD MOVEABLE MULTIPLE
HEAPSIZE    4096
STACKSIZE   8192
```

Listing X5.2. The source code for the CLSXPR1A.H header file.

```
#if !defined(__clsxpr1a_h)      // Sentry, use file only if
                                // it's not already included.
#define __clsxpr1a_h
/*  Project clsxprt1

    Copyright © 1993. All Rights Reserved.
    SUBSYSTEM:    clsxprt1.exe Application
    FILE:         clsxpr1a.h
    AUTHOR:

    OVERVIEW
    ========
    Class definition for clsxprt1App (TApplication).
*/

#include <owl\owlpch.h>
#pragma hdrstop
#include <owl\editfile.h>
#include <owl\opensave.h>
#include "clsxpr1a.rh"             // Definition of all resources.

//{{TApplication = clsxprt1App}}
class clsxprt1App : public TApplication {
private:
    TEditFile *Client; // Client window for the frame.
    TOpenSaveDialog::TData FileData;  // Data to control
                                      // open/saveas standard dialog.
public:
    clsxprt1App ();
    virtual ~clsxprt1App ();
    void OpenFile (const char *fileName = 0);
//{{clsxprt1AppVIRTUAL_BEGIN}}
public:
    virtual void InitMainWindow();
//{{clsxprt1AppVIRTUAL_END}}
//{{clsxprt1AppRSP_TBL_BEGIN}}
protected:
    void CmFileNew ();
    void CmFileOpen ();
    void CmFileClose ();
    void CmHelpAbout ();
    void CmUppercase ();
    void CmLowercase ();
    void CmInsertDate ();
    void CmInsertTime ();
    void CmInsertDateTime ();
    void CmReverse ();
//{{clsxprt1AppRSP_TBL_END}}
```

```
    DECLARE_RESPONSE_TABLE(clsxprt1App);
};    //{{clsxprt1App}}

#endif                          // __clsxpr1a_h sentry.
```

Notice that the header file in Listing X5.2 contains the protected member functions `CmUppercase`, `CmLowercase`, `CmInsertDate`, `CmInsertTime`, `CmInsertDateTime`, and `CmReverse`, which handle the Windows commands emitted by the new menu options. The ClassExpert utility added these member functions. The remaining declarations are the product of AppExpert.

Listing X5.3. The source code for the CLSXPR1A.RH header file.

```
//#if !defined(__clsxpr1a_rh)    // Sentry use file only if
                                 // it's not already included.
//#define __clsxpr1a_rh
/*  Main clsxprt1

    Copyright © 1993. All Rights Reserved.
    SUBSYSTEM:    clsxprt1.exe Application
    FILE:         clsxpr1a.rh
    AUTHOR:

    OVERVIEW
    ========
    Constant definitions for all resources defined in clsxpr1a.rc.
*/

//
// IDHELP BorButton for BWCC dialogs.
//
#define IDHELP                   998        // Id of help button

//
// Application specific definitions:
//
#define IDI_SDIAPPLICATION       1001       // Application icon
#define SDI_MENU                 100        // Menu resource ID and
                                            // Accelerator IDs
#define CM_REVERSE
106
#define CM_INSDATETIME
105
#define CM_INSTIME
104
```

continues

Listing X5.3. continued

```
#define CM_INSDATE
103
#define CM_LOWERCASE
102
#define CM_UPPERCASE
101
//
// CM_FILEnnnn commands (include\owl\editfile.rh
// except for CM_FILEPRINTPREVIEW)
#define CM_FILENEW                24331           // SDI New
#define CM_FILEOPEN               24332           // SDI Open
#define CM_FILECLOSE              24339
#define CM_FILESAVE               24333
#define CM_FILESAVEAS             24334

//
// Window commands (include\owl\windows.rh)
//
#define CM_EXIT                   24310

//
// CM_EDITnnnn commands (include\owl\edit.rh)
//
#define CM_EDITUNDO               24321
#define CM_EDITCUT                24322
#define CM_EDITCOPY               24323
#define CM_EDITPASTE              24324
#define CM_EDITDELETE             24325
#define CM_EDITCLEAR              24326

//
// Search menu commands (include\owl\editsear.rh)
//
#define CM_EDITFIND               24351
#define CM_EDITREPLACE            24352
#define CM_EDITFINDNEXT           24353

//
// Help menu commands.
//
#define CM_HELPABOUT              24389

//
// About Dialogs
//
#define IDD_ABOUT             22000
#define IDC_VERSION               22001
#define IDC_COPYRIGHT             22002
#define IDC_DEBUG                 22003
//
```

```
// OWL defined strings
//
// Statusbar
#define IDS_MODES                 32530
// EditFile
#define IDS_UNTITLED              32550
#define IDS_UNABLEREAD            32551
#define IDS_UNABLEWRITE           32552
#define IDS_FILECHANGED           32553
#define IDS_FILEFILTER            32554

// EditSearch
#define IDS_CANNOTFIND            32540

//
// General & application exception messages
// (include\owl\except.rh)
//
#define IDS_UNKNOWNEXCEPTION      32767
#define IDS_OWLEXCEPTION          32766
#define IDS_OKTORESUME            32765
#define IDS_UNHANDLEDXMSG         32764
#define IDS_UNKNOWNERROR          32763
#define IDS_NOAPP                 32762
#define IDS_OUTOFMEMORY           32761
#define IDS_INVALIDMODULE         32760
#define IDS_INVALIDMAINWINDOW     32759
//
// Owl 1 compatibility messages
//
#define IDS_INVALIDWINDOW         32756
#define IDS_INVALIDCHILDWINDOW    32755
#define IDS_INVALIDCLIENTWINDOW 32754
//
// TXWindow messages
//
#define IDS_CLASSREGISTERFAIL     32749
#define IDS_CHILDREGISTERFAIL     32748
#define IDS_WINDOWCREATEFAIL      32747
#define IDS_WINDOWEXECUTEFAIL     32746
#define IDS_CHILDCREATEFAIL       32745
#define IDS_MENUFAILURE           32744
#define IDS_VALIDATORSYNTAX       32743
#define IDS_PRINTERERROR          32742
#define IDS_LAYOUTINCOMPLETE      32741
#define IDS_LAYOUTBADRELWIN       32740
//
// TXGdi messages
//
#define IDS_GDIFAILURE            32739
```

continues

Listing X5.3. continued

```
#define IDS_GDIALLOCFAIL          32738
#define IDS_GDICREATEFAIL         32737
#define IDS_GDIRESLOADFAIL        32736
#define IDS_GDIFILEREADFAIL       32735
#define IDS_GDIDELETEFAIL         32734
#define IDS_GDIDESTROYFAIL        32733
#define IDS_INVALIDDIBHANDLE      32732

// TInputDialog DIALOG resource (include\owl\inputdia.rh)
#define IDD_INPUTDIALOG           32514
#define ID_PROMPT                 4091
#define ID_INPUT                  4090

// TSlider bitmaps (horizontal and vertical)
// (include\owl\slider.rh)
#define IDB_HSLIDERTHUMB          32000
#define IDB_VSLIDERTHUMB          32001

// Validation messages (include\owl\validate.rh)
#define IDS_VALPXPCONFORM         32520
#define IDS_VALINVALIDCHAR        32521
#define IDS_VALNOTINRANGE         32522
#define IDS_VALNOTINLIST          32523

//#endif          // __clsxpr1a_rh sentry.
```

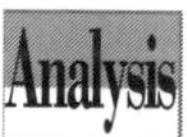

The resource header file in Listing X5.3 shows the `CM_XXXX` constants for the new menu options that were added by the Resource Workshop. The remaining statements are the product of AppExpert.

Listing X5.4. The script of the CLSXPR1A.RC resource file.

```
/*  Main clsxprt1

    Copyright © 1993. All Rights Reserved.
    SUBSYSTEM:    clsxprt1.exe Application
    FILE:         clsxpr1a.rc
    AUTHOR:

    OVERVIEW
    ========
    All resources defined here.
*/
#if !defined(WORKSHOP_INVOKED)
#include <windows.h>
#endif
```

```
#include "clsxpr1a.rh"
SDI_MENU MENU
{
 POPUP "&File"
 {
  MENUITEM "&New", CM_FILENEW
  MENUITEM "&Open...", CM_FILEOPEN
  MENUITEM "&Close", CM_FILECLOSE
  MENUITEM SEPARATOR
  MENUITEM "&Save", CM_FILESAVE, GRAYED
  MENUITEM "Save &As...", CM_FILESAVEAS, GRAYED
  MENUITEM SEPARATOR
  MENUITEM "E&xit\tAlt+F4", CM_EXIT
 }
 POPUP "&Edit"
 {
  MENUITEM "&Undo\tAlt+BkSp", CM_EDITUNDO, GRAYED
  MENUITEM SEPARATOR
  MENUITEM "Cu&t\tShift+Del", CM_EDITCUT, GRAYED
  MENUITEM "&Copy\tCtrl+Ins", CM_EDITCOPY, GRAYED
  MENUITEM "&Paste\tShift+Ins", CM_EDITPASTE, GRAYED
  MENUITEM SEPARATOR
  MENUITEM "Clear &All\tCtrl+Del", CM_EDITCLEAR, GRAYED
  MENUITEM "&Delete\tDel", CM_EDITDELETE, GRAYED
 }
 POPUP "&Search"
 {
  MENUITEM "&Find...", CM_EDITFIND, GRAYED
  MENUITEM "&Replace...", CM_EDITREPLACE, GRAYED
  MENUITEM "&Next\aF3", CM_EDITFINDNEXT, GRAYED
 }
 POPUP "S&pecial"
 {
  MENUITEM "&Uppercase", CM_UPPERCASE
  MENUITEM "&Lowercase", CM_LOWERCASE
  MENUITEM "&Reverse", CM_REVERSE
  MENUITEM SEPARATOR
  MENUITEM "Insert &Date", CM_INSDATE
  MENUITEM "Insert &Time", CM_INSTIME
  MENUITEM "Insert D&ate/Time", CM_INSDATETIME
 }
 POPUP "&Help"
 {
  MENUITEM "&About...", CM_HELPABOUT
 }
}

// Accelerator table for short-cut to menu commands.
// (include\owl\editfile.rc)
SDI_MENU ACCELERATORS
```

continues

Listing X5.4. continued

```
BEGIN
  VK_DELETE, CM_EDITCUT, VIRTKEY, SHIFT
  VK_INSERT, CM_EDITCOPY, VIRTKEY, CONTROL
  VK_INSERT, CM_EDITPASTE, VIRTKEY, SHIFT
  VK_DELETE, CM_EDITCLEAR, VIRTKEY, CONTROL
  VK_BACK,   CM_EDITUNDO, VIRTKEY, ALT
  VK_F3,     CM_EDITFINDNEXT, VIRTKEY
END

//
// Table of help hints displayed in the status bar.
//
...

// About box.
IDD_ABOUT DIALOG 12, 17, 204, 65
STYLE DS_MODALFRAME | WS_POPUP | WS_CAPTION | WS_SYSMENU
CAPTION "About clsxprt1"
FONT 8, "MS Sans Serif"
BEGIN
    CTEXT "Version", IDC_VERSION, 2, 14, 200, 8, SS_NOPREFIX
    CTEXT "My Application", -1, 2, 4, 200, 8, SS_NOPREFIX
    CTEXT "", IDC_COPYRIGHT, 2, 27, 200, 17, SS_NOPREFIX
    RTEXT "", IDC_DEBUG, 136, 55, 66, 8, SS_NOPREFIX
    ICON IDI_SDIAPPLICATION, -1, 2, 2, 16, 16
    DEFPUSHBUTTON "OK", IDOK, 88, 48, 28, 12
END

// TInputDialog class dialog box.
IDD_INPUTDIALOG DIALOG 20, 24, 180, 64
STYLE WS_POPUP | WS_CAPTION | DS_SETFONT
FONT 8, "Helv"
BEGIN
    LTEXT "", ID_PROMPT, 10, 8, 160, 10, SS_NOPREFIX
    CONTROL "", ID_INPUT, "EDIT", WS_CHILD | WS_VISIBLE |
          WS_BORDER | WS_TABSTOP | ES_AUTOHSCROLL, 10, 20, 160, 12
    DEFPUSHBUTTON "&OK", IDOK, 47, 42, 40, 14
    PUSHBUTTON "&Cancel", IDCANCEL, 93, 42, 40, 14
END

...
#endif
```

The resource file in Listing X5.4 shows the pop-up menu Special and its nested menu options. The Resource Workshop has inserted these script statements. The remaining script statements are the product of AppExpert.

Listing X5.5. The source code for the CLSXPR1A.CPP implementation file.

```
/*  Project clsxprt1

    Copyright © 1993. All Rights Reserved.
    SUBSYSTEM:    clsxprt1.exe Application
    FILE:         clsxpr1a.cpp
    AUTHOR:

    OVERVIEW
    ========
    Source file for implementation of clsxprt1App (TApplication).
*/

#include <owl\owlpch.h>
#pragma hdrstop

#include "clsxpr1a.h"
#include "clsxp1ad.h"            // Definition of about dialog.
#include <stdio.h>
#include <string.h>
#include <dos.h>
//{{clsxprt1App Implementation}}

//
// Build a response table for all messages/commands handled
// by the application.
//
DEFINE_RESPONSE_TABLE1(clsxprt1App, TApplication)
//{{clsxprt1AppRSP_TBL_BEGIN}}
    EV_COMMAND(CM_FILENEW, CmFileNew),
    EV_COMMAND(CM_FILEOPEN, CmFileOpen),
    EV_COMMAND(CM_FILECLOSE, CmFileClose),
    EV_COMMAND(CM_HELPABOUT, CmHelpAbout),
    EV_COMMAND(CM_UPPERCASE, CmUppercase),
    EV_COMMAND(CM_LOWERCASE, CmLowercase),
    EV_COMMAND(CM_INSDATE, CmInsertDate),
    EV_COMMAND(CM_INSTIME, CmInsertTime),
    EV_COMMAND(CM_INSDATETIME, CmInsertDateTime),
    EV_COMMAND(CM_REVERSE, CmReverse),
//{{clsxprt1AppRSP_TBL_END}}
END_RESPONSE_TABLE;

//
// FrameWindow must be derived to override Paint for Preview
// and Print.
//
class SDIDecFrame : public TDecoratedFrame {
public:
```

continues

Listing X5.5. continued

```
    SDIDecFrame (TWindow *parent,
                 const char far *title,
                 TWindow *clientWnd,
                 BOOL trackMenuSelection = FALSE,
                TModule *module = 0) :
           TDecoratedFrame(parent, title, clientWnd,
                           trackMenuSelection, module)
      {  }
    ~SDIDecFrame ()
      {  }
};

////////////////////////////////////////////////////////////
// clsxprt1App
// =====
//
clsxprt1App::clsxprt1App () : TApplication("clsxprt1")
{
    // Common file flags and filters for Open/Save As
    // dialogs. Filename and directory are computed in the
    // member functions CmFileOpen, and CmFileSaveAs.
    FileData.Flags = OFN_FILEMUSTEXIST ¦ OFN_HIDEREADONLY ¦
                     OFN_OVERWRITEPROMPT;
    FileData.SetFilter("All Files (*.*)¦*.*¦");
    // INSERT>> Your constructor code here.
}

clsxprt1App::~clsxprt1App ()
{
    // INSERT>> Your destructor code here.
}

////////////////////////////////////////////////////////////
// clsxprt1App
// =====
// Application initialization.
//
void clsxprt1App::InitMainWindow ()
{
    Client = new TEditFile(0, 0, 0);
    SDIDecFrame *frame = new SDIDecFrame(0, GetName(), Client,
                                         FALSE);
    nCmdShow = nCmdShow != SW_SHOWMINIMIZED ?
                              SW_SHOWNORMAL : nCmdShow;
    //
    // Assign ICON w/ this application.
    //
    frame->SetIcon(this, IDI_SDIAPPLICATION);
    //
    // Menu associated with window and accelerator table
```

```
    // associated with table.
    //
    frame->AssignMenu(SDI_MENU);

    //
    // Associate with the accelerator table.
    //
    frame->Attr.AccelTable = SDI_MENU;

    MainWindow = frame;
}

//////////////////////////////////////////////////////////
// clsxprt1App
// ===========
// Menu File New command
void clsxprt1App::CmFileNew ()
{
    Client->NewFile();
}

//////////////////////////////////////////////////////////
// clsxprt1App
// ===========
// Menu File Open command
void clsxprt1App::CmFileOpen ()
{
    //
    // Display standard Open dialog box to select a file name.
    //
    *FileData.FileName = 0;
    if (Client->CanClose())
        if (TFileOpenDialog(MainWindow, FileData).Execute() ==
            IDOK)
            OpenFile();
}

void clsxprt1App::OpenFile (const char *fileName)
{
    if (fileName)
        lstrcpy(FileData.FileName, fileName);
    Client->ReplaceWith(FileData.FileName);
}

//////////////////////////////////////////////////////////
// clsxprt1App
// =====
// Menu File Close command
void clsxprt1App::CmFileClose ()
{
```

continues

Listing X5.5. continued

```
 if (Client->CanClose())
        Client->DeleteSubText(0, UINT(-1));
}

////////////////////////////////////////////////////////////
// clsxprt1App
// ===========
// Menu Help About clsxprt1.exe command
void clsxprt1App::CmHelpAbout ()
{
    //
    // Show the modal dialog.
    //
    clsxprt1AboutDlg(MainWindow).Execute();
}

int OwlMain (int , char* [])
{
    clsxprt1App     App;
    int             result;
    result = App.Run();
    return result;
}
void clsxprt1App::CmUppercase ()
{
  UINT startPos, endPos;
  int numChars;
  char* pszStr;
  Client->GetSelection(startPos, endPos);
  // is there selected text
  if (startPos < endPos) {
    numChars = endPos - startPos + 1;
    pszStr = new char[numChars+1];
    Client->GetSubText(pszStr, startPos, endPos);
    strupr(pszStr);
    Client->Insert(pszStr);
    Client->SetSelection(startPos, endPos);
    delete [] pszStr;
  }
  else {
    numChars = Client->GetWindowTextLength();
    pszStr = new char[numChars+1];
    Client->GetSubText(pszStr, 0, (UINT)numChars);
    strupr(pszStr);
    Client->DeleteSubText(0, (UINT)numChars);
    Client->SetSelection(0, 0);
    Client->Insert(pszStr);
    delete [] pszStr;
  }
}
```

```

void clsxprt1App::CmLowercase ()
{
  UINT startPos, endPos;
  int numChars;
  char* pszStr;
  Client->GetSelection(startPos, endPos);
  // is there selected text
  if (startPos < endPos) {
    numChars = endPos - startPos + 1;
    pszStr = new char[numChars+1];
    Client->GetSubText(pszStr, startPos, endPos);
    strlwr(pszStr);
 Client->Insert(pszStr);
    Client->SetSelection(startPos, endPos);
    delete [] pszStr;
  }
  else {
    numChars = Client->GetWindowTextLength();
    pszStr = new char[numChars+1];
    Client->GetSubText(pszStr, 0, (UINT)numChars);
    strlwr(pszStr);
    Client->DeleteSubText(0, (UINT)numChars);
    Client->SetSelection(0, 0);
    Client->Insert(pszStr);
    delete [] pszStr;
  }
}

void clsxprt1App::CmInsertDate ()
{
  struct date dt;
  char szStr[41];
  getdate(&dt);
  sprintf(szStr, "%02d/%02d/%4d",
          dt.da_mon, dt.da_day, dt.da_year);
  Client->Insert(szStr);
}

void clsxprt1App::CmInsertTime ()
{
  struct time tm;
  char szStr[41];
  gettime(&tm);
  sprintf(szStr, "%02d:%02d:%02d",

 tm.ti_hour, tm.ti_min, tm.ti_sec);
  Client->Insert(szStr);
}

```

continues

Listing X5.5. continued

```
void clsxprt1App::CmInsertDateTime ()
{
  struct date dt;
  struct time tm;
  char szStr[41];
  getdate(&dt);
  sprintf(szStr, "%02d/%02d/%4d ",
          dt.da_mon, dt.da_day, dt.da_year);
  Client->Insert(szStr);
  gettime(&tm);
  sprintf(szStr, "%02d:%02d:%02d",

 tm.ti_hour, tm.ti_min, tm.ti_sec);
  Client->Insert(szStr);
}

void clsxprt1App::CmReverse ()
{
  UINT startPos, endPos;
  int numChars;
  char* pszStr;
  char swapChar;
  Client->GetSelection(startPos, endPos);
  // is there selected text
  if (startPos < endPos) {
    numChars = endPos - startPos + 1;
    pszStr = new char[numChars+1];
    Client->GetSubText(pszStr, startPos, endPos);
    for (int i = 0, j = strlen(pszStr)-1; i < j ; i++, j--) {
      swapChar = pszStr[i];
      pszStr[i] = pszStr[j];
      pszStr[j] = swapChar;
    }
    Client->Insert(pszStr);
    Client->SetSelection(startPos, endPos);
    delete [] pszStr;
  }
  else {
    numChars = Client->GetWindowTextLength();
    pszStr = new char[numChars+1];
    Client->GetSubText(pszStr, 0, (UINT)numChars);
    for (int i = 0, j = strlen(pszStr)-1; i < j ; i++, j--) {
      swapChar = pszStr[i];
      pszStr[i] = pszStr[j];
      pszStr[j] = swapChar;
    }
    Client->DeleteSubText(0, (UINT)numChars);
    Client->SetSelection(0, 0);
    Client->Insert(pszStr);
```

```
297:        delete [] pszStr;
298:     }
299:  }
```

Analysis The implementation file in Listing X5.5 shows the definitions of the `CmXXXX` member functions that handle the new menu options. The file contains the `#include` statements that we added to include the header files STDIO.H, STRING.H, and DOS.H. Also, notice the response table macros that were inserted by the ClassExpert utility. We added the code for the following member functions:

1. The member function `CmUppercase` (defined in lines 171 to 197) responds to the Uppercase menu option by performing the following tasks:

    - Obtains the currently selected text (if any). This task involves sending the C++ message `GetSelection` (in line 176) to the client window (accessed by the application's member `Client`). The arguments for this message are the local variables `startPos` and `endPos`.

    - Performs the following sequence of subtasks (found in line 179 to 185) if the value in variable `startPos` is less than that in `endPos` (which indicates that there is selected text):

        - Calculates the number of characters in the selected text and assigns this number to the local variable `numChars`.

        - Creates a dynamic string with `numChars+1` characters and assigns the address of that string to the local pointer `pszStr`.

        - Copies the selected text into the dynamic string. This task involves sending the C++ message `GetSubText` to the client window. The arguments for this message are `pszStr`, `startPos`, and `endPos`.

        - Converts the characters of the dynamic string to uppercase by using the string function `strupr`.

        - Replaces the selected text with the contents of the dynamic string. This task involves sending the C++ message `Insert` to the client window. The argument for this message is the pointer `pszStr`.

        - Selects the newly inserted text by sending the C++ message `SetSelection` to the client window. The arguments for this message are the local variables `startPos` and `endPos`.

- ☐ Deletes the dynamic string accessed by pointer `pszStr`.

☐ If there is no selection, the function converts all of the characters in the file to uppercase by performing the following subtasks (using the statements in lines 188 to 195):

- ☐ Obtains the size of the edited text by sending the C++ message `GetWindowTextLength` to the client window. This task assigns the result of the message to the local variable `numChars`.
- ☐ Creates a dynamic string with `numChars+1` characters and assigns the address of that string to the local pointer `pszStr`.
- ☐ Obtains the entire edited text by sending the C++ message `GetSubText` to the client area. The arguments for this message are `pszStr` (the text copy buffer), `0`, and `(UINT)numChars`.
- ☐ Converts the characters of the dynamic string to uppercase by using the string function `strupr`.
- ☐ Deletes the entire edited text by sending the C++ message `DeleteSubText` to the client window. The arguments for this message are `0` and `(UINT)numChars`.
- ☐ Selects the start of the file as the insertion point by sending the C++ message `SetSelection` to the client window. The arguments for this message are the integers 0 and 0.
- ☐ Inserts the characters of the dynamic string into the client window. This task involves sending the C++ message `Insert` to the client area. The argument for this message is the pointer `pszStr`.
- ☐ Deletes the dynamic string accessed by pointer `pszStr`.

Note: The program implements the various text-edit operations using the data member `Client`, which is a pointer to the class `TEditFile`. This class is a descendant of the class `TEditSearch`, which in turn is a descendant of the class `TEdit`. This lineage enables the pointer `Client` to receive C++ editing messages implemented by the member functions of class `TEdit`.

2. The member function `CmLowercase` (defined in lines 199 to 225) responds to the menu option Lowercase. The function is very similar to the function `CmUppercase` and differs only by its use of the string function `strlwr` instead of the function `strupr`.

3. The member function `CmInsertDate` (defined in lines 227 to 235) responds to the Insert Date menu option by performing the following options:

   - Obtains the current system date by calling the function `getdate` (prototyped in the DOS.H header file). The argument for this function call is the address of the structured variable `dt`. This variable has the date structure.

   - Creates a formatted string image of the month number, day number, and year number. This task uses the function `sprintf` and assigns the formatted string to the local string variable `szStr`.

   - Inserts the string image into the client window by sending that window the C++ message `Insert`. The argument for this message is the variable `szStr`.

4. The member function `CmInsertTime` (defined in lines 237 to 246) responds to the Insert Time menu option by performing the following options:

   - Obtains the current system time by calling the function `gettime` (prototyped in the DOS.H header file). The argument for this function call is the address of the structured variable `tm`. This variable has the time structure.

   - Creates a formatted string image of the hour, minute, and second. This task uses the function `sprintf` and assigns the formatted string to the local string variable `szStr`.

   - Inserts the string image into the client window by sending that window the C++ message `Insert`. The argument for this message is the variable `szStr`.

5. The member function `CmInsertDateTime` responds to the Insert Date/Time menu option. This function combines the tasks of the member functions `CmInsertDate` and `CmInsertTime`.

6. The member function `CmReverse` (defined in lines 264 to 299) responds to the Reverse menu option. This function performs the following tasks:

    - Obtains the currently selected text (if any). This task involves sending the C++ message `GetSelection` to the client window (accessed by the application's member `Client`). The arguments for this message are the local variables `startPos` and `endPos`.
    - Performs the following sequence of subtasks (in lines 273 to 283) if the value in variable `startPos` is less than that in `endPos` (which indicates that there is selected text):
        - Calculates the number of characters in the selected text and assigns this number to the local variable `numChars`.
        - Creates a dynamic string with `numChars+1` characters and assigns the address of that string to the local pointer `pszStr`.
        - Copies the selected text into the dynamic string. This task involves sending the C++ message `GetSubText` to the client window. The arguments for this message are `pszStr`, `startPos`, and `endPos`.
        - Reverses the characters in the dynamic string. This task involves using a `for` loop with two control variables: `i` and `j`. The loop statements swap characters using the local variable `swapChar`. The loop initializes the variable `i` and `j` to `0` and `strlen(pszStr)-1`, respectively, and iterates until variable `i` is equal to or is greater than variable `j`.
        - Replaces the selected text with the contents of the dynamic string. This task involves sending the C++ message `Insert` to the client window. The argument for this message is the pointer `pszStr`.
        - Selects the newly inserted text by sending the C++ message `SetSelection` to the client window. The arguments for this message are the local variables `startPos` and `endPos`.
        - Deletes the dynamic string accessed by pointer `pszStr`.

- If there is no selection, the function converts all of the characters in the file to uppercase by performing the following subtasks (using the statements in lines 286 to 293):
    - Obtains the size of the edited text by sending the C++ message `GetWindowTextLength` to the client window. This task assigns the result of the message to the local variable `numChars`.
    - Creates a dynamic string with `numChars+1` characters and assigns the address of that string to the local pointer `pszStr`.
    - Obtains the entire edited text by sending the C++ message `GetSubText` to the client area. The arguments for this message are `pszStr` (the text copy buffer), `0`, and `(UINT)numChars`.
    - Reverses the characters in the dynamic string. This task involves using a `for` loop with two control variables: `i` and `j`. The loop statements swap characters using the local variable `swapChar`. The loop initializes the variable `i` and `j` to `0` and `strlen(pszStr)-1`, respectively, and iterates until variable `i` is equal to or is greater than variable `j`.
    - Deletes the entire edited text by sending the C++ message `DeleteSubText` to the client window. The arguments for this message are `0` and `(UINT)numChars`.
    - Selects the start of the file as the insertion point by sending the C++ message `SetSelection` to the client window. The arguments for this message are the integers 0 and 0.
    - Inserts the characters of the dynamic string into the client window. This task involves sending the C++ message `Insert` to the client area. The argument for this message is the pointer `pszStr`.
    - Deletes the dynamic string accessed by pointer `pszStr`.

Compile and run the program CLSXPRT1.EXE. Load a small text file and experiment with converting and reversing the characters of selected text and of the entire file. In addition, experiment with inserting the date, the time, or both. When you are done experimenting, exit the file without saving it. Figure X5.2 shows a sample session with the CLSXPRT1.EXE program.

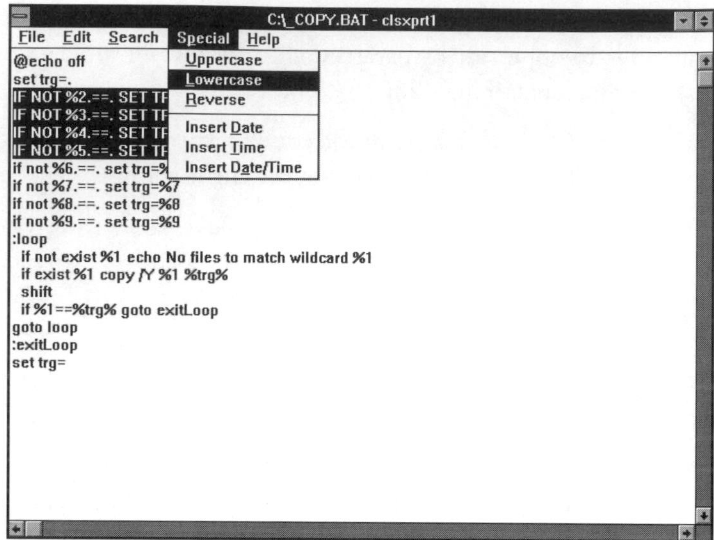

Figure X5.2. *A sample session with the CLSXPRT1.EXE program.*

Adding a Class

Let's develop the preceding programming project to create program CLSXPRT2.EXE by adding a new menu option in the Special menu selection. This option pops up a dialog box that permits you to select the date format (MM/DD/YYYY, DD/MM/YYYY, or YYYY/MM/DD) and time format (24 hours or AM/PM). The new program supports this dialog box by first creating its resource, then declaring its class, and finally adding the various member functions and declarations to breathe life into the new dialog box.

Here are the general steps to create the project files:

1. Create the files of project CLSXPRT2, using AppExpert as in project CLSXPRT1.

2. Use the Resource Workshop to add the menu selection Special and its menu options: Lowercase, Uppercase, Reverse, Insert Date, Insert Time, Insert Date/Time, and Preferences.... The last menu option is the one that invokes the dialog box with the date and time format selection. Use the identifiers `CM_LOWERCASE`, `CM_UPPERCASE`, `CM_REVERSE`, `CM_INSDATE`, `CM_INSTIME`,

CM_INSDATETIME, and CM_FORMATDATETIME, respectively, for the preceding menu options. Insert a separator menu item after the menu options Reverse and Insert Date/Time.

3. Use the Resource Workshop to create the new Borland-style dialog box resource IDD_DATETIME_DLG, which contains the following controls:
   - The OK and Cancel pushbuttons, which are automatically inserted by the Resource Workshop.
   - The Date Format group box (with the ID IDD_DATE_GRP), which contains the following Borland-style radio buttons:
     - The MM/DD/YYYY radio button (with the ID IDC_MMDDYY_RBT)
     - The DD/MM/YYYY radio button (with the ID IDC_DDMMYY_RBT)
     - The YYYY/MM/DD radio button (with the ID IDC_YYMMDD_RBT)
   - The Time Format group box (with the ID IDC_TIME_GRP), which contains the following Borland-style radio buttons:
     - The 24-hour radio button (with the ID IDC_24HR_RBT)
     - The AM/PM radio button (with the ID IDC_AMPM_RBT)
4. Use the ClassExpert to add the member functions CmLowercase, CmUppercase, CmReverse, CmInsertDate, CmInsertTime, CmInsertDateTime, and CmPreferences to handle the preceding new menu options, respectively.
5. Use the ClassExpert to create the new dialog box class TFrmtDialog. To perform this task, move the mouse to the Classes pane of the ClassExpert window, select the class clsxprt2AboutDlg, and then click the right mouse button to view the pop-up menu. Select the Create New Class… menu option. This option brings up the Add New Class dialog box, which has the following controls:
   - The Base Class drop-down combo list, which enables you to choose the base class for the new class. Accept the default selection of TDialog as the base class.
   - The Class Name edit box, in which you enter the name of the new class. Enter TFrmtDialog.
   - The Source File edit box, which contains the name of the implementation file.

- The Header File edit box, which contains the name of the header file for the new class.
- The Dialog Id drop-down combo list, which enables you to choose the ID of the new dialog box.

When you type in the class name, the Add New Class dialog box automatically forms the names of the implementation and header files. When you are done, click the OK pushbutton. Figure X5.3 shows a sample session with the Add New Class dialog box. It is worth noting that the Add New Class dialog box is context-sensitive. If you select the application class and then invoke it, you see slightly different controls, because ClassExpert assumes you wish to create a window or a control.

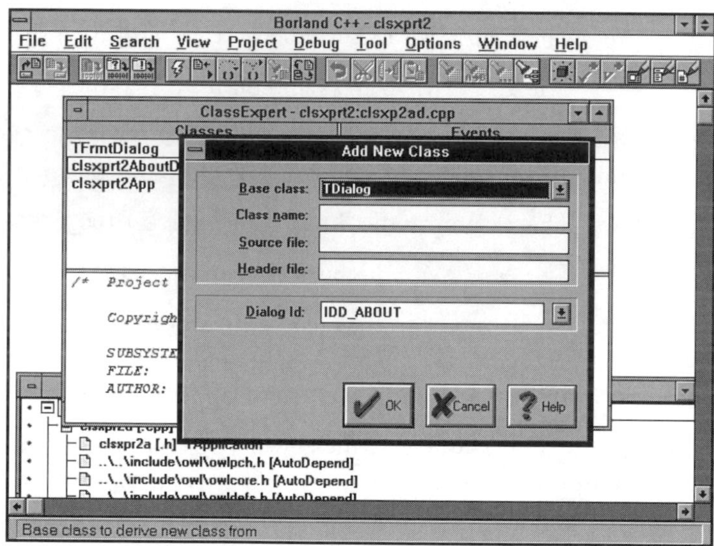

Figure X5.3. *A sample session with the Add New Class dialog box.*

Listing X5.6 contains the contents of the CLSXPR2A.DEF definition file. Listing X5.7 contains the source code for the TFRMTDLG.H header file. Listing X5.8 contains the source code for the CLSXPR2A.H header file. Listing X5.9 contains the source code for the CLSXPR2A.RH header file. Listing X5.10 contains the partial script of the CLSXPR2A.RC resource file. Listing X5.11 contains the source code for the TFRMTDLG.CPP implementation file. Listing X5.12 contains the source code for the CLSXPR2A.CPP implementation file. (We will discuss the customization process for each listing later in this section.)

Listing X5.6. The contents of the CLSXPR2A.DEF definition file.

```
;-------------------------------------------------
;   Main clsxprt2
;
;   Copyright © 1993. All Rights Reserved.
;
;   SUBSYSTEM:    clsxprt2.exe Module Definition File
;   FILE:         clsxpr2a.def
;   AUTHOR:
;
;-------------------------------------------------
NAME clsxprt2
DESCRIPTION 'clsxprt2 Application - Copyright © 1993. All Rights
                Reserved.'
EXETYPE      WINDOWS
CODE         PRELOAD MOVEABLE DISCARDABLE
DATA         PRELOAD MOVEABLE MULTIPLE
HEAPSIZE     4096
STACKSIZE    8192
```

Listing X5.7. The source code for the TFRMTDLG.H header file.

```
#if !defined(__tfrmtdlg_h)          // Sentry, use file only if
                                    // it's not already included.
#define __tfrmtdlg_h
/*  Project clsxprt2

    Copyright © 1993. All Rights Reserved.
    SUBSYSTEM:    clsxprt2.exe Application
    FILE:         tfrmtdlg.h
    AUTHOR:

    OVERVIEW
    ========
    Class definition for TFrmtDialog (TDialog).
*/
#include <owl\owlpch.h>
#pragma hdrstop
#include <owl\dialog.h>
#include "clsxpr2a.rh"              // Definition of all resources.
#include "clsxpr2a.h"
//{{TDialog = TFrmtDialog}}
class TFrmtDialog : public TDialog {
public:
```

continues

Listing X5.7. continued

```
23:     TFrmtDialog (TWindow* parent, TResId resId = IDD_ABOUT,
24:                 TModule* module = 0);
25:     virtual ~TFrmtDialog ();
26:     BOOL IsAmPm;
27:     clsxprt2App::dateFormat df;
28: //{{TFrmtDialogVIRTUAL_BEGIN}}
29: public:
30:     virtual BOOL EvInitDialog (HWND hWndFocus);
31:     void CmOk();
32: //{{TFrmtDialogVIRTUAL_END}}
33:  // insert declaration of response table
34:  DECLARE_RESPONSE_TABLE(TFrmtDialog);
35: };    //{{TFrmtDialog}}
36:
37: #endif                          // __tfrmtdlg_h sentry.
```

Listing X5.7 shows the header file TFRMTDLG.H, which contains the declaration for the date/time format dialog box class, `TFrmtDialog`. The ClassExpert utility generated this header file when we created the class `TFrmtDialog`. In addition, we used ClassExpert to add the member function `EvInitDialog` to handle initializing the dialog box. We manually added the following:

1. The statement `#include "clsxpr2a.h"` in line 19, which enables the class `TFrmtDialog` to access a nested enumerated type in the application class.
2. The declaration of the member function `CmOk` in line 31, to handle pressing the OK button of the dialog box.
3. The Boolean data member `IsAmPm` in line 26, which stores the selection of the time format.
4. The enumerated data member `df` in line 27, which stores the date format. Notice that the enumerated type is `clsxprt2App::dateFormat`, an export of class `clsxprt2App`.
5. The declaration of the message response table in line 34.

Listing X5.8. The source code for the CLSXPR2A.H header file.

```
#if !defined(__clsxpr2a_h)            // Sentry, use file only if
                                      // it's not already included.
#define __clsxpr2a_h
/*  Project clsxprt2

```

```
    Copyright © 1993. All Rights Reserved.
    SUBSYSTEM:    clsxprt2.exe Application
    FILE:         clsxpr2a.h
    AUTHOR:

    OVERVIEW
    ========
    Class definition for clsxprt2App (TApplication).
*/

#include <owl\owlpch.h>
#pragma hdrstop
#include <owl\editfile.h>
#include <owl\opensave.h>
#include "clsxpr2a.rh"            // Definition of all resources.

//{{TApplication = clsxprt2App}}
class clsxprt2App : public TApplication {
  // declare friend class
private:
    TEditFile *Client; // Client window for the frame.
    TOpenSaveDialog::TData FileData;  // Data to control
                                      // open/saveas standard dialog.
public:
    // new nested enumerated type
    enum dateFormat { mmddyy, ddmmyy, yymmdd };
    clsxprt2App ();
    virtual ~clsxprt2App ();
    void OpenFile (const char *fileName = 0);
//{{clsxprt2AppVIRTUAL_BEGIN}}
public:
    virtual void InitMainWindow();
//{{clsxprt2AppVIRTUAL_END}}
//{{clsxprt2AppRSP_TBL_BEGIN}}
protected:
    BOOL IsAmPm;
    dateFormat df;
    void CmFileNew ();
    void CmFileOpen ();
    void CmFileClose ();
    void CmHelpAbout ();
    void CmInsertDateTime ();
    void CmInsertTime ();
    void CmLowercase ();
    void CmReverse ();
    void CmUppercase ();
    void CmDateTimeFormat ();
    void CmPreferences ();
    void CmInsertDate ();
//{{clsxprt2AppRSP_TBL_END}}
```

continues

Listing X5.8. continued

```
    DECLARE_RESPONSE_TABLE(clsxprt2App);
};    //{{clsxprt2App}}

#endif                                      // __clsxpr2a_h sentry.
```

Listing X5.8 shows the CLSXPR2A.H header file, which contains the declaration of the application class `clsxprt2App`. The AppExpert utility generated most of the statements in this file. The ClassExpert utility inserted the member functions `Cm`*XXXX*, which deal with the options of the Special menu selection. We manually added the following items:

1. The public declaration of the nested enumerated type `dateFormat`. This type models the three date formats.
2. The Boolean data member `IsAmPm`, which stores the time format.
3. The enumerated data member `df`, which stores the date format.

Listing X5.9. The partial source code for the CLSXPR2A.RH header file.

```
//#if !defined(__clsxpr2a_rh)       // Sentry use file only if
                                    // it's not already included.
//#define __clsxpr2a_rh

/*  Main clsxprt2

    Copyright © 1993. All Rights Reserved.

    SUBSYSTEM:    clsxprt2.exe Application
    FILE:         clsxpr2a.h
    AUTHOR:


    OVERVIEW
    ========
    Constant definitions for all resources defined in clsxpr2a.rc.
*/


//
// IDHELP BorButton for BWCC dialogs.
//
#define IDHELP                    998        // Id of help button


```

```
//
// Application specific definitions:
//
#define IDI_SDIAPPLICATION      1001       // Application icon

#define SDI_MENU                100        // Menu resource ID
                                           // and Accelerator IDs

//
// CM_FILEnnnn commands (include\owl\editfile.rh except for
// CM_FILEPRINTPREVIEW)
//
#define CM_FILENEW              24331           // SDI New
#define CM_FILEOPEN             24332           // SDI Open
#define CM_FILECLOSE            24339
#define CM_FILESAVE             24333
#define CM_FILESAVEAS           24334


//
// Window commands (include\owl\windows.rh)
//
#define CM_EXIT                 24310


//
// CM_EDITnnnn commands (include\owl\edit.rh)
//
#define CM_EDITUNDO             24321
#define CM_EDITCUT              24322
#define CM_EDITCOPY             24323
#define CM_EDITPASTE            24324
#define CM_EDITDELETE           24325
#define CM_EDITCLEAR            24326


//
// Search menu commands (include\owl\editsear.rh)
//
#define CM_EDITFIND             24351
#define CM_EDITREPLACE          24352
#define CM_EDITFINDNEXT         24353

//
// Special menu commands
//
#define CM_LOWERCASE            300
#define CM_UPPERCASE            301
#define CM_REVERSE              302
#define CM_INSDATE              303
```

continues

Listing X5.9. continued

```
#define CM_INSTIME                   304
#define CM_INSDATETIME               305
#define CM_DATETIMEFORMAT            306

#define IDD_DATETIME_DLG             400
#define IDC_MMDDYY_RBT               401
#define IDC_DDMMYY_RBT               402
#define IDC_YYMMDD_RBT               403
#define IDC_24HR_RBT                 404
#define IDC_AMPM_RBT                 405
#define IDC_TIME_GRP                 406
#define IDC_DATE_GRP                 407


//
// Help menu commands.
//
#define CM_HELPABOUT                 24389
...
//#endif          // __clsxpr2a_rh sentry.
```

The resource header file in Listing X5.9 (which is a *partial* listing) shows the `CM_XXXX`, `IDD_DATETIME_DLG`, `IDC_XXXX_RBT`, and `IDC_XXXX_GRP` identifiers for the new menu options and the new dialog box resource. The Resource Workshop added these identifiers. The remaining statements are the product of AppExpert.

Listing X5.10. The partial script of the CLSXPR2A.RC resource file.

```
/*  Main clsxprt2

    Copyright © 1993. All Rights Reserved.

    SUBSYSTEM:    clsxprt2.exe Application
    FILE:         clsxpr2a.rc
    AUTHOR:


    OVERVIEW
    ========
    All resources defined here.
*/

#if !defined(WORKSHOP_INVOKED)
#include <windows.h>
```

```
#endif
#include "clsxpr2a.rh"

SDI_MENU MENU
{
 POPUP "&File"
 {
  MENUITEM "&New", CM_FILENEW
  MENUITEM "&Open...", CM_FILEOPEN
  MENUITEM "&Close", CM_FILECLOSE
  MENUITEM SEPARATOR
  MENUITEM "&Save", CM_FILESAVE, GRAYED
  MENUITEM "Save &As...", CM_FILESAVEAS, GRAYED
  MENUITEM SEPARATOR
  MENUITEM "E&xit\tAlt+F4", CM_EXIT
 }

 POPUP "&Edit"
 {
  MENUITEM "&Undo\tAlt+BkSp", CM_EDITUNDO, GRAYED
  MENUITEM SEPARATOR
  MENUITEM "Cu&t\tShift+Del", CM_EDITCUT, GRAYED
  MENUITEM "&Copy\tCtrl+Ins", CM_EDITCOPY, GRAYED
  MENUITEM "&Paste\tShift+Ins", CM_EDITPASTE, GRAYED
  MENUITEM SEPARATOR
  MENUITEM "Clear &All\tCtrl+Del", CM_EDITCLEAR, GRAYED
  MENUITEM "&Delete\tDel", CM_EDITDELETE, GRAYED
 }

 POPUP "&Search"
 {
  MENUITEM "&Find...", CM_EDITFIND, GRAYED
  MENUITEM "&Replace...", CM_EDITREPLACE, GRAYED
  MENUITEM "&Next\aF3", CM_EDITFINDNEXT, GRAYED
 }

 POPUP "S&pecial"
 {
  MENUITEM "&Uppercase", CM_UPPERCASE
  MENUITEM "&Lowercase", CM_LOWERCASE
  MENUITEM "&Reverse", CM_REVERSE
  MENUITEM SEPARATOR
  MENUITEM "Insert &Date", CM_INSDATE
  MENUITEM "Insert &Time", CM_INSTIME
  MENUITEM "Insert Date/Time", CM_INSDATETIME
  MENUITEM SEPARATOR
  MENUITEM "&Preferences...", CM_DATETIMEFORMAT
 }

 POPUP "&Help"
```

continues

Listing X5.10. continued

```
  {
   MENUITEM "&About...", CM_HELPABOUT
  }

}
...
//
// Misc application definitions
//

// Application ICON
IDI_SDIAPPLICATION ICON "applsdi.ico"


// About box.
IDD_ABOUT DIALOG 12, 17, 204, 65
STYLE DS_MODALFRAME | WS_POPUP | WS_CAPTION | WS_SYSMENU
CAPTION "About clsxprt2"
FONT 8, "MS Sans Serif"
BEGIN
    CTEXT "Version", IDC_VERSION, 2, 14, 200, 8, SS_NOPREFIX
    CTEXT "My Application", -1, 2, 4, 200, 8, SS_NOPREFIX
    CTEXT "", IDC_COPYRIGHT, 2, 27, 200, 17, SS_NOPREFIX
    RTEXT "", IDC_DEBUG, 136, 55, 66, 8, SS_NOPREFIX
    ICON IDI_SDIAPPLICATION, -1, 2, 2, 16, 16
    DEFPUSHBUTTON "OK", IDOK, 88, 48, 28, 12
END


// TInputDialog class dialog box.
IDD_INPUTDIALOG DIALOG 20, 24, 180, 64
STYLE WS_POPUP | WS_CAPTION | DS_SETFONT
FONT 8, "Helv"
BEGIN
    LTEXT "", ID_PROMPT, 10, 8, 160, 10, SS_NOPREFIX
    CONTROL "", ID_INPUT, "EDIT", WS_CHILD | WS_VISIBLE |
    WS_BORDER | WS_TABSTOP | ES_AUTOHSCROLL, 10, 20, 160, 12
    DEFPUSHBUTTON "&OK", IDOK, 47, 42, 40, 14
    PUSHBUTTON "&Cancel", IDCANCEL, 93, 42, 40, 14
END
...

IDD_DATETIME_DLG DIALOG 55, 37, 189, 124
STYLE DS_MODALFRAME | WS_POPUP | WS_VISIBLE | WS_CAPTION |
      WS_SYSMENU
CLASS "bordlg"
CAPTION "Date & Time Formats"
FONT 8, "MS Sans Serif"
{
 CONTROL "", -1, "BorShade", BSS_HDIP | BSS_LEFT | WS_CHILD |
```

```
    WS_VISIBLE, 0, 83, 189, 3
  CONTROL "", IDOK, "BorBtn", BS_DEFPUSHBUTTON ¦ WS_CHILD ¦
    WS_VISIBLE ¦ WS_TABSTOP, 48, 92, 37, 25
  CONTROL "", IDCANCEL, "BorBtn", BS_PUSHBUTTON ¦ WS_CHILD ¦
    WS_VISIBLE ¦ WS_TABSTOP, 104, 92, 37, 25
  CONTROL "&mm/dd/yyyy", IDC_MMDDYY_RBT, "BorRadio",
    BS_AUTORADIOBUTTON ¦ BBS_PARENTNOTIFY ¦ WS_CHILD ¦ WS_VISIBLE ¦
    WS_TABSTOP, 13, 27, 57, 12
  CONTROL "&dd/mm/yyyy", IDC_DDMMYY_RBT, "BorRadio",
    BS_AUTORADIOBUTTON ¦ BBS_PARENTNOTIFY ¦ WS_CHILD ¦ WS_VISIBLE ¦
    WS_TABSTOP, 13, 44, 57, 12
  CONTROL "&yyyy/mm/dd", IDC_YYMMDD_RBT, "BorRadio",
    BS_AUTORADIOBUTTON ¦ BBS_PARENTNOTIFY ¦ WS_CHILD ¦ WS_VISIBLE ¦
    WS_TABSTOP, 13, 60, 57, 12
  GROUPBOX " Time Format", IDC_TIME_GRP, 97, 13, 63, 60,
    BS_GROUPBOX
  GROUPBOX " Date Format", IDC_DATE_GRP, 9, 9, 69, 73,
    BS_GROUPBOX
  CONTROL "24 Hour", IDC_24HR_RBT, "BorRadio", BS_AUTORADIOBUTTON ¦
    BBS_PARENTNOTIFY ¦ WS_CHILD ¦ WS_VISIBLE ¦ WS_TABSTOP,
    108, 32, 44, 11
  CONTROL "AM/PM", IDC_AMPM_RBT, "BorRadio", BS_AUTORADIOBUTTON ¦
    BBS_PARENTNOTIFY ¦ WS_CHILD ¦ WS_VISIBLE ¦ WS_TABSTOP,
    108, 55, 44, 11
}
```

Listing X5.10 shows the partial script statements of the resource file CLSXPR2A.RC. The listing shows the menu resource and the custom dialog box resource.

Listing X5.11. The source code for the TFRMTDLG.CPP implementation file.

```
/*  Project clsxprt2

    Copyright © 1993. All Rights Reserved.
    SUBSYSTEM:    clsxprt2.exe Application
    FILE:         tfrmtdlg.cpp
    AUTHOR:

     OVERVIEW
    ========
    Source file for implementation of TFrmtDialog (TDialog).
*/
#include <owl\owlpch.h>
#pragma hdrstop
#include "tfrmtdlg.h"
```

continues

Listing X5.11. continued

```

//{{TFrmtDialog Implementation}}
DEFINE_RESPONSE_TABLE1(TFrmtDialog, TDialog)
    EV_COMMAND(IDOK, CmOk),
END_RESPONSE_TABLE;

TFrmtDialog::TFrmtDialog (TWindow* parent, TResId resId,
                           TModule* module):
    TDialog(parent, resId, module)
{
    // INSERT>> Your constructor code here.
}

TFrmtDialog::~TFrmtDialog ()
{
    Destroy();
    // INSERT>> Your destructor code here.
}

BOOL TFrmtDialog::EvInitDialog (HWND hWndFocus)
{
    BOOL result;

 result = TDialog::EvInitDialog(hWndFocus);
    // INSERT>> Your code here.
    CheckRadioButton(IDC_MMDDYY_RBT, IDC_YYMMDD_RBT,
                     IDC_MMDDYY_RBT);
    CheckRadioButton(IDC_24HR_RBT, IDC_AMPM_RBT,
                     IDC_24HR_RBT);
    return result;
}
void TFrmtDialog::CmOk()
{
    // save date format
    if (IsDlgButtonChecked(IDC_MMDDYY_RBT))
      df = clsxprt2App::mmddyy;
    else if (IsDlgButtonChecked(IDC_DDMMYY_RBT))
      df = clsxprt2App::ddmmyy;
    else
      df = clsxprt2App::yymmdd;
    // save time format
    IsAmPm = (IsDlgButtonChecked(IDC_AMPM_RBT)) ?
                                      TRUE : FALSE;
    TDialog::CmOk();
}
```

Listing X5.11 shows the source code for the TFRMTDLG.CPP implementation file. The ClassExpert utility created this file and added the empty definition of the member function `EvInitDialog`. We manually added the definition of the event response table, the statements in function `EvInitDialog`, and the entire member function `CmOk`.

The member function `EvInitDialog` initializes the dialog box by performing the following tasks:

- Invokes the function `EvInitDialog` of the parent class and assigns its result to the local Boolean variable `result`.
- Clears the radio buttons in the Date Format group box and checks the MM/DD/YYYY radio button. This task uses the member function `CheckRadioButton`, which is inherited from class `TWindow`.
- Clears the radio buttons in the Time Format group box and checks the 24-hour radio button. This task uses the inherited member function `CheckRadioButton`.
- Returns the value in the local variable result.

The member function `CmOk` responds to clicking the OK pushbutton of the dialog box by performing the following tasks:

- Saves the date format in the data member `df`. This task uses a multiple-decision `if` statement to examine each radio button control in the Date Format group box. The `if` statement invokes the inherited member function `IsDlgButtonChecked` to determine which radio button is checked.
- Saves the time format in the data member `IsAmPm`. This task invokes the inherited member function `IsDlgButtonChecked` to determine if the AM/PM radio button is checked.
- Invokes the function `CmOk` of the parent class.

Listing X5.12. The source code for the CLSXPR2A.CPP implementation file.

```
/*  Project clsxprt2

    Copyright © 1993. All Rights Reserved.
    SUBSYSTEM:    clsxprt2.exe Application
    FILE:         clsxpr2a.cpp
    AUTHOR:
```

continues

Listing X5.12. continued

```

    OVERVIEW
    ========
    Source file for implementation of clsxprt2App (TApplication).
*/

#include <owl\owlpch.h>
#pragma hdrstop

#include "clsxpr2a.h"
#include "clsxp2ad.h"           // Definition of about dialog.
#include "tfrmtdlg.h"
#include <stdio.h>
#include <string.h>
#include <dos.h>
//{{clsxprt2App Implementation}}

//
// Build a response table for all messages/commands handled
// by the application.
//
DEFINE_RESPONSE_TABLE1(clsxprt2App, TApplication)
//{{clsxprt2AppRSP_TBL_BEGIN}}
    EV_COMMAND(CM_FILENEW, CmFileNew),
    EV_COMMAND(CM_FILEOPEN, CmFileOpen),
    EV_COMMAND(CM_FILECLOSE, CmFileClose),
    EV_COMMAND(CM_HELPABOUT, CmHelpAbout),
    EV_COMMAND(CM_INSDATETIME, CmInsertDateTime),
    EV_COMMAND(CM_INSTIME, CmInsertTime),
    EV_COMMAND(CM_LOWERCASE, CmLowercase),
    EV_COMMAND(CM_REVERSE, CmReverse),
    EV_COMMAND(CM_UPPERCASE, CmUppercase),
    EV_COMMAND(CM_DATETIMEFORMAT, CmPreferences),
    EV_COMMAND(CM_UPPERCASE, CmUppercase),
    EV_COMMAND(CM_REVERSE, CmReverse),
    EV_COMMAND(CM_LOWERCASE, CmLowercase),
    EV_COMMAND(CM_INSTIME, CmInsertTime),
    EV_COMMAND(CM_INSDATE, CmInsertDate),
    EV_COMMAND(CM_INSDATETIME, CmInsertDateTime),
//{{clsxprt2AppRSP_TBL_END}}
END_RESPONSE_TABLE;

//
// FrameWindow must be derived to override Paint for Preview
// and Print.
//
class SDIDecFrame : public TDecoratedFrame {
public:
    SDIDecFrame (TWindow *parent,
                 const char far *title,
```

```
                        TWindow *clientWnd,
                        BOOL trackMenuSelection = FALSE,
                        TModule *module = 0) :
                TDecoratedFrame(parent, title, clientWnd,
                        trackMenuSelection, module)
        { }
      ~SDIDecFrame ()
        { }
};

//////////////////////////////////////////////////////////////
// clsxprt2App
// =====
//
clsxprt2App::clsxprt2App () : TApplication("clsxprt2")
{
    // Common file  flags and filters for Open/Save As
    // dialogs. Filename and directory are computed in the
    // member functions CmFileOpen, and CmFileSaveAs.
    FileData.Flags = OFN_FILEMUSTEXIST | OFN_HIDEREADONLY |
                     OFN_OVERWRITEPROMPT;
    FileData.SetFilter("All Files (*.*)|*.*|");
    // INSERT>> Your constructor code here.
    IsAmPm = FALSE;
    df = mmddyy;
}

clsxprt2App::~clsxprt2App ()
{
    // INSERT>> Your destructor code here.
}

//////////////////////////////////////////////////////////////
// clsxprt2App
// =====
// Application initialization.
//
void clsxprt2App::InitMainWindow ()
{
    Client = new TEditFile(0, 0, 0);
    SDIDecFrame *frame = new SDIDecFrame(0, GetName(),
                                          Client, FALSE);
    nCmdShow = nCmdShow != SW_SHOWMINIMIZED ?
                               SW_SHOWNORMAL : nCmdShow;
    //
    // Assign ICON w/ this application.
    //
    frame->SetIcon(this, IDI_SDIAPPLICATION);
    //
    // Menu associated with window and accelerator table
```

continues

Listing X5.12. continued

```
    // associated with table.
    //
    frame->AssignMenu(SDI_MENU);

    //
    // Associate with the accelerator table.
    //
    frame->Attr.AccelTable = SDI_MENU;

    MainWindow = frame;
}

//////////////////////////////////////////////////////////
// clsxprt2App
// ===========
// Menu File New command
void clsxprt2App::CmFileNew ()
{
    Client->NewFile();
}

//////////////////////////////////////////////////////////
// clsxprt2App
// ===========
// Menu File Open command
void clsxprt2App::CmFileOpen ()
{
    //
    // Display standard Open dialog box to select a file name.
    //
    *FileData.FileName = 0;
    if (Client->CanClose())
        if (TFileOpenDialog(MainWindow, FileData).Execute() ==
            IDOK)
            OpenFile();
}

void clsxprt2App::OpenFile (const char *fileName)
{
    if (fileName)
        lstrcpy(FileData.FileName, fileName);
    Client->ReplaceWith(FileData.FileName);
}

//////////////////////////////////////////////////////////
// clsxprt2App
// =====
// Menu File Close command
void clsxprt2App::CmFileClose ()
{
```

```
 if (Client->CanClose())
        Client->DeleteSubText(0, UINT(-1));
}

////////////////////////////////////////////////////////////
// clsxprt2App
// ===========
// Menu Help About clsxprt2.exe command
void clsxprt2App::CmHelpAbout ()
{
    //
    // Show the modal dialog.
    //
    clsxprt2AboutDlg(MainWindow).Execute();
}

int OwlMain (int , char* [])
{
    clsxprt2App     App;
    int             result;
    result = App.Run();
    return result;
}
void clsxprt2App::CmInsertTime ()
{
  struct time tm;
  char szStr[41];
  gettime(&tm);
  if (IsAmPm) {
    if (tm.ti_hour == 12)
      sprintf(szStr, "12:%02d:%02d p.m.",

     tm.ti_min, tm.ti_sec);
    else if (tm.ti_hour > 12)
      sprintf(szStr, "%2d:%02d:%02d p.m.",

 tm.ti_hour - 12, tm.ti_min, tm.ti_sec);
    else
       sprintf(szStr, "%2d:%02d:%02d a.m.",

 tm.ti_hour, tm.ti_min, tm.ti_sec);
  }
  else
    sprintf(szStr, "%2d:%02d:%02d",

 tm.ti_hour, tm.ti_min, tm.ti_sec);
  Client->Insert(szStr);
}

void clsxprt2App::CmLowercase ()
```

continues

Listing X5.12. continued

```
{
  UINT startPos, endPos;
  int numChars;
  char* pszStr;
  Client->GetSelection(startPos, endPos);
  // is there selected text
  if (startPos < endPos) {
    numChars = endPos - startPos + 1;
    pszStr = new char[numChars+1];
    Client->GetSubText(pszStr, startPos, endPos);
    strlwr(pszStr);
 Client->Insert(pszStr);
    Client->SetSelection(startPos, endPos);
    delete [] pszStr;
  }
  else {
    numChars = Client->GetWindowTextLength();
    pszStr = new char[numChars+1];
    Client->GetSubText(pszStr, 0, (UINT)numChars);
    strlwr(pszStr);
    Client->DeleteSubText(0, (UINT)numChars);
    Client->SetSelection(0, 0);
    Client->Insert(pszStr);
    delete [] pszStr;
  }
}

void clsxprt2App::CmReverse ()
{
  UINT startPos, endPos;
  int numChars;
  char* pszStr;
  char swapChar;
  Client->GetSelection(startPos, endPos);
  // is there selected text
  if (startPos < endPos) {
    numChars = endPos - startPos + 1;
    pszStr = new char[numChars+1];
    Client->GetSubText(pszStr, startPos, endPos);
    for (int i = 0, j = strlen(pszStr)-1; i < j ; i++, j--) {
      swapChar = pszStr[i];
      pszStr[i] = pszStr[j];
      pszStr[j] = swapChar;
    }
 Client->Insert(pszStr);
    Client->SetSelection(startPos, endPos);
    delete [] pszStr;
  }
  else {
    numChars = Client->GetWindowTextLength();
```

```
    pszStr = new char[numChars+1];
    Client->GetSubText(pszStr, 0, (UINT)numChars);
    for (int i = 0, j = strlen(pszStr)-1; i < j ; i++, j--) {
      swapChar = pszStr[i];
      pszStr[i] = pszStr[j];
      pszStr[j] = swapChar;
    }
    Client->DeleteSubText(0, (UINT)numChars);
    Client->SetSelection(0, 0);
    Client->Insert(pszStr);
    delete [] pszStr;
  }
}

void clsxprt2App::CmUppercase ()
{
  UINT startPos, endPos;
  int numChars;
  char* pszStr;
  Client->GetSelection(startPos, endPos);
  // is there selected text
  if (startPos < endPos) {
    numChars = endPos - startPos + 1;
    pszStr = new char[numChars+1];
    Client->GetSubText(pszStr, startPos, endPos);
    strupr(pszStr);
    Client->Insert(pszStr);
    Client->SetSelection(startPos, endPos);
    delete [] pszStr;
  }
  else {
    numChars = Client->GetWindowTextLength();
    pszStr = new char[numChars+1];
    Client->GetSubText(pszStr, 0, (UINT)numChars);
    strupr(pszStr);
    Client->DeleteSubText(0, (UINT)numChars);
    Client->SetSelection(0, 0);
    Client->Insert(pszStr);
    delete [] pszStr;
  }
}
void clsxprt2App::CmPreferences ()
{
  TFrmtDialog* pDlg = new TFrmtDialog(Client,
                              TResID(IDD_DATETIME_DLG));
  pDlg->EnableTransfer();
  if (pDlg->Execute() == IDOK) {
    // save time format
    IsAmPm = pDlg->IsAmPm;
    // save date format
```

continues

Listing X5.12. continued

```
      df = pDlg->df;
    }
}
void clsxprt2App::CmInsertDateTime ()
{
  struct date dt;
  struct time tm;
  char szStr[41];
  getdate(&dt);
  switch (df) {
    case mmddyy:
       sprintf(szStr, "%2d/%02d/%4d ",
           dt.da_mon, dt.da_day, dt.da_year);
       break;
    case ddmmyy:
       sprintf(szStr, "%2d/%02d/%4d ",
           dt.da_day, dt.da_mon, dt.da_year);
       break;
    default:
       sprintf(szStr, "%4d/%02d/%02d ",
           dt.da_year, dt.da_day, dt.da_mon);
       break;
  }
  Client->Insert(szStr);
  gettime(&tm);
  if (IsAmPm) {
    if (tm.ti_hour == 12)
      sprintf(szStr, "12:%02d:%02d p.m.",
     tm.ti_min, tm.ti_sec);
    else if (tm.ti_hour > 12)
      sprintf(szStr, "%2d:%02d:%02d p.m.",
 tm.ti_hour - 12, tm.ti_min, tm.ti_sec);
    else
       sprintf(szStr, "%2d:%02d:%02d a.m.",
 tm.ti_hour, tm.ti_min, tm.ti_sec);
  }
  else
    sprintf(szStr, "%2d:%02d:%02d",
 tm.ti_hour, tm.ti_min, tm.ti_sec);
  Client->Insert(szStr);
}
void clsxprt2App::CmInsertDate ()
{
  struct date dt;
  char szStr[41];
```

```
357:     getdate(&dt);
358:     switch (df) {
359:       case mmddyy:
360:          sprintf(szStr, "%2d/%02d/%4d",
361:              dt.da_mon, dt.da_day, dt.da_year);
362:          break;
363:       case ddmmyy:
364:          sprintf(szStr, "%2d/%02d/%4d",
365:              dt.da_day, dt.da_mon, dt.da_year);
366:          break;
367:       default:
368:          sprintf(szStr, "%4d/%02d/%02d",
369:              dt.da_year, dt.da_day, dt.da_mon);
370:          break;
371:     }
372:     Client->Insert(szStr);
373:   }
```

Analysis Listing X5.12 shows the CLSXPR2A.CPP implementation file. The AppExpert utility generated this file. The ClassExpert utility added the response-table macro and the empty definitions of the `CmXXXX` member functions, which respond to the options of the Special menu selection. We inserted the statements in these member functions and added the `#include` directives to include files TFRMTDLG.H, STDIO.H, STRING.H, and DOS.H.

The member functions `CmLowercase`, `CmUppercase`, and `CmReverse` are identical to those in the file CLSXPR1A.CPP (in Listing X5.5). The member functions `CmInsertTime`, `CmInsertDate`, and `CmInsertDateTime` are expanded versions of their counterparts in Listing X5.5. This extension is due to the fact that these member functions use the data members `IsAmPm` and `df` to select the time and date format and create the string image of the date and/or time accordingly.

The most relevant member function in Listing X5.12 is `CmPreferences`. This function, which is defined in lines 298 to 309, performs the following tasks:

- Creates the instance `pDlg` of class `TFrmtDialog`. The parent window of this dialog box is the member `Client` (which accesses the client window). The resource ID for this dialog box is `IDD_DATETIME_FLG`.
- Executes the dialog box instance by sending it the C++ message `Execute`, and performs the subsequent tasks if the message returns `IDOK`.
- Copies the value of the dialog's data member `IsAmPm` to the application's data member `IsAmPm`.

- Copies the value of the dialog's data member `df` to the application's data member `df`.

Compile and run the CLSXPRT2.EXE program. Invoke the dialog box for selecting the date and time formats (see Figure X5.4). Then create a new text file and try inserting the date and/or time.

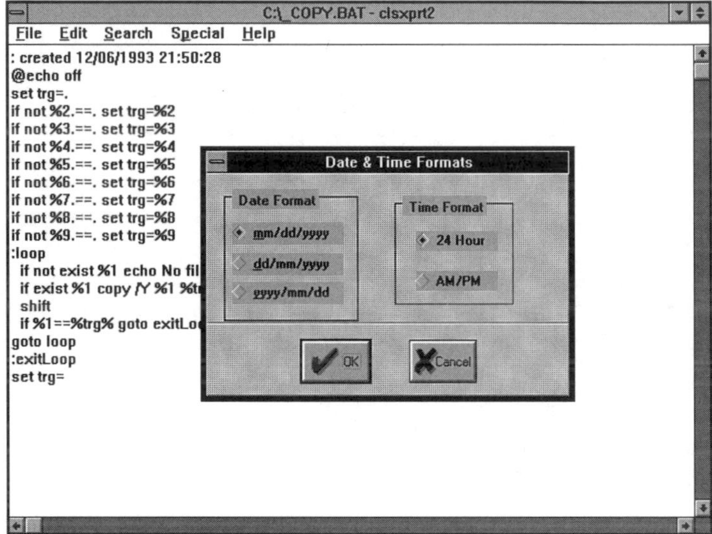

Figure X5.4. *A sample session with program CLSXPRT2.EXE.*

Summary

This chapter presented the ClassExpert utility, which enables you to fine-tune and customize OWL-based Windows applications generated by AppExpert. You learned about the following:

- Invoking the ClassExpert utility from an option in the View menu selection. The ClassExpert displays a window with the Classes pane, the Events pane, and the editor pane. The Classes pane lists the current project classes. The Events pane shows an outline for the various events related to the currently selected class. The editor pane lists the implementation file for the current class.

- ClassExpert enables you to add new member functions to a class created by AppExpert. This task involves adding the declaration of the member functions in the targeted class, adding the response table macros for the new functions, and inserting empty definitions of these functions.
- ClassExpert enables you to add a new class to the project created by AppExpert. This task involves creating the header and implementation files for the new class and placing the declaration and definition of the class in these files, respectively.

Q&A

Q Does ClassExpert generate source code that supports OLE 2.0?

A No.

Q Does ClassExpert generate source code that supports VBX (Visual Basic) controls?

A No, but you can use OWL classes to support VBX controls.

Q Does ClassExpert generate source code that supports ODBC (Open Database Connectivity)?

A No.

Exercises

1. Create a version of the program CLSXPRT1.EXE that adds the capability to write a block of selected text to a file and to insert text from a file.
2. Create a version of program CLSXPRT2.EXE that sorts the lines either in the selected text or in the entire file.

Common Dialog Boxes

The lesson for Day 20 introduced you to building your own dialog boxes. In this extra-credit chapter, we present three of the five common dialog boxes supported by both Windows and the ObjectWindows library. In addition, we present the input dialog box supported by the ObjectWindows library. In this extra-credit chapter, you will learn about the following topics:

- Software requirements for using the common dialog boxes.
- The ObjectWindows `TInputDialog` class.
- The file-selection dialog box class `TFileOpenDialog`. This class creates dialog boxes that support opening a file.
- The file-selection dialog box class `TFileSaveDialog`. This class creates dialog boxes that support saving a file.
- The color-selection dialog box class `TChooseColorDialog`.
- The text-search dialog box class `TFindDialog`. This class creates dialog boxes that support finding text.
- The text-replacement dialog box class `TReplaceDialog`. This class creates dialog boxes that support replacing text.

We would like to emphasize that the common dialog boxes merely offer the user interfaces for the respective tasks of the common dialog boxes. You are responsible for providing the associated operations based on the information supplied or selected by the user of these common dialog boxes. Many of the examples in this chapter are kept short to focus on creating, invoking, and accessing the data of the common dialog boxes.

Software Requirements

The use of the common dialog boxes requires Windows 3.1 COMMDLG functions in order to compile. However, these dialog boxes do not require Windows 3.1 to run. You need to observe the following when incorporating the common dialog box into your Windows applications:

- Ensure that the project's .DEF file assigns at least 16 KB of stack space.
- Include the corresponding header file in the client source files.
- Ensure that the COMMDLG.DLL file is present in the Windows system directory.

DO	DON'T

DO allow a minimum stack space of 16 KB in the project's .DEF file.

DON'T forget to ensure that your Windows programs that use common dialog boxes have a copy of the file COMMDLG.DLL in the Windows directory of the system running these programs.

The *TInputDialog* Class

Some of the programs that we presented in earlier chapters required input dialog boxes to obtain your input. These programs executed instances of the ObjectWindows `TInputDialog` class. This class declares three data members, a constructor, and a set of member functions. The declaration of class `TInputDialog` is as follows:

```
class _OWLCLASS TInputDialog : public TDialog {
  public:
    char far* Prompt;
    char far* Buffer;
    int       BufferSize;

    TInputDialog(TWindow*        parent,
                 const char far* title,
                 const char far* prompt,
                 char far*       buffer,
                 int             bufferSize,
                 TModule*        module = 0,
                 TValidator*     valid = 0);  // Optional validator

   ~TInputDialog();

    //
    // Override TWindow virtual member functions
    //
    void TransferData(TTransferDirection);


  protected:
    //
    // Override TWindow virtual member functions
    //
    void SetupWindow();
```

```
  private:
    //
    // hidden to prevent accidental copying or assignment
    //
    TInputDialog(const TInputDialog&);
    TInputDialog& operator=(const TInputDialog&);

  DECLARE_STREAMABLE(_OWLCLASS, TInputDialog, 1);
};
```

The data members `Buffer` and `Prompt` are pointers to the text buffer and prompting string, respectively. The data member `BufferSize` stores the size of the buffer that returns the user's input.

The class constructor requires the parameters for the parent window, the pointer to the dialog box title, the pointer to the prompt string, the pointer to the text buffer, and the buffer size. The constructor calls the `TDialog` constructor to pass the parameter `parent`, the resource identifier `SD_INPUTDIALOG`, and the `AModule` parameter. The identifier `SD_INPUTDIALOG` is the name of the dialog box resource defined in the INPUTDIA.RC resource file, supplied by Borland. You need to include this recource file in your resource file using a `#include` directive.

Perhaps the most noteworthy `TInputDialog` member function is the `TransferData` function. This function transfers the data between the edit control of the input dialog box and the text buffer. If the caller passes the argument `tdSetData` to the `direction` parameter, the function transfers data from the text buffer to the edit control. The function moves data in the reverse direction when a caller passes the `tdGetData` argument.

Let's look at a simple number-guessing game that uses the input dialog box to prompt you for a new guess. The game has a main menu along with the Exit and Game menu items. To start the game, run file INPUTDLG.EXE and then click the Game menu item or press the Alt+G keys. The program generates a secret number between 0 and 1,000 and enables you make up to 10 guesses. To assist you in refining your guess, the program displays hints in the dialog box that tell you whether your last guess was higher or lower than the secret number. You can stop the game at any time by clicking the Cancel button. If you do stop the game, the program displays the secret number. If you fail to guess the number after 10 trials, the program also displays the secret number. If you do manage to guess the number, the program displays a congratulatory message. Figure X6.1 shows a sample session with the INPUTDLG.EXE application.

Let's look at the source code for the number guess game. Listing X6.1 shows the contents of the INPUTDLG.DEF definition file. Listing X6.2 shows the source code for the INPUTDLG.H header file, which contains a single constant declaration.

Listing X6.3 shows the script for the INPUTDLG.RC resource file. The file includes the INPUTDIA.DLG resource file required to define the ObjectWindows input dialog box. Listing X6.4 shows the source code for the INPUTDLG.CPP program file.

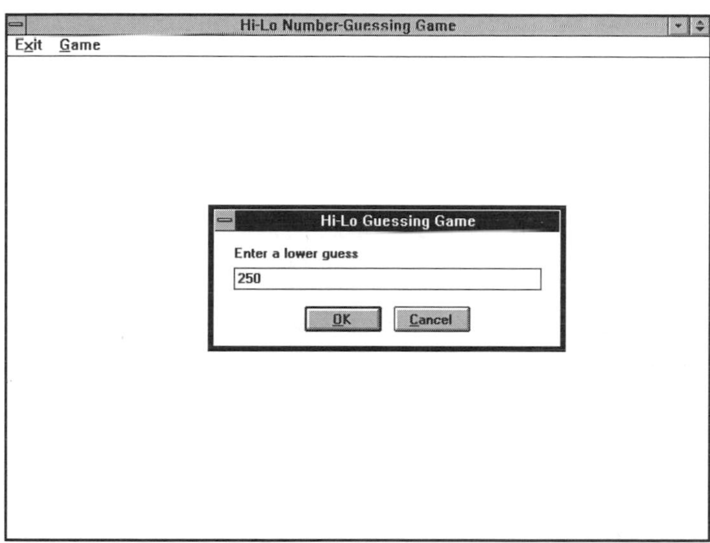

Figure X6.1. *A sample session with the INPUTDLG.EXE application.*

Listing X6.1. The contents of the INPUTDLG.DEF definition file.

```
NAME         InputDlg
DESCRIPTION  'An OWL Windows Application'
EXETYPE      WINDOWS
CODE         PRELOAD MOVEABLE DISCARDABLE
DATA         PRELOAD MOVEABLE MULTIPLE
HEAPSIZE     1024
STACKSIZE    8384
```

Listing X6.2. The source code for the INPUTDLG.H header file.

```
#define CM_GAME      101
#define IDM_MAINMENU 400
```

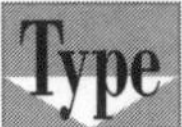

Listing X6.3. The script for the INPUTDLG.RC resource file.

```
#include <windows.h>
#include <owl\window.rh>
#include <owl\inputdia.rh>
#include <owl\inputdia.rc>
#include "inputdlg.h"

IDM_MAINMENU MENU LOADONCALL MOVEABLE PURE DISCARDABLE
BEGIN
    MENUITEM "E&xit", CM_EXIT
    MENUITEM "&Game", CM_GAME
END
```

Listing X6.4. The source code for the INPUTDLG.CPP program file.

```
/*
  Program illustrates using the input dialog box in a
  number-guessing game
*/
#include <owl\applicat.h>
#include <owl\framewin.h>
#include <owl\inputdia.h>
#include "inputdlg.h"
#include <stdlib.h>
#include <stdio.h>
#include <string.h>

const MaxBuffer = 81;

// declare the custom application class as
// a subclass of TApplication
class TWinApp : public TApplication
{
public:
  TWinApp() : TApplication() {}

protected:
  virtual void InitMainWindow();
};

// expand the functionality of TWindow by deriving class
// TMainWindow
class TMainWindow : public TWindow
{
public:

```

```
  TMainWindow() : TWindow(0, 0, 0) {}

protected:

  // handle the Game menu item
  void CMGame();

  // handle closing the window
  virtual BOOL CanClose();

  DECLARE_RESPONSE_TABLE(TMainWindow);
};

DEFINE_RESPONSE_TABLE1(TMainWindow, TWindow)
  EV_COMMAND(CM_GAME, CMGame),
END_RESPONSE_TABLE;

void TMainWindow::CMGame()
{
  char s[MaxBuffer];
  int n, m;
  int MaxIter = 10;
  int iter = 0;
  BOOL ok = TRUE;
  TInputDialog* pDlg;

  randomize();
  n = random(1001);

  strcpy(s, "500");
  // execute the opening dialog box
  pDlg = new TInputDialog(this, "Hi-Lo Guessing Game",
                        "Enter a number between 0 and 1000",
                        s, sizeof(s));
  if (pDlg->Execute() == IDOK) {
       m = atoi(s);
       iter++;
       // loop to obtain the other guesses
       while (m != n && iter < MaxIter && ok == TRUE) {
         // is the user's guess higher?
         if (m > n) {
           pDlg = new TInputDialog(this,
                           "Hi-Lo Guessing Game",
                           "Enter a lower guess",
                            s, sizeof(s));
           ok = (pDlg->Execute() == IDOK) ? TRUE : FALSE;

        }
         else {
           pDlg = new TInputDialog(this,
                           "Hi-Lo Guessing Game",
```

continues

Listing X6.4. continued

```
                              "Enter a higher guess",
                               s, sizeof(s));
            ok = (pDlg->Execute() == IDOK) ? TRUE : FALSE;
         }
          m = atoi(s);
          iter++;
        }

        // did the user guess the secret number
        if (iter < MaxIter && ok == TRUE) {
          MessageBeep(MB_ICONEXCLAMATION);
          MessageBeep(MB_ICONEXCLAMATION);
          sprintf(s, "You guess it! It's %d", n);
          MessageBox(s, "Congratulations!", MB_OK);
        }
        else {
          MessageBeep(-1);
          sprintf(s, "The secret number is %d", n);
          MessageBox(s, "Sorry!", MB_OK);
        }
  }
}

BOOL TMainWindow::CanClose()
{
  return MessageBox("Want to close this application",
                    "Query", MB_YESNO ¦ MB_ICONQUESTION) == IDYES;
}

void TWinApp::InitMainWindow()
{
  MainWindow = new TFrameWindow(0, "Hi-Lo Number-Guessing Game",
                                new TMainWindow);
  // load the menu resource
  MainWindow->AssignMenu(TResID(IDM_MAINMENU));
}

int OwlMain(int /* argc */, char** /*argv[] */)
{
  TWinApp app;
  return app.Run();
}
```

The program in Listing X6.4 declares two classes: the application class, `TWinApp`, and the main window class, `TMainWindow`.

The most relevant part of the program is the member function `CMGame`, which executes the number-guess game. The function, whose definition starts at line 48, performs the following tasks:

- Randomizes the seed for the random-number generating function, using the statement at line 57.
- Obtains a random number in the range of 0 to 1,000 and stores that number in the local variable `n`.
- Assigns the string `"500"` to the text buffer (implemented using the local variable `s`).
- Executes the opening dialog box by calling the `Execute` member function, at line 62, to create an instance of the `TInputDialog` class. If the function `Execute` returns `IDOK`, the game resumes by executing the next tasks.
- Converts the contents of the text buffer into an `int` and stores that value in the local variable `m`. This task calls the function `atoi` at line 66.
- Increments the iteration counter variable `iter`.
- Loops to obtain other guesses while the following conditions are true:
    - The contents of variables `m` and `n` differ.
    - The number of iterations is less than the maximum limit.
    - The Boolean `ok` flag is `TRUE` to indicate that you did not click the Cancel button of the dialog box.

  The loop, which starts at line 69, displays one of two dialog box versions, depending on whether the last number you entered is less than or greater than the secret number. The loop also converts your input into the integer stored in variable `m` and increments the loop iteration counter.
- Displays a congratulatory message (in lines 92 to 95) if you guessed the secret number within the allowed number of iterations. Otherwise, the program displays the secret number using the statements at lines 98 to 100.

The *TCommonDialog* Class

The classes that model the common dialog boxes in this chapter are descendants of the class `TDialog`. In addition, these classes (except `TInputDialog`) are also descendants of the class `TCommonDialog`. Here is the declaration of the class `TCommonDialog`:

```
class _OWLCLASS TCommonDialog : public TDialog {
  public:
    TCommonDialog(TWindow* parent, const char far* title = 0,
                  TModule* module = 0);

    HWND DoCreate()
          { return 0; }
    int DoExecute()
         { return IDCANCEL; }

  protected:
    const char far* CDTitle;

    void SetupWindow();

    // Default behavior inline for message response functions
    //
    void CmOkCancel()
          { DefaultProcessing(); } // EV_COMMAND(IDOK or IDCANCEL)
    void EvClose()
          { DefaultProcessing(); } // EV_CLOSE
    void CmHelp()
          { DefaultProcessing(); } // EV_COMMAND(pshHelp,

  private:
    TCommonDialog(const TCommonDialog&);
    TCommonDialog& operator=(const TCommonDialog&);

  DECLARE_RESPONSE_TABLE(TCommonDialog);
  DECLARE_CASTABLE;
};
```

The `TCommonDialog` class is the root of the common dialog class subhierarchy that models color selection, font selection, input-file selection, output-file selection, printing, text search, and text-replacement dialog boxes.

The File Dialog Classes

The ObjectWindows library offers the classes `TOpenSaveDialog`, `TFileOpenDialog`, and `TFileSaveDialog` to implement the common modal dialog boxes that support opening a file and saving data in a file. The class `TOpenSaveDialog` is a descendant of class `TCommonDialog` and the parent of classes `TFileOpenDialog` and `TFileSaveDialog`. Figure X6.2 shows a standard File dialog box in the open file mode. The Open and Save As dialog boxes have the following controls:

- A filename combo box
- A file-filter combo box

- A current directory static-text control
- A directory list box that shows the current directory, its sibling directories, and its parent directory
- A drives combo box
- An OK pushbutton
- A Cancel pushbutton
- A Help pushbutton
- A read-only check box to select read-only files

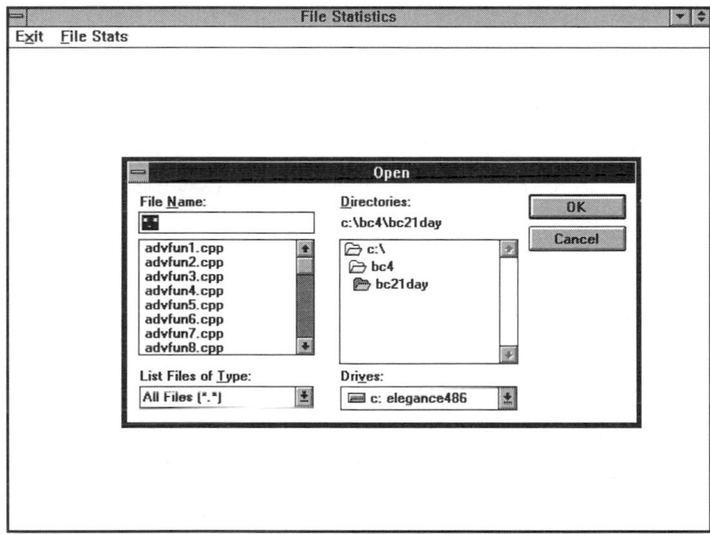

Figure X6.2. *A sample session with the COMMDLG1.EXE program.*

The Supporting Classes and Structures

The `TOpenSaveDialog` class encapsulates the `OPENFILENAME` structure and the Windows API functions `GetOpenFileName` and `GetSaveFileName`. The `OPENFILENAME` structure is declared as follows:

```
typedef struct tagOFN
{
    DWORD   lStructSize;
    HWND    hwndOwner;
    HINSTANCE hInstance;
```

```
        LPCSTR   lpstrFilter;
        LPSTR    lpstrCustomFilter;
        DWORD    nMaxCustFilter;
        DWORD    nFilterIndex;
        LPSTR    lpstrFile;
        DWORD    nMaxFile;
        LPSTR    lpstrFileTitle;
        DWORD    nMaxFileTitle;
        LPCSTR   lpstrInitialDir;
        LPCSTR   lpstrTitle;
        DWORD    Flags;
        UINT     nFileOffset;
        UINT     nFileExtension;
        LPCSTR   lpstrDefExt;
        LPARAM   lCustData;
        UINT     (CALLBACK *lpfnHook)(HWND, UINT, WPARAM, LPARAM);
        LPCSTR   lpTemplateName;
    }   OPENFILENAME;
```

The `OPENFILENAME` structure and its related Windows API functions use the following `OFN_`*`XXXX`* constants:

```
    #define OFN_READONLY                  0x00000001
    #define OFN_OVERWRITEPROMPT           0x00000002
    #define OFN_HIDEREADONLY              0x00000004
    #define OFN_NOCHANGEDIR               0x00000008
    #define OFN_SHOWHELP                  0x00000010
    #define OFN_ENABLEHOOK                0x00000020
    #define OFN_ENABLETEMPLATE            0x00000040
    #define OFN_ENABLETEMPLATEHANDLE      0x00000080
    #define OFN_NOVALIDATE                0x00000100
    #define OFN_ALLOWMULTISELECT          0x00000200
    #define OFN_EXTENSIONDIFFERENT        0x00000400
    #define OFN_PATHMUSTEXIST             0x00000800
    #define OFN_FILEMUSTEXIST             0x00001000
    #define OFN_CREATEPROMPT              0x00002000
    #define OFN_SHAREAWARE                0x00004000
    #define OFN_NOREADONLYRETURN          0x00008000
    #define OFN_NOTESTFILECREATE          0x00010000
```

The declaration of the `TOpenSaveDialog` class is as follows:

```
class _OWLCLASS TOpenSaveDialog : public TCommonDialog {
  public:
    class _OWLCLASS TData {
      public:
        DWORD      Flags;
        DWORD      Error;
        char*      FileName;
        char*      Filter;
        char*      CustomFilter;
        int        FilterIndex;
```

```
    char*      InitialDir;
    char*      DefExt;

    TData(DWORD flags=0, char* filter=0, char* customFilter=0,
          char* initialDir=0, char* defExt=0);
    ~TData();

    void     SetFilter(const char* filter = 0);

    void     Write(opstream& os);
    void     Read(ipstream& is);
  };

  TOpenSaveDialog(TWindow*        parent,
                  TData&          data,
                  TResId          templateId = 0,
                  const char far* title = 0,
                  TModule*        module = 0);

  static int GetFileTitleLen(const char far* fileName)
       { return ::GetFileTitle((LPSTR)fileName, 0, 0);  //Win32 cast

  static int GetFileTitle(const char far* fileName,
                          char far* fileTitle,
                          int fileTitleLen) //Win32 casts
       { return ::GetFileTitle((LPSTR)fileName,
                               fileTitle,(WORD)fileTitleLen); }

protected:
  OPENFILENAME ofn;
  TData&       Data;

  TOpenSaveDialog(TWindow* parent, TData& data, TModule* module = 0);
  void Init(TResId templateId);
  BOOL DialogFunction(UINT message, WPARAM, LPARAM);

  //
  // override TWindow & TDialog virtuals
  //
  int DoExecute() = 0;

  //
  // Virtual function called when a share violation occurs in dlg
  //
  virtual int ShareViolation();

  //
  // Messages registered by the common dialog DLL
  //
  static UINT ShareViMsgId;
```

```
    // Default behavior inline for message response functions
    //
    void CmOk()
          { DefaultProcessing(); } // EV_COMMAND(IDOK,
    void CmLbSelChanged()
          { DefaultProcessing(); } // EV_COMMAND(lst1 or lst2)

  private:
    TOpenSaveDialog(const TOpenSaveDialog&);
    TOpenSaveDialog& operator =(const TOpenSaveDialog&);

  DECLARE_RESPONSE_TABLE(TOpenSaveDialog);
};
```

The class `TOpenSaveDialog` declares the nested class `TData`. This nested class contains data members that store information related to the selected file and other information used in the file-selection process. The class `TOpenSaveDialog::TData` works with both descendants, `TFileOpenDialog` and `TFileSaveDialog`.

Typically, you create an instance of the class `TData` and initialize it when you create the main window. The creation of the `TData` instance involves specifying the values for the `TData` members `Flags`, `Filter`, `CustomFilter`, `InitialDir`, and `DefExt`.

The argument for parameter flags in the `TData` constructor can have one or more `OFN_`*`XXXX`* constants to fine-tune various aspects of the File dialog box. In the case of multiple `OFN_`*`XXXX`* constants, you need to use the bitwise OR operator to combine their effect. For example, the following expression

```
OFN_HIDEREADONLY | OFN_NOCHANGEDIR | OFN_FILEMUSTEXIST
```

performs the following dialog box operations:

1. Hides the read-only check box in the dialog box.
2. Sets the current directory back to the original one when the dialog box was opened.
3. Permits the user to type in only names of existing files. If this condition is violated, the dialog box displays a warning-message dialog box.

The argument for the parameter filter (in the `TData` constructor) is a specially-formatted string. It contains pairs of substrings. The first pair member contains the wording of the filter—for example, the string `C++ file (*.CPP)`. This wording is selected by the dialog box user and need not include any filename wildcard. The second pair member contains the actual wildcard used in filtering the selected files—for example, `*.CPP`. The formatting rules to observe are as follows:

- ☐ Use the bar character, `|`, to separate the substrings.

- Use pairs of strings—one for wording and one for the corresponding wildcard. The latter is actually used to filter the file selection.
- The string must end with an empty substring. That is, the last two string characters must be a pair of bar characters, ¦¦.

An example of the argument for `lpszFilter` is the following string:

```
char szFilter[] =
"All files (*.*)¦*.*¦C++ files¦*.cpp¦Header files (*.h)¦*.h¦¦";
```

The preceding string displays three file selections. The first one enables you to select all of the files, the second enables you to choose the *.CPP files, and the last one enables you to pick the header files.

The argument for the parameter `customFilter` (in the `TData` constructor) is a string that represents a user-specified file filter, such as `*.CPP`. The argument for the parameter `initialDir` can specify an initial directory other than the current one. The argument for the parameter `defExt` indicates the default file extension. The data member `Error` contains a `CDERR_XXXX` value that identifies the kind of error involved in creating the dialog box.

The declaration of the `TFileOpenDialog` is as follows:

```
class _OWLCLASS TFileOpenDialog : public TOpenSaveDialog {
  public:
    TFileOpenDialog(TWindow*        parent,
                    TData&          data,
                    TResId          templateId = 0,
                    const char far* title = 0,
                    TModule*        module = 0);

    //
    // override TDialog virtual functions
    //
    int  DoExecute();

  private:
    TFileOpenDialog(const TOpenSaveDialog&);
    TFileOpenDialog& operator=(const TOpenSaveDialog&);
};
```

The class `TFileOpenDialog` declares a constructor that has a list of five parameters. The parameter `parent` is the pointer to the parent window. The parameter `data` is the reference to the `TData` structure that passes the information for the file I/O operation. The `templateId` is the resource ID for a dialog box. The parameter `title` specifies the dialog box title.

The declaration of class `TFileSaveDialog` is as follows:

```
class _OWLCLASS TFileSaveDialog : public TOpenSaveDialog {
  public:
    TFileSaveDialog(TWindow*        parent,
                    TData&          data,
                    TResId          templateId = 0,
                    const char far* title = 0,
                    TModule*        module = 0);

    //
    // override TDialog virtual functions
    //
    int  DoExecute();

  private:
    TFileSaveDialog(const TFileSaveDialog&);
    TFileSaveDialog& operator=(const TFileSaveDialog&);
};
```

The `TFileOpenDialog` class constructor creates a dialog box object defined by the various parameters. These parameters are similar to those in the class `TFileSaveDialog`.

Invoking the File Dialog Box

After the `TFileOpenDialog` instance is created by the constructor, you can invoke the dialog box using the member function `Execute`. To accept the dialog box, selection click the OK button. This action makes the function `Execute` return the `IDOK` result. To close the dialog box without accepting the current selection, click the Cancel button or select the Close system-menu command. Either action causes the function Execute to return `IDCANCEL`.

The File Statistics Program

Next is a program that enables you to obtain file statistics (file size and date/time stamp) using the standard file dialog box. Listing X6.5 the contents of the COMMDLG1.DEF definition file. Listing X6.6 the COMMDLG1.H header file. Listing X6.7 shows the script for the COMMDLG1.RC resource file. Listing X6.8 shows the source code for the COMMDLG1.CPP program file.

Compile and run the COMMDLG1.EXE program. Click the File Stats menu item to invoke the Open dialog box. The file-filter combo box has two items: all the files and the .CPP files. You can select a file from the current directory or move to another directory. When you have selected a file, click the OK button. The Open dialog box

disappears and a message box appears with the selected filename, size, and date/time stamp.

Listing X6.5. The contents of the COMMDLG1.DEF definition file.

```
NAME          CommDlg1
DESCRIPTION   'An OWL Windows Application'
EXETYPE       WINDOWS
CODE          PRELOAD MOVEABLE DISCARDABLE
DATA          PRELOAD MOVEABLE MULTIPLE
HEAPSIZE      1024
STACKSIZE     16384
```

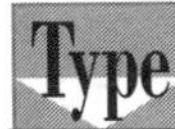

Listing X6.6. The source code for the COMMDLG1.H header file.

```
#define CM_FILESTAT  100
#define IDM_MAINMENU 400
```

Listing X6.7. The script for the COMMDLG1.RC resource file.

```
#include <windows.h>
#include <owl\window.rh>
#include "commdlg1.h"

IDM_MAINMENU MENU LOADONCALL MOVEABLE PURE DISCARDABLE
BEGIN
    MENUITEM "E&xit", CM_EXIT
    MENUITEM "&File Stats", CM_FILESTAT
END
```

Listing X6.8. The source code for the COMMDLG1.CPP program file.

```
/*
  Program to test the Open File common dialog box. The program
  displays the basic statistics for the file you select
*/

#include <owl\applicat.h>
```

continues

Listing X6.8. continued

```
#include <owl\framewin.h>
#include <owl\opensave.h>
#include "commdlg1.h"
#include <stdlib.h>
#include <stdio.h>
#include <string.h>
#include <dos.h>
#include <dir.h>

const MaxStringLen = 256;

// declare the custom application class as
// a subclass of TApplication
class TWinApp : public TApplication
{
public:
  TWinApp() : TApplication() {}

protected:
  virtual void InitMainWindow();
};

// expand the functionality of TWindow by
// deriving class TMainWindow
class TMainWindow : public TWindow
{
public:

  TMainWindow();

protected:

  // the pointer to the data for the File Open dialog box
  TOpenSaveDialog::TData *FileData;

  // handle the calculation
  void CMFileStat();

  // handle exiting the program
  void CMExit();

  // handle closing the window
  virtual BOOL CanClose();

  // declare the message map macro
  DECLARE_RESPONSE_TABLE(TMainWindow);

};

```

```
DEFINE_RESPONSE_TABLE1(TMainWindow, TWindow)
  EV_COMMAND(CM_FILESTAT, CMFileStat),
  EV_COMMAND(CM_EXIT, CMExit),
END_RESPONSE_TABLE;

TMainWindow::TMainWindow()
  : TWindow(0, 0, 0)
{
  FileData = new TOpenSaveDialog::TData(
       DWORD(OFN_HIDEREADONLY | OFN_OVERWRITEPROMPT),
       "All Files (*.*)|*.*|"
       "C++ Programs (*.cpp)|*.cpp|"
       "Batch files (*.bat)|*.bat||",
       "*.cpp", "", "*.cpp");
}

void TMainWindow::CMFileStat()
{
  char selFile[MaxStringLen];
  char s[MaxStringLen];
  char format[MaxStringLen];
  ffblk fileInfo;
  unsigned Hour, Minute, Second, Day, Month, Year,
       uDate, uTime;
  TFileOpenDialog* FileDialog;

  FileDialog = new TFileOpenDialog(this, *FileData);

  if (FileDialog->Execute() == IDOK) {
    // get the file information
    strcpy(selFile, FileData->FileName);
    findfirst(selFile, &fileInfo, FA_ARCH);
    // build the format string
    strcpy(format, "Filename: %s\n");
    strcat(format, "Time Stamp: %02u:%02u:%02u\n");
     strcat(format, "Date Stamp: %02u/%02u/%u\n");
     strcat(format, "Size: %ld bytes\n");
    uTime = (unsigned)fileInfo.ff_ftime;
    // get the seconds
    Second = 2 * (uTime & 0x1f);
    // get the minutes
    Minute = (uTime >> 5) & 0x3f;
    // get the hours
    Hour = (uTime >> 11) & 0x1f;
    uDate = (unsigned)fileInfo.ff_fdate;
    // get the day
    Day =  uDate & 0x1f;
    // get the month
     Month = (uDate >> 5) & 0xf;
    // get the year
```

continues

Listing X6.8. continued

```
106:       Year = (uDate >> 9) & 0x7f;
107:       sprintf(s, format, fileInfo.ff_name, Hour, Minute, Second,
108:           Month, Day, Year + 1980U, fileInfo.ff_fsize);
109:        MessageBox(s, "File Statistics",
110:                             MB_OK ¦ MB_ICONINFORMATION);
111:     }
112: }
113:
114: void TMainWindow::CMExit()
115: {
116:   Parent->SendMessage(WM_CLOSE);
117: }
118:
119: BOOL TMainWindow::CanClose()
120: {
121:   return MessageBox("Want to close this application?",
122:                     "Query", MB_YESNO ¦ MB_ICONQUESTION) == IDYES;
123: }
124:
125: void TWinApp::InitMainWindow()
126: {
127:   MainWindow = new TFrameWindow(0, "File Statistics",
128:                     new TMainWindow);
129:   // load the menu resource
130:   MainWindow->AssignMenu(TResID(IDM_MAINMENU));
131:   // enable the keyboard handler
132:   MainWindow->EnableKBHandler();
133: }
134:
135: int OwlMain(int /* argc */, char** /*argv[] */)
136: {
137:   TWinApp app;
138:   return app.Run();
139: }
```

Analysis Now let's examine the code for the program in Listing X6.4. The window class `TMainWindow` declares a constructor, a data member, and three member functions. The data member `FileData` is a pointer to the supporting structure `TOpenSaveDialog::TData`. The `TMainWindow` constructor initializes member `FileData`, at line 64, by dynamically allocating a new instance of `TOpenSaveDialog::TData`. This instance is initialized using the ORed constants `OFN_HIDEREADONLY` and `OFN_OVERWRITEPROMPT`. In addition, the creation of the preceding instance specifies the arguments for the parameters `filter` (the long string that spans over three lines), `customFilter` (the string `"*.cpp"`), `initialDir` (the empty string), and `defExt` (the string `"*.cpp`").

The most relevant component of the class is the `CMFileStat` member function, whose definition starts at line 72. The function declares a number of local variables. The function also declares the `ffblk`-typed `fileInfo` variable, in line 72. This variable contains the structure for the DOS file data. In addition, the function declares, in line 80, the `FileDialog` object as a pointer to `TFileOpenDialog`. The function `CmFileStat` creates a dynamic instance of `TFileOpenDialog` using the arguments `this` and `*FileData`. The latter argument passes information to and from the dialog box.

The `CMFileStat` function sends the C++ message `Execute` to the dialog box object in an `if` statement (located at line 84) that compares the result of `Execute` with `IDOK`. If the two values match, the function obtains the full name of the selected file by using the expression `FileData->FileName` (`FileName` is a member of the structure `TOpenSave::TData`). The result of this function is assigned to the string variable `selFile`. The function `CMFileStat` then uses this string variable in the function `findfirst` to obtain the information for the selected file and stores it in the `fileInfo` variable. The rest of the statements, in the `if` statement, obtain the file statistics and build the output string. The function then displays the text of this output string in a call to function `MessageBox`.

The *TChooseColorDialog* Class

The `TChooseColorDialog` class supports the color-selection common dialog box. Figure X6.3 shows the Color dialog box. The dialog box contains various controls to select colors, define custom colors, and add to custom colors. As with every other dialog box, the Color dialog box has OK and Cancel buttons.

Supporting Classes and Structures

The `TChooseColorDialog` class encapsulates the `CHOOSECOLOR` structure and the Windows API function `ChooseColor`. The declaration of the `CHOOSECOLOR` structure is as follows:

```
typedef struct tagCHOOSECOLOR
{
    DWORD   lStructSize;
    HWND    hwndOwner;
    HWND    hInstance;
    COLORREF rgbResult;
    COLORREF FAR* lpCustColors;
    DWORD   Flags;
    LPARAM  lCustData;
```

```
    UINT    (CALLBACK* lpfnHook)(HWND, UINT, WPARAM, LPARAM);
    LPCSTR  lpTemplateName;
} CHOOSECOLOR;
```

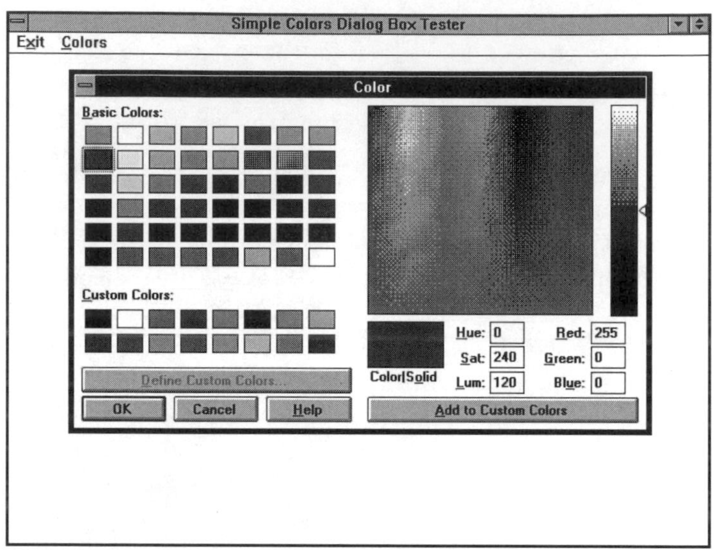

Figure X6.3. *A sample session with the COMMDLG2.EXE program.*

The `CHOOSECOLOR` structure uses the following `CC_XXXX` constants:

```
#define CC_RGBINIT                  0x00000001
#define CC_FULLOPEN                 0x00000002
#define CC_PREVENTFULLOPEN          0x00000004
#define CC_SHOWHELP                 0x00000008
#define CC_ENABLEHOOK               0x00000010
#define CC_ENABLETEMPLATE           0x00000020
#define CC_ENABLETEMPLATEHANDLE     0x00000040
```

The `TChooseColorDialog` class, a descendant of `TCommonDialog`, is declared as follows:

```
class _OWLCLASS TChooseColorDialog : public TCommonDialog {
  public:
    class _OWLCLASS TData {
      public:
        DWORD       Flags;
        DWORD       Error;
        TColor      Color;
        TColor*     CustColors;
    };
```

```
    TChooseColorDialog(TWindow*          parent,
                       TData&            data,
                       TResId            templateId = 0,
                       const char far*   title = 0,
                       TModule*          module = 0);

    //
    // Set the current RGB color in this dialog
    //
    void SetRGBColor(TColor color)
         { SendMessage(SetRGBMsgId,0,color); }

  protected:
    CHOOSECOLOR  cc;
    TData&       Data;

    int DoExecute();
    BOOL DialogFunction(UINT message, WPARAM, LPARAM);

    //
    // Registered messages this class sends (to itself)
    //
    static UINT SetRGBMsgId;

    //
    // Default behavior inline for message response functions
    //
    LPARAM EvSetRGBColor(WPARAM, LPARAM) // EV_REGISTERED(SETRGBSTRING,
             { return DefaultProcessing(); }

  private:
    TChooseColorDialog(const TChooseColorDialog&);
    TChooseColorDialog& operator=(const TChooseColorDialog&);

  DECLARE_RESPONSE_TABLE(TChooseColorDialog);
  DECLARE_CASTABLE;
};
```

The constructor has five parameters that customize the Color dialog boxes. The parameter `parent` is the pointer to the parent window. The parameter `data` is a reference to a `TChooseColorDialog::TData` structure. The parameter `templateId` is the dialog box resource ID. The parameter `title` specifies the title of the Color dialog boxes.

The `TChooseColorDialog` declares the protected data members `cc` and `Data`. The member `cc` has the `CHOOSECOLOR` structure type. This data member enables the class instances to exchange data with the supporting API function. The data member `Data`

is a reference to the `TData` structure. This structure contains data members that set and query the color in the dialog box, and it sets the flags that fine-tune the appearance and operations of the dialog box. The data member `Error` contains a `CDERR_XXXX` value that identifies the kind of error involved in creating the dialog box.

Invoking a Color dialog box is very similar to invoking an Open or Save As dialog box. The OK button, the Cancel button, and the Close System menu item play the same role in influencing the result returned by the `Execute` member function. The Windows API function `CommDlgExtendedError` can also be used to detect errors when the `Execute` function returns `IDCANCEL`.

A Sample Program

The following is a simple program that invokes the Color dialog box and then displays the numeric value for the selected color. Listing X6.9 shows the contents of the COMMDLG2.DEF definition file. Listing X6.10 shows the COMMDLG2.H header file. Listing X6.11 contains the script for the COMMDLG2.RC resource file. Listing X6.12 contains the source code for the COMMDLG2.CPP program file.

Compile and run the COMMDLG2.EXE program. Click the Colors menu item to invoke the Color dialog box. Experiment with selecting different colors. Click the OK button to close the dialog box. The program then displays a message box that contains the integer code for the currently selected color.

Listing X6.9. The contents of the COMMDLG2.DEF definition file.

```
NAME         CommDlg2
DESCRIPTION  'An OWL Windows Application'
EXETYPE      WINDOWS
CODE         PRELOAD MOVEABLE DISCARDABLE
DATA         PRELOAD MOVEABLE MULTIPLE
HEAPSIZE     1024
STACKSIZE    16384
```

Listing X6.10. The source code for the COMMDLG2.H header file.

```
#define CM_COLORCHANGE 100
#define IDM_MAINMENU   400
```

Listing X6.11. The script for the COMMDLG2.RC resource file.

```
NAME           CommDlg2
DESCRIPTION    'An OWL Windows Application'
EXETYPE        WINDOWS
CODE           PRELOAD MOVEABLE DISCARDABLE
DATA           PRELOAD MOVEABLE MULTIPLE
HEAPSIZE       1024
STACKSIZE      16384
```

Listing X6.12. The source code for the COMMDLG2.CPP program file.

```
/*
  Program to test the Choose Color common dialog box.
*/

#include <owl\applicat.h>
#include <owl\framewin.h>
#include <owl\chooseco.h>
#include "commdlg2.h"
#include <stdio.h>
#include <string.h>

const int MaxStrLen = 31;
const int MaxLongStrLen = 1024;

// declare the custom application class as
// a subclass of TApplication
class TWinApp : public TApplication
{
public:
  TWinApp() : TApplication() {}

protected:
  virtual void InitMainWindow();
};

// expand the functionality of TWindow by
// deriving class TMainWindow
class TMainWindow : public TWindow
{
public:

  TMainWindow();

```

continues

Listing X6.12. continued

```
protected:

  // the data for the color dialog box
  TChooseColorDialog::TData ColorData;

  // handle invoking the color dialog box
  void CMColors();

  // handle exiting the program
  void CMExit();

  // handle closing the window
  virtual BOOL CanClose();

  // declare the message map macro
  DECLARE_RESPONSE_TABLE(TMainWindow);

};

DEFINE_RESPONSE_TABLE1(TMainWindow, TWindow)
  EV_COMMAND(CM_COLORCHANGE, CMColors),
  EV_COMMAND(CM_EXIT, CMExit),
END_RESPONSE_TABLE;

TMainWindow::TMainWindow()
  : TWindow(0, 0, 0)
{
}

void TMainWindow::CMColors()
{
  char ColorStr[MaxStrLen];
  static TColor CustColors[16] =
  {
    TColor(0,0,0), TColor(255, 255, 255), TColor(128, 128, 128),
    TColor(255, 0, 0), TColor(0, 255, 0), TColor(0, 0, 255),
    TColor(255, 128, 0), TColor(128, 255, 0), TColor(128, 0, 255),
    TColor(255, 0, 128), TColor(0, 255, 128), TColor(0, 128, 255),
    TColor(255, 128, 128), TColor(128, 255, 128),
    TColor(128, 128, 255), TColor(64, 64, 64)
  };
  TChooseColorDialog* ColorDialog;

  ColorData.Color = TColor(255, 0, 0);
  ColorData.Flags = CC_FULLOPEN | CC_SHOWHELP | CC_RGBINIT;
  ColorData.CustColors = CustColors;
  ColorDialog = new TChooseColorDialog(this, ColorData);

```

```
82:     if (ColorDialog->Execute() == IDOK) {
83:        sprintf(ColorStr,
84:           "Hexadecimal color code: %lX\nDecimal color code: %lu",
85:           COLORREF(ColorData.Color),
86:           COLORREF(ColorData.Color));
87:        MessageBox(ColorStr, "Color Metrics",
88:                          MB_OK ¦ MB_ICONINFORMATION);
89:     }
90:   }
91:
92:   void TMainWindow::CMExit()
93:   {
94:     Parent->SendMessage(WM_CLOSE);
95:   }
96:
97:   BOOL TMainWindow::CanClose()
98:   {
99:     return MessageBox("Want to close this application?",
100:                "Query", MB_YESNO ¦ MB_ICONQUESTION) == IDYES;
101:  }
102:
103:  void TWinApp::InitMainWindow()
104:  {
105:    MainWindow = new TFrameWindow(0,
                       "Simple Colors Dialog Box Tester",
106:                   new TMainWindow);
107:    // load the menu resource
108:    MainWindow->AssignMenu(TResID(IDM_MAINMENU));
109:    // enable the keyboard handler
110:    MainWindow->EnableKBHandler();
111:  }
112:
113:  int OwlMain(int /* argc */, char** /*argv[] */)
114:  {
115:    TWinApp app;
116:    return app.Run();
117:  }
```

Analysis

Let's examine the source code shown in Listing X6.12. The window class `TMainWindow` declares a constructor, a data member, and a number of member functions. The data member `ColorData` is a `TChooseColorDialog::TData` structure and is involved in passing information to and from the color-selection dialog box.

The relevant member function is `CMColor`, whose definition starts at line 63. This function declares a local string variable; the `TColor`-typed static array, `CustColors`; and `ColorDialog`, a pointer to the class `TChooseColorDialog`. The function initializes the array `CustColors`. The function invokes the Color dialog box by sending it the C++

message `Execute` in an `if` statement (located at line 82). The `if` statement compares the value returned by the function `Execute` with `IDOK`. If the two values match, the `CMColors` function converts the numeric value (both the hexadecimal and decimal values) of the expression `ColorData.Color` into a string and then displays that string in a message box.

The Find and Replace Dialog Classes

The ObjectWindows library offers the classes `TFindReplaceDialog`, `TFindDialog`, and `TReplaceDialog` to support modeless dialog boxes that are involved in finding and replacing text. Figure X6.4 shows the Find dialog box, which contains the following controls:

- Find What edit control, which contains the search text
- Match Whole Word Only check box
- Match Case check box
- Direction group box, which contains the Up and Down radio buttons
- Find Next pushbutton, which acts like the OK button of a typical modal dialog box
- Cancel pushbutton
- Help pushbutton

Figure X6.5 shows a sample Replace dialog box, which contains the following controls:

- Find What edit control, which contains the search text
- Replace With edit control, which contains the replacing text
- Match Whole Word Only check box
- Match Case check box
- Find Next pushbutton, which acts like the OK button of a typical modal dialog box
- Replace pushbutton

- Replace All pushbutton
- Cancel pushbutton

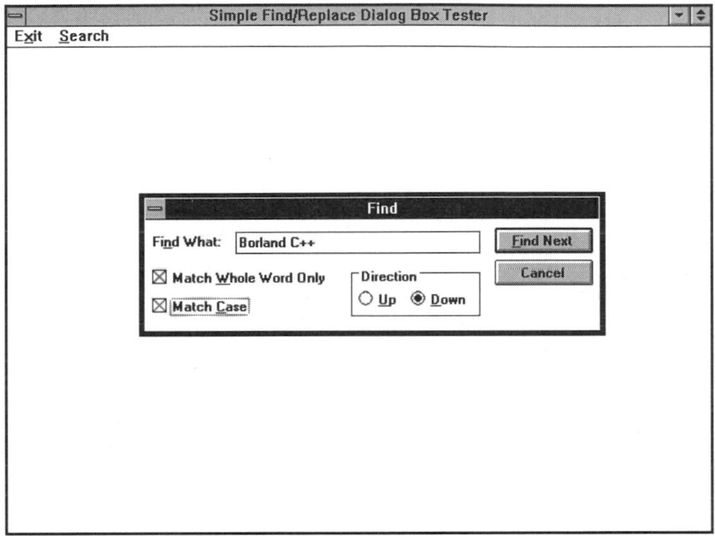

Figure X6.4. *A sample Find dialog box.*

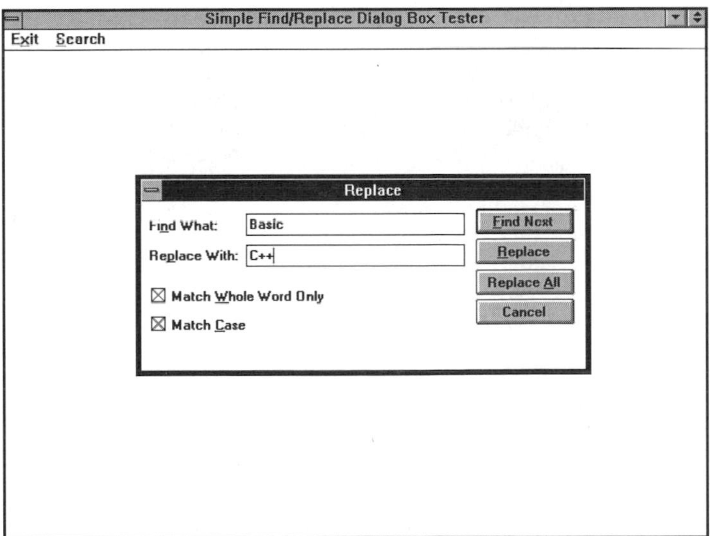

Figure X6.5. *A sample Replace dialog box.*

Supporting Classes and Structures

The `TFindReplaceDialog` class encapsulates the `FINDREPLACE` structure and the Windows API functions `FindText` and `ReplaceText`. The declaration of the `FINDREPLACE` structure is as follows:

```
typedef struct tagFINDREPLACE
{
    DWORD lStructSize; /* size of this struct 0x20 */
    HWND hwndOwner; /* handle to owner's window    */
    HINSTANCE hInstance; /* instance handle of.EXE that
                         contains  cust. dlg. template */

    DWORD Flags; /* one or more of the FR_?? */
    LPSTR lpstrFindWhat; /* ptr. to search string */
    LPSTR lpstrReplaceWith; /* ptr. to replace string */
    UINT wFindWhatLen; /* size of find buffer */
    UINT wReplaceWithLen;  /* size of replace buffer */
    LPARAM lCustData; /* data passed to hook fn. */
    UINT (CALLBACK* lpfnHook)(HWND, UINT, WPARAM, LPARAM);
          /* ptr. to hook fn. or NULL    */
    LPCSTR lpTemplateName; /* custom template name */
} FINDREPLACE;
```

The `FINDREPLACE` structure and the related Windows API functions use the following `FR_`*`XXXX`* constants:

```
#define FR_DOWN                    0x00000001
#define FR_WHOLEWORD               0x00000002
#define FR_MATCHCASE               0x00000004
#define FR_FINDNEXT                0x00000008
#define FR_REPLACE                 0x00000010
#define FR_REPLACEALL              0x00000020
#define FR_DIALOGTERM              0x00000040
#define FR_SHOWHELP                0x00000080
#define FR_ENABLEHOOK              0x00000100
#define FR_ENABLETEMPLATE          0x00000200
#define FR_NOUPDOWN                0x00000400
#define FR_NOMATCHCASE             0x00000800
#define FR_NOWHOLEWORD             0x00001000
#define FR_ENABLETEMPLATEHANDLE    0x00002000
#define FR_HIDEUPDOWN              0x00004000
#define FR_HIDEMATCHCASE           0x00008000
#define FR_HIDEWHOLEWORD           0x00010000
```

The *TFindReplaceDialog* Class

The `TFindReplaceDialog` class, a descendant of the class `TCommonDialog`, supports the modeless dialog boxes that are typically used to find and replace text. The descendant

classes, `TFindDialog` and `TReplaceDialog`, offer more specialized operations for searching and replacing text. Making the instances of class `TFindDialog` modeless makes them easier to use, because their dialog boxes remain visible while the text search takes place. As modeless dialogs, the Find and Replace dialog boxes enable the focus to be shifted to the related window that contains the edited text. You can reselect these dialog boxes at any time and resume another round of text search. There is no need to reinvoke the dialog box from a menu, because the dialog boxes are on stand-by. This flexibility comes at a price—a slightly more elaborate coding requirement. The declaration of the `TFindReplaceDialog` class is as follows:

```
class _OWLCLASS TFindReplaceDialog : public TCommonDialog {
  public:
    class _OWLCLASS TData {
      public:
        DWORD     Flags;
        DWORD     Error;
        char*     FindWhat;
        char*     ReplaceWith;
        int       BuffSize;

        TData(DWORD flags = 0, int buffSize = 81);
        ~TData();

        void      Write(opstream& os);
        void      Read(ipstream& is);
    };

    TFindReplaceDialog(TWindow*         parent,
                       TData&           data,
                       TResId           templateId = 0,
                       const char far* title = 0,
                       TModule*         module = 0);

    void UpdateData(LPARAM lParam = 0);

  protected:
    FINDREPLACE  fr;
    TData&       Data;

    HWND DoCreate() = 0;

    TFindReplaceDialog(TWindow*         parent,
                       TResId           templateId = 0,
                       const char far* title = 0,
                       TModule*         module = 0);

    void Init(TResId templateId);
    BOOL DialogFunction(UINT message, WPARAM, LPARAM);
```

```
    //
    // Default behavior inline for message response functions
    //
    void CmFindNext()
          { DefaultProcessing(); }    // EV_COMMAND(IDOK,
    void CmReplace()
          { DefaultProcessing(); }     // EV_COMMAND(psh1,
    void CmReplaceAll()
          { DefaultProcessing(); }     // EV_COMMAND(psh2,
    void CmCancel()
          { DefaultProcessing(); }      // EV_COMMAND(IDCANCEL,

    void EvNCDestroy();

  DECLARE_RESPONSE_TABLE(TFindReplaceDialog);
  DECLARE_CASTABLE;
};
```

The class `TFindReplaceDialog` declares the nested class `TData`. This nested class contains data members that store the dialog box flags, search string, replacement string, error flag, and buffer size. The dialog box flags fine-tune the appearance and operations of the Find and Replace dialog boxes. The class `TFindReplaceDialog` declares a constructor with five parameters. The parameter `parent` is the pointer to the parent window. The parameter `data` is the reference to the nested class `TData`. The parameter `templateID` specifies the resource ID for the dialog box. The default argument for this parameter invokes the standard resource for the Find or Replace dialog box. The parameter `title` designates the title of the dialog box. The default argument for this parameter invokes the standard title for the Find or Replace dialog box. The member function `UpdateData` updates the protected data member `Data`, which is a reference to the nested class TData.

The class `TFindReplaceDialog` declares a set of protected member functions—`CmFindNext`, `CmReplace`, `CmReplaceAll`, and `CmCancel`—to handle clicking the Find Next, Replace, Replace All, and Cancel buttons (respectively) in the Find and/or the Replace dialog boxes.

The *TFindDialog* Class

The declaration of class `TFindDialog` is as follows:

```
class _OWLCLASS TFindDialog : public TFindReplaceDialog {
  public:
    TFindDialog(TWindow*        parent,
                TData&          data,
                TResId          templateId = 0,
                const char far* title = 0,
                TModule*        module = 0);
```

```
  protected:
    HWND DoCreate();

  private:
    TFindDialog();
    TFindDialog(const TFindDialog&);

  DECLARE_CASTABLE;
};
```

The class `TFindDialog` constructor has the same number and type of parameters as the constructor of its parent class, `TFindReplaceDialog`. The class also declares two additional private constructors. One is the default constructor and the other is a copy constructor. They are private to prevent copying.

The *TReplaceDialog* Class

The class `TReplaceDialog`, which models the modeless Replace dialog box, has the following declaration:

```
class _OWLCLASS TReplaceDialog : public TFindReplaceDialog {
  public:
    TReplaceDialog(TWindow*        parent,
                   TData&          data,
                   TResId          templateId = 0,
                   const char far* title = 0,
                   TModule*        module = 0);

  protected:
    HWND     DoCreate();

  private:
    TReplaceDialog(const TReplaceDialog&);
    TReplaceDialog& operator=(const TReplaceDialog&);

  DECLARE_CASTABLE;
};
```

The `TReplaceDialog` class constructor has the same number and type of parameters as the constructor of its parent class, `TFindReplaceDialog`. The class also declares two additional private constructors. One is the default constructor and the other is a copy constructor. They are private to prevent copying.

Notifying the Parent Window

In order for the instances of classes `TFindDialog` and `TReplaceDialog` to notify the parent window, you need to define the following:

- ☐ A data member that is an instance of the class `TFindReplaceDialog::TData`.
- ☐ A data member that is a pointer to the class `TFindDialog`. The window class should initialize this data member to `NULL` or 0.
- ☐ A data member that is a pointer to class `TReplaceDialog`. The window class should initialize this data member to `NULL` or 0.

In addition, include in your main window class the following member functions:

1. A member function to handle the command that invokes the Find dialog box. This function examines the data member that points to the class `TFindDialog` to determine whether to create the Find dialog box.
2. A member function to handle the command that invokes the Replace dialog box. This function examines the data member that points to class `TReplaceDialog` to determine whether to create the Replace dialog box.
3. A member function that handles the messages sent by the Find and Replace dialog boxes. The function examines the pointers to both classes `TFindDialog` and `TReplaceDialog` in order to determine which dialog box is sending messages to the main window.

The following code fragment represents a general idea of how to code and initialize the preceding members:

```
class TMainWindow : public TWindow
{
public:
     // member declarations

protected:
     TFindReplaceDialog::TData FRdata;
     TFindDialog* pFindDlg;
     TReplaceDialog* pReplaceDlg;


     // other declarations

     // handle invoking the Find dialog box
     void CMFind();

     // handle invoking the Replace dialog box
     void CMReplace();

     // handle the messages
     LRESULT EvFindMsg(WPARAM, LPARAM lParam);

     DECLARE_RESPONSE_TABLE(TMainWindow);
};
```

```
DEFINE_RESPONSE_TABLE1(TMainWindow, TWindow)
...
     EV_COMMAND(CM_FIND, CMFind),
     EV_COMMAND(CM_REPLACE, CMReplace),
     EV_REGISTERED(FINDMSGSTRING, EvFindMsg),
END_RESPONSE_TABLE;


TMainWindow::TMainWindow()
     : TWindow(0, 0, 0)
{
     pFindDlg = NULL;
     pReplaceDlg = NULL;
     // other statements
}

void TMainWindow::CMFind()
{
     if (!pFindDlg && !pReplaceDlg) {
          // create the Find dialog box
     }
}

void TMainWindow::CMReplace()
{
     if (!pReplaceDlg && !pReplaceDlg) {
          // create the Replace dialog box
     }
}


LRESULT TMainWindow::EvFindMsg(WPARAM, LPARAM lParam)
{
     // handle the Find dialog box
     if (pFindDlg) {
          pFindDlg->UpdateData(lParam);
          // is dialog box terminating?
          if (FRdata.Flags & FR_DIALOGTREM) {
               // statements for dialog box cleanup
          }
          else {
               // statements for continual usage
          }
     }

     // handle the Replace dialog box
     if (pReplaceDlg) {
          pReplaceDlg->UpdateData(lParam);
          // is dialog box terminating?
          if (FrData.Flags & FR_DIALOGTREM) {
               // statements for dialog box cleanup
```

```
            }
            else {
                  // clicked Replace button?
                  if (FRdata.Flags & FR_REPLACE) {
                        // handle Replace button
                  }
                  // clicked Replace All button?
                  else if (FRdata.Flags & FR_REPLACEALL) {
                        // handle Replace All button
                  }
                  else {
                        // handle Find Next button
                  }
            }

      }
      return 0;
}
```

The preceding code segment shows the class `TMainWindow` declaring the following three data members:

1. The member `FRdata`, an instance of the class `TFindReplaceDialog::TData`.
2. The member `pFindDlg`, a pointer to the class `TFindDialog`.
3. The member `pReplaceDlg`, a pointer to the class `TReplaceDialog`.

The preceding pointers access their respective dynamic dialog boxes. The main window class also declares the member functions `CMFind`, `CMReplace`, and `EvFindMsg`. The first two functions handle the commands that invoke the Find and Replace dialog boxes. The third member function handles the messages sent by either dialog box to the main window. Notice that the response table contains the `EV_COMMAND` entries to map the commands `CM_FIND` and `CM_REPLACE` with member functions `CMFind` and `CMReplace`. In addition, the response table contains the registered message map entry `EV_REGISTERED` to map the message `FINDMSGSTRING` with the member function `EvFindMsg`. This is how the main window is able to respond to the clicking of the various buttons in the Find and Replace dialog boxes.

The constructor for the class `TMainWindow` initializes the pointers `pFindDlg` and `pReplaceDlg` with `NULL`s or zeros. The member function `CMFind` creates the Find dialog box only if neither the Find nor Replace dialog boxes are nonexistent. This condition assumes that the two modeless dialog boxes antagonize each other and should not coexist. If your program can tolerate both dialog boxes (assuming each has its own `TData` instance), then you can replace the current tested condition with `!pFindDlg`. The code fragment defines the member function `CMReplace` in a manner similar to the function `CMFind`.

The member function `EvFindMsg` handles responding to the buttons of the Find and Replace dialog boxes. The function takes a `WPARAM`-type parameter and an `LPARAM`-type parameter. The latter parameter contains a pointer that must be passed to the `Updatedata` member function of the dialog box instance. The function returns a `LRESULT` type. The function has two main `if` statements that determine if the Find or Replace dialog box is active. If the Find dialog box is active, the function performs the following tasks:

- Sends the C++ message `UpdateData` to the Find dialog box. The parameter of this message is the argument for the `LPARAM`-type parameter.
- Determines if the dialog box is not terminating by performing a bitwise AND operation between the `Flags` member and the predefined constant `FR_DIALOGTERM`. If the result is not zero, the statements in the `if` clause handle the cleanup operation before closing the dialog box. Otherwise, the function `EvFindMsg` executes the statements in the `else` clause to support the ongoing operations of the dialog box.

If the Replace dialog box is active, the function performs the following tasks:

- Sends the C++ message `UpdateData` to the Replace dialog box. The parameter of this message is the argument for the `LPARAM`-type parameter.
- Determines if the dialog box is not terminating by performing a bitwise AND operation between the `Flags` member and the predefined constant `FR_DIALOGTERM`. If the result is not zero, the statements in the `if` clause handle the cleanup operation before closing the dialog box.
- If the function `EvFindMsg` executes the `else` clause, it uses an `if-elseif-else` statement to determine if you clicked the Replace, Replace All, or the Find Next buttons in the Replace dialog box.

Remember that the preceding code segment is just one way of managing the Find and Replace dialog boxes. Your application may warrant changing and fine-tuning this code. (In fact, the next programming example does just that.)

A Sample Program

Let's put all of the preceding information to work in a test program. Here we present a simple menu-driven program that enables you to invoke a Find or Replace dialog box. Listing X6.13 shows the contents of the COMMDLG3.DEF definition file. Listing X6.14 shows the COMMDLG3.H header file. Listing X6.15 contains the script for the COMMDLG3.RC resource file. Listing X6.16 contains the source code for the COMMDLG3.CPP program file.

Compile and run the COMMDLG3.EXE test program. The program has two main menu items, Exit and Search. When you select the Search menu item, a pull-down menu appears with the Find... and Replace... options. The first option invokes the Find dialog box; the second one invokes the Replace dialog box. Select either option and experiment with making new selections and typing new text in the corresponding dialog box. Click the Find Next button (available in both the Find and Replace dialog boxes) and watch the program display a message box that contains the data for the Find or Replace dialog box. When you finish experimenting with one dialog box, select the other. When you are done testing the program, click the Cancel button of the current dialog box to exit. Figure X6.6 illustrates a sample session with program COMMDLG3.EXE showing the Find dialog box. Figure X6.7 illustrates a sample session with program COMMDLG3.EXE displaying the Replace dialog box.

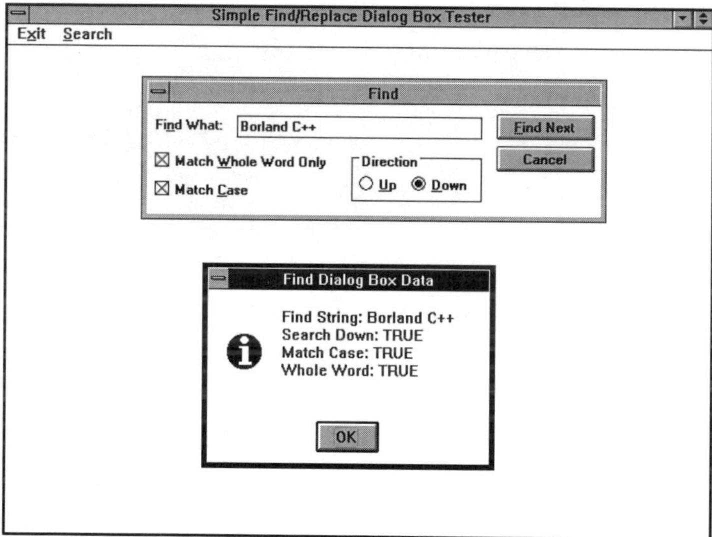

Figure X6.6. *A sample session with program COMMDLG3.EXE showing the Find dialog box.*

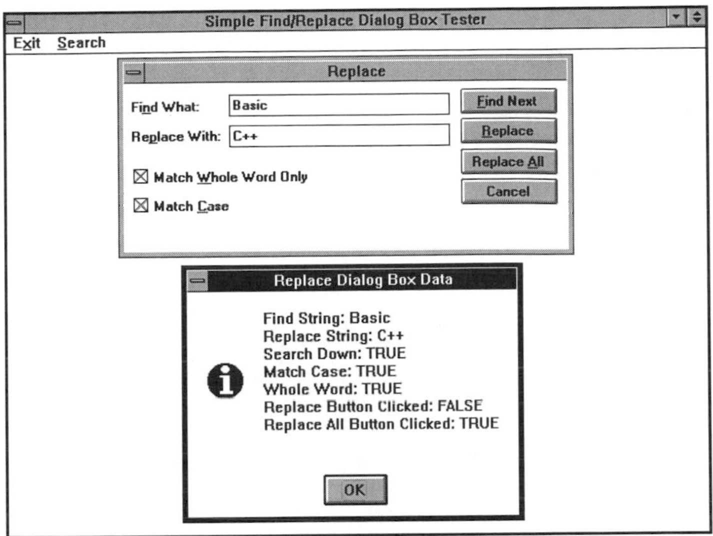

Figure X6.7. *A sample session with program COMMDLG3.EXE showing the Replace dialog box.*

Listing X6.13. The contents of the COMMDLG3.DEF definition file.

```
NAME           CommDlg3
DESCRIPTION    'An OWL Windows Application'
EXETYPE        WINDOWS
CODE           PRELOAD MOVEABLE DISCARDABLE
DATA           PRELOAD MOVEABLE MULTIPLE
HEAPSIZE       1024
STACKSIZE      16384
```

Listing X6.14. The source code for the COMMDLG3.H header file.

```
#define CM_FIND       100
#define CM_REPLACE    101
#define IDM_MAINMENU  400
```

Listing X6.15. The script for the COMMDLG3.RC resource file.

```
#include <windows.h>
#include <owl\window.rh>
#include "commdlg3.h"

IDM_MAINMENU MENU LOADONCALL MOVEABLE PURE DISCARDABLE
BEGIN
    MENUITEM "E&xit", CM_EXIT
    POPUP "&Search"
    BEGIN
      MENUITEM "&Find...", CM_FIND
      MENUITEM "&Replace...", CM_REPLACE
    END
END
```

Listing X6.16. The source code for the COMMDLG3.CPP program file.

```
/*
  Program to test the Find and Replace common dialog boxes.
*/

#include <owl\applicat.h>
#include <owl\framewin.h>
#include <owl\findrepl.h>
#include "commdlg3.h"
#include <stdio.h>
#include <string.h>

const int MaxStrLen = 31;
const int MaxLongStrLen = 1024;

// declare the custom application class as
// a subclass of TApplication
class TWinApp : public TApplication
{
public:
  TWinApp() : TApplication() {}

protected:
  virtual void InitMainWindow();
};

// expand the functionality of TWindow by
// deriving class TMainWindow
class TMainWindow : public TWindow
{
```

```
public:

  TMainWindow();

protected:

  TFindReplaceDialog::TData FRdata;
  TFindDialog* pFindDlg;
  TReplaceDialog* pReplaceDlg;

  // handle invoking the Find dialog box
  void CMFind();

  // handle clicking the Find Next button
  LRESULT EvFindMsg(WPARAM, LPARAM);

  // handle the Replace menu item
  void CMReplace();

  // handle exiting the program
  void CMExit();

  // handle closing the window
  virtual BOOL CanClose();

  // write "TRUE" or "FALSE" in string
  void BoolToStr(DWORD Flag, char* s);

  // declare the message map macro
  DECLARE_RESPONSE_TABLE(TMainWindow);

};

DEFINE_RESPONSE_TABLE1(TMainWindow, TWindow)
  EV_COMMAND(CM_FIND, CMFind),
  EV_COMMAND(CM_REPLACE, CMReplace),
  EV_COMMAND(CM_EXIT, CMExit),
  EV_REGISTERED(FINDMSGSTRING, EvFindMsg),
END_RESPONSE_TABLE;

TMainWindow::TMainWindow()
    : TWindow(0, 0, 0)
{
  pFindDlg = NULL;
  pReplaceDlg = NULL;
}

void TMainWindow::CMFind()
{
```

continues

Listing X6.16. continued

```
  if (!pFindDlg && !pReplaceDlg) {
     FRdata.Flags ¦= FR_DOWN;
     pFindDlg = new TFindDialog(this, FRdata);
     pFindDlg->Create();
  }
}

LRESULT TMainWindow::EvFindMsg(WPARAM, LPARAM lParam)
{
  char s[256];
  char s2[11];
  if (pFindDlg) {
     pFindDlg->UpdateData(lParam);
     // is the dialog box still opened
     if (!(FRdata.Flags & FR_DIALOGTERM)) {
         strcpy(s, "Find String: ");
         strcat(s, FRdata.FindWhat);
         strcat(s, "\nSearch Down: ");
         BoolToStr(DWORD(FRdata.Flags & FR_DOWN), s2);
         strcat(s, s2);
         strcat(s, "Match Case: ");
         BoolToStr(DWORD(FRdata.Flags & FR_MATCHCASE), s2);
         strcat(s, s2);
         strcat(s, "Whole Word: ");
         BoolToStr(DWORD(FRdata.Flags & FR_WHOLEWORD), s2);
         strcat(s, s2);
         MessageBox(s, "Find Dialog Box Data",
                          MB_OK ¦ MB_ICONINFORMATION);
     }
     else
         pFindDlg = NULL;
  }

  if (pReplaceDlg) {
      pReplaceDlg->UpdateData(lParam);
     // is the dialog box still opened
     if (!(FRdata.Flags & FR_DIALOGTERM)) {
         strcpy(s, "Find String: ");
         strcat(s, FRdata.FindWhat);
         strcat(s, "\nReplace String: ");
         strcat(s, FRdata.ReplaceWith);
         strcat(s, "\nSearch Down: ");
         BoolToStr(DWORD(FRdata.Flags & FR_DOWN), s2);
         strcat(s, s2);
         strcat(s, "Match Case: ");
         BoolToStr(DWORD(FRdata.Flags & FR_MATCHCASE), s2);
         strcat(s, s2);
         strcat(s, "Whole Word: ");
         BoolToStr(DWORD(FRdata.Flags & FR_WHOLEWORD), s2);
         strcat(s, s2);
```

```
        strcat(s, "Replace Button Clicked: ");
        BoolToStr(DWORD(FRdata.Flags & FR_REPLACE), s2);
        strcat(s, s2);
        strcat(s, "Replace All Button Clicked: ");
        BoolToStr(DWORD(FRdata.Flags & FR_REPLACEALL), s2);
        strcat(s, s2);
        MessageBox(s, "Replace Dialog Box Data",
                          MB_OK ¦ MB_ICONINFORMATION);
    }
    else
        pReplaceDlg = NULL;
  }
  return 0;
}

void TMainWindow::CMReplace()
{
  if (!pFindDlg && !pReplaceDlg) {
    FRdata.Flags = FR_DOWN ¦ FR_MATCHCASE ¦ FR_WHOLEWORD;
    pReplaceDlg = new TReplaceDialog(this, FRdata);
    pReplaceDlg->Create();
  }
}

void TMainWindow::CMExit()
{
  Parent->SendMessage(WM_CLOSE);
}

void TMainWindow::BoolToStr(DWORD Flag, char* s)
{
  strcpy(s, (Flag != 0) ? "TRUE\n" : "FALSE\n");
}

BOOL TMainWindow::CanClose()
{
  return MessageBox("Want to close this application?",
                "Query", MB_YESNO ¦ MB_ICONQUESTION) == IDYES;
}

void TWinApp::InitMainWindow()
{
  MainWindow = new TFrameWindow(0,
                    "Simple Find/Replace Dialog Box Tester",
               new TMainWindow),
  // load the menu resource
  MainWindow->AssignMenu(TResID(IDM_MAINMENU));
  // enable the keyboard handler
  MainWindow->EnableKBHandler();
}

```

continues

Listing X6.16. continued

```
180:  int OwlMain(int /* argc */, char** /*argv[] */)
181:  {
182:    TWinApp app;
183:    return app.Run();
184:  }
```

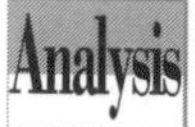

The COMMDLG3.CPP source code in Listing X6.16 declares the main window class `TMainWindow` and the application class `TWinApp`. The main window class has the following three protected data members:

1. The member `FRdata` (declared in line 36) is an instance of the class `TFindReplaceDialog::TData`. This member is commonly used by the Find and Replace dialog boxes. This program feature requires that the dialog boxes should not coexist.

2. The member `pFindDlg` (declared in line 37) is a pointer to the class `TFindDialog`. This member is a pointer to the Find dialog box instance that is dynamically created.

3. The member `pReplaceDlg` (declared in line 38) is a pointer to the class `TReplaceDialog`. This member is a pointer to the Replace dialog box instance that is dynamically created.

The `TMainWindow` constructor assigns `NULL`s to the data members `pFindDlg` and `pReplaceDlg`. The class declares the following relevant member functions:

1. The member function `CMFind` (whose definition starts at line 77) handles invoking the Find dialog box. The function performs the following tasks:

   - Verifies that both pointers `pFindDlg` and `pReplaceDlg` are `NULL`s. If this condition is true, the function `CMFind` proceeds with the remaining tasks, located in lines 80 to 82.

   - Includes the downward search flag `FR_DOWN` to the current set of flags, stored in the member `FRdata.Flags`.

   - Creates a dynamic instance of the class `TFindDialog` and assigns its pointer to the member `pFindDlg`. The creation of this instance specifies the pointers `this` and `FRdata` as the arguments for the parent window and the `TData` reference.

   - Invokes the modeless Find dialog box by sending the C++ message `Create` to the dialog box object.

2. The member function `CMReplace` (whose definition starts at line 144) handles invoking the Replace dialog box. The function performs the following tasks:

   - Verifies that both pointers `pFindDlg` and `pReplaceDlg` are `NULL`s. If this condition is true, the function `CMReplace` proceeds with the remaining tasks, located in lines 147 to 149.
   - Assigns the `FR_XXXX` flags for downward replacement, case-sensitive replacement, and the replacement of whole words to the member `FRdata.Flags`.
   - Creates a dynamic instance of the class `TReplaceDialog` and assigns its pointer to the member `pReplaceDlg`. The creation of this instance specifies the pointers `this` and `FRdata` as the arguments for the parent window and the `TData` reference.
   - Invokes the modeless Replace dialog box by sending the C++ message `Create` to the dialog box object.

3. The member function `EvFindMsg` (whose definition begins at line 86) handles the messages sent by the Find and Replace dialog boxes to the main window. This function uses two main `if` statements to handle messages sent by either dialog box. If the member `pFindDlg` is not `NULL`, the function carries out the following tasks:

   - Sends the C++ message `UpdateData` to the Find dialog box. The argument for this message, located at line 91, is the parameter `lParam`.
   - Determines if the Find dialog box is not terminating, using the `if` statement at line 93. If this condition is true, the function `EvFindMsg` performs the next tasks. Otherwise, the function executes the `else` clause statement, which assigns `NULL` to the member `pFindDlg`. This assignment enables the program to properly invoke the Find dialog box the next time you invoke the Find option.
   - Builds the multiline string `s`, which contains information about the search string, the search direction, the match-case state, and the whole word state. This task, which uses the statements in lines 94 through 104, involves the member function `BoolToStr`, which converts integers into a `"TRUE"` or `"FALSE"` string.
   - Displays the dialog box data string, `s`, in a message dialog box.

If the member `pReplaceDlg` is not `NULL`, the function carries out the following tasks:

- Sends the C++ message `UpdateData` to the Replace dialog box. The argument for this message is the parameter `lParam`.
- Determines if the Replace dialog box is not terminating, using the `if` statement in line 115. If this condition is true, the function `EvFindMsg` performs the next tasks. Otherwise, the function executes the `else` clause statement, which assigns `NULL` to the member `pReplaceDlg`. This assignment enables the program to properly invoke the Replace dialog box the next time you invoke the Replace option.
- Builds the multiline string `s`, which contains information about the search string, the replacement string, the search direction, the match-case state, the whole-word state, whether the user clicked the Replace button, and whether the user clicked the Replace All button. This task, which uses the statements in lines 116 through 134, involves the member function `BoolToStr`, which converts integers into a `"TRUE"` or `"FALSE"` string.
- Displays the dialog box data string, `s`, in a message dialog box.

The `if` statement that handles the message sent by the Replace dialog box is simpler than the code fragment we presented earlier. This is due to the fact that the program does not take alternate action if you click the Replace or Replace All buttons.

Summary

This chapter presented you with powerful dialog boxes that serve as input tools. You learned about the following:

- The ObjectWindows `TInputDialog` class, which enables you to prompt the user for an input.
- Software requirements for using the common dialog boxes. These include adequate stack space in the .DEF file, making sure that the COMMDLG.DLL file is in the Windows system directory, and including the corresponding header files.
- The file-selection dialog box classes `TSaveOpenDialog`, `TFileOpenDialog`, and `TFileSaveDialog`. These classes create dialog boxes that support either opening or saving a file.
- The color-selection dialog box class `TChooseColorDialog`.

- The text find/replace dialog box classes `TFindReplaceDialog`, `TFindDialog`, and `TReplaceDialog`. These classes create dialog boxes that support either finding or replacing text.

Q&A

Q What are the other two common dialog boxes not presented in this chapter?

A The other common dialog boxes are the font-selection and Print common dialog boxes. The font-selection dialog box enables you to select a font. The Print dialog box enables you to print or set up your printer.

Q Is it easy to access the folder bitmaps that appear in the File Open/Save dialog box?

A No. Accessing these bitmaps requires advanced programming skills.

Q Can I use the Find and Replace dialog boxes to search for text patterns?

A Yes. However, using such patterns may not be obvious to the dialog box user. Using a check box that indicates whether to use pattern search is highly recommended. This additional control requires that you create your own version of the Find and Replace dialog boxes.

Exercises

1. Extend the class `TInputDialog` to create the class `TIntegerInput`. The new class supports integer input with validation.
2. Use the class `TIntegerInput` to replace the class `TInputDialog` in the number-guessing game, program INPUTGLD.EXE.
3. Write a program that uses the File dialog box to copy a file, possibly using a different name for the copy.

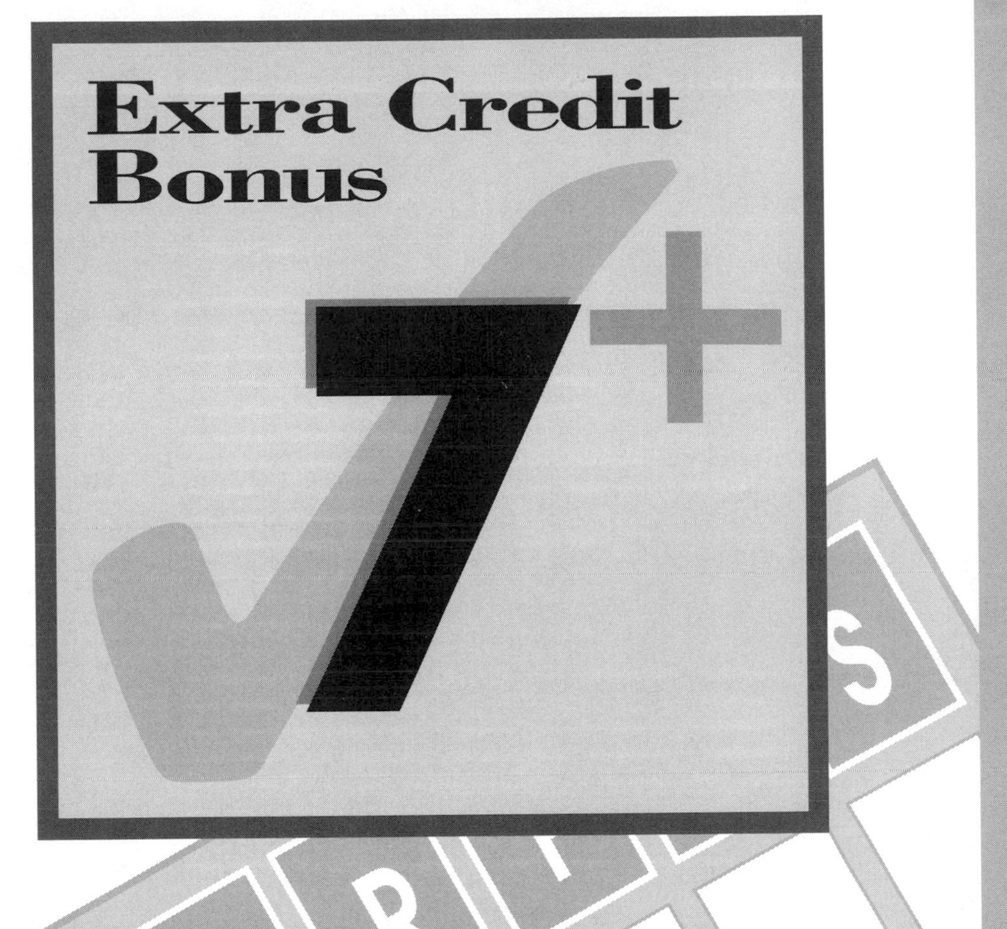

OLE 2

Object Linking and Embedding (OLE) is the Windows system for enabling several programs to work together, and OLE 2 represents a further degree of refinement and increase in function over the original OLE system. With Borland C++ 4.5, new classes have been provided to support OLE 2. Today, you explore the following topics:

- The Borland solution to implementing OLE 2
- Embedding objects the OWL way
- Passing data between programs—OLE Automation

What Is OLE 2?

New Term: With *object linking and embedding*, objects can be linked together. Thus, a document or other object can be composed of many objects from different applications, and the data that represents the objects can be embedded into the document.

A *linked* object holds sufficient information in the client to invoke another application with the reference for the data to be operated on.

An *embedded* object has the data of the object held in the client.

Before going into detail, let's examine why a user would want linking and embedding. From the early days of PC programs, users wanted the capability of joining information from different applications. For example, every word-processed sales report needs that sales-up-in-the-third-quarter pie chart. The original solutions of integration, such as Lotus Symphony, tried to do everything in one large application. Similarly, most of the industry-standard word processors, spreadsheets, and presentation graphics programs have a tremendous overlap of function—in Excel, you can draw on your spreadsheet; in Word, you can make a simple spreadsheet in a word processing table. Of course, the user does not want cut-down functionality in these add-on features. The solution in Windows is to provide the capability of inserting the output from other applications into documents.

OLE 2 is not just about providing the user with desktop publishing, however. The question could better be phrased "What *are* OLE 2?" OLE 2 comes in two forms:

- A system of data exchange called *Automation* that enables programs to pass data between themselves
- A system of joining programs and data together to create a compound document

New Term: Throughout the rest of the day, the term *OLE* means OLE 2 unless explicit reference is made to OLE 1.

There is a significant difference between the two activities. With Automation, the two programs must have a defined interface and know about the data that is being passed between them, as with DDEML. The client transaction processes the data provided by the Automation server. With object linking and embedding, the principle is that the container knows nothing about the object being contained; rather, it interacts with the OLE system only. However, an OLE container must provide certain features to enable an object to cohabit.

New Term: The correct terminology for the user of an OLE object is a *container*. The provider of an OLE object is a *server*.

To the user, OLE means being able to edit a document or graphic and place other objects on the screen. An object is inserted into a container either by an Insert Object command, the Clipboard using the special OLE options, or drag-and-drop. The container is responsible for providing the space for the object; the object's server is responsible for drawing it. Similarly, when saving an embedded object, the server is responsible for writing the object to the file provided by the container.

Note: Once an OLE object has been linked or embedded, the server is no longer required. The OLE container keeps an image of the object (drawn using a Windows metafile) so it can reproduce the object. This includes scaling to fit the page and printing it—true WYSIWYG fashion.

There are two different processes. In linking, the container stores a reference to another application with instructions as to how to access the server. One linked document can be shared among several containers. A change to a linked document can be updated across several containers—and, if the document is moved to another machine, the linked document needs to go with it and the links may need to be reestablished. In embedding, all the data is held in the container document. This means that the object is safely owned by the document, and it can be copied from one place to another without losing the embedded data. Only one document owns the data, however—other documents are not kept up to date. The appropriate method for linking is a user decision, depending on why the object is being inserted.

OLE gets in everywhere. OLE 2 defines a standard for the format for storing objects. The storage is divided into compartments, which can contain other compartments. The main document contains a subcompartment for each embedded object. The advantages of the standardization of the storage are that containers can identify the server data mixed in with its own data and that the container can use the OLE file structure so that it reads only objects that are needed. For example, if the object is a 24-bit screen print that is displayed on the second page of a document, it may not be necessary to read the picture when opening a document to view the first page. More importantly, the storage structure is hierarchical and can be used by an object to contain other objects. Finally, the storage concept is independent of the medium in which the objects are saved; a storage can be on disk or memory or held in a blob on a Paradox database, for example.

New Term: The OLE name for a compartment is a *storage*.

An OLE object is made of two separate components: the data and the view. As you have seen, the data can be stored separately from the application that displays the object. An object also can be viewed in a number of different ways, as with Clipboard formats. So, for an extreme (but actual) example, an embedded wave file may provide a visual "view" for its representation in a document and a sound "view" to play it.

The level of integration in OLE is very high. A true OLE 2 container embedding or linking an OLE object enables its menu, toolbar, and status bar to be taken over by the server for in-place editing, effectively appearing to be the server application. The object, when activated (when it has focus, rather than being edited), can add options to menus, provides for pop-up menus over the object, and can be moved and sized within a document. Originally, OLE 1 enabled embedded objects, but, to edit them, a separate application window had to be opened. Figure X7.1 shows an ancient Word 2 processor doing simple embedding.

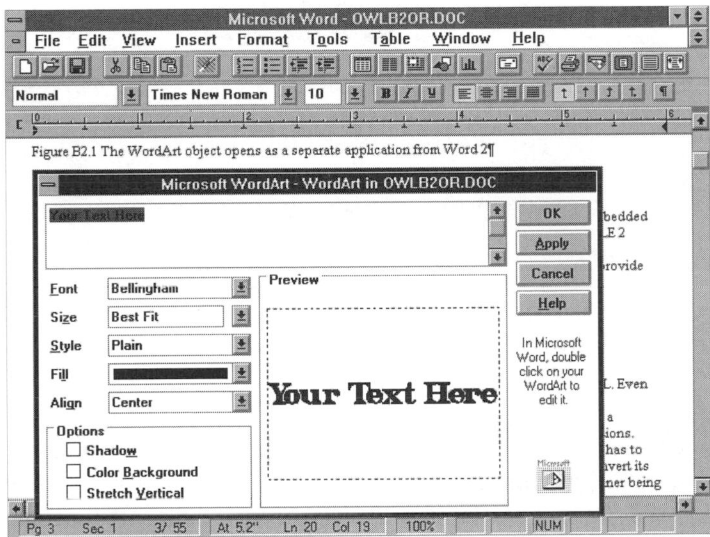

Figure X7.1. *The WordArt object opens as a separate application from Word 2.*

OLE applications can work as containers, servers, or both. Even more confusing is that an OLE embedded object with in-place editing can itself open an in-place edited object, as in Figure X7.2. OLE 2 provides backwards compatibility with OLE 1 so that you can embed OLE 2 objects in an OLE 1 application (without in-place editing). Similarly, OLE 2 can insert OLE 1 objects; they just cannot provide in-place editing.

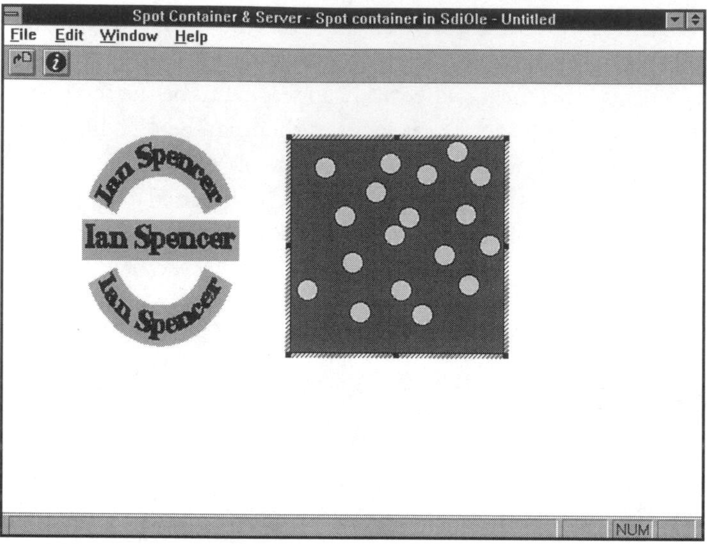

Figure X7.2. *The OLE 2 way of embedding.*

There are two ways you can provide an OLE server: as an executable and as a DLL. Even as an executable, you may not want to provide your object as a stand-alone application—to save implementing the stand-alone requirements of printing and file management, for example. Providing a server as a DLL has large performance improvements. This enables OLE to call server functions directly. With an OLE executable, OLE has a problem. Because OLE is designed for true multitasking systems, it has to organize calls between tasks properly; it cannot simply send messages. Therefore, OLE has to convert its commands into task-independent messages to ensure that it can edit the object without having the container aware of the object implementation. Furthermore, the intention is that the OLE implementation can be extended to enable objects to be implemented across networks so that the OLE tasks might run on different computers—all transparent to the user and the programmer.

How Does Borland Implement OLE 2?

New Term: *OCF* stands for *Object Components Framework*. This is Borland's high-level C++ wrapper around OLE, which converts between a

> simplified C++ OOP interface and the OLE API. It is similar to the ObjectWindows Library that acts as a wrapper around the standard Windows API.

OLE contains many features. However, "there ain't no such thing as a free lunch." To provide all these features, a container application must provide the correct interaction with OLE. This, as you might imagine, is hard work, considering the tremendous number of different situations with which the application has to cope. OCF simplifies the work required by providing a number of classes that support the basic function in the same way that OWL supports the Windows API. Aside from the classes, OCF provides a number of macros to simplify the definition of the OLE registration data and class definitions. It does so in a way similar to the way that OWL uses macros for the response tables, and it also defines its own special messages to enable a simplified OCF event to be handled.

> **Note:** OCF is a separate set of classes from OWL. OWL 2.5 provides classes that make use of OCF to build OLE applications, but OCF does not require the use of OWL.

OCF provides class support for OLE servers, OLE containers, and OLE Automation. OCF helps implement the following:

- *Linking and embedding.* OCF provides support for both server and container.
- *The Clipboard.* OCF provides all the cut-and-paste options.
- *Drag-and-drop.* This is the capability of dragging an object and, when placed in a drag-and-drop enabled window, placing the object in that window.
- *OLE interface.* OCF provides standard components to build OLE dialog boxes, and also provides the capability of modifying the container window if it is written to conform to OCF's requirements.
- *OLE compound files.*

OCF places a layer of abstraction over the standard Microsoft OLE interface. If you were to program in straight C++ without OWL, OCF would provide a simplified way of programming OLE. For OLE Automation, OCF provides all the function required to pass data between a client and server object. OCF also provides additional help to the application to enable it to handle the command line correctly, which is used to instruct an OLE application as to the mode in which it should run. However, there still is a lot of work to do in managing a linking and embedding application.

Building on the OCF classes, OWL then provides a number of classes to ease the programming of OLE via OCF. There are OLE-enabled frames, `TOleFrame` and `TOleMDIFrame`, and OLE container windows—for example, `TOleWindow`. `TOleDocument` and `TOleView` represent the container and views of the container. There also have been some modifications to the `TApplication` class to enable it to run in the different ways required by OLE.

OWL provides support for these OCF functions, but wraps them still further to the point that you need very little code in your program to support OLE.

AppExpert has been revised to support the OLE classes and you can quickly generate the framework of an OLE application for both an OLE container and server.

OLE *Doc/View*

For the rest of the look at OLE linking and embedding, you study the `TOleDocument` and `TOleView` implementation of OLE. The `Doc/View` model has been present in OWL 2 since its original release. The principle of the `Doc/View` model is that the storing of data and the presentation of data are two different tasks.

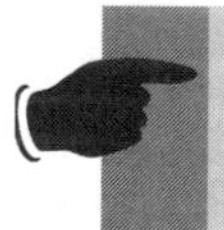

New Term: For simplicity, *`Doc/View`* refers to `TOleDocument` and `TOleView` throughout the rest of today's lesson.

Defining a *TOleDocument* Class

There are several steps to follow in defining a `TOleDocument` class.

Step 1: Define the Document Storage

`TOleDocument` understands how to store OLE documents and provides the container with access to the storage medium so that the programmer can easily add specific data to the document.

OWL Note: Transparently, you write to the special OLE storage format. This means you do not need to do anything special to store data in either embedded or stand-alone file format.

Normally, you derive a class and provide `Open` and `Commit` functions to enable the document to read and write its data. You also provide a `Close` function to clear the document, and you may want to provide a `Revert` function to reset your document to a cleared or as-originally-read state. In each of these, you need to call the base `TOleDocument` function. You access the file by using the `Instream` function to return a `TInStream` for reading and the `OutStream` function for getting a `TOutStream`. When writing the file, you should place markers or read a fixed number of objects, which you note before writing so that you can safely reread the data.

Caution: At the end of writing out data in the `Commit` function, make sure you call `TOleDocument::CommitTransactedStorage`, which updates the storage to disk. If you do not do this, the file you write will be incomplete and cannot be opened.

Step 2: Define Notifications to Tell Views to Update Themselves

You are likely to need some notifications to tell the document views of any changes to the document that might affect them. At any time, a document may have several views open, although only one will be active. When a document changes, it uses the `NotifyViews` function, which sends the notification to all the views that are open via the standard message response table. There are a number of standard notifications. Additionally, you can define your own document-specific notifications for which you need to define a notification value, a response function signature (via a macro that OWL provides), and a response table entry. For example, this code snippet defines document notifications for when the document has been added to or been cleared:

```
//
// Custom Doc/View notifications
//
const int vnDrawAppend = vnCustomBase+0;
const int vnDrawClear = vnCustomBase+1;
//
```

```
// Custom Doc/View signatures
//
NOTIFY_SIG(vnDrawAppend, uint)
NOTIFY_SIG(vnDrawClear, void)
//
// Response table macros
//
#define EV_VN_DRAWAPPEND  VN_DEFINE(vnDrawAppend,  VnAppend,  int)
#define EV_VN_DRAWCLEAR  VN_DEFINE(vnDrawClear,  VnClear,  void)
```

Step 3 is to provide data access functions for views.

Defining a *TOleView* Class

Next, you need to provide access functions so that the various views can get at the data. Their exact form is up to you, but, normally, you require at least something to add data and to get the data from the document. More sophisticated applications provide more functions.

Creating a `TOleView` class requires a bit more work. How much work depends on whether the view is intended to contain OLE objects (remember that an OLE server can itself contain objects if you want). `TOleView` contains all the work to contain objects.

OWL Note: When building your `TOleView` class, you should store a pointer or reference to your document class. There is already such a pointer, but it is of the generic `TOleDocument` type and needs downcasting to use.

Step 1: Define the Presentation

Defining the presentation is based on accessing data from the document. Generally, this consists of having the `Paint` function retrieve data from the document. You may have more than one method of presenting the data. If so, you can either create separate `TOleView` classes or, more likely, derive further classes from a common class of your own devising. The special trick to an OLE server is that the view may not be presented in device units. OWL looks after the scaling, but it means that any interaction you have with the screen needs to be managed in logical window units—not pixels as you would expect.

Step 2: Add Data Editing Methods

How the view accepts data is up to the view. However, because there may be several views open on the document at once, take care as to how you handle this. The general approach is to handle the editing in the view, and when the object is complete, store it in the document, using the document access functions you provide. The document accepts the data and sends a notification message. For example, in a PaintBrush example, you might type text on the picture only in the active view and when the text is accepted by the user, add the text to the document. Then, in the notification response, invalidate the window to ensure that the screen is redisplayed. By using custom notifications, you can refine the process so that when adding data, all the views can, if possible, modify their screen rather than entirely redrawing it.

Step 3: Add Notification Responses

The view should handle all document notifications to ensure that the display matches the document data. The normal response often is to invalidate the screen (by calling `Invalidate`), but, if the object is a server, the view should also call `InvalidatePart` to ensure that the container is kept in step with the editing.

Note: It's important to remember that if you edit an OLE object (rather than opening for in-place editing), you can observe your embedded object being updated as you edit the object in a separate application.

Step 4: Support Embedded Objects, if Required

OWL supports embedded objects for you in `TOleView`. However, you need to avoid interfering with how it works. Essentially, OWL provides a default place to dump new objects, then uses `EvLButtonDown`, `EvMouseMove`, and `EvLButtonUp` to manage moving and sizing the embedded objects. There are a few traps to mouse handling:

- You need to enable the mouse messages to be responded to by the base class to enable contained objects to be handled.
- The `EvLButtonDown` and `EvMouseMove` messages convert the `TPoint` mouse position parameter into logical units, dependent on the view. The DC view

is provided by the `DragDC` member of the view. The mouse down always creates a `DragDC` for you. If you are drawing on the view, you need to use the `DragDC` to get the correct scaling for an embedded edit. If you are storing the position of the object based on the `EvLButtonUp`, you need to convert the mouse coordinates to logical units yourself.

- You should use the mouse only if the mouse hasn't selected an embedded object. You can test for this by testing whether a `DragDC` exists (it will unless your mouse has been moved over the window, having first been pressed outside). Then you should check whether the mouse is holding the object. You do this by calling `SelectEmbedded`, which returns `true` if the `TOleView` is currently handling an embedded object.

By default, you have no control over the placement of the objects (which is normal for many embedding applications). You can provide a current position for insertion by providing a `GetInsertPosition` function (for example, this might return the current cursor position in a word processor).

You provide the rest of the OLE container functionality by giving the appropriate menu options—all the OLE function is built in whether you are building a server or a container.

As you can see, the steps using the `Doc/View` model are nearly identical for a container or server.

The OLE Registry

The first thing an OLE application does when it starts up is to register itself with Windows, letting the operating system know just what parts of OLE the program can handle. The standard method has been to fill in all sorts of long complicated parameters to all manner of OLE API functions. With OCF, however, the information can still be rather complicated; the information is created in a structure with the aid of special registration macros. The structure is then passed into the OCF object constructors, which make sure that your application's program is registered properly with the operating system.

Note: The actual registry information is stored in the REG.DAT file in Windows 3.1. In Windows NT and Windows 95, the information is stored in the system registry.

Although there are several registry functions, the most common ones—the ones in which you're interested—are listed in Table X7.1. These are used to build the registration structures that describe both the application and the various document formats.

Table X7.1. OCF registry macros.

Macro	Meaning
`BEGIN_REGISTRATION`	This is used to start defining a structure. This is similar to the `DEFINE_RESPONSE_TABLE`*x* macro used in OWL. The single parameter to this macro is the name of the structure to be defined.
`END_REGISTRATION`	This is used to end the definition of a structure. It is similar to OWL's `END_RESPONSE_TABLE` macro.
`REGDATA`	This is the main workhorse macro that adds a keyed entry to the structure. The first parameter to this macro is the key. The second parameter is a value to associate with the key.
`REGDOCFLAGS`	This adds an entry containing flags for a document template. These flags are used in the Doc/View model of OLE programming. The parameter is an ORed together bunch of `dt`*XXX* flags.
`REGFORMAT`	Each document needs to let the OLE registry know what formats, such as metafiles, bitmaps, and so on, it can handle. This adds information regarding a document's capabilities to the structure.
`REGISTRATION_FORMAT_BUFFER`	Some of the macros used to create the registration structure require some temporary space in order to properly expand. This macro provides that temporary space, the size of which is based on its single parameter.

In the description of the REGDATA macro, I mentioned that it registers keyed entries. There are quite a number of keys available to be registered, some of which are required for various structures. Table X7.2 describes some of the keys.

Table X7.2. OCF registry keys.

Key Name	Entry Value
clsid	This defines the Globally Unique Identifier (GUID) needed to differentiate each OLE application from one another. The GUIDs are generated automatically by the IDE's AppExpert. If you create an OLE application on your own, you can use the GUIDGEN.EXE program supplied with the compiler to generate a GUID for this field.
progid	This is a string that identifies the structure. This is used for both documents and for applications, and it typically consists of three parts: a program name, an object name, and a version number.
description	When OLE puts up a string for the user to see, it shows the contents of this entry, which can be up to 40 characters long.
cmdline	This describes the arguments that OLE should place on the program's command line when OLE starts the application. It's often just an empty string.
appname	This is usually the title that shows up in the application's main window.
docfilter	This is represented as a file mask, such as *.SPT, and generally uses the same letters as in the document's extension. That file mask is used in the common dialogs, along with a file type (see menuname and description) when OLE asks the user to open or save files.
usage	This is a flag that lets OLE know whether or not it should start up a new instance of the application server for each client that requests it. If ocrSingleUse is used here, the application will be started once for each OLE client that needs it. ocrMultipleUse means that the server application will be opened only once, no matter how many clients ask for it.

Key Name	Entry Value
`insertable`	The key for this entry is always an empty string; its presence is used in a structure to identify a document as one that can be inserted into other container documents. It will appear in the list of available documents when the user selects the `Insert Object` menu item.
`menuname`	This is a short name that shows up as a menu item in container programs. In order to keep menu sizes short and readable, the suggested maximum length for this entry is 15 characters.
`verbN`	This describes the verbs used for documents, ones that will appear in popup menus. *N* represents a number that should begin with 0 and go no further than 7. Typical entries are &Edit and &Open.
`extension`	This is used to identify filename extensions for OLE documents. When OLE is asked to open a file, it matches the extension of the file with the various servers associated with extensions and then uses the matching one.

It's important to note that this list is by no means complete. There are a number of other keys that can be used, but the ones listed so far are enough to get a program up and running with full OLE functionality.

Creating an OLE Application

The previous discussion has created only the `Doc/View` components and described the registry in general terms, but this has not explained how documents and views are managed. OWL provides a document manager, called `TDocManager`. It is this class (which you normally don't need to amend in any way) that looks after documents and views. There are a few simple steps that you take to enable the document manager to understand your class.

Step 1: Declare a *Doc/View* Template and Register its Details

You do not need to worry about the internals of declaring a `Doc/View` template. There are three components you need to define. (You don't use these yourself, they are used by the `TDocManager`.) The `DEFINE_DOC_TEMPLATE_CLASS` macro associates the documents and the views. You declare one of these for each combination:

```
DEFINE_DOC_TEMPLATE_CLASS(SpotDoc, SpotView, SpotTemplate);
```

Then you need to declare some important OLE registration details for each document.

```
BEGIN_REGISTRATION(__SpotRegistration)
    REGDATA(progid, "Spot.Container.1")
    REGDATA(description, "Spot Container Version 1")
    REGDATA(extension, "SPT")
    REGDATA(docfilter, "*.SPT")
    REGDOCFLAGS(dtAutoDelete ¦ dtUpdateDir
                ¦ dtAutoOpen ¦ dtRegisterExt)
    REGDATA(menuname, "Spot container")
    REGDATA(insertable, "")
    REGDATA(verb0, "&Edit")
    REGDATA(verb1, "&Open")
    REGFORMAT(0, ocrEmbedSource,  ocrContent,
                 ocrIStorage, ocrGet)
    REGFORMAT(1, ocrMetafilePict, ocrContent,
                 ocrMfPict ¦ ocrStaticMed, ocrGet)
    REGFORMAT(2, ocrBitmap, ocrContent,
                 ocrGDI ¦ ocrStaticMed, ocrGet)
    REGFORMAT(3, ocrDib, ocrContent,  ocrHGlobal
                 ¦ ocrStaticMed, ocrGet)
    REGFORMAT(4, ocrLinkSource, ocrContent,
                 ocrIStream, ocrGet)
END_REGISTRATION
```

This table is passed to Windows so that your application is entered into the system. This enables other applications to know of your existence. Important entries (well, they are all important!) are the `progid` and `description`, which appear when the user accesses the object (for example, via Insert Object). `insertable` is a placeholder to indicate that this object can be inserted—that is, the document is an OLE server. `extension`, `docfilter`, and the `REGDOCFLAGS` line all tell the document manager (and OLE) what files can be handled by the `Doc/View` combination. The `REGFORMAT`s tell OLE what formats the server can produce for linking and embedding. OWL `Doc/View` can provide all these formats for you.

Having created this information, you then declare a global static instance of the `Doc/View` template. The instance looks after associating itself with the manager, so you can call it what you like. It takes the registration information as a parameter (you pass the registration details even if you decide not to provide OLE support):

```
SpotTemplate __spotTemplate(__SpotRegistration);
```

You have now created your `Doc/View` classes.

Step 2: Add the Application Registration Details

Next, you need to sort out the application. There are a number of new features for this. First, you need a static `TAppDictionary`. This manages OWL internal information. This must be called `AppDictionary` to ensure that certain OWL features work.

Second, you need to register the application (by the way, place this before your `Doc/View` registration):

```
//
// Ole 2 linking and embedding apps need a TOcRegistrar
//
static TPointer<TOcRegistrar> Registrar;

REGISTRATION_FORMAT_BUFFER(100)

BEGIN_REGISTRATION(ApplicationReg)
//
// The following must be unique per Ole 2 application
//
    REGDATA(clsid, "{FE91A8E0-DBDA-101B-A585-040224007802}")
    REGDATA(appname, "Spot Container & Server")
    REGDATA(description, "Spot Container & Server Application")
    REGDATA(cmdline, "")
    REGDATA(usage, ocrMultipleUse)
END_REGISTRATION
```

Create a `TOcRegistrar` pointer, which must be called `Registrar`. OCF uses templates that rely on this. You will set up the `Registrar` in `OwlMain`.

Note: The `TPointer` class is a cunning ruse to ensure that dynamically allocated objects get cleaned up. It accepts a pointer of the type of the object specified and deletes the object if the instance goes out of scope, a new object is assigned to it, or zero is assigned to it. This improves the capability of cleaning up objects if something goes wrong. You can use this class yourself. Typically, you use it where you would declare a variable, but, because of size, you want to declare it using `new`. One place it works well is where an exception may be thrown—objects declared on the stack are cleaned up, but dynamically allocated objects are not. By wrapping the pointer in an object, dynamically allocatable objects can now be cleaned up.

Next, create the application registration. `appname` and `description` are self-explanatory. `usage` enables multiple clients to use the same application, and `cmdline` indicates that there are no arguments needed on the command line. The important one is `clsid`.

Caution: The class id must be absolutely unique to ensure that OLE starts the correct program. The Globally Unique Identifier is unique around the world, and you should never copy someone else's—especially if you are going to distribute your application.

This horrible long number can easily be generated. Merely run GUIDGEN (which lives in your Borland C++ BIN directory). This places a new GUID in your Clipboard and you can then paste it into your code.

Step 3: Implement the Application Class

You now can move and look at the class. A `Doc/View` application handles a couple of responses for the document manager:

```
DEFINE_RESPONSE_TABLE1(SpotApp, TApplication)
    EV_OWLVIEW(dnCreate, EvNewView),
    EV_OWLVIEW(dnClose,  EvCloseView),
    EV_COMMAND(CM_HELPABOUT, CmHelpAbout),
END_RESPONSE_TABLE;
```

The application itself is multi-derived from `TApplication` and `TOcModule`. The `TOcModule` is transparent, but you do need to use a special `TApplication` constructor:

```
SpotApp::SpotApp () : TApplication
   (::ApplicationReg["description"], ::Module, &::AppDictionary)
{
    SetDocManager(new TDocManager(dmSDI ¦ dmMenu, this));
}
```

The constructor is identical for any OLE application you write, using the global objects you created earlier. In the constructor, set up the document manager. This needs to be set for whether you are using SDI or MDI (it controls whether multiple documents can be open).

`InitMainWindow` is fairly standard, except that you cannot create a client at this point; OLE is not yet ready. You use a `TOleFrame`, which is a special `TDecoratedFrame` that can handle the OLE toolbar interface. You would create your toolbar for a stand-alone application here, setting the toolbar's `Attr.Id` to `IDW_TOOLBAR`. This enables OWL to swap it if another application takes over your application.

In `TApplication::InitInstance`, the application can now have its client window set up if required. If the application is not embedding, you can open the file based on the command line, or you can open a blank document. To open files, you ask the document manager. In the following snippet, if not embedding, the application finds out whether the document manager recognizes the filename that has been sent via `MatchTemplate`. If so, it attempts to open the file by creating a document. It uses the document template to construct an empty document, then uses the document manager to initialize it, which, in turn, opens a view. Similarly, if there is no document, the application merely opens a new view:

```
    if (!::Registrar->IsOptionSet(amEmbedding))
      {
         TDocTemplate* tpl = GetDocManager()
             ->MatchTemplate(GetCmdLine().c_str());
         if (tpl)
           {
             TDocument* doc = tpl->ConstructDoc();
             if (doc)
               {
                 doc->SetTemplate(tpl);
                 GetDocManager()->InitDoc(doc,
                        GetCmdLine().c_str(), 0);
                 return;
               }
           }
         GetDocManager()->CreateAnyDoc(0, dtNewDoc);
      }
```

The document manager opens the view. Recall that the application response table defined two document notifications. Once a view has been created, it has to be associated with a window. Because the application may operate in an embedded mode, this view may be a window in the container document. So, to handle the notification, the application needs to test whether the document is embedded. If the document is embedded, it creates a view parented to a special window; otherwise, the view is created as a standard client (in this case, an SDI client):

```
TOleView* ov = dynamic_cast<TOleView*>(&view);
if (ov && view.GetDocument().IsEmbedded() &&
    !ov->GetOcRemView()->IsOpenEditing())
  {
    //
    // Embedded view window
    //
    TWindow* vw = view.GetWindow();
    vw->SetParent(dynamic_cast<TOleFrame*>(GetMainWindow())
                  ->GetRemViewBucket());
    vw->Create();
  }
 else
  {
    //
    // Normal window - associate with MainWindow
    //
    GetMainWindow()->SetClientWindow(view.GetWindow());
    if (!view.IsOK())
      GetMainWindow()->SetClientWindow(0);
    else
      if (view.GetViewMenu())
        GetMainWindow()->MergeMenu(*view.GetViewMenu());
  }
```

Note: In `Doc/View`, menu merging is used even in an SDI application, because different views can be placed as a client.

Step 4: Implement an OLE *OwlMain*

The `OwlMain` is changed around. This is to enable the OLE system to call your application correctly. When you run an OLE application, it receives a variety of command-line options. It is responsible for registering and unregistering itself, and also for interpreting the command-line options that OLE might have passed. OWL strips these out for you, leaving a simplified command line with only non-OLE

information. This saves you from having to decode the flags yourself. You can interrogate the flags by calling `TRegistrar::IsOptionSet`. This tests for any flags you send, which are enumerated. The main test you need is to decide whether your application is operating in embedded mode. Normally, the command line can contain the filename to enable File Manager to start your application via its associations. It also normally passes the filename and a flag to request printing a document:

```
int OwlMain (int , char* [])
{
    try
      {
        ::Registrar = new TOcRegistrar(::ApplicationReg,
                              TOleDocViewFactory<SpotApp>(),
                              TApplication::GetCmdLine(),
                              ::DocTemplateStaticHead);
        if (!::Registrar->IsOptionSet(amAnyRegOption))
          ::Registrar->Run();
        ::Registrar = 0;
        return 0;
      }
    catch (xmsg& x)
      {
        ::MessageBox(0, x.why().c_str(), "Exception", MB_OK);
      }
    return -1;
}
```

The main trick here is the use of the `::Registrar` object. For an OLE application that does linking and embedding, you need a `TOcRegistrar` object. The `::ApplicationReg` and `TApplication::GetCommandLine()` are all standard objects that you use. `::DocTemplateStaticHead` represents a special link for the registration to find the document template registration details. The special part is the `TOleDocViewFactory`. This is a template class that generates a hidden callback function. This callback function is what is actually called by the `::Registrar->Run()` call. OWL provides a number of different callbacks depending on the sort of application you are building. The name `Factory` implies that this is the OLE object generator. When building an OLE application, your target needs to include the OCF libraries. (When distributing an OLE application, you also need to distribute the OLE libraries.)

Put all that together; then run your application. However, before you run an OLE-enabled server, you should run it in register mode. The proper way to do this is to run it with a `-RegServer` command line. The IDE makes this easy for you; there are two special commands on the SpeedMenu for a target node. Choose SpeedMenu ¦ Special ¦ Register or Unregister, and the IDE will run your application in registration mode. In this mode, it does not create windows; it merely performs the registration and then immediately exits.

Creating OLE Applications with AppExpert

The following application was initially generated using AppExpert, although it has been substantially tidied up. With Borland C++ 4.5, AppExpert is OLE-enabled. You can create `Doc/View` servers or containers with all the usual features that you would expect to be able to generate. ClassExpert understands the OLE `Doc/View` model. You are familiar with AppExpert (having studied Bonus Day 3), so you will find it simple to amend OLE applications. At the time of writing, AppExpert gives a derived `TOleView` object to work with, but does not provide a derived `TOleDocument` class. This always is required for all but trivial examples. This can easily be derived by using ClassExpert. (Remember to use the SpeedMenu from the class pane; this enables you to derive from any class that the ClassExpert knows about.)

Another suggestion is to amend the derived `TOleView` class manually so that it accepts a derived `TOleDocument` as a parameter rather than the `TOleDocument` set as the parameter. This saves down-casting the document each time you access it.

If you want to create an OLE container to play with, press the generate button and compile the result. You will find that you can make an application that provides a nearly complete OLE implementation. AppExpert is useful, because an OLE application normally needs to support toolbars and status bars, and it will generate all the different menus and registration tables.

Note: Do not select Automation support in the OLE 2 options yet. This option is covered in the second part of today's lesson.

Listings X7.1 through X7.12, SPOT.EXE, provide a practical and stimulating example.

Listing X7.1. STOPAPP.H.

```
#if !defined(__spotapp_h)
#define __spotapp_h

//    Class definition for SpotApp (TApplication).

#include <owl\owlpch.h>
```

```
#pragma hdrstop


#include "spotapp.rh"
//
// For OLE2 linking & embedding, need TOcModule,
// which coordinates with OCF
//
class SpotApp : public TApplication, public TOcModule
  {
    public:
      SpotApp ();
      virtual void InitMainWindow ();
      virtual void InitInstance ();
    protected:
      void EvNewView (TView& view);
      void EvCloseView (TView& view);
      void CmHelpAbout ();
    DECLARE_RESPONSE_TABLE(SpotApp);
};

#endif
```

Type Listing X7.2. SPOTAPP.CPP.

```
#include <owl\owlpch.h>
#pragma hdrstop
#include "spotdoc.h"
#include "spotapp.h"
#include "spotview.h"
#include "sptabtdl.h"
//
// Ole 2 linking & embedding apps (may need to) use a special
// dictionary.
//
DEFINE_APP_DICTIONARY(AppDictionary);
//
// Ole 2 linking and embedding apps need a TOcRegistrar
//
static TPointer<TOcRegistrar> Registrar;

REGISTRATION_FORMAT_BUFFER(100)

BEGIN_REGISTRATION(ApplicationReg)
//
// The following must be unique per Ole 2 application
// Use GUIDGEN to make one.
//
```

continues

Listing X7.2. continued

```
        REGDATA(clsid, "{FE91A8E0-DBDA-101B-A585-040224007802}")
        REGDATA(appname, "Spot Container & Server")
        REGDATA(description, "Spot Container & Server Application")
        REGDATA(cmdline, "")
        REGDATA(usage, ocrMultipleUse)
    END_REGISTRATION

    //
    // This builds the relationship between the document
    // and the view.
    //
    DEFINE_DOC_TEMPLATE_CLASS(SpotDoc, SpotView, SpotTemplate);

    BEGIN_REGISTRATION(__SpotRegistration)
        REGDATA(progid, "Spot.Container.1")
        REGDATA(description, "Spot Container Version 1")
        REGDATA(extension, "SPT")
        REGDATA(docfilter, "*.SPT")
        REGDOCFLAGS(dtAutoDelete ¦ dtUpdateDir ¦ dtAutoOpen ¦
                    dtRegisterExt)
        REGDATA(menuname, "Spot container")
        REGDATA(insertable, "")
        REGDATA(verb0, "&Edit")
        REGDATA(verb1, "&Open")
        REGFORMAT(0, ocrEmbedSource,  ocrContent,  ocrIStorage,
                  ocrGet)
        REGFORMAT(1, ocrMetafilePict, ocrContent,  ocrMfPict ¦
                  ocrStaticMed, ocrGet)
        REGFORMAT(2, ocrBitmap, ocrContent,  ocrGDI ¦ ocrStaticMed,
                  ocrGet)
        REGFORMAT(3, ocrDib, ocrContent,  ocrHGlobal ¦ ocrStaticMed,
                  ocrGet)
        REGFORMAT(4, ocrLinkSource, ocrContent,  ocrIStream, ocrGet)
    END_REGISTRATION
    SpotTemplate __spotTemplate(__SpotRegistration);


    //
    // Build a response table for all messages/commands handled
    // by the application.
    //
    DEFINE_RESPONSE_TABLE1(SpotApp, TApplication)
        EV_OWLVIEW(dnCreate, EvNewView),
        EV_OWLVIEW(dnClose,  EvCloseView),
        EV_COMMAND(CM_HELPABOUT, CmHelpAbout),
    END_RESPONSE_TABLE;

    //
    // Note the special constructor
```

```
//
SpotApp::SpotApp () : TApplication
   (::ApplicationReg["description"], ::Module, &::AppDictionary)
{
    //
    // Tell the doc manager what sort of application it is
    // dealing with - SDI in this case
    //
    SetDocManager(new TDocManager(dmSDI ¦ dmMenu, this));
}


//
// Application intialization.
//
void SpotApp::InitMainWindow ()
{
//
// AppExpert likes to set this in a complicated way...
//
    if (nCmdShow != SW_HIDE)
      nCmdShow = (nCmdShow != SW_SHOWMINNOACTIVE) ?
                              SW_SHOWNORMAL : nCmdShow;

    TOleFrame *frame = new TOleFrame(GetName(), 0, false, this);
    //
    // Assign ICON w/ this application.
    //
    frame->SetIcon(this, IDI_SDIAPPLICATION);
    //
    //  Menu and accelerator
    //
    frame->AssignMenu(SDI_MENU);
    frame->Attr.AccelTable = SDI_MENU;

    SetMainWindow(frame);
    //
    // OLE 2 needs to use menu descriptors for
    // easy merging of menus
    //
    frame->SetMenuDescr(TMenuDescr(SDI_MENU));
    EnableCtl3d(true);
    }
void SpotApp::InitInstance ()
{
    TApplication::InitInstance();

    if (!::Registrar->IsOptionSet(amEmbedding))
      {
          TDocTemplate* tpl = GetDocManager()
            ->MatchTemplate(GetCmdLine().c_str());
```

continues

Listing X7.2. continued

```
            if (tpl)
              {
                TDocument* doc = tpl->ConstructDoc();
                if (doc)
                  {
                    doc->SetTemplate(tpl);
                    GetDocManager()->InitDoc(doc,
                          GetCmdLine().c_str(), 0);
                    return;
                  }
                }
            GetDocManager()->CreateAnyDoc(0, dtNewDoc);
        }

  }
  // Response Table handlers:
  //
  void SpotApp::EvNewView (TView& view)
  {
     //
     // When a new view is opened - need to associate with
     // correct window. If the object is embedded and is
     // using in-place editing - get the in-place window.
     // (Can be embedded and do full-screen editing)
     //
     // Only OLE servers need this test
     //
     TOleView* ov = dynamic_cast<TOleView*>(&view);
     if (ov && view.GetDocument().IsEmbedded() &&
         !ov->GetOcRemView()->IsOpenEditing())
       {
         //
         // Embedded view window
         //
         TWindow* vw = view.GetWindow();
         vw->SetParent(dynamic_cast<TOleFrame*>(GetMainWindow())
                        ->GetRemViewBucket());
         vw->Create();
       }
      else
        {
         //
         // Normal window - associate with application
         // main window frame.
         //
         GetMainWindow()->SetClientWindow(view.GetWindow());
         if (!view.IsOK())
           GetMainWindow()->SetClientWindow(0);
```

```
        else
          if (view.GetViewMenu())
            GetMainWindow()->MergeMenu(*view.GetViewMenu());
      }
}


void SpotApp::EvCloseView (TView&)
{
    GetMainWindow()->SetClientWindow(0);
    //
    // Set caption back to just title
    //
    GetMainWindow()->SetCaption("Spot");
}
//
// Menu Help About spot.exe command
void SpotApp::CmHelpAbout ()
{
    //
    // Show the modal dialog.
    //
    // Note the special parenting command
    //
    SpotAboutDlg(&TWindow(GetMainWindow()->
         GetCommandTarget())).Execute();
}


int OwlMain (int , char* [])
{
    try
      {
        ::Registrar = new TOcRegistrar(::ApplicationReg,
                            TOleDocViewFactory<SpotApp>(),
                            TApplication::GetCmdLine(),
                            ::DocTemplateStaticHead);
        if (!::Registrar->IsOptionSet(amAnyRegOption))
        // If this is an exe server normal run, run the app now.
          ::Registrar->Run();
        ::Registrar = 0; // Explicitly free registrar
        return 0;
      }
    catch (xmsg& x)
      {
        ::MessageBox(0, x.why().c_str(), "Exception", MB_OK);
      }
    return -1;
}
```

Type

Listing X7.3. SPOTDOC.H.

```
#if !defined(__spotdoc_h)
#define __spotdoc_h

//    Class definition for SpotDoc (TOleDocument).

#include <owl\owlpch.h>
#pragma hdrstop
#include "spotapp.rh"
//
// Custom Doc/View notifications
//
const int vnDrawAppend = vnCustomBase+0;
const int vnDrawClear  = vnCustomBase+1;
//
// Custom Doc/View signatures
//
NOTIFY_SIG(vnDrawAppend, uint)
NOTIFY_SIG(vnDrawClear, void)
//
// Response table macros
//
#define EV_VN_DRAWAPPEND VN_DEFINE(vnDrawAppend,  VnAppend,  int)
#define EV_VN_DRAWCLEAR  VN_DEFINE(vnDrawClear,  VnClear,  void)

typedef TArray<TPoint> Points;
//
// Underlying OLE-capable document - uses OLE2 storage
// format
//
class SpotDoc : public TOleDocument
  {
    public:
      SpotDoc (TDocument* parent = 0);
      virtual ~SpotDoc ();
//
// SpotView helper functions
//
      TPoint* GetSpot(uint index);
      void    AddSpot(TPoint& point);
      void    Clear();
//
// Document manager functions
//
      virtual bool Open (int mode, const char far* path = 0);
      virtual bool Commit (bool force);
      virtual bool Close ();
    protected:
      Points* points;
  };
#endif
```

Listing X7.4. SPOTDOC.CPP.

```
#include <owl\owlpch.h>
#pragma hdrstop
#include "spotdoc.h"
SpotDoc::SpotDoc (TDocument* parent):
    TOleDocument(parent)
{
    points = new Points(10,0,10);
}


SpotDoc::~SpotDoc ()
{
    delete points;
}
//
// Warning! Open is called and path is never
// populated!
//
bool SpotDoc::Open (int mode, const char far* path)
{
    points->Flush();
    //
    // If new - GetDocPath() will return 0
    //
    if (GetDocPath())
      {
        //
        // Read base storage for any contained
        // objects
        //
        TOleDocument::Open(mode,path);
        //
        // Get the file stream
        //
        TInStream* is = (TInStream*)InStream(ofRead);
        //
        // If cannot open file, will be zero
        //
        if (!is)
          return false;
        // reference for convenience
        TInStream& in = *is;
        //
        // Check how many points to read
        //
        //
        uint pointCount;
        in >> pointCount;
```

continues

Listing X7.4. continued

```
            //
            // Read specified number of points
            //
            TPoint p;
            for (int i = 0; i < pointCount; i++)
             {
               in >> p;
               points->Add(p); // Add to container
             }
            delete is;
         }
        SetDirty(false);        // Mark as unchanged
        return true;
      }
    bool SpotDoc::Commit (bool force)
    {
        bool result;
        //
        // Write out contained objects
        //
        result = TOleDocument::Commit(force);
        //
        // Get output stream to write own data
        //
        TOutStream* os = OutStream(ofWrite);
        if (!os)
          return false;
        TOutStream& out = *os; // reference for convenience
        //
        // Write out number of points
        //
        out << points->GetItemsInContainer();
        //
        // For each point, write out to stream
        //
        for (int i = 0; i < points->GetItemsInContainer();i++)
          out << (*points)[i];
        delete os;
        //
        // Mark document as matching
        //
        SetDirty(false);
        //
        // Very important line! This forces write to disk;
        // without this, the file IS created but is corrupt.
        //
        TOleDocument::CommitTransactedStorage();
```

```
    return true;
}

//
// Close document
//
bool SpotDoc::Close()
  {
    points->Flush();
    return TOleDocument::Close();
  }
//
// View service functions
//
//  GetSpot returns a point at index
//
TPoint* SpotDoc::GetSpot(uint index)
  {
    if (points && index < points->GetItemsInContainer())
      return &(*points)[index];
    else
      return 0;
  }
//
// Add spot to collection
//
void SpotDoc::AddSpot(TPoint& point)
  {
    points->Add(point);
    // Picture has changed - set dirty flag
    SetDirty(true);
    //
    // Notify all views that the view has changed
    // Pass the index of the new point so that the
    // views can draw the new spot without redrawing
    // the entire screen.
    //
    // vnDrawAppend is defined in the header
    //
    NotifyViews(vnDrawAppend, points->GetItemsInContainer() - 1);
  }
//
// Entirely clear document
//
void SpotDoc::Clear()
  {
    //
    // Clear the document data
    //
```

continues

Listing X7.4. continued

```
    points->Flush();
    SetDirty(true);
    //
    // Tell view to empty container
    //

    NotifyViews(vnDrawClear,0);
  }
```

Listing X7.5. SPOTVIEW.H.

```
#if !defined(__spotview_h)
#define __spotview_h
#include <owl\owlpch.h>
#pragma hdrstop


#include "spotapp.rh"              // Definition of all resources.
#include "spotdoc.h"
//
// View class (may be several instances of this per
// document)
//
class SpotView : public TOleView
  {
    public:
      SpotView (SpotDoc& doc, TWindow* parent = 0);
      virtual ~SpotView ();
      virtual void Paint (TDC& dc, bool erase, TRect& rect);
      virtual const char far* GetViewName ();
      static const char far* StaticName ();
    protected:
      SpotDoc& spotDoc;  // Parent document
      TBrush* backBrush;
      TBrush* spotBrush;
      TPoint storePoint;
      TControlBar * toolBar;
      //
      // Draw a spot from a view
      //
      void SpotView::DrawSpot(TDC& dc, const TPoint& point);
      void EvLButtonDown (uint modKeys, TPoint& point);
      void EvMouseMove (uint modKeys, TPoint& point);
      void EvLButtonUp (uint modKeys, TPoint& point);
      void CmClear ();
      void CmEditCopy ();
```

```
        void CmEditCut ();
        bool EvOcViewPartSize(TOcPartSize far& ps);
        bool EvOcViewShowTools(TOcToolBarInfo far& tbi);

    // Document notifications
        bool VnCommit(bool force); // Document saved
        bool VnRevert(bool clear); // Document restored
        bool VnAppend(uint index); // Document amended
        bool VnClear();            // document blanked
        DECLARE_RESPONSE_TABLE(SpotView);
};

#endif
```

Listing X7.6. SPOTVIEW.CPP.

```
#include <owl\owlpch.h>
#pragma hdrstop

#include "sptabtdl.h"
#include "spotapp.h"
#include "spotview.h"
#include "spotapp.rh"
#include <stdio.h>

const int spotRadius = 10; // Spot size
//
// Build a response table for all messages/commands handled
// by the application.
//
DEFINE_RESPONSE_TABLE1(SpotView, TOleView)
  //
  // Standard messages
  //
  EV_WM_LBUTTONDOWN,
  EV_WM_MOUSEMOVE,
  EV_WM_LBUTTONUP,
  EV_COMMAND(CM_EDITCLEAR, CmClear),
  EV_COMMAND(CM_EDITCOPY, CmEditCopy),
  EV_COMMAND(CM_EDITCUT, CmEditCut),
  //
  // View notifications
  //
  EV_VN_COMMIT,
  EV_VN_REVERT,
  EV_VN_DRAWAPPEND,
  EV_VN_DRAWCLEAR,
```

continues

Listing X7.6. continued

```
    //
    // OCF notifications
    //
    EV_OC_VIEWPARTSIZE,
    EV_OC_VIEWSHOWTOOLS,
END_RESPONSE_TABLE;

// SpotView
// ==========
// Construction/Destruction handling.
SpotView::SpotView (SpotDoc& doc, TWindow* parent)
    : TOleView(doc, parent),
      spotDoc(doc)
{
    backBrush = new TBrush(TColor::LtMagenta);
    spotBrush = new TBrush(TColor::LtYellow);
    toolBar = 0;
}


SpotView::~SpotView ()
{
    delete backBrush;
    delete spotBrush;
    delete toolbar;    // Just in case
}
//
// Class and View names
//
const char far* SpotView::GetViewName ()
{
    return "SpotViewClass";
}
const char far* SpotView::StaticName ()
{
    return "Spot View";
}
//
// Paint is not only called for window, but also to update
// OLE2 metafile
//
void SpotView::Paint (TDC& dc, bool erase, TRect& rect)
{
    TPoint* spot;
    //
    TRect clientRect(0,0,GetSystemMetrics(SM_CXSCREEN),
                         GetSystemMetrics(SM_CYSCREEN));
```

```
    dc.FillRect(clientRect,*backBrush);

    //
    // This line paints the OLE embedded objects
    // (note: OLE objects are painted from a metafile and
    // do not require the server to be present)
    //
    TOleView::Paint(dc, false, rect);
    //
    // Spots before your eyes...
    //
    dc.SelectObject(*spotBrush);
    int i = 0;
    do
      {
        spot = spotDoc.GetSpot(i++);
        if (spot)
          DrawSpot(dc,*spot);
      }
    while (spot);

    dc.RestoreBrush();
}
void SpotView::DrawSpot(TDC& dc, const TPoint& point)
  {
    int radius = spotRadius;
    TRect spotRect(point.x - radius,
                   point.y - radius,
                   point.x + radius,
                   point.y + radius);
    dc.Ellipse(spotRect);

  }


void SpotView::EvLButtonDown (uint modKeys, TPoint& point)
{
    //
    // Base call sets up DragDC - it also modifies point
    // to be in logical units. This enables in-place editing
    // to work when the window has been stretched
    //
    TOleView::EvLButtonDown(modKeys, point);
    if (DragDC && !SelectEmbedded())
      {
        //
        // If haven't hit an OLE object -
        // capture mouse and draw temporary spot
        //
```

continues

Listing X7.6. continued

```
            SetCapture();
            DragDC->SetROP2(R2_XORPEN);      // Invert drawing
            storePoint = point;              // store point
            DragDC->SelectObject(*spotBrush);
            DrawSpot(*DragDC,storePoint);   // Draw spot inverted
          }
    }


void SpotView::EvMouseMove (uint modKeys, TPoint& point)
{
    TOleView::EvMouseMove(modKeys, point); // point modified
    if (DragDC&& !SelectEmbedded())  // If not dragging OLE object
      {
        DrawSpot(*DragDC,storePoint); // Clear up spot
        storePoint = point;
        DrawSpot(*DragDC,storePoint); // Spot breaks out again
      }

}


void SpotView::EvLButtonUp (uint modKeys, TPoint& point)
{
    if (DragDC && !SelectEmbedded()) // Not OLE2 object
      {
        DrawSpot(*DragDC,storePoint); // Clear up spot
        storePoint = point;           // Store point
        DragDC->DPtoLP(&storePoint);  // Convert to LPs
        ReleaseCapture();
        spotDoc.AddSpot(storePoint);
      }
                                      // Inconsistent:
    TOleView::EvLButtonUp(modKeys, point);
                                      // Does not convert point
                                      // except if using itself
}
//
// Let container know about the server view size in pixels
//
bool
SpotView::EvOcViewPartSize(TOcPartSize far& ps)
{
  TClientDC dc(*this);
  // Set minimum size...
  TRect rect(0, 0, 0, 0);
  // a 2" x 2" extent for server
  //
  rect.right  = dc.GetDeviceCaps(LOGPIXELSX) * 2;
```

```
  rect.bottom = dc.GetDeviceCaps(LOGPIXELSY) * 2;
  //
  // Note: this would be better calculated on open of
  // view and when data changed - but for simplicity, I have
  // just done it a nasty way.
  //
  // Declare picture size to be a minimum of 2" x 2"
  // but enable user to add more points for scaling
  //
  // Iterate through all the points and calculate the
  // most extreme
  //
  uint i = 0;
  TPoint* point = spotDoc.GetSpot(i++);
  while (point)
    {
      if (point->x > rect.bottom)
        rect.bottom = point->x;
      if (point->y > rect.right)
        rect.right = point->y;
      point = spotDoc.GetSpot(i++);
    }
  ps.PartRect = rect;
  return true;
}
//
// Give toolbar to container application.
// Note: to emphasize the point, when executing, the
// server does not have a toolbar - only when embedding.
// For the application, create a toolbar in the standard
// fashion. (Give it an Attr.Id of IDW_TOOLBAR)
//
bool
SpotView::EvOcViewShowTools(TOcToolBarInfo far& tbi)
{
  //
  // Construct & create a control bar for show;
  // destroy our bar for hide
  //
  if (tbi.Show)
    {
      if (!toolBar)
        {
          toolBar = new TControlBar(this);
          toolBar->Insert(*new TButtonGadget(CM_EDITCLEAR,
                       CM_EDITCLEAR, TButtonGadget::Command));
          toolBar->Insert(*new TSeparatorGadget);
          toolBar->Insert(*new TButtonGadget(CM_HELPABOUT,
                       CM_HELPABOUT, TButtonGadget::Command));
        }
    toolBar->Create();
```

continues

Listing X7.6. continued

```
      tbi.HTopTB = (HWND)*toolBar;
    }
    else
      {
        if (toolBar)
          {
            toolBar->Destroy();
            delete toolBar;
            toolBar = 0;
          }
      }
    return true;
}


bool SpotView::VnCommit(bool /*force*/)
{
  // nothing to do here; no data held in view
  return true;
}

bool SpotView::VnRevert(bool /*clear*/)
{
  Invalidate();  // force full repaint
  return true;
}
//
// View notification that the document has been
// emptied
//
bool SpotView::VnClear()
  {
  Invalidate();  // force full repaint
  //
  // Component parts are held in a collection
  // iterate the collection to remove the data
  //
  for (TOcPartCollectionIter i(GetOcDoc()->GetParts()); i; i++)
    {
      TOcPart* p = i.Current();
      TOcPartChangeInfo changeInfo(p, invData¦invView);
      EvOcViewPartInvalid(changeInfo);
      GetOcDoc()->GetParts().Detach(p,true);
    }
  InvalidatePart(invData¦invView);
  return true;
}
//
// View notiification that the document has been added to
//
```

```
bool SpotView::VnAppend(uint index)
{
  //
  // Append a spot onto current views - could be a metafile
  //
  // Get a dc for the view window
  TClientDC dc(*this);
  //
  // Get the spot notified at index
  //
  const TPoint* spot = spotDoc.GetSpot(index);
  bool metafile = dc.GetDeviceCaps(TECHNOLOGY) == DT_METAFILE;
  //
  // If drawing to metafile, need to scale
  //
  SetupDC(dc, !metafile);
  dc.SelectObject(*spotBrush);
  DrawSpot(dc,*spot);
  //
  // Tell container to redraw
  //
  InvalidatePart(invView);
  return true;
}


void SpotView::CmClear ()
{
    //
    // Tell document to clear down
    //
    spotDoc.Clear();
}


void SpotView::CmEditCopy ()
{
  //
  // Supposed to be able to copy view to Clipboard
  //
  // Not implemented at time of writing
  //
    TOcRemView* orv = GetOcRemView();
  //  if (orv)
  //     orv->Copy();
}


void SpotView::CmEditCut ()
{
    // Do nothing... nothing sensible to do
}
```

Listing X7.7. SPOTAB.H.

```
#if !defined(__sptab_h)
#define __sptab_h

#include <owl\owlpch.h>
#pragma hdrstop

#include "spotapp.rh"
class SpotAboutDlg : public TDialog
 {
  public:
    SpotAboutDlg (TWindow *parent, TResId resId = IDD_ABOUT,
                  TModule *module = 0);
    virtual ~SpotAboutDlg ();
  public:
    void SetupWindow ();
};
// Reading the VERSIONINFO resource.
class ProjectRCVersion
  {
    public:
      ProjectRCVersion (TModule *module);
      virtual ~ProjectRCVersion ();

      bool GetProductName (LPSTR &prodName);
      bool GetProductVersion (LPSTR &prodVersion);
      bool GetCopyright (LPSTR &copyright);
      bool GetDebug (LPSTR &debug);

    protected:
      LPBYTE      TransBlock;
      void FAR    *FVData;

    private:
    // Don't enable this object to be copied.
    ProjectRCVersion (const ProjectRCVersion &);
    ProjectRCVersion & operator =(const ProjectRCVersion &);
  };

#endif
```

Type Listing X7.8. SPOTAB.CPP.

```
#include <owl\owlpch.h>
#pragma hdrstop

#if !defined(__FLAT__)
#include <ver.h>
#endif

#include "spotapp.h"
#include "spotab.h"
//
// AppExpert generated About box
//
ProjectRCVersion::ProjectRCVersion (TModule *module)
{
    char    appFName[255];
    char    subBlockName[255];
    DWORD   fvHandle;
    UINT    vSize;

    FVData = 0;

    module->GetModuleFileName(appFName, sizeof(appFName));
    DWORD dwSize = ::GetFileVersionInfoSize(appFName,&fvHandle);
    if (dwSize)
     {
        FVData  = (void FAR *)new char[(UINT)dwSize];
        if (::GetFileVersionInfo(appFName, fvHandle, dwSize,
                                 FVData))
          {
            strcpy(subBlockName, "\\VarFileInfo\\Translation");
            if (!::VerQueryValue(FVData, subBlockName,
                          (void FAR* FAR*)&TransBlock, &vSize))
              {
                delete FVData;
                FVData = 0;
              }
            else
                *(DWORD *)TransBlock =
                             MAKELONG(HIWORD(*(DWORD *)TransBlock),
                             LOWORD(*(DWORD *)TransBlock));
          }
     }
  }


ProjectRCVersion::~ProjectRCVersion ()
  {
    if (FVData)
```

continues

Listing X7.8. continued

```
        delete FVData;
  }


bool ProjectRCVersion::GetProductName (LPSTR &prodName)
  {
    UINT    vSize;
    char    subBlockName[255];

    wsprintf(subBlockName, "\\StringFileInfo\\%08lx\\%s",
      *(DWORD *)TransBlock, (LPSTR)"ProductName");
    return FVData ? ::VerQueryValue(FVData, subBlockName,
                        (void FAR* FAR*)&prodName, &vSize) : false;
  }


bool ProjectRCVersion::GetProductVersion (LPSTR &prodVersion)
  {
     UINT    vSize;
     char    subBlockName[255];

     wsprintf(subBlockName, "\\StringFileInfo\\%08lx\\%s",
            *(DWORD *)TransBlock, (LPSTR)"ProductVersion");
     return FVData ? ::VerQueryValue(FVData, subBlockName,
            (void FAR* FAR*)&prodVersion, &vSize) : false;
  }


bool ProjectRCVersion::GetCopyright (LPSTR &copyright)
  {
    UINT    vSize;
    char    subBlockName[255];

    wsprintf(subBlockName, "\\StringFileInfo\\%08lx\\%s",
            *(DWORD *)TransBlock, (LPSTR)"LegalCopyright");
    return FVData ? ::VerQueryValue(FVData, subBlockName,
           (void FAR* FAR*)&copyright, &vSize) : false;
  }


bool ProjectRCVersion::GetDebug (LPSTR &debug)
{
    UINT    vSize;
    char    subBlockName[255];

    wsprintf(subBlockName, "\\StringFileInfo\\%08lx\\%s",
            *(DWORD *)TransBlock, (LPSTR)"SpecialBuild");
    return FVData ? ::VerQueryValue(FVData, subBlockName,
```

```
            (void FAR* FAR*)&debug, &vSize) : false;
}


SpotAboutDlg::SpotAboutDlg (TWindow *parent, TResId resId,
                            TModule *module)
    : TDialog(parent, resId, module)
 {
 }

SpotAboutDlg::~SpotAboutDlg ()
  {
    Destroy();
  }

void SpotAboutDlg::SetupWindow ()
{
    LPSTR prodName = 0, prodVersion = 0, copyright = 0, debug = 0;

    // Get the static text for the value based on VERSIONINFO.
    TStatic *versionCtrl = new TStatic(this, IDC_VERSION, 255);
    TStatic *copyrightCtrl = new TStatic(this, IDC_COPYRIGHT,
                                         255);
    TStatic *debugCtrl = new TStatic(this, IDC_DEBUG, 255);
    TDialog::SetupWindow();
    // Process the VERSIONINFO.
    ProjectRCVersion applVersion(GetModule());
    // Get the product name and product version strings.
    if (applVersion.GetProductName(prodName) &&
        applVersion.GetProductVersion(prodVersion)) {
        char    buffer[255];
        char    versionName[128];
        buffer[0] = '\0';
        versionName[0] = '\0';
        versionCtrl->GetText(versionName, sizeof(versionName));
        wsprintf(buffer, "%s %s %s", prodName,
                 versionName, prodVersion);
        versionCtrl->SetText(buffer);
    }
    //Get the legal copyright string.
    if (applVersion.GetCopyright(copyright))
        copyrightCtrl->SetText(copyright);
    if (applVersion.GetDebug(debug))
        debugCtrl->SetText(debug);
  }
```

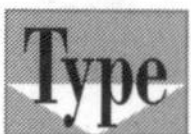

Listing X7.9. SPOTAPP.RH.

```
//#if !defined(__spotapp_rh)
//#define __spotapp_rh
//
// IDHELP BorButton for BWCC dialogs.
//
#define IDHELP      998              // Id of help button


//
// Application-specific definitions:
//
#define IDI_SDIAPPLICATION      1001  // Application icon

#define SDI_MENU                100   // Menu and Accelerator IDs

#define IDM_DOCMANAGERFILE      32401
                               // Menu for DocManager merging.

//
// OleView merged menus (include\owl\oleview.rh)
//
#define IDM_OLEPOPUP            32405
#define IDM_OLEVIEW             32406


//
// CM_FILEnnnn commands
//  (include\owl\editfile.rh except for CM_FILEPRINTPREVIEW)
//
#define CM_FILENEW              24331           // SDI New
#define CM_FILEOPEN             24332           // SDI Open
#define CM_FILECLOSE            24339
#define CM_FILESAVE             24333
#define CM_FILESAVEAS           24334
#define CM_FILEREVERT           24335
#define CM_VIEWCREATE           24341


//
// Window commands (include\owl\window.rh)
//
#define CM_EXIT                 24310


//
// CM_EDITnnnn commands (include\owl\window.rh)
//
```

```
#define CM_EDITUNDO              24321
#define CM_EDITCUT               24322
#define CM_EDITCOPY              24323
#define CM_EDITPASTE             24324
#define CM_EDITDELETE            24325
#define CM_EDITCLEAR             24326
#define CM_EDITADD               24327
#define CM_EDITEDIT              24328
#define CM_EDITPASTESPECIAL      24311
#define CM_EDITPASTELINK         24312
#define CM_EDITINSERTOBJECT      24313
#define CM_EDITLINKS             24314

#define CM_EDITOBJECT            24370
#define CM_EDITFIRSTVERB         24371        // 20 verbs at most
#define CM_EDITLASTVERB          24390

#define CM_EDITCONVERT           24391
#define CM_EDITSHOWOBJECTS       24392


//
// Search menu commands (include\owl\editsear.rh)
//
#define CM_EDITFIND              24351
#define CM_EDITREPLACE           24352
#define CM_EDITFINDNEXT          24353


//
// Help menu commands.
//
#define CM_HELPABOUT             2009


//
// About Dialogs
//
#define IDD_ABOUT                22000
#define IDC_VERSION              22001
#define IDC_COPYRIGHT            22002
#define IDC_DEBUG                22003


//
// OWL defined strings
//

// Status bar
#define IDS_MODES                32530
```

continues

Listing X7.9. continued

```
#define IDS_MODESOFF              32531


// EditFile
#define IDS_UNABLEREAD            32551
#define IDS_UNABLEWRITE           32552
#define IDS_FILECHANGED           32553
#define IDS_FILEFILTER            32554

// EditSearch
#define IDS_CANNOTFIND            32540


//
// General & application exception messages
//  (include\owl\except.rh)
//
#define IDS_UNKNOWNEXCEPTION      32767
#define IDS_OWLEXCEPTION          32766
#define IDS_OKTORESUME            32765
#define IDS_UNHANDLEDXMSG         32764
#define IDS_UNKNOWNERROR          32763
#define IDS_NOAPP                 32762
#define IDS_OUTOFMEMORY           32761
#define IDS_INVALIDMODULE         32760
#define IDS_INVALIDMAINWINDOW     32759
#define IDS_VBXLIBRARYFAIL        32758

//
// Owl 1 compatibility messages
//
#define IDS_INVALIDWINDOW         32756
#define IDS_INVALIDCHILDWINDOW    32755
#define IDS_INVALIDCLIENTWINDOW   32754

//
// TXWindow messages
//
#define IDS_CLASSREGISTERFAIL     32749
#define IDS_CHILDREGISTERFAIL     32748
#define IDS_WINDOWCREATEFAIL      32747
#define IDS_WINDOWEXECUTEFAIL     32746
#define IDS_CHILDCREATEFAIL       32745

#define IDS_MENUFAILURE           32744
#define IDS_VALIDATORSYNTAX       32743
#define IDS_PRINTERERROR          32742

#define IDS_LAYOUTINCOMPLETE      32741
```

```
#define IDS_LAYOUTBADRELWIN     32740

//
// TXGdi messages
//
#define IDS_GDIFAILURE          32739
#define IDS_GDIALLOCFAIL        32738
#define IDS_GDICREATEFAIL       32737
#define IDS_GDIRESLOADFAIL      32736
#define IDS_GDIFILEREADFAIL     32735
#define IDS_GDIDELETEFAIL       32734
#define IDS_GDIDESTROYFAIL      32733
#define IDS_INVALIDDIBHANDLE    32732


// ListView (include\owl\listview.rh)
#define IDS_LISTNUM             32584


// DocView (include\owl\docview.rh)
#define IDS_DOCMANAGERFILE      32500
#define IDS_DOCLIST             32501
#define IDS_VIEWLIST            32502
#define IDS_UNTITLED            32503
#define IDS_UNABLEOPEN          32504
#define IDS_UNABLECLOSE         32505
#define IDS_READERROR           32506
#define IDS_WRITEERROR          32507
#define IDS_DOCCHANGED          32508
#define IDS_NOTCHANGED          32509
#define IDS_NODOCMANAGER        32510
#define IDS_NOMEMORYFORVIEW     32511
#define IDS_DUPLICATEDOC        32512
#define IDS_EDITOBJECT          32600
#define IDS_EDITCONVERT         32601
#define IDS_CLOSESERVER         32602
#define IDS_EXITSERVER          32603

// Text for Clipboard format names
#define IDS_CFTEXT              32610
#define IDS_CFBITMAP            32611
#define IDS_CFMETAFILE          32612
#define IDS_CFSYLK              32613
#define IDS_CFDIF               32614
#define IDS_CFTIFF              32615
#define IDS_CFOEMTEXT           32616
#define IDS_CFDIB               32617
#define IDS_CFPALETTE           32618
#define IDS_CFPENDATA           32619
#define IDS_CFRIFF              32620
#define IDS_CFWAVE              32621
```

continues

Listing X7.9. continued

```
#define IDS_CFUNICODETEXT       32622
#define IDS_CFENHMETAFILE       32623

#define IDS_IN                  32700


//#endif
```

Listing X7.10. SPOTAPP.RC.

```
#if !defined(WORKSHOP_INVOKED)
#include <windows.h>
#endif
#include "spotapp.rh"
//
// Standard application menu
//
SDI_MENU MENU
{
 POPUP "&File"
 {
  MENUITEM "&New", CM_FILENEW
  MENUITEM "&Open...", CM_FILEOPEN
  MENUITEM SEPARATOR
  MENUITEM "&Save", CM_FILESAVE, GRAYED
  MENUITEM "Save &As...", CM_FILESAVEAS, GRAYED
  MENUITEM SEPARATOR
  MENUITEM "E&xit\tAlt+F4", CM_EXIT
 }

 MENUITEM SEPARATOR
 POPUP "&Edit"
 {
  MENUITEM "&Undo\tAlt+BkSp", CM_EDITUNDO, GRAYED
  MENUITEM SEPARATOR
  MENUITEM "Cu&t\tShift+Del", CM_EDITCUT, GRAYED
  MENUITEM "&Copy\tCtrl+Ins", CM_EDITCOPY, GRAYED
  MENUITEM "&Paste\tShift+Ins", CM_EDITPASTE, GRAYED
  MENUITEM "Paste &Special...",    CM_EDITPASTESPECIAL
  MENUITEM "Paste &Link",          CM_EDITPASTELINK
  MENUITEM SEPARATOR
  MENUITEM "Clear &All\tCtrl+Del", CM_EDITCLEAR, GRAYED
  MENUITEM Separator
  MENUITEM "&Insert Object...",    CM_EDITINSERTOBJECT
  MENUITEM "&Links...",            CM_EDITLINKS
  MENUITEM "&Object",              CM_EDITOBJECT
```

```
  MENUITEM Separator
  MENUITEM "&Show Objects",        CM_EDITSHOWOBJECTS
 }

 MENUITEM SEPARATOR
 MENUITEM SEPARATOR
 MENUITEM SEPARATOR
 MENUITEM SEPARATOR
 POPUP "&Help"
 {
  MENUITEM "&About...", CM_HELPABOUT
 }

}


// Accelerator table for short-cut to menu commands.
(include\owl\editfile.rc)
SDI_MENU ACCELERATORS
BEGIN
  VK_DELETE, CM_EDITDELETE, VIRTKEY
  VK_DELETE, CM_EDITCUT, VIRTKEY, SHIFT
  VK_INSERT, CM_EDITCOPY, VIRTKEY, CONTROL
  VK_INSERT, CM_EDITPASTE, VIRTKEY, SHIFT
  VK_DELETE, CM_EDITCLEAR, VIRTKEY, CONTROL
  VK_BACK,   CM_EDITUNDO, VIRTKEY, ALT
  VK_F3,     CM_EDITFINDNEXT, VIRTKEY
END


// DocManager File menu

IDM_DOCMANAGERFILE MENU LOADONCALL MOVEABLE PURE DISCARDABLE
BEGIN
    MENUITEM "&New", CM_FILENEW
    MENUITEM "&Open...", CM_FILEOPEN
    MENUITEM "&Close", CM_FILECLOSE
    MENUITEM SEPARATOR
    MENUITEM "&Save", CM_FILESAVE, GRAYED
    MENUITEM "Save &As...", CM_FILESAVEAS, GRAYED
    MENUITEM SEPARATOR
    MENUITEM "E&xit\tAlt+F4", CM_EXIT
END


// Menu merged in when TOleView is active;
// notice the extra MENUITEM SEPARATORs, which are
// for menu negotation.  These separators are used as group
// markers by OWL.
IDM_OLEVIEW MENU
{
```

continues

Listing X7.10. continued

```
 MENUITEM SEPARATOR
 POPUP "&Edit"
 {
  MENUITEM "&Undo\aCtrl+Z", CM_EDITUNDO
  MENUITEM SEPARATOR
  MENUITEM "&Cut\aCtrl+X", CM_EDITCUT
  MENUITEM "C&opy\aCtrl+C", CM_EDITCOPY
  MENUITEM "&Paste\aCtrl+V", CM_EDITPASTE
  MENUITEM "Paste &Special...", CM_EDITPASTESPECIAL
  MENUITEM "Paste &Link", CM_EDITPASTELINK
  MENUITEM "Clear &All\aCtrl+Del", CM_EDITCLEAR
  MENUITEM Separator
  MENUITEM "&Insert Object...",    CM_EDITINSERTOBJECT
  MENUITEM "&Links...",            CM_EDITLINKS
  MENUITEM "&Object",              CM_EDITOBJECT
  MENUITEM Separator
  MENUITEM "&Show Objects",        CM_EDITSHOWOBJECTS

 }

 MENUITEM SEPARATOR
 MENUITEM SEPARATOR
 MENUITEM SEPARATOR
 MENUITEM SEPARATOR
 POPUP "&Help"
 {
  MENUITEM "&About...", CM_HELPABOUT
 }

}
//
// OLE pop-up
//

IDM_OLEPOPUP MENU LOADONCALL MOVEABLE PURE DISCARDABLE
BEGIN
    POPUP "OLE"
    BEGIN
        MENUITEM "&Cut\aCtrl+X", CM_EDITCUT
        MENUITEM "C&opy\aCtrl+C", CM_EDITCOPY
        MENUITEM "&Delete\aDel", CM_EDITDELETE
        MENUITEM SEPARATOR
        MENUITEM "&Object", CM_EDITOBJECT
    END
END


//
// Table of help hints displayed in the status bar.
//
```

```
STRINGTABLE
BEGIN
    -1,             "File/document operations"
    CM_FILENEW,     "Creates a new document"
    CM_FILEOPEN,    "Opens an existing document"
    CM_VIEWCREATE,  "Creates a new view for this document"
    CM_FILEREVERT,  "Reverts changes to last document save"
    CM_FILECLOSE,   "Closes this document"
    CM_FILESAVE,    "Saves this document"
    CM_FILESAVEAS,  "Saves this document with a new name"
    CM_EXIT,        "Quits Spot and prompts to save the documents"
    CM_EDITUNDO-1,  "Edits operations"
    CM_EDITUNDO,    "Reverses the last operation"
    CM_EDITCUT,  "Cuts the selection and puts it on the Clipboard"
    CM_EDITCOPY,  "Copies selection and puts it on the Clipboard"
    CM_EDITPASTE, "Inserts clipboard contents at insertion point"
    CM_EDITPASTESPECIAL, "Selects paste option and format"
    CM_EDITPASTELINK,    "Links with object on the clipboard"
    CM_EDITDELETE,  "Deletes the selection"
    CM_EDITCLEAR,   "Clears the document"
    CM_EDITLINKS,   "Edit links to the document"
    CM_EDITINSERTOBJECT,     "Inserts an object into the document"
    CM_EDITOBJECT,  "Asks the selected object to perform an action"
    CM_EDITSHOWOBJECTS,      "Hilights selected object"
    CM_EDITADD,     "Inserts a new line"
    CM_EDITEDIT,    "Edits the current line"
    CM_EDITFIND-1,  "Search/replace operations"
    CM_EDITFIND,    "Finds the specified text"
    CM_EDITREPLACE, "Finds the specified text and changes it"
    CM_EDITFINDNEXT,"Finds the next match"
    CM_HELPABOUT-1, "Access About"
    CM_HELPABOUT,   "About the Spot application"
END

//
// OWL string table
//

// EditFile (include\owl\editfile.rc and include\owl\editsear.rc)
STRINGTABLE LOADONCALL MOVEABLE DISCARDABLE
BEGIN
    IDS_CANNOTFIND,  "Cannot find ""%s""."
    IDS_UNABLEREAD,  "Unable to read file %s from disk."
    IDS_UNABLEWRITE, "Unable to write file %s to disk."
    IDS_FILECHANGED, "The text in the %s file has changed."
                     "\n\nDo you want to save the changes?"
    IDS_FILEFILTER,  "Text files (*.TXT)¦*.TXT¦AllFiles
                     "(*.*)¦*.*¦"
END
```

continues

Listing X7.10. continued

```
// ListView (include\owl\listview.rc)
STRINGTABLE LOADONCALL MOVEABLE DISCARDABLE
BEGIN
  IDS_LISTNUM,  "Line number %d"
END


// Doc/View (include\owl\docview.rc)
STRINGTABLE LOADONCALL MOVEABLE DISCARDABLE
BEGIN
    IDS_DOCMANAGERFILE,          "&File"
    IDS_DOCLIST,                 "--Document Type--"
    IDS_VIEWLIST,                "--View Type--"
    IDS_UNTITLED,                "Document"
    IDS_UNABLEOPEN,              "Unable to open document."
    IDS_UNABLECLOSE,             "Unable to close document."
    IDS_READERROR,               "Document read error."
    IDS_WRITEERROR,              "Document write error."
    IDS_DOCCHANGED,              "The document has been"
            "changed.\n\nDo you want to save the changes?"
    IDS_NOTCHANGED,        "The document has not been changed."
    IDS_NODOCMANAGER,            "Document Manager not present."
    IDS_NOMEMORYFORVIEW,         "Insufficient memory for view."
    IDS_DUPLICATEDOC,            "Document already loaded."
END


// OLEView (include\owl\oleview.rc)
STRINGTABLE LOADONCALL MOVEABLE DISCARDABLE
BEGIN
     IDS_EDITOBJECT,             "&Object"
     IDS_EDITCONVERT,            "Convert..."
     IDS_CLOSESERVER,            "Close and Return to "
     IDS_EXITSERVER,             "Exit and Return to "
END

STRINGTABLE LOADONCALL MOVEABLE DISCARDABLE
BEGIN
    IDS_CFTEXT,                  "Text\nplain text"
    IDS_CFBITMAP,                "Bitmap\na bitmap image"
    IDS_CFMETAFILE,              "Metafile Picture\na static picture"
    IDS_CFSYLK,                  "Sylk\na spreadsheet"
    IDS_CFDIF,                   "DIF\na document"
    IDS_CFTIFF,                  "Tagged Image File Format\na "
                                 "TIFF image file"
    IDS_CFOEMTEXT,               "OEM Text\nan OEM text"
    IDS_CFDIB,                   "DIB\na device independent bitmap"
                                 "image"
```

```
    IDS_CFPALETTE,              "Palette\na color palette"
    IDS_CFPENDATA,              "Pen Data\npen data"
    IDS_CFRIFF,                 "RIFF\na RIFF media file"
    IDS_CFWAVE,                 "Wave\na sound wave file"
    IDS_CFUNICODETEXT,          "UniCode Text\nUnicode text"
    IDS_CFENHMETAFILE,          "Enhanced Metafile\nan "
                                "enhanced metafile picture"
    IDS_IN,                     " in "
END


// Exception string resources (include\owl\except.rc)
STRINGTABLE LOADONCALL MOVEABLE DISCARDABLE
BEGIN
    IDS_OWLEXCEPTION,           "ObjectWindows Exception"
    IDS_UNHANDLEDXMSG,          "Unhandled Exception"
    IDS_OKTORESUME,             "OK to resume?"
    IDS_UNKNOWNEXCEPTION,       "Unknown exception"

    IDS_UNKNOWNERROR,           "Unknown error"
    IDS_NOAPP,                  "No application object"
    IDS_OUTOFMEMORY,            "Out of memory"
    IDS_INVALIDMODULE,      "Invalid module specified for window"
    IDS_INVALIDMAINWINDOW,      "Invalid MainWindow"
    IDS_VBXLIBRARYFAIL,         "VBX Library init failure"

    IDS_INVALIDWINDOW,          "Invalid window %s"
    IDS_INVALIDCHILDWINDOW,     "Invalid child window %s"
    IDS_INVALIDCLIENTWINDOW,    "Invalid client window %s"

    IDS_CLASSREGISTERFAIL,
             "Class registration fail for window %s"
    IDS_CHILDREGISTERFAIL,
             "Child class registration fail for window %s"
    IDS_WINDOWCREATEFAIL,       "Create fail for window %s"
    IDS_WINDOWEXECUTEFAIL,      "Execute fail for window %s"
    IDS_CHILDCREATEFAIL,        "Child create fail for window %s"

    IDS_MENUFAILURE,            "Menu creation failure"
    IDS_VALIDATORSYNTAX,        "Validator syntax error"
    IDS_PRINTERERROR,           "Printer error"

    IDS_LAYOUTINCOMPLETE,
         "Incomplete layout constraints specified in window %s"
    IDS_LAYOUTBADRELWIN,
        "Invalid relative window specified in layout constraint
         in window %s"

    IDS_GDIFAILURE,             "GDI failure"
    IDS_GDIALLOCFAIL,           "GDI allocate failure"
    IDS_GDICREATEFAIL,          "GDI creation failure"
```

continues

Listing X7.10. continued

```
    IDS_GDIRESLOADFAIL,             "GDI resource load failure"
    IDS_GDIFILEREADFAIL,            "GDI file read failure"
    IDS_GDIDELETEFAIL,              "GDI object %X delete failure"
    IDS_GDIDESTROYFAIL,             "GDI object %X destroy failure"
    IDS_INVALIDDIBHANDLE,           "Invalid DIB handle %X"
END


// General Window's status bar messages. (include\owl\statusba.rc)
STRINGTABLE
BEGIN
    IDS_MODES                       "EXT¦CAPS¦NUM¦SCRL¦OVR¦REC"
    IDS_MODESOFF                    "   ¦    ¦   ¦    ¦   ¦   "
    SC_SIZE,                "Changes the size of the window"
    SC_MOVE,                "Moves the window to another position"
    SC_MINIMIZE,            "Reduces the window to an icon"
    SC_MAXIMIZE,            "Enlarges the window to its maximum size"
    SC_RESTORE,             "Restores the window to its previous size"
    SC_CLOSE,                       "Closes the window"
    SC_TASKLIST,                    "Opens task list"
    SC_NEXTWINDOW,                  "Switches to next window"
END



//
// Misc application definitions
//

// Application ICON
IDI_SDIAPPLICATION ICON "applsdi.ico"


// About box.
IDD_ABOUT DIALOG 12, 17, 204, 65
STYLE DS_MODALFRAME ¦ WS_POPUP ¦ WS_CAPTION ¦ WS_SYSMENU
CAPTION "About Spot"
FONT 8, "MS Sans Serif"
BEGIN
    CTEXT "Version", IDC_VERSION, 2, 14, 200, 8, SS_NOPREFIX
    CTEXT "Expert OWL Application", -1, 2, 4, 200, 8, SS_NOPREFIX
    CTEXT "", IDC_COPYRIGHT, 2, 27, 200, 17, SS_NOPREFIX
    RTEXT "", IDC_DEBUG, 136, 55, 66, 8, SS_NOPREFIX
    ICON IDI_SDIAPPLICATION, -1, 2, 2, 34, 34
    DEFPUSHBUTTON "OK", IDOK, 82, 48, 40, 14
END

CM_EDITCLEAR BITMAP LOADONCALL MOVEABLE
{
```

```
 '42 4D 66 01 00 00 00 00 00 00 76 00 00 00 28 00'
 '00 00 14 00 00 00 14 00 00 00 01 00 04 00 00 00'
 '00 00 F0 00 00 00 00 00 00 00 00 00 00 00 00 00'
 '00 00 00 00 00 00 00 00 00 00 00 00 80 00 00 80'
 '00 00 00 80 80 00 80 00 00 00 80 00 80 00 80 80'
 '00 00 80 80 80 00 C0 C0 C0 00 00 00 FF 00 00 FF'
 '00 00 00 FF FF 00 FF 00 00 00 FF 00 FF 00 FF FF'
 '00 00 FF FF FF 00 88 88 88 88 88 88 88 88 88 88'
 '40 00 88 88 88 88 88 88 88 88 88 88 90 00 88 88'
 '88 88 88 88 88 88 88 88 20 00 88 88 88 88 88 88'
 '88 88 88 88 40 18 88 88 88 88 88 88 88 88 88 88'
 '00 00 88 88 88 88 88 88 88 88 88 88 00 00 88 88'
 '88 88 88 88 88 88 88 88 00 00 88 88 88 88 88 88'
 '88 88 88 88 0B 00 88 80 08 88 88 88 88 88 88 88'
 '00 00 88 80 08 88 88 88 88 88 88 88 00 00 88 80'
 '08 88 88 84 44 44 44 48 00 00 88 80 08 80 88 84'
 'EF EF EF 48 0B 00 88 80 07 80 08 84 FE FE FE 48'
 '00 00 88 87 00 00 00 84 EF EF EF 48 00 00 88 88'
 '70 00 00 84 FE FE FE 48 00 00 88 88 88 80 08 84'
 'EF EF EF 48 0B 00 88 88 88 80 88 84 FE FE 44 48'
 'FF FF 88 88 88 88 88 84 EF EF 44 88 FF FF 88 88'
 '88 88 88 84 44 44 48 88 00 00 88 88 88 88 88 88'
 '88 88 88 88 0B 00'
}
CM_HELPABOUT BITMAP
{
'42 4D 66 01 00 00 00 00 00 00 76 00 00 00 28 00'
'00 00 14 00 00 00 14 00 00 00 01 00 04 00 00 00'
'00 00 F0 00 00 00 00 00 00 00 00 00 00 00 00 00'
'00 00 00 00 00 00 00 00 00 00 00 00 80 00 00 80'
'00 00 00 80 80 00 80 00 00 00 80 00 80 00 80 80'
'00 00 80 80 80 00 C0 C0 C0 00 00 00 FF 00 00 FF'
'00 00 00 FF FF 00 FF 00 00 00 FF 00 FF 00 FF FF'
'00 00 FF FF FF 00 88 88 88 88 88 88 88 88 88 88'
'00 00 88 88 88 84 44 44 48 88 88 88 00 00 88 88'
'84 44 44 44 44 48 88 88 00 00 88 88 44 46 FF 64'
'44 44 88 88 00 00 88 84 44 4F FF F6 44 44 48 88'
'00 00 88 44 44 4F F6 48 44 44 44 88 00 00 88 44'
'44 46 FF 44 44 44 44 88 01 01 84 44 44 44 FF 64'
'44 44 44 48 08 33 84 44 44 44 6F F4 44 44 44 48'
'00 00 84 44 44 44 4F F6 44 44 44 48 00 00 84 44'
'44 48 46 FF 44 44 44 48 00 00 84 44 44 46 FF FF'
'44 44 44 48 00 00 84 44 44 44 6F F6 44 44 44 48'
'00 00 88 44 44 44 44 44 44 44 44 88 00 00 88 44'
'44 44 44 66 44 44 44 88 00 00 88 84 44 44 46 FF'
'64 44 48 88 00 00 88 88 44 44 46 FF 64 44 88 88'
'00 00 88 88 84 44 44 66 44 48 88 88 00 00 88 88'
'88 84 44 44 48 88 88 88 00 00 88 88 88 88 88 88'
'88 88 88 88 00 00'
}
// Version info.
```

Listing X7.10. continued

```
//
#if !defined(__DEBUG_)
// Non-Debug VERSIONINFO
1 VERSIONINFO LOADONCALL MOVEABLE
FILEVERSION 1, 0, 0, 0
PRODUCTVERSION 1, 0, 0, 0
FILEFLAGSMASK 0
FILEFLAGS VS_FFI_FILEFLAGSMASK
FILEOS VOS__WINDOWS16
FILETYPE VFT_APP
BEGIN
    BLOCK "StringFileInfo"
    BEGIN
        // Language type = U.S. English (0x0409) and
        // Character Set = Windows, Multilingual(0x04e4)
        BLOCK "040904E4"
            // Matches VarFileInfo Translation hex value.
        BEGIN
            VALUE "CompanyName", "Honor Oak Systems\000"
            VALUE "FileDescription", "Spot for Windows\000"
            VALUE "FileVersion", "1.0\000"
            VALUE "InternalName", "Spot\000"
            VALUE "LegalCopyright",
              "Copyright   1994 by Honor Oak Systems. \000"
            VALUE "LegalTrademarks", "Windows (TM)\000"
            VALUE "OriginalFilename", "Spot.EXE\000"
            VALUE "ProductName", "Spot\000"
            VALUE "ProductVersion", "1.0\000"
        END
    END

    BLOCK "VarFileInfo"
    BEGIN
        VALUE "Translation", 0x0409, 0x04e4
   // U.S. English(0x0409) & Windows Multilingual(0x04e4) 1252
    END

END
#else

// Debug VERSIONINFO
1 VERSIONINFO LOADONCALL MOVEABLE
FILEVERSION 1, 0, 0, 0
PRODUCTVERSION 1, 0, 0, 0
FILEFLAGSMASK VS_FF_DEBUG ¦ VS_FF_PRERELEASE ¦ VS_FF_PATCHED ¦
VS_FF_PRIVATEBUILD ¦ VS_FF_SPECIALBUILD
FILEFLAGS VS_FFI_FILEFLAGSMASK
FILEOS VOS__WINDOWS16
```

```
FILETYPE VFT_APP
BEGIN
    BLOCK "StringFileInfo"
    BEGIN
        // Language type = U.S. English (0x0409)
        // and Character Set = Windows, Multilingual(0x04e4)
        BLOCK "040904E4"
        // Matches VarFileInfo Translation hex value.
        BEGIN
            VALUE "CompanyName", "Honor Oak Systems\000"
            VALUE "FileDescription", "Spot for Windows\000"
            VALUE "FileVersion", "1.0\000"
            VALUE "InternalName", "Spot\000"
            VALUE "LegalCopyright",
               "Copyright 1994 by Honor Oak Systems.  \000"
            VALUE "LegalTrademarks", "Windows (TM)\000"
            VALUE "OriginalFilename", "Spot.EXE\000"
            VALUE "ProductName", "Spot\000"
            VALUE "ProductVersion", "1.0\000"
            VALUE "SpecialBuild", "Debug Version\000"
            VALUE "PrivateBuild", "Built by Ian Spencer\000"
        END
    END

    BLOCK "VarFileInfo"
    BEGIN
        VALUE "Translation", 0x0409, 0x04e4
    // U.S. English(0x0409) & Windows Multilingual(0x04e4) 1252
    END

END
#endif

IDM_OLEVIEW ACCELERATORS
{
 VK_DELETE, CM_EDITDELETE, VIRTKEY, CONTROL
}
```

Type

Listing X7.11. SPOTAPP.DEF.

```
NAME spot

DESCRIPTION 'Spot - Copyright 1994 by Honor Oak Systems.'
EXETYPE     WINDOWS
CODE        PRELOAD MOVEABLE DISCARDABLE
DATA        PRELOAD MOVEABLE
HEAPSIZE    4096
STACKSIZE   20000
```

Type **Listing X7.12. SPOT.IDE.**

```
SPOT[.EXE] OWL + OCF LIBRARIES
  SPOTAPP[.CPP]
  SPOTDOC[.CPP]
  SPOTVIEW[.CPP]
  SPOTAB[.CPP]
  SPOTAPP[.RC]
  SPOTAPP[.DEF]
```

Analysis First, ensure that you have registered the server. You may want to build some of the OLE samples in the EXAMPLES directory to give you a test bed, unless you have a modern application. Running it as a stand-alone application might give you a result like the one in Figure X7.3. Running in another OLE application, STEP14.EXE (provided as an example in the OWL tutorial directory), gives the appearance shown in Figure X7.4.

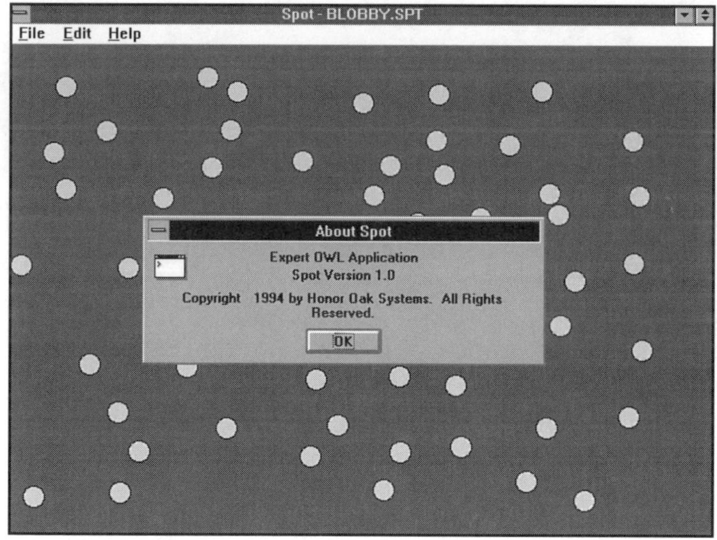

Figure X7.3. *The SPOT application running as a stand-alone application.*

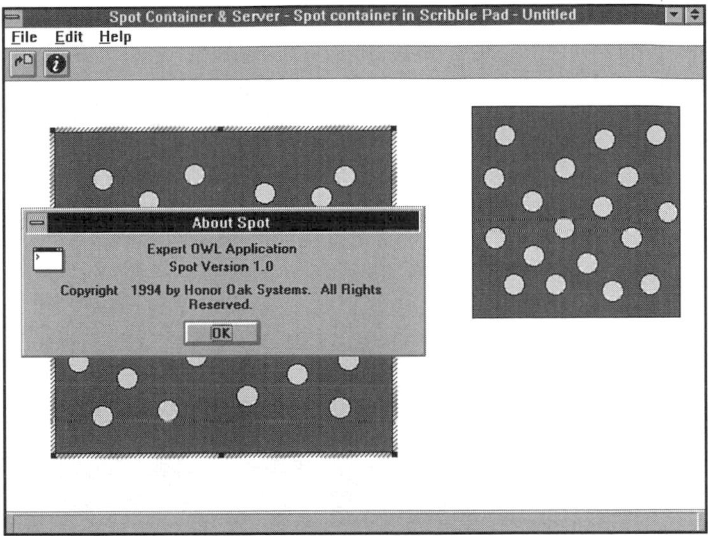

Figure X7.4. *The SPOT application running with in-place editing.*

Looking first to the application class in Listing X7.2 (SPOTAPP.CPP), you see that there was no toolbar created in the `InitMainWindow`. This emphasizes that, when running as an in-place editor, you provide a toolbar specifically for the application. In fact, if you can guarantee that the instance will be only single-use (set by the registration option `usage` for the application), you can borrow the control bar for your main application. OWL `TOleView` does this by default in response to `EvOcShowTools`. You should always provide a toolbar—if you don't, the screen jumps about while switching in the container application as the client window is repositioned.

Note also that OWL expects to use menu merging even for an SDI application. For OWL to manage the menus for you, you merely need to create menus of the correct identity. OWL creates the `TMenuDescr` objects for you, except for the main menu, as long as you use the predefined menu identifiers.

Take a look at the `InitInstance`. If the application starts as an embedding application, OWL looks after creating the view. In this SDI application, there should always be a client view by first attempting to open a command-line document (this could be optimized to avoid opening for obviously invalid command lines).

The trivialities of the About box bring out an important point about embedded objects. You may want to bring up dialogs. `GetCommandTarget` can be used to provide a suitable parent in place of `GetMainWindow`, which may, in fact, be hidden during embedding. This should ensure that the dialog stays modal over the container application.

In Listing X7.4 (SPOTDOC.CPP), the first catch is in writing the `Open` function. Although the path appears to be passed in as a parameter, it is not used. You should use `GetDocPath`, which is filled in before `Open` is called in `TOleDocument::InitDoc`.

You can detect a failure to open a file by using the result of the `InStream` function. In `SpotDoc`, the spots are held in a `TArray` container. They can easily be read in from and out to this container.

Caution: Failure to read a document can occur because the document was improperly written. Check that the `Commit` function is properly structured and ends with a call to `TOleDocument::CommitTransactedStorage`.

`AddSpot` uses a custom notification to get the views updated. This is a good optimization, because, for this application, the views need to add the item to their current display, rather than redrawing the entire screen. Note the interaction of the view and the document. The view captures the data and passes it to the document, which then tells the view to draw it.

Moving on to `Paint` in Listing X7.6 (SPOTVIEW.CPP), the drawing here requires care. Your `Paint` functions up to now have almost always been able to rely on having the mapping mode be `MM_TEXT` when drawing to a window. Because the OLE container may have scaled the image, when you edit in place, your window may not be pixel-based. OWL sorts out the scaling for you. However, this means that you must be careful that you draw in logical units, not pixels. The `Paint` function is also called by OWL to create the metafile that OLE stores in the embedded document for viewing and printing. This does not provide the usual functions you might expect to determine the drawing area—it is up to you to define the drawing area. The view always obtains its data from the document; it does not store its own data. The other unusual thing to note is the call to `TOleView::Paint`. This is how the embedded objects that are not active get redisplayed. (Therefore, it is not required for a server-only application.)

The mouse handling needs consideration. `TOleView` handles matching the mouse with the current display mapping mode. To handle its embedded objects, it provides a DC to enable it to draw and to scale its mouse movements. The tricky part is in the use of the `EvLButtonUp` response. Unlike the other two mouse events, `TOleView` does not scale the mouse coordinates. Also unlike the other two responses, your code needs to happen before the base class processing so that you can test for the presence of the DC. (Again, if the application is not a container, it does not need to worry about the base class processing.)

There are two OCF events you might like to handle, which are specific for an OLE server.

The first is declaring the size of your view to OLE with `EvOcViewPartSize`. The implementation here is quick and dirty. Normally, good programming practice dictates avoiding recalculating the view size each time the message is called. In this case, the view expands if data is placed outside the declared bounds. To avoid problems, the minimum view is declared to be a two-inch square.

New Term: In OCF, the embedded objects are known as *parts*.

Second, there is the placing of the toolbar. This is requested when OLE opens the object for in-place editing. You create a standard toolbar. (By default, `TOleView` assumes it can borrow the application `MainWindow` toolbar on the assumption that the application instance is single-use.) This toolbar is likely to be slightly different from a normal stand-alone application toolbar, leaving out File Save and other items. Hidden away is the OWL processing, which updates the menu and manages the status bar. Much of the processing is enabled merely by placing the correct options on the menu and toolbar.

There is a whole raft of functions that OWL provides. You should spend some time experimenting with the effects of the different embedding options. Try dragging objects around, resizing their borders when selected, resizing when open for editing, pasting links and so on. It is worth remembering that, in OWL, most of the `Doc/View` control is provided by the document manager (`TDocManager`). The controlling of the window is mainly provided by `TOleView` through `TOleWindow`. With luck, investigating these classes should provide you with the information you need to go beyond this quick look at OLE linking and embedding.

Consider what the changes would be to take away the container functionality—a very few statements, removing a few menu items and a few base class calls. Consider what it would take to take away server function—some registration options and some spare notifications. Finally, compare that with a stand-alone application—using the `Doc/View` model. OLE `Doc/View` provides a surprisingly high degree of implementation independence. It is possible to write OWL OLE applications without the `Doc/View` model; however, your application needs to be quite specialized to make it worthwhile.

There is a wealth of issues not covered here. OLE 2 provides language independence for the interface. `Doc/View` is a very high-level abstraction—OWL does enable closer control of the OLE process. You can go on to explore enabling your application to control object positioning or laying out objects around the embedded parts. Finally, don't get so involved with providing OLE support that you forget to develop a useful application. There already are a lot of container applications out there—what is needed are useful servers.

OLE Automation

As the final part of your tour of OLE, you look at OLE Automation. OLE Automation provides a method of linking application data across the OLE interface. This acts as a replacement for DDEML. When you study Automation, the most noticeable thing you find in the OCF implementation is the ease of use of these objects—unlike the low level of DDEML. The big difference is that Automation understands classes. Using OCF, your server provides a C++ class that can use all the usual features. The client uses another C++ class that maps onto the server class behind the scenes, using OCF magic. In both applications, the class is handled the same way as a normal C++ class. An Automation object interface is not limited in the same way as VBX. You can call functions and pass data, which includes your own C++ classes.

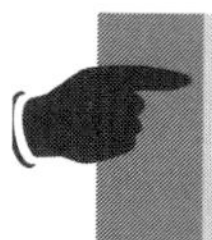

New Term: Under Automation, you provide an *Automation server* to supply services and an *Automation controller* to ask for them.

A server can provide methods (or callable functions), properties (data members accessed by function), direct access to data members, or even automated objects it is accessing from another server.

New Term: Declaring a member, function, or class to be visible via Automation is called *exposing*.

Using Automation is surprisingly simple. Just follow a few simple steps.

Step 1: Design the Server Class

The server class may be a new class especially designed for the Automation server, or you can provide some elements of an existing class or a whole new class. You should design it in the first instance without consideration of having it operated remotely.

Step 2: Declare the Class to Be Automatic

Note: It is recommended that the class be derived from `TAutoClass`, which merely ensures that OLE is notified of the class' destruction if the class instance is deleted when still in use by OLE. This is not essential.

Within the class declaration, a series of macros are used to declare the services to be exposed. For example, this code snippet:

```
DECLARE_AUTOCLASS(DataServer)
  AUTOPROPRO(Value, GetValue, int,)
  AUTOPROPRO(Text, GetText, TAutoString,)
  AUTOFUNC0(Throw,Throw,int,)
```

exposes two read-only properties and a function with no parameters that returns an `int`. There are a set of macros that include the following:

Declaration Macro	Member
AUTODATA	Data
AUTODATARO	Data, read-only
AUTOFLAG	A bit flag
AUTOFUNC*n*	Function returning a value with *n* parameters
AUTOFUNC*n*V	Function returning void with *n* parameters
AUTOITERATOR	Iterator object
AUTOPROP	Property
AUTOPROPRO	Property, read-only
AUTOPROXY	Property containing an automated object
AUTOSTAT	Static member function or global function
AUTOTHIS	*this

Caution: These macros look similar but are organized differently from response tables. In particular, note that there is no comma at the end of the line and that there is an optional last parameter, where you must specify the comma that precedes it even if you do not give the final parameter.

For example, `AUTOFUNC1(OleFunction,CalledFuction,int,bool,)` calls the class member function `int CalledFunction(bool)`. The first parameter of the macro represents the OLE name for the object and is used by the controlling application. The only rule on types is that if the type is a character array, declare it as a `TAutoString`, and if the object is a pointer or reference to a C++ object, wrap it up in a `TAutoObject<>` wrapper.

Note: OCF uses the `TAuto...` templates to enable it to convert types using RTTI (Run Time Type Information). RTTI gets the type information from the actual object, not from pointers and references, so it is hard to handle. The special auto classes, therefore, create an actual object of a known type that contains a pointer or reference of a type known by template generation.

These macros allow an option to be their last parameter to enable you to hook the command—that is, execute some action when the OLE accesses the exposed member. These are quite complicated except for `AUTOVALIDATE`. This enables you to place a boolean expression, which is called whenever the function or data is accessed. *`Val`* is used to represent the value when a member is accessed, *`Arg1`*, *`Arg2`*, and so forth are used to represent function parameters. For example, if the valuc of one pair of dice is exposed, this snippet:

```
AUTODATA(DiceValue,value,int,
                   AUTOVALIDATE(Val>0 && Val <= 6))
```

ensures that a value between 1 and 6 is set; otherwise, an OLE error occurs in the controlling application.

Step 3: Define the Automatic Methods and Properties

Having exposed the members, it is necessary to describe the members to OLE:

```
DEFINE_AUTOCLASS(DataServer)
  EXPOSE_METHOD(Throw,TAutoShort,"Throw","Throw the dice",)
  EXPOSE_PROPRO(Value,TAutoShort,"Value","Last throw",)
  EXPOSE_PROPRO(Text,TAutoString,"Text","Last throw as text",)
  EXPOSE_APPLICATION(DataServer,"Dice","Dice application",)
  EXPOSE_QUIT("Quit","Quit",)
END_AUTOCLASS(DataServer,"Dice","Dice throwing class",0)
```

Note: Exposing methods enables multilingual support. This is beyond the scope of this book.

The `END_AUTOCLASS(`*`cls`*`, `*`name`*`, `*`desc`*`, `*`help`*`)` defines that the C++ class *`cls`* is given to OLE as *`name`*, described as *`desc`*, with a help index of *`help`*.

Note: You can provide a help interface by registering a help file. The identifier on the macro enables the controlling application to request context-sensitive help from WinHelp.

The macros implement methods for a class nested within your automated class, which OCF uses to communicate with the class.

Macro	Member Declaration
`EXPOSE_APPLICATION`	Automated application name—just for interest
`EXPOSE_METHOD`	Method
`EXPOSE_PROPRO`	Read-only property
`EXPOSE_PROPRW`	Read-write property
`EXPOSE_PROPWO`	Write-only property
`EXPOSE_QUIT`	Shutdown method (provided by `TAutoBase`)

In addition, functions with parameters need to be followed with `REQUIRED_ARG` and `OPTIONAL_ARG` macros. Remember that required arguments cannot follow optional arguments. The data types in the table must be special `TAuto...` data types. Refer to your ObjectWindows Programmers Guide, Chapter 4, to understand the conversion table.

Step 4: Build the Application Engine

Having built the table, all that remains is to build the server application. Because this does not require object linking and embedding, the registration is much simpler. The key item is registering the application with the command-line flag of `-Automation`. The application also can use a simple hidden window so the OWL bit is trivial.

OWL doesn't provide a `ComponentFactory` macro that works with a plain `TApplication` object. Take an opportunity to write one. A `ComponentFactory` is a callback that is called three times in an executing server: to register, run, and shut down the application. However, it may also have to cope with a standard execution. The example that follows shows a simple callback. It uses a static member to store the data server object between callbacks and uses the application to run the message loop. Note that the registrar is a `TRegistrar` and that the includes required are simple, too. You also must include a `TOleAllocator(0)` object in your `OwlMain` procedure. Your target needs to include the OCF libraries.

Step 5: Build a Type Library and C++ Class

It is almost time to move on to building the controller, but first you build and run the controller with a parameter of `-TypeLib`. This does two things. It registers the automatic objects with OLE, and it builds a type library in the directory of the executable. Then, by running AutoGen (provided with Borland C++ 4.5) and picking up the type library (selecting the Automation option), you can generate a C++ class, which can be used by the Automation controller. These are given in a C++ source and header that you can include directly in your project.

Step 6: Use the C++ Class

The AutoGen application produces a C++ class with names taken from the exposed functions. You normally can use this class without amendment merely by including the generated code in your application. AutoGen does an excellent job of generating function names, because it can take the name that you declared for each member and use that as a proxy class member. The salient points are that the class is derived from `TAutoProxy`. The function calls and class members are declared as normal C++ members. OCF then provides some simple `AUTO...` macros that combine to translate the calling function into a call to OCF. For example, here is the other end of the `DataServer` class—note that the class declaration is simple:

```
class Dice : public TAutoProxy {
  public:
    Dice() : TAutoProxy(0x409) {}
    // Throw the dice
    short Throw(); // [id(1), method]
    // Last throw of the dice
    short GetValue(); // [id(2), propget]
    // Last throw of dice in text
    TAutoString GetText(); // [id(3), propget]
    // Dice-throwing application
    void GetDice(Dice&); // [id(4), propget]
    // Quit
    void Quit(); // [id(5), method]
};
short Dice::Throw()
{
  AUTONAMES0("Throw")
  AUTOARGS0()
  AUTOCALL_METHOD_RET
}

short Dice::GetValue()
{
  AUTONAMES0("Value")
  AUTOARGS0()
  AUTOCALL_PROP_GET
}
```

```
TAutoString Dice::GetText()
{
  AUTONAMES0("Text")
  AUTOARGS0()
  AUTOCALL_PROP_GET
}
```

New Term: A class used by an Automation controller that is supplied by an Automation server is called a *proxy class.*

Don't worry about the `TAutoString`; it converts quite nicely to a `char *`. The types aren't quite identical at the other end of the OLE conversation, but they are compatible.

To use a proxy class, you merely declare it; call the `TAutoProxy::Bind` member with the name of the application—which AutoGen even supplies at the top of the include file if you've forgotten it. Having included the CXX file in your application, use the class as a normal class. The only change required to the rest of the application is to declare a `TOleAllocator(0)` in `OwlMain`. You also need to include the OCF libraries.

Here are the applications; one will be very familiar. The first one, Listing X7.13, is DICESVR.EXE.

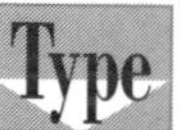

Listing X7.13. DICESVR.CPP.

```
#include <owl\applicat.h>
#include <ocf/appdesc.h>
#include <ocf/automacr.h>
#include <ocf/ocreg.h>
#include <owl\framewin.h>

TPointer<TRegistrar> Registrar;

REGISTRATION_FORMAT_BUFFER(100)
BEGIN_REGISTRATION(AppReg)
  REGDATA(clsid,"{82F153C0-DCB6-101B-A585-040224007802}")
  REGDATA(progid,"Dice.Server")
  REGDATA(description,"Dice Thrower")
  REGDATA(cmdline, "-Automation")
END_REGISTRATION

class OleServerApp;

class DataServer: public TAutoBase
   {
```

```
    public:
    DataServer();
    ~DataServer();
    int GetValue() {return value;}
    const char* GetText();
    int Throw();
    private:
      int value;
    DECLARE_AUTOCLASS(DataServer)
      AUTOPROPRO(Value, GetValue, int,)
      AUTOPROPRO(Text, GetText, TAutoString,)
      AUTOFUNC0(Throw,Throw,int,)
   };
 DEFINE_AUTOCLASS(DataServer)
   EXPOSE_METHOD(Throw,TAutoShort,"Throw","Throw the dice",)
   EXPOSE_PROPRO(Value,TAutoShort,"Value","Last throw of the dice",)
   EXPOSE_PROPRO(Text,TAutoString,"Text","Last throw of dice in text",)
   EXPOSE_APPLICATION(DataServer,"Dice","Dice throwing application",)
   EXPOSE_QUIT("Quit","Quit",)
 END_AUTOCLASS(DataServer,"Dice","Dice throwing class",0)

 DataServer::DataServer():TAutoBase()
   {
     value = 0;
     randomize();
   }
 DataServer::~DataServer()
   {
     ::GetAppDescriptor()->InvalidateObject(this);
   }
 const char* DataServer::GetText()
   {
     const char * throwText[] =
{"","One","Two","Three","Four","Five","Six"};
     return throwText[value];
   }
int DataServer::Throw()
  {
   value = rand() % 6 + 1;
   return value;
  }


class OleServerApp:public TApplication
  {
    public:
      void InitMainWindow()
        {
          SetMainWindow(new TFrameWindow(0,"Dice Throw"));
          if (Registrar->IsOptionSet(amAutomation))
            nCmdShow = SW_HIDE;
```

continues

Listing X7.13. continued

```
        }
  };
IUnknown* ComponentFactory(IUnknown* outer, uint32 options, uint32 /
➥*id*/ = 0)
{
  static DataServer* dataServer = 0;     // used to hold EXE object
➥until OLE factory call
  IUnknown* ifc = 0;
  if (options & amShutdown)
      return (options & amServedApp) ? 0 : outer;
  //
  // Must be first time through - make server App
  // or we are going through once and running
  //
  if (!dataServer)
    dataServer = new DataServer();

  //
  // If not Automation (so is going to drop through to run)
  // or callback, is request to register use
  //

  if (!(options & amAutomation) ||(options & amServedApp))
  //
  // Do OLE stuff
  //
    ifc = *::Registrar->CreateAutoApp
          (TAutoObjectDelete<DataServer>(dataServer),
          options, outer); // does an AddRef
  //
  // If this is a call to just run the app
  //
  if (options & amRun)
      OleServerApp().Run();
  return ifc;
}
int OwlMain(int,char*[])
  {
    TOleAllocator oleAllocator(0);
    try
      {
       Registrar = new TRegistrar(AppReg, ComponentFactory,
                                  TApplication::GetCmdLine());
       if (!Registrar->IsOptionSet(amAnyRegOption))
         Registrar->Run();
       Registrar = 0;
      }
    catch(...)
```

```
      {
      }
    return 0;
  }
```

Finally, here are Listings X7.14 through X7.19, DICECLIE.EXE, which is a client that uses an OLE-served dice throw.

Type

Listing X7.14. DICE.H.

```
#ifndef _DICE_H
#define _DICE_H
#include <owl\owlall.h>
// stdio for sprintf
#include <stdio.h>
#include "dice.rh"
#include "dicedlg.h"

#endif
```

Type

Listing X7.15. DICE.CPP.

```
#include "dice.h"
//
//  The usual TApplication derivative, this time
//  putting in the dice client
//
class DiceApp:public TApplication
  {
   public:
   void InitMainWindow()
          {
            TDialog* dice = new DiceDialog();
            //
            // The proper way to handle MainWindow...
            //
            SetMainWindow(new TFrameWindow(0,"Dice",dice,TRUE));
            GetMainWindow()->SetIcon(this,IDI_DICE);
            GetMainWindow()->Attr.Style
                &= ~WS_THICKFRAME & ~WS_MAXIMIZEBOX;

          }
  };
int OwlMain(int,char*[])
  {
```

continues

Listing X7.15. continued

```
    TOleAllocator oleAlloc(0); // NEW!
    DiceApp diceApp;
    try
      {
         return diceApp.Run(); // Standard TApplication::Run
       }
    catch (TXBase be)
      {
        MessageBox(0,be.why().c_str(),0,MB_OK);
      }
    return 0;
  }
```

Type **Listing X7.16. DICEDLG.H.**

```
#ifndef _DICEDIAL_H
#define _DICEDIAL_H
// Forward declaration for Dice pointer
class Dice;
class DiceDialog:public TDialog
  {
   public:
   DiceDialog();
   // new destructor
   ~DiceDialog();
   protected:
   Dice* diceThrow; // Pointer to proxy class
   TStatic* dice1;
   TStatic* dice2;
   TStatic* diceText1;
   TStatic* diceText2;
   TEdit* sum;
   TButton* pushButton;
    void SetupWindow();
   void PushButton();
   void EvTimer(UINT timerId);
   void EvPaint();
   void Paint(TDC&,BOOL,TRect&);

   private:
   BOOL roll;
   int sumValue;
   int diceValue1;
   int diceValue2;
   TRect rectDice1;
   TRect rectDice2;
```

```
   TDib* dice;
   DECLARE_RESPONSE_TABLE(DiceDialog);
  };

#endif
```

Listing X7.17. DICEDLG.CPP.

```
#include "dice.h"
// Include dicesvr source code
#include "dicesvr.cxx"
DEFINE_RESPONSE_TABLE1(DiceDialog,TDialog)
  EV_WM_TIMER,
  EV_WM_PAINT,
  EV_BN_CLICKED(IDC_PUSHBUTTON1,PushButton),
END_RESPONSE_TABLE;
DiceDialog::DiceDialog()
  :TDialog(0,DICE)
  {
     diceThrow = new Dice();          // Create proxy class
//
// Declare the controls - add some text this time
//
    dice1 = new TStatic(this,IDC_DICE1);
    diceText1 = new TStatic(this,IDC_DICETEXT1);
    dice2 = new TStatic(this,IDC_DICE2);
    diceText2 = new TStatic(this,IDC_DICETEXT2);
    sum = new TEdit(this,IDC_EDIT3);

    pushButton = new TButton(this,IDC_PUSHBUTTON1);
//
// Initialize the dice
//
    roll = FALSE;
    sumValue = 0;
    dice = new TDib(TBitmap(GetModule()->GetInstance(),
           IDB_DICE));
    diceValue1 = 0;
    diceValue2 = 0;
  };
//
// Destructor - called when instance deleted
//
DiceDialog::~DiceDialog()
  {
//
// Delete some brushes
```

continues

Listing X7.17. continued

```
//
    delete dice;
    diceThrow->Quit(); // Force the closure of the proxy
                       // object
    delete diceThrow;
  }
void DiceDialog::SetupWindow()
  {
   TDialog::SetupWindow();
   rectDice1 = dice1->GetWindowRect();
   rectDice2 = dice2->GetWindowRect();
   dice1->Destroy();
   dice2->Destroy();
   ScreenToClient(rectDice1.TopLeft());
   ScreenToClient(rectDice2.TopLeft());
   ScreenToClient(rectDice1.BottomRight());
   ScreenToClient(rectDice2.BottomRight());
   diceThrow->Bind("Dice.Server"); // bind to server
                                   // throws an exception
                                   // if fails
}

void DiceDialog::PushButton()
  {
   if (roll)
    {
      char diceString[5];
      KillTimer(1);
      roll = FALSE;
      pushButton->SetCaption("&Spin");
      sprintf(diceString,"%i",sumValue);
      sum->SetText(diceString);
    }
   else
    {
      roll = TRUE;
      pushButton->SetCaption("&Stop");
      sum->SetText("");
      SetTimer(1,100);
      EvTimer(1);
    }

  }
void DiceDialog::EvTimer(UINT /*timerId*/)
  {
   TClientDC dc(*this);
   //
   // Four calls to the proxy class - that's
```

```
    // all that is new, replacing the call to
    // the local random number generator.
    //
    diceValue1 = diceThrow->Throw();
    diceText1->SetText(diceThrow->GetText());
    diceValue2 = diceThrow->Throw();
    diceText2->SetText(diceThrow->GetText());
    sumValue = diceValue1 + diceValue2;
    Paint(dc,TRUE,TRect(0,0,0,0));
   };
void DiceDialog::EvPaint()
   {
    TPaintDC dc(*this);
    TRect&   rect = *(TRect*)&dc.Ps.rcPaint;
    Paint(dc, dc.Ps.fErase, rect);
   }
void DiceDialog::Paint(TDC& dc,BOOL,TRect&)
   {
     TRect source1(0,0,dice->Height(),dice->Height());
     source1.Offset(dice->Height()*diceValue1,0);
     dc.StretchDIBits(rectDice1,source1,*dice);
     TRect source2(0,0,dice->Height(),dice->Height());
     source2.Offset(dice->Height()*diceValue2,0);
     dc.StretchDIBits(rectDice2,source2,*dice);
   }
```

Type

Listing X7.18. DICE.RH.

```
#define IDI_DICE  1
#define IDB_DICE  1
#define DICE  1
#define IDC_EDIT3  103
#define IDC_PUSHBUTTON1  104
#define IDC_DICE1  120
#define IDC_DICE2  121
#define IDC_DICETEXT1  131
#define IDC_DICETEXT2  132
```

Listing X7.19. DICE.RC.

```
#include "dice.rh"
DICE DIALOG 7, 15, 85, 58
STYLE WS_CHILD ¦ WS_VISIBLE ¦ WS_BORDER
FONT 8, "MS Sans Serif"
{
 EDITTEXT IDC_EDIT3, 60, 6, 16, 12, ES_READONLY ¦
```

continues

Listing X7.19. continued

```
            NOT WS_TABSTOP ¦ WS_BORDER
   LTEXT "+", -1, 25, 8, 6, 8
   LTEXT "=", -1, 52, 9, 7, 8
   DEFPUSHBUTTON "&Spin", IDC_PUSHBUTTON1, 17, 39, 50, 14
   CONTROL "", IDC_DICE1, "static", SS_BLACKFRAME ¦ WS_CHILD
          ¦ WS_VISIBLE, 6, 6, 16, 17
   CONTROL "", IDC_DICE2, "static", SS_BLACKFRAME ¦ WS_CHILD
          ¦ WS_VISIBLE, 35, 6, 16, 17
   CTEXT "", IDC_DICETEXT1, 2, 25, 25, 8
   CTEXT "", IDC_DICETEXT2, 30, 26, 25, 8
  }

  IDB_DICE BITMAP
  {
   '42 4D F6 03 00 00 00 00 00 00 76 00 00 00 28 00'
   '00 00 70 00 00 00 10 00 00 00 01 00 04 00 00 00'
   '00 00 80 03 00 00 00 00 00 00 00 00 00 00 00 00'
   '00 00 10 00 00 00 00 00 00 00 00 BF 00 00 BF'
   '00 00 00 BF BF 00 BF 00 00 00 BF 00 BF 00 BF BF'
   '00 00 C0 C0 C0 00 80 80 80 00 00 00 FF 00 00 FF'
   '00 00 00 FF FF 00 FF 00 00 00 FF 00 FF 00 FF FF'
   '00 00 FF FF FF 00 91 11 11 11 11 11 11 11 91 11'
   '11 11 11 11 11 11 91 11 11 11 11 11 11 11 91 11'
   '11 11 11 11 11 11 91 11 11 11 11 11 11 11 91 11'
   '11 11 11 11 11 11 91 11 11 11 11 11 11 11 79 99'
   '99 99 99 99 99 91 79 99 99 99 99 99 99 91 79 99'
   '99 99 99 99 99 91 79 99 99 99 99 99 99 91 79 99'
   '99 99 99 99 99 91 79 99 99 99 99 99 99 91 79 99'
   '99 99 99 99 99 91 79 99 99 99 99 99 99 91 79 99'
   '99 99 99 99 99 91 79 99 99 99 99 9B BB 91 79 99'
   '99 99 99 9B BB 91 79 BB B9 99 99 9B BB 91 79 BB'
   'B9 99 99 9B BB 91 79 BB B9 99 99 9B BB 91 79 99'
   '99 99 99 99 99 91 79 99 99 99 99 99 99 91 79 99'
   '99 99 99 9B BB 91 79 99 99 99 99 9B BB 91 79 BB'
   'B9 99 99 9B BB 91 79 BB B9 99 99 9B BB 91 79 BB'
   'B9 99 99 9B BB 91 79 99 99 99 99 99 99 91 79 99'
   '99 99 99 99 99 91 79 99 99 99 99 9B BB 91 79 99'
   '99 99 99 9B BB 91 79 BB B9 99 99 9B BB 91 79 BB'
   'B9 99 99 9B BB 91 79 BB B9 99 99 9B BB 91 79 99'
   '99 99 99 99 99 91 79 99 99 99 99 99 99 91 79 99'
   '99 99 99 99 99 91 79 99 99 99 99 99 99 91 79 99'
   '99 99 99 99 99 91 79 99 99 99 99 99 99 91 79 99'
   '99 99 99 99 99 91 79 99 99 99 99 99 99 91 79 99'
   '99 99 99 99 99 91 79 99 99 99 99 99 99 91 79 99'
   '99 99 99 99 99 91 79 99 99 99 99 99 99 91 79 99'
   '99 99 99 99 99 91 79 99 99 99 99 99 99 91 79 99'
   '99 99 99 99 99 91 79 99 99 9B BB 99 99 91 79 99'
   '99 99 99 99 99 91 79 99 99 9B BB 99 99 91 79 99'
```

```
 '99 99 99 99 99 91 79 99 99 9B BB 99 99 91 79 BB'
 'B9 99 99 9B BB 91 79 99 99 99 99 99 99 91 79 99'
 '99 9B BB 99 99 91 79 99 99 99 99 99 99 91 79 99'
 '99 9B BB 99 99 91 79 99 99 99 99 99 99 91 79 99'
 '99 9B BB 99 99 91 79 BB B9 99 99 9B BB 91 79 99'
 '99 99 99 99 99 91 79 99 99 9B BB 99 99 91 79 99'
 '99 99 99 99 99 91 79 99 99 9B BB 99 99 91 79 99'
 '99 99 99 99 99 91 79 99 99 9B BB 99 99 91 79 BB'
 'B9 99 99 9B BB 91 79 99 99 99 99 99 99 91 79 99'
 '99 99 99 99 99 91 79 99 99 99 99 99 99 91 79 99'
 '99 99 99 99 99 91 79 99 99 99 99 99 99 91 79 99'
 '99 99 99 99 99 91 79 99 99 99 99 99 99 91 79 99'
 '99 99 99 99 99 91 79 99 99 99 99 99 99 91 79 99'
 '99 99 99 99 99 91 79 99 99 99 99 99 99 91 79 99'
 '99 99 99 99 99 91 79 99 99 99 99 99 99 91 79 99'
 '99 99 99 99 99 91 79 99 99 99 99 99 99 91 79 99'
 '99 99 99 99 99 91 79 BB B9 99 99 99 99 91 79 BB'
 'B9 99 99 99 99 91 79 BB B9 99 99 9B BB 91 79 BB'
 'B9 99 99 9B BB 91 79 BB B9 99 99 9B BB 91 79 99'
 '99 99 99 99 99 91 79 99 99 99 99 99 99 91 79 BB'
 'B9 99 99 99 99 91 79 BB B9 99 99 99 99 91 79 BB'
 'B9 99 99 9B BB 91 79 BB B9 99 99 9B BB 91 79 BB'
 'B9 99 99 9B BB 91 79 99 99 99 99 99 99 91 79 99'
 '99 99 99 99 99 91 79 BB B9 99 99 99 99 91 79 BB'
 'B9 99 99 99 99 91 79 BB B9 99 99 9B BB 91 79 BB'
 'B9 99 99 9B BB 91 79 BB B9 99 99 9B BB 91 77 77'
 '77 77 77 77 77 79 77 77 77 77 77 77 77 79 77 77'
 '77 77 77 77 77 79 77 77 77 77 77 77 77 79 77 77'
 '77 77 77 77 77 79 77 77 77 77 77 77 77 79 77 77'
 '77 77 77 77 77 79'
}


IDI_DICE ICON
{
 '00 00 01 00 01 00 20 20 10 00 00 00 00 00 E8 02'
 '00 00 16 00 00 00 28 00 00 00 20 00 00 00 40 00'
 '00 00 01 00 04 00 00 00 00 00 80 02 00 00 00 00'
 '00 00 00 00 00 00 00 00 00 00 00 00 00 00 00 00'
 '00 00 00 00 BF 00 00 BF 00 00 00 BF BF 00 BF 00'
 '00 00 BF 00 BF 00 BF BF 00 00 C0 C0 C0 00 80 80'
 '80 00 00 00 FF 00 00 FF 00 00 00 FF FF 00 FF 00'
 '00 00 FF 00 FF 00 FF FF 00 00 FF FF FF 00 00 00'
 '00 00 00 00 00 00 00 00 00 00 00 00 00 00 00 00'
 '00 00 00 00 00 00 00 00 00 00 00 00 00 00 00 00'
 '00 00 00 00 00 00 00 00 00 00 00 00 00 00 00 00'
 '00 00 00 00 00 00 00 00 00 00 00 00 00 00 00 00'
 '00 00 01 11 11 11 11 11 11 11 33 31 00 00 00 00'
 '00 01 11 11 11 11 33 31 11 11 11 11 10 00 00 00'
 '00 11 33 31 11 11 11 11 11 11 11 11 10 00 00 00'
 '00 19 99 99 99 99 99 99 99 99 91 11 10 00 00 00'
```

continues

Listing X7.19. continued

```
    '0D 99 99 99 99 99 99 99 99 99 99 11 10 00 00 00'
    '0D 99 99 99 99 99 99 99 9B B9 99 11 10 00 00 00'
    '0D 99 99 99 99 99 99 99 BB BB 99 11 10 00 00 00'
    '0D 99 99 99 99 99 99 99 BB BB 99 11 10 00 00 00'
    '0D 99 99 99 99 99 99 99 9B B9 99 11 10 00 00 00'
    '0D 99 99 99 99 99 99 99 99 99 99 11 10 00 00 00'
    '0D 99 99 99 99 99 99 99 99 99 99 13 10 00 00 00'
    '0D 99 99 99 99 99 99 99 99 99 99 13 10 00 00 00'
    '0D 99 99 99 99 99 99 99 99 99 99 13 10 00 00 00'
    '0D 99 99 99 99 99 99 99 99 99 99 11 10 00 00 00'
    '0D 99 99 99 99 99 99 99 99 99 99 11 10 00 00 00'
    '0D 99 99 99 99 99 99 99 99 99 99 11 10 00 00 00'
    '0D 99 99 99 99 99 99 99 99 99 99 11 10 00 00 00'
    '0D 99 99 99 99 99 99 99 99 99 99 11 10 00 00 00'
    '0D 99 BB 99 99 99 99 99 99 99 99 11 10 00 00 00'
    '0D 9B BB B9 99 99 99 99 99 99 99 11 10 00 00 00'
    '0D 9B BB B9 99 99 99 99 99 99 99 11 00 00 00 00'
    '0D 99 BB 99 99 99 99 99 99 99 99 11 00 00 00 00'
    '0D D9 99 99 99 99 99 99 99 99 99 10 00 00 00 00'
    '00 DD DD DD DD DD DD DD DD DD D0 00 00 00 00 00'
    '00 00 00 00 00 00 00 00 00 00 00 00 00 00 00 00'
    '00 00 00 00 00 00 00 00 00 00 00 00 00 00 00 00'
    '00 00 00 00 00 00 00 00 00 00 00 00 00 00 00 00'
    '00 00 00 00 00 00 00 00 00 00 00 00 00 00 FF FF'
    'FF FF FF FF FF FF FF FF FF FF FF FF FF FF FF 80'
    '00 0F FE 00 00 07 FC 00 00 07 FC 00 00 07 F8 00'
    '00 07 F8 00 00 07 F8 00 00 07 F8 00 00 07 F8 00'
    '00 07 F8 00 00 07 F8 00 00 07 F8 00 00 07 F8 00'
    '00 07 F8 00 00 07 F8 00 00 07 F8 00 00 07 F8 00'
    '00 07 F8 00 00 07 F8 00 00 07 F8 00 00 07 F8 00'
    '00 0F F8 00 00 0F F8 00 00 1F FC 00 00 7F FF FF'
    'FF FF FF FF FF FF FF FF FF FF FF FF FF FF'
}
```

The application appears in Figure X7.5.

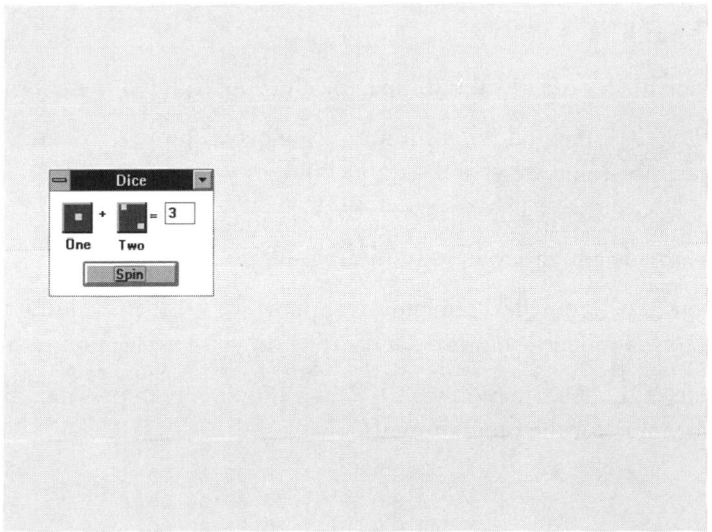

Figure X7.5. *The automatic dice.*

Analysis

I am sure you are surprised at how easy it is to use a proxy class with the help of OCF. Assuming that OLE can find the server, you should have no difficulty using the class. The `Bind` statement makes the connection through OLE. The destructor of the object should disconnect, but it is safest to call the `Quit` method to ensure that OLE disconnects the server. The function calls themselves are almost transparent.

For the server, the hard work is not in defining the class, but in matching up the OCF macros to the server class. This is a tedious rather than difficult task.

Whither Automation?

This was a simple example. Obviously, data exchange using Automation through OCF is simplicity itself compared to DDEML. However, at the time of writing, there isn't a proper way to send notifications back to the proxy object. Automation objects are the core of OCX, the replacement for VBX controls for 32-bit Windows. OLE defines quite a number of other features for Automation, including help file support and international translation via resources. OLE embedding servers can also provide automation.

Summary

Today, you got a taste of OLE 2. Specifically, you explored these topics:

- OLE 2 as a method for communicating between programs and for linking and embedding views and data
- How ObjectWindows and Object Components Framework work together to provide a high-level programming solution to OLE 2
- How OWL provides tremendous support for OLE embedding via its OLE `Doc/View` model—you can concentrate on your application rather than OLE
- Using OLE Automation via OCF as a simple way to pass data between programs (for the programmer!)

Q&A

Q Can an OLE Automation server pass across more than one class?

A Yes, by using aggregation. Effectively, this means defining a controlling class that inherits or contains other classes. The aggregate class can then delegate the task of responding to requests to its component classes.

Q How do I set up an advise loop as I would in DDEML?

A The interface for notifying events is not supported yet. Eventually, this will be part of the emerging capabilities of the specification of OCX.

Q How do I find out more about OLE?

A If possible, work through the examples in the Borland manuals on OCF that do not use the OWL classes. These highlight some of the mechanics of OLE. I recommend that you avoid books on pure OLE as these will not explain the OCF interface. There is a full tutorial included with the Borland package; it is well worth working through it. The OWL manuals and online help are full of information about OLE and OCF.

Workshop

The Workshop provides quiz questions to help you consolidate your understanding of the material covered, and exercises to provide you with experience in using what you've learned. Try to understand the quiz and exercise answers before continuing on to the next day's lesson. Answers are provided in Appendix A, "Answers."

Quiz

1. What method of joining documents should a user use to place a document in several other documents?
2. What OWL class is responsible for managing the display of embedded objects?
3. What must you do before you can access an OLE 2 server from a container?
4. Did you enjoy working through this book?

Exercise

Generate a copy of the SPOT application with AppExpert with all the decorations.

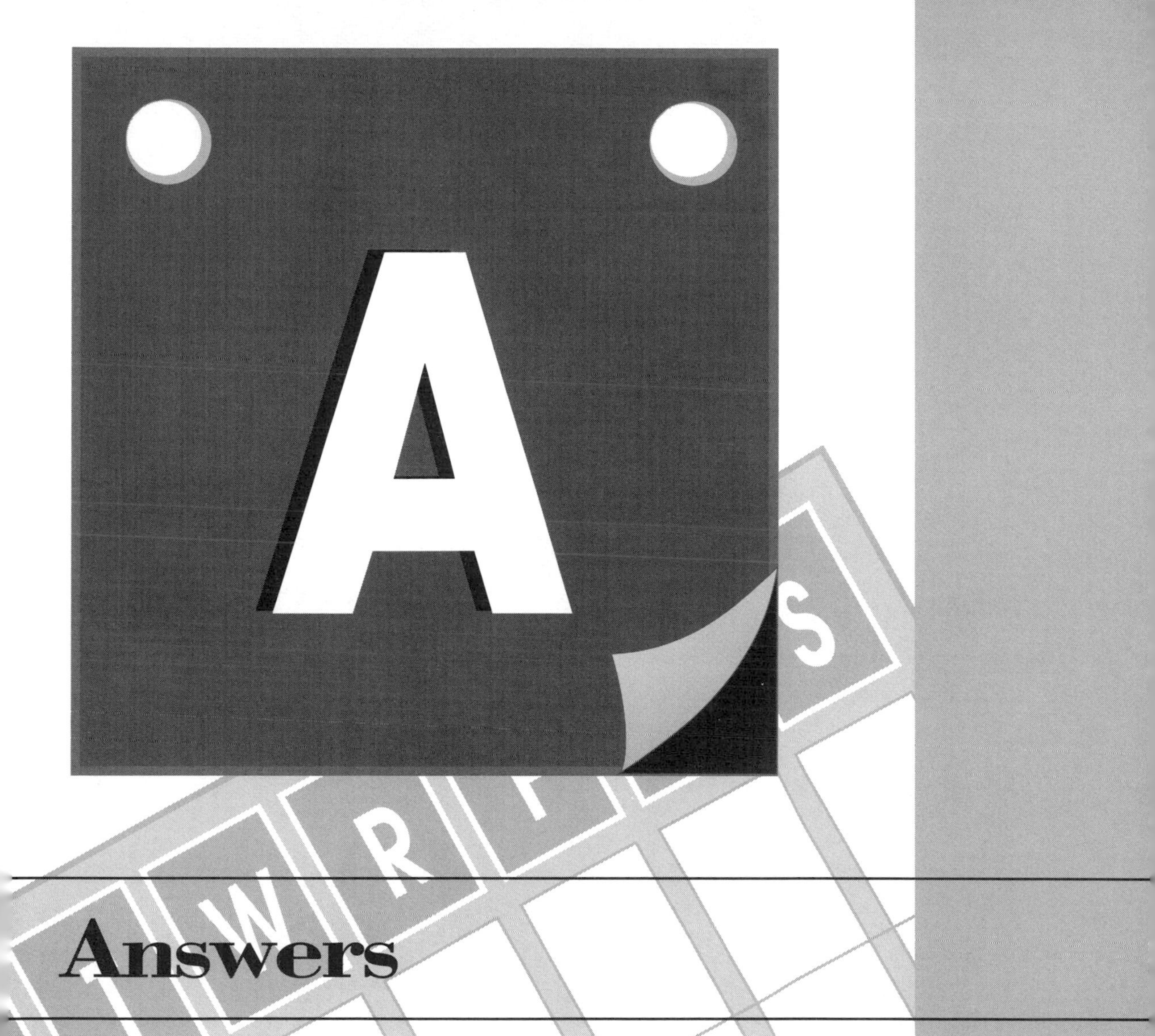

Answers

Note: Because of space limitations, not every Exercise has an answer presented here.

Answers to Day 1, "Getting Started"

Quiz

1. The program generates the string `C++ in 21 Days?`.
2. The program generates no output because the `cout` statement appears inside a comment! The function `main` simply returns 0.
3. The `cout` statement is missing the semicolon.

Exercise

```
// Exercise program

#include <iostream.h>

main()
{
  cout << "I am a C++ Programmer";
  return 0;
}
```

Answers to Day 2, "C++ Program Components"

Quiz

1. The following table indicates which identifiers are valid and which are not (and why).

Identifiers	Valid?	Reason (If Invalid)
`numFiles`	Yes	
`n0Distance_02_Line`	Yes	
`0Weight`	No	Starts with a digit
`Bin Number`	No	Contains a space

Identifiers	Valid?	Reason (if Invalid)
`static`	No	Reserved keyword
`Static`	Yes	

2. The output of the program is

   ```
   a = 10 and b = 3
   ```

   The function `swap` fails to swap the arguments `a` and `b` because it only swaps a copy of their values.

3. The output of the program is

   ```
   a = 3 and b = 10
   ```

   The function `swap` succeeds in swapping the arguments `a` and `b` because it uses reference parameters. Consequently, the changes in the values of parameters `i` and `j` go beyond the scope of the function itself.

4. The second version of function `inc` has a default argument, which, when used, hinders the compiler from determining which version of `inc` to call. The compiler flags a compile-time error for such functions.

5. Because the second parameter has a default argument, the third one must also have a default argument. Here is one version of the correct definition of function `volume`:

   ```
   double volume(double length, double width = 1, double height = 1)
   {
     return length * width * height
   }
   ```

6. The parameter `i` is a lowercase letter. However, the function uses the uppercase `I` in the assignment statement. The compiler complains that the identifier `I` is not defined.

7. The function `main` requires a prototype of function `sqr`. The correct version of the program is

   ```
   #include <iostream.h>

   // declare prototype of function sqr
   double sqr(double);
   ```

```
main()
{
  double x = 5.2;

  cout << x << "^2 = " << sqr(x);
  return 0;
}

double sqr(double x)
{ return x * x ; }
```

Exercise

Here is my version of program OVERLOD2.CPP:

```
// C++ program illustrates function overloading
// and default arguments

#include <iostream.h>

// inc version for int types
void inc(int& i, int diff = 1)
{
  i = i + diff;
}

// inc version for double types
void inc(double& x, double diff = 1)
{
  x = x + diff;
}

// inc version for char types
void inc(char& c, int diff = 1)
{
  c = c + diff;
}

main()
{
  char c = 'A';
  int i = 10;
  double x = 10.2;

  // display initial values
  cout << "c = " << c << "\n"
```

A

```
        << "i = " << i << "\n"
        << "x = " << x << "\n";
    // invoke the inc functions using default arguments
    inc(c);
    inc(i);
    inc(x);
    // display updated values
    cout << "After using the overloaded inc function\n";
    cout << "c = " << c << "\n"
        << "i = " << i << "\n"
        << "x = " << x << "\n";
     return 0;
}
```

Answers to Day 3, "Operators and Expressions"

Quiz

1. The output is

```
12
8
2
3.64851
150.5
```

2. The output is

```
12
8
2
```

3. The output is

```
12
27
```

4. The output is

```
TRUE
TRUE
TRUE
FALSE
```

Exercises

1. Here is my version of the function max:

```
int max(int i, int j)
{
  return (i > j) ? i : j;
}
```

2. Here is my version of the function min:

```
int min(int i, int j)
{
  return (i < j) ? i : j;
}
```

3. Here is my version of the function abs:

```
int abs(int i)
{
  return (i > 0) ? i : -i;
}
```

4. Here is my version of the function isOdd:

```
int isOdd(int i)
{
  return (i % 2 != 0) ? 1 : 0;
}
```

Answers to Day 4, "Managing I/O"

Quiz

1. The output statement cannot contain the inserter operator >>. The statement can be corrected as follows:

```
cout << "Enter a number ";
cin >> x;
```

2. Because the variable x appears in the first and last items, the last number overwrites the first number.

Exercises

1. Here is my version of program OUT3.CPP:

```
// C++ program uses the printf function for formatted output

#include <stdio.h>
#include <math.h>

main()
{
  double x;

  // display table heading
  printf("      X          Sqrt(X)\n");
  printf("------------------------\n");
  x = 2;
  printf("    %3.0lf          %3.4lf\n", x, sqrt(x));
  x++;
  printf("    %3.0lf          %3.4lf\n", x, sqrt(x));
  x++;
  printf("    %3.0lf          %3.4lf\n", x, sqrt(x));
  x++;
  printf("    %3.0lf          %3.4lf\n", x, sqrt(x));
  x++;
  printf("    %3.0lf          %3.4lf\n", x, sqrt(x));
  x++;
  printf("    %3.0lf          %3.4lf\n", x, sqrt(x));
  x++;
  printf("    %3.0lf          %3.4lf\n", x, sqrt(x));
  x++;
  printf("    %3.0lf          %3.4lf\n", x, sqrt(x));
  x++;
  printf("    %3.0lf          %3.4lf\n", x, sqrt(x));
  return 0;
}
```

2. Here is my version of program OUT4.CPP:

```
// C++ program which displays octal and hexadecimal integers
```

```
#include <iostream.h>
#include <stdio.h>

main()
{
  long i;
  cout << "Enter an integer : ";
  cin >> i;

  printf("%ld = %lX (hex) = %lo (octal)\n", i, i, i);
  return 0;
}
```

Answers to Day 5, "The Decision-Making Constructs"

Quiz

1. The simpler version is

```
if (i > 0 && i < 10)
  cout << "i = " << i << "\n";
```

2. The simpler version is

```
if (i > 0) {
  j = i * i;
  cout << "j = " << j << "\n";
}
else if (i < 0) {
  j = 4 * i;
  cout << "j = " << j << "\n";
}
else {
  j = 10 + i;
  cout << "j = " << j << "\n";
}
```

3. False. When the variable `i` stores values between -10 and -1, the statements in the clauses of the two `if` statements execute. In this case, all the

assignment statements are executed. By contrast, it is impossible to execute the statements in both the `if` and `else` clauses of the supposedly equivalent `if-else` statement.

4. The simplified version is

```
if (i > 0 && i < 100)
     j = i * i;
else if (i >= 100)
     j = i;
else
     j = 1;
```

   Noticc that I eliminate the original first `else if` clause because the tested condition is a subset of the first tested condition. Consequently, the condition in the first `else if` never gets examined and the associated assign statement never gets executed. This is an example of what is called *dead code*.

5. The tested condition is always false. Consequently, the statements in the clause are never executed. This is another example of dead code.

Exercises

1. Here is my version of program IF5.CPP:

```
// C++ program to solve quadratic equation

#include <iostream.h>
#include <math.h>

main()
{
  double A, B, C, discrim, root1, root2, twoA;

  cout << "Enter coefficients for equation A*X^2 + B*X + C\n";
  cout << "Enter A: ";
  cin >> A;
  cout << "Enter B: ";
  cin >> B;
  cout << "Enter C: ";
  cin >> C;
```

```
    if (A != 0) {
       twoA = 2 * A;
       discrim = B * B - 4 * A * C;
       if (discrim > 0) {
         root1 = (-B + sqrt(discrim)) / twoA;
         root2 = (-B - sqrt(discrim)) / twoA;
         cout << "root1 = " << root1 << "\n";
         cout << "root2 = " << root2 << "\n";
       }
       else if (discrim < 0) {

         discrim = -discrim;
         cout << "root1 = (" << -B/twoA
              << ") + i (" << sqrt(discrim) / twoA <<")\n";
         cout << "root2 = (" << -B/twoA
              << ") - i (" << sqrt(discrim) / twoA << ")\n";
       }
       else {
         root1 = -B / 2 / A;
         root2 = root1;
         cout << "root1 = " << root1 << "\n";
         cout << "root2 = " << root2 << "\n";
       }
    }
    else
      cout << "root = " << (-C / B) << "\n";


    return 0;
  }
```

2. Here is my version of program SWITCH2.CPP:

```
// C++ program which uses the switch statement to implement
// a simple four-function calculator program

#include <iostream.h>

const int TRUE = 1;
const int FALSE = 0;
```

```
main()
{
  double x, y, z;
  char op;
  int error = FALSE;

  cout << "Enter the first operand: ";
  cin >> x;
  cout << "Enter the operator: ";
  cin >> op;
  cout << "Enter the second operand: ";
  cin >> y;

  switch (op) {
    case '+':
      z = x + y;
      break;
    case '-':
      z = x - y;
      break;
    case '*':
      z = x * y;
      break;
    case '/':
      if (y != 0)
        z = x / y;
      else
        error = TRUE;
      break;
    default:
      error = TRUE;
  }

  if (!error)
    cout << x << " " << op << " " << y << " = " << z << "\n";
  else
    cout << "Bad operator or division-by-zero error\n";

  return 0;
}
```

Answers to Day 6, "Loops"

Quiz

1. The statements inside the loop fail to alter the value of `i`. Consequently, the tested condition is always true and the loop iterates endlessly.
2. The output of the program consists of the numbers 3, 5, and 7.
3. The output of the program is an endless sequence of lines that display the value of 3. The reason for the indefinite looping is that the loop control variable is not incremented.
4. The nested `for` loops use the same loop control variable. This program will not run.
5. Both `for` loops declare the variable `i` as their loop control variable. The compiler generates an error for this duplication.
6. The condition of the `while` loop is always true. Therefore, the loop iterates endlessly.
7. The program lacks a statement which explicitly initializes the variable `factorial` to 1. Without this statement, the program automatically initializes the variable `factorial` to 0—the wrong value. Consequently, the `for` loop ends up assigning 0 to the variable `factorial` in every iteration. Here is the correct version of the code:

```
int n;
double factorial = 1;
cout << "Enter positive integer : ";
cin >> n;
for (int i = 1; i <= n; i++)
  factorial *= i;
cout << n << "!= " << factorial;
```

Exercises

1. Here is my version of program FOR5.CPP:

```
// Program calculates a sum of odd integers in
// the range of 11 to 121

#include <iostream.h>
```

```
const int FIRST = 11;
const int LAST = 121;

main()
{
    double sum = 0;
    for (int i = FIRST; i <= LAST; i += 2)
      sum += (double)i;

    cout << "Sum of odd integers from "
         << FIRST << " to " << LAST << " = "
         << sum << "\n";
    return 0;
}
```

2. Here is my version of program WHILE2.CPP:

```
// Program calculates a sum of squared odd integers in
// the range of 11 to 121

#include <iostream.h>

const int FIRST = 11;
const int LAST = 121;

main()
{
    double sum = 0;
    int i = FIRST;
    while (i <= LAST) {
      i += 2;sum += double(i * i);
    }
    cout << "Sum of squared odd integers from "
         << FIRST << " to " << LAST << " = "
         << sum << "\n";
    return 0;
}
```

3. Here is my version of program DOWHILE2.CPP:

```
// Program calculates a sum of squared odd integers in
// the range of 11 to 121
```

```
#include <iostream.h>

const int FIRST = 11;
const int LAST = 121;

main()
{
    double sum = 0;
    int i = FIRST;
    do {
      sum += double(i * i);
    } while ((i += 2) <= LAST);
    cout << "Sum of squared odd integers from "
         << FIRST << " to " << LAST << " = "
         << sum << "\n";
    return 0;
}
```

Answers to Day 7, "Arrays"

Quiz

1. The program displays the factorials for the numbers 0 to 4:

```
x[0] = 1
x[1] = 1
x[2] = 2
x[3] = 6
x[4] = 24
```

2. The program displays the square roots for the numbers 0 to 4:

```
x[0] = 0
x[1] = 1
x[2] = 1.41421
x[3] = 1.73205
x[4] = 2
```

3. The first `for` loop should iterate between `1` and `MAX-1` and not between `0` and `MAX-1`. The first loop iteration uses an out-of-range index.

Exercise

Here is my version of program ARRAY7.CPP:

```
// C++ program that sorts arrays using the Comb sort method
 #include <iostream.h>

 const int MAX = 10;
 const int TRUE = 1;
 const int FALSE = 0;

 int obtainNumData()
 {
   int m;
   do { // obtain number of data points
     cout << "Enter number of data points [2 to "
         << MAX << "] : ";
     cin >> m;
     cout << "\n";
   } while (m < 2 || m > MAX);
   return m;
 }

 void inputArray(int intArr[], int n)
 {
   // prompt user for data
   for (int i = 0; i < n; i++) {
     cout << "arr[" << i << "] : ";
     cin >> intArr[i];
   }
 }

 void showArray(int intArr[], int n)
 {
   for (int i = 0; i < n; i++) {
     cout.width(5);
     cout << intArr[i] << " ";
   }
   cout << "\n";
 }

 void sortArray(int intArr[], int n)
 {
   int offset, temp, inOrder;

   offset = n;
   while (offset > 1) {
     offset /= 2;
     do {
       inOrder = TRUE;
       for (int i = 0, j = offset; i < (n - offset); i++, j++) {
```

```
        if (intArr[i] > intArr[j]) {
          inOrder = FALSE;
          temp = intArr[i];
          intArr[i] = intArr[j];
          intArr[j] = temp;
        }
      }
    } while (!inOrder);
  }
}

main()
{
  int arr[MAX];
  int n;

  n = obtainNumData();
  inputArray(arr, n);
  cout << "Unordered array is:\n";
  showArray(arr, n);
  sortArray(arr, n);
  cout << "\nSorted array is:\n";
  showArray(arr, n);
  return 0;
}
```

Answers to Day 8, "User-Defined Types and Pointers"

Quiz

1. The enumerated values `on` and `off` appear in two different enumerated types. Here is a correct version of these statements:

   ```
   enum Boolean { false, true };
   enum State { state_on, state_off };
   enum YesNo { yes, no };
   enum DiskDriveStatus { drive_on , drive_off };
   ```

2. False. The enumerated type `YesNo` is correctly declared.
3. The program lacks a delete statement before the return statement. Here is the correct version:

   ```
   #include <iostream.h>
   main()
   {
   ```

```
  int *p = new int;
  cout << "Enter a number : ";
  cin >> *p;
  cout << "The square of " << *p << " = " << (*p * *p);
  delete p;
  return 0;
}
```

Exercises

1. Here is my version of PTR6.CPP:

```
/* C++ program that demonstrates pointers to structured types */

#include <iostream.h>
#include <stdio.h>
#include <math.h>

const MAX_RECT = 4;
const TRUE = 1;
const FALSE = -1;

struct point {
  double x;
  double y;
};

struct rect {
  point ulc; // upper left corner
  point lrc; // lower right corner
  double area;
  int id;
};

typedef rect rectArr[MAX_RECT];

main()
{
  rectArr r;
  rect temp;
  rect* pr = r;
```

```
rect* pr2;
double length, width;
int offset;
int inOrder;

for (int i = 0; i < MAX_RECT; i++, pr++) {
  cout << "Enter (X,Y) coord. for ULC of rect. # "
       << i << " : ";
  cin >> pr->ulc.x >> pr->ulc.y;
  cout << "Enter (X,Y) coord. for LRC of rect. # "
       << i << " : ";
  cin >> pr->lrc.x >> pr->lrc.y;
  pr->id = i;
  length = fabs(pr->ulc.x - pr->lrc.x);
  width = fabs(pr->ulc.y - pr->lrc.y);
  pr->area = length * width;
}

// sort the rectangles by areas
offset = MAX_RECT;
do {
  offset = (8 * offset) / 11;
  offset = (offset == 0) ? 1 : offset;
  inOrder = TRUE;
  pr = r;
  pr2 = r + offset;
  for (int i = 0;
       i < MAX_RECT - offset;
       i++, pr++, pr2++)
    if (pr->area > pr2->area) {
      inOrder = FALSE;
      temp = *pr;
      *pr = *pr2;
      *pr2 = temp;
    }
} while (!(offset == 1 && inOrder));

pr = r; // reset pointer
// display rectangles sorted by area
```

A

```
  for (i = 0; i < MAX_RECT; i++, pr++)
    printf("Rect # %d has area %5.4lf\n", pr->id, pr->area);
  return 0;
}
```

2. Here is my version of structure `intArrStruct`:

```
struct intArrStruct {
  int* dataPtr;
  unsigned size;
};
```

3. Here is my version of structure `matStruct`:

```
struct matStruct {
  double* dataPtr;
  unsigned rows;
  unsigned columns;
};
```

Answers to Day 9, "Strings"

Quiz

1. The string `s1` is smaller than string `s2`. Consequently, the call to function `strcpy` causes a program bug.

2. Using the function `strncpy` to include the constant `MAX` as the third argument ensures that string `s1` receives `MAX` characters (excluding the null terminator) from string `s1`:

```
#include <iostream.h>
#include <string.h>
const in MAX = 10;
main()
{
  char s1[MAX+1];
  char s2[] = "123456789012345678901234567890";
  strncpy(s1, s2, MAX);
  cout << "String 1 is " << s1
       << "\nString 2 is " << s2;
  return 0;
}
```

3. Because the string in variable s1 is lesser than that in variable s2, the statement assigns a negative number in variable i.
4. The call to function strcmp compares the substrings "C++" with "Pascal" because the arguments include an offset value. Because "C++" is lesser than "Pascal", the statement assigns a negative number in variable i.
5. False! Although the basic idea for the function is sound, dimensioning the local variable requires a constant. One solution is to use the same constant, call it MAX_STRING_SIZE, to size up the arguments of parameter s:

```
int hasNoLowerCase(const char* s)
{
  char s2[MAX_STRING_SIZE+1];
  strcpy(s2, s);
  strupr(s2);
  return (strcmp(s, s2) == 0) ? 1 : 0);
}
```

The other solution uses dynamic allocation to create a dynamic local string that stores a copy of the argument of parameter s. This solution works with all arguments of parameter s:

```
int hasNoLowerCase(const char* s)
{
  char *s2 = new char[strlen(s)+1];
  int i;
  strcpy(s2, s);
  strupr(s2);
  // store result in variable i
  i = (strcmp(s, s2) == 0) ? 1 : 0);
  delete [] s2; // first delete local dynamic string
  return i; // then return the result of the function
}
```

Exercises

1. Here is my version of function strlen:

```
int strlen(const char* s)
{
  int i = 0;
```

```
  while (s[i] != '\0')
    i++;
  return i;
}
```

2. Here is the other version of function `strlen`:

```
int strlen(const char* s)
{
  char *p = s;
  while (p++ != '\0')
    /* do nothing */;
  return p - s;
}
```

3. Here is my version of program STRING5.CPP:

```
#include <stdio.h>
#include <string.h>

main()
{
   char str[] = "2*(X+Y)/(X+Z) - (X+10)/(Y-5)";
   char strCopy[41];
   char* tkn[3] = { "+-*/ ()", "( )", "+-*/ " };
   char* ptr;

   strcpy(strCopy, str); // copy str into strCopy
   printf("%s\n", str);
   printf("Using token string %s\n", tkn[0]);
   // the first call
   ptr = strtok(str, tkn[0]);
   printf("String is broken into: ");
   while (ptr) {
     printf(", %s", ptr);
     // must make first argument a NULL character
     ptr = strtok(NULL, tkn[0]);
   }

   strcpy(str, strCopy); // restore str
   printf("\nUsing token string %s\n", tkn[1]);
   // the first call
```

```
    ptr = strtok(str, tkn[1]);
    printf("String is broken into: ");
    while (ptr) {
      printf(", %s", ptr);
      // must make first argument a NULL character
      ptr = strtok(NULL, tkn[1]);
    }

    strcpy(str, strCopy); // restore str
    printf("\nUsing token string %s\n", tkn[2]);
    // the first call
    ptr = strtok(str, tkn[2]);
    printf("String is broken into: ");
    while (ptr) {
      printf(", %s", ptr);
      // must make first argument a NULL character
      ptr = strtok(NULL, tkn[2]);
    }
    printf("\n\n");
    return 0;
}
```

Answers to Day 10, "Advanced Function Parameters"

Quiz

1. The function is

   ```
   double factorial(int i)
   { return (i > 1) ? double(i) * factorial(i-1) : 1; }
   ```

2. At first glance, the function may seem correct, though somewhat unusual. The `case` labels offer quick results for arguments of 0 to 4. However, the catch-all `default` clause traps arguments that are greater than 4 *and* are negative values! The latter kind of arguments causes the recursion to overflow the memory resources. Here is a corrected version that returns a very large negative number when the argument is a negative number:

```
double factorial(int i)
{
  if (i > -1)
    switch (i) {
         case 0:
         case 1:
             return 1;
              break;
         case 2:
              return 2;
              break;
         case 3:
              return 6;
              break;
         case 4:
              return 24;
              break;
         default:
              return double(i) * factorial(i-1);
    }
  else
    return -1.0e+30; // numeric code for a bad argument
}
```

3. The nonrecursive version of function `Fibonacci` is

```
double Fibonacci(int n)
{
  double Fib0 = 0;
  double Fib1 = 1;
  double Fib2;

  if (n == 0)
    return 0;
  else if (n == 1 || n == 2)
    return 1;
  else
    for (int i = 0; i <= n; i++) {
      Fib2 = Fib0 + Fib1;
      Fib0 = Fib1;
```

```
            Fib1 = Fib2;
          }
          return Fib2;
      }
```

4. True. The first function uses a formal reference parameter, whereas the second parameter uses a pointer parameter.

Exercise

Here is my version of program ADVFUN9.CPP:

```
/*
   C++ program that uses pointers to functions to implement a
   a linear regression program that supports temporary
   mathematical transformations.
*/

#include <iostream.h>
#include <math.h>

const unsigned MAX_SIZE = 100;

typedef double vector[MAX_SIZE];

struct regression {
   double Rsqr;
   double slope;
   double intercept;
};

// declare array of function pointers
double (*f[2])(double);

// declare function prototypes
void initArray(double*, double*, unsigned);
double linear(double);
double sqr(double);
double reciprocal(double);
void calcRegression(double*, double*, unsigned, regression&,
                    double (*f[2])(double));
int select_transf(const char*);

main()
{
    char ans;
    unsigned count;
    vector x, y;
    regression stat;
    int trnsfx, trnsfy;
```

```
do {
    cout << "Enter array size [2.."
         << MAX_SIZE << "] : ";
    cin >> count;
} while (count <= 1 || count > MAX_SIZE);

// initialize array
initArray(x, y, count);
// transform data
do {
  // set the transformation functions
  trnsfx = select_transf("X");
  trnsfy = select_transf("Y");
  // set function pointer f[0]
  switch (trnsfx) {
   case 0 :
      f[0] = linear;
      break;
   case 1 :
      f[0] = log;
      break;
   case 2 :
      f[0] = sqrt;
      break;
   case 3 :
      f[0] = sqr;
      break;
   case 4 :
      f[0] = reciprocal;
      break;
   default :
      f[0] = linear;
      break;
  }
  // set function pointer f[1]
  switch (trnsfy) {
   case 0 :
      f[1] = linear;
      break;
   case 1 :
      f[1] = log;
      break;
   case 2 :
      f[1] = sqrt;
      break;
   case 3 :
      f[1] = sqr;
      break;
   case 4 :
      f[1] = reciprocal;
      break;
```

```
        default :
           f[1] = linear;
           break;
      }

      calcRegression(x, y, count, stat, f);

      cout << "\n\n\n\n"
           << "R-square = " << stat.Rsqr << "\n"
           << "Slope = " << stat.slope << "\n"
           << "Intercept = " << stat.intercept << "\n\n\n";
      cout << "Want to use other transformations? (Y/N) ";
      cin >> ans;
    } while (ans == 'Y' || ans == 'y');
  return 0;
}

void initArray(double* x, double* y, unsigned count)
// read data for array from the keyboard
{
    for (unsigned i = 0; i < count; i++, x++, y++) {
       cout << "X[" << i << "] : ";
       cin >> *x;
       cout << "Y[" << i << "] : ";
       cin >> *y;
    }
}

int select_transf(const char* var_name)
// select choice of transformation
{

   int choice = -1;
   cout << "\n\n\n";
   cout << "select transformation for variable " << var_name
        << "\n\n\n"
        << "0) No transformation\n"
        << "1) Logarithmic transformation\n"
        << "2) Square root transformation\n"
        << "3) Square transformation\n"
        << "4) Reciprocal transformation\n";
   while (choice < 0 || choice > 4) {
      cout << "\nSelect choice by number : ";
      cin >> choice;
   }
   return choice;
}

double linear(double x)
{ return x; }
```

```
double sqr(double x)
{ return x * x; }

double reciprocal(double x)
{ return 1.0 / x; }

void calcRegression(double* x,
                    double* y,
                    unsigned count,
                    regression &stat,
                    double (*f[2])(double))

{
     double meanx, meany, sdevx, sdevy;
     double sum = (double) count, sumx = 0, sumy = 0;
     double sumxx = 0, sumyy = 0, sumxy = 0;
     double xdata, ydata;

     for (unsigned i = 0; i < count; i++) {
         xdata = (*f[0])(*(x+i));
         ydata = (*f[1])(*(y+i));
         sumx += xdata;
         sumy += ydata;
         sumxx += sqr(xdata);
         sumyy += sqr(ydata);
         sumxy += xdata * ydata;
     }

     meanx = sumx / sum;
     meany = sumy / sum;
     sdevx = sqrt((sumxx - sqr(sumx) / sum)/(sum-1.0));
     sdevy = sqrt((sumyy - sqr(sumy) / sum)/(sum-1.0));
     stat.slope = (sumxy - meanx * meany * sum) /
                  sqr(sdevx)/(sum-1);
     stat.intercept = meany - stat.slope * meanx;
     stat.Rsqr = sqr(sdevx / sdevy * stat.slope);
}
```

Answers to Day 11, "Object-Oriented Programming and C++ Classes"

Quiz

1. By default, the members of a class are protected. Therefore, the class declaration has no public member and cannot be used to create instances.

2. The third constructor has a default argument, which makes it redundant with the fourth constructor. The C++ compiler detects such an error.

3. True. `String("Hello Borland C++")` creates a temporary instance of class `String` and then assigns it to the instance `s`.

4. Yes. The new statements are valid.

Exercise

Here is the implementation of function `main` in my version of program CLASS7.CPP:

```
main()
{

  Complex c[5];
  c[1].assign(3, 5);
  c[2].assign(7, 5);
  c[4].assign(2, 3);

  c[3] = c[1] + c[2];
  cout << c[1] << " + " << c[2] << " = " << c[3] << "\n";
  cout << c[3] << " + " << c[4] << " = ";
  c[3] += c[4];
  cout << c[3] << "\n";
  return 0;
}
```

Answers to Day 12, "Basic Stream File I/O"

Quiz

1. False. The `read` and `write` functions cannot store and recall the dynamic data, which is accessed by a pointer member of a structure or a class.

2. True.

3. True.

4. False.

Exercise

Here is the code for member function `binSearch` and the updated function `main` in program IO4.CPP (the output also shows the new global constant `NOT_FOUND` and the updated class declaration):

```
const unsigned NOT_FOUND = 0xffff;

class VmArray
{
   protected:
     fstream f;
     unsigned size;
     double badIndex;

   public:
     VmArray(unsigned Size, const char* filename);
     ~VmArray()
       { f.close(); }
     unsigned getSize() const
       { return size; }
     boolean writeElem(const char* str, unsigned index);
     boolean readElem(char* str, unsigned index);
     void Combsort();
     unsigned binSearch(const char* search);
};

unsigned VmArray::binSearch(const char* search)
{
  unsigned low = 0;
  unsigned high = size - 1;
  unsigned median;
  char str[STR_SIZE+1];
  int result;

  do {
    median = (low + high) / 2;
    readElem(str, median);
    result = strcmp(search, str);
    if (result > 0)
      low = median + 1;
    else
      high = median - 1;
  } while (result != 0 && low <= high);
  return (result == 0) ? median : NOT_FOUND;
}

main()
{
  const unsigned NUM_ELEMS = 10;
  char* data[] = { "Michigan", "California", "Virginia", "Main",
                   "New York", "Florida", "Nevada", "Alaska",
                   "Ohio", "Maryland" },
  VmArray arr(NUM_ELEMS, "arr.dat");
  char str[STR_SIZE+1];
  char c;
  unsigned index;
```

```
    // assign values to array arr
    for (unsigned i = 0; i < arr.getSize(); i++) {
      strcpy(str, data[i]);
      arr.writeElem(str, i);
    }
    // display unordered array
    cout << "Unsorted arrays is:\n";
    for (i = 0; i < arr.getSize(); i++) {
      arr.readElem(str, i);
      cout << str << "\n";
    }
    // pause
    cout << "\nPress any key and then Return to sort the array...";
    cin >> c;
    // sort the array
    arr.Combsort();
    // display sorted array
    cout << "Sorted arrays is:\n";
    for (i = 0; i < arr.getSize(); i++) {
      arr.readElem(str, i);
      cout << str << "\n"
    }
    // pause
    cout << "\nPress any key and then Return to search the array...";
    cin >> c;
    // search for array elements using the pointer data
    for (i = 0; i < NUM_ELEMS; i++) {
      index = arr.binSearch(data[i]);
      if (index != NOT_FOUND)
        cout << "Found " << data[i]
             << " at index " << index << "\n";
      else
        cout << "No match for " << data[i] << "\n";
    }
    return 0;
}
```

Answers to Day 13, "The C++ *string* Class"

Quiz

1. CSTRING.H must be included to use the C++ string class.
2. A string class variable can be declared either with or without an initial value, for example:

   ```
   string s1;
   string s2("Initial Value");
   ```

3. The string class includes functions for comparing it to a C-style string.

   Operators ==, >, <, >=, <= and != have versions that compare string class variables to C-style strings.

   Another way is to compare the C-style element of the string class variable to the C-string, as in the following:

   ```
   result = strcmp(CStyleStr, stringClassVar.c_str());
   ```

4. The task performed by the `replace` member function finds text and substitutes for it in one call.
5. The second character in a string class variable is at index 1. Addressing is the same as with any array, with index 0 being the first item.
6. Given string `s1` = "11"; string `s2` = "2112";
   a. The result of `s1 + s2` is "112112"
   b. `s2.contains(s1);` returns 1 because "11" is found in "2112"
   c. `s1 > s2` is false
   d. `s2.find(s1, 0);` returns 1 because "11" is located beginning at index 1 in "2112"

Exercises

1. C-style string of value "12"

   ```
   char myCStyleString[] = "12";

   C++ string class item of value "12";
   ```

   either one of the following:

   ```
   string myString("12");
   string myString = "12";
   ```

2. The following is a function that accepts a C++ string as a calling argument and that writes its value to the computer screen:

   ```
   void MyFunction(string& myString)

     {
     cout << myString;
     }
   ```

3. The following function writes out each character of the passed string individually and then returns the size of the string:

```
size_t MyFunction(string& myString)
{
size_t index;
size_t len = myString.length();

// write each char from the string to the screen
// one for each pass through the loop

for (index = 0; index < len; ++index)
  cout << myString[index];

return len; // return the length of the string
}
```

4. The first thing to remember is that a C++ string is quite different from a C character array. The problem with using `strrev` on the direct result of the `c_str` member function is that `c_str` returns a `const char*` while `strrev` requires a `char*`. This can easily be taken care of with a cast:

```
strrev((char*)myString.c_str());
```

This, of course, is overriding the regular type-checking that lets C++ help to prevent programmers from making bad mistakes. It works, but it bypasses some potential problems. In order to do things properly, one should do something like the following:

```
char* temp=new char*[myString.length()+1];
strcpy(temp,myString.c_str());
myString=strrev(temp);
delete[] temp;
```

It's a bit more complicated, but it's a little safer than blindly casting the results of a `c_str`. The main problem with a blind cast is that we don't know (aren't supposed to know) how the C++ `string` class works and, therefore, whether simply casting is dangerous or not.

Answers to Day 14, "Programming Windows with OWL 2.5"

Quiz

1. False. Templates aren't magic; the compiler still has to be able to figure out how to execute each statement in a template exactly as if it weren't a template. For example, the < comparisons in the `Low()` template function don't make sense for classes:

```
template <class T> const T& Low(const T& a, const T& b, const T& c)
       {
       if (a < b)
         {
         if (a < c)
             return a;
         }
       else if (b < c)
         return b;
         return b;
       return c;
       }
```

   What does the < operator mean for a class? There are two solutions:

   - Write versions of the template that know how to deal with specific classes (which almost defeats the purpose of using templates).
   - Write operators for those classes. (For example, if you wanted to use `Low()` with a class of your own, you'd need to provide an operator < function that would figure out what makes one class less than another.)

2. False. The types already changed between Windows 3.1 and Windows NT, for example. (WORD, for example, changed from an unsigned `int` to an unsigned `short`.) The idea, though, is that if you use the Windows types, you won't have to make any changes to your own code.

3. True. Even though OWL uses C++ classes, OWL itself is still written using the same functions that a C program would. Using OWL, you get to let the Borland programmers do the work for you.

Answers to Day 15, “Basic Windows”

Quiz

1. True.
2. True.
3. False.

Answers to Day 16, “OWL Controls”

Quiz

1. False. Only the text for controls with `SS_SIMPLE` style are unchangeable.
2. True.
3. True.
4. True.
5. True, because every control is a window.
6. True, but the OWL-prescribed method is to use the `EV_BN_CLICKED` macro.

Answers to Day 17, “Grouped Controls”

Quiz

1. False. The check box can replace the two radio buttons only if these buttons offer opposite alternatives.
2. True.
3. True. Each check box can be independently toggled.
4. False.

Answers to Day 18, "List Box Controls"

Quiz

1. True.
2. True.
3. False. LBN_SELCHANGE indicates that a new item is selected.
4. False. LBN_DBLCLICK indicates that a list item is selected with a double mouse click.
5. False. LBS_STANDARD includes the LBS_SORT style and therefore creates sorted list boxes.

Answers to Day 19, "Scroll Bars and Combo Boxes"

Quiz

1. True.
2. False. You need to respond to the CBN_EDITUPDATE message.
3. False. The items are sorted, but not unique. You can insert multiple copies of the same string.
4. True. In order to maintain a chronological order, you must prevent automatic sorting.
5. False.
6. True.
7. False.

Answers to Day 20, "Dialog Boxes"

Quiz

1. False. You don't need the .RES file until after linking the object modules and libraries.
2. False. There does, however, need to be a method by which the user can signal the dialog box to close itself. This is often done with buttons that, though labeled differently, return `IDOK` and `IDCANCEL`.
3. True.
4. False. The best examples of nested dialogs are those related to setting up the printer.
5. False. Dialog boxes can be stand-alone windows.

Answers to Day 21, "MDI Windows"

Quiz

1. False. MDI child windows cannot have their own menus.
2. False. MDI child windows are confined to the frame area of their parent window.
3. False. You cannot nest MDI child windows.
4. True. Now you can move on to the extra-credit chapters to further sharpen your Windows programming skills.

Index

Symbols

A

B

D

Sams
Learning
Center

SAMS
PUBLISHING

E

F

SAMS
PUBLISHING

G

H

I–J

K

L

M

N

O

P

Q-R

S

SAMS
PUBLISHING

T

SAMS
PUBLISHING

U

V

W

X-Z

Book ISBN 0-672-30598-4

Disk Offer

The programs in *Teach Yourself Borland C++ 4.5 in 21 Days, Second Edition* are available on disk from the authors. Fill out this form and enclose a check for only $10.00 to receive a copy. Outside the U.S., please enclose a check for $14.00 in U.S. currency, drawn on a U.S. bank. Please make the check payable to **Namir C. Shammas**. Sorry, no credit card orders. Mail this form to

Namir C. Shammas
3928 Margate Drive
Richmond, VA 23235

Name ____

Company (for company name) __________________________

Street ____

City ____

State/Province _______________________________________

ZIP or Postal Code ____________________________________

Country (outside the USA) _____________________________

Disk format (check one):

5.25 inch__________ 3.5 inch__________